Ethnic American Food Today

A Cultural Encyclopedia

Volume I: A–K

Edited by Lucy M. Long

ROWMAN & LITTLEFIELD

Lanham • Boulder • New York • London

Published by Rowman & Littlefield
A wholly owned subsidiary of The Rowman & Littlefield Publishing Group, Inc.
4501 Forbes Boulevard, Suite 200, Lanham, Maryland 20706
www.rowman.com

Unit A, Whitacre Mews, 26-34 Stannary Street, London SE11 4AB

Copyright © 2015 by Rowman & Littlefield

All rights reserved. No part of this book may be reproduced in any form or by any electronic or mechanical means, including information storage and retrieval systems, without written permission from the publisher, except by a reviewer who may quote passages in a review.

British Library Cataloguing in Publication Information Available

Library of Congress Cataloging-in-Publication Data

Ethnic American food today : a cultural encyclopedia / edited by Lucy M. Long.
   pages cm
 Includes bibliographical references and index.
 ISBN 978-1-4422-2730-9 (cloth : alk. paper) — ISBN 978-1-4422-2731-6 (electronic) 1. Cooking, American—Encyclopedias. 2. International cooking—Encyclopedias. I. Long, Lucy M., 1956–
 TX349.E86 2015
 641.59—dc23   2015000433

∞™ The paper used in this publication meets the minimum requirements of American National Standard for Information Sciences—Permanence of Paper for Printed Library Materials, ANSI/NISO Z39.48-1992.

Printed in the United States of America

Contents

List of Nations by Continent	vii
List of Maps	xi
List of Contributors	xxiii
Acknowledgments	xxxi
Introduction	1

Afghanistan	15	Bosnia and Herzegovina	76
African American	18	Botswana	81
Albania	23	Brazil	82
Algeria	24	British Virgin Islands	85
American Samoa	28	Brunei Darussalam	86
Amish	28	Bulgaria	86
Andorra	30	Burkina Faso	88
Angola	31	Burma	89
Anguilla	32	Burundi	89
Antigua and Barbuda	32	Cajun	91
Argentina	32	Cambodia	94
Armenia	35	Cameroon	98
Aruba	38	Canada	102
Australia	38	Cape Verde	105
Austria	41	Caribbean (Americas)	106
Azerbaijan	44	Caribbean, Dutch	107
Bahamas	47	Cayman Islands	109
Bahrain	50	Central African Republic	109
Bangladesh	50	Central Asia	110
Barbados	55	Chad	115
Basque	56	Chile	117
Belarus	61	China	121
Belgium	63	Colombia	129
Belize	66	Comoros	132
Benin	68	Congo	133
Bermuda	69	Cook Islands	133
Bhutan	71	Cornwall	133
Bolivia	73	Costa Rica	135
Bonaire, Saint Eustatius, and Saba	76	Côte d'Ivoire	137

Creole	138	Guadeloupe	237
Croatia	142	Guam	237
Cuba	145	Guatemala	237
Curaçao	152	Guernsey	241
Cyprus	152	Guinea	241
Czechoslovakia	152	Guinea-Bissau	242
Democratic Republic of Congo	157	Guyana	243
Denmark	159	Gypsy	248
Djibouti	164	Haiti	255
Dominica	165	Hawaiian	260
Dominican Republic	165	Hmong	263
Ecuador	171	Honduras	266
Egypt	173	Hong Kong	270
El Salvador	175	Hungary	274
England	179	Iceland	283
Equatorial Guinea	183	India	285
Eritrea	184	Indonesia	293
Estonia	186	Iran	297
Ethiopia	187	Iraq	300
Falkland Islands/Malvinas	195	Ireland	305
Federated States of Micronesia	195	Isle of Man	309
Fiji	195	Israel	311
Finland	195	Italy	314
France	200	Jamaica	325
French Guiana	206	Japan	327
French Polynesia	207	Jersey	337
Gabon	209	Jewish-Ashkenazi	337
Gambia	211	Jewish-Sephardic	341
Georgia	211	Jordan	346
German-Russian	214	Kazakhstan	351
Germany	217	Kenya	351
Ghana	221	Kiribati	354
Gibraltar	225	Korea, North	354
Greece	225	Korea, Republic of (South Korea)	354
Greenland	234	Kuwait	358
Grenada	235	Kyrgyzstan	359

List of Nations by Continent

AFRICA—EASTERN
Burundi
Comoros
Djibouti
Eritrea
Ethiopia
Kenya
Madagascar
Malawi
Mauritius
Mayotte
Mozambique
Reunion
Rwanda
Seychelles
Somalia
Tanzania, United Republic of
Uganda
Zambia
Zimbabwe

AFRICA—MIDDLE
Angola
Cameroon
Central African Republic (CAR)
Chad
Congo, Republic of
Democratic Republic of Congo
Equatorial Guinea
Gabon
São Tomé and Príncipe

AFRICA—NORTHERN
Algeria
Egypt
Libya
Morocco

South Sudan
Sudan
Tunisia
Western Sahara

AFRICA—SOUTHERN
Botswana
Lesotho
Namibia
South Africa
Swaziland

AFRICA—WESTERN
Benin
Burkina Faso
Cape Verde
Côte d'Ivoire
Gambia
Ghana
Guinea
Guinea-Bissau
Liberia
Mali
Mauritania
Niger
Nigeria
Senegal
Sierra Leone
Togo

AMERICA—CARIBBEAN
Anguilla
Antigua and Barbuda
Aruba
Bahamas
Barbados
Bonaire, Saint Eustatius, and Saba

British Virgin Islands
Cayman Islands
Cuba
Curaçao
Dominica
Dominican Republic
Grenada
Guadeloupe
Haiti
Jamaica
Martinique
Montserrat
Puerto Rico
Saint-Barthélemy
Saint Kitts and Nevis
Saint Lucia
Saint Maarten—Dutch
Saint Martin—French
Saint Vincent and the Grenadines
Trinidad and Tobago
Turks and Caicos Islands
United States Virgin Islands

AMERICA—CENTRAL
Belize
Costa Rica
El Salvador
Guatemala
Honduras
Mexico
Nicaragua
Panama

AMERICA—NORTH
African American
Amish
Bermuda
Cajun
Canada
Creole
Greenland
Hawaiian
Jewish—Ashkanazi
Jewish—Sephardic
Mennonite

Native American: Eastern Woodlands
Native American: Pacific Northwest
Native American: Plains
Native American: Southwest
Pennsylvania Dutch
Roma
Saint Pierre and Miquelon

AMERICA—SOUTH
Argentina
Bolivia
Brazil
Chile
Colombia
Ecuador
Falkland Islands (Malvinas)
French Guiana
Guyana
Paraguay
Peru
Suriname
Uruguay
Venezuela

ASIA—CENTRAL
Kazakhstan
Kyrgyzstan
Tajikistan
Turkmenistan
Uzbekistan

ASIA—EASTERN
China
Hong Kong
Japan
Korea, North
Korea, Republic of (South)
Macau
Mongolia
Taiwan

ASIA—SOUTHERN
Afghanistan
Bangladesh
Bhutan

India
Iran
Maldives
Nepal
Pakistan
Sri Lanka
Tibet

ASIA—SOUTHEASTERN
Brunei Darussalam
Cambodia
Hmong
Indonesia
Laos
Malaysia
Myanmar (Burma)
Philippines
Singapore
Thailand
Timor-Leste
Vietnam

ASIA—WESTERN
Armenia
Azerbaijan
Bahrain
Cyprus
Georgia
Iran
Iraq
Israel
Jordan
Kuwait
Lebanon
Oman
Palestine
Qatar
Saudi Arabia
Syria
Turkey
United Arab Emirates
Yemen

EUROPE—EASTERN
Belarus
Bosnia and Herzegovina
Bulgaria
Czechoslovakia
German-Russian
Hungary
Moldova
Poland
Romania
Russia
Slovakia
Ukraine

EUROPE—NORTHERN
Cornwall
Denmark (Faroe Islands)
England
Estonia
Finland
Guernsey
Iceland
Ireland
Isle of Man
Jersey
Latvia
Lithuania
Norway
Scotland
Sweden
Wales

EUROPE—SOUTHERN
Albania
Andorra
Basque
Bosnia and Herzegovina
Croatia
Gibraltar (UK)
Greece
Italy (Sardinia and Sicily)
Macedonia
Malta and Gozo
Montenegro (with Serbia)
Portugal
San Marino
Serbia (with Montenegro)

Slovenia
Spain
Vatican City

EUROPE—WESTERN
Austria
Belgium
France
Germany
Liechtenstein
Luxembourg
Monaco
Netherlands
Switzerland

OCEANIA—AUSTRALIA AND NEW ZEALAND
Australia
New Zealand

OCEANIA—MELANESIA
Fiji
New Caledonia
Papua New Guinea
Solomon Islands
Vanuatu

OCEANIA—MICRONESIA
Guam
Kiribati
Marshall Islands
Micronesia (Federated States of)
Nauru
Northern Mariana Islands
Palau

OCEANIA—POLYNESIA
American Samoa
Cook Islands
French Polynesia
Niue
Pitcairn
Samoa
Tokelau
Tonga
Tuvalu
Wallis and Futuna Islands

List of Maps

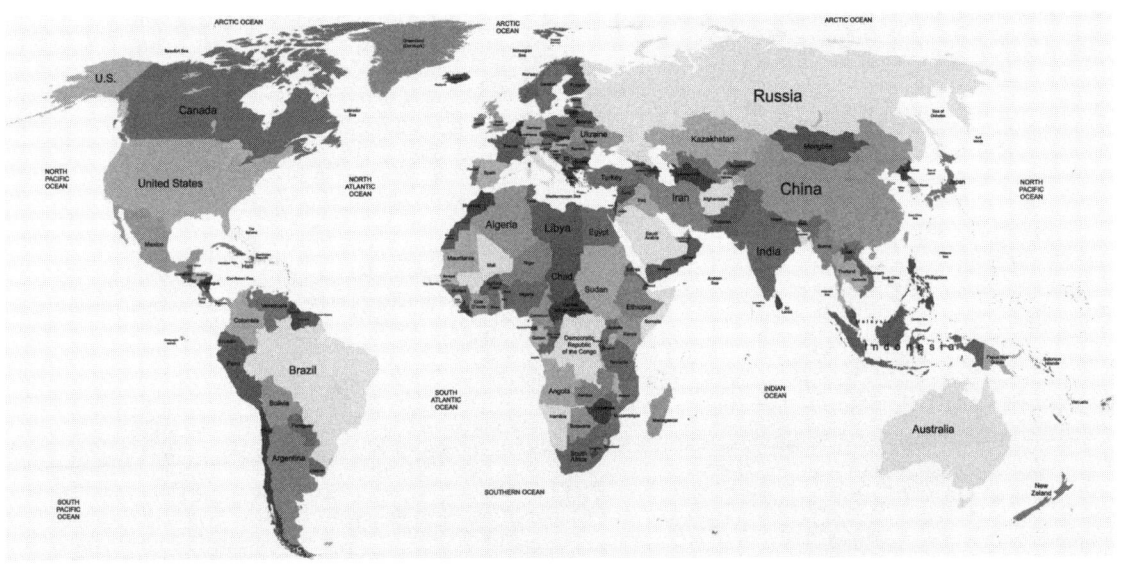

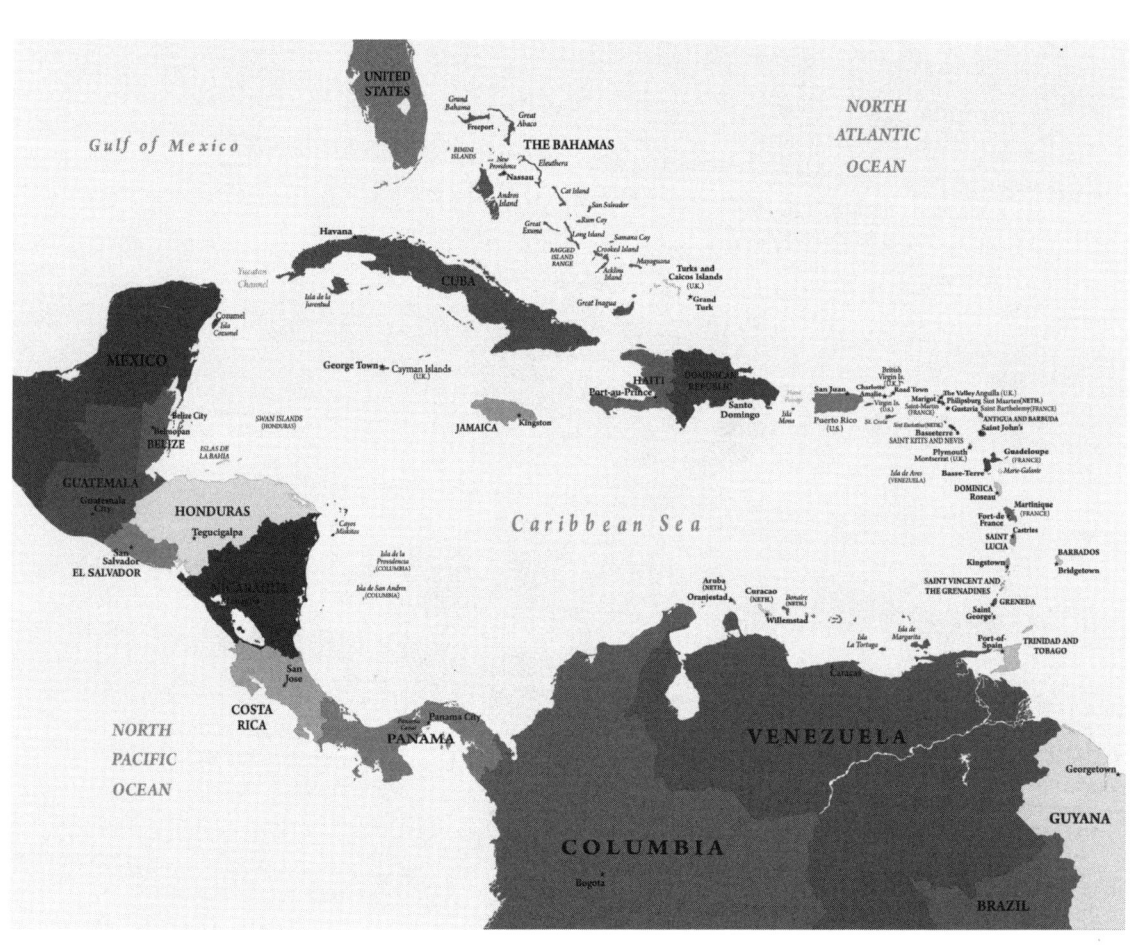

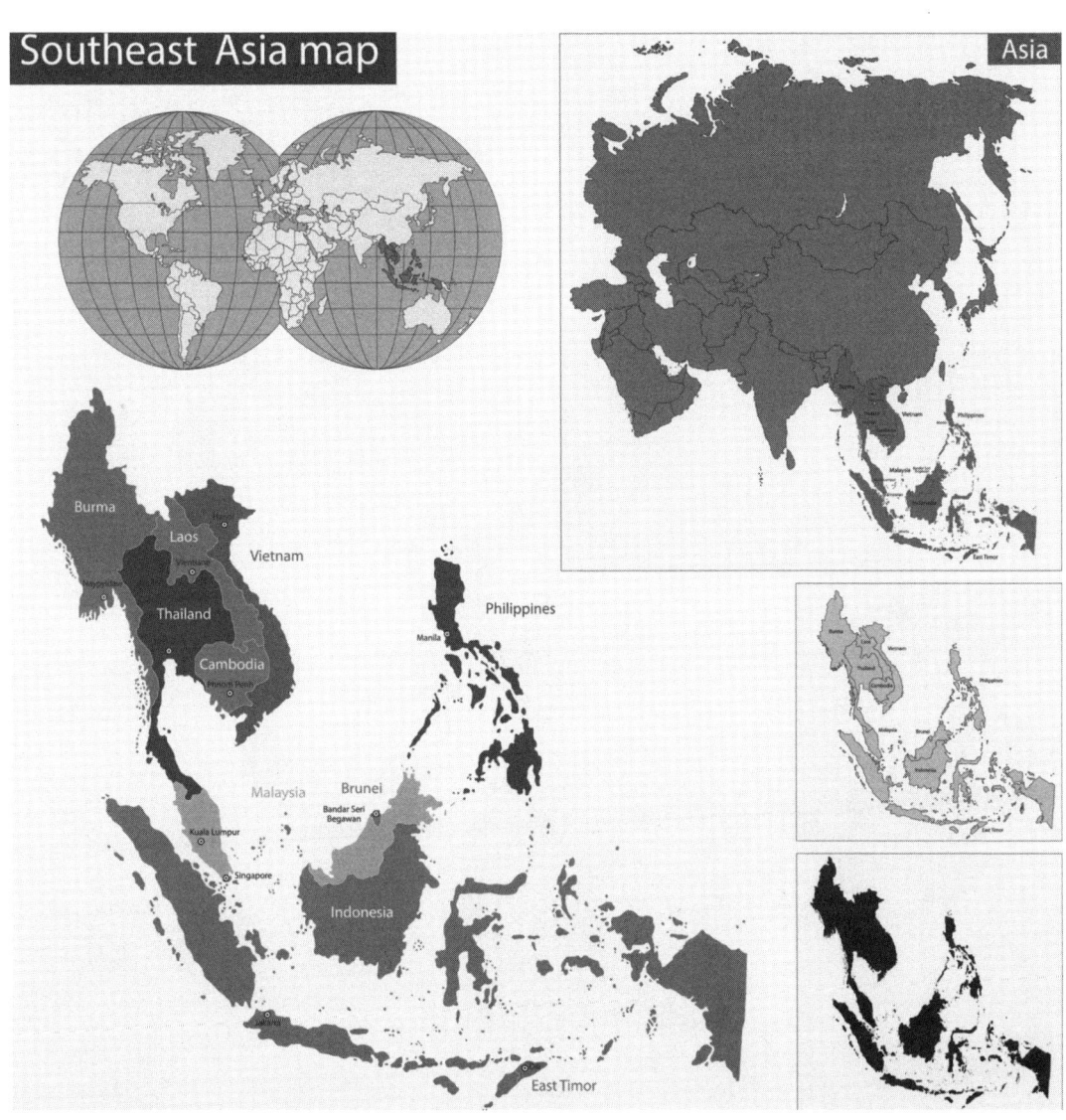

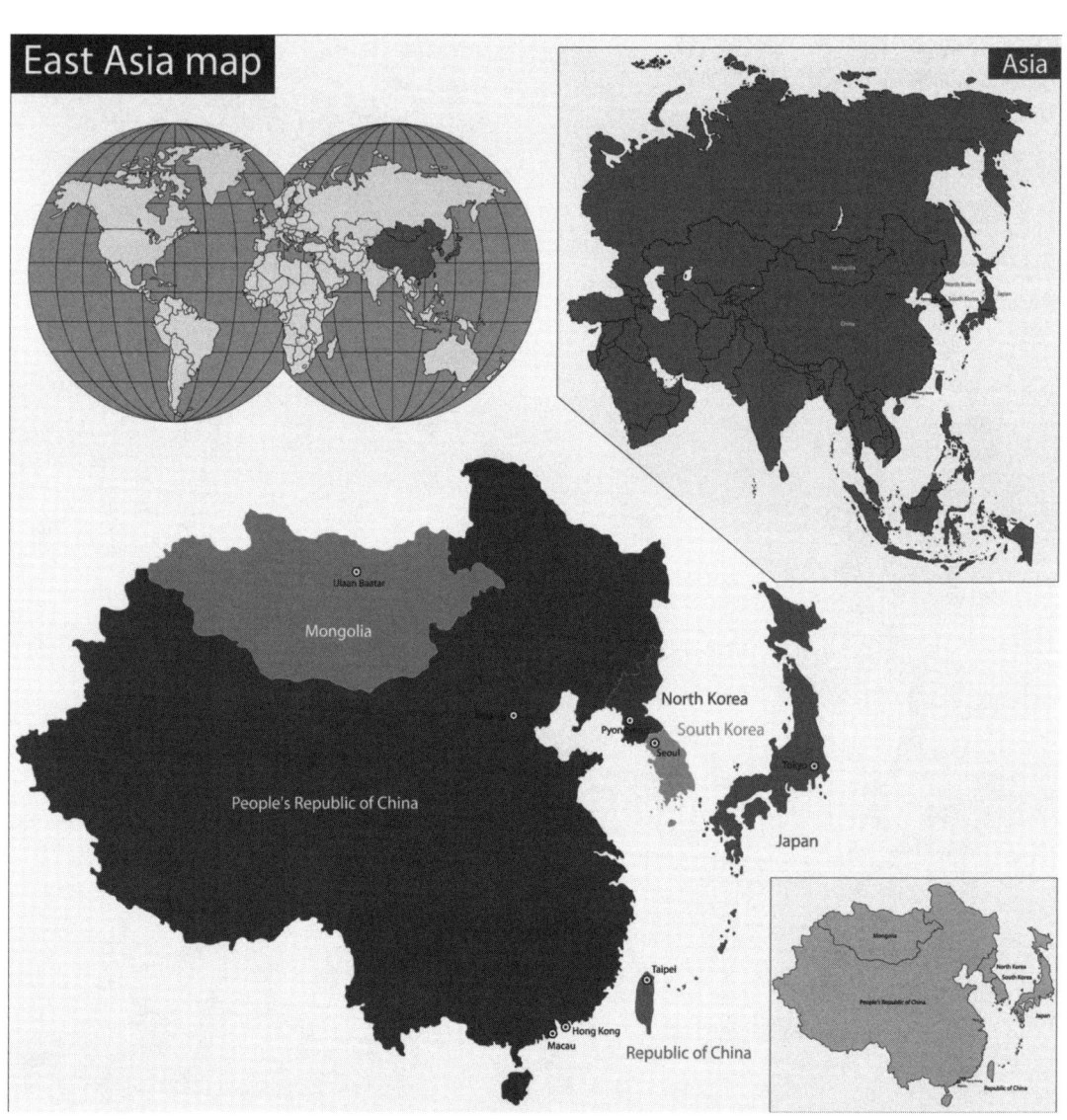

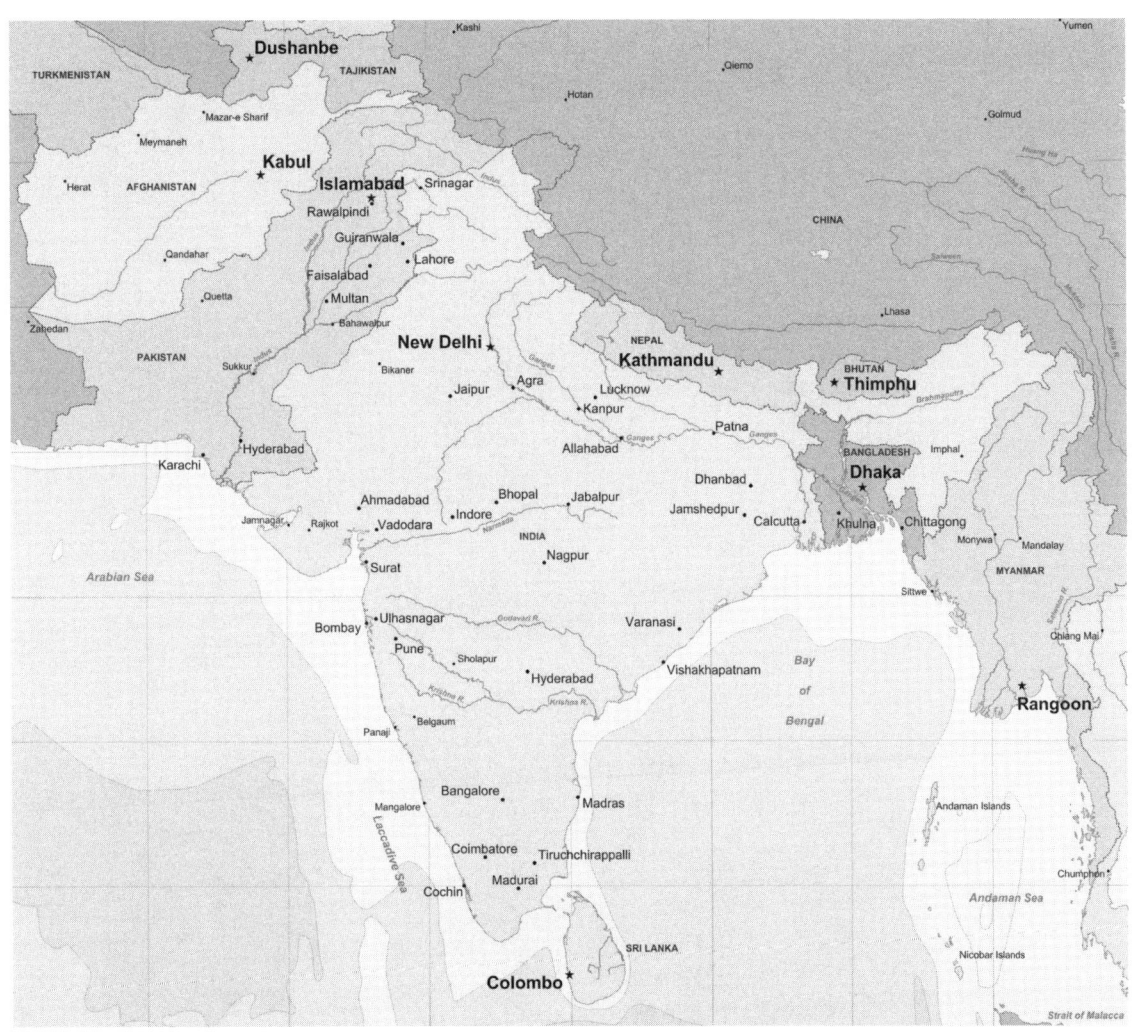

Ethnic American Food Today xvii

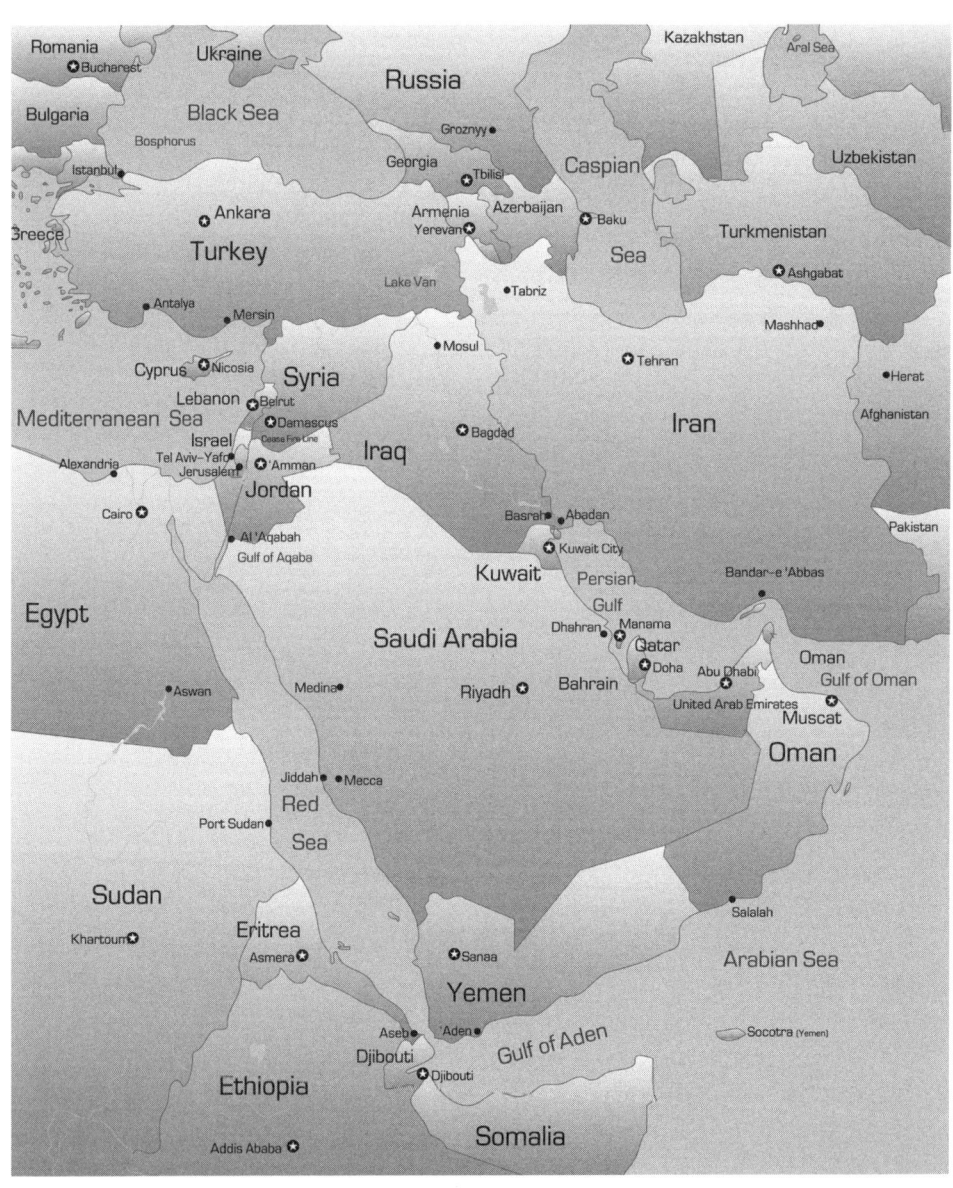

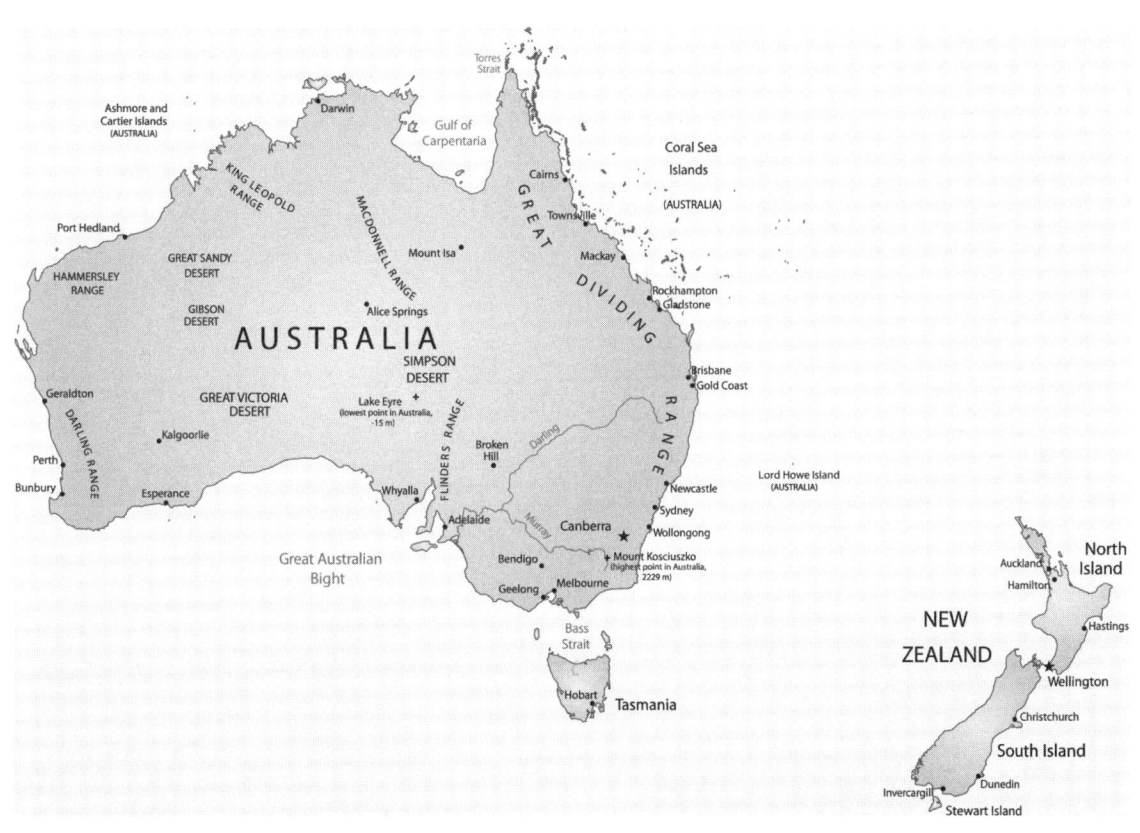

List of Contributors

EDITOR

Lucy M. Long, PhD, is a folklorist, adjunct assistant professor, and founder/director of the Center for Food and Culture in Bowling Green, Ohio. She has taught food studies, among other subjects, since the mid-1990s.

CONTRIBUTORS

Shamsa Ahmed is a Somali henna artist and health care professional living in Portland, Maine. (Somalia)

Narwan Aimen, a home cook and recent graduate at George Mason University in Virginia, is an Afghan American whose parents emigrated from Afghanistan in 1981. (Afghanistan)

Ken Albala is professor of history at the University of the Pacific. (Jewish-Sephardic)

Suleiman Almulhem, from Saudi Arabia, is a tourism student at Bowling Green State University in Ohio.

Alexandria Ayala is a graduate of Florida Gulf Coast University, studying and working with populations from Latin America and the Caribbean. (Dominican Republic, Grenada, United States Virgin Islands)

Sally M. Baho is Syrian American and an aspiring food scholar. Her interests include food as it relates to identity, culture, immigrants and diaspora communities, memory and nostalgia, and its dynamic nature in the twenty-first century. (Syria)

Charles A. Baker-Clark is an associate professor of hospitality and tourism management at Grand Valley State University, Michigan. He is currently working in the Balkans as a Fulbright Scholar, where he is teaching about food and culture. (Albania, Azerbaijan, Belarus, Lithuania, Moldova, Romania, Serbia and Montenegro, Vatican)

Puja Batra-Wells is a doctoral candidate in the Department of Comparative Studies at The Ohio State University. She holds a master's degree in Popular Culture from Bowling Green State University and researches material and visual cultures. (Pakistan)

Betty J. Belanus, PhD, is a folklorist at the Smithsonian Center for Folklife and Cultural Heritage. She has conducted fieldwork and presented programs with numerous ethnic groups for the Smithsonian Folklife Festival. (Botswana, Isle of Man, Namibia, South Africa, Swaziland, Wales)

David Beriss is associate professor of anthropology at the University of New Orleans. (Creole)

Christopher B. Bolfing is a PhD candidate in anthropology at the University of Arkansas. His dissertation research addresses phenomenology, identity, ceremonialism, and traditional ecological knowledge among Muskogee Creeks in Florida. (Native American: Eastern Woodlands)

Katherine Borland, PhD, is a folklorist teaching at The Ohio State University in Columbus, Ohio. (Nicaragua)

Matt Branch is a geography PhD student at Pennsylvania State University. He is a Himalayan scholar working in Nepal and Bhutan. (Nepal)

Whitney E. Brown is an independent folklorist and dry-stone waller who completed her master's degree at the University of North Carolina–Chapel Hill in 2010. (Spain)

xxiii

Anthony F. Buccini is an independent researcher and writer in the fields of linguistics and food studies in Chicago. (Italy)

Tina Bucuvalas, PhD, and folklorist, is curator of arts and historical resources for the City of Tarpon Springs, Florida. (Greece)

Heidi Busse is a researcher at the University of Wisconsin School of Medicine and Public Health, where she manages global health partnerships with Ethiopian academic and NGO collaborators that emphasize health and food systems strengthening. (Ethiopia)

Bailey M. Cameron is a recent graduate from the University of Alberta with a bachelor of arts in social anthropology and an intern at the Smithsonian Institute Center for Folklife and Cultural Heritage. (Canada, Kenya)

Kathryn Clune is currently a graduate student at University of North Carolina Chapel Hill, where she studies food and culture, among other subjects. (Hmong)

Emily H. J. Contois, MPH, MLA, is a doctoral student in American Studies at Brown University. (New Zealand)

Mary Lynn Crowley has an MA in food science, University of Akron. (Native American: Southwest)

Amy Dahlstrom is associate professor of linguistics at the University of Chicago. (Sweden)

Shannon Davis is an anthropologist and intern at the Smithsonian Center for Folklife and Cultural Heritage, Washington, DC. (Yemen)

Carmen Sofia Dence is artist-educator with the Missouri Folk Arts Program; founder and artistic director of Grupo Atlántico Inc., a traditional dance troupe presenting Caribbean folklore; and a native of Barranquilla, Colombia. (Colombia)

James I. Deutsch is a program curator at the Smithsonian Center for Folklife and Cultural Heritage in Washington, DC. In 1998–1999, he served as a Fulbright Senior Scholar at Veliko Turnovo University in Bulgaria. (Bulgaria)

Alan Deutschman is professor of journalism at the University of Nevada, Reno. (Chad, Eritrea, Tanzania)

M. Ruth Dike is a PhD anthropology student at the University of Kentucky, where her research focuses on the anthropology of food, gender, identity, globalization, diasporic studies, and applied anthropology in Morocco, the Moroccan diaspora, and beyond. (Morocco)

Jane Dusselier, PhD, teaches in the Asian American studies program in the Department of History at Iowa State University. (Sri Lanka)

Ryan S. Eanes is a media studies PhD candidate at the University of Oregon's School of Journalism and Communication. (Brazil)

Nicholas Eaton is a culinary educator in secondary and postsecondary education. (Slovenia)

Elaine Eff is a Maryland folklorist and cofounder of Maryland Traditions, Baltimore, Maryland. (England)

Susan Eleuterio is a professional folklorist, ethnic foods scholar, educator, and consultant to nonprofits. Her paternal grandparents immigrated to the United States from St. Miguel, the Azores. (Angola, Belize, Cape Verde, Central African Republic, Guinea-Bissau, Laos, Maldives, Mauritius, Mexico, Portugal, São Tomé and Príncipe, Slovakia)

Nailam Elkhechen has a master's degree in educational technology and a bachelor's in dietetics. She is currently an adjunct instructor at Bowling Green State University, teaching food and culture in the dietetics program. (Libya, Oman, Palestine, Saudi Arabia, Tunisia)

Zilia Estrada, PhD, is a folklorist living in Bloomington, Indiana, where she works with community gardens and local food initiatives. (Tibet)

Tricia T. Ferdinand is a doctoral candidate in folklore from the Department of Folklore and Ethnomusicology at Indiana University in Bloomington, Indiana. Tricia was born and spent much of her childhood in Trinidad and

Tobago, and she is now a proud Trinidadian American! (Trinidad and Tobago)

Anne Flannery has studied and taught Austrian culture for over ten years, where she developed an appreciation for Austrian pastries. She currently teaches German and works in the digital humanities in Chicago. (Austria)

Kristie Foell is associate professor of German at Bowling Green State University, Ohio, the descendant of at least four German American great-grandparents, an avid student of Arabic and all things Egyptian, and a pretty good cook. (Egypt, Germany)

Mary Gee is a doctoral candidate in sociology at the University of California, San Francisco. (Hong Kong, Macau)

Janet C. Gilmore is an associate professor of folklore and landscape architecture at the University of Wisconsin–Madison, where she teaches foodways courses and is affiliated with the Center for the Study of Upper Midwestern Cultures. (Ethiopia)

Alexandra Gouirand teaches French in Olympia, Washington. (France)

Liora Gvion is a senior lecturer of sociology at the Kibbutzim College of Education in Tel Aviv, Israel. (Israel)

Laura K. Hahn, PhD, is a professor of communication at Humboldt State University. (Iraq)

Adrienne Hall is assistant teaching professor at Drexel University, Philadelphia, Pennsylvania. (Macedonia, Malta and Gozo)

Gregory Hansen is professor of folklore and English at Arkansas State University. His grandparents immigrated into America from Denmark at the turn of the century. (Denmark)

Nicholas Hartmann is a graduate student at Memorial University and a folklorist-in-residence at the Southwest Folklife Alliance in Tucson, Arizona. A lifelong lover of Nordic and Baltic culture, he became interested in Estonian food following a study-abroad term in Tartu, Estonia. (Estonia)

Dana Hercbergs is an independent folklorist whose research focuses on Arab and Jewish residents' narratives about Jerusalem, as well as ephemera associated with travel and tourism in Palestine/Israel. (Lebanon)

Emily Hilliard is a folklorist and writer. She works at Smithsonian Folkways and writes the pie blog www.nothinginthehouse.com. (Algeria, Democratic Republic of Congo, Republic of Congo)

Graham Hoppe is a master's candidate in the folklore program at the University of North Carolina at Chapel Hill. He lives in Chapel Hill with his wife, Amy. (Cajun)

Holly Howard is an independent scholar and research assistant with Panamanian heritage. (Panama)

Tony Howard is a video producer/director with an interest in foodways. (Panama)

Katherine C. Hysmith, MLA, is a freelance writer and food scholar living in the Greater Boston Area. (Russia)

Eve Jochnowitz is a culinary ethnographer specializing in Jewish food and the Yiddish language. (Jewish-Ashkenazi)

Catherine Hiebert Kerst is a folklife specialist and archivist in the American Folklife Center, Library of Congress, whose heritage, on both sides of her family, is Russian Mennonite. (Mennonite)

Seema Khan is a Pakistani American and financial analyst who likes to cook for family and friends, fusing American and Pakistani recipes and spices. (Pakistan)

Timothy J. Kloberdanz, PhD, is a folklorist and professor emeritus of anthropology at North Dakota State University (Fargo). He has published numerous articles about the Germans from Russia. (German-Russian)

M. Dustin Knepp is an assistant professor of Spanish and the director of Latin American and Latino Studies at the University of Central Arkansas. (Honduras)

Lili Kocsis, BA in linguistics from Harvard University, devotes most of her time to traveling the world and exploring the history behind the regional cuisines she encounters. She shares her culinary adventures on her website, under the penname MyAmusedBouche. (Hungary)

Elinor Levy, PhD, is an independent folklorist as well as an adjunct in anthropology at Raritan Valley Community College and Fairleigh Dickinson University. (Barbados, Cameroon, Zimbabwe)

Mathilde Frances Lind is a student at the University of Oregon. (Bermuda)

Ray P. Linville has taught in the North Carolina Community College System as a professor of English and humanities, served on the board of the NC Folklore Society, and written about Burmese refugees in North Carolina for the NC Folklife Institute. (Myanmar)

Arthur Lizie, PhD, is chair of the Department of Communication Studies and associate professor of media studies and communication technologies at Bridgewater State University. (Armenia, Ireland)

William G. Lockwood is emeritus professor of anthropology at the University of Michigan in Ann Arbor, Michigan. (Bosnia and Herzegovina, Gypsy)

Yvonne R. Lockwood is emerita, curator of folklife, Michigan State University Museum, East Lansing, Michigan. (Bosnia and Herzegovina, Finland)

Andrea M. Lubrano is a freelance gastronome, photographer, and writer. (Venezuela)

Margaret Magat, PhD, is a cultural researcher and writer based in Hawaii and Los Angeles. (Hawaii, Philippines, Tonga)

Richard March, folklorist and ethnomusicologist, grew up in a household where the cuisine of the northern Adriatic was frequently everyday fare. (Croatia)

Elena Martínez is a folklorist at City Lore in New York and artistic codirector of the Bronx Music Heritage Center. (Puerto Rico)

Nomvula Mashoai-Cook is founder and executive director of Mpumalanga Traditional Art Market (MTAM). South African by birth, she was raised in Lesotho due to apartheid during the 1970s and currently lives in Johannesburg, South Africa. (South Africa)

Amanda Mayo is a PhD candidate in American and New England studies at Boston University and a lecturer in the gastronomy program at Boston University. (Korea)

Melissa McGovern is a sociology and anthropology student affiliated with Le Moyne College in Syracuse, New York. (Costa Rica)

Felicia McMahon, research associate in anthropology at Syracuse University, earned a PhD in folklore and folklife studies from the University of Pennsylvania and is the author of the award-winning book *Not Just Child's Play: Emerging Tradition and the Lost Boys of Sudan*, which won the 2008 Chicago Folklore Prize. (South Sudan)

C. McNabb has an MA in folklore, MLIS, independent scholar. (Ukraine)

John Melgnailis, an emeritus professor of electrical engineering at the University of Maryland, is the owner of Black Rooster Food, a small company that markets Latvian rye bread. (Latvia)

Debra Merskin is associate professor of media studies at the University of Oregon. (Czechoslovakia)

W. Gabriel Mitchell is a recent graduate of Boston University's MLA gastronomy program and CEO of Maison Mitchell, a boutique gourmet pâtisserie in Hamburg. (Peru)

Eric César Morales is a PhD candidate in the Department of Folklore and Ethnomusicology at Indiana University, Bloomington. (Micronesia, Polynesia)

Deeksha Nagar is an independent folklorist and education consultant. (India, Pakistan)

Shelia Navalia Onzere, formerly an extension educator in community food systems at the University of Minnesota, is currently a sociologist and research associate at the University of South Carolina. (Kenya)

Jacqueline M. Newman, PhD and professor emeritus at Queens College, the City University of New York, is editor of *Flavor and Fortune*, a publication dedicated to Chinese cuisine, and she has published extensively on Asian food. (Mongolia)

Justin M. Nolan is associate professor and vice chair of anthropology at the University of Arkansas. His research examines medical ethnobotany, the cultural conservation of food customs, health beliefs, and folklife in North American cultures. (Native American: Eastern Woodlands)

Zachary Nowak is assistant director for the Food Studies Program at the Umbra Institute in Perugia, Italy. (Poland)

Carlos C. Olaechea is an MLA candidate in gastronomy at Boston University and received a BA in anthropology and sociology from Florida International University in Miami, Florida, where he was exposed to the cultures and cuisines of the Caribbean and studied under Dr. Alex Stepick, a pioneer in the study of Haitians in the United States, as well as other social scientists specializing in Caribbean studies. (Bahamas, Haiti)

Alyce Ornella is an independent filmmaker and ethnographer based in Harpswell, Maine. (Somali)

Maggie Ornstein is a doctoral candidate at the Graduate Center, City University of New York, and a part-time lecturer in food studies at the New School. (Iceland)

Cecilia Peterson is an archivist at the Ralph Rinzler Folklife Archives and Collections at the Smithsonian Center for Folklife and Cultural Heritage. (Jordan)

Anne Pryor is a folklorist and education specialist working for the Wisconsin Arts Board, Madison, Wisconsin. (Belgium, Togo)

Shahla Ray, PhD in biochemistry, teaches nutrition science and obesity and health-related courses in the School of Public Health at Indiana University. (Iran)

Amy Reddinger is associate professor of English and women's studies at the University of Wisconsin–Marinette. (Cornwall, Pennsylvania Dutch)

Matthew Reger is an attorney who lived for one year in Tbilisi, Georgia, while working for the American Bar Association Rule of Law Initiative. (Georgia)

Gillian Richards-Greaves is a visiting assistant professor in the Department of History. She is an anthropologist and ethnomusicologist whose research interests include the musical, cultural, linguistic, and ritual expressions of the African Diaspora, particularly of the English-speaking Caribbean. (Guyana)

Emily Ridout is a graduate student in the University of Oregon Folklore Program. (Argentina, Thailand)

Kristina Roque is a professional fundraiser and activist who believes that all children should have access to a quality public education. She was born and raised in Chicago by her Polish American father and Mexican mother, who immigrated to the United States as a teenager. (Mexico)

Annu Ross, MLA in gastronomy from Boston University, is an independent food scholar and writer. (El Salvador)

Puja Sahney has a PhD in folklore from Indiana University, Bloomington. She is lecturer in the writing and critical inquiry program at University at Albany–State University of New York. (Bangladesh)

Rachelle H. Saltzman, PhD, is a folklorist, adjunct assistant professor, and executive director of the Oregon Folklife Network at University of Oregon. (Cambodia, Thailand)

Hannah M. Santino is an independent researcher specializing in Celtic diasporic identity and traditional Irish dance. (Greenland, Liechtenstein, Luxembourg, Monaco, Senegal)

Amy B. Santos is a freelance writer who received her MA in folklore studies from the University of Oregon. (Jamaica)

Y. Ozan Say is assistant professor of anthropology at Bridgewater State University. (Turkey)

Linda E. Schiesser is a retired home economics teacher and associate of the Swiss Center of North America. (Switzerland)

Ethnic American Food Today xxvii

Dillon Tautunu Smith is a master's student in the Department of Linguistics at Hawaii University at Mānoa. (Polynesia)

Robert James Smith is a professor of education at Southern Cross University. (Australia)

Esther Spencer, PhD student at Florida State University in the English department, majoring in African American literature and minoring in folklore, is Nigerian with Sierra Leonean ancestry and part of a vibrant African community. (Liberian, Nigerian, Sierra Leone)

Stephanie St. Pierre, MDiv, MPH, DPHc, is a lecturer, writer, and consultant. (Native American: Pacific Northwest, Native American: Plains)

Lois Stanford, PhD, is associate professor of anthropology and advisor for food studies, New Mexico State University. (Bolivia, Chile, Ecuador, Guatemala, Paraguay, Uruguay)

Aliza H. Stark is senior tenured faculty at the Hebrew University of Jerusalem, the Robert H. Smith Faculty of Agriculture, Food and Environment, and the School of Nutritional Sciences. (Israel)

Sally Anna Steiner is a Norwegian American and a graduate student in folklore specializing in art traditions and material culture at the University of Wisconsin–Madison. (Norway)

Ceci Tchakounte Tadfor was born in Cameroon, where she learned to cook from her grandmother. She attended college in South Carolina but settled in Santa Fe, New Mexico, where she runs a catering service and cooking classes and is writing a cookbook on Cameroonian food. (Cameroon)

Pat Tanumihardja is a food and travel writer and author of *The Asian Grandmothers Cookbook: Home Cooking from Asian American Kitchens*, and she blogs at theasiangrandmotherscookbook.wordpress.com. Pat was born in Jakarta, Indonesia; grew up in Singapore; and now lives in the Washington, DC, metro area. (Indonesia, Singapore)

Sarah Tekle is an educator born in Uganda to parents from Eritrea and is currently pursuing a graduate degree in public administration from Bowling Green State University in Ohio. (Chad, Tanzania)

Jacqueline S. Thursby is a professor of English and folklore at Brigham Young University and has written a book and several articles about the Basque American people in the United States. (Basque)

Michael W. Twitty is a culinary historian and food writer from Washington, DC, and he is the webmaster of www.Afroculinaria.com, a site devoted to historic African American foodways and contemporary black food culture.

Claire Y. van den Broek is a doctoral candidate in comparative literature and German studies at Indiana University. She became enthusiastic about Bhutanese cuisine while sharing an apartment with a Bhutanese friend in London. (Bhutan)

Karin Vaneker is an independent food scholar and writer based in the Netherlands who has published extensively on ethnic food, including two cookbooks of immigrant cuisines in western Europe. (Dutch Caribbean, Gabon, Ghana, Madagascar, Melanesia, Netherlands, Rwanda, Suriname, Uganda)

Marisella Veiga, MFA, was born in Havana, Cuba, and was raised in the United States. She is a freelance writer and adjunct professor at Flagler College. (Cuba)

Howie Velie is a certified executive chef, certified hospitality educator, and associate dean of culinary specializations at the Culinary Institute of America, Hyde Park, New York. (Malaysia)

Ričardas Vidutis, PhD, is an ethnographer and historian and director of Recordations, LLC. (Lithuania)

Joseph Vuskovich was born and raised in New Orleans. He has translated his passion and enthusiasm for his native cuisine into Yats, a Midwest-based restaurant group. (Cajun)

Michaele Weissman is a journalist and author who writes about food. Her most recent book, *God in a Cup: The Obsessive Quest for Perfect Coffee*, was published in 2008. (Latvia)

Sarah Wyer is a graduate student in folklore and arts management at the University of Oregon. (Côte d'Ivoire)

Mulusew Yayehirad is a student at the University of Wisconsin School of Medicine and Public Health. (Ethiopia)

Almaz Yimam is a student at the University of Wisconsin–Madison. (Ethiopia)

Ayako Yoshimura is a PhD candidate in folklore at the University of Wisconsin–Madison. Since coming to the United States, she has continued to savor the rich food culture of her native Japan while exploring ethnic foods of other cultures. (Japan)

Russell Zanca, PhD, is a Central Asia specialist and professor of anthropology at Northeastern Illinois University. (Central Asia)

Willa Zhen is lecturing instructor of liberal arts at the Culinary Institute of America in Hyde Park, New York. She is Chinese American by heritage, and her research focuses on cuisine, culinary training, and identity among southern Chinese cooks. (China, Taiwan)

Acknowledgments

Many people have contributed to this encyclopedia. Individuals who worked behind the scenes include Melissa Hill, Holly Howard, and Hannah Santino, who did some of the tedious work that goes into producing such a publication. They have been tremendously helpful. Among authors of the individual entries, several stand out in contributing additional entries, editing others, or doing research that was helpful to other writers—Susan Eleuterio, Karin Vaneker, Betty Belanus, Charles Baker-Clark, and Nailam Elkhechen receive special gratitude.

Introduction to Ethnic American Food Today

The United States has been called a melting pot, a salad bowl, a buffet, even a potluck of cultures.[1] Each of those images carries different approaches to what it means to be American, but all of them suggest the significance of food in defining who we are. Food and foodways play a role in our daily lives. We structure our time around the production, procurement, preparation, and consumption of food, and we frequently schedule our socializing around it as well. Our cultural as well as personal histories shape the ways in which we eat, so that, frequently without realizing it, we express those histories through the ways we eat, defining what can or should be eaten as well as determining what tastes we find desirable. Our physical environments also shape our food resources, although they have less influence as the modern food system takes over more and more.

Memories become attached to food, creating emotional attachments to a particular food or food activity and giving us a sense of connection through food to particular places or people. A central feature of contemporary American foodways is the variety from which Americans can pick and choose for their own eating enjoyment.

This encyclopedia offers an overview and introductions to the diversity of food cultures existing within the United States. Some of them have become an integral part of mainstream foodways; others are not known apart from the individuals who maintain some aspect of them. The size of an ethnic group or its longevity in the United States does not always match with its impact on how and what Americans eat, but all ethnic food cultures add to the melting pot, tossed salad, smorgasbord, buffet of "American food." This encyclopedia cannot possibly cover all the subtleties of these ethnic food cultures, but it tries to at least give a sense of the diversity available. It is my hope that it will inspire more research, more studies, and more attention to an often overlooked but significantly meaningful aspect of our lives.

DEFINITIONS

Ethnic American Food Today raises numerous questions about what is ethnicity, what is American, and even what is food. The emphasis on contemporary food shows the complexity of identity in the "space-time compression"[2] of the modern, globalized world in which we are all connected through mass media and the Internet, yet frequently physically isolated and socially distanced. At what point do a group of immigrants become "ethnic"? How much can a dish be adapted before it no longer represents an ethnic heritage? And aren't all Americans—and American food—essentially immigrants and ethnic? (Except, of course, Native Americans, whose food is included here.) Food can actually help us answer some of these questions, or at least, recognize their complexity.

Ethnic food is food belonging to "groupings that were culturally distinguishable from a larger social system of which they formed some part."[3] This is significantly different from a group or individual being defined by race or nationality, and it suggests the complexity—and fluidity—of ethnic identity in a modern, multicultural society, such as the United States. Race and nationality obviously do play a role in defining Americans, but the ways in which those shape our food habits and our interactions with others around foodways is only part of being ethnic. Many Americans have a family history from a country (or multiple countries) that they do not draw upon as part of their food traditions or their concept of self. For example, an individual may have ancestors from both Ireland and Italy but identify only with the Irish heritage and participate in Irish American food traditions rather than Italian ones. Family dynamics, particularly in terms of gender roles, also play a significant role in ethnicity and foodways, complicating the ways in which they are related, since both are frequently passed down through family customs and relationships.

Ethnic identity, then, "is the intellectual and emotional sense that an individual has of his relationship to the behaviors, ideas, and values of an ethnic group," and that identity can be expressed through speech, artistic performances, everyday practices (such as food), and any social interaction or individual creation.[4] The fact that individuals can pick and choose when to emphasize their ethnicity means that ethnic identity is a "situational identity," one dependent on specific contexts and expressed differently according to each context.

This notion of ethnicity as a perception of self and group belonging separates ethnic groups from immigrant groups. Immigrants are new to a culture and are having to learn new ways of eating and thinking. Their foodways have not yet had time to adapt to or be adapted by the larger American culture.

Another important aspect of ethnicity is that it exists only within a larger social or cultural system. For example, an individual from Japan is ethnic when he or she comes to the United States. In their own country, they might be identified by religion, socioeconomic class, or family history, but all of those distinctions are merged into being simply Japanese American in the United States. Distinctions in food habits and traditions in their own country are similarly ignored, and all of the variations existing in Japan become one category of Japanese American food. Ethnicity tends to homogenize the diversity of a culture, and this happens to ethnic food as well.

Some of that is changing, however. Since the turn of the millennia, there has been a growing trend in awareness and knowledge of regional (or other) variations within the numerous food cultures that have been brought to the United States. Chinese American food, for example, was known primarily by southern Chinese (Cantonese) food culture from its introduction in the 1860s until the 1960s and 1970s, when American tastes began expanding and consumers developed interests in the regional variations found within China. Now, Chinese restaurants offer Szechuan, Peking, and other regional Chinese cuisines.

Another definition needed is that of food. Seemingly self-evident, food is actually a concept constructed by each culture—matter considered appropriate for ingestion. This means that every culture has different ideas of what can and should be eaten, as well as when, where, with whom, how, and why it is eaten. Food can be viewed as three types of construct. As a cultural one, it reflects the worldview, history, physical and natural environment, and values of the culture within which it develops. Cultural construct tends to shape notions of edibility, while taste—palatability—are shaped more by hierarchies of power, such as socioeconomic class and social status, making food a social construct. However, food is also a personal construct in that every individual has his or her own taste preferences, circumstances, interests, and values as well as memories attached to food. Thinking of food constructed at these three levels helps to understand how individuals fit into larger groups and histories.

Ethnicity brings together these diverse constructions of food and requires a certain amount of juggling and negotiating by individuals and groups as to what aspects of their food culture they want to (and are able to) continue. For example, foods with strong odors might cause offense to their new neighbors. Do they then leave out the ingredients or preparation methods that cause those odors, stop eating that food, or change neighbors? Also, some foods seem to be integral to a food culture but simply cannot be obtained in the United States. What happens when this type of food is something those ethnic groups feel is essential for their food culture to be fully maintained and to their sense of cultural identity? What does it mean for an individual from an ethnic background to personally dislike a food considered integral to that ethnicity? Is he or she no longer a representative of that group?

These are all complex questions that literature on ethnicity in general has attempted to address. The entries in this encyclopedia do not attempt to answer them, but they do shed light on how these processes affect the individuals and groups going through them.

Several terms are used in this encyclopedia when discussing food. *Foodways* refers to the total system of actions, practices, concepts, beliefs, and contexts surrounding eating. This can be further divided into *product* (ingredients, recipes, meals), *processes* (production, procurement, preservation, preparation, presentation, consumption, cleanup, and disposal), *performances* (symbolism, rituals), and *concepts-contexts*.[5] Foodways gives a framework for looking at all the different aspects of activities around food and helps us understand these as interconnected. For example, changes in physical environments between the home country and the United States will mean that only certain foods can be grown, shaping the recipes for traditional dishes. Similarly, the standard American nine-to-five workday means that individuals coming from the many Hispanic and Mediterranean food cultures that allow for a late, leisurely lunch with later work hours have to shift their cooking and eating patterns, perhaps changing the food itself.

Food culture is similar to *foodways* but tends to be larger and more encompassing of the historical forces shaping eating patterns. Culture, in general, can be seen as a resource from which individuals and groups make selections for their practices. *Food system* refers to the "food chain" of how food gets from the producer to the consumer and is also part of the larger food culture. The modern industrial food system prevalent in the United States includes a number of links in the chain—producer, processor, packager, and distributor—before food gets to the consumer and has allowed for Americans to have access to a wide variety of foods regardless of season and place, but it also has turned food into a commodity rather than a carrier of meaningfulness and memories. It has also enabled immigrants to frequently have access to more varieties food; made ethnic foodways more available to a wider number of Americans, not only members of ethnic groups; and has brought selected versions of ethnic food into the national palate.

The word *cuisine* is used here in a specific way to refer to a public and officially articulated set of ingredients, recipes, dishes, flavorings, preservation, preparation, cooking methods, and serving styles felt to represent the best of a group's food culture.[6] Cuisine is usually presented (and created) through sites such as restaurants, in cookbooks, and in public forums, such as websites and Internet chat rooms, but they also tend to be controlled by individuals or institutions who have some degree of power in defining culinary identity, such as governmental agencies, tourism boards, schools, churches, and so on. The concept of cuisine is useful in representing the role of power and status on the ways in which we eat, and it is a reminder that not all subgroups within an ethnic group have the same foodways. It also helps distinguish between the occasions in which groups are intentionally using their food to express identity and to create images associated with that identity from those in which people participate in their food practices out of comfort, nostalgia, taste, health, nutrition, hunger, or any of the myriad of other reasons for eating.

Fusion cuisines are those in which chefs, cooks, and/or eaters knowingly and purposefully combine elements from different cuisines, experimenting with novel tastes and experiences. Cuisines, like food cultures, constantly evolve, oftentimes calling into question the definition of that cuisine. Individuals also combine cuisines out of necessity, such as the lack of availability or a prohibitive expense of an ingredient, out of personal taste or health needs, and for other reasons, creating what are referred to as *hybrid* or *creolized cuisines*. The latter term is probably a more accurate one to use, since, as Lockwood and Lockwood point out, hybrids cannot reproduce. Creolized dishes and creolized cuisines continue to adapt and evolve.

A final definition is that of "American" food culture. Rather than debate the existence, the makeup, or the quality of such an idea, this encyclopedia adds to the knowledge of, as folklorist Don Yoder refers to it, one of the multiple layers making up that culture, contributing to as well as borrowing from the other components of localized, regional foodways and the mass-reproduced and nationally distributed foods that serve as a common binder familiar to almost all residents of the country.[7] Entries do refer to "mainstream" American food, by which is meant the publicly known and generally accepted ways of defining what constitutes the menus and styles of eating of people who think of themselves as American. This is a rather circular definition, but it acknowledges that we all have notions—stereotypes, perhaps—of what represents American rather than "ethnic" food. Whether or not that notion accurately reflects reality, we use it to evaluate the identity of the foods we encounter. Like culture itself, our notions can change, and what was "mainstream" fifty years ago is not mainstream today. Similarly, what is considered the normative national food culture can differ between regions of the country, as well as between other divisions, such as urban and rural, generational, socioeconomic class, and even between individuals.[8]

NAMES OF ETHNIC GROUPS AND ENCYCLOPEDIA ENTRIES

The encyclopedia is organized according to nationality, and each entry is identified primarily by the official name of the nation. The geographic region follows along with the adjective by which that cultural group is known in the United States. Following that information is a "see also" pointing readers to other ethnic groups that share similar food cultures and experiences in the United States. Some entries are very brief, but more extensive information is available in other entries.

In some cases, the names of nations have changed, but immigrants use other names to identify themselves (such as Burmese Americans from the nation of Myanmar). Also, some groups identify with a cultural identity rather than a national one, and they historically or currently have lived in several nations (such as the Hmong or Palestinians).

Nationality is oftentimes an identity imposed by political powers and needs, and it frequently does not accurately represent cultural, ethnic, or tribal identities. Groups have overpowered other groups since the beginning of human history, oftentimes due to territorial disputes and conflicts over access to resources. Empires throughout the world have expanded, imposing religion, language, worldviews, and culinary practices on conquered peoples and complicating cultural identities. European colonization established the notion of nation-states and divided up geographic regions according to the convenience and interests of the colonizers. Much of Africa, for example, was historically divided among these colonialist powers according to geographic features rather than native cultural ones.

Nationality as the designation for ethnicity is used here for several reasons. Immigrants are initially identified in the United States by their citizenship and by who issued their passports. This means that immigration and census statistics oftentimes reflect the country of origin, not the cultural identity of an individual, although the census does record that information. Also, nationality means a shared sociopolitical history that oftentimes provides a common motivation for immigration. Such things as wars, interactions between nations, and trade agreements are shaped partly by national boundaries, however imposed those are, and those all affect the daily lives of individuals living within those boundaries. Similarly, environmental events, such as droughts or floods, affect people, regardless of their cultural identity, forcing them to adapt their food traditions to those new conditions or even to leave their homes. Such external forces create a shared foundation for immigration and for constructing new lives in the United States.

Colonization histories also shape the food culture of each nation, introducing ingredients, recipes, cooking styles, and customs and attitudes surrounding foodways and eating. Nations that share a history of colonization therefore also frequently share some similarities in food culture. This means that when immigrants from those nations in the United States are looking for familiar ingredients, dishes, contexts, or ways of eating, they can oftentimes find them with each other, so that colonization history can cut across religious or language barriers to create a common culture in the United States. Groups historically colonized by a particular nation frequently find each other and settle in geographic proximity in the United States. The coastal areas of New England, for example, host a number of Portuguese-speaking ethnic groups, such as Cape Verdean, as well as communities of Portuguese Americans. Another example is the Arabic language offering a common foundation in the Detroit, Michigan, area for the many diverse ethnic groups from parts of western Asia and northern Africa.

Similarly, food cultures frequently cut across national boundaries and even religious and language ones. Jewish and Muslim immigrants from northern Africa ("the middle East") share many dietary restrictions, so that they tend to frequent stores in the United States recognizing those restrictions. Butcher shops, in particular, may offer both halal and kosher products. Such cross-exchanges create food communities in the United States that transcend ethnic identity. This is part of how ethnicity works. Groups find each other according to certain similarities and oftentimes "join forces," so to speak, in order to be large enough to sustain groceries and restaurants. Also, these larger groups can become a homogenized identity by which individuals are known, regardless of their distinctive and unique ethnicity, such as "Middle Eastern," "Asian," or "Latino."

The encyclopedia entries attempt to address these complexities by identifying similarities in history and food habits as well as actual communities that have developed in the United States.

LENGTH OF ENCYCLOPEDIA ENTRIES

The length of an entry ideally represents the extent of the impact on American food culture and the size of the population in the United States. Some smaller ethnic groups are simply mentioned, and readers are referred to other similar groups. The length of entries also reflects the quality and quantity of information available. Some ethnicities and some ethnic food cultures have been documented more than others, while some have received very little attention. Not surprisingly, given the historical roots of many Americans working in scholarly or professional fields attending to food, European ethnic food cultures have been studied the most, while ethnic groups from Africa have barely had the surface scratched. Also, some groups are more visible than others, and that visibility sometimes depends on the initiative of individuals or organizations from that group, their access to media, and their own interests. The backgrounds of contributors and their own familiarity with both food studies and the specific group also impact the length.

ORGANIZATION OF ENCYCLOPEDIA ENTRIES

The entries follow a set outline that was given to each contributor and were then followed to varying degrees according to the contributor's background and knowledge as well as the resources available for specific groups. Also, ethnic groups vary in their maintenance of traditional foodways and in the place of their cuisine in mainstream American culture, and the outlines of the entries reflect those variations.

Some entries begin with an *introductory statement* summarizing the significance of the impact on American food culture and the extent of the continuation of traditional food traditions by the ethnic group.

1. Background

This section answers questions such as: when did this group began immigrating to the United States; why and under what circumstances; and where are they distributed in the United States? Is there any information on whether or not they created and stayed in ethnic neighborhoods or dispersed, and any information on common occupations and general economic well-being?

The background of a nation is relevant to understanding its citizens as an ethnic group in another country because the geography and social-political-economic history shaped the food culture they come from. Colonization and international trade relations is particularly significant, since these introduced food—ingredients, recipes, preparation methods—as well as language, social institutions, cutural practices, religions, and value systems. From a pragmatic perspective, the languages imposed by colonization frequently became the national language for official business between tribal languages within that country. The language then brought to the United States with immigration has implications for how those individuals assimilate and integrate into American society and find a place within the workforce and economic system. For example, immigrants from former British colonies have generally learned English and therefore can immediately attend schools in the United States and join the workforce. Furthermore, colonization shapes immigration patterns, with immigrants frequently going to those countries that colonized them. Many Vietnamese, for example, went to France during the war, where they were versatile in the language and shared other cultural forms. Also, colonizers brought particular food cultures that then translated into particular culinary skills being learned. The French colonies, for example, developed bread and pastry baking; immigrants from those countries thus have a marketable skill for work in bakeries and restaurants in the United States.

2. Foodways

This section oftentimes gives a comparison of foodways activities, customs, and beliefs in the home country with those in the United States. The emphasis is on more traditional ethnic-American homes, but the typical amount of assimilation is also discussed as well as what other ethnicities a particular group might associate with through foodways.

The section is further broken into smaller sections.

Foodstuffs—Discussion of typical staples and the cast of that cuisine as changed in the United States. What are the basic, common foods in their home country? What has been changed, adapted, or dropped here in the United States? Are any of these foods borrowed from other ethnic groups in the United States? Are there any American foods that they have adopted in a particular way? Ingredients and foods are broken into the following categories:

Starches and carbohydrates (for example, rice, potato, cassava, bread, etc.)
Proteins (for example, fish, meats, beans, vegan substitutes, milk and dairy products)
Vegetables (root, leafy, other)
Fruits
Liquids/Drinks (milks, fruit drinks, alcoholic)
Flavorings/Spices (herbs, spices, sweeteners)

Procurement and Preparation—Are there any distinctive cooking techniques or equipment used? Are traditional gender roles continued or adapted in the United States? If so, how and why?

How are ingredients, foods, and cooking equipment obtained? Are there any specialty groceries or farms specific to this ethnic group? Do they shop at stores for other groups, and if so, which ones? Are they part of a larger, more generic category of store, such as "Asian" or "international"? Are certain items imported or borrowed from other ethnic groups?

Meals—How are meals usually put together; for example, a starch and a protein? What are the "signature dishes," those that in some way represent that ethnicity to the American public or that are considered essential by members of that group to a meal being traditional? Also, what dishes do people miss the most if they are recent immigrants, or feel carry the most meaningful memories? Have those dishes been adapted, and in what ways?

Recipes—These are usually of the dishes described in the above section, but they might also be holiday foods. The recipes are adapted by contributors to show how that dish would be made in the United States.

Meal System—This refers to the ways in which meals are organized over the span of a day or week (for example, in the United States, the typical breakfast, lunch, dinner, and snacks). What are the usual times of day, contexts, and typical menus for meals in the home country, and how has that been changed in the United States? Also, are there any special consumption styles (utensils, eating out of the same bowl, seating arrangements, etc.) that are unique to that culture and stand out as different from mainstream American food culture?

Holiday Feasts—What traditional holidays featuring food or rituals surrounding food are celebrated in the United States? Are these celebrated publicly at festivals, churches, or ethnic institutions; are some private family traditions? How have they been adapted in the United States? Has this ethnic group adapted mainstream American holiday traditions in any way?

3. Place in American Culture

This section focuses on how well known an ethnic cuisine or food is in mainstream American food culture and what kinds of associations are usually attached to it. Has any of the food become "Americanized" to the point that it is no longer thought of as ethnic or appears throughout the United States and across menus? How is this food presented in cookbooks? Has it assimilated completely; is it designated as ethnic and referred to as "foreign"?

Also, does this ethnic culture or its food appear in any American films, television shows, literature, or music? Are there any pieces from these expressive forms created outside the United States that have had a significant impact on American food culture? What seems to be the popular image and stereotypes of this cuisine? Do any dishes have specific associations?

4. Noted Restaurants and Chefs

This section looks at the overall patterns for eating outside the home within a particular ethnic group. What types of restaurants offer this ethnic food? Are there restaurants specializing in it; is it commonly included in panethnic establishments or with another ethnic food? Are any of the traditional ethnic ingredients or dishes being celebrated in fusion cooking today or being adapted somehow in the American restaurant scene?

Are any individuals with some degree of this ethnicity as part of their heritage recognized or celebrated as chefs? Have they had an impact on the American (or international) culinary world or food scene in any way? Have well-known or influential chefs from other ethnicities adopted this cuisine?

5. Further Reading

Each entry includes a list of books, articles, or Internet sources for more information about the ethnic foodways. Many entries included in this section the references used as resources for information.

CONTRIBUTORS AND RESOURCES

Contributors to the encyclopedia represent a variety of scholarly disciplines, professions, and personal backgrounds. Different disciplines take different approaches to food, to ethnicity, and to research on the two, as well as to writing about them. Those disciplines emphasizing ethnography, such as folklore and anthropology, tend to give insights into the ways in which individuals actually eat and think about food in specific contexts. History tends to emphasize written accounts of ethnic foodways in the past, while cultural studies emphasize the external political forces shaping those foodways. Sociology tends to seek the overall patterns and movements of social groups. Area studies, such as American studies, Asian studies, Latino studies, and others, tend to be interdisciplinary and draw from most of the humanities disciplines, while the emerging field of food studies combines the humanities and social sciences as well as theory and applied skills in order to study all aspects of food. Scholars did their research and wrote their entries from those disciplinary perspectives, with contributions reflecting those perspectives.

Contributors also come from a variety of professions, not only academia. Some work in K–12 educational settings, but also museums, state arts and humanities councils, the hospitality and tourism industry, food-related businesses, the culinary arts, and writing, specializing in travel, food, and culture. Collaborations were encouraged, particularly ones between a professional or scholar and a member of the ethnic community being studied. In this way, the entries attempt to include perspectives on a group's foodways from both the insider's and outsider's perspective. The latter tells us larger patterns along with the perceptions of that culture by other ethnicities and by the mainstream; the former gives a sense of what food traditions actually mean to that group of people.

Not all academic disciplines or professions pay attention to food—even those in industries surrounding the production and selling of it. In some cases, it just has not occurred to scholars that food can be a rich subject for study. Some tend to think of it as a domestic or women's domain and outside the realm of important subjects or activities, such as politics or economics. Also, some geographic regions and their food cultures have been studied more than others. European culinary traditions and their ethnic foodways in the United States have received a good deal of attention, while those of the continent of Africa have received very little. Explanations for such discrepancies go beyond the scope of this encyclopedia, but it is hoped that it will stimulate more research that will then make up for what is lacking.

SOURCES

Contributors were encouraged to use a variety of sources, academic and popular, as well as fieldwork and personal experience. Books, articles in scholarly journals, encyclopedias, even cookbooks provided data, interpretations, and insights into specific food cultures, the experiences of that group as immigrants to the United States, and the various networks, practices, and culinary traditions that have developed as they have become established as ethnic groups.

The Internet proved to be a rich resource for finding information as well as organizations, individuals, and other publications relevant to specific groups. The US census posts information online, and many ethnic associations and societies have websites, offering a glimpse into the activities of specific ethnic groups around food, as do most governments, national tourism boards, and businesses and entrepreneurs involved in travel and food industries. These sites, of course, are understood to be marketing tools that are presenting selected information in the best light possible, but they provide useful indicators of a group's perception of their place in the larger culture. Similarly, restaurant websites oftentimes give excellent descriptions of the cuisine, and some restaurant review sites were extremely useful in locating establishments for particular ethnic groups and for gaining a sense of the place of that cuisine in mainstream food culture. Food sites now abound also, many giving descriptions, photographs, and recipes for ethnic dishes. These are frequently "signature dishes" that stand out as either favorites within mainstream American food culture or are perhaps too exotic for that culture. Individuals and organizations from an ethnic group maintain many websites, however, and they represent their own perceptions of their food traditions and of their place within the larger culture. For that reason, personal blogs are oftentimes excellent sources for accounts of individual's experiences around food and ethnicity. This is especially important since this encyclopedia focuses on contemporary ethnic food—on what, when, where, how, and why Americans claiming an ethnic heritage or identity are eating today.

Much of that type of information comes only from talking to people within an ethnic group. Many contributors to the encyclopedia had previously done extensive fieldwork in specific ethnic communities, and so they were familiar with everyday foodways practices—and the variations within those communities across the nation. Some contributors drew upon their own experiences, either as a member of an ethnic group or as an interested observer and, oftentimes, eater, who informally visited restaurants, grocery stores, festivals, homes, and other venues where ethnic foods were being presented. These observations may reflect only a small part of the experiences of ethnic groups, so they are presented in a larger context, but they do help to point out patterns as well as to remind readers that individuals all approach food and ethnicity in their own ways.

CONCLUSION

The history of the world can be read through food. Even a single dish can give such a window. The ingredients used, the adaptations made to them or to cooking techniques, the contexts for consuming that dish, the customs surrounding who prepares it and serves it, and more—all are shaped by historical factors as well as contemporary conditions. Food similarly is a window into the complexities of ethnicity—the processes, contradictions, confusions of becoming and being ethnic—as well as the richness and complexities of specific cultural and national groups in the United States today. Ethnic food, though, is perhaps best thought of as a mirror. It shows the contrasts and differences between a group's foodways and that of the surrounding culture. In doing so, it also suggests the ways in which individuals and groups respond to and address those differences, not only constructing new food identities for themselves but also adding to—stretching and maybe even challenging—the broader spectrum of foods making up the mainstream food culture.

This encyclopedia introduces readers to ethnic food and foodways as both a window and a mirror. It points out those culinary practices that are significant to a particular ethnic group in defining, presenting, and maintaining their cultural identity and also those that make them stand out from—or help them blend in with—American society. It likewise offers a foundation for further research, both scholarly and personal, and for inspiration to explore some of the many ethnic food cultures existing in the United States. Ultimately, it is about much more than food; it is about the people who make and eat that food and the ways in which they create lives for themselves—work, identity, communities, meaningfulness—through the food traditions they have inherited and constructed.

NOTES

1. For an excellent discussion of the need to recognize the complexity of ethnicity in American culture and a history from the perspective of several ethnic groups, see Ronald Takaki, *A Different Mirror: A History of Multicultural America* (New York: Little, Brown, 1993).
2. The phrase comes from geographer David Harvey's *The Condition of Postmodernity: An Enquiry into the Origins of Cultural Change* (Cambridge, MA: Blackwell, 1990).
3. As defined by the Oxford Dictionary, quoted by Elliott Oring, "Ethnic Groups and Ethnic Folklore," in *Folk Groups and Folklore Genres: An Introduction* (Logan: University of Utah Press, 1986), 24.
4. Oring, "Ethnic Groups and Ethnic Folklore," 24.
5. See Lucy M. Long (*Food and Folklore Reader*, Berg Press, 2015) for a fuller description of the concept of foodways and how it developed in the field of folklore. For application of the concept, see Lucy Long, "Foodways: Using Food to Teach Folklore Theories and Methods," *Digest* 19 (1999): 32–36.
6. Warren Belasco gives other definitions of cuisine in his *Food: The Key Concepts* (Oxford: Berg, 2008). Anthropologist Sidney Mintz also explores the question of whether or not the United States has a cuisine in his article, "Eating American," in *Food in the USA: A Reader*, edited by Carole M. Counihan (New York: Routledge, 2002), 23–33.
7. See Don Yoder, "Folk Cookery," in *Folklore and Folklife, an Introduction*, edited by Richard M. Dorson (Chicago: University of Chicago Press, 1972), 325–50. For more on regional food cultures in the United States and the ways in which they interact with ethnic cuisines, see Lucy M. Long, *Regional American Food Culture* (Santa Barbara, CA: Greenwood, 2009). For a summary of approaches and opinions on the idea of an American cuisine, see Lucy M. Long, "Foodways," in *Encyclopedia of American Cultural and Intellectual History*, edited by Mary Kupiec Clayton and Peter W. Williams (Oxford: Oxford University Press, 2013), and Long, "Existence of American Cuisine," in *Encyclopedia of Food and Agricultural Ethics*, edited by Paul B. Thompson and David M. Kaplan (New York: Springer Reference, 2014).
8. For more on perspectives on understanding and defining American food, see Counihan, *Food in the USA*; Harvey Levenstein, *Paradox of Plenty: A Social History of Eating in Modern America* (New York: Oxford University Press, 1993); Richard Pillsbury, *No Foreign Food: The American Diet in Time and Place* (Boulder, CO: Westview Press, 1998); and Jennifer Jensen Wallach, *How America Eats: A Social History of U.S. Food and Culture* (Lanham, MD: Rowman & Littlefield, 2013).

FURTHER READING

Alperson, Myra. *Nosh New York: The Food Lover's Guide to New York City's Most Delicious Neighborhoods*. New York: St. Martin's Griffin, 2003.

Anderson, Lynne Christy. *Breaking Bread: Recipes and Stories from Immigrant Kitchens*. Berkeley: University of California Press, 2010.

Belasco, Warren J. "Ethnic Fast Foods: The Corporate Melting Pot." *Food and Foodways* 2 (1987): 1–30.

Belasco, Warren J., and Philip Scranton. *Food Nations: Selling Taste in Consumer Societies*. New York: Routledge, 2002.

Berzok, Linda Murray. *American Indian Food*. Westport, CT: Greenwood, 2005.

Bonacich, Edna, and John Modell. *The Economic Basis of Ethnic Solidarity: Small Business in the Japanese American Community*. Berkeley: University of California Press, 1980.

Bower, Anne L. "Community Cookbooks." *The Oxford Encyclopedia of Food and Drink in America*, volume 1, 312–15. Edited by Andrew F. Smith. Oxford: Oxford University Press, 2004.

Brown, Linda Keller, and Kay Mussell, eds. *Ethnic and Regional Foodways in the United States: The Performance of Group Identity*. Knoxville: University of Tennessee Press, 1984.

Cinotto, Simone. *The Italian American Table: Food, Family, and Community in New York City*. Urbana: University of Illinois Press, 2013.

Coe, Andrew. *Chop Suey: A Cultural History of Chinese Food in the United States*. New York: Oxford University Press, 2009.

Collingham, Lizzie. *Curry: A Tale of Cooks and Conquerors*. Oxford: Oxford University Press, 2006.

Counihan, Carole, and Penny Van Esterik, eds. *Food and Culture: A Reader*. New York: Routledge, 1997.

Denker, Joel. *The World on a Plate: A Tour through the History of America's Ethnic Cuisines*. Boulder, CO: Westview, 2003.

Diner, Hasia R. *Hungering for America: Italian, Irish, and Jewish Foodways in the Age of Migration*. Cambridge, MA: Harvard University Press, 2001.

Gabaccia, Donna R. *We Are What We Eat: Ethnic Food and the Making of Americans*. Cambridge, MA: Harvard University Press, 1998.

Goode, Judith, Karen Curtis, and Janet Theophano. "Meal Formats, Meal Cycles, and Menu Negotiation in the Maintenance of an Italian-American Community." *Food in the Social Order: Studies of Food and Festivities*. Ed. Mary Douglas. New York: Russell Sage Foundation, 1984.

Haber, Barbara. *From Hardtack to Home Fries: An Uncommon History of American Cooks and Meals*. New York: Free Press, 2002.

Hafner, Dorinda. *United Tastes of America*. New York: Ballantine, 1998.

Hauck-Lawson, Annie, and Jonathan Deutsch. *Gastropolis Food and New York City*. New York: Columbia University Press, 2009.

Hyde, Alan. "Offensive Bodies." *The Smell Culture Reader*, first edition, 53–58. By Jim Drobnick. Oxford: Berg, 2006.

Inness, Sherrie A., ed. *Kitchen Culture in America: Popular Representations of Food, Gender, and Race*. Philadelphia: University of Pennsylvania Press, 2001.

Inness, Sherrie A., ed. *Pilaf, Pozole, and Pad Thai: American Women and Ethnic Food*. Amherst: University of Massachusetts Press, 2001.

Inness, Sherrie A. *Secret Ingredients: Race, Gender, and Class at the Dinner Table*. New York: Palgrave Macmillan, 2006.

Jung, John. *Sweet and Sour: Life in Chinese Family Restaurants*. Cypress, CA: Yin and Yang, 2010.

Kalcik, Susan. "Ethnic Foodways in America: Symbol and Performance of Identity." *Ethnic and Regional Foodways in the United States: The Performance of Group Identity*. Edited by Linda Keller, 37–65. Brown and Kay Mussell. Knoxville: University of Tennessee Press, 1984.

Kaplan, Anne R., Marjorie A. Hoover, and Willard B. Moore. *The Minnesota Ethnic Food Book*. St. Paul: Minnesota Historical Society, 1986.

Kirlin, Katherine S., and Thomas M. Kirlin. *Smithsonian Folklife Cookbook*. Washington: Smithsonian Institution, 1991.

Kirshenblatt-Gimblett, Barbara. "Recipes for Creating Community: The Jewish Charity Cookbook in America." *Jewish Folklore and Ethnology* 9 (1987): 8–20.

Ku, Robert Ji-Song, Martin F. Manalansan IV, and Anita Mannur. "An Alimentary Introduction." *Eating Asian America: A Food Studies Reader*, 1–12. Edited by Robert Ji-Song et al. New York: New York University Press, 2013.

Ku, Robert Ji-Song, Martin F. Manalansan IV, and Anita Mannur, eds. *Eating Asian America: A Food Studies Reader*. New York: New York University Press, 2013.

Levenstein, Harvey A. *Paradox of Plenty: A Social History of Eating in Modern America*. New York: Oxford University Press, 1993.

Levenstein, Harvey. "The American Response of Italian Food, 1880–1930." *Food in the USA: A*

Lockwood, William G. "United States: Ethnic Cuisines." *Encyclopedia of Food and Culture*, volume 3, 442–46. Edited by Solomon H. Katz and William Woys Weaver. New York: Charles Scribner's Sons, 2003.

Lockwood, Yvonne H., and William G. Lockwood. "Pasties in Michigan: Foodways, Interethnic Relations, and Cultural Dynamics." *Creative Ethnicity: Symbols and Strategies of Contemporary Ethnic Life*. Edited by Stephen Stern and John Allan Cicala. Logan: Utah State University Press, 1991.

Long, Lucy M. *Culinary Tourism*. Lexington: University of Kentucky Press, 2004.

Long, Lucy M. *Food and Folklore Reader*. New York: Berg Press, 2015.

Magliocca, Sabina. "Playing with Food: The Negotiation of Identity in the Ethnic Display Event by Italian Americans in Clinton, Indiana." *Studies in Italian American Folklore*. Edited by Luisa Del Giudice. Logan: Utah State University Press, 1993.

Manalansan, Martin F. "Immigrant Lives and the Politics of Olfaction in the Global City." *The Smell Culture Reader*, first edition, 41–52. By Jim Drobnick. Oxford: Berg, 2006.

McCann, James. *Stirring the Pot: A History of African Cuisine*. Athens: Ohio University Press, 2009.

Nabhan, Gary Paul. *Arab/American: Landscape, Culture, and Cuisine in Two Great Deserts*. Tucson: University of Arizona Press, 2008.

Oring, Elliott. "Ethnic Groups and Ethnic Folklore." *Folk Groups and Folklore Genres: An Introduction*, 23–44. Edited by Elliott Oring. Logan: Utah State University Press, 1986.

Pilcher, Jeffrey M. "Industrial Tortillas and Folkloric Pepsi: The Nutritional Consequences of Hybrid Cuisines in Mexico." *Food Nations: Selling Taste in Consumer Societies*, 222–39. By Warren James Belasco and Philip Scranton. New York: Routledge, 2002.

Pillsbury, Richard. *No Foreign Food: The American Diet in Time and Place*. Boulder, CO: Westview, 1998.

Ray, Krishnendu. *The Migrant's Table: Meals and Memories in Bengali-American Households*. Philadelphia: Temple University Press, 2004.

Richards-Greaves, Gillian. "Cookup Rice: Guyana's Culinary 'Dougla' and Ethnic Identity Negotiations." *Rice and Beans: A Unique Dish in a Hundred Places*, 192–225. Edited by Richard Wilk and Livia Barbosa. Oxford: Berg, 2012.

Royce, Anya Peterson. *Ethnic Identity: Strategies of Diversity*. Bloomington: Indiana University Press, 1982.

Smith, Jeff. *The Frugal Gourmet on Our Immigrant Ancestors: Recipes You Should Have Gotten from Your Grandmother*. New York: William Morrow, 1990.

Spivey, Diane M. *The Peppers, Cracklings, and Knots of Wool Cookbook: The Global Migration of African Cuisine*. New York: State University of New York Press, 1999.

Stern, Stephen, and John Allan Cicala, eds. *Creative Ethnicity Symbols and Strategies of Contemporary Ethnic Life*. Logan: Utah State University Press, 1991.

Sutton, David E. *Remembrance of Repasts: An Anthropology of Food and Memory*. Oxford; New York: Berg, 2001.

Tanumihardja, Patricia. *The Asian Grandmothers Cookbook: Home Cooking from Asian American Kitchens*. Seattle, WA: Sasquatch, 2009.

Wells, Troth. *The Food Book: Recipes from Africa, Asia and Latin America for Western Kitchens with Country Information and Food Facts*. Oxford: New Internationalist, 1995.

Wilk, Richard R. *Home Cooking in the Global Village: Caribbean Food from Buccaneers to Ecotourists*. Oxford: Berg, 2006.

Wilson, David Scofield, and Angus K. Gillespie, eds. *Rooted in America: Foodlore of Popular Fruits and Vegetables*. Knoxville: University of Tennessee Press, 1999.

Wu, David Y. H., and Sidney C. H. Cheung. *The Globalization of Chinese Food*. Honolulu: University of Hawaii Press, 2002.

Zanger, Mark H. *The American Ethnic Cookbook for Students*. Phoenix, AZ: Oryx, 2001.

Zanger, Mark H. "Ethnic Foods." *The Oxford Encyclopedia of Food and Drink in America*, volume 1, 429–46. Edited by Andrew F. Smith. Oxford: Oxford University Press, 2004.

Ziegelman, Jane. *97 Orchard: An Edible History of Five Immigrant Families in One New York Tenement*. New York: Smithsonian/HarperCollins, 2010.

Zubaida, Sami, and Richard Tapper, eds. *Culinary Cultures of the Middle East*. London: I. B. Tauris, 1994.

ENCYCLOPEDIAS AND REFERENCE WORKS

Albala, Ken, ed. *Food Cultures of the World Encyclopedia, Volume 2: Americas*. Westport, CT: Greenwood Press, 2008.

Handlin, Oscar, Ann Orlov, and Stephan Thernstrom, eds. *Harvard Encyclopedia of American Ethnic Groups*. Cambridge: The Belknap Press of Harvard University, 1980.

Katz, Solomon H., and William Woys Weaver, eds. *Encyclopedia of Food and Culture*. 3 vols. New York: Charles Scribner's Sons, 2003.

Kiple, Kenneth F., and Kriemhild Coneè Ornelas, eds. *The Cambridge World History of Food*. 2 vols. Cambridge: Cambridge University Press, 2000.

Lee, Jonathan H. X., and Kathleen M. Nadeau, eds. *Encyclopedia of Asian American Folklore and Folklife*. Santa Barbara, CA: ABC-CLIO, 2011.

Newman, Jacqueline M. *Melting Pot: An Annotated Biography and Guide to Food and Nutrition Information for Ethnic Groups in America*, second edition. New York: Garland, 1993.

Smith, Andrew F., ed. *The Oxford Encyclopedia of Food and Drink in America*. 2 vols. Oxford: Oxford University Press, 2004.

Thernstrom, Stephan, Ann Orlov, and Oscar Handlin. *Harvard Encyclopedia of American Ethnic Groups*. Cambridge, MA: Belknap of Harvard University, 1980.

Vecoli, Rudolph J., Judy Galens, Anna J. Sheets, and Robyn V. Young, eds. *Gale Encyclopedia of Multicultural America*. Detroit, MI: Gale Research, 1995.

Wilson, Charles Reagan, James G. Thomas, and Ann J. Abadie, eds. *The New Encyclopedia of Southern Culture*. Chapel Hill: University of North Carolina Press, 2006.

WEBSITES

http://www.foodbycountry.com.

http://www.inmamaskitchen.com/index.html. Recipes from mothers around the nation.

http://www.everyculture.com.

http://www.census.gov. US Census data.

http://www.census.gov/acs/www/. American Community Surveys based on the US Census.

http://www.celtnet.org.uk/recipes. Foods from around the world.

A

AFGHANISTAN
(Southern Asia) Afghan American
See also: Pakistan.

Background
The largest migration in the history of Afghanistan took place after the 1979 invasion by the neighboring Soviet Union. Realizing their homeland and Islamic culture was being threatened by the communist Soviet Union, the Afghan-supported *mujahedeen*, or freedom fighters, began a war of independence that lasted for eight years and resulted in the death of over two million Afghans. The increasingly bloody, violent fighting prompted more than six million Afghans to leave the country. The vast majority settled first in neighboring Pakistan, taking odd jobs in an effort to support themselves. Some recognized opportunities in the Pakistani food industry and opened Afghan restaurants and bakeries.

From Pakistan, thousands of Afghans obtained refugee visas and scattered throughout Europe and America. Many settled in New York, Washington, DC, and San Francisco—which is home to over 50 percent of all Afghan refugees living in the United States. As in Pakistan, refugees once again found themselves struggling to find their roles in a new environment. This influx of Afghans resulted in a new crop of restaurants, markets, and bakeries throughout the country. In an attempt to appeal to the large Indian and Pakistani populations in the United States, the Afghan cuisine served in these restaurants evolved to include flavors and seasonings popular in Indian and Pakistani foods. As a result, the food at many Afghan restaurants has changed somewhat from traditional Afghan cooking.

Food Preparation and Staples
Traditionally, Afghanistan is a patriarchal society, and the women of the household do the majority of the cooking. Dinnertime is an especially important meal in Afghanistan. Great care is taken to prepare delicious, yet elaborate, meals for the men returning home from work. While women cook at home, it is typically only men who cook in public restaurants and food stands. These gender roles have relaxed some in America, and it is not uncommon for men in Afghan American households to help prepare meals.

Rice
Traditionally, the primary staples of food in Afghanistan are those that are inexpensive, readily available, and filling. Despite the fact that Afghans living in America have an exhaustive variety of produce and ingredients at their disposal, many continue to rely on the same staples as those used in their homeland. Rice is one such example, and it is prepared in an extensive multitude of ways. It is often served as a *chalow*, which is white basmati rice; or as a *palow*, which contains meat and stock. A fixture at most mealtimes, rice is also a staple at special gatherings, such as weddings. On such occasions, several different varieties can be expected. *Kabuli palow*, which is a rice dish traditionally made with lamb and studded with raisins and generous slivers of almonds and carrots, is most popular for special occasions. This dish reflects positively on the preparer

because it contains multiple ingredients—thus indicating the preparer's wealth in acquiring the ingredients—and requires extensive preparation as the rice, meat, and vegetables must all be seasoned and cooked separately, before finally being combined to steam in the oven.

Bread

Bread, or *naan*, is another important staple in the Afghan diet. Typically eaten at every mealtime in Afghanistan, it is used as a side for vegetable *kormas*, stews, meat dishes, and rice, or can be eaten on its own. As is custom in Afghanistan, some Afghans typically forgo silverware in favor of using their hands to eat. Consequently, bread is an important accoutrement for scooping up food.

Most families prepare their own simple dough using yeast, warm water, flour, and salt. Oil is added to this dough for *naan roghani*, or bread with oil, which is served for breakfast with butter and preserves and is accompanied by cups of sweet, black tea. In Afghanistan, those without *tandoor*, or clay ovens used for baking and cooking, can have their dough baked in the *tandoor* of local bakeries for a small fee.

For most Afghan Americans living in the United States, bread remains an important staple at mealtimes. It is still served as a side to traditional dishes, such as *bomiyah*, which is a *korma* made with okra. Many Afghan restaurants in America prepare bread the traditional way, using *tandoor* ovens to achieve the same chewy, airy consistency of flatbread that one would find back home. Furthermore, many Afghan markets bake their own bread so that Afghan Americans can continue to obtain traditional Afghan bread.

Kormas

Served alongside rice and bread, flavorful *kormas* are another staple of Afghan meals. These are traditional Afghan curries consisting of braised meats or vegetables, like *korma gosht* (lamb *korma*) or *korma kachaloo* (potato *korma*). To create the base for *kormas*, onions and tomatoes are seasoned with salt, pepper, and turmeric, and fried to create a sauce. *Kormas* are often served with *mast*, or a homemade yogurt sauce accented with lemon, salt, and crushed mint leaves; or alongside with bowls of Afghan *salata*, which is a salad of diced tomatoes, cucumbers, and onions, drizzled with lemon juice and mixed with fresh mint leaves.

Tea

Tea is yet another favorite staple and serves as an important ritual in Afghan households across the world. This custom also serves a significant social function as it provides the opportunity for friends and loved ones to visit one another and socialize during teatime. Served at all hours of the day, the preparation of tea involves steeping loose green or black tea leaves with cardamom seeds. It is then served with raisins and nuts, or traditional Afghan sweets such as butter cookies and *sheerpira*, which is similar to fudge. Though far from their homeland, most Afghans living in America continue to follow the conventional methods of preparing and serving tea.

Holidays

Nowruz, the Persian New Year, and the Islamic religious holiday, *Eid al-Fitr*, are just two occasions on which holiday feasts can be expected in Afghan homes all over the world. In Afghanistan, these two holidays are typically celebrated with visits to loved ones' homes for tea and sweets throughout the day, or for dinner in the evening. *Nowruz*, which heralds the start of spring, also entails festivals, picnics, and concerts in parks. While a plentitude of Afghan specialties—including a variety of meats, *palows*, and *kormas*—are prepared for these feasts, these holidays also call for some specific foods as well. These traditions are still upheld among Afghan Americans, who continue to make these dishes.

Nowruz

One popular food item shared on *Nowruz* is *Aft Meywa*, or Seven Fruits, which is believed to bring good luck and prosperity in the New Year. Similar to the idea of fruit salad, the dish consists of a variety of raisins, dried apricots, walnuts, almonds, pistachios, and oleaster fruit in a naturally sweetened syrup. Several days before *Nowruz*, the nuts and fruits are separated and soaked in warm water in order to soften the nuts and to allow the fruits' natural sugars to become syrupy. In time for the holiday, the nuts are first shelled, mixed with the fruit, and then served to visiting friends and family members.

In Afghanistan, women traditionally hold festive gatherings to create another *Nowruz* favorite, *samanak*, which is a sweet, wheat-based pudding. To prepare this dish, wheat germ is arranged on a damp towel and watered every other day for several days. This allows the wheat to sprout. Once the sprouts grow to about two inches, the wheat grains are ground; mixed with flour, water, and walnuts; and placed in an oversized pot several feet high. The pot is positioned over an outdoor fire and stirred for about eight to ten hours until the mixture reaches the right consistency.

Due to the time-intensive process of making samanak, female family members and friends join together to sing celebratory songs, dance, and gossip while taking turns to stir the pot. Once the pudding is ready, the gathered women make wishes before enjoying the final product. While this process is less social in America and samanak parties are rare, this dish is still an especially popular one and enjoyed by many Afghan Americans, especially on *Nowruz*.

Eid al-Fitr

Marking the end of fasting during Ramadan, an abundant spread of food is especially important on *Eid al-Fitr*, which is celebrated for three days. On these three days, a plethora of rice and meat dishes, like *kabuli palow*, are prepared and served. Another favorite is *mantu*. *Mantu* are dumplings filled with onions and ground beef and drizzled with *mast*, or yogurt sauce. Preparing these dumplings is a time-consuming affair. First, the onions and ground beef must be cooked, then sealed in wonton wrappers and shaped into tiny parcels, which are then steamed. In Afghanistan, and oftentimes in America, women gather together in groups to prepare the *mantu*, sharing the labor and using this time to gossip and socialize with one another.

There is also a special emphasis on sweets during *Eid*. Desserts such as Afghan tea biscuits; *firni*, or rice pudding; and *jalebi*, a syrupy, crunchy cake equivalent to funnel cake, are prepared well in advance. As families gather together to celebrate and pass out gifts and money to the younger members of the family, these desserts are served with steaming cups of tea.

Traditional Afghan *Roht*

Roht is a thick and hearty cake that is often served with tea. This family recipe was brought to the United States in 1981 and evokes memories of the weekly Sunday ritual of the grandmother making these by hand while children played alongside her in the kitchen.

3 cups all-purpose flour
1 cup vegetable oil
2 eggs
3 tablespoons full-fat plain yogurt
1 cup sugar
½ cup of warm water
8-ounce packet yeast
1 teaspoon cardamom

Note: This recipe can be made using a food processor, but it is traditionally mixed by hand.

Thoroughly mix the flour, sugar, yeast, and cardamom together. Gradually add yogurt, eggs, oil, and warm water to the mixture. Knead for about 15 to 20 minutes until a smooth dough forms. Shape the dough into a ball and place in a large bowl. Cover with a dishtowel and let rest for two hours until the dough has adequately risen. Splitting the dough into two parts, roll out each section of the dough into an oblong shape with a thickness of about one-half inch.

Bake at 400 degrees for about 20 to 25 minutes until the *roht* achieves a golden color. Cool before cutting. Can be sprinkled with powdered sugar and served with tea.

Place in American Culture: Ethnic Markets

While the diversity of the United States has encouraged many Afghan Americans to veer out of their comfort zones and to explore foods from other cultures, the accessibility of ethnic food stores in the country has also helped them maintain close ties with their roots. Modeled after markets in Afghanistan, the primary focus of these stores is to supply customers with *halal* meats, which are prepared following strict Islamic regulations. These shops also provide an extensive range of difficult-to-find ingredients, such as cardamom seeds and ground turmeric, as well as fresh Afghan bread, baked goods, specialty cheeses, loose teas, and different varieties of rice.

Socializing is another important aspect of ethnic food stores. These stores help foster connections between members of the Afghan community. Following traditional behavior patterns, fellow Afghans are greeted like family with hearty handshakes, kisses on the cheek, and hugs. Shopping trips are used to make plans with fellow shoppers, to catch up with one another, or simply to share recipes and tips. This socializing further reinforces the ties between Afghan Americans and helps strengthen their sense of identity and community while living away from Afghanistan.

American Consumers and Noteworthy Establishments

Given the US appreciation for diversity, it is no secret that many Americans enjoy exploring foods from different cultures. As there are no famous Afghan chefs in America, and because Afghan food is not represented on American cooking shows, the majority of Afghan restaurants in the country rely on word-of-mouth marketing to encourage American guests to try their food. The breadth of Afghan restaurants throughout the country invites many to experience a culture that is so often misrepresented in the media. Some noteworthy restaurants include the De Afghanan Kabob House in Fremont, California's "Little Kabul" section; Chopahn Restaurant in San Diego, California; and the Afghan Restaurant in Alexandria, Virginia.

Further Reading

Afghan Culture Unveiled. http://www.afghancooking.net/.

Eigo, Tim. "Afghan Americans." *Countries and Their Cultures*, accessed June 3, 2014, http://www.everyculture.com/multi/A-Br/Afghan-Americans.html.

Saberi, Helen. *Noshe Djan: Afghan Food & Cookery*. Devon, England: Prospect Books, 1986.

Kitchen Recipes. http://www.afghankitchenrecipes.com/.

Narwan Aimen

AFRICAN AMERICAN

(North America) Black American Food, African American Food

Background

African Americans are the descendants of (mostly) enslaved West, Central, and Southeast Africans brought to what is now the United States between the sixteenth and nineteenth centuries. The genetic and cultural base of African American history and culture is centered on interactions between Africans, Western Europeans, and Native Americans along the eastern seaboard, and it is most pronounced in the colonial and antebellum South. The definition of who is African American includes those individuals grandfathered into this ethnic group by historical or family connection and by choice, and it often excludes self-identified African immigrants, Afro-Latinos, and West Indian or Afro-Caribbean, who are often misidentified as African Americans based on phenotype. To be certain, the interaction between these different parts of the African Diaspora in the United States has informed, encouraged, and enriched African American foodways and how African Americans view their own foodways in a global context. Contemporary African American foodways have deep connections with southern, Creole, and Cajun cooking, but it has a reach beyond regions given the migratory patterns of African Americans in the late nineteenth through mid-twentieth centuries.

Historically, African American cuisine was largely centered on West and Central African foodways—a large swath of the African coastline with a remarkably similar culinary pattern based on starches, leafy greens, fresh fruit, soups, stews, and roasted or fried foods. Yams, millet, bananas, plantains, *fonio*, sorghum, rice, and later cassava, corn, and sweet potatoes formed the starchy base with which the other foods enumerated were enjoyed as a relish. At the time of the trans-Atlantic slave trade, West and Central Africa were the crossroads of foods from those indigenous to the continent, to Europe, the Middle East, Southeast Asia, and the Americas. Unlike other enslaved Africans brought to locations in the New World, enslaved Africans in what would become the United States lived in fairly temperate rather than tropical locales, further shaping the development of the cuisine. Enslavement by largely Northern European slaveholders—predominately from the British Isles with a minority held in bondage by others from Western Europe—further shaped the taste and tenor of African American foodways.

Enslaved Africans preserved and passed on a remarkable number of ingredients and recipes. From the cornucopia of global gardens and fields of African towns and villages came seeds and tastes that came to mark a distinct African American diet. Indigenous species such as guinea fowl, sesame (benne), okra, cowpeas or black-eyed peas, sorghum, watermelon, muskmelon, millet, Bamana groundnut, and varieties of yam and naturalized taro crossed the Atlantic while African cultigens of hot peppers, tomatoes, peanuts, and sweet potatoes became naturalized in the South via the slave trade. The American plantation absorbed these foods into a diet largely based on a fusion of foods central to the Eastern and Southern Native American diet—such as corn, beans, and squash, with wild plants, fruits, and game—and Northern European foodways—with their cold and temperate fruits; brassicas such as cabbage, kale, and colewort or collards; root vegetables; and reliance upon wheat, pork, and beef.

On southern plantations and small eastern farms and urban locales, enslaved African Americans were actively engaged in preparing their own meals and well as those of their captors. Although the moniker "soul food" has come to signify this tradition, this proto-Southern food was far from a unified tradition, and African American food traditions differed greatly from region to region—namely, the northeastern seaboard and mid-Atlantic, the Chesapeake and Tidewater, the Lowcountry, Southern Uplands and Frontier, the Gulf Coast, and Lower Mississippi Valley. After slavery, these food traditions spread as African Americans moved from the South in search of opportunity and greater social freedom and political mobility. The Great Migration—a period of a series of mass exodus from the Old South—roughly from 1910 to 1945 saw the move of African American foodways to Harlem and Boston in the east, to Oakland and Los Angeles in the west, and to Chicago, Detroit, Cleveland, and other urban centers far removed from the traditional geographic centers. This situation proved definitive in shaping the culture of African American foodways.

Ethnic American Food Today

Foodways

Contemporary African American food culture is largely based on the southern soul tradition, but it is highly absorbent of other culinary traditions. That said, many other traditions often mix in the contemporary African American kitchen, significantly diversifying the larder. Corn is still king of starches—and it makes its appearance in the form of cornbread, grits (eaten by themselves or with gravy, shrimp, or cutlets such as grillades), cornmeal for frying and coating, and other preparations such as succotash and Lousiana *maque choux*, fried or cream corn, corn on the cob, and dishes where corn is a component, such as in salads like Texas caviar or okra, and corn and tomatoes cooked together. Wheaten bread follows a close second. Early adopted along the African coast, West Indies, and in the plantation days, wheaten bread often means hot biscuits or hot rolls lavished with butter or jams and preserves—especially those made from fruits endemic to southern farms—grapes, blackberries, peaches, and apples. Rice is another key staple, especially important in cuisines based out of the Lowcountry or Lower Mississippi Valley.

Favored produce includes tomatoes; fresh fruit; hot peppers; bell peppers; sweet potatoes; melons; peaches; apples; berries; collard, turnip, or mustard greens; cabbage; kale; green beans; okra; field peas; squash; onions (especially green onions); potatoes; and peanuts—which in the South are prepared "green" by boiling, frying, or roasting. Pork, despite several black religious movements bound and determined to replace it, remains a key meat after chicken—the African American protein par excellence. Beef, lamb, goat, and seafood such as shrimp, crab, oysters, and crawfish have their place, largely determined by regional availability and locale. Dairy is limited in the African American foodways tradition predominately because of the high rate of lactose intolerance imported from West Africa during the slave trade. Spices and seasonings are very important—and hot sauces, barbecue sauce, soy sauce, vinegar, molasses, and brown sugar, as well as spice mixtures such as seasoning salt, seafood boiling spice, and Creole seasoning, are usually ubiquitous in African American households. Smoked meat and fish still figure prominently in how pots of vegetables and sauces are flavored.

In many African American households there is often a jar or coffee can filled with cooking grease left over from frying bacon, fish, or chicken sitting on the kitchen counter. This grease, especially bacon grease, is often reused or is an additive to other dishes, and it sometimes coats cast iron pans used for baking. Cornstarch, liquid hickory smoke, corn syrup, vanilla, lemons, cinnamon, nutmeg, cayenne pepper, sage, and black pepper are important flavor additives to the diet. Gravies, glazes, homemade sauces, and other preparations depend on the skillful hand of the cook in determining what proportions of those flavors need to be used when finishing off a dish.

With the increased presence of other members of the African Diaspora and mixing with other ethnic groups over the past century, African Americans have joined the rest of the United States in happily incorporating foods and flavors from across the globe. Jerk rubs and spices from Jamaica and the West Indies are delighted in, not to mention dishes based on Italian, Chinese, and Mexican cooking. Spaghetti, stir fries, or noodle dishes such as *yaka* or *ya mein*, and burritos or tacos are as much part of the African American pantry as any other culture—from Indian-style curries to foods and dishes from Brazil, Ethiopia, or West Africa, such as *joloff rice* and groundnut stew.

In traditional West and Central African cultures, women do almost all of the domestic cookery. In the acclimation to Northern European culture, similar patterns relegating women to home cooking dictated who did the cooking. However, the number of trained male cooks in plantation days interrupted this pattern, and men became cooks, bakers, and especially barbecue masters of renown. Food is not heavily gendered in traditional African American cooking, but it is still largely a female badge of identity, honor, and familial pride if a daughter grows up to be a good cook and passes on the family recipes.

African American foodways have retained an emphasis on one-pot or composite meals where multiple ingredients combine to make a complex, flavorful whole. Rice and bean dishes, leafy greens eaten with starches or proteins, and soups and stews such as jambalaya, okra soup, or gumbo apply here. Often they begin with a sauté, followed by a gravy starter like a *roux* or a sauce that helps bind everything together. Another classic model is the "meat and three," where a protein like a slow-cooked or roasted or fried protein such as pork, chicken, or beef is accompanied by a bread and three side dishes, often cooked in one large pot with a piece of smoked meat or two. Special occasions, discussed below, often require special preparations such as the making of a large pot of shellfish, corn, potatoes, and sausage for a seafood boil, or ribs or shoulders for a barbecue, or large pots of Brunswick stew, jambalaya, *perlou*, or gumbo.

Holiday Feasts

The African American culture has several key points of culinary celebration—the spring and winter civil religious holidays—Easter, Thanksgiving, Christmas, and New Year's; the summer holidays—July 4th and Labor Day; and various indigenous cultural commemorations like the contemporary rituals of Kwanzaa or the celebration of Juneteenth—a stand-in for the day on which all enslaved blacks were effectively freed after the Civil War.

As the movie *Soul Food* suggests, African American holidays are shaped by big meals prepared collectively, often by the women of the family. Fried or baked chicken, okra, black-eyed peas, macaroni and cheese, greens, hot rolls or biscuits, candied sweet potatoes, coleslaw, potato salad, sweet potato pie, peach or berry cobbler, and fried apple pies might make an appearance. Barbecues feature slow-cooked pork, chicken, and sometimes beef with baked beans, salads, corn, and cold watermelon. Juneteenth is marked in Texas with red foods—including barbecue and red soda and red velvet cake. Kwanzaa, a pan-African holiday begun in the late 1960s by Dr. Maulana Karenga, is celebrated by thousands of African Americans and has encouraged more African Americans to embrace African recipes from across the continent as well as West Indian and Brazilian foodways. On New Year's day, black-eyed peas and greens are eaten for good luck and cash, and pigs' feet, cornbread, sweet potatoes, and other foods have symbolic meanings meant to usher in a year with good tidings and glee.

Place in American Culture

African American foodways unfortunately enjoy much acclaim against much criticism. Watermelon, fried chicken, sweet drinks, and collard greens have been used to poke fun or even embarrass or belittle African American culture as grotesque, simple, or backward. Such stereotypes harken back to the turn of the twentieth century when similar images were used to sell food products by recalling the presumed docility or buffoonery of African American cooks or people. Fried chicken chains often sell their authenticity on the presence of African American actors fronting as expert cooks trained in the southern cooking tradition. Food has been used to mark or designate African Americans as different—such as the comment that star golf player Tiger Woods might want "collard greens or whatever the hell *they* eat" for his banquet after winning the Masters. In the contemporary era, soul food has become synonymous with both black ethnic pride and a shameful past. Soul food is really the "memory cuisine of the grandchildren of enslaved African Americans," not a direct pass-down from slavery. It was immortalized in the 1960s to 1970s musical *Hair* with a melodic litany, "Colored Spade," celebrating and derisively mocking "watermelon, hominy grits, shortening bread, alligator ribs . . . pig tails . . . black-eyed peas . . . chitlins . . . collard greens," which followed a musical list of epithets and insults for African Americans. This was not by accident, as some from the Great Migration's success stories felt a sense of embarrassment at the rural and humble origins from which their families came.

In the early twenty-first century, African American food came under attack as a predominant source of the chronic health ailments faced by African Americans. To be fair, African American celebratory food was never meant to be eaten every day, and the traditional fare of leafy greens, sweet potatoes, legumes, and fresh fruit is a fairly healthy, natural diet. However, tastes for deep-fried, sugary, or starchy foods—and not just those desired in soul food but also those from other ethnic cuisines gone Americanized or junk or fast food—accompanied by lack of access to places where whole or healthy foods could be purchased, equally contributed to the decline in health as the American lifestyle became more sedentary.

Films such as *Soul Food Junkies* joined a plethora of books, talks, and classes celebrating the African American food tradition while calling into question issues of health, food security, and food and culinary justice. African American foodways could easily be considered the most academically discussed and debated ethnic food tradition of them all, with reaches into racial politics, environmental justice, intergroup relations, and ethnic and cultural heritage. The overarching verdict has been that African American food has the makings of a healthy, sustainable tradition with room for some indulgence, but not much. To that end, community gardens have sprung up, often cultivating heritage or heirloom crops that are a part of the African American culinary tradition, and edible schoolyards are encouraging African American youth to take ownership of their diets and learn to grow, prepare, and consume healthier alternatives to junk or fast food.

Noted Restaurants and Chefs
The older generation of African American master chefs is slowly passing into time, as Austin Leslie, Edna Lewis, Sylvia Lewis, and others have passed away. There are, however, many restaurants that purport to give an authentic taste of African American ethnic cuisine. Many are of the "soul food" variety where a meat and three sides, usually vegetables and starches, are presented alongside a quick bread such as rolls, biscuits, or cornbread. Such establishments are found from the Northeast to the cities of the Midwest, West Coast, and throughout the southern United States. Examples include Amy Ruth's and Sylvia's in Harlem or Weaver D's in Athens, Georgia. Some businesses such as Ronnie's Ribs offer similar fare in Richmond, Virginia, and more African American entrepreneurs are taking up the food truck model. Other restaurants feature a more upscale or gourmet version of African American food; for example, Sweet Potatoes in Winston-Salem or Harold and Belle's in the Watts neighborhood of Los Angeles offering both soul and Creole cuisine. Still others build on pan-African models and use common elements to draw out traditions from across the globe at a high-price point, such as Red Rooster, Marcus Samuelsson's restaurant in Harlem. Pop-up restaurants and events by chefs such as vegan master chef Bryant Terry or French-meets-soul chef Jennifer Booker are other examples of newer and more recent innovations in how African American foodways are becoming familiar to a wider and more informed food public of all backgrounds.

Further Reading
Bower, Anne L., ed. *African American Foodways: Explorations of History and Culture*. Urbana: University of Illinois Press, 2007.

Harris, Jessica B. *High on the Hog: A Culinary Journey from Africa to America*. New York: Bloomsbury, 2011.

Lewis, Edna, and Evangeline Peterson. *The Edna Lewis Cookbook*. Indianapolis: Bobbs-Merrill, 1972.

Miller, Adrian. *Soul Food: The Surprising Story of an American Cuisine, One Plate at a Time*. Chapel Hill: University of North Carolina, 2013.

Opie, Frederick Douglass. *Hog & Hominy Soul Food from Africa to America*. New York: Columbia University Press, 2008.

Terry, Bryant. *Afro-Vegan: Farm-Fresh African, Caribbean & Southern Flavors Remixed*. Berkeley, CA: Ten Speed Press, 2014.

Williams-Forson, Psyche A. *Building Houses Out of Chicken Legs: Black Women, Food, and Power*. Chapel Hill: University of North Carolina, 2006.

Michael Twitty

ALBANIA

(southern Europe) Albanian American
See also: Turkey, Italy, Greece.

Background

Albanians represent a relatively small group of immigrants in America. They did not begin to arrive in America in significant numbers until the end of the nineteenth century and the early years of the twentieth century. Many were escaping harsh economic conditions or were young men fleeing conscription into the Turkish military. Another wave of Albanians arrived after their country was taken over by communists. After the fall of the communist bloc, another wave arrived as immigration and travel restrictions eased. Currently, there are between 75,000 and 150,000 Albanian Americans in America, and the majority have settled on the Eastern Seaboard.

Foodways

Traditional Albanian foodways have been strongly influenced by the food traditions of Greece and Turkey. A number of Albanian Americans are descended from Albanians who initially fled their homeland after Turkish invasions and settled in parts of southern Italy, including Sicily. Many of these Albanian Italians then immigrated to America. This adds an Italian element to Albanian American foodways.

Albanian Americans are strongly influenced by life in the larger American culture. Meals consist of visits to food service establishments and the preparation of food at home, including from-scratch cookery as well as the use of value-added products.

For Albanian Americans, shopping for traditional foods involves a few specialty shops including meat markets. It is probable, however, that most retail grocery stores and specialty markets used by Albanian Americans are associated with similar ethnic groups such as Serbian Americans or can be described as offering Mediterranean foods. Ingredients used in typical Albanian American households include cabbage, onions, root vegetables, peppers, and olives. Feta is a popular cheese, and other sources of protein include beef, lamb, chicken, and fish.

Traditional Albanian dishes include salads, stuffed dishes, savory pies, soups, and a variety of sweets. Albanians are known for welcoming guests with food, a tradition that is reflected in a wide variety of cold and hot *mezze*, or appetizers. These are typically offered along with *raki*, a national distilled spirit.

Holiday Feasts

The Easter celebrations of Albanian Americans include foods similar to those associated with other Balkan cultures: red eggs, a variety of cookies, holiday breads, cucumber and tomato salad, roast lamb, and wine.

Meat and Potatoes in Sauce

    1 pound beef, pork, or lamb
    1 onion, medium, chopped
    1 green bell pepper, chopped

1 rib celery, fine dice
6 garlic cloves, minced
¼ cup olive oil
¾ cup dry red wine
1 tablespoon tomato paste
¾ cup low-sodium beef or chicken broth
3 pounds redskin potatoes, cut into 1-inch cubes
2 tablespoons chopped parsley
salt and black pepper to taste

Cut meat into large cubes and season with salt and pepper and set aside in a small bowl. Sauté onion, bell pepper, and celery in oil until they begin to soften. Add garlic and continue to sauté until it begins to change color. Add meat and brown. Add tomato paste. Deglaze the pan with wine and add the parsley. Transfer ingredients to an ovenproof dish; cover and bake for 30 minutes at 325 F. Heat the broth and add it, along with the potatoes, to the dish. Season with salt and pepper and continue baking until potatoes are tender.

Place in American Culture

Albanians constitute a small population in America, and their place in American food culture is not prominent. Most Albanian Americans tend to blend in with the overall American culture.

Restaurants

Many restaurants claiming to represent Albanian American cuisine fall into the category of Mediterranean. An example of this is a restaurant named Pita Palace in Carol Stream, Illinois.

Further Reading

Hysa, K., and R. J. Hysa. *The Best of Albanian Cooking: Favorite Family Recipes.* New York: Hippocrene Books, 1998.

Jurgens, G. "Albanian Americans." In *Gale Encyclopedia of Multicultural America*, second edition. Pp. 55–66. Detroit: Gale, 2000.

Charles Baker-Clark

ALGERIA

(North Africa) Algerian American Food
See also: Tunisia, Morocco, Libya.

Background

It is difficult to know how many Algerians immigrated to the United States prior to 1975, as it was not used as an immigrant record category until that year. In the late 1990s, a group of Algerians came to the United States to work and study with the Algerian director of the National Institute of Health, Elias Zerhouni. This is a typical example of Algerian immigration to the United States—many Algerians come for work or to further their education.

From the late 1990s through the early 2000s, many Algerian refugees, including journalists, immigrated to the United States due to the civil war. However, because of the lack of a language barrier in French-speaking Canada, many Algerians in North America reside in Quebec. In the United States, enclaves of Algerian immigrants are based in New Jersey, Philadelphia, and Boston, largely because of the availability of jobs in those urban areas.

Foodways

Algerian cuisine is an amalgam of Turkish, Berber, French, and Islamic influences. The Ottoman influence is more prominent in the eastern half of the country, with the Moroccan and Spanish bearing more influence on the western part of the country.

Couscous is the national dish of Algeria. It is eaten every Friday—the day of the big family meal—and at any big celebration such as weddings or funerals, but it is also a primary daily food item. *Mechoui*, roasted lamb, is just as important as *couscous*. The head is removed, and the lamb is spiced and slow-roasted on a spit. The meat is then served with *harissa*, bread, fries, and salad, and occasionally with vegetables and *couscous*. This is done for the big *Eid* holiday, or any big celebrations such as weddings, graduations, or circumcision ceremonies.

Stews, consisting of a vegetable sauce and usually lamb but occasionally chicken, are also popular dishes. Common vegetables include turnips, carrots, pumpkins, summer squash, and potatoes.

Semolina is a staple grain in Algeria, dating back to when the Romans took over North Africa and found that Algeria had fertile conditions for growing semolina. Today Algeria consumes so much semolina that they need to import it from other countries. Semolina is used in almost all traditional Algerian breads and pastas. Algeria is home to over a dozen varieties of pasta dishes, the origin of which dates back to the era when the Mongols were making their way through North Africa. One of the khans served a noodle dish to a North African leader, who brought it back to the Berber world.

All Algerian pasta dishes are made with homemade noodles and are steamed (not boiled) in a steamer called a *couscousiere*. After the noodles are steamed, some dishes are served with a stewlike sauce ladled over the top, and others are cooked like a risotto, with sauce added gradually until incorporated with the noodles. Most sauces are generally rather basic and are either white or red with vegetables. Red sauce contains tomatoes, but unlike the Italian pasta dishes most Americans are familiar with, Algerian white sauce does not contain cream or milk but is referred to as "white" merely because it does not contain tomatoes. Chickpeas are prevalent in most pasta sauces. *Rechta* is perhaps the most common pasta dish and is specific to Algeria. A specialty of Algiers, the noodles are thin—almost as thin as vermicelli—and once steamed, they are cooked in a spiced broth with chicken or lamb, chickpeas, and vegetables, and topped with halved hard-boiled eggs.

Other popular items include *chakhchouka*, a dish of eggs poached in a spicy tomato sauce; *karantita*, a savory chickpea-based flan; *kesra*, a traditional flatbread that is the basis for most meals; *sharbats*, fruit- or nut-flavored milk drinks; and *harissa*, a spicy red chili sauce. Due to the prevalence of the Islamic faith in Algerian culture, pork is not served, but lamb, chicken, fish, and other seafood are common.

Ras el hanout is a major spice in Algerian cuisine (though in the United States it is always labeled as Moroccan, it is particular to Algeria). Like a curry powder, *ras el hanout*, meaning "head of the shop," is a blend. While you can buy it premixed, chefs and home cooks often create their own mixtures, which can include a handful of different spices, up to thirty.

Traditionally, the biggest meal is eaten at midday, and the big family meal is eaten on Friday, as it is the Islamic holy day. Due to the importance of the Islamic faith in Algeria, the weekend was previously Thursday and Friday, but recently it was switched to Friday and Saturday to be more in accordance with the international schedule. A typical Friday dinner might consist of the following.

The meal begins with a variety of cold salads, generally highlighting one vegetable. These could be grilled pepper salads with garlic and extra virgin olive oil, a cold carrot salad, beet salad, or a fennel salad.

The salad course is followed by soup, served with traditional Algerian semolina bread or a French *baguette*. The soup could be an Algerian style *harira*, made with a number of different vegetables and varying drastically from the Moroccan version with the inclusion of more vegetables such as potatoes, carrots, and zucchini. Another popular soup is called *garri* and is made with *frikeh*—a smoked, green wheat grain—and tomatoes, onion, spices, and beef or lamb. During Ramadan, the fast is broken with one of these soups.

The main entree consists of a pasta course, which could be *couscous* or other Algerian noodles. This is followed by a sweet tagine (*ham l'ahlou*), made with meat, prunes, and other fruits such as pears, apples, dried figs, apricots, and *nèfle*, which are sliced thin (never cubed—every slice retains the shape of the original fruit). The tagine is usually brown or black in color due to the prunes. The sauce is thick and syrupy, and the meat is used to flavor the fruits, but it is generally not consumed. The sauce is finished with slivered almonds and served with traditional semolina bread, similar to a brioche.

Other meals might include salads, soups, and a savory tagine of spiced meatballs and olives; chicken thighs or drumsticks; or a cauliflower tagine consisting of cauliflower beignets, dipped in batter and deep fried and served with a nondairy white sauce, stewed lamb chops, and chickpeas.

The dinner ends with dessert, always consisting of fresh fruit. The variety of fruit is generally dictated by the seasons, but it could include dates, apricots, Barbary figs, watermelon, honeydew melon, peaches, oranges, clementines (which were created in Algeria by a French monk), pears, apples, strawberries, and/or grapes.

Dates are a main Algerian crop and export. The Deglet D'noor date is native to Algeria, although it is now more popularly known across the world as Tunisian.

Breakfast is generally a typical French breakfast with warm (not cold) milk, espresso or tea, and French pastries such as *pain au chocolate*, *croissants* or palmers, or Algerian bread or a French *baguette* with salted butter and jams. *Crepes* are occasionally eaten for breakfast on weekends.

Adults may take another espresso break at 10 a.m. with a French or Algerian pastry. Algerian pastries are similar to *baklava* and generally contain almond paste or walnuts with honey and/or orange blossom water syrup. Lunch, generally eaten between noon and 1 p.m., is more substantial than dinner (see above for a Friday lunch/dinner menu). A 4 p.m. afternoon snack is common and might include coffee and milk or traditional Algerian mint tea with pine nuts, along with pastry or bread and butter with apricot jam.

Dinner is taken around 8 p.m. and usually is smaller than lunch, consisting of leftovers, French fries (frites), or large salads. These could be rice salads and/or green salads with hard-boiled eggs. It also might include grilled meats, *chakhchoukha* (especially in summer when tomatoes are in season), and Algerian-style pancakes made with semolina and served with butter and sugar or honey.

Holiday Feasts

At Ramadan, the food becomes much more traditional. During this month, a fast is observed from sunrise to sunset and is always broken with dates. The pits are removed and replaced with a walnut or almond or pistachio paste. Sometimes they are dusted with ground almonds or coconut, and are served with a glass of cold milk, buttermilk, or yogurt.

The breaking of the fast is followed by a prayer. Then around normal dinnertime, typically 8 p.m., a full meal is served. This includes soup and salad—during Ramadan, pasta dishes are reserved for ceremonial occasions to celebrate the fifteenth day of the fast and the twenty-seventh day, as that's when the Koran was believed to have been revealed. This meal also usually includes *bourek*, a roll similar to Asian spring rolls, with a semolina wrapper (in the United States, Filipino *lumpia* wrappers or other wonton wrappers are often substituted). Those dishes are followed by a tagine with bread. This meal is typically not followed with fresh fruit as it would be normally be.

Following the meal, families attend mosque for prayer and a reading of the Koran. Upon returning, dessert—consisting of Turkish-style rice pudding called *m'helbi*, and/or pastries—is served with sugared tea. Just before sunrise, families wake up to take a light snack, generally eggs, bread with cheese or butter, jam, milk, and coffee.

During the last week of Ramadan, women in the family begin to prepare for the feast of *Eid* by baking cookies and pastries. On the morning of *Eid*, the men go to mosque, followed by a big family breakfast, including the traditional pastries the women have been preparing for the past week. Then families visit neighbors, friends, and family, bringing along the homemade cookies and pastries. The visiting is followed by a lunch, always consisting of *couscous*, usually with cold salads. Then the visiting recommences in the afternoon.

Two months after the *Eid* (which means "holiday") of Ramadan, another "Big *Eid*" is observed. This three-day-long holiday celebrates the end of the pilgrimage to Mecca and Medina. Following the story of the prophet of Abraham and his two sons, a lamb is sacrificed. One lamb is for consumption by families, and another is anonymously donated to personal friends or acquaintances in need.

Breakfast on the first day of this *Eid* is similar to the other *Eid*, with pastries, though usually a few less in number. For the main meal of the day, lamb is the centerpiece of the meal, and no *couscous* is served. In Algeria, a whole *halal* lamb would be used, but in the United States, my consultant, Lamia, said she buys a smaller portion of *halal* lamb from the grocery store and roasts it. In Algeria, the organs are generally eaten on the first day, often as *boulfef*—liver wrapped in intestines, cubed, and fried or grilled—and served with fries, green tossed salad, and sometimes *harissa* and bread.

For the main meal on the second day, the head of the lamb and limbs are chopped and stewed in a tagine with spices, onions, and aromatic vegetables. This is generally served with *couscous* or another traditional pasta dish and shared with visiting friends.

In the weeks that follow, leftover lamb is grilled or seared with mashed potatoes or fries. It might also be prepared into *chakhchoukha*, a uniquely Algerian dish made with layers of thin semolina phyllo baked on a thin, cast iron griddle. The phyllo is shredded and then cooked with a spicy tomato sauce, stewed vegetables, and lamb.

Many Algerian dishes, or dishes common among Algeria, Morocco, and Tunisia, are labeled as "Moroccan" in the United States. Some examples include *merguez*, a spicy lamb sausage; *couscous*; and *harissa*, all of which are prevalent across North Africa and have recently experienced increasing popularity in the United States.

Place in the American Culture

Algerian Americans generally blend in with other groups from North Africa. Also, because many come from cosmopolitan cities in Algeria, they tend to integrate easily with the multiculturalism of the urban United States. Most Algerian food here is prepared and eaten in family homes.

Noted Restaurants and Chefs

Many Algerian immigrants work in professional occupations rather than the food service industry, and few open restaurants of any cuisine. When Algerian food is found in the United States, it is often grouped with or labeled as Moroccan cuisine, which is more widely known in this country, or as Mediterranean. An example is the Zuzu Café, run by an Algerian family but offering a variety of casual, "healthy," and innovative dishes, along with a few Algerian specialties, such as tomato pasta soup, bean soups, and a "North African Breakfast," a traditional bowl of beans stew topped with a fried egg and *harissa* sauce.

Further Reading

Chef Zadi: http://chefzadi.com/, the website of Farid Zadi, an Algerian French chef who lives and works in Los Angeles.

Koehler, Jeff. *Rice Pasta Couscous*. New York: Chronicle Books, 2009.

Nana's Tasty Traditions: www.nanastastytraditions.com, an extensive blog written by an Algerian American.

http://thezuzucafe.com.

Emily Hilliard

AMERICAN SAMOA
(Polynesia, Oceania)
See entry on Polynesia.

AMISH
(North America) Amish Foodways
See also: Pennsylvania Dutch, Mennonite

Background

The Amish originated in Switzerland with roots in the Protestant Reformation, specifically in the Anabaptist movement starting in 1525 that emphasized the need for adult rather than infant baptism. Differences in doctrine lead to a split in 1693 within the Swiss Anabaptists into Mennonite and the followers of Jacob Ammann, the Amish. Religious persecution caused the Amish to leave their homeland in Switzerland and the lower Rhine valley and, eventually, Europe altogether.

The Amish came to North America in two waves, the first in the mid-1700s and again in the early 1800s. The first Amish immigrants seem to have been in 1737, when twenty-one Amish families left Europe from the Netherlands for the "new world." In 1749, an Amish bishop was established in a village north of Philadelphia, Pennsylvania. Between 1807 and 1857, over three thousand Amish came to the United States, settling primarily in Pennsylvania and eastern Ohio. In 1865 a dispute over doctrine caused the Amish community to split, with the more conservative branch becoming known as "old-order" Amish who believed in upholding the *Ordnung*, rules for each community that maintained separation from modern technological developments and non-Amish society. The less insular branch rejoined with the Mennonite church. The Amish, meanwhile, moved further west, establishing farming communities, particularly in central Ohio and eastern and northern Indiana, the two states that today have the largest populations of Amish out of the total of around 261,000 individuals. Amish communities can now be found in twenty-eight states and the province of Ontario in Canada, with significant populations in Iowa, Michigan, Missouri, New York, and Wisconsin. There are no congregations left in Europe.

Amish communities display various differences over rules for maintaining separation from the "English," as the non-Amish are known, from the federal government, particularly over education of Amish children, and from acceptance of modern lifestyles. Many still speak the dialect of Swiss German brought in the 1700s that became known as Pennsylvania German or Pennsylvania Dutch (a misspelling and misinterpretation of the German word for *German*, "Deutsch"). Also central to the culture is a set of values referred to as *Gelassenheit*, meaning "submission," that emphasizes obedience, contentment with one's place and fortune, self-denial, modesty, and a "quiet spirit."[1]

Disputes over differences in adherence to traditional values and lifestyles, particularly the adoption of technological developments, led in the 1960s to the establishment of "new order Amish," groups that accepted some modern ways. These individuals and groups now use electricity, telephones, farm equipment, and, for some, even automobiles, and allow more contact with the outside world for the families. Old order Amish are most recognizable today by their dress ("plain" and modest, in blacks and grays, with long sleeves and long pants and skirts) and their use of horse-drawn buggies rather than automobiles. New order Amish maintain some of these customs to varying degrees and, drawing upon their traditional foodways, have made significant inroads into the food and tourism industries. Farming remains the primary occupation and defines the lifestyle of the culture.

Foodways

The Amish brought with them the food traditions common in Switzerland and Germany during the 1700s and 1800s. In the United States, they maintained those traditions but adapted the ingredients available in colonial and pioneer America, particularly corn, molasses, apples, cabbage, and meat and other products from pigs, cows, and chickens. Amish cuisine features potatoes, noodles, hearty soups, sausages, root vegetables, sauerkraut and other pickled vegetables (beets, green beans, cucumbers), bread, and cheese. Cream-based gravies moisten the food, and sweet and sour (sugar and vinegar) flavors appear frequently in pickles and salads. Pies, both savory and dessert, are popular. Chicken "pot pies" are common, as are a molasses pie, called "shoofly pie," and a dried apple one, known as *snitz* pie. Pickles and relishes are standard accompaniments to meals, and "chow-chow" has become an iconic Amish dish, as have apple butter, sweet and sour cabbage, and meat products, such as bologna and scrapple, a "pudding" made from ground beef and pork heart, liver, and kidneys mixed with cornmeal. The Amish diet includes plentiful sweets—cakes, sweet rolls, and specialties, such as the regional Pennsylvania "whoopee pie," two rounds of small chocolate cake around a crème filling.

Place in American Culture

The Amish are well known in the United States as a distinctive subculture. A number of films and literature have romanticized them, playing up their ethos of simplicity and their anti-technology lifestyle. The award-winning 1985 movie, *Witness*, about a policeman protecting a young Amish boy who witnessed a crime, brought Amish culture to mainstream attention, but it was not well received by the Amish community itself.

Amish food today is known as plain but wholesome, frequently homegrown without chemicals and technology, and handmade rather than factory produced. Amish-raised chickens are marketed in numerous supermarkets, and Amish-labeled canned products—preserves, jams, jellies, pickles, and relishes—are frequently sold at farmers' markets, roadside stands, tourist shops, and any venue evoking earlier times, regardless of any actual cultural or geographic connection of those venues to the Amish. Many of the dishes in Amish tradition are also thought of as Midwestern or basic American comfort foods, the type that is found in many farming communities throughout the country, such as fried chicken, meatloaf, mashed potatoes and gravy, noodles and gravy, white bread and rolls, and lots of cakes and pies, washed down with coffee.

Amish communities have become significant tourist destinations. Frequently referred to as "Amish country," areas with large populations of Amish have tended to retain their older rural, pastoral character, which is part of their attraction along with their air of being old-fashioned and representing "simpler" times. Inns, restaurants, and shops have been established in these areas and bring in money from tourists that frequently enable the local residents to maintain that lifestyle. Some Amish towns, such as Intercourse, Pennsylvania, and Shipshewana, Indiana, have become tourism destinations and have developed museums along with shops and inns for visitors.

Noted Restaurants and Chefs

Just as the word *Amish* has become a marketing image attached to home-canned goods, it is also used in restaurants attached to ingredients, dishes, and to the idea of buffets full of hearty comfort foods. These restaurants are frequently also associated with the Pennsylvania Dutch, such as the Dutchman Hospitality group that runs restaurants, inns, and shops in Pennsylvania, Ohio, and Florida. Using the name "Der Dutchman" for most of their establishments, they advertise "hearty, home-style Amish Kitchen Cooking."[2] Their menus include foods that are traditional to the Amish but are also accepted and liked by the mainstream clientele that frequents these establishments (the Amish themselves mostly eat at home): fried chicken, mashed potatoes with gravy, stewed beef or chicken over homemade noodles, pot pies, sauerkraut and sweet and sour pickled beets, rolls and butter with homemade jams and apple butter, and plentiful pies and cakes. Cookbooks featuring Amish recipes are carried in the shops accompanying the restaurants, and they are also offered at other venues featuring regional or pioneer-era-style goods. Similarly, the Das Dutchman Essenhaus in Middlebury, Indiana, offers a restaurant, shop, inn, performance venue, and conference center and advertises "family-style dining" with "home-style food."[3] It also evokes the Amish values of contentment and obedience in their call for guests to come there and "enjoy the quiet serenity that surrounds you." The Blue Gate Restaurant and Bakery in Shipshewana, Indiana, is also typical of many other Amish restaurants in that it is family run, serves both family-style and a la carte meals, and includes a shop next to the restaurant.[4] Their website shows the usual abundance of hearty, comfort foods.

Popular alternatives to restaurants are family-style dinners served in Amish homes. These are usually organized through Amish-run tourist businesses, and tourists must sign up in advance for the limited number of spaces. Traditional iconic dishes are prepared, usually by the female members of the family, and are served with the patriarch of the family presiding over the meal.

Notes

1. EveryCulture.com, Countries and Their Culture, "Amish," http://www.everyculture.com/multi/A-Br/Amish.html.
2. Dutchman Hospitality, http://www.dhgroup.com/en/seg/restaurants.php.
3. Das Dutchman Essenhaus, http://www.essenhaus.com.
4. Blue Gate Restaurant, http://www.riegsecker.com/shipshewana/bluegaterestaurant/menus/.

Further Reading

American Experience. "The Amish." http://www.pbs.org/wgbh/americanexperience/features/timeline/amish/.

AmishAmerica.com. http://amishamerica.com/the-top-ten-amish-settlements/.

EveryCulture.com, Countries and Their Culture. "Amish." http://www.everyculture.com/multi/A-Br/Amish.html.

Gus, Jon. "Amish History: A Timeline." http://pabook.libraries.psu.edu/palitmap/AmishHistoryTimeline.html.

Hostetler, John. *Amish Society*, 4th edition. Baltimore, MD; London: Johns Hopkins University Press, 1993.

Kraybill, Donald B., Karen M. Johnson-Weiner, and Steven M. Nolt, eds. *The Amish*. Johns Hopkins University Press, 2013.

Kraybill, Donald B., and Marc A. Olshan, eds. *The Amish Struggle with Modernity*. Hanover, NH: University Press of New England, 1994.

Nolt, Steven M. *A History of the Amish*. Intercourse: Good Books, 1992.

Nolt, Steven M., and Thomas J. Myers. *Plain Diversity: Amish Cultures and Identities*. Baltimore: Johns Hopkins University Press, 2007.

Umble, Diane Zimmerman, and David L. Weaver-Zercher, eds. *The Amish and the Media*. Johns Hopkins University Press, 2008.

Weaver-Zercher, David L. *The Amish in the American Imagination*. Baltimore: Johns Hopkins University Press, 2001.

Lucy M. Long

ANDORRA

(Southern Europe)

See also: Spain.

Andorra is a tiny country in the Pyrenees Mountains between Spain and France. Its population of approximately eighty-five thousand people speaks Spanish, Portuguese, French, and Catalan, which is the official language. It is known for tourism, financial prosperity, and having the second-highest life expectancy in the world. With free education, health care, and social services, Andorrans have little reason to emigrate, and Americans are more likely to move there to join the vibrant ex-pat community.

Andorran culture and food is traditionally Catalan, an ethnic group prevalent in northeastern Spain.

Lucy M. Long

ANGOLA
(Middle Africa) Angolan American Foodways
See also: Cape Verde, Congo, and Brazil.

Background
Located in the southwestern part of middle Africa, the Republic of Angola is situated on the Atlantic Coast and is bordered by Namibia, the Democratic Republic of the Congo, and Zambia. Colonized by the Portuguese beginning in the 1500s, Angola has been home to a number of African tribes, particularly the Bantu, but also the Mbunda. Angola gained independence in 1975 but has been devastated by civil wars.

Under the Portuguese, Angola became a center of the trans-Atlantic slave trade. Estimates put the number of slaves coming from Angola to North and South America (Brazil) as more than five million.[1] Angolan Americans are Americans descended from Angolan slaves or contemporary immigrants from Angola. In the 1990 census, over two thousand immigrants to Philadelphia listed Angola as their country of origin, but the 2008–2012 "Foreign Born Population from Africa Brief" lists only 0.4 percent of African immigrants to the United States coming from Angola.[2] St. Louis, Philadelphia, Chicago, and Phoenix have been areas of settlement.[3]

Foodways
Basic ingredients include flour made from cassava or corn depending on the region, beans and rice, fish and chicken, various sauces, and vegetables such as sweet potato, tomatoes, onions, and okra.[4] Porridges, such as *funge*, made with cassava, manioc, or corn flour, are common. The Portuguese-influenced spices and seasonings mean that tomatoes, vinegar, onions, and garlic are added to sauces.

Place in American Culture
While the number of immigrants directly identified as Angolan in the United States is small, the influence of Angolan culture is quite historical and dates back to the importation of slaves during US colonial times.[5] In both the United States and Brazil, slaves were frequently connected to Angola both directly and as a reference; for instance, the term *Gullah* may be a form of *Angola*.[6] It would be interesting to connect contemporary immigrants from Angola with these historical roots in America and to further investigate which food traditions may be interrelated.

Notes
1. US Census Bureau, "The Foreign-Born Population from Africa, 2008–2012," http://www.census.gov/content/dam/Census/library/publications/2014/acs/acsbr12-16.pdf, and Henry Louis Gates and Jason Amos, "My Slave Ancestors: From Angola?" The Root.com, http://www.theroot.com/articles/world/2013/06/where_did_slaves_come_from_in_africa_angola_is_one_place.html.
2. U.S. Census Bureau, "The Foreign-Born Population from Africa, 2008–2012."
3. Encyclopedia of Chicago, "Angolans," http://www.encyclopedia.chicagohistory.org/pages/51.html.
4. Wikipedia, "Angolan Cuisine," http://en.wikipedia.org/wiki/Angolan_cuisine.
5. Wikipedia, "Angolan American," http://en.wikipedia.org/wiki/Angolan_American.
6. New Georgia Encyclopedia, "Geechee and Gullah Culture," http://www.georgiaencyclopedia.org/articles/arts-culture/geechee-and-gullah-culture.

Further Reading
Embassy of Angola. http://www.angola.org/index.php?page=history.
EveryCulture.com. "Angola." http://www.everyculture.com/A-Bo/Angola.html#ixzz375FFGaJC.

Faus, Mark, and Jana Faus. Angola Rising. http://angolarising.blogspot.com/2009/11/angolan-food-yum.html.

Gates, Henry Louis, and Jason Amos. "My Slave Ancestors: From Angola?" http://www.theroot.com/articles/world/2013/06/where_did_slaves_come_from_in_africa_angola_is_one_place.html.

Oyebade, Adebayo. *Culture and Customs of Angola*. New York: Greenwood, 2007, 109.

Poe, Tracy N. "Angolans." *The Electronic Encyclopedia of Chicago*. Chicago Historical Society. 2005.

Wikipedia. "Angolan American." http://en.wikipedia.org/wiki/Angolan_American.

Wikipedia. "Angolan Cuisine." http://en.wikipedia.org/wiki/Angolan_cuisine.

Susan Eleuterio and Lucy M. Long

ANGUILLA

(America—Caribbean)

A British territory in the Caribbean along with the Bahamas, Cayman Islands, Grenada, Turks and Caicos Islands, British Virgin Islands, and Montserrat.

See entries for the Bahamas and Grenada.

ANTIGUA AND BARBUDA

(America—Caribbean)

English-speaking but independent nation in the Caribbean along with Bahamas, Barbados, Dominica, Jamaica, Saint Kitts and Nevis, Saint Lucia, Saint Vincent and the Grenadines, and Trinidad and Tobago. See full entries on Bahamas, Barbados, Jamaica, and Trinidad and Tobago.

For similar food cultures, see the British territories in the Caribbean, particularly the entries for the Bahamas and Grenada.

ARGENTINA

(South America) Argentine American Food
See also: Brazil, Chile.

Background

Argentina (Argentine Republic) covers most of the southern cone of South America and is bordered by Bolivia, Paraguay, Brazil, Uruguay, Chile, and the Atlantic Ocean. Indigenous food traditions, sixteenth-century Spanish conquistadors, settlers, and then nineteenth- and twentieth-century waves of European immigrants, most notably Italian, French, and German, have affected Argentine foodways. Argentina has a distinct blend of local and Mediterranean flavors that characterize its culinary traditions. Those flavor combinations have migrated to various locations in the United States where Argentine immigrants and chefs have settled.

The largest Argentine populations are in Los Angeles and New York. Educated professionals make up the bulk of the more recent residents.

Foodways

Argentina's history of colonialism and immigration as well as its climate have affected its foodways. It is second to the United States in the number of immigrants it has taken it, giving it a widely diverse culinary culture, and its varied landscape, renowned for its cattle ranches, also produces abundant grains, vegetables, and fruits. In general, Argentine cuisine is characterized by heavy beef consumption, although lamb and goat are favored in the Patagonian region, and freshwater and ocean fish and other seafood are also abundant. Staple dishes include savory meat-based ones (*asado, empanadas, locro*); Italian-influenced pastas, pizzas, and focaccia bread; sweet desserts featuring dulce de leche, a sweet caramel; and full-bodied teas and wines. Basic starches include corn and potatoes (used for ñoquis and tortillas) as well as wheat (used for breads and pastas). Fruits are generally eaten often and include peaches, plums, apricots, grapes, cherries, and prickly pear. Argentine cuisine is not generally spiced; however, five key spices influence many dishes: nutmeg, bay leaf, oregano, paprika, and cayenne. Particularly notable dishes include *empanadas*, a half-moon-shaped hand pie typically filled with meat and vegetables, and *asado*, and it is often accompanied by a chimichurri sauce of vinegar, herbs, and garlic. Dulce de leche, a sweetened and carmelized goat milk spread, is Argentina's most prominent sweet, often eaten by itself or combined with other ingredients. A favorite treat is alfajor, a cookie sandwich filled with dulce de leche. Argentines also enjoy the sweet spread on toast.

Yerba mate is made from the infused leaves of the Southern American holly tree, *Ilex paraguariensis*. According to tradition, the Guarani people of northeast Argentina, Brazil, Uruguay, and Paraguay were the first to make it, and it is featured in folk tales, with one version describing how the moon gave the beverage to a good, hospitable couple, and another explaining it as the discovery of adventurers. It is also known as the favorite drink of Argentine *gauchos* (cowboys), who regard the tea as liquid vegetables. Today, yerba mate is served to guests upon their arrival, and it is highly valued in Argentine culture.

There are regional differences in the preparation of the drink, but it is typically served from a gourd or *mate*, from which the tea derives its name, and sipped through a straw filter called a *bombilla*. Preparation involves filling the gourd with mate, tilting the gourd so the mate is on one side, splashing a bit of cold water into the gourd, then filling the gourd with hot water and some sugar. The host or hostess consumes the first cup, fills it again, and passes it to the next person. This continues until all present have enjoyed a cup of yerba mate. In some locations, people equate good mate with good hospitality and bad mate with bad hospitality. In the United States, people drink mate in teashops or purchase it in specialty grocery stores. Most Americans approach the drink as they approach other teas; however, so much of yerba mate's customs remain local to Argentina.

Wine, particularly Malbec, a deep purple wine known for its intensely fruity flavor and velvety texture, is another popular drink. Argentina's provincial governor, agronomist Michel Pouget, invented it, and then other nineteenth-century French immigrants brought over vine cuttings from the Bordeaux region. They flourished in the lower Andes, particularly in Mendoza, which provides a hospitable home for this varietal. Frost and the phylloxera aphid destroyed many of the original vines back in France. In Argentina, Malbec is so popular that the country declared the varietal their national grape. A small number of Malbec vines can be found in Bordeaux and in California, but the climate is such that these vines are now primarily associated with Argentina.

In the United States, Argentine immigrants favor many of their traditional foods that are similar to mainstream American and other ethnic foods, such as rich coffee, tea, beer, wine, *fugazzeta* (pizza), ñoquis (gnocchi-potato dumplings), pastas, steaks and ribs, salads, French fries, ham and cheese sandwiches, *fugazza* (Argentine focaccia bread), *sorrentinos* (ravioli with ham and cheese), and sausages.

In Argentina, women traditionally prepare most of the food, particularly for family gatherings. One important exception to this rule is *asado*, which men usually grill, just as mainstream American men dominate the barbecue realm. However, many middle-class and upper-class Argentine families have cooks and never learned to prepare traditional dishes. In Argentina, professional chefs are usually male, which is also true for most Argentine chefs in the United States.

Typically, Argentine people eat a small breakfast and a substantial lunch and dinner. A siesta follows lunch, and many people simply shut their businesses from noon to four. Dinner is eaten much later in the evening, around eight or nine, which is common in many South American countries. Simple meat and vegetable dishes are usual, as are pasta dishes and *empanadas*. Mealtime sociability is a significant value, so that Argentines take their time eating and generally dine with family and friends, and the pace of meals is much more relaxed in the typical Argentine home than in its American counterpart.

Beef *Empanadas*

Makes eighteen *empanadas*

   750 grams all-purpose flour
   1 cup beef fat
   coarse salt
   boiling water
   1½ kilo of a flesh-cut rump or sirloin
   2 onions
   3 cloves of garlic
   1 handful of green onions
   4 hardboiled eggs
   1½ cups green olives
   salt and pepper
   chili powder
   paprika
   cumin
   2½ tablespoons olive oil
   1 egg yolk

Dough: Place flour on counter with an indention in the middle. Prepare a brine of boiling water with 1 to 2 tablespoons of salt and let cool. Melt fat in a frying pan and let cool slightly (but not until it is solid). Pour fat and a few tablespoons of brine into the flour. Add brine as necessary until the flour is all worked in and you have a fairly stiff dough. Roll dough out with a rolling pin, and cut discs four inches in diameter. Allow dough to cool.

Filling: Dice meat and chop the onions, green onions, and garlic. Julienne the green olives. Sauté onions, garlic, and green onions in oil. In a separate bowl, mix one teaspoon paprika, one teaspoon chili powder, two and a half tablespoons of cumin, and three tablespoons of cold water. Add spice paste to the sautéed onions. Add meat and sauté, stirring occasionally. Remove from heat when the meat is cooked but still juicy. Add seasoning to taste. Let cool 2 hours in the refrigerator.

Fill *empanada* pastry circles with a heaping tablespoon of filling, an olive, and an eighth of an egg. Fold the pastry over and seal edges with a bit of water. At this point, either paint the pies with egg yolk and bake in a hot oven until golden brown or fry pies in a deep pan.

Eat *empanadas* hot with red wine.

Holiday Feasts

Notable Argentine holidays include Christmas and Epiphany, as well as Sundays, all of which are traditionally enjoyed with family. Holiday foods often include heavier, meaty dishes. Often this includes *lorco*, a beef stew that incorporates all parts of the cow. Families typically serve *asado* as well. Argentines observe *la sobremesa* after both holiday feasts and everyday meals.

Place in American Culture

Americans frequently equate Argentine cuisine with cowboy culture and grilled beef, and they are not familiar with other typically Argentine foods, partly because these closely resemble Italian or Spanish dishes, such as pasta and pizza. *Empanadas* and *asado* stand out as iconic Argentine. Argentine steakhouses in Miami, Los Angeles, New York, and other cities have familiarized Americans with the variety of grilled meats known as *asado*. Less formal restaurants, shop fronts, and food carts in major cities sell *empanadas*, which appeal to the American appreciation for flavorful, hand-held fast food. Yerba mate is found in health food stores, and the United States imports most of its Malbec from Argentina.

Noted Restaurants and Chefs

Increasingly, in the United States Argentine steakhouses and restaurants are emerging in most major cities like Los Angeles, Chicago, New York, and Miami. Current popular choices include La Cabana Argentinian Steakhouse, Pampas Argentinas, La Fusta Restaurant, and Puerto Madero Steakhouse in New York City; Carlitos Gardel Restaurant, Lala's Grill, ACA Grill, and Ushuaia Argentinean Steakhouse in Los Angeles; Tango Sur, El Nandu, Folklore Argentine Grill, and Caminito Argentinian Grill in Chicago; Knife Argentinian Steakhouse, La Patagonia Argentina, Graziano's Restaurant, and Rincon Argentino in Miami. These restaurants serve traditional Argentine food with a flair. Reviewers particularly appreciate the *asado* at many of these restaurants.

Further Reading

Brooks, Shirley Lomax. *Argentina Cooks!: Treasured Recipes from the Nine Regions of Argentina.* New York: Hippocrene Books, 2003.

Mallmann, Francis. *Seven Fires: Grilling the Argentine Way.* New York: Artisan, 2009.

Pite, Rebekah E. *Creating a Common Table in Twentieth-Century Argentina: Dona Petrona, Women, and Food.* Chapel Hill: University of North Carolina Press, 2013.

Emily Ridout

ARMENIA

(Western Asia) Armenian American Food
See also: Turkey, Iran.

Background

Prior to the 1890s, there were very few Armenians in the United States. Since then, there have been three major waves of Armenian immigration to the United States, all predicated more on avoiding harsh conditions in the homeland rather than any intrinsic lure of American culture. The first wave of immigration began in the 1890s as the Ottoman Empire was collapsing and the persecution of the Christian Armenians increased. Over sixty thousand Armenians settled in the United States from this time until the beginning of World War I, primarily around Boston and New York City.

The second wave took place as a result of the Ottoman-organized Armenian Genocide, which lasted from 1915 to 1920 and resulted in more than a million ethnic Armenian deaths. During the period of 1920–1924, thirty thousand Armenians immigrated to the United States. In 1924 a yearly immigration quota of 150 was set. This second wave saw settlement primarily in greater New England and New York State.

The third wave took place after World War II as numerous upheavals affected Armenian communities in the diaspora and the homeland, including the Lebanese Civil War, the Iranian Revolution of the 1970s, and the collapse of the Soviet Union in the early 1990s. Most of these immigrants settled in the Los Angeles area, which houses more than a quarter-million Armenian Americans, and many of those settled in Glendale, which is almost 10 percent Armenian.

Foodways

Christian Armenia sits, often uncomfortably, at the gateway between the East and the West, and its cuisine, which runs along a continuum of Mediterranean, Turkish, Arab, and Persian tastes, reflects its location. Lacking Armenian American grocers beyond Boston and Los Angeles, many Armenian foods find a home in Middle Eastern and Eastern Mediterranean food stores.

Perhaps the defining aspect of Armenian American foodways is not any specific food, per se, but the emphasis on abundance as a baseline for any meal, especially any family gathering or feast. This, not surprisingly, is a result of the memories and fears of hunger and starvation brought about by the genocide, a subject never forgotten or, at least mentally, set too far in the past. While the responsibility for preparing this abundance historically has fallen to women in the home (and home-cooked meals are still common), it has been in service of a patriarchal culture. This, as in most continually assimilating cultures, is constantly changing.

Armenian American food is heavy on small dishes, appetizers, side dishes, and desserts, but it does include a number of signature main dishes.

While beef and chicken have made their way onto the Armenian American menu, the preferred main dish meat is lamb. Lamb features in *shish kebab* (grilled, marinated chunks), *lulu* or *luleh kebabs* (grilled ground lamb), *kalajosh* (roast, seasoned leg), *tass kebab* (roasted, marinated leg), and Armenian lamb shanks (boiled with vegetables).

Inevitably accompanying these dishes, or roast beef or roast chicken dishes, is *pilaf*. Armenian *pilaf* is rice sautéed with broken bits of long pasta such as vermicelli, cooked with a meat broth, and then finished with butter and parsley.

Armenian *Pilaf*

This *pilaf* typically accompanies Armenian meat and vegetable dishes, but it can be used as a side dish for almost any occasion.

- 8 ounces butter (4 ounces melted)
- 8 ounces thin spaghetti or vermicelli, broken into 1-inch lengths
- 2½ cups long grain white rice (Carolina brand, if possible)
- 2 quarts (8 cups) chicken stock
- minced parsley
- nuts (pine nuts, walnuts, or almonds) for sprinkling (optional)

1. Melt half the butter over medium heat in a large pot. Add the pasta and brown, being careful not to burn it. Add the rice and stir to coat, about one minute.
2. Add the stock and bring to a boil. Adjust heat to very low. Cover and cook, checking for desired consistency after 20 minutes. Cook longer if too soupy.
3. Let sit five minutes, fluff with fork, and then turn out onto a plate. Top with melted butter, parsley, and optional nuts, then serve.

Lamb also features in what is perhaps the best-known Armenian American dish: *lamejun* or *lahmahjoon*, also known as Armenian pizza. *Lamejun* is a quick snack, appetizer, or lunch. It consists of a flatbread base (typically store-bought *lavash* or pita bread, although a home-cooked base can tend more toward tortilla consistency) covered by a well-seasoned, tomato-based mixture of ground lamb. As with pizza, there are topping variations, including beef.

In addition to *lamejun*, Armenian American food relies heavily on small dishes or *meza*. The most popular includes *yalanchi* (rice-stuffed grape leaves, a.k.a. *dolmades*), *mutabel* (eggplant, *tahini*, and yogurt dip, a.k.a. *baba ganoush*), *hummus* (chickpea and *tahini* dip), *boreg* or *beureg* (spinach and cheese-filled phyllo, similar to *spanakopita*), and *basturma* (a cured, dried meat similar to pastrami). These are typically served with *lavash*, the soft flatbread that can double as a wrap. Desserts tend toward pastry with honey and nuts, with *baklava*, claimed by many cultures in the region, being the most popular.

Place in American Culture

Armenian American food has tended to stay in the home and is available outside the home primarily in those areas of the country in proximity to large Armenian American populations (near Boston, parts of New York City, and Los Angeles). However, mainstays of Armenian American cuisine shared with other regional cuisines, such as shish kebab, can be found at many Greek, Turkish, and Middle Eastern restaurants. In terms of home preparation, shish kebabs turn up at many family cookouts, and *hummus* has become a ubiquitous picnic appetizer.

Perhaps the most well-known Armenian food preparation is Rice-a-Roni. This boxed side dish classic was created in the 1940s by the Golden Grain Macaroni Company based on a *pilaf* recipe by Armenian American Pailadzo Captanian. This "The San Francisco Treat" from an Italian American company is really an Armenian dish.

Noted Restaurants and Chefs

Restaurants have been less important to the Armenian American Diaspora than access to quality grocers, as the important meals are eaten around the family dinner table. An early example of a popular grocer is the Ararat Grocery Company, founded in 1910 and located in the Boston and Worcester, Massachusetts, markets. The most successful of these early grocers was Stephen Mugar's Star Market, which became a major New England supermarket chain and now exists, in name only, at about twenty locations as part of the Jewel-Osco Company.

Popular long-serving grocers in the Boston area include Massis Bakery, Arax Market, and Sevan Bakery (all in Watertown) and Eastern Lamejun Bakers (Belmont).

The pre-genocide period also saw the publication of what are likely the earliest Armenian American cookbooks, the English-language *The Oriental Cook Book* (*Oriental* being used in its former sense of "Near Eastern") by Ardashes Keolian and the Armenian-language *Khohanotsi Girk* (literally "Book of the Kitchen") by V. H. Barakian.

Near East Foods, which manufactures *couscous*, *pilaf*, and pasta, was established by Hannah Kalajian in 1962 in Worcester, Massachusetts, and is perhaps the best-known packaged store brand featuring Armenian food.

The most famous Armenian American restaurateur was George Mardikian. Mardikian was an Armenian patriot who immigrated to the United States and opened Omar Khayyam's in San Francisco in 1938. The restaurant existed into the 1980s, when it was destroyed by fire, and Mardikian's 1944 cookbook, *Dinner at Omar Khayyam's*, went through numerous printings through the 1960s.

The leading contemporary Armenian American chefs are Geoffrey Zakarian and George Duran (born Guldalian in Venezuela); both have enjoyed success on the Food Network, but neither centrally features Armenian food in their work. Duran achieved a level of notoriety in 2011 in a failed attempt to secretly convince healthy food bloggers to endorse unhealthy corporate food.

Further Reading

Advocates for Human Rights. "Waves of Armenian Immigration." http://www.energyofanation.org/waves_of_armenian_immigration.html.

Avakian, Arlene Voski. "The Triumph of Fassoulia, or Aunt Elizabeth and the Beans." In *Pilaf, Pozole, and Pad Thai: American Women and Ethnic Food*. Edited by Sherrie A. Inness. Amherst: University of Massachusetts Press, 2001.

Avakian, Arlene Voski. "Shish Kebab Armenians? Food and the Construction and Maintenance of Ethnic and Gender Identities Among Armenian American Feminists." In *From Betty Crocker to Feminist Food Studies: Critical Perspectives on Women and Food*. Edited by Arlene Voski Avakian and Barbara Haber. Amherst: University of Massachusetts Press, 2005.

Kitchen Sisters. "Birth of Rice-a-Roni: The Armenian-Italian Treat." http://www.npr.org/2008/07/31/93067862/birth-of-rice-a-roni-the-armenian-italian-treat, July 31, 2008.

Mamigonian, Marc A. "An Armenian Business: The Case of the Ararat Grocery Company." In *The Armenians of New England*. Edited by Marc A. Mamigonian. Belmont, MA: Armenian Heritage Press, 2004.

Newman, Andrew Adam. "Bloggers Don't Follow the Script, to ConAgra's Chagrin." *New York Times*, September 6, 2011.

Arthur Lizie

ARUBA
(America—Caribbean)
See Caribbean, Dutch.

AUSTRALIA
(Oceania) Australian American Food
See also: New Zealand.

Background
Australian immigration into the United States is comparatively small, but it has been long running and with some peaks in numbers. The mid-nineteenth-century gold rushes of both countries caused cross-Pacific migration in both directions. The next sizeable movement of groups was in 1942, when American service personnel arrived in Australia in large numbers. Subsequently, there was movement in the reverse direction across the Pacific by Australian war brides. Since the affluence of the 1960s, the steadily increasing travel of youth has brought a broader awareness of Australia to Americans. Adding to this, since the opening of Australian financial markets in the 1980s there has been a steadily increasing migration of Australian businesspeople, many of whom have now made the United States their home.

In 2009 there were two hundred thousand Australian-born people permanently residing in the United States.[1] Their main locations are Los Angeles, San Francisco, Washington, DC, and New York.[2] In addition to this established base, are the large numbers of shorter-term visitors, either as tourists or due to family links—a product of the increasing national affluence. These visitors totaled just short of one million in 2013 alone.[3] While this comprises a tiny proportion of the US population, it is a high proportion of Australia's population (currently twenty-three million). This movement and its large scale indicate a fascination of that country's people with the United States and also of their broad awareness and appreciation of American culture. Among each other, this experience also engenders a sense of expatriate fellowship and shared delight in aspects of their original culture—especially as its scale is so small as to be underacknowledged in their new surroundings.

Foodways
The Australian reliance upon primary production has long meant a ready availability of meat as a staple. Lamb, beef, pork, and chicken are all plentiful and affordable there. Of the native sources, only kangaroo meat has found a small place on the supermarket displays.

The most marked of Australian foods in the United States are particular commercial products available in only a few specialty stores but largely brought by visiting Australians as a "gift from home." The predominant example is a black, thick, yeast-based spread with the proprietary name Vegemite. So ubiquitous is this food, it is likely to be found in the cupboard of any home of Australian origin. Its high salt content makes it long lasting, and it is an excellent source of vitamin B. It is considered an "acquired taste," however, and appreciation of it is considered a matter of ethnic pride. The original advertising jingle from the mid-twentieth century is likely to be sung at expatriate gatherings with misty-eyed glee: "We're happy little Vegemites."[4]

Almost as popular is a chocolate-layered and -coated biscuit, known by its proprietary name of Tim Tams. The name alone is near synonymous with the concept of "comfort food." Among the young, these rectangular biscuits are often adapted as a treat for drinking coffee. Two corners are bitten off, at diagonal opposites, and then the biscuit is used like a "straw" to draw up the coffee. This infuses the beverage with chocolate, until eventually the biscuit crumbles and is consumed. This food may be found in refrigerators, but, understandably, it disappears quickly, and it is a praised treat if brought by visitors from Australia.

Small, individual-serve meat pies are widely considered to be distinctively Australian, but these are rarely prepared in homes, being too demanding of one's pastry skills. Two home-baked foods regularly prepared when Australianness needs to be stressed are the lamington ("cubes" of sponge cake, dipped first in chocolate and then in desiccated coconut) and pavlova (a large meringue pie base filled with fresh strawberries, peaches, and cream). French fries are also enjoyed, but the Australian "chips" are larger and readily prepared at home.

While Australians had long been characterized as beer drinkers, today they are more likely to be imbibing wine, either red or white, and to be quite familiar with the varietal names and their personal preferences among these.

A similar change has occurred away from tea drinking and especially from instant coffee. There is a broad preference for espresso coffee prepared in the Italian way but almost always with milk. Unlike the Italian pattern, this coffee may be consumed at any time of the day. Many Australians have small, domestic espresso machines.

The most distinctive of Australian food preparation is the "barbie," a barbecue or grill of beefsteak and sausages that are less spiced than is usual in the United States. The male of the household cooks these, and the cook is often assisted by bearers of beer or red wine. The barbecue is marked by casualness and is used for minor celebrations, and, while considered distinctively Australian, much is borrowed from American practices of home grilling.

Salads, vegetables, and a little meat are now characteristic of everyday meals for Australians. Often nowadays, vegetables and the meat are prepared in Asian style as a stir fry, accompanied by noodles or rice.

For everyday meals, lamb is much more common in the Australian diet, and its comparative unavailability in the United States is cause for some consternation among Australian Americans, who will travel "cross town" to access a butcher who stocks lamb, particularly if it is for a special meal for a visiting Australian. The following is a traditional and now typical recipe:

Roast Lamb (Leg or Shoulder)
Method:
1. Prepare oven.
2. Prepare joint and remove knuckle.
3. Weigh the joint and allow 30 minutes for each pound.
4. Place in baking dish fat side up. If lean add 1 or 2 level tablespoons fat.
5. Place into a moderate oven. Cook gently for the required time.
6. Vegetables may be baked in the dish, allowing ½ to ¾ of an hour.
7. When cooked, carve and serve onto individual plates.
8. Meat should be accompanied by thin, brown gravy, and by mint sauce; also baked vegetables.

Australians rarely use serving dishes; rather, the food is arrayed onto each individual's plate and presented to them complete. In eating, they would not use a fork alone (that seen as a childlike lack of dexterity); yet for dessert they would themselves ignore the fork and use the spoon alone.

Christmas feasts in Australia have long followed the northern hemisphere's hot meal base, despite its awkwardness in the heat of an Australian Christmas. While there has been a considerable change in Australia toward a Christmas feast of seafood, salads, and chilled wine, in the United States, Australians readily return to the hot traditional meals.

Australian public holidays are often cause for a celebratory feast among ex-pats, but since these dates are more likely to occur on working days in the United States, any acknowledgment or celebration is likely to be more muted. Anzac Day (April 25) is the Memorial Day for all who have died in wars for Australia and New Zealand. The distinctive foods for this day are Anzac biscuits—large, oat-based cookies (originally sent to serving soldiers) and beer. Australia Day (January 26) is the national day. This occurs in the Australian late summer and is usually celebrated wherever possible around the world with a barbecue. Lamb is often part of that barbecue. With some Australian self-mockery, former Australian Rules footballer Sam Kekovich is in his tenth year as Australia Day "Lambassador."[5]

Barbecues may also be held for significant sporting events, such as cricket "Test" matches (especially against England), football World Cup matches, or for Rugby League or Rugby Union finals.

Place in American Culture

Commercial interests have driven much of the still small awareness of Australian food and drink among Americans. Foster's beer garnered some prominence in the 1980s, at the same time as the *Crocodile Dundee* movies. From those movies, part of their rugged individualism in the approach to life has helped to shape an American view of Australian food. More recently, Australian wines, with the varietal descriptions now common across the New World, have a reasonable level of recognition. Best known for their high-volume wine products, the "cheap and cheerful" section of the market, Australians themselves largely search out midrange wines from their homeland. Almost any Shiraz-Cabernet blend will draw gasps of recognition from Australians and surprise American hosts or guests with its pleasing flavor. The impression is as if the "Crocodile Dundees" are becoming civilized.

Noted Restaurants and Chefs

An Australian-themed restaurant chain in the United States is the Outback restaurants, which primarily operates as a steakhouse. There are occasional Australian bars and restaurants, where the food is described as "pub grub"—cheap, accessible, fresh, and friendly.[6] These individual efforts usually have an authenticity that is often lost by the franchise efforts for other nationalities. Even rarer are the "pie shops" (such as one in Greenwich Village). Although not marked as Australian, coffee shops are keenly sought after, and Australians will discuss "where one can get a good coffee"—that is, a milk-based espresso, without the milk being "burnt."

Although there are not many such establishments in the United States, fine dining restaurants serving contemporary Australian food or promoting an Australian chef typically emphasize freshness of ingredients and creativity, and they frequently display an Asian influence upon a Western base.

Notes

1. See Australian Consulate-General, New York, http://newyork.usa.embassy.gov.au/nycg/ANY1Wi09.html.
2. See Southern Cross Group, http://www.southern-cross-group.org/archives/Statistics/Numbers_of_Australians_Overseas_in_2001_by_Region_Feb_2002.pdf.
3. See Australian Government, Department of Foreign Affairs and Trade, http://www.dfat.gov.au/geo/us/us_brief.html.
4. Hear this song, within the original television advertisement, https://www.youtube.com/watch?v=0yA98MujNeM.
5. Sam Kekovich, "Australia Day," https://www.youtube.com/playlist?list=PL7RgGl9hEueV6hbImDyik3t_8jV2hhA5h.
6. Zabar's *New York City Restaurants 2010* lists six as Australian (the same number listed as Ethiopian).

Further Reading

Alexander, Stephanie. *The Cook's Companion: The Complete Book of Ingredients and Recipes for the Australian Kitchen*, photography by Earl Carter, 2nd edition. Camberwell, Vic: Penguin Books, Australia, 2004.

Fahey, Warren. *When Mabel Laid the Table: The Folklore of Eating and Drinking in Australia.*

Sydney, NSW: State Library of New South Wales Press, 1992.

Santich, Barbara. *Bold Palates: Australia's Gastronomic Heritage.* Kent Town, SA: Wakefield Press, 2012.

Symons, Michael. *One Continuous Picnic: A Gastronomic History of Australia,* 2nd edition. Carlton, Vic: Melbourne University Press, 2007.

Robert James Smith

AUSTRIA

(Western Europe) Austrian American Foodways
See also: Germany, Italy, Hungary, Switzerland.

Background

Austria's geographic position as a bridge between Eastern and Western Europe provides it with an interesting cultural landscape that has shaped all aspects of its culture, especially food, and contributes not only to a distinct national pride but also to unique provincial identities. Austria is bordered by Germany, the Czech Republic, Slovakia, Hungary, Slovenia, Italy, and Switzerland. Depending on the province, Austrian cuisine is heavily influenced by different combinations of these countries. This broad cultural spectrum is acutely apparent in its signature provincial dishes. Americans are familiar with only a few common Austrian dishes, but the growing influence of the cuisine is becoming clear as more and more Austrian cafés and restaurants emerge in major US cities such as New York, Chicago, and Los Angeles.

The largest wave of Austrian emigration to the United States occurred during the waning years of the Austro-Hungarian Empire (1890–1918), at which time over one million Austrians left central Europe for the United States. The second-largest wave (eighty-one thousand Austrians) took place in the decade following World War II (1950–1959) during a difficult reconstruction effort that stretched across war-ravaged Europe. According to the *2008 Yearbook of Immigration Statistics* from the Department of Homeland Security, determining the exact numbers of Americans with Austrian heritage is difficult because of the historically complex cultural and political associations of Austria and Hungary before 1918, and Austria and Germany from 1938 to 1945.

During these periods of time, many Austrians were counted as either Hungarians or Germans as they entered the United States. At these key twentieth-century moments the term *Austrian* did not denote the discrete national identity we think of today since Austria has only officially existed since 1955. Currently, it is estimated that more than seven hundred thousand Americans claim Austrian heritage (approximately .3 percent of the population). The United States and Austria have, for the most part, enjoyed stable relations with the exception of periods of conflict surrounding and including World War I and World War II, during which the United States withdrew diplomatic relations from Austria. However, since 1955 and the signing of the Austrian Treaty, both countries have shared a harmonious political association.

Foodways

Austrian food culture has a long tradition of *Gemütlichkeit* (coziness) that is embodied by Viennese café culture, as well as the traditions of the *Beisl* (pub) and *Heuriger* (wine tavern). There is an intrinsic hominess that is cultivated, and this atmosphere has been characteristic of Austrian food culture for centuries. There are nine provinces in Austria: Burgenland, Carinthia, Lower Austria, Upper Austria, Salzburgerland, Styria, Tyrol, Vorarlberg, and Vienna, and each has its own regional dishes, such as the *Tiroler Gröstl* that consists of fried ham and potatoes with a fried egg on top and the Salzburg *Nockerln* (a sweet egg soufflé). These regional cuisines are indicative of the culinary landscape of the Austro-Hungarian Empire with all of its intersecting national cultures. Hungary has proven to be a strong influence with the prevalence of gulash, *Palatschinken* (*crepes*), and Esterhazy torte (an intricate layer cake with hazelnut cream named after the Estserhazy noble family). The *Knödl* (dumpling) reveals a strong Czech influence, and if one were to go all the way back to the sixteenth century and the Turkish siege on Vienna, one would find the roots of two of the most well-known culinary traditions in all of Austria, coffee and apple strudel.

Austria is a global leader in organic farming, and there is strong, national support for eating locally and sustaining traditional agriculture practices. Staple foods include: meat (pork, beef, poultry, and fish); dairy (cheese, eggs, milk); field crops; specialty crops; honey; and wine. In fact, according to the Austrian National Tourist Office, Vienna is the only world capital to have a notable number of vineyards within its city limits. The country's wine culture, particularly the delicious *Grüner Veltliner*, is essential to its national cuisine. Beer is also produced within the city limits at the Ottakringer Brewery. Hans C. Kordik, counselor for Agriculture and Environment at the Austrian Embassy in Washington, DC, has written about Austria's commitment to organic farming. According to the embassy's website, Austria registered the first organic farm in 1927, and currently 16 percent of Austrian farmers and 20 percent of their farmland adhere to strict environmental standards of organic farming. Austria also forbids the use of hormones, growth substances, and radiation, as well as biotechnology. More recently, movements such as "slow food" have taken root. This is a natural progression of the understanding of food in Austria since 1891 when, under the Austro-Hungarian Empire, a scientific commission was appointed to research and record the standards used in food cultivation and traditional food products of the Empire. This same commission (the Austrian Codex Commission) still advises the Ministry of Health, and the Austrian Food Codex is still an active document under the auspices of the Ministry of Agriculture, Forestry Management, and Water Management according to the Austrian government's website for the Ministry of Life.

In Austrian culture there has always been an emphasis on women preparing the meals. However, with the increase of interest in how food is prepared in recent years, Austrians claim that these traditional gender roles are slowly changing among the younger generations.

Everyday Meals

The commensality of food consumption is valued in Austria, and although holidays bring seasonal fare to the table, everyday meals are no less important. Generally, the daily menu consists of four meals: *Fruhstück* (breakfast), *Mittagessen* (lunch), the largest meal of the day, a *Kaffeejause* (coffee break), and *Abendbrot* (dinner), which has similar components to breakfast with the addition of a soup or salad. Breakfast can be a simple case of *Kaiser Semmeln* (round, *baguette*-like rolls) with butter, jam, or cheese and meat with coffee or tea. There is also an extended version that includes an assortment of jams, cheeses, and meats, rolls of all varieties, *croissants*, *Kipferl* (a crescent-shaped butter treat that is much more breadlike than *croissants* and is often stuffed with a nut or poppy seed filling), soft-boiled egg, and coffee and tea. The largest meal is served midday and consists of an entree, vegetable, and potato/dumpling with possibly a soup to start. The afternoon brings a coffee break with or without a famous pastry. The evening meal is similar to the English tea and consists of dark bread, cheese, and meats, as well as pickled vegetables or a salad. Wine or beer is always an acceptable addition to the midday and evening meals. Recipes for two quintessential Austrian dishes, specifically Viennese specialties, are found below.

Sachertorte

Preheat oven to 325°F and have a 9-inch, ungreased, removable-rim pan.

Ingredients:

    5 to 6 ounces semisweet chocolate
    ½ cup sugar
    ½ cup butter
    6 egg yolks
    ¾ cup dry breadcrumbs
    ¼ cup finely ground blanched almonds
    ¼ teaspoon salt
    6 to 7 egg whites
    apricot preserves
    strong coffee

Begin by grating 5 to 6 ounces of semisweet chocolate and set aside. Cream ½ cup of granulated sugar with ½ cup butter. Beat in 6 egg yolks, one at a time, until the mixture is light and fluffy. Add grated chocolate to this mixture as well as ¾ cup dry bread crumbs and ¼ cup finely ground blanched almonds, along with ¼ teaspoon of salt. Beat until stiff, but not dry, and fold in 6 egg whites. Pour into ungreased pan and bake for 50 minutes to an hour. When cool, slice the torte horizontally through the middle and place 1 cup apricot preserves between the layers.

To make the glaze, melt 7 ounces of semisweet chocolate in a double boiler with 1 tablespoon of butter. Bring to a boil ¾ cup of sugar and ⅓ cup of water (3 tablespoons of which should be strong coffee) and then pour this syrup into the chocolate slowly while stirring constantly. Pour this mixture over the cake. Be careful to pour the glaze all at once as it hardens immediately. Serve cake slices with whipped cream.

Wiener Schnitzel

Ingredients:

    6- to 8-ounce pieces of veal (as many as are needed)
    salt and pepper
    flour for dusting
    2 eggs, plus 2 tablespoons milk, beaten, for egg wash
    breadcrumbs
    lard or butter for frying

To prepare: Take veal pieces and pound with a meat cleaver until they are as thin as possible without tearing. Season them with salt and pepper. Lay flat on both sides in the flour. Dip in egg wash and coat with breadcrumbs. Deep fry in hot lard until golden brown on both sides and cooked all the way through. Transfer to paper towels to blot for excess grease. Garnish with lemon wedges and parsley.

Holiday Feasts

Holidays in Austria are celebrated differently according to region; however, there are still cherished traditions that are a part of the country's national identity. Austrians celebrate *Heiligabend* (Christmas Eve) to a much greater extent than *Weihnachten* (Christmas Day). On December 24, traditional celebrations will often include carp or some sort of fried fish with traditional potato salad (using a vinegar base as opposed to the broth base of traditional German potato salad, or mayonnaise as encountered in American potato salad) and *Vogerlsalat* (lambs lettuce). Beer and wine will normally accompany the meal, and it is preceded by coffee and cake in the late afternoon. On Christmas Day, festivities are not as elaborate. The main meal might include baked fish, goose, or perhaps a turkey. New Year celebrations are based around traditional *Brötchen* (open-faced sandwiches) that are topped with a variety of local cheeses, salami, and ham, as well egg or tuna salad accompanied by *Sekt* (champagne). Fondue is sometimes a tradition, especially in Western Austria. A typical dessert on *Silvester* (New Year's Eve) is a *Bisquitfische* (fish-shaped cookies) that is dunked in champagne (tail first) after midnight. *Ostern* (Easter) consists of an *Ostershinken* (Easter ham). This is sometimes covered in a *Blätterteigmäntelung* (phyllo pastry wrapping) and paired with fresh horseradish sauce and *Erdäpfelschmarrn* (boiled potatoes that are then pan fried). Broth from the ham is often poured over the potatoes. A common dessert is the *Osterlamperl* (Easter lamb), a lamb-shaped, sandy sweet cake that is distributed among family and friends.

Place in American Culture

Austria is oftentimes thought of as part of Germany in the United States, even though the coffee culture of Vienna; the 1965 musical, *The Sound of Music*; and the classical music of Mozart and Beethoven have made an indelible mark on the cultural landscape of the United States. Culinary influences are not overwhelmingly pervasive but reside deep within the United States vocabulary when it comes to food. *Wiener schnitzel* is a commonly known, if not made, dish. Recipes for Austrian classics like the *sachertorte* and *linzertorte* are found in the classic American cookbook, *The Joy of Cooking*. The American coffee culture, though very different in tone, still mimics an attention to detail bordering on obsession, which is similar to that which is found in Viennese coffee traditions. Wolfgang Puck is a world-renowned Austrian chef who has even forayed into the packaged food industry, and his name is routinely seen on grocery store shelves. Recently, the famous chef and Travel Channel regular, Anthony Bourdain, featured Vienna on his hit show *No Reservations* in 2011.

Noted Restaurants and Chefs

There are a few very notable Austrian restaurants, such as Café Sebarsky, Wallse, and Café Steinhof in New York City, Kafé Leopold in Washington, DC, and BierBeisl in Los Angeles, and chef Julius Meinl in Chicago. The list is not long, but these restaurants are doing traditional and innovative things with Austrian cuisine in the United States. There are numerous German or Bavarian restaurants that are worth mentioning, but they do not capture or play with the particular elements that make Austrian cuisine one of a kind.

Further Reading

Beer, Gretel. *Austrian Cooking and Baking*. New York: Dover, 1954.

Beilenson, Edna. *Simple Viennese Cookery*. White Plains, NY: Peter Pauper Press, 1960, 2012.

Bouley, David, and Melissa Clark. *East of Paris: The New Cuisines of Austria and the Danube*. New York: Ecco, 2003.

Fercher, Dietmar, and Andrea Karrer. *Austrian Desserts and Pastries*. New York: Skyhorse, 2011.

Grunauer, Peter, and Andreas Kisler with Donald Flanell Friedman. *Viennese Cuisine: The New Approach*. New York: Doubleday, 1981.

Gutenbrenner, Kurt, and Jane Sigal. *Neue Cuisine: The Elegant Tastes of Vienna: Recipes from Cade Sabarsky, Wallse, and Blue Gans*. New York: Rizzoli International, 2011.

Hughes, Helga. *Cooking the Austrian Way (Easy Menu Ehtnic Cookbooks)*. Minneapolis, MN: Lerner, 2003.

Langseth-Christensten, Lillian. *Gourmet's Old Vienna Cookbook: A Viennese Memoir*. New York: Gourmet Distributing Corporation, 1959.

Rombauer, Irma S., and Marion Rombauer Becker. *The Joy of Cooking*. New York: Penguin Group, 1997.

Sedlnitzky, Sylvia. *Köstliches Österreich: Die 100 besten Gourmandisen*. Vienna: Brandstätter Verlag, 2011.

Wechsberg, Joseph. *Cooking of Vienna's Empire*. New York: Time Life Books, 1970.

Anne Flannery

AZERBAIJAN

(Western Asia) Azerbaijani Americans
See also: Armenia, Georgia, Iran, Russia.

Background

Although technically part of western Asia, Azerbaijan shares little in common with the cultures of the Arabian peninsula. It is part of the Caucasus region is bordered by Armenia,

Georgia, Iran, and Russia, with an extensive coast on the Caspian Sea. As such, Azerbaijani Americans identify more with those cultures than those thought of in the United States as typical Middle Eastern ones. The languages spoken also indicate cultural affiliations: American English, Azerbaijani, Russian, Persian, and Turkish.

Immigrants from Azerbaijan began coming to the United States in the 1910s, but most came in the 1940s and 1950s as a result of World War II. Many settled initially in New York City but later moved to Massachusetts and New Jersey, where the Azerbaijani Society of America was founded in 1957. Later migrations and immigrations went to Miami, Florida, where another association was founded in 2006,[1] and in Houston, Texas, and Los Angeles, California. The 2000 census estimated 14,205 Azerbaijani Americans, with the majority in New York and others in New Jersey, Texas, California, and Minnesota. A small but active community is also in Cleveland, Ohio, where they established an Azerbaijani Park in 2008 as part of the city's Cultural Gardens.[2]

Foodways

The Azerbaijani diet traditionally emphasizes meats including lamb and mutton, beef and poultry. Vegetables include roots such as potatoes as well as cabbage, beet, and cabbage. Rice is also a popular ingredient that is prepared as a *pilaf* and served fried with various meats.

Azerbaijani dishes tend to be included in the food cultures of the general Caucasus region, although they may be spelled distinctively. Common dishes found there include *dolma*, *bozbash*, *bozartma*, *chikhirtma*, *khashil*, *piti*, and *pilau govurma*.

Azerbaijani Americans can find similar dishes in the United States at Mediterranean, Turkish, and other western Asian restaurants and grocery stores. Russian and eastern European specialty shops also offer these foods for them, as well as online sources.

Chyghyrtma

Ingredients:
  1 chicken, frying, whole
  1 tablespoon peppercorns
  2 onions, yellow, medium size
  juice of one lemon
  2 eggs, large
  4 tablespoons milk, whole
  2 tablespoons butter, whole
  2 tablespoons olive oil, extra virgin
  salt and pepper to taste

Procedure:
Place whole chicken in a large saucepan and cover with cold water. Add peppercorns. Poach the chicken in the water until nearly done. Remove from heat and permit chicken to cool. When the chicken has cooled, cut it into quarters, pat dry with a paper towel, and reserve. Reserve the cooking liquid. In a medium-size bowl, lightly beat the eggs and mix in the milk. Peel and slice the onions. Heat butter and olive oil in a large skillet. When butter and oil begin to sizzle, add the sliced onions a handful at a time. As the onions begin to change color, add the chicken pieces and brown on all sides. Sprinkle the chicken with lemon juice. Pour the egg and milk mixture over the chicken and onion and add ½ cup of the reserved poaching liquid. Continue to sauté until the eggs are finished to desired consistency, stirring as needed.

Serve with warm bread and roasted potatoes.

Place in American Culture

Azerbaijan is probably best known among Americans for its centarians, who have been written up extensively. Their longevity is frequently associated with their food and eating habits. Be that as it may, Azerbaijani food is not well known as a distinctive cuisine.

Restaurants

Like many other ethnic cuisines, restaurants specializing in Azerbaijani food and identifying themselves as Azerbaijani are found only where large communities can support them. An example is the Azerbaijan Grill in Westbury, New York.

Notes

1. Azerbaijani American Cultural Association, http://azerbaijaniamerican.com.
2. Cleveland Cultural Gardens, http://www.culturalgardens.org.

Further Reading

Azerbaijani American Cultural Association, http://azerbaijaniamerican.com.

Azerbaijan Travel, http://www.azerbaijan.travel/en/cusine-main/116.

Azeri Food, http://www.azerb.com/az-food.html.

Charles Baker-Clark and Lucy M. Long

B

BAHAMAS

(Americas—Caribbean) Bahamian American Food

See also: Jamaica, Trinidad and Tobago.

In 1646, a company called Eleutheran Adventures was founded in London, England, with the intent of establishing a colony in what is now known as the Bahamas; shortly afterward, Captain William Sayle landed there with a group of English settlers. The colony became a haven for those seeking greater religious freedom than what was available in England, and it later attracted revolutionaries and other English defectors. Many of the early English settlers to the Bahamas were Cockney and involved in the fishing trade, making a livelihood from the capture and sale of turtles and conch, the latter becoming a nickname by which white Bahamians were known. The colony also offered a safe haven for runaway slaves from plantations in other parts of the West Indies, and when Britain abolished slavery in 1807, the human cargo of intercepted slave ships was brought to the Bahamas, further adding to the colony's black population.

In the 1800s, a few Conchs (white Bahamians) decided to establish pineapple plantations in the Florida Keys, with the largest on Elliott Key and Key Largo, and they employed large numbers of black Bahamians as laborers. By 1875, these Bahamian-owned plantations shipped a million crates of fruit annually to markets in the northeastern United States. Shortly after, the crops died due to overuse of the land, and the Conchs were put out of business. Around that time, white American farmers were beginning to arrive in the area around Biscayne Bay, which would later become the city of Miami, Florida. The collapse of the Bahamian economy and the truck farming system that paid labor in commodities rather than cash led to an influx of black Bahamian migrants to South Florida to work in these farms. By the time that Miami was officially incorporated as a city, 40 percent of the area's black residents were Bahamians.

In South Florida, Bahamians established enclaves in Lemon City, Cutler, Overtown, and Coconut Grove. Coconut Grove now serves as the center of the Bahamian community in South Florida and hosts the popular Goombay Festival in June, a traditional Bahamian carnival that has been celebrated there since the late 1800s and features masked and costumed dancers and traditional junkanoo music. Today it serves as a showcase of Bahamian and Caribbean culture and has become an institution not only for the Bahamian community but for the larger local black community as well.

Immigration to the United States slowed around 1917 and then picked up again around 1943 when over five thousand Bahamians were employed as temporary workers on US farms in the northern United States. Most came to the United States with the intent to save money and move back to the Bahamas, which many did following improved economic conditions in the colony and greater involvement of blacks in Bahamian politics in the 1950s and 1960s. Following full independence from British rule in 1973, emigration from the Bahamas greatly slowed, and by 1980 no more than nine thousand Bahamian nationals lived in the United States, and over five thousand of them had become US citizens.

There are currently an estimated 48,043 people in the United States who claim Bahamian ancestry. While South Florida is host to the majority of Bahamians and Bahamian Americans, many also immigrated to New York City and settled in Harlem, where they established the Nassau Bahamas Association of New York in 1912, which was later rebranded in 2002 as the Bahamian American Association Incorporated (BAAI). New York is also home to a Bahamian consulate, and together with the BAAI, they organize cultural programs for the community.

Foodways

In 1889, L. D. Poules wrote an account of the colony of the Bahamas and noted that meat, peaches, apples, and pears seemed to all be imported from the United States. However, bananas, watermelon, potatoes, and onions were abundant, and fish, grits, sugarcane, and oranges appeared to play central roles in the local diet. Not much has changed in that regard in over one hundred years. The size of the Bahamian islands prohibits extensive agriculture or livestock production. As a result, many products are still imported from the United States, and this has had an influence on the local cuisine, with many American dishes becoming rooted in Bahamian foodways.

Nevertheless, Bahamian cuisine does retain its own character. There are similarities between it and other Anglo-Caribbean cuisines, although flavors can be subtler, and there is not as much of an Indian culinary influence as is seen in Jamaica and Trinidad and Tobago. Seafood features prominently in the cuisine and is a staple, especially fish and conch, for which the Bahamas is famous, but also crab and a clawless breed of spiny lobster native to the Caribbean. Rice, as well as grits (ground corn), make up most of the starches in Bahamian meals. Potatoes also feature sporadically. Pigeon peas are the preferred legume and are often cooked together with rice. Seasonings include allspice, garlic, onions, cilantro, and chilies in savory dishes and cinnamon, coconut, and rum in sweet dishes. Tropical fruits including mango, pineapple, guava, soursop, sapodilla, and papaya are also regularly consumed as is or in beverages or desserts.

Bahamian cuisine is perhaps most famous for its preparations of conch, a large mollusk with a spiral shell. The variety consumed in the Bahamas is the queen conch, and it must be tenderized or "cracked" before consuming by pounding it. The two favorite preparations are conch fritters, in which the meat is finely diced and mixed into a seasoned batter with onions and herbs before being fried in small balls, and conch salad, in which it is chopped and mixed with citrus juice and chopped vegetables. Conch also features in stews, soups, and a popular chowder. Grouper is the most popular fish and can be served fried or grilled, although it is most popular boiled and served with grits as a breakfast dish. Also popular for breakfast is johnnycake, consisting of wheat flour, butter, milk, sugar, and baking powder baked in a large, round pan and sliced. Pork chops, oxtails, and goat also make appearances on the Bahamian table. Popular side dishes include a mayonnaise-based potato salad, baked macaroni and cheese, and fried sweet plantains.

Cornmeal pudding and bread pudding are popular desserts, but perhaps the most distinctive Bahamian sweet dish is the guava duff, a type of dumpling made from wheat flour dough filled with guava pulp and served with a sweet rum sauce. This dessert features prominently during celebrations like Bahamian Independence Day. Jams are also made from a variety of tropical fruit, including "goombay" marmalade made with papaya, pineapple, and green ginger. Nonalcoholic beverages include tropical fruit drinks, a sweetened malt beverage, and switcha, a drink made from a local variety of limes, sugar, and water. Favorite alcoholic drinks include the national lager, Kalik, and sky water (or sky juice), a combination of coconut water, condensed milk, and gin.

Conch Salad

    1 pound chopped raw conch meat
    1 cup chopped white onion
    1 cup chopped green bell pepper
    ½ cup chopped celery
    ½ cup peeled and chopped tomato
    ½ cup lime juice
    ¼ cup olive oil (optional)
    1 tablespoon Worcestershire wauce
    salt, pepper, hot sauce to taste

Combine all ingredients in a large bowl. Let marinade for at least 3 hours, but preferably overnight. This keeps in the refrigerator for 4 to 5 days.

Holiday and Festive Foods

The majority of Bahamians are Protestant, and Christmas is the most important festive holiday in the Bahamian calendar. It is typically celebrated with a breakfast of boiled fish, a dish of simmered grouper, snapper, mahi mahi, or cod with sliced potatoes, onions, and celery and a subtle seasoning of salt and black pepper so as to preserve the flavor of the fish. Christmas dinner is consumed later in the evening and traditionally consists of European- or American-influenced dishes like roasted turkey, baked ham with pineapple rings and maraschino cherries, and side dishes of baked macaroni and cheese, potato salad, and rice cooked with green pigeon peas. Junkanoo is celebrated the day after Christmas on December 26 and again on New Year's Eve. The celebration includes costumed dancers, parades, and carnivals throughout the islands. Typical Bahamian favorites like conch fritters, cracked conch, and conch salad are consumed during Junkanoo, as well as alcoholic beverages like sky water and fruit daiquiris. Good Friday sees the consumption of another European dish, hot cross buns, and baked ham is repeated on Easter Sunday.

Place in American Culture

The significant role that conch plays in Bahamian cuisine has made the mollusk almost synonymous with the Bahamas in the minds of many Americans. Because of the Bahamas' proximity to Florida, and the city of Miami having one of the largest commercial cruise ports in the world, the Caribbean nation is a popular cruise destination, and conch dishes are one of the most sought-out culinary attractions when passengers arrive at port.

    Conch dishes are also popular dishes throughout Florida, where Bahamian cuisine has had the most influence in the United States and where the same types of seafood are available. In South Florida and the Florida Keys, especially, conch fritters, cracked conch, and conch salad feature prominently on many restaurant menus, particularly those that specialize in seafood. Kalik beer is available in many, if not most, grocery stores in South Florida. Of particular interest is the influence that Bahamian cuisine has had on South Floridian black American cuisine (soul food). Many Bahamian descendants have assimilated into the general black American community, and there has been an interchange of foodways to the point that many black American restaurants, such as People's Bar-B-Que in Overtown, feature conch salad along with black American staples.

Notable Restaurants and Chefs

Most of the Bahamian restaurants in the United States are located in South Florida. Bahamian Connection Grill in Miami was originally founded in Broward County in 1978 and is one of the most prominent Bahamian establishments in the region. In addition to serving favorite native dishes, the restaurant also serves as a nightclub and hosts a weekly Friday night Junkanoo rush-out party, as well as

Ethnic American Food Today   49

other Bahamian-themed events. Other Bahamian restaurants in Miami include Bahamian Pot Restaurant, Conch Heavens, and Take Me Three Bahamian Restaurant. Spread out north of Miami in Broward County are Lynn's Bahamian Kitchen in West Park, Bahamian Flavors in Hollywood, Bahamian Conch Shell Restaurant in Fort Lauderdale, and Bahamian Reef Seafood Restaurant in Sunrise.

Bahama Breeze is a popular chain of casual restaurants owned by the Darden restaurant group and founded in Orlando, Florida, in 1996. Despite making reference to the Bahamas, the restaurant has used the archipelago and popular American perceptions of it as an inspiration for their Caribbean- and Latin American–themed restaurant that features Americanized interpretations of foods and beverages from throughout the region, with few traditional Bahamian dishes appearing on the menu.

Further Reading

Beard, Kathryn. "Bahamian Immigrants." In *Multicultural America: An Encyclopedia of the Newest Americans*, 79. Edited by Ronald H. Bayor. Santa Barbara: ABC-CLIO, 2011.

Dunn, Marvin. *Black Miami in the Twentieth Century*. Gainesville: University Press of Florida, 1997.

Johnson, Howard. "Bahamian Labor Migration to Florida in the Late Nineteenth and Early Twentieth Centuries." *International Migration Review* 22 (1988): 84–103.

Mohl, Raymond A. "Black Immigrants: Bahamians in Early Twentieth-Century Miami." *Florida Historical Quarterly* 65, no. 3 (1987): 271–97.

Carlos C. Olaechea

BAHRAIN

(Western Asia) (Bahraini American)
See also: Saudi Arabia, Oman, Kuwait, United Arab Emirates, Qatar.

The Kingdom of Bahrain is an archipelago of thirty-three arid islands in the Persian Gulf. It is connected by a causeway to Saudi Arabia, and it is in close proximity to Iran and Qatar. Islam was established there in the seventh century (AD 628). It has been ruled by Arabs, Bedouins, Portuguese (1521–1602), and Persians; then it became British Protectorate in late 1880s until 1971 when it declared independence. The official language is Arabic, and the economy, based primarily banking and tourism, supports a high quality of life and students attending American universities. Very few Bahrainis have immigrated permanently to the United States, and they are not identified in the US census. Most are professionals and generally have not maintained distinctive Bahraini food traditions.

Bahraini food culture is similar to that of Saudi Arabia and other Gulf countries, but it also makes heavy use of the fish and seafood from the surrounding waters. It also relies on rice, meat (beef and chicken), dates, and the spices usually found in this region—cardamom, saffron, cloves, black pepper, and cinnamon.

Further Reading

Bahrain Embassy. http://www.bahrainembassy.org.

Lucy M. Long

BANGLADESH

(Southern Asia) Bangladeshi American Food, Bengali American Food
See also: India.

Background

Bangladesh, the country of the Bengali language, has a rich culinary culture that it shares with the state of West Bengal in India. According to the US Census in 2010, the approximate population of Bangladeshis in the United States is 142,080. New York City, particularly Jackson Heights in Queens, has the largest settlement of Bangladeshis in the United States followed by New Jersey. Most immigration from Bangladesh to the United States started in the early 1970s, gradually increasing in the 1980s and reaching its peak in the 1990s. Most immigrants moved to the United States in search of better work opportunities. While some joined the industry as white-collared professionals, many found jobs as cab drivers or waiters in Bangladeshi and other South Asian restaurants in New York City.

In addition to language, Bengali food is an important aspect of the Bengali identity both among Bangladeshi Muslims and their Hindu neighbors in India. One of the primary reasons for this is the importance of fish in the Bengali diet. Availability of traditional fish is one of the striking features that distinguish Bangladeshi ethnic stores from Indian grocery stores in the United States. Large refrigerators filled with frozen fish line a large portion of Bangladeshi grocery stores frequented by Bangladeshi and Bengali Indians in search for traditional fish. Jackson Heights in Queens, New York City, has the largest number of Bangladeshi grocery stores that receive daily shipments of traditional fish from Bangladesh due to high demand. For many suburbanites living around New York City and New Jersey, a visit to Queens means a stop to one of these ethnic stores to stock up on fish that is preserved for many months in the refrigerator.

Foodways

Fish, usually cooked in a gravy sauce called *jhol* or *jhaal* (if spicy hot), is the staple food of Bangladesh, provided by the river Padma, known as the Ganges in India. Fish is consumed every day for lunch and dinner in Bangladesh, and the types are considered appropriate for different occasions. The most popular fish eaten in Bangladesh are hilsha, baim, boal, magoor/shing, tengra, tilapia, chitol, kechki, pabda, koiee, pangas, puti, ruie, shoul, taki, and many others.

Fish remains a staple for Bengalis who live abroad, but many of these varieties are not easily available in the United States. Although Bangladeshi-populated areas such as Jackson Heights in Queens, New York, have Bangladeshi stores where these fish, frozen and shipped from Bangladesh, can be bought, others, especially those living in suburbs where these ethnic stores are fewer, frequently substitute fish that is bought from regular American stores or Asian markets run by Chinese and Korean immigrants. Preference for the kind of fish depends on their similarities to the Bengali fish. Catfish is considered very close in taste to the Bengali magur. Similarly, bighead and buffalo are considered similar to the Bengali rahu. These fish, easily available in Chinese and Korean markets, are therefore popular among Bengalis.

Tilapia is a fish eaten in both Bangladesh and the United States, and it is one of the most popular fish among the Bangladeshi and Indian Bengali immigrants. Back home it is considered inferior in taste compared to the expensive hilsha. However, the trend changes in the United States, where preference and value for tilapia increases due to its easy availability, good quality, and expensive price. Bengalis like their fish "boney," which is an aspect they miss in the United States, where fish like the tilapia are usually sold as fillets. In spite of this, another important reason for tilapia's popularity is that Bengali children raised in the United States are not habituated to eating boney fish, which is a technique they fail to master growing up in the United States. As a result, Bengalis prefer buying tilapia fillets in American grocery stores so that it is easier for children to eat.

Everyday Meals

A typical lunch and dinner of upper-class Bangladeshis is fish, meat, vegetables, *dal*, and rice eaten with some chutney, and all items are served at the same time rather than course by course. The most popular chutneys eaten are *khajur* (dates), *boroi* (*jujubi*), *jolpai* (olive), *tetul* (tamarind), and mango. Rice is one of the most important parts of a Bengali meal. In Bangladesh the most popular rice consumed on a daily basis is boiled rice, which includes *biroi*, *aush*, *amon*, and *boro*. However, this trend changes in the United States where boiled rice is not as easily available and is more expensive than basmati rice (basmati rice has a longer grain than boiled rice, which is smaller in size). As a result, for many Bengalis basmati frequently becomes the more popular rice consumed on a daily basis at home rather than boiled rice. Others continue to eat boiled rice on a daily basis but reserve basmati rice for special dishes such as *biryani*.

Rice is such an important part of the Bengali diet that it is also used to make several other dishes. For example, *jorda* is sweet rice, red in color, made with sugar and saffron, with small pieces of *golap jamon* (sweet fried dumplings) and *kheer* (Indian rice pudding eaten as a sweet dish and prepared with rice, milk, sugar, and cardamom, raisins, cashew nuts, pistachios, or almonds and saffron put on top of it). The dish is popularly served during weddings due to the sweetness and attractive presentation. *Biryani* is one of the most popular dishes prepared with rice and usually associated with Muslim countries such as Bangladesh and Pakistan, even though the dish is also popular in India. *Biryani* is rice cooked with meat and other spices. Traditionally, in Bangladesh, *biryani* is prepared in a large, deep-dish pot, where the rice and meat are allowed to cook together so that the flavors mix well. In the United States, with easier provisions to kitchen comforts, some Bangladeshis also prepare *biryani* in the oven, where they alternatively layer the rice and meat one on top of the other in a large glass dish and bake at 350 degrees rather than cook it on a flame.

The most popular *biryanis* are made with chicken, goat, and beef. Goat meat *biryani* is preferred during weddings along with chicken roast, kebabs, salad, and *borhani*, a yogurt-based drink with salt and pepper, resembling the Indian *lassi*, which helps in the digestion of rich foods. Another popular rice dish is called *tehari*, which is very spicy *biryani*, mostly consisting of beef. Yellow rice made with turmeric, *pulao*, which is rice cooked with vegetables and without meat, and *khichuri*, rice and *dal* cooked together, are other popular rice dishes. Bengali *payesh*, a type of sweet rice pudding, is also frequently prepared during festivals, weddings, and other auspicious events. Although variations of *payesh*, known by different names, are popularly prepared throughout India and other South Asian countries, Bengali *payesh* is prepared with sugar as well as *jaggery* and is much thicker in texture than that used in other parts of South Asia.

In addition to rice, Bangladeshis eat all kinds of breads. *Loochi* is one of the most popular and resembles the Indian bread called *poori*, which are small, deep-fried, circular bread made with wheat dough. However, Bangladeshis make their *loochi* with *maida* (all-purpose flour) rather than wheat. *Loochi* is generally eaten at breakfast rather than lunch and dinner, or at weddings and festivals where they are a part of a large feast. In addition to *loochi*, Bangladeshis also eat *chapati* or *porota*, which is similar to the Indian *roti* and is prepared with wheat flour. Once again the consumption of *chapati* or *porota* is restricted to a traditional breakfast or dinner in Bangladesh. However, in the United States, due to lack of time and domestic help, the most preferred breakfast is cereal and rice, which is frequently substituted for *chapati* at dinner. As a result, the consumption of breads such as *loochi*, *chapati*, and *porota* are pushed to the weekend where women, who are usually the cooks in the house, have more time to devote to the preparation of these breads, which are more time-consuming than the preparation of rice.

Desserts are an important part of the Bengali diet and are eaten after the meal. Bengali sweets are very popular in India. They are prepared using dairy products such as milk and are generally not deep fried like the famous Indian *gulab jamun*. Resembling the *rasagulla* are other desserts such as *chomchom*, *rasmalai*, and *shondesh*, which are also popular sweets consumed after meals and during festivals and weddings.

In the United States, Bangladeshis prefer to buy their sweets from their own ethnic stores where they get their *halal* meat. In the absence of these stores, most Bangladeshi immigrants make their own sweets at home.

Preparation

Most Bengali food does not consist of too many spices. The most commonly used spices in Bengali food are turmeric, red chili, and coriander powder. Ginger and garlic are used in some dishes. One of the most traditional dishes in Bengali cuisine is fish fry. Fish is first cleaned and then skinned. In the United States, where fish is commonly sold as fillets, fish is cleaned and then marinated with salt and turmeric. Then it is shallow-fried in a little oil and kept aside. For the *jhol*, also referred to as gravy in English, tomatoes are blended with ginger, red chili powder, oil, and a little water. Then it is left to boil so that the flavors mix well. Fish is then added and cooked in the *jhol* for some time and served hot.

Rasagulla is a dessert that is frequently cooked at home. While in Bangladesh or India, this dish may be bought from a sweetshop, but most Bengalis in the United States prefer cooking it at home, since the quality of *rasagulla* in the United States is inferior to the one found in markets in Bangladesh or India. *Rasagulla* is prepared from *paneer* (fresh cheese made by curdling boiling milk with lemon) using full-fat milk, then steamed in a pressure cooker with sugared water and chilled in the refrigerator for several hours before serving.

Payesh is another popular dessert cooked at home. Bengali *payesh* tends to be a little different from other versions found across the country because of its thick texture and addition of *jaggery*. Whole milk and uncooked rice are boiled together until the rice becomes soft. Sugar and *jaggery* are later added and continuously stirred until the *payesh* becomes thick in texture. Cashews, raisins, almonds, and green cardamom powder are also added for flavor. It is usually served cool.

Women are the primary cooks in the family in both Bangladesh and the United States. While in India, all meals consist of either *loochi* or rice along with some vegetables and meat, the trend changes in the United States, where many women work. As a result, breakfast and lunch tend to be more American to save women time who are usually rushed in the morning. Although dinner tends to be traditional, the quality of food tends to be lesser than food consumed in Bangladesh. For instance, dinner in the United States usually consists of either fish or meat rather than both, which is usually the case in Bangladesh. If women are preparing pasta for children at dinner, many do not cook a separate traditional meal for adults since it takes more time to cook two different cuisines. Lack of domestic help in the form of personal maids is also considered another reason that daily food is not as elaborate as it is in Bangladesh. Furthermore, breads such as *loochi* or *porota*, which are usually eaten daily at breakfast in Bangladesh, get pushed to the weekends when women have more time to devote to their preparation, which is considered tedious.

A distinguishing factor of Bengali cuisine is a unique combination of spices used in Bengali food called *panch phoran*, which translates as five seeds—fenugreek, nigella, cumin, black mustard, and fennel in equal parts. This mixture of *panch phoran* is fried in oil and commonly added to *dal* at the very end of its preparation, a culinary gesture popularly called *baagaar*. Vegetables are also an important part of the Bangladeshi diet and are traditionally consumed at breakfast, lunch, and dinner. Vegetables are eaten in many forms, such as fried, called *bhaja* (potato, eggplant, bitter gourd, and so on), and mashed, called *bhortha*. Bangladeshis eat a lot of *bhortha* of various vegetables such as eggplant, potato, spinach, beans, and others. In the United States, with the abundant availability of vegetables such as broccoli, broccoli *bhortha* is also popularly consumed.

Bengali children growing up in the United States bring about many changes in the daily diet of Bengalis. For instance, many children complain about the strong smell of fish cooked in the house. They also prefer to eat chicken, considered by Bengalis as more American, rather than traditional fish. As a result, daily consumption of fish reduces to twice or three times a week for many Bengalis and is usually eaten at dinner. American dishes such as pasta, lasagna, and spaghetti increase in consumption as children request them, especially for lunch, which is a meal consumed outside the house. Dinner, on the other hand, is generally Bengali, consisting of fish, rice, *dal*, and vegetables, and cooked using traditional methods and spices.

Holiday Feasts

Food constitutes an important part of Bengali festivals both among Hindus in India and Muslims in Bangladesh. *Durga puja* (a communal worship of Goddess Durga, one of the most important deities in West Bengal) by Hindus in Bengali and Ramadan by Bangladeshi Muslims are two of the most important Bengali events celebrated in the United States. Ramadan, a month-long festival, is one of the most popular religious festivals celebrated in Bangladesh and among immigrants in the United States. Food plays a particularly important role because during the month of Ramadan, Muslim adults maintain a daylong fast. At Ramadan, Muslims wake up before sunrise and eat a series of foods called *sohur*. Commonly eaten foods at *sohur* are *porota*, egg, and *halwa*, which are filling and able to sustain people for the daylong fasting ahead. At sundown Muslims break their fasts and eat a meal that is called *iftar*. Commonly eaten foods at *iftar* are dates, *piyaji* (made of lentil paste, like falafel), *beguni* (made of thin-sliced eggplant), *chola* (cooked chickpeas), *moglai porota* (stuffed *pita* bread), *samosa* (fried dumplings), fruits, Bengali sweets, and a drink called lemon *shorbot* (a sweet drink). Both in Bangladesh and the United States, Muslims begin preparing these foods at home at least a month prior to the start of Ramadan and store them in the refrigerator. During Ramadan, portions of the food are laid out every day to break the fast. In addition to homes, markets and restaurants in Bangladesh also begin to prepare for Ramadan since people frequently like to eat out then. While Ramadan festivities are rarely noticed on the streets in the United States, the celebration of Ramadan in Bangladesh is met with foods such as *jilapi*, *piyaji*, and *beguni* prepared fresh in stores, streets, and restaurants to attract huge crowds breaking their fasts.

Durga puja is the most popular festival celebrated by Bengali Hindus in India. The celebration of *Durga puja* is equally popular and festive in the United States. However, unlike India where the festival is celebrated outside on the streets, the festival is generally celebrated indoors inside temples or large halls inside school buildings. *Bhog*, which refers to a feast blessed by the goddess, consists of a variety of vegetable dishes, curries, rice, and sweets and is cooked, served, and consumed with equal enthusiasm by Bengali immigrants in the United States. Unlike Ramadan, meat is generally avoided on the menu as it is considered inappropriate to offer the goddesses. Hindus believe that meat and eggs associated with death are inauspicious food items during religious events. Unlike West Bengal, where the festival may last for a week, the *Durga puja*, like many Hindu festivals in the United States, is celebrated over the weekend.

Place in American Culture

In the United States, the uniqueness of Bengali cuisine does not get recognized outside the house. Most South Asian restaurants cater to a pan-Indian cuisine that is generally North Indian and consists of *naans*, curries, meat, and vegetables. Most food served at Bengali Hindu weddings in the United States is catered by

North Indian restaurants and mainly consists of an array of vegetable dishes, curries, lentils, rice, and *naan*. On the other hand, most Bangladeshis prefer to cater food from Bangladeshi-run restaurants mainly due to a variety of *halal* meat that is served as a symbol of prestige and status at Bangladeshi weddings.

One of the unique features of Indian and Bangladeshi weddings in the United States is the presence of at least one Italian pasta dish or Chinese noodles such as *lo mein* for the US-born children attending the wedding who do not like to eat "Indian" food.

Noted Restaurants and Chefs

Ali Baba, Haat Bazaar, and Khaabar Baari are some of the most popular Bangladeshi restaurants in New Jersey and New York. One of the most distinguishing features of a Bangladeshi restaurant is the variety of *halal* meat and fish options on the menu. There is also the option of eating more Bengali sweets such as *shondesh* and *rasagulla* that are generally not found in Indian or Pakistani restaurants. The focus on *biryani*, a variety of beef options, and kebabs are also a distinguishing feature of Bangladeshi restaurants.

Further Reading

One of the most popular books on Bengali cuisine in the United States is *The Migrant's Table: Meals and Memories in Bengali-American Households* written by Krishnendu Ray. While the focus of the book is on the Hindu Bengali Indian immigrants living in the United States, it also outlines important aspects of Bengali culinary adaptation in the United States that could be extended to Bangladeshi immigrant food.

Puja Sahney

BARBADOS

(Americas—Caribbean) Barbadian American Food, Bajan American Food
See also: British Caribbean.

Background

Barbados is a Caribbean island with a contested history. According to the CIA, it was uninhabited until the British settled the island in 1627. They brought in African slaves to work on the sugar plantations. Other sources (including Barbados.org) claim that it was inhabited by Amerindians from Venezuela who settled along the coast; however, there is little archaeological evidence of that.

The US census estimates that approximately sixty-two thousand Barbadians (or Bajans) reside in the country as of 2013. The Bajan American community dates back to the first decades of the twentieth century with the first wave of West Indian immigrants. Bajans seem to follow the jobs rather than residing in Bajan enclaves in the United States.

Foodways

Bajan food is similar to that of other Caribbean cultures as well as to that of West Africa. Meats include fish, pork, and chicken, and other staples include rice, okra, papaya, mangoes, and other tropical fruits. Some dishes emanate from sugar plantation slave times, using salt beef or fish and cornmeal, ingredients that were supplied to slaves. Given that Barbados was under British rule and the plantations had African slaves, it is not surprising to find those influences mixing with indigenous foodways.

The national dish is *cou-cou*, a blend of cornmeal and okra, served with flying fish. Souse, or head cheese, is a dish served on special occasions with pudding, a mixture of sweet potatoes and seasonings stuffed into pig intestines. According to a number of websites, no Bajan Christmas would be complete without *jug-jug*, a dish composed of pigeon peas and salt meat and pork. Pigeon peas are boiled with the meat and then the stock is poured off. What is left is minced, and guinea corn flour is added and the mixture is cooked for thirty minutes.

November 30 is Independence Day in Barbados, and it would not be complete without serving *conkies*, a sweet, steamed melding of cornmeal, coconut, pumpkin, raisins, sweet potatoes, and spices wrapped in banana leaves.

Place in American Culture, Restaurants and Chefs

While there is only one restaurant in New York City dedicated to Bajan food, Cock's Bajan Restaurant and Bakery, one might find Bajan dishes on the menu of pan-Caribbean restaurants, particularly in cities in Florida.

Further Reading

"Barbados." http://www.everyculture.com/A-Bo/Barbados.html.

Barbados Pocket Guide. "Bajan Food and Drinks." http://www.barbadospocketguide.com/eat-and-drink-in-barbados/bajan-food-and-drinks.html.

Barbados Tourism Encyclopedia. "History." http://www.barbados.org/history1.htm.

Callaghan, Brett. "Top 10 Barbados Delicacies." Totally Barbados. http://www.totallybarbados.com/barbados/About_Barbados/Local_Information/Barbados_Food/Top_10_Barbados_Delicacies/.

CIA. "Barbardos." The World Factbook. https://www.cia.gov/library/publications/the-world-factbook/geos/bb.html.

Hagan. "Cock's Bajan Restaurant & Bakery." Wandering Foodie. http://wanderingfoodie.com/2011/cocks-bajan-restaurant-and-bakery/#.

McCabe, Kristen. "Caribbean Immigrants in the United States." Migration Policy Institute. http://www.migrationpolicy.org/article/caribbean-immigrants-united-states.

Nation Publishing. "Traditional Bajan Christmas: Jug-Jug Completes Menu." Nation News.com. http://www.nationnews.com/articles/view/traditional-bajan-christmas-jug-jug-completes-menu/#.

"#7 Barbados: I like Cock's." United Nations of Food. http://www.unitednationsoffood.com/2010/03/barbadian-food-nyc/.

US Census. "Caribbean-American Heritage Month: June 2013." Facts for Features. http://www.census.gov/newsroom/facts-for-features/2013/cb13-ff16.html.

Elinor Levy

BASQUE

(Southern Europe) Basque American Foodways
See also: Spain.

Background

On the Sea of Biscay, nestled in the inner elbow between northeastern Spain and southwestern France, is the autonomous Basque Country. Only around one hundred miles long and eighty miles wide, with three distinct geographical regions (seaside, mountains, and plains), this ancient civilization is home to a unique, pre-Indo-European language and some of the earliest cave paintings in Europe. Invasion and migration have been familiar dynamics of the Basque history, and some Basques claim that the early Basques, shipbuilders and veteran cod fishermen, sailed with the great ships of Christopher Columbus. Descendants of the earliest Basques to arrive in America settled in South America and eventually established themselves as ranchers in the Pampas region.

Mark Kurlansky, author of several books including *Cod* (1997) and *The Basque History of the World* (1999), described the early North Atlantic Basque fishermen and their inventive fishing and fish preservation methods (including the fishing dory). The dory, a small boat launched from the larger ships, was still in use for cod fishing until the mid-twentieth century. Kurlansky also stated that the early Basques learned that low-fat cod could be preserved indefinitely by salting and drying. Those methods are still in use today, and in markets in the Basque Country one can still purchase a large, flat cod, salted and dried and ready for the soaking process that prepares it for cooking.

According to the 2000 US Census, there are approximately fifty-eight thousand Americans of full or part Basque descent, of both Spanish and French heritage, living in the United States today. The largest Basque American populations are in California, Idaho, Nevada, Washington, and Oregon, though they are present in all of the states. Idaho is the state with the highest Basque population. Many Basques migrated to South America at the time the Spanish were building colonies in the New World. Because they had never been conquered by any invader, the Spanish Crown respected them as noblemen and gave them government posts in South America. They later turned to ranching. Further migrations to South America occurred in the 1830s after the Spanish Carlist Wars. Later in the century, the gold strikes in California tempted them to find their fortunes in California. Finding themselves unwelcome as sojourners, they became sheepherders, and that began the call for migration from the Old Country. Herding in America became an opportunity to earn a living. Most young Basque men came from varied rural occupations, but they quickly mastered the art of herding.

By networking, relatives invited relatives so that hundreds of rooming houses and Basque hotels were established in Nevada, Idaho, and California. José Aguirre established the earliest hotel in San Francisco as early as 1866, and there are still several Basque hotels operating in towns throughout Nevada. The Star Hotel in Elko was established in 1910 and still serves as a home for retired herders. The Basque sheepherders became a strong presence in Western America, and the hotels provided Basque meals, their home language, games, and camaraderie, and a place to receive mail from home. If they became sick, there was a place to rest and receive medical care. Young Basque women were imported from the Old Country to tend the rooms and cook, and it wasn't long before the hotels were nicknamed "marriage mills." There are only a few Basque sheepherding operations today, and most of the hotels have vanished over time. Herding provided a way into the American economy, but great majorities of the descendants of these early herders have attended universities and subsequently have entered a variety of professions.

Foodways (Particularly in More Traditional Basque Homes)

Traditional Basque American homemakers serve a large variety of dishes. Common ingredients are lamb, beans, fresh vegetables, tomatoes, garlic, garbanzos, peppers, bread, and wine. For decades there were few written recipes, and they were passed by word of mouth through family members. Since the publication of several excellent Basque American cookbooks in the last twenty years or so, younger cooks have turned to proven recipes for guidance in the more complicated dishes.

Where the Basque Americans have active sheep operations, there is often a cookhouse where the hired men take three meals a day if they are not out with the sheep. The hearty lunches and dinners are usually accompanied by red wine, water, and long loaves of white bread usually purchased at a local supermarket. A typical breakfast is scrambled eggs, chorizo sausage or ham, and fresh fruit. These days there may be cartons of yogurt on the table as well as cereal options. *Café con leche*, strong coffee with heavy cream, is popular at breakfast for many. The cooks are usually women. For lunch, a bean soup is usually standard. It may be red bean, garbanzo, lentil, or pinto bean flavored with other vegetables. Sometimes a more elaborate leek and potato, fish-based soup, or chicken and vermicelli noodle soup is prepared. The soup is accompanied by the bread and wine, and there are usually assorted sandwich makings available on the table: sliced meat (often ham), assorted cheeses, sliced tomatoes, leafy greens, and condiments. Fruit, usually apples, bananas, and sometimes grapes, are available at lunch. There is seldom a dessert served at the midday meal.

Dinner is often started with a soup and followed by a variety of meat (not always including lamb), potatoes or rice, vegetables, a leafy salad (served with a simple oil and vinegar dressing flavored with garlic and a little sugar), and the ubiquitous bread and red wine. Dessert might be as simple as seasonal fruit served with heavy cream to caramel custard (flan), rice pudding, or a variety of cakes. Main dishes such as *paella* (saffron rice with chicken and/or seafood), leg of lamb, and other more complex dishes are served on weekends or holidays. Pasta, scrambled eggs with fresh mushrooms, potato tortillas, pan-fried meats, and fresh vegetables are prepared and served with a minimum of seasoning. Garlic, pimentos, salt, and pepper are standard flavorings. Basque Americans generally enjoy fresh ingredients and simple, straightforward cooking methods.

Preparation

Most at-home evening dinners are prepared by women, but there are exceptions. Many Basque men have a particular interest in the dishes of the Old Country, and gourmet cooking has become a popular hobby for many. The meal styles in traditional Basque American homes are greatly varied and depend on the interest and skill of the cook(s). On a smaller scale, they are similar to the meals described above as served in the cookhouse, but the dishes are often prepared with more expensive ingredients and more time-intensive methods. A Basque cook who came to the United States as a young woman said that she simply looks in the refrigerator, thinks it, and cooks it. She was trained to cook in a four-star Michelin restaurant, without recipes. Convenience foods, with the exception of bread, are seldom used in traditional Basque homes.

The North American Basque Association has chapters in many American cities, and one of the options for adult members is to become a part of a Basque cooking club. These are Basque American–only clubs, and the men often pride themselves on cooking the meals for their group. Women, wives and friends, also cook for the group. There are traditions of men's private gastronomique clubs in many of the cities in the Basque Country, and the adaption of that gourmet tradition has become popular among the Basque cooking clubs in the United States. Specialized dishes such as bream (a rich fish), *bacalao a la viscaya* (cod in tomato sauce), *chipirones a su tinta* (an appetizer—squid in ink sauce), and rich desserts are often prepared and served by both men and women in the American cooking clubs.

Bereakasopia (Garlic Soup)

Many Basques believe that this simple garlic soup is a common cure for a head cold or the flu. Another highly recommended use is to relieve a hangover the morning after.

   1 to 2 tablespoons mild vegetable or olive oil
   1 or 2 cloves of garlic, chopped
   ¼ teaspoon ground chili pepper
   2 to 3 cups water
   2 to 3 slices dried bread
   optional chorizo sausage

Brown the chopped garlic in the hot oil. Add the bread and water; let it soak. Add chili pepper and stir gently. Serve hot. Chorizo may be added if desired.

Paella (Saffron Rice and Seafood and/or Chicken)

There are many variants of this recipe, and the meat and/or seafood are the cook's choice.

¼ cup mild olive oil
2 cups rice
1 cup peas
1 cup thinly sliced carrots
2 cloves garlic, sliced
4 cups of hot water in which saffron (to taste) has been dissolved
Several thin slices of chorizo or hard Spanish sausage, or other cooked meat or raw seafood

Heat the oil and lightly brown the garlic. Remove the garlic. Add the rice and stir over medium heat until lightly browned. Stir in the saffron-flavored water and add peas, carrots, chorizo, and other cooked meat and/or raw seafood (shrimp, clams, lobster) as desired. Stir, cover, and cook over low to medium heat according to the length of time it takes for the rice to absorb the liquid.

Bacalao a la Viscaya (Cod in Tomato Sauce)

True codfish, or *bacalao*, inhabit the North Atlantic waters. Basque fishermen have caught, consumed, and sold this fish for centuries, and the Basque cooks have a two-part preparation for this authentic Basque main dish. The method may also be used with thawed, frozen cod.

1½ pound dried salted codfish
mild olive oil
1 clove garlic, minced
1 large onion, sliced
canned tomato sauce
purchased hot or sweet pepper sauce

Desalt the codfish by soaking for 24 hours in water. Change the water as often as possible. Drain the cod and press firmly to remove the water. To cook: Brown the garlic and onion in oil, add the cod, and cook slowly. When the cod has cooked for about 10 minutes, serve with tomato sauce that has been flavored with the red pepper seasoning.

Tortilla de Patatas (Potato Omelette)

In Spain an omelet is called a tortilla, with a rolled "r" pronunciation. The Mexican tortilla is pronounced flatly, and the two are very different dishes. In Mexico, the tortilla is a flat round of cornmeal or flour. In Spain, the tortilla is varied, but a favorite is the potato omelet often served with slices of toasted baguette.

4 large or 5 small eggs
2 cups of diced or thinly sliced potatoes
salt and pepper
½ onion, finely chopped
1 clove garlic, crushed
½ cup cooking oil

Prepare the potatoes, onion, and garlic and set aside. Heat oil in sauté or omelette pan. Cook at a medium heat. Add the potatoes and cook until partially soft, and then add onion and garlic. Salt to taste. Beat the eggs well, add salt and pepper to taste and add to the potato mixture. Continue to cook, jiggling the pan a little to make sure it is not sticking. When the bottom of the mixture is slightly browned, place a plate over the top of the pan and turn the tortilla onto the plate. Slide the upturned tortilla back into the pan and cook slowly until the vegetable and egg mixture is firm. Serves two.

Holiday Feasts

A Basque American holiday feast includes many traditional dishes such as roasted chestnuts served warm and enjoyed throughout the fall and at Christmastime. A simple garlic-flavored cabbage soup is a traditional Christmas Eve dish among some Basque Americans. Most Basque Americans are Roman Catholics, so their holidays tend to follow the church calendar. Peeled apples and pears, cut in half and softened in simmering red burgundy wine seasoned with cinnamon and sugar, is another Basque Christmas favorite. At the Christmas Day feast, there may be a garbanzo and vermicelli soup followed by a fine rib roast flavored with bacon, a leg of lamb, or even a roasted suckling pig as a main dish. The table is always heavy with bean dishes, succulent vegetables, roasted potatoes, selections of breads and rolls, and a variety of condiments such as dates, figs, and other dried fruits, jams, and jellies. Though most meals for Basque Americans end with fruit, holiday sweets are always welcome. The Basque tart (*gateau Basque*), popular in the Southern France Basque region, is more of a tart than a cake. It is sweet custard baked in a pie dish between two layers of rich dough.

Another favorite, often served at Easter feasts, is a sweet, fried custard tostada. For this dish, sweet, cooked custard is made with cornstarch to allow it to set up firmly, and then it is carefully cut into squares. The squares are dipped into beaten eggs, covered with flour, and then browned gently in oil. A traditional leg of lamb is served at Easter along with roasted potatoes and a variety of vegetables and salads, rolls, sweet breads, and cakes.

Through the late spring and summer, NABO (North American Basque Organization) holds regional festivals throughout the West. Typical foods at the festivals are chorizo, barbecued beef, chicken, and pork along with roasted lamb. Beans and fried potatoes are popular, and tossed salads with a variety of dressings are served along with kaiser rolls, butter, and a variety of jellies and jams. Pies and cakes of all flavors are available as well as generous bowls of rice pudding.

Because the Basque Americans consider themselves Americans, their celebration of Thanksgiving is very much the same as the traditional Thanksgiving meal served throughout the United States: turkey, stuffing, sweet potatoes, mashed potatoes, gravy, cranberry sauce, green vegetables, fine rolls, homemade pumpkin and apple pies, a bowl of assorted salted or candied nuts, and boxes of fine chocolate candy (often imported) make up a typical Thanksgiving dinner. Now and then the Basque American cook will add chorizos and garlic to the stuffing to give it a bit of Basque flavor. Some Basque cooks prefer to serve dishes such as rabbit in wine or creamed pheasant or Cornish hens, common celebratory dishes in the Old Country. The majority of the Basque American Thanksgiving meals, however, celebrate the survival of the Founding Fathers and the roots of American culture.

Place in American Culture

Many Americans outside of the West are not familiar with Basque culture. Chorizo sausage has become popular in the United States, as well as flan, sweetened rice with cream, hearty bean soups, and delicate fish soups. These dishes are often attributed solely to the Spanish, but they are also ancient foodways of the people who migrated from the Pyrenees region. Once straddling the border between France and Spain, the ancient Basques did not believe in rulership by kings and priests, feeling that "the people" should have a strong voice in government. John Adams, second president of the United States, admired their historical form of government and love of liberty enough to mention it in his own writing. The Basque Americans are family centered, often deeply religious, and although scattered throughout the United States, they are a culturally proud people. Although spirited Americans, many have worked hard to maintain their Basque cultural heritage, and the traditional foods are constant reminders of the ancient palate of their ancestors.

When Idaho celebrated its one-hundredth-year celebration of statehood, Boise and Guernica, an ancient governmental seat in the Basque Country, became sister cities. Every five years the Basques hold an international festival in Boise called *Jaialdi*, which means "celebration." The weeklong festivities include a scholarly conference, film showings, games and competitions, craft booths, dance demonstrations, and delicious traditional foods. The public is invited, and people come from as far away as the Basque Country for cultural celebration and renewal. One visiting Basque from San Sebastian in the Basque Country remarked that he felt the *Jaialdi* celebration was more Basque than anything he could find at home.

As time and generations passed, Basque Americans sent their children to fine universities, among which are Notre Dame, Gonzaga, St. Louis University, the University of San Francisco, and other well-known Catholic schools. Basques have entered many professions and political venues, and many have become well known in America including, David Archuleta, American singer; Pete T. Cenarrusa, former secretary of the state of Idaho; John Garamendi, lieutenant governor of California; Jose Iturbi, composer, conductor, and pianist; Paul Laxalt, US senator and former governor of Nevada; Jedediah Smith, explorer of the American West; and Ted Williams, Baseball Hall of Fame.

Noted Restaurants and Chefs

A popular custom in Basque American restaurants is sharing the meal "family style" around a large table, though this is not the custom in restaurants in the Basque Country. Two restaurants in Reno, the Santa Fe Hotel and Louis' Basque Corner, serve "family style." Dinner is served in courses: soup, salad, beans, potatoes, a meat or fish entrée (your choice), bread, and a house red wine. Ice cream is the usual dessert. The meal is heavy, but the price is moderate.

A few of the noted Basques chefs in American cities have opened restaurants well worth visiting. San Francisco chef Gerald Hirigoyen opened the restaurant Fringale (which means "the urge to eat" in French), with J. B. Lorda. In 2002 he opened Piperade, named for a signature Basque dish of peppers, tomatoes, ham, eggs, and garlic. Hirigoyen has also established a wine and tapas (finger food) bar, Bocadillos, near the place of the original San Francisco Basque hotels.

Two authentic Basque restaurants located in Boise are the Gernika (owned by Dan Ansotegui) and the Leku Ona, both on Grove Street, Boise's Basque block. In Meridian, a suburb of Boise, is Epi's, also owned by Dan Anesotegui. According to the Spanish National Board of Tourism, chef Teresa Barrenechea serves the most authentic Spanish food in the United States. Her Marichu restaurants are located in Manhattan and in Bronxville, New York.

Further Reading

Barrenechea, Teresa, with Mary Goodbody. *The Basque Table: Passionate Home Cooking from One of Europe's Great Regional Cuisines*. Boston: Boston Common Press, 1998.

Hirigoyen, Gerald. *The Basque Kitchen: Tempting Food from the Pyrenees*. New York: William Morrow Cookbooks, 1999.

Hirigoyen, Gerald, and Lisa Weiss. *Pintxos: Small Plates in the Basque Tradition*. Berkeley, CA: Ten Speed Press, 2009.

For an up-to-date listing of Basque restaurants, see Buber's Basque Page: Basque Restaurants of the United States (http://www.buber.net/Basque/Food/charley.html). It is maintained by Charles L. Shaffer and lists restaurants state by state.

Jacqueline S. Thursby

BELARUS

(Eastern Europe) Belarusian American Food
See also: Russia, Poland, Lithuania.

Background

While immigrants from Belarus have arrived in America since the colonial period, definite numbers are difficult to track because Belarusians have often been associated with other cultures such as Russia. Waves of immigrants from this country have arrived during the early twentieth century, before and after World War II and following the collapse of the Soviet Union.

Concentrations of Belarusian Americans have settled in areas proximal to New York City and New Jersey as well as Detroit. There is a Belarusian American Association that helps maintain social networks and also a Belarusian cultural center in Strongsville, Ohio.

Foodways

The traditional diets of Belarus strongly reflect the influence of surrounding powerful cultures such as Russia, Poland, and Lithuania. Traditional dishes enjoyed by Belarusian Americans include pork stew, *machanka*, and a variety of sausages, *vereshchaka*. As with other Eastern Europeans, the diet of Belarusian Americans includes potatoes, vegetables, and greens. Cabbage is a popular vegetable. Their diet also includes pulses and grains.

Traditional preparation methods of Belarus are distinguished from other surrounding food cultures by lengthy and complicated cooking and the frequent inclusion of a variety of flours other than wheat, such as buckwheat and rye. One prominent food of Belarus is a heavy, dark rye bread. It has a sour flavor akin to sourdough and often contains a variety of seeds such as caraway. Another popular Belarusian food is a soup, *zhur*, which contains a variety of vegetables and, at times, meats.

While these dishes and ingredients reflect traditional food preferences, most Belarusian Americans have probably become assimilated into mainstream American food culture. Belarusian Americans likely enjoy a wider variety of meats, and some traditional foods have incorporated ingredients that resonate more readily with American tastes. One example is a greater reliance on refined wheat flours for baking. Traditional foodways are oftentimes maintained by older generations and reserved for holidays and special occasions.

Draniki (Potato Pancakes)

Ingredients:
    6 potatoes, russet or Idaho, medium size
    1 onion, yellow, medium size
    2 garlic cloves
    vegetable oil for frying
    salt and pepper to taste

Procedure:
Peel and grate potatoes and onions. Peel and mince garlic. Combine ingredients. Add salt and pepper to taste. Heat a small quantity of oil in a skillet. Place small quantities of the mixture on the skillet and shape into small pancakes. Fry until brown on one side and turn to brown the other, approximately 2 to 3 minutes per side. Adjust seasoning with salt and pepper as needed.

These may be served warm or included in other dishes such as meat stews.

Holiday Meals

Belarusian Americans celebrate Christmas Eve with a twelve-course dinner similar to that enjoyed by Lithuanian Americans.

Place in American Culture

It is probably best to include the food heritage of Belarusian Americans with similar cultures that have settled in America.

Restaurants

Most Belarusian dishes are likely to be offered by restaurants that feature foods of different Eastern European cultures. An example of this is the Belarussian Baker in Higginsville, Missouri.

Further Reading

Belarusan-American Association, Inc., http://www.bazahq.org.

Belarusian Diaspora in the USA, http://www.belarus-misc.org/bel-dusa.htm.

Cuisine of Belarus, http://www.belarus.by/en/about-belarus/cuisine.

Kipel, V. EveryCulture.com, Countries and Their Cultures. "Belarusan Americans." http://www.everyculture.com/multi/A-Br/Belarusan-Americans.html.

Republic of Belarus, The Cuisine of Belarus, http://www.belarus.by/en/about-belarus/cuisine.

Charles Baker-Clark

BELGIUM

(Western Europe) Belgian American Foodways
See also: France.

Background

Belgium comprises three regions: Dutch-speaking Flanders to the north, French-speaking Wallonia to the south, and between them bilingual Brussels, the capital. There is also a small German-speaking community on the eastern border of the Walloon Region. The regions share common foodways as well as embracing regional variations, reflecting centuries of inspiration and exchange with neighboring states.

Significant Belgian immigration to the United States began in the nineteenth century, peaking in the 1850s to the 1910s. Wisconsin has the largest Belgian settlement in the country, located to the north and east of Green Bay; rural isolation helped to keep the Walloon culture there strong, evidenced in town names, characteristic architecture, Walloon language, and persistent lifeways, including food traditions. A National Historic Landmark designation in 1990 officially recognized the area.

Flemish settlement was particularly strong on the eastern side of Lake Michigan near Detroit; Michigan has the country's second-largest population of Belgian Americans. Elsewhere, Belgian American clubs exist in twenty-nine states, some spanning one hundred years, as in Illinois and California. Rural Belgian enclaves and urban Belgian American enthusiasts maintain and modify traditional foodways and food-related holiday practices.

Foodways

Rural Belgian American foodways are seasonal and regional. Favorite meats are roast chicken, veal, sausages, and beef served as stew, meatloaf or meatballs (*boulettes*); shellfish and fish such as smoked herring or fried perch, the latter with a sauce made of the fond (the pan remains); and vegetables that feature potatoes, root crops, leeks, and cabbage. Yeasted specialties include breads, pies, waffles, and beer. Fruits such as apples and cherries, both locally grown in the Upper Midwest, are in pies and other cooked sweets. Urban Belgian American foodways emphasize mussels, *frites* (double-fried potatoes), and fine chocolate imported from Belgium.

Foodstuffs

Belgian food is linked to French and Dutch cuisine, with German influences, featuring meat, seafood, leeks, asparagus, potatoes, cheese, and beer as favorite ingredients, with waffles and chocolate as featured desserts. The food can be both hearty and fine.

In Wisconsin's Belgian settlement, both men and women fished in Green Bay for home use, though men were the commercial fishers before that industry collapsed in the late twentieth century. Women raised vegetables in a home garden and baked in large outdoor brick ovens, still evident in the area. Men butchered the beef and pork.

A popular harvest festival is Kermis, at which men are the public cooks. In the 1990s, each town in the Belgian settlement area celebrated successively, from the fourth weekend of August to the third weekend of October. A Catholic Mass (sometimes a "polka Mass," in which the sacred music is set to polka tempo or existing polka songs are adapted to sacred purpose) would be one element, followed by a community meal with vegetable dishes, salads, chicken *booyah*, Belgian tripe, beef stew, baked chicken, buns, cakes, tortes, and Belgian pies. The festivities would include music, singing, dancing, and storytelling. At the start of the twenty-first century, fewer towns and parishes hold Kermis events. Kermis is now also a homecoming festival, drawing back people who have left the area.

Booyah is a chicken stew, with the name possibly derived from *bouillon*, a typical addition, or *bouilli*, implying a boiled, souplike dish. Made at home, *booyah* can be simply stewed chicken with carrots, celery, onion, leek, and noodles in a broth. Public *booyah* is dense, with additional vegetables such as cabbage, chopped tomatoes, potatoes, green beans, corn, and peas. It is made gallons at a time, cooked outdoors in a large metal kettle over an open flame fueled by wood or propane, and stirred with paddles.

Belgian pie is another important menu item for family, parish, or community gatherings with recipes designed for large yields of multiple pies. Belgian pie is an open-faced tart with a yeast crust with fillings such as apple, prune, raisin, or poppy seed that are topped with a sweet custard or cottage cheese baked with the pie, or a rice filling that receives a whipped cream topping after baking.

Everyday Meals

The main meal of the day in Belgian American households is the evening meal, served in one course at a table. If the gathering is large, the meal will be served as a buffet. Many everyday meal items reflect the hearty side of Belgian American fare. For example, cabbage is a key ingredient in several signature dishes. *Trippe* (also *tripe*) is savory Belgian sausage, the most popular variety of which includes cabbage. Boiled and ground cabbage is mixed with ground pork, onion, salt, pepper, cloves, nutmeg, and thyme, which are stuffed into casings to form three-inch-long sausages. To serve, the *trippe* is boiled and then browned in a pan or on a grill.

Jut or *djote* is a simple cabbage side dish using savoy cabbage. To prepare, boil the cabbage until tender and allow it to cool; drain all liquid. Cut into thin slices and sauté in a pan with side pork drippings and butter. Season with salt, pepper, and nutmeg. A common variation is to mix the cooked cabbage with mashed potatoes, called *stoemp* in Flemish. Other vegetables are often substituted for the cabbage, including head lettuce, endive, celery root, leeks, or carrots. One variant recipe follows:

Boil 5 large potatoes cut into chunks and 1 medium cauliflower broken into florets. When soft, drain and mash. Sauté 1 diced fennel bulb and 3 leeks in 4 tablespoons of butter. Add cream to taste and ½ cup vegetable broth. Simmer for about 10 minutes to reduce liquid. Add to potatoes and cauliflower. Mix. Add salt, pepper, and nutmeg to taste.

Jut and *stoemp* are served with *trippe* or a beef stew. *Carbonade flamande* is a classic Belgian beef and onion stew in which the beef chunks are slowly browned in butter then transferred to a Dutch oven. Next, sliced onions are slowly carmelized in butter and then combined with the meat. Using a Belgian Abbey beer to deglaze the skillet, the beer is then poured over the meat and onions and left to simmer 1.5 to 2 hours until the meat is very tender and the liquid has thickened. Season with salt, pepper, and thyme. The Walloon recipe ends here, while the Flemish version adds vinegar and brown sugar to the thickened liquid before serving, for a sweet/sour flavor.

Holiday Feasts

Belgian Americans celebrate St. Nicholas Day, December 6. Legend relates that kindly St. Nicholas travels from house to house visiting children, protecting them from his companion *Père Fouettard* (the Whipping Father), and leaving them gifts, fruit, nuts, and sweets.

Special among the sweets is *speculoos*, a spice cookie formed in the shape of the saint. *Speculoos* are thin, crunchy, and slightly browned. The cookie's distinctive taste comes from the spice blend (cinnamon, cloves, nutmeg, coriander and cardamom, and sometimes white pepper). Ground or slivered almonds are optional ingredients.

Christmas is a day for families to gather and celebrate with a traditional meal that often includes roast turkey, chestnut stuffing, goose or duck *pâté*, and chocolate truffles. Special baked desserts are *cramique,* a rich raisin bread or top-knotted brioche roll; *Buche de Noel*, a Yule log cake decorated with seasonal symbols; and *cougnou*, a sweet bread with distinct shape, also called "bread of Jesus."

Place in American Culture

Belgium claims as its creation *frites* or *frieten* ("French fries"), now considered a thoroughly American food. Belgian *frites* are freshly cut potatoes fried twice, which yields a crisp outer coating and soft inside. Served in a paper cone as street food in Belgium or as the perfect accompaniment to steamed mussels (*moules-frites*), *frites* are enjoyed with a variety of dipping sauces such as plain or flavored mayonnaise or aioli, Ghent sauce (chives and shallots in mayonnaise), Andalouse sauce (onion, bell pepper and tomato paste in mayonnaise), and many creative variations.

"Belgian waffles" offered for breakfast in American pancake houses are an American invention of soft, thick batter with large indentations topped with whipped cream and strawberries. These stand in contrast to the waffles that are a staple street food in Belgium or a favorite dessert in Belgian American cuisine. There are multiple types of these waffles, many of which use yeast as the leavening. One favorite is the Liege waffle, which has a caramelized texture due to pearl sugar in the dough. Belgian American households serve waffles, or *galettes* (also *gället*), as a special New Year's Day dish served with a buttermilk sauce. A waffle iron is a required tool.

Brussels sprouts and Belgian endive carry the name of their Belgian origin but are grown in American gardens and farms without much association with Belgium. Belgian-style beer has been adapted to mass marketing, with New Belgium Brewing of Fort Collins, Colorado, leading the way in the United States. In general, these beers are ales and include unique combinations of yeasts, spices, and fruits. Imported Belgian beers are valued for their wide variety in types and consistent high quality.

Belgian spice cookies, *speculoos*, are available on American grocery store shelves without being identified as such. They are recognizable as thin, lightly browned, crunchy cookies with an image such as a windmill imprinted on the front. Delta Airlines serves a version of *speculoos* as an in-flight snack, specifically offering the Biscoff brand from Belgium. As of 2007, a spreadable version of the cookie has been marketed, similar in consistency to peanut butter and consisting of crushed cookies mixed with vegetable oil.

Noted Restaurants and Chefs

Belgian restaurants exist in American cities with lively food scenes. Both New York City and Washington, DC, host Belgian Restaurant Weeks. Bistros or taverns that claim Belgian roots feature *moules-frites* and an extensive selection of draft Belgian beers. Full-fledged Belgian restaurants include other Belgian fare such as *carbonnade flamande*, various fish and shellfish preparations, *frites* with multiple dipping sauces, endive salad, cheeses, and use of beer as a cooking ingredient.

Along with classic Belgian dishes served with distinctive touches, some of these restaurants also offer interesting experiments. Chef Claudio Pirollo of Et Voila! in DC fuses American and Belgian favorites in the mussels burger.

In Cincinnati, Taste of Belgium owner Jean-Francois Flechet expands waffles as in the "wafflegato," a waffle topped with gelato with hot espresso poured on top. Washington, DC, has several notable Belgian American restaurants thanks to chefs such as Robert Wiedmaier, Bart Vandaele, and Jan Van Haute.

Further Reading

"Belgian-American Research Collection." *State of Wisconsin Collection.* Madison: Board of Regents of the University of Wisconsin System, 2011. http://digital.library.wisc.edu/1711.dl/WI.BelgAmrCol.

Cook, Jane Stewart. EveryCulture.com, Countries and Their Cultures. "Belgian Americans." http://www.everyculture.com/multi/A-Br/Belgian-Americans.html#ixzz2z7De9nw0, 2009.

Draize, Margaret. *Belgian American Heritage Customs and Cookbook.* Luxemburg, Wisconsin, 1996.

Anne Pryor

BELIZE

(Central America) Belizean American Food

Background

Emigration from Belize to the United States began during World War II, with the majority of Belizeans settling in New York, Chicago, Los Angeles, Miami, Houston, and New Orleans. Population estimates vary widely because a number of immigrants remain undocumented. In the 2011 US Community Survey, 1 percent of the 3.1 million Central American immigrants in the United States were born in Belize. English-speaking Creoles (who also speak Kriol), Afro-Belizeans (both Creole and Garifuna), and Garifuna (descendents of Caribbean indigenous and African slaves, also called Black Caribs) make up the majority of the US population of Belizeans. Known as British Honduras from the 1860s until 1973, Belize remained under British control until it gained full independence in 1981. As with other Central and South American groups, Belizean foodways, restaurants, and cafes reflect a mixture of culinary traditions. Belizean American restaurants almost always include Mayan foodways and influences such as the use of corn as well as Afro-Caribbean spices and hot sauces, Anglo-influenced cakes and pies, and specific ingredients and dishes from the Garifuna culture.

Foodways and Foodstuffs

Traditionally women have been the cooks in Belize, and there are numerous references in Belizean and Belizean American culture to the power of being able to cook well.[1]

The basics of Belizean cuisine are rice and beans, or rice with beans (the difference being whether the rice is cooked with the beans or separately) frequently spiced up with Marie Sharpe's™ or other hot sauces and often served with a stew, meat, or fish with ingredients depending on which culture's influence dominates the particular dish. Garifuna foodways are centered on cassava, coconut, plantains, bananas, poultry, and seafood, particularly conch. Kriol-Belizean food reflects a reliance on meat, usually beef or chicken but pork as well, along with starches—primarily yams and plantains—and, of course, fish, especially king fish. Belizean restaurants feature all of these along with oxtail, jerk, and curry chicken, conch fritters, cow foot soup, *garnaches* (fried corn tortillas served with beans and cheese, and ketchup sauce in Chicago), *panades* (corn patties served with cheese, cabbage, and onion), *salbutes* (fried tortillas topped with chicken), and chicken tamales. Ripe and green plantains are boiled to create "*hudut* (or *judutu*)," a bready sauce served with fish or soup.[2] *Boil ups*, a kind of stew like a New England boiled dinner but with tropical ingredients, might include pig tails, fish, yams, plantains, and hard-boiled eggs. Breakfast foods include fry jacks (fried dough) with eggs and refried beans.

Ethnic American Food Today

Desserts include sweet potato pound cake or "pone" made with coconut milk and ginger, and other cakes and baked goods such as coconut tarts. Beverages include juices, (mixes of mango carrot, guava carrot, pineapple ginger, sorrel ginger, and pineapple guava), ginger tea, black tea, and imported Caribbean sodas including ginger beer and Ting (Jamaican grapefruit).

Holiday Feasts

Like many Central American immigrants, Belizeans gather for festivals, including the celebration of Belize's independence from England, picnics, fund-raisers, and community potlucks. Immigrants and their descendants often use these occasions to raise funds and collect supplies for communities in Belize. Belizeans in Chicago have established an annual festival, the first Sunday in August, where traditional foods are featured. The Evangelical Garifuna Council of Churches in the Bronx hosts an annual Garifuna Day, which focuses on desserts, including banana, sweet potato, and corn cakes as well as *hudut* and other specialties. In Los Angeles, the Belizean Fish Market and Restaurant has held sway for over thirty years serving one of the larger Belizean diaspora populations as well as those who discover a taste for Caribbean food on the West Coast. Inglewood, California, holds a music festival, Caye Fest, that includes Caribbean music, food, and dancing. In Houston, the Belize Association features traditional dishes including tamales, rice and beans, and stewed chicken at its annual Family Fun Day. In Florida, there are several Belizean associations that host dances, festivals, and picnics. Louisiana's Belize Association holds an annual tea party along with other celebrations.

Place in American Culture

While many Americans are unfamiliar with Belizean foodways, the example of Garifuna Flava, a small restaurant located on the South Side of Chicago, provides a potential glimpse of a future where those who follow food television programs, such as on the Food Network, watch the YouTube Belize in America Channel, or visit Facebook will at least virtually learn about the dishes, seasonings, and traditions of this multifaceted food culture. Social media also highlights the various Belizean associations' annual picnics, festivals, and feasts.

Notes

1. "We all born cooking and dancing, honey. Yes, we all born cooking and dancing," said Enid Patton, playfully winding her hips as her sister, Leta Flowers, busily kneads dough for powder buns (sweet scones). Quoted in Lucille Renwick, "Home Away from Home: Belizeans Bring Sights, Sounds, Smells of Their Native Country to South-Central," July 3, 1994, *Los Angeles Times*, http://articles.latimes.com/1994-07-03/news/ci-11433_1_south-los-angeles/2.
2. Garifuna Flava, Chicago menu.

Further Reading and Watching

Burum, Linda. "The Find: Flavors of Belize." *New York Times*, March 10, 2011. http://articles.latimes.com/2011/mar/10/food/la-fo-find-flavors-of-belize-20110310.

Crowley, Chris E. "Finding Hudutu at the Bronx's Garifuna Day," April 24, 2013. http://newyork.seriouseats.com/2013/04/finding-hudutu-at-the-bronxs-garifuna-day.html.

LA Eater. "Belizean Fish Market: A Central American Seafood Gem." la.eater.com/archives/2014/07/08/belizean_fish_market_a_central_american_seafood_gem.php#more.

McKinstry, Nicole. *Being Belizean: A Story of 2 Cultures*. http://www.discoveringbelize.com/being_belizean_american.php.

Merrill, Tim, ed. "Migration." *Belize: A Country Study*. Washington: GPO for the Library of Congress, 1992. http://countrystudies.us/belize/22.htm.

Morrissey, Robert. "Belizeans." *Encyclopedia of Chicago History*. The Chicago Historical Society. http://www.encyclopedia.chicagohistory.org/pages/127.html.

Straughan, Jerome. "Emigration from Belize since 1981." *Taking Stock: Belize at 25 Years of Independence.* By Jaime J. Awe et al. Belize: Cubola Productions, 2007.

Wilk, Richard R. "'Real Belizean Food': Building Local Identity in the Transnational Caribbean." *American Anthropologist*, New Series, 101, no. 2. (June 1999): 244–55.

Wilk, Richard R. *Home Cooking in the Global Village.* Oxford: Berg, 2006.

YouTube. *Chicago's Best: Garifuna Flava.* https://www.youtube.com/watch?v=V0HuLhLEn1A.

Sue Eleuterio

BENIN

(Western Africa) Beninese American Food
See also: Gambia, Ghana, Nigeria, Senegal, and Guinea.

Background

Located on the western coast of Africa, the Republic of Benin shares cultural, geographic, and historical commonalities with other West African countries, particularly those that were colonized by France. It has a tropical climate and five distinctive geographic regions: seacoast, fertile plateau, wooded savanna, mountains, and river basin (Niger River). It also has cultural diversity, hosting fifty languages and dialects. Fon is spoken by half of its 4.5 million population, although French is the national language, reflecting Benin's status as a French colony (Dahomey) from the late 1800s to 1960. English is now also taught in school. Benin is world renowned for its art—specifically brass, ivory, wooden carvings, and sculptures—and woven cloth. Benin's economy is largely agricultural, and it is self-sufficient in its food supply.

The first Beninese came to the United States as slaves, some of whom helped bring voodoo beliefs and practices to New Orleans. In the 1980s, immigrants from Benin came to New York City for educational and employment opportunities. Many worked as hair braiders or made and sold African clothing. In 1984, the Association of Beninese Nationals in the United States (ARBEUA) was established in Washington, DC. In the 1990s, a community developed in Chicago, and many moved there from other parts of the United States. In the late 1990s, another wave of immigration occurred, again with employment and education as the impetus. A 2000 census counted only 605 individuals of Beninese descent, but in 2001 they were instrumental in founding the African Hairbraiding Association of Illinois, which called for licensing of the occupation. Today, small communities are found in Chicago, Washington, DC, and New York City.

Foodways

Beninese American food shares much in common with other West African ethnic groups, with the basic meals being a starch served with sauces and stews. Couscous is also a staple, as are plentiful tropical fruits and vegetables. Three meals a day are standard, with a breakfast of leftovers or street food and food prepared at home, usually by women, for midday and evening.

There is also regional diversity within Benin, however, where it is divided into northern and southern foods. In the south, the primary staple is maize (corn) along with rice and manioc as staples, eaten with peanut- or tomato-based sauces. The basic meats are chicken (grilled) and fish (smoked), but also beef, goat, and bush rat. Palm oil and peanut oil are used for cooking, as in fried plantains. Also significant are beans, usually cooked as a side dish, tomatoes, and fruit, such as oranges, bananas, kiwi, avocado, and pineapples.

In the North, yams are usually pounded into *fufu*, and millet and sorghum are the basic staple grains. Beef and pork are staple meats, and a soft, mild, cow's milk cheese (*wagasi*) is made by the Fulani people and used in cooking. Fruits include mangos, oranges, and avocados, and vegetables include okra, tomatoes, pumpkin seeds, peanuts, eggplants, and peppers.

Millet beer (*choukachou* or *chouk*) is common, particularly in the north, while palm wine liquor (*sodabi*) is consumed more in the south and is used in ceremonies.

Popular dishes include *ago glain*, a stew of shellfish, tomato, and onions, which is considered the national dish, and is served with a local hot sauce, *pilipili*. This sauce is oftentimes sold in the United States in African groceries as well as the occasional Asian or Hispanic market. Another popular dish is *acaraje*, black-eyed peas peeled and formed into ball, then deep fried in palm oil. This dish is also found in Ghana and Nigeria.

Holidays are frequently celebrated with feasts, with Muslims oftentimes consuming roasted whole sheep, and Christians consuming pork.

Place in American Culture

The Beninese American population is very small and, if known at all, is best known for its applique cloth, stores selling African clothing, and hairbraiding rather than its food.

Restaurants

In Benin itself, restaurants usually serve French cuisine. There seem to be no specifically Beninese restaurants in the United States, although the food can be found in West African restaurants, particularly those of other French-speaking nations.

Further Reading

The Association of Beninese of Illinois. http://www.benineseofillinois.org/aboutus.html.

EveryCulture.com, Countries and Their Cultures. "Benin." http://www.everyculture.com/A-Bo/Benin.html.

Steffes, Tracy. "Beninese (in Chicago)." http://www.encyclopedia.chicagohistory.org/pages/2491.html.

Lucy M. Long

BERMUDA
(North America) Bermudian American Food
See also: Belize.

Background

A small series of islands located in the Atlantic Ocean, but often mistakenly associated with the Caribbean, Bermuda is a British Overseas Territory with a diverse population. The islands were uninhabited at the time of European contact in 1503, with the first English settlement established in 1609, and the current population reflects the legacy of two hundred years of slavery. The population is multiethnic, including people of African, Native American, and European descent, but it continues to diversify through a steady rate of immigration and the widespread employment of foreign workers. Emigration from the islands has increased in recent years, and Bermuda's census organization warns of a "brain drain" effect as more educated individuals move away at a disproportionately rapid rate. In 2010, 39 percent or 380 of these emigrants went to the United States. Many Bermudians have settled in Florida, but families have not followed a tight dispersion pattern and may be found throughout the country.

Foodways

Like Belize, Bermuda's long history of British rule has influenced its foodways. Much of Bermuda's cuisine has British origins, including dishes ranging from Christmas puddings to fish chowders. Although Bermuda is surrounded by the sea and has a subtropical climate, 80 percent of Bermuda's food is imported, mostly from the United States. While local fruits, vegetables, and seafood are available and play an important part in the cuisine, the high rate of food importation along with European influence has created a cuisine that contains a fusion of foreign and local ingredients. Imported salted codfish is one of the most common ingredients, featured in fishcakes and fried for the traditional Sunday breakfast, but local seafood, such as spiny lobster and wahoo, is also abundant. Local fruits and vegetables are featured in many recipes, with the Bermudian sweet onion as one of the most recognizable, to the point that Bermudians themselves are sometimes known as "onions." Among Bermudian immigrants in the United States, the dishes that persist in daily and holiday menus often include ingredients that are more commonly found in supermarkets or ethnic markets, such as codfish, cassava, potatoes, rice, and black-eyed peas.

Cod fishcakes are a much-loved dish, as is fish chowder served with sherry pepper, a condiment made from hot peppers soaked in sherry. Hoppin' John, a dish made of black-eyed peas and rice that is found through much of the South, is also a part of the everyday cuisine of Bermudian Americans. Sunday breakfast is a weekly occasion celebrated with a large family meal, and the traditional menu consists of fried codfish and potatoes, often served with hard-boiled eggs, bananas, onions, and avocado.

Major holiday feasts include Easter, when the traditional foods include hot cross buns and fishcakes, and Christmas, celebrated with cassava cake. As in parts of the southern United States, Hoppin' John may be eaten on New Year's Day to give good luck, although it is also common to eat it throughout the year.

Cod Fish Cakes

1 pound frozen cod fillets
2 large potatoes peeled and chopped
1 clove of garlic, crushed
1 tablespoon grated sweet onion
1 tablespoon butter
1 egg
1 teaspoon thyme
pinch of seasoning salt
pinch of black pepper
flour (white or potato) for coating
oil sufficient for pan frying

Directions:
1. Boil the potatoes until soft.
2. Steam the cod with the onion and garlic until the cod becomes opaque and begins to flake apart.
3. Thoroughly drain potatoes.
4. Mash or rice potatoes with egg, butter, and seasonings.
5. Fold cod into the potato mixture. Chunks of cod should be visible throughout the mix.
6. Chill the mixture in the refrigerator for an hour before handling.
7. Form fishcakes and coat in flour.
8. Pan fry in oil or bake at 400° until golden brown.

Place in American Culture

Bermuda's cuisine does not have the same presence in the United States as those from the Caribbean. One of the few Bermudian food items known in the United States is an alcoholic drink containing dark rum and spicy ginger beer that is on many menus in South Florida restaurants. When made from Gosling's Dark Rum, it is called by the trademarked name Dark and Stormy®. Other brands of rum may be substituted, but the emphasis in substitution is on using a very dark rum with a strong molasses overtone to complement the zesty ginger.

Noted Restaurants and Chefs

Bermudian cuisine is uncommon in American restaurants. Frozen, salted cod is sometimes available through Asian markets, and cassava may be found in both Asian and Latin American markets. Many Bermudians report bringing back key ingredients after visiting the islands due to difficulty finding them in the United States.

Further Reading

Bermuda Junior Service League. *Island Thyme: Tastes and Traditions of Bermuda*. Nashville: Favorite Recipes Press, 2005.

Forbes, Keith Archibald. "Bermuda Cuisine." *Bermuda Online.* The Royal Gazette Ltd., October 29, 2014. http://www.bermuda-online.org/cuisine.htm.

The Lion and the Mouse: The Story of America and Bermuda. Dir. Lucinda Spurling. Afflare Films, 2009. Film.

Mathilde Frances Lind

BHUTAN

(Southern Asia) Bhutanese American Food
See also: Nepal, Tibet, India.

Background

The Himalayan nation of Bhutan is not well known to Americans, even though an estimated sixty thousand Bhutanese refugees live in the United States. Ethnic Nepalese whose families had lived in Bhutan for centuries were driven out of the kingdom and stripped of their nationality as part of an ethnic cleansing movement in the early 1990s. After more than a decade in Nepalese refugee camps, many came to America to rebuild their communities and start anew, primarily in New York, Chicago, and San Francisco.

Foodways

The ingredients dominating Bhutanese cuisine are largely limited to produce able to be grown at the high altitudes of the Himalayas, such as onions, tomatoes, and potatoes. Rice is a staple at every meal, and buckwheat and barley are also cultivated and consumed in different regions of the country. Dishes typically feature a combination of these, with fiery red and green chilies called *ema*, yak's or cow's cheese and butter, and chopped chicken, beef, and pork. Common spices include cardamom, ginger, chili, garlic, turmeric, and caraway. Most dishes are variations on Bhutanese curry, *tshoem*, served with Bhutan's famous red rice, which has a strong, nutty flavor. A common snack found at Bhutanese markets is *chugo*, a protein-rich yak cheese, which is dried until it is rock solid. Desserts and sweets are less popular in Bhutan, although meals may be followed with fruits such as peaches and pears. Bhutan's national drink, *ara*, is a home-brewed, rice-based beverage that can be fermented or distilled, and which is typically served hot with butter and scrambled or poached egg added for texture. During morning and afternoon tea, the Bhutanese drink *suja* is consumed, a hot drink made by churning salted tea together with yak butter.

Preparation

Bhutanese food was traditionally prepared in earthenware, and older generations ate with their fingers instead of utensils, although modern cookware has now replaced these customs. Bhutanese meals are typically boiled rather than fried, with copious amounts of butter and chilies, which are used as a vegetable rather than a spice, making Bhutanese food some of the spiciest in the world. The Bhutanese use few additives and condiments, and Bhutan has pledged to become the world's first entirely organic country.

Traditionally, men are the providers of food in Bhutan while women stay at home and take care of the household and the children. The Bhutanese take pride in sharing and will offer generous amounts of food to guests. The polite response, when first offered food, is to place your hand over your mouth and say *meshu meshu* as a refusal, before accepting the second or third offer.

Everyday Meals

The Bhutanese often eat red rice with curries or stews three times a day. *Jasha maroo* is a curry made from diced chicken, tomatoes, onions, garlic, ginger, and plenty of chilies, and it is typically served with red rice. Another popular dish consists of hand-pulled buckwheat noodles, *puta*, served with meat, turnip leaves, and gravy. Side dishes include *khule* (buckwheat pancakes), *momo* (dumplings), and a salsa-like dish called *ezay*.

Bhutan's national dish, *ema datshi*, is a simple stew made from chilies and cheese. The following recipe serves two to four people.

Ema Datshi
- 8 ounces of Bhutanese peppers (substitute jalapeños)
- 1 onion, coarsely chopped
- 2 tomatoes, diced
- 8 ounces of Bhutanese farmer's cheese (substitute feta or queso fresco)
- 4 cloves of garlic, crushed
- 4 cilantro leaves
- 2 teaspoons of vegetable oil

Slice the peppers into strips. Fill a saucepan with 12 ounces of water, and boil the chilies and onion until soft (10 minutes). Add the oil, onion, tomato, and garlic, and simmer for two minutes. Add cheese and cilantro, and allow to simmer for another two minutes. Serve with red rice.

Holiday Feasts

Food plays a prominent role in Bhutanese festivals, and sharing food is a symbol of brotherhood. During the Bhutanese New Year, different regions prepare special foods, such as *hoentey*, a dumpling made with sweet buckwheat flower, turnips, cottage cheese, and amaranth seeds. A common festival dish is *jomja*, a Bhutanese "pizza" made from rice dough and covered with a walnut, chili, ginger, and onion spread. *Daisi*, a ceremonial dish, is made with rice, butter, sugar, and saffron, topped with raisins and chestnuts.

Place in American Culture

The Bhutanese are best known to Americans for their concept of "gross national happiness," a concept coined by the Bhutanese as a way to measure the happiness and health of the nation in terms of quality of life, rather than GDP. Bhutanese cuisine, however, is little known and represented primarily by the Himalayan snack known as *momo*, which has become a common sight in the contemporary food scene in urban America. This dumpling stuffed with meat is common in Bhutan, Tibet, and Nepal, and the Bhutanese version, served with a fiery chili dipping sauce, oftentimes also features a cheese filling.

Bhutanese restaurants have not yet made a mark on the American scene, and immigrants often prefer to eat at home, seeing mealtimes as a family occasion. Food is central to social activities in Bhutanese American communities, being used as an opportunity to preserve cultural traditions and to share stories about the homeland with younger generations. Festivals are often celebrated together with local Nepalese communities in America.

Bhutanese ingredients can be difficult to locate in America, although Bhutanese red rice can be found at some Asian food stores, and yak products are gaining popularity in the United States. American perceptions of Bhutanese food are limited, since most Bhutanese people in America only arrived in or after 2008, but American food critic Ruth Reichl famously remarked that Bhutan has "the world's worst cuisine." Conversely, the 2008 Smithsonian Folk Festival in Washington, DC, offered an opportunity for Americans to experience Bhutanese culture, with exhibits on Bhutanese life and food cooked by Bhutanese chefs.

Adjustments to American food have been difficult for many Bhutanese immigrants, who are used to the starchy Bhutanese diet high in carbohydrates and fat but are unaccustomed to the large portion sizes and reliance on packaged food in America. Obesity, hypertension, and diabetes are high in the Bhutanese American community as a result. Traditional Bhutanese gender roles have also changed for Bhutanese immigrants, as many find that both partners need to work in order to support their family in the United States.

Noted Restaurants and Chefs

Few Bhutanese restaurants currently exist in America, but several restaurants feature Bhutanese dishes, such as the Himalaya Restaurant in Plattsburgh, New York, which is run by Bhutanese owner-chef Tenzin Dorjee. Their menu includes *suja*, *ema datshi*, and *tsipha pa*, a pork rib dish often served at festivals, all prepared from scratch. Some of their ingredients are sourced directly from Bhutan, where Dorjee's cousin grows them on his farm. Himalayan Yak in Jackson Heights serves *ema datshi*, *phaksha pa*, and momo. Wasabi Point in nearby Elmhurst features Bhutanese dishes as well, prepared by chef-owner Jimmy Thonsur, who spent his formative years in Bhutan. In the Bay Area, Bhutanese food can be found in El Cerrito at Tashi Delek, or Himalayan Flavors in Berkeley, which serves *jasha maroo*, *momo*, a goat curry dish, and buckwheat pancakes.

Further Reading

Choden, Kunzang. *Chilli and Cheese: Food and Society in Bhutan*. Bangkok: White Lotus Press, 2008.

Halpern, Sue, and Bill McKibben. "How Manchester's Burgeoning Bhutanese Population Is Pursuing the American Dream." *Smithsonian Magazine*, April 2014.

Leaming, Linda. *Married to Bhutan*. Carlsbad, CA: Hay House, 2011.

Nagamatsu, Ernest, and Erik Nagamatsu. *Foods of the Kingdom of Bhutan*. Thimphu: Kuensel, 2010.

Rennie, Frank, and Robin Mason. *Bhutan: Ways of Knowing*. Charlotte, NC: IAP, 2008.

Claire Y. van den Broek

BOLIVIA

(South America) Bolivian American Food

Bolivia's cuisine is influenced by regional variations that characterize two different cooking styles: altiplano or lowlands. Most meals include meat, usually served with potatoes, rice, or both. Bolivian immigrants from the highlands eat mostly potatoes, while those from the lowlands consider rice, plantains, and yuccas to be staples. The number of Bolivian immigrants to the United States is small, and most tend to adapt their foodways and lifestyles to life in the United States.

Background

The US Census Bureau only began recording nation of origin for Latin American immigrants in 1960. During the second half of the twentieth century, there were two waves of Bolivian immigrants, the first following the 1952 National Revolution, and the second during the economic hyperinflation of the 1980s. The first immigrants were predominately upper-middle-income professionals or political dissidents, while the second tended to be lower-income mestizos in service and manual labor. Historically US immigration has been limited, ranging between three hundred to five hundred individuals per year between 1980 and the mid 1990s. Total numbers of Bolivian Americans are undoubtedly greater, as immigrants may arrive with tourist visas but overstay their visas. In general, Bolivian Americans constitute a small percentage of the Latin American immigrant pool, reaching a total estimated population of eighty-two thousand in 2006.

Although Bolivians represent a small percentage of Latin American immigrants to the United States, immigrants are predominately educated workers and professionals. They tend to settle in urban centers on the West or East Coast, concentrated primarily in Los Angeles, Chicago, and Washington, DC.

Foodways

The Bolivian cuisine reflects the influence of two major ecological zones: altiplano and lowlands. Highland residents include the majority of highland Indians, both Aymara and Quechua, and Bolivians of Spanish descent, known as *blancos*, or white. Despite the long Spanish occupation, Highland Bolivians tended to maintain their traditional prehistoric diet based on potatoes, quinoa, and beans, with the addition of corn, throughout the colonial period. In the lowlands, residents grew a wider variety of vegetables and fruits, such as tomatoes, chili pepper, peanuts, squash, chocolate, and avocados, expanding their cuisine. Spaniards introduced both new foods, such as wheat, rice, pigs, chicken, and vegetables, including cilantro, limes, garlic, carrots, and olives, as well as new forms of cooking, such as the more common Spanish soups, stews, and sautéed dishes.

In general, the cuisine is represented by numerous stews, including *silpancho*, pounded beef with a fried egg on top; *thimphu*, a spicy vegetable stew; and *fricase*, a pork stew seasoned with yellow hot pepper. Another stew, *changa*, is made of chicken or guinea pig, potato, peas, and green onions. In general, these stews are spicy, flavored by local chilies, *ají*, that warm up consumers in the high, cold altiplano. Indigenous Bolivians developed and adapted different kinds of chilies, following the prehistoric domestication of chilies in Mesoamerica. South Americans prefer a small, spicy chili pepper, known as *ají*, from the Taino (indigenous Caribbean) word *ají*. In contrast with Mexicans, South Americans prefer the smaller finger peppers, called *ají de montaña* or *ají entero*, hot chilies that are usually combined with herbs and onions. In Latino specialty groceries, Bolivian Americans purchase imported *locoto* chilies frozen or in brine that can be stuffed or used to flavor other dishes. *Locotos* form the base of *llajua*, a sauce made with ground *locotos*, tomatoes, and onions, and flavored with Bolivian herbs. In the United States, more readily available herbs, such as mint, basil, or cilantro, often substitute the less available Bolivian herbs.

First domesticated in the Andean highlands, potatoes appeared early in the Lake Titicaca basin from where they were spread throughout South America. There are hundreds of different potato varieties, mostly consumed by the indigenous Quechua and Aymara. Different dishes draw on the specific qualities of these different kinds of potatoes, but in the United States, Bolivian American must use the limited number of varieties available domestically. Bolivians who immigrate to the United States often must substitute more common varieties of US potatoes—for example, russets or Yukon gold—when faced with the challenge of finding specialty potatoes in US markets. This is particularly a problem for recipes that call for *chuño*, the freeze-dried potato produced in the altiplano.

Meat dishes are also common. Preferred meats include pork, particularly in roast suckling pig, although chicken or turkey may be substituted for pork. An indigenous delicacy, *charque de llama*, or dried llama meat, is often fried by Bolivian cooks and served with stewed corn, hard-boiled eggs, and cheese. *Charque de llama* is much more difficult to locate in American groceries.

Fricase (Pork Stew)

2 teaspoons oil
2½ pounds pork cubes
1 cup white onion, cut into thin strips
1 teaspoon cumin
½ teaspoon ground black pepper
1 teaspoon oregano (crushed)
2 cloves garlic, minced
½ cup cayenne pepper
1 teaspoon salt
½ cup scallions, cut into thin strips
8 cups water, boiling
½ cup plain breadcrumbs

To serve:
4 cups cooked white corn
8 potatoes, peeled, cooked separately, and in chunks

Heat oil in large pot over medium heat. Add pork and fry until golden. Add onion, cumin, pepper, oregano, garlic, cayenne pepper, salt and scallions. Stir and add 8 cups of boiling water.

Cook for 2 hours, until meat is tender and shredding. Add water if needed, to maintain amount of broth.

Before serving, add breadcrumbs to thicken. Serve in a deep plate with broth. Garnish with pieces of cooked potato and cooked white corn.

For Bolivians, street food also comprises an important part of the daily diet. Particularly common are *salteñas*, a pastry similar to *empanadas*, filled with different meats, potato, or cheese with onion fillings. *Salteñas* are spiced with *locoto*. *Humitas* are similar to tamales in shape, made with corn and cheese, and then wrapped in corn leaves before steaming. Made with fresh corn, these are more similar to Mexican *uchepos*, common in the central western highlands, than tamales, made with the *masa* of dried corn.

Bolivians generally start the day with a light breakfast that includes coffee or hot tea and a small pastry. After this, many Bolivians snack or eat at various times throughout the day, starting at mid-morning with a *salteña*, or *empanada*. Lunch is the largest meal of the day, and in Bolivia many offices or departments close midday to allow workers to return home for the midday meal. This meal would be comprised of soup, a meat dish, rice, potatoes, beans, and a dessert, followed inevitably by a break before returning to work. For Bolivian Americans, the midday meal has been reduced to the American lunch hour, and the main meal has shifted to the evening dinner. Traditionally, Bolivians would take tea around 4:00 p.m., comprised of a pastry and either tea or coffee. In addition to black tea, Bolivians also serve *api*, a Bolivian tea that is made from lemon, corn, cloves, and cinnamon. In Bolivia, tearooms often provide both tea and pastries. Dinner is usually lighter than the midday meal, consisting of soup or *empanadas*. Typical soups can include ground peanut soups or more stewlike soups, known as *chupes*, based on fish and stewed tubers of chopped meats.

Holiday Feasts

Most Bolivians are Catholic, although traditionally indigenous Ayamara and Quechua practice a form of popular Catholicism that reflects the religious syncretism of colonial Catholic practices with indigenous pre-Hispanic religions. Bolivians traditionally celebrate Christmas Eve with the *picana de Navidad*, a stew made with lamb, beef, chicken, carrots, turnips, onions, tomatoes, raisins, prunes, potatoes, and fresh corncobs. Seasoned with black pepper, cloves, bay leaves, cumin, oregano, and red wine, the *picana* closely mirrors the *puchero*, a Spanish stew introduced during the colonial period. Bolivians prepare *buñuelos*, a wheat flour fried pastry, seasoned with anise seeds or chocolate. Following Christmas, Bolivians adhere to the sacrifices of the Lenten period with a traditional fish broth, known in the Aymaran language as *challwa-wallakhes*. Abstinence continues through the Holy Week period, when on Holy Thursday Bolivians traditionally prepare a cod stew. On Good Friday, they eat dried cod again, as *bacalao a la vizcaína*, a dried cod and rice dish prepared in the Basque style. The calendar closes in the fall with All Souls' Day and All Saints' Day, on November 1 and 2, during which devout Catholics go to church and to the cemeteries to venerate their dead ancestors. Bolivians traditionally prepare *uchu de Todos los Santos*, All Saints' chili, made up of beef tongue, guinea pig, red chili pepper, onions, garlic, cumin, and parsley, along with potatoes and hard-boiled eggs. In the United States, Bolivian Americans can usually locate the ingredients required for the traditional feast foods, although the guinea pig may often be left out of the *uchu de Todos los Santos*.

Place in American Culture and Restaurants

Earlier Bolivian immigrants were mostly upper middle class but lived dispersed in the United States and faced challenges to maintain traditional foodways. In the United States, they adapted to the broader Latino culture and adapted Bolivian recipes with available ingredients. With increased migration in the 1990s and a concentration of immigrants in certain East Coast centers, particularly around Washington, DC, it is becoming more common to see Bolivian restaurants or to find certain ingredients, such as different kinds of potatoes or chilies, in Latino groceries. Bolivian American restaurants tend to be casual, family-style eateries.

Further Reading

Boliva Web. "Recipes Gallery: Traditional Bolivian Cooking." http://www.boliviaweb.com/recipes/english/.

Carnegie Library of Pittsburgh. "Latin American Food & Cooking." http://www.carnegielibrary.org/research/food/cuisines/latin.html.

Janer, Zilkia. *Latino Food Culture*. Westport, CT: Greenwood Press, 2008.

Lovera, José Rafael. *Food Culture in South America*. Westport, CT: Greenwood Press, 2005.

Ortiz, Elizabeth Lambert. *The Book of Latin American Cooking*. New York: Alfred A. Knopf, 1979.

Presilla, Maricel. *Gran Cocina Latina: The Food of Latin America*. New York: W. W. Norton, 2012.

Sánchez, José. *My Mother's Bolivian Kitchen: Recipes and Recollections*. New York: Hippocrene Books, 2005.

Sarmiento de Dupleich, Magaly. *Bolivian Food Andean Flavor: Sabor Andino Comida Boliviana*. La Paz, Bolivia: Sierpe, 2004.

Lois Stanford

BONAIRE, SAINT EUSTATIUS, AND SABA

(America—Caribbean)
See Caribbean, Dutch.

BOSNIA AND HERZEGOVINA

(Eastern Europe) Bosnian American
See also: Serbia and Montenegro, Croatia.

Background

The great waves of Bosnian refugees who arrived during and after the war offer an opportunity to observe the earliest stages of an ethnic cuisine in the making and provide insights on the importance, persistence, and malleability of traditional food and foodways.

The wave of war refugees in 1945 and subsequent economically motivated migration beginning in the 1960s revitalized the original Chicago community. There was by this time a smattering of Bosnians elsewhere in the United States, but not enough to establish viable communities until the large migration following the Bosnian civil war. Chicago is still a principal community, but Bosnians now live everywhere in America, and a number of other large communities have developed, including St. Louis, New York, Detroit, and Oakland. After two decades in America, Bosnian Americans have established an impressive ethnic infrastructure, and larger communities easily support businesses serving Bosnians, including grocery stores, meat markets, bakeries, restaurants, and coffee houses.

There is considerable overlap between Bosnian food and that of Serbia and Croatia, particularly along border areas. Borders have never been stable for very long in the Balkans, and all three groups speak the same language, further facilitating cultural exchange. This is the first time in history that Bosnian Muslims have constituted a country of their own.

Exact population figures are unavailable, but according to an estimate from the Bosnian-Herzegovinan Embassy, there are some 350,000 Bosnian Muslims in the United States.

Foodways

Food prepared in the kitchen is exclusively by women. Men do all the cooking outdoors, usually meaning grilling or spit roasting meat, but including on occasion the preparation of a fish stew or goulash prepared over a wood fire. Bosnian food is not particularly spicy, although jars of medium-hot pickled peppers are sometimes seen.

As in Bosnia, the most common food in Bosnian America is *pita*. Phyllolike dough (*jufka*) is rolled around filling, then baked. The filling is most often ground meat or white cheese but can vary widely, including spinach and cheese, potatoes, winter squash, wild nettles, and, in a sweet version, apples. Innovation is always possible. At least one Bosnian American has experimented with mushrooms. Bosnian American cooks from the Tuzla area have learned to use leeks from a woman from Prijedor, where they are traditional. *Pita* is baked in a specific pan about one-and-a-half inches high and up to eighteen inches in diameter. These are available in Near Eastern or Balkan markets or brought back from Bosnia-Herzegovina, to which most families make regular trips.

Bread is the constant and essential component of every meal in Bosnia and Bosnia America. There is a maxim in Bosnia: "We don't even eat bread without bread." Several big slabs of bread are laid by the plate as part of the place setting at both family and festive occasions. In America, the daily bread is usually loaves of unsliced white bread obtained at Bosnian bakeries, if available, otherwise at grocery stores. A special bread, *lepinje* (also called *samun*), eight-inch-diameter rounds of a puffy white yeast bread, is essential when eating *ćevapčići*, the popular uncased, grilled sausage. Every larger Bosnian American community has one or more bakeries producing *lepinje*, and usually also loaves of daily bread. *Ćevapčići* and *lepinje* are the most common foods, sometimes the only foods, offered in Bosnian American restaurants. *Lepinje* is split and laid over the *ćevapčići* as they fry on the grill so as to soak up grease and meat juices. *Ćevapčići* are traditionally served in groups of five or ten in a *lepinje* with chopped onions on the side and eaten not as a sandwich but by hand, one by one, with a piece torn from the bread. *Lepinje* is produced only in bakeries, never at home, because it necessitates a bakery oven. A number of commercial bakers learned to produce *lepinje* only after emigration. Reviewers of Bosnian restaurants invariably enthuse about the bread, and restaurants catering to non-Bosnians have come to serve *lepinje* with everything. Loaves of daily bread are sometimes baked at home, but less so now than when Bosnians first arrived because most women now work outside the home and have less time for baking.

Meat is more commonly eaten in America than in Bosnia. Fish, because it is more available, and chicken, probably because it is the least expensive meat, are more frequently eaten. Lamb is much less common, even among those Bosnians from sheepherding regions, because of its relative high cost. Veal is highly ranked but less eaten than in Bosnia-Herzegovina for the same reason. Beef has become the most commonly eaten meat. In Bosnia and elsewhere in former Yugoslavia, spit roasting a whole sheep is part of festive occasions. The act, itself, usually accompanied by visiting, drinking, and singing, is as important as the food prepared. It is no wonder that Bosnians recently arrived in America, with a job that affords some luxuries, are roasting sheep much more frequently than they ever did in Bosnia. Always a joyous act, in the United States it takes on an additional meaning, filled with nostalgia and symbolism of all those happier times in the homeland. In addition to *ćevapčići*, *pljeskavica* (patties traditionally made of a mixture of ground meats but now all beef), chicken, offal, and, most common, thin beefsteaks are cooked on backyard grills or over campfires. Mixed grill (*mešano meso*) is a popular combination of grilled meats. In Bosnia *ćevapčići* are considered restaurant food and are not prepared at home. In America, uncooked *ćevapčići* are available from every Bosnian butcher and frozen from every Bosnian market.

Smoked meat (*suho meso*), either beef or lamb, and smoked beef or lamb sausage (*sudžuk*) are much appreciated snacks, usually served as appetizers (*meze*), especially with drinks. They are produced by Bosnian butchers (who were not necessarily butchers in Bosnia-Herzegovina) in a number of communities scattered across the United States and Canada. Smoked meat and, less commonly, sausage are also often home produced. Men have constructed their own backyard smokehouses, and smoked meat and cheese are frequent gifts between men. Although most Bosnian Americans observe the Islamic prohibition of pork, they, like many Muslims in Bosnia, do drink, preferring beer or *šljivovica* (plum brandy).

Vegetables are little eaten, both in Bosnia and Bosnia America, except in combinations such as spinach *pita* or stuffed vegetables. The primary exception is salad. Onions are essential to the cuisine. It is said that in preparation of a meal, a Bosnian will chop onions and then decide what to cook. Cabbage rolls (*sarma*), meat and rice wrapped usually in home-cured sauerkraut leaves, and peppers (*punjeni paprike*) stuffed with the same filling are common favorites. Stuffed onions (*sogan dolma*) are a Muslim specialty. Bean soup, sometimes prepared with a bit of fresh meat or *suho meso*, is frequently prepared. Paprika is the primary spice.

Filled Peppers (*Punjene Paprike*)

    6 to 8 green Balkan peppers (NOT bell peppers)
    1 onion
    ¼ cup rice
    1 pound ground beef (ground lamb would be even better)
    1 egg
    1 teaspoon *vegeta*
    salt and pepper
    1 can tomatoes or 5 to 6 large, ripe, chopped tomatoes
    3 tablespoons oil
    3 to 4 tablespoons flour
    paprika
    sour cream

Cut off stems of peppers, remove seeds, and rinse. Sauté finely chopped onion in 1 tablespoon oil until transparent. Add rice and sauté until rice is coated. Cool. Add meat, egg, *vegeta*, salt, and pepper. Fill peppers. Place in heavy pot with peppers upright. Add canned tomatoes with juice or ripe tomatoes with a little water. Cover and simmer; add water when necessary. This is done when the peppers are tender.

Make a *roux*: In a heavy skillet, heat 2 tablespoons oil, and add 3 to 4 tablespoons flour over a low heat. Stir the flour continually until golden brown. Add paprika. Add cold water slowly to bubbling flour mixture and cook for about 10 to 15 minutes. Stir continually or the flour will lump. The desired consistency is a thick but not stiff sauce. While stirring slowly add some liquid from the pot of peppers to dilute it so that it can be poured back into the pepper pot. Shake the pot to distribute *roux*. Cook for another 10 minutes. Serve on a platter with the juice from the pan; pour sour cream over the peppers.

Trahana (in some regions, *tarhana* or *tarana*) is an ancient food introduced during the Ottoman period. In Bosnia-Herzegovina, it is associated with, and usually only produced by, Muslims.

It is a popular home-processed food, a sort of granular dumpling used in soup. It had disappeared from the active repertoire of recipes in many regions of Bosnia-Herzegovina even prior to the civil war, but many from regions where it had persevered continue to make it now. Its traditional production involves at least a week of fermentation, then forcing the dough through a traditional sieve (*sito*) to form the grains. These sieves are unavailable in America; consequently, housewives have developed different methods of achieving similar results, working on an experimental basis. One, for example, substitutes an American strainer. Another dries the dough and grates it. Unless someone starts importing the traditional sieves, one or another alternative method will eventually be accepted by the community as best for doing the job.

Another specialized Bosnian cooking implement is a certain type of earthenware pot (*lonac*). The national dish of Bosnia, *Bosanski lonac*, is a stew of combined meats (traditionally three) and vegetables slow cooked in this covered pot.

Turkish-style Bosnian coffee is still the norm, though now often served in American coffee cups or demitasse instead of the tiny handless cups (*findžani*) that were traditional. It is sometimes made in the traditional *djezva*, but now more often a larger metal pot. Coffee is made repeatedly during the day. As one Bosnian from the St. Louis community stated, "We have Turkish coffee maybe three or four times a day, but it's not like in the United States where you use coffee to wake up. We use coffee to socialize." This last point is important. When guests arrive, coffee is immediately made. It is served with sugar cubes on the saucer to be dipped or drunk through along with two or three pieces of sweet pastry, even if the coffee service is preliminary to a large meal.

Holiday Feasts

The most important feasts are the two *Bajrams* (Arabic, *Eid*) held each year according to the lunar calendar. *Ramazanski Bajram* consists of three days of feasting, visiting, and prayer following the Ramadan fast. Sometimes one home will host an evening of prayer, including a local Imam, followed by a feast, the men and women eating separately. Two lunar months later, *Kurban Bajram* is centered on the ritual killing of a sacrificial animal (*kurban*), usually a sheep that should be pure white and lacking imperfections. According to the Koran, the meat should be distributed to the poor, but, as one member of the Detroit area community said, "In America there are no poor"—that is, no poor Bosnians. Instead, small packages of raw meat are given to friends and relatives, who return packages of their own *kurban* in a round of gift giving lasting over a three-day period. Some families, in the years following their arrival in America, sent money back to a relative in Bosnia to purchase, kill, and distribute a *kurban* in their name. All religious holidays are according to the lunar calendar.

Thanksgiving is also observed. Like so many other immigrant and ethnic communities in America, the Thanksgiving feast consists of a turkey surrounded by Bosnian dishes.

Improvements in international marketing have made it much easier to replicate Bosnian food in America. Bosnian markets, and sometimes non-Bosnian markets with a partial clientele of Bosnians, stock imports from Bosnia-Herzegovina and parallel products from Croatia, Macedonia, and Serbia. As a result, it is less necessary to find or concoct substitutes. Earlier Balkan immigrants, and those Bosnians without access to such markets, found it necessary to construct a substitute for *kajmak*, a partially fermented cultured cream product similar to clotted cream that is much used throughout the Balkans, eaten both fresh and in cooking. Some stores import a credible factory-made version from Bosnia-Herzegovina, but most families have substituted American sour cream for the purposes of cooking. So common is its use that some purchase sour cream in five-pound cartons.

Bosnian markets import a number of products either unavailable in America or preferred by Bosnians to their American counterparts. Sugar cubes are imported because the large rectangular, rough-edged Bosnian cubes are more familiar than American ones, even if the taste is no different. *Vegeta*, considered essential by Bosnian cooks, is always on the shelves in great supply. It is a flavor enhancer composed primarily of salt, dehydrated vegetables, and monosodium glutamate, and Bosnians use it in most savory dishes, such as stews and meats to be grilled. Also common are jars of *ajvar*, a relish made of pepper paste sometimes diluted with eggplant puree, and *pekmez*, a fruit spread most commonly made of the same plums used for šljivovica. Both can be homemade, producing a superior product. *Travnički sir* (cheese from Travnik) is a fetalike white cheese but creamier, less crumbly, and less salty. It is sometimes imported but difficult to find and not as good as the bulk product in Bosnia. Bosnians much prefer it, but they have largely replaced it with feta. Bosnian coffee, paprika, jams, and herbal teas from one or another of the post-Yugoslav nations, small cans of Croatian or Bosnian *paté*, *jufka*, imported thin noodles as used in soup, shrink-wrapped packages of *suho meso*, frozen and/or fresh *ćevapčići*, and *lepinje* are usually available. Sometimes one can purchase chunks of freshly roasted lamb. Usually, no effort is made to obtain *halal* meats, even when these are available in nearby Arab markets.

Place in American Culture

Other Americans, unless they have traveled to Bosnia or have Bosnian American friends, have little, if any, knowledge of Bosnian food. Most would assume it to be "spicy," which it is not.

Noted Restaurants and Chefs

Bosnian American restaurants tend to be of two types: those catering to fellow Bosnians and those primarily serving Bosnian food to the general public. The proprietors of either type were almost never restaurateurs in Bosnia-Herzegovina. The clientele of the former are almost exclusively men. They usually offer little other than *ćevapčići* and other grilled meat, coffee, and perhaps beer. Roasted lamb may be available on weekends. The social function of such establishments is more important than the food. They are a feature of the earlier days of the Bosnian community and have declined in number over time.

The greatest changes in Bosnian food are found in those Bosnian restaurants catering to a non-Bosnian clientele. The food is frequently a fanciful version of traditional Bosnian food—whatever the proprietor thinks will appeal to Americans. Thus, it is the public face of Bosnian food that is the least Bosnian. There has been a craze in New York City in recent years for "Bosnian hamburgers," by which is meant an oversized *pljeskavica*, usually filled with mozzarella cheese, served in *lepinje* and eaten like a sandwich. There is even in New York City a Bosnian food truck. Catering to contemporary American tastes, much more chicken is offered in Bosnian American restaurants than would be in Bosnia. At least one restaurant has added Greek-style gyros to its menu. One has added Arabic hummus. Another, in a neighborhood shared with Albanians, has included "Kosovski *sudžuk*." While in Bosnia, *ćevapčići* are served only with *lepinje* and chopped onions, but some restaurateurs in America will serve both *kajmak* and *ajvar* as well, with a green salad on the side.

All Bosnian American restaurants are small and relatively rare. No chefs of note have yet developed.

Further Reading

Bringa, Tone. *Being Muslim the Bosnian Way: Identity and Community in a Central Bosnian Village*. Princeton, NJ: Princeton University Press, 1995.

Franz, Barbara. *Refugees in Flux. Bosnian Refugees in Austria and the United States, 1992–2000*. PhD Dissertation, SUNY, 2002.

Franz, Barbara. "Bosnian Refugees and Socio-Economic Realities: Changes in Refugee and Settlement Policies in Austria and the United States." *Journal of Ethnic and Migration Studies* 29 (2003): 5–25.

Gilliland, Mary Kay, Sonja Spoljar-Vrzina, and Vlasta Rudan. "Reclaiming Lives: Variable Effects of War on Gender and Ethnic Identities in the Narratives of Bosnian and Croatian Refugees." *Anthropology of East Europe Review* 13 (1995): 30–39.

Lockwood, William G. *European Moslems: Economy and Ethnicity in Western Bosnia.* New York: Academic Press, 1975.

Lockwood, William G., "Bosnian Muslims." In *Harvard Encyclopedia of American Ethnic Groups.* Edited by Stephen Thernstrom. Cambridge, MA: Harvard University Press, 1980.

Lockwood, William G., and Yvonne R. Lockwood. "Bosnia-Herzegovina." In *Food Cultures of the World Encyclopedia*, vol. 4, 51–60. Edited by Kenneth Albala. Santa Barbara: Greenwood Press, 2001.

Lockwood, William G., and Yvonne R. Lockwood. "The Transformation of Traditional Foodways in the Bosnian American Community." In *The Return of Traditional Food.* Edited by Patricia Lysaght, Proceedings of the 19th International Commission for Ethnological Food Research. Lund, Sweden, 2013.

Puskar, Samira, *Bosnian Americans of Chicagoland.* Charleston, SC: Arcadia, 2007.

Zulfic, Muharem. *100 Godina Bošnjaka u Ćikagu* (100 Years of Bosnians in Chicago). Chicago: Džemijetul Hajrije, 2003.

William G. Lockwood and Yvonne R. Lockwood

BOTSWANA

(Southern Africa) Botswanan American Food
See also: South Africa, Lesotho, Namibia, Swaziland, Zambia.

Background

Botswana (the Republic of Botswana, or in Tswana, *Lefatshe la Botswana*, formerly Bechuanaland) is a flat, landlocked country bordered by South Africa to the south and southeast, Namibia to the west and north, and Zimbabwe to the northeast. Up to 70 percent of its territory, which is approximately the size of the combined states of Nebraska, Kansas, and Oklahoma, is made up of the Kalahari Desert. The citizens refer to themselves as *Batswana* (singular: *Motswana*). Formerly a British protectorate, Botswana gained independence on September 30, 1966.

With just over two million people within its fairly large borders, Botswana is one of the most sparsely populated nations in the world. About 10 percent of the population lives in the capital and largest city, Gaborone. Once one of the poorest countries in the world, Botswana now enjoys relative prosperity compared to most of the rest of Africa. The country became known to many Western audiences through a popular series of novels by Scottish author Alexander McCall Smith featuring Mma Precious Ramotswe, who runs the fictional "No. 1 Ladies' Detective Agency."

Foodways

The national dish of Botswana is called *seswaa*, a meat stew made of goat, beef, or chicken served over a thick, cornmeal staple called *pap*. The stew is made by boiling meat with onion and pepper, which is then shredded and pounded with salt. A leafy green called *morogo* is a popular vegetable. For breakfast, maize or sorghum porridge called *bogobe* is common.

Afrikaans, though a small portion of the population, have influenced the cuisine as well. Botswanans enjoy barbecues featuring grilled meats, which often mark a special occasion. *Vetkoek*, a deep-fried dough, is cut in half and filled with curried meat. Beans and peas grown in the country and enjoyed in dishes include cowpeas and *ditloo*, an African legume. The main meal is traditionally eaten at lunchtime, and leftovers or bread and tea are eaten at dinner.

A relatively small number of immigrants from Botswana live in the United States, and no specifically Botswanan restaurants or food shops in the United States are listed on the Internet. A number of Botswana recipes for such dishes as *seswaa* and *morogo* are available online, however, and Botswanans in the United States may find familiar dishes and food products at South African restaurants and shops. The organization Southern African Community USA includes Botswanans in its numbers.

Further Reading

English, Michael. "Culture and Traditions of Botswana: Local Cuisine." http://www.botswana.co.za/Cultural_Issues-travel/food-of-botswana.html.

Southern African Community USA. http://southernafricancommunity.org/who-we-are/about-sacu/.

Wikipedia, "Botswana." http://en.wikipedia.org/wiki/Botswana.

Betty J. Belanus

BRAZIL

(South America) Brazilian American Food

Background

Brazil's long colonial history began in 1500, when Portuguese explorer and nobleman Pedro Álvares Cabral landed on what is now Brazil's eastern coast. Less than sixty years later, the Portuguese established their first colony in Brazil: Salvador, located on *Baía de Todos os Santos* (All Saints Bay), which also served as the first colonial capital of Brazil. It also became an important seaport, financial center, and Catholic bishopric within a few years of its establishment. Over the following centuries, additional colonies and cities followed, with cane sugar becoming a major export in large part because of Brazil's heavy importation of slaves. Brazil was ruled as a colony until 1822, when Dom Pedro I, the son of Portuguese king Dom João VI and regent of Brazil, declared the country's independence from Portugal. A series of Brazilian governments rose and fell over the centuries that followed, with military coups often serving to overthrow elected presidents and installing dictators. Brazil's democratic structure finally stabilized in the early 1990s with the legitimate election of Fernando Henrique Cardoso as president.

The US Immigration and Naturalization Service did not differentiate Brazilians from other South Americans until the mid-twentieth century, so it is difficult to determine exactly how many Brazilians immigrated to the United States prior to 1960. The largest recorded wave of immigrants to the United States from Brazil occurred in the mid-1980s through the early 1990s, when 1.4 million Brazilians left their homeland thanks to massive inflation, economic depression, and falling household incomes. Today, the US Census Bureau estimates that there are more than 350,000 Brazilian Americans living in the United States, although there are likely a large number of undocumented Brazilians living and working in the United States for which this population figure does not account.

There are significant numbers of Brazilian Americans in the New York metropolitan area, with West 46th Street between Fifth and Sixth avenues known as "Little Brazil." There are other large enclaves of Brazilian Americans in Newark, Chicago, and the Miami metropolitan area, and significant populations living in towns in Massachusetts and Connecticut.

Foodways

The ingredients that are often found in Brazilian dishes are evidence of the country's colonial past and tropical climate, although specific preparations of particular recipes can vary from one region to the next. Ingredients commonly used in Brazilian cuisine include root vegetables (e.g., manioc, cassava, yams), tropical fruits (e.g., mango, guava, passion fruit), rice, beans, fish, beef, chicken, and pasta. Sausage is also commonly encountered, especially *linguiça*, a mild, cured pork sausage. Pastries and desserts are a perpetual favorite, with some food writers claiming that Brazilians all seem to have a massive sweet tooth. Coffee is the national beverage of Brazil, while the national spirit is *cachaça*, a type of liquor similar to rum that is distilled from sugar cane. The *caipirinha*, Brazil's national cocktail, is made from *cachaça* poured over muddled lime, brown sugar, and ice. *Capifrutas* are similar in preparation, though they are made with fruits other than limes (e.g., tangerine, pineapple).

In years past, slaves were largely responsible for cooking, particularly on larger plantations; indeed, slaves are credited with concocting the national dish known as *feijoada*. While slavery was abolished in the nineteenth century, household employees are still relatively common, particularly among upper-middle-class and wealthy families; in many cases, these domestic employees handle most of the day-to-day household cooking. In less wealthy households, women often handle most of the cooking, though this is far from a hard and fast rule. Indeed, family is a priority for Brazilians, with food often taking center stage at family events and responsibility for the preparation shared by family members. Food is a Brazilian social lubricant, and it is not uncommon for extra portions to be made just in case family members or friends stop by to say hello.

Generally speaking, the midday dinner or lunch is the largest meal consumed by Brazilians, with a smaller meal of leftovers eaten later in the evening. A typical Brazilian dinner often comprises beans and rice, a protein, and a vegetable, with some variation in meal sizes depending upon the socioeconomic status of the individual or family.

The national dish, known as *feijoada*, a type of beef stew with beans, is commonly encountered, served with a variety of side dishes that can include rice, sausages, polenta, and salad. A recipe for *feijoada* follows, which can be made ahead and will feed approximately eight.

Feijoada

1 smoked ham hock or shank
½ pound thick-sliced bacon, diced
2 large yellow onions, chopped
½ cup green onions, chopped
2 cloves garlic, chopped
1 12-ounce package dry black beans, soaked in water overnight
1 pound boneless pork shoulder or boneless beef, any cut
olive oil
2 bay leaves
pinch of ground coriander
½ cup chopped fresh parsley
½ cup chopped fresh cilantro

Boil ham hock in salted water and bring to a simmer until the meat pulls away from the bone, approximately 1 hour. Meanwhile, in a pot or Dutch oven over medium-high heat, cook the bacon until crisp and the fat has rendered. Add the onions, green onions, and garlic, and cook until softened and barely translucent, approximately 4 minutes. Cut the pork or beef into 1 to 2 inch cubes and add to the onion mixture; cook on all sides until browned. Add the ham hock to the mixture, along with the beans, salt, pepper, bay leaves, and coriander, and cover with water. Simmer for 45 minutes to 1 hour, stirring often; if the mixture appears too thick, add additional water as needed. Add cilantro and parsley prior to serving.

Pastries and desserts are not difficult to find in Brazil. *Brigadeiro*, or chocolate balls, similar to bonbons, are a perpetual Brazilian favorite and are easy to make. A simple recipe follows, which makes approximately two-dozen small balls.

Brigadeiro

1 14-ounce can sweetened condensed milk
1 tablespoon unsalted butter
3 to 4 tablespoons cocoa powder
variety of coatings of choice (chocolate sprinkles, coconut, crushed nuts, etc.)

Over medium heat, combine the condensed milk, butter, and cocoa powder; cook, stirring often, until the mixture thickens. Allow mixture to rest until cool. Form into balls, rolling in various coatings. Eat immediately or chill for a firmer texture.

Holiday Feasts

Brazilians are known for their parties and parades—these are people who love to have a good time! Brazilian Carnival, in particular, is pegged to the Catholic calendar, beginning on Ash Wednesday and running through the week that follows. Carnival is essentially a weeklong party that includes parades, masquerades, dances, and feasts that often feature heavily spiced foods, with many dishes served that can be greasy and heavily meat based. Street foods are also commonplace during Carnival; these include *espetinho* (grilled meat kebabs), *pasteís* (cheese or meat pastries), *empadas* (miniature meat pies), *coxinha* (chicken croquettes), and *paõ de queijo* (cheese bread). Massive amounts of *cerveja* (beer) are also consumed during Carnival, with some estimating that as many as four hundred million liters of beer are consumed by Brazilians in a single week.

Place in American Culture

Thanks to the ready assimilation of second- and third-generation Brazilians into mainstream American culture, Brazilian food is not frequently encountered in the United States, and seldom is it celebrated in any notable way in America. Indeed, journalist Kelly Senyei of *Gourmet* describes the dearth of Brazilian cuisine in the United States as "bleak at best." Despite the rich and delicious array of foods available across Brazil itself, there have been virtually no emergent "celebrity" chefs in that country in recent history, but that may be changing, particularly as the country prepares to host the 2016 Summer Olympics.

Brazilian cuisine has not been totally absent from American cultural imagination, though one could be forgiven for failing to notice it. The 2000 film *Woman on Top*, directed by Fina Torres, starred Penélope Cruz as Isabella, a Brazilian chef who flees Brazil for the United States, where she finds success as the host of a popular food TV show titled *Passion Food*. The film, however, was far from a box office success; it ranked tenth of all films that opened the weekend of September 22, 2000, and ultimately it grossed only $10.2 million worldwide.

Cookbooks focusing on Brazilian cuisine have been a bit more successful and routinely top booksellers' best-sellers lists. As of this writing, for example, Fernando Farah's *The Food and Cooking of Brazil* was ranked number 5 in Amazon.com's Latin American cookbooks category and number 9 in Amazon's international cookbooks category. Indeed, a search on Amazon for "Brazilian cooking" produced nearly three hundred results. This may speak more to the American obsession with cookbooks than the popularity of Brazilian food; however, paper cookbooks continue to sell particularly well, especially when compared to sales of other types of printed books.

As mentioned previously, the 2016 Summer Olympics will be held in Rio de Janeiro, Brazil. This massive spectacle, heavily covered by world media, will doubtless draw renewed attention to Brazilian customs and cuisine, particularly in America where the Olympics are heavily televised, promoted, and viewed. While it is difficult to estimate what the impact of this major sporting event might be on American culture, it is entirely possible that interest in Brazilian cuisine in America will see an uptick during and immediately following the Olympic games. If ever there were an ideal time for Brazilian cuisine to assert itself in the United States, the 2016 Olympics would seem to be it.

Noted Restaurants and Chefs

Despite the fact that there are relatively few Brazilian Americans in the United States, particularly when compared to other ethnic groups, Brazilians have still managed to make their mark on the American restaurant scene when it comes to grilled meat. Most people could likely identify the *churrascaria*, sometimes referred to as a "Brazilian steakhouse," as Brazilian in origin. These types of establishments specialize in meats that are prepared in the *churrasco* style, which roughly translates from the Portuguese as "grilled" or "barbecued," usually over charcoal. Typically speaking, *churrascarias* tend to offer an "all you can eat" menu, with meats usually served *rodízio*, or carved tableside from skewers by *passadores*, or waiters. While beef is perhaps the most common meat prepared and served at a typical *churrascaria*, pork, sausage, lamb, duck, or chicken may be offered. More exotic meats, including chicken hearts and other types of offal, might also be on offer, depending upon the specific establishment and its clientele. Diners are often instructed to use a signal of some kind—usually either a two-sided card, red on one side and green on the other, or a red/green light—to indicate whether they desire additional portions (green) or if they've had enough (red).

Curiously enough, despite the fact that *churrascarias* are popular dining destinations, particularly in larger cities, there are virtually no Brazilian celebrity chefs of note in the United States. Perhaps even more telling, Wikipedia, as of this writing, lists only three names under its categorical listing of "Brazilian chefs." However, that is not to say that Brazilian chefs lack influence or that they do not exist. In fact, Alex Atala is identified by *Forbes* magazine as one of the world's most influential chefs; he owns two restaurants in São Paulo, Dalva e Dito and D.O.M., the latter having been been named one of the best restaurants in the world repeatedly by "The World's 50 Best Restaurants" over the past decade. Nevertheless, Atala does not own or operate a restaurant in the United States, nor has he indicated any plans to do so.

If one searches hard enough, however, it is entirely possible to find Brazilian restaurants hiding in plain sight in the United States, many of which are rated quite highly by reviewers and patrons alike. BarBossa in Manhattan, for example, is highly rated on Yelp.com (4 of 5 stars at this writing) and has received positive write-ups from both the *New York Times* and *New York* magazine. Big cities are not the only places you'll find Brazilian fare; Amor de Brazil, for example, located in Matthews, North Carolina (population 28,699, as of this writing), boasts a Yelp.com rating of 4 of 5 stars and positive recognition from local media, including the *Charlotte Observer*. Despite the Brazilian tendency to assimilate into the American landscape, it seems apparent that Brazilian recipes continue to live on—if you know where to look.

Further Reading

Dória, Carlos A. "Beyond Rice Neutrality: Beans as *Patria*, *Locus*, and *Domus* in the Brazilian Culinary System." In *Rice and Beans: A Unique Dish in a Hundred Places*. Edited by Richard Wilk and Livia Barbosa. Oxford: Berg, 2011.

Farah, Fernando. *The Food and Cooking of Brazil: Traditions, Ingredients, Tastes, Techniques, 65 Classic Recipes*. London: Anness, 2012.

Ferro, Jennifer. *Brazilian Foods and Culture*. Vero Beach, FL: Rourke, 1999.

Hamilton, Cherie. *Brazil: A Culinary Journey*. New York: Hippocrene, 2005.

Idone, Christopher. *Brazil: A Cook's Tour*. New York: Clarkson N. Potter, 1995.

Oths, Kathryn S., Adriana Carolo, and Jose Ernesto Dos Santos. "Social Status and Food Preference in Southern Brazil." *Ecology of Food and Nutrition* 42, nos. 4–5 (2003): 303–24.

Ryan S. Eanes

BRITISH VIRGIN ISLANDS
(Americas—Caribbean)

A British territory in the Caribbean along with Anguilla, the Bahamas, Cayman Islands, Grenada, Montserrat, and Turks and Caicos Islands.

See entries for the Bahamas and Grenada.

BRUNEI DARUSSALAM

(Southeastern Asia) Bruneian American Food
See also: Indonesia, Malaysia, Singapore.

Background

Brunei Darussalam is on the island of Borneo, bordering the South China Sea and surrounded by Malaysia. Its people are Malay, and Malay is the official language, but many residents also speak English and Chinese. It is officially Muslim and has recently adopted sharia law, but it also includes Christian and Buddhist populations. Although it was a British Protectorate from 1888 to 1984, Brunei Darussalam has been ruled by the same family for six centuries! In the fifteenth to seventeenth centuries, they controlled all of northwest Borneo and some of the Philippines.

The country has coastal plains with heavily forested mountains inland. It also has oil and natural gas resources. With one of the highest GNPs in Asia, Brunei Darussalam is more likely to take in immigrants than to lose citizens to emigration. Bruneians seem to come to the United States primarily for educational opportunities.

Foodways

Bruneian food and foodways are similar to those of Malaysia, with rice and noodles being staples and the liberal use of hot peppers. Malay names of dishes are identical to those found in Malaysia and Indonesia, such as *rending* (stews) and *nasi* (rice). Coconut milk is frequently used for cooking, as in *nasi lemak* (rice cooked in coconut milk), and for a refreshing drink. Tea and coffee are also popular. Chinese and Indian cuisines are also common in Brunei, but the *halal* dietary guidelines of Islam mean that alcohol and pork are not used.

The national dish is *ambuyat*, sago starch made from the trunk of the Rumbia palm tree that is dipped into various sauces. Two favorites are made of fruit, a sour one from *binjai* fruit, and one from durian, infamous for its strong odor. The starch is wrapped around a specialized bamboo fork before being dipped. Fish, meat, and vegetables are also served with it. An article in the *Brunei Times* in 2011 called for *ambuyat* to be recognized as an intangible cultural heritage of the nation.[1]

Note

1. Jessica Tiah and Bandar Seri Begawan, "Ambuyat—Our Iconic Heritage," http://web.archive.org/web/20140404182236/http://www.bt.com.bn/art-culture/2011/01/08/ambuyat-our-iconic-heritage, accessed November 14, 2014.

Further Reading

1UpTravel.com, http://www.1uptravel.com/international/asia/brunei/cuisine.html.
CIA, World Factbook, https://www.cia.gov/library/publications/the-world-factbook/geos/bx.html.
Embassy of Brunei Darussalam, http://www.bruneiembassy.org.
iFoodTV.com, Cuisine of Brunei, "Brunei," http://ifood.tv/other/43254-cuisine-of-brunei.

Lucy M. Long

BULGARIA

(Eastern Europe) Bulgarian American Foodways
See also: Turkey.

Background

Bulgarians have never received much recognition in the United States. One reason is that their numbers have been relatively small, with fewer than one thousand Bulgarians immigrating in the nineteenth century to the United States, and approximately one hundred thousand persons of Bulgarian heritage currently residing here. Another reason is Bulgaria's relative obscurity—it was occupied by the Ottoman Empire from the fourteenth century until 1878 and was subsequently subsumed by communist regimes during the second half of the twentieth century. As a result, Bulgarian identity—and especially Bulgarian cuisine—has had relatively little visibility in the United States, even in some of the large, industrial cities such as Chicago and Cleveland where many Bulgarian immigrants settled. As is the case with many immigrant groups, Bulgarian Americans have maintained many of their ancestors' foodways, while also assimilating to conditions and customs in their new home.

Foodways

A wide variety of fruits and vegetables thrive in Bulgaria, thanks to its location on fertile lands between the Danube River and Balkan Mountains. Accordingly, Bulgarians and Bulgarian American cuisine make extensive use of apples, carrots, cherries, eggplant, garlic, grapes, melons, onions, peppers, spinach, and tomatoes in salads and soups. Meat is often a secondary ingredient in vegetable stews, but it is also featured in grilled kebabs made from lamb, veal, and pork. Milk and dairy products are important elements in Bulgarian cuisine, particularly a type of salty, soft white cheese known as *sirene* (similar to and resembling Greek feta cheese), a hard, yellow cheese known as *kashkaval*, and fermented milk known in Bulgarian as *kiselo mlyako* (literally, sour milk), but it is much better known worldwide as yogurt, its name in Turkish. *Kiselo mlyako* is made thanks to *Lactobacillus bulgaricus*, a bacterium first identified in 1905 by the Bulgarian doctor Stamen Grigorov.

The Turkish influence is profound in many areas of the Balkans where the Ottomans were present for centuries. Bulgarian dishes such as *ayran* (a chilled yogurt drink), *baklava* (thin layers of pastry drenched in sugar syrup with chopped walnuts and cashews), *guvech* (a spicy vegetable stew cooked in a clay pot), and *moussaka* (minced meat with sautéed onions, peppers, potatoes, and tomatoes) all bear the mark of Ottoman influence. Similarly, many Bulgarians and Bulgarian Americans favor strong Turkish coffee, especially in small coffeehouses, which are known in Bulgarian as *kafene*. For instance, as early as 1910 in the Bulgarian American community of Granite City, Illinois (informally known as Hungry Hollow), Bulgarian immigrants gathered in the *kafene*, not only to enjoy familiar dishes and drinks but also to play cards, read newspapers from home, socialize with their compatriots, and learn about employment opportunities.

Signature Dish—*Tarator*

   1 pound of cucumbers
   2 or 3 cloves of garlic
   3 cups of yogurt
   2 tablespoons of sunflower or olive oil
   salt and chopped dill to taste

Peel and chop the cucumbers into small cubes. Mince or press the cloves of garlic. Dilute the yogurt with one cup of water. Combine all ingredients and stir well. Cool in refrigerator for 30 minutes before serving.

Holiday Feasts

Bulgarian American homes—rather than coffeehouses or other public spaces—are the scenes for holiday feasts and celebrations. Most distinctive are Christmas and New Year's Eve, when *banitsa* are filled with good-luck charms, and St. George's Day (May 6), when lamb meat is roasted or barbecued. On such occasions, the food is almost always accompanied by Bulgarian *rakia*—a clear, potent liquor made from fermented fruits—most often grapes or plums, but occasionally cherries, pears, and other fruits. Easter, also, is celebrated with a feast, usually of roasted lamb, and with colored, hard-boiled eggs.

Noted Restaurants and Chefs

Bulgarian restaurants in the United States serve similar functions today. Centers of Bulgarian American population are the natural locations for such eating establishments, including Avenue BG in Elk Grove Village (a suburb of Chicago), Bistro Bulgari in Arlington (a suburb of Washington, DC), and Mehanata on New York's Lower East Side. Typical dishes in these restaurants include the *banitsa*, a breakfast pastry made by filling a mixture of eggs, white cheese, and yogurt among layers of phyllo; *kebapche*, a grilled, minced meat in the shape of a hot dog; *lukanka*, a spicy salami of minced beef and pork, stuffed into a casing of cow's intestine and coated with a powder of white fungus; *lyutenitsa*, a puree of tomatoes, red peppers, and carrots, often served on bread and topped with white cheese; *pulneni chushki*, a mixture of minced meat, rice, onions and spices stuffed into bell peppers; *shkembe chorba*, a spicy soup made from the tripe of various animals; *shopska* salad, a combination of chopped cucumbers, onions, peppers, and tomatoes sprinkled with Bulgarian white cheese; and *tarator*, a cold soup made of finely chopped cucumbers, garlic, yogurt, and dill.

Further Reading

Altankov, Nikolay G. *The Bulgarian-Americans*. Palo Alto, CA: Racusan Press, 1979.

Bulgarian and Other Favorite Recipes. Washington, DC: St. George Ladies Society, 1991.

"Bulgarian Diet Stresses Variety of Vegetables." *Los Angeles Times*, October 26, 1938, B6.

Cassens, David E. "The Bulgarian Colony of Southwestern Illinois, 1900-1920." *Illinois Historical Journal* 84 (Spring 1991): 15–24.

DeChenne, David. "Hungry Hollow: Bulgarian Immigrant Life in Granite City, Illinois, 1904–1921." *Gateway Heritage* 11 (Summer 1990): 52–61.

Philpott, Don. *The Wine and Food of Bulgaria*. London: Mitchell Beazley, 1989.

Smith, Stuart S. "Cuisine Combination: Bulgarian Cooking Based on Seasonal Food." *Baltimore Sun*, January 11, 1968, D1.

Spieler, Marlena. *Jewish Traditions Cookbook*. London: Lorenz Books, 2005.

James I. Deutsch

BURKINA FASO

(Western Africa) Burkinabe American Food
See also: Ghana, Benin, Mali, Côte d'Ivoire, Niger, Togo.

Formerly called Upper Volta and Burkina, and landlocked in West Africa, Burkina Faso borders Ghana, Benin, Mali, Côte d'Ivoire, Niger, and Togo and shares food cultures with those nations. It has a tropical climate, but it suffers from droughts and has limited natural resources. Slightly larger than the state of Colorado, it has a population of over eighteen million and high birth rates, and it is one of the poorest nations in Africa. It was a French colony until late 1960s, and the official language is French, with two major native languages spoken, Moore and Dioula. It is a secular state, with over half the population Muslim, but it also has a strong Catholic tradition as well as animist belief systems and practices. Two major ethnic groups are the Voltaic and the Mande.

Poverty has driven emigration from the nation, and the United States hosts approximately five thousand to six thousand Burkinabe Americans, most of whom have settled in New York City, Washington, DC, and a community in Texas.

Burkinabe food is typical of other West African cuisines, with yams, sorghum, millet, rice, and corn being the basic staples accompanied by potatoes, beans, tomatoes, peppers, and okra. Protein is primarily from beans, chicken meat and eggs, and freshwater fish. Goat and mutton is also consumed. Palm sap is fermented into wine (*banji*). *Fufu* is the common basis of a meal, with various sauces accompanying it. European, particularly French, influence is seen in some of the cooking, such as green beans, *poulet bicyclette* (a grilled chicken dish popular throughout West Africa), and *ragout*.

Further Reading

Debrevic, Liza. "Burkina Faso." In *Food Cultures of the World*. By Ken Albala. Santa Barbara: ABC-CLIO, 2011.

McCann, James C. *Stirring the Pot: A History of African Cuisine*. Athens: Ohio University Press, 2009.

Osseo-Asare, Fran. *Food Culture in SubSaharan Africa*. Westport, CT: Greenwood, 2005.

Lucy M. Long

BURMA

(Southeastern Asia) Burmese American Food
See entry for Myanmar.

BURUNDI

(Eastern Africa) Burundian American Food
See also: Democratic Republic of Congo, Rwanda, and Tanzania.

Background

Landlocked in central Africa between the Democratic Republic of Congo, Rwanda, and Tanzania, Burundi's topography includes forests, rivers, savannas, and mountains. The country grows coffee and tea, but it also has mineral deposits. It was a German colony from 1890 to 1919, then was overseen by Belgium through the League of Nations until 1962 when it became independent. French and Kirundi are the official languages. According to Internet sources, it is one of only a few African countries to have cultural and linguistic homogeneity, with Kirundi the commonly spoken language.

Burundi is densely populated, and it went through a major civil war between the Hutus and Tutsis ethnic groups. The war devastated the economy as well as the population, and Burundi is one of the top five African countries with immigrants seeking refugee asylum, with an estimate of over 4,500 settling in the United States through an official resettlement program. There is an active Burundian American community association based in Silver Spring, Maryland, that assists community members with practical matters, sponsors cultural events, and also helps members maintain a social network. Active communities are also located in Vermont; Chicago; Louisville, Kentucky; and Portland, Maine.

Foodways

Burundi's land and climate are good for agriculture. Their cuisine relies on beans (peas), corn, manioc, cassava, wheat, plantains, and yams as staples. Little meat is eaten, but goats and sheep are the primary meat sources. Cows are very scarce. A special dish is red kidney beans with fried onions and bananas, and a banana wine (*urwarwa*) is used for special occasions. Coffee and tea are also consumed and are locally grown. There is also a good deal of Asian influence on the food, particularly from India, and *chipattis* (a flat bread of Indian origin and made from flour, water, salt, and oil), rice dishes, and "Indian" curry spices are popular.

The nation celebrates Christian holidays—Easter, All Saint's Day, Christmas, and other Roman Catholic holy days. Burundi Americans recognize these holidays and participate in mainstream American foodways traditions associated with them, but they also use them as times to gather with each other and share their traditional ethnic foods.

Burundi American food is typical of that of other central African cultures in the United States, but it differs in its Catholic affiliations and its history as a German colony, which did not seem to actively influence the cuisine. It might also share some ethnic food culture in the United States with other Francophone African nations.

Further Reading

Burundi Embassy, http://www.burundiembassy-usa.org.

Immigration Policy Center, http://immigrationpolicy.org/just-facts/african-immigrants-america-demographic-overview.

Recipes Wikia, "Burundi," http://recipes.wikia.com/wiki/Burundian_Cuisine.

United Burundian-American Community Association, Inc. (UBACA), https://www.facebook.com/pages/United-Burundian-American-Community-Association-Inc-UBACA/103661263067208.

Lucy M. Long

C

CAJUN
(North America) Cajun Food
See also: Creole, France.

Background
Cajuns are descended from the Acadians, French colonists who initially settled in the Maritime Provinces in eastern Canada and then immigrated in the mid-1700s to the southern United States (most notably, southern Louisiana). The heart of "Cajun Country" is Acadiana, twenty-two Louisiana parishes that stretch along the Gulf Coast from New Orleans to the Texas border. Many Cajuns preserve their culture and folkways through a distinctive French dialect, music, dance, and cuisine, celebrating it at home and through numerous festivals.

With the exception of its most famous dish, gumbo, Cajun cuisine as we know it today largely coalesced in the twentieth century. Foods that are now deeply ingrained with Cajun culture, such as crawfish and other seafood, gained popularity among Cajuns after refrigeration. It is probable that many of the distinctive elements that developed over the last century were consciously cultivated in an assertion of a unique Cajun identity.

Historically, there was a distinct divide between Cajun and Creole cuisine: Cajun was the rustic food of the country, and Creole was the urban food of New Orleans. Today the two cuisines overlap, and the differences between them are relatively minor.

Foodways
At the heart of many Cajun dishes are the central ingredients of pork, rice, and vegetables (particularly bell peppers, onions, and celery—known as the "trinity" when used together in a similar fashion to the French *mirepoix*). Fish and shellfish are favorites in dishes such as blackened redfish and crawfish *étouffée*. Poultry and game birds are also quite common on the Cajun table.

Sausage and cured meats often play significant roles in Cajun cooking. A smoked pork sausage may be added as either a central protein ingredient or a seasoning in iconic dishes such as jambalaya, gumbo, or red beans and rice. The three most commonly prepared meats are *andouille*, *tasso*, and *boudin*. The first is a coarse-ground pork sausage influenced by not just the French Acadians but also the Rhinelander Germans who settled in the eastern parishes of Acadiana. *Andouille* is often heavily spiced with garlic and black pepper. Traditionally, the word refers to sausages that are thick in diameter and short in length, but it has increasingly become a catch-all term for any Louisiana-inspired smoked sausage.

Tasso refers to Cajun ham that is dried and smoked in a manner resembling smoked jerky. *Tasso* has a powerful, rich taste and is used as a flavoring agent as opposed to a main ingredient—particularly for gumbos, jambalayas, and bean dishes. Where *andouille* was largely the product of German and Acadian influences, *tasso* is the product of Spanish and Acadian blending. The word itself is a Cajun derivation of the Spanish word *tasajo*, meaning smoked or dried meat. Unlike *andouille*, *tasso* has not been as widely recognized or exported outside of Cajun country.

Similarly, *boudin* has remained a local phenomenon in Louisiana and parts of Texas, but many Cajuns consider it their most distinctive food. *Boudin* is usually a fresh sausage made with cooked rice and pork. It is usually served poached in its casing, but it can also be smoked or even rolled into balls, breaded, and deep fried. There are two key types: *boudin rouge*, which contains pork blood, and *boudin blanc*, which does not. Both can also be made with shrimp, crawfish, or alligator meat, although these varieties are less common.

Jambalaya, gumbo, and *maque choux* are three quintessential Cajun dishes. Jambalaya is a one-pot rice dish prepared with a variety of meat or seafood, and various vegetables. Traditional "Cajun jamabalya" is a brown jambalaya, in that it does not contain tomatoes, unlike "Creole jambalaya" or "red jambalaya" found in the immediate area around New Orleans. Jambalaya has a long list of culinary cousins, some of which may or may not be antecedents to the dish we know today. Given the demographics of southern Louisiana, the three most likely antecedents are Spanish *paella*, West African *jollof* rice, and Indian *biryani*.

Cajun gumbo is defined by *roux*, a browned blend of flour and either butter or oil used to thicken the gumbo broth. There are as many varieties of ingredients and combinations to Louisiana gumbos as there are gumbo cooks, but the most common are chicken and sausage, or seafood. Creole gumbos are less reliant on *roux*; they often use okra or other vegetables as a thickener. Gumbo *z'herbes* is another variant, similar to southern collard greens, sometimes served as a vegetarian option during lent. *Filé* gumbo has roots among the Choctaw Native Americans in the Mississippi valley. *Filé* is made from ground sassafras leaves that are sprinkled as a finishing spice to thicken and add an herbaceous flavor to the soup.

Maque choux (also spelled *machoux*) is sweet corn–based, and it largely owes its origins to the Native American cooks who predated the Acadians in the region. Corn kernels are cooked with bell peppers, onions, and other vegetables. Some Cajun chefs will also add cream or sugar to further enrich the flavor. Unlike jambalaya, which is cooked with rice at the same time, both gumbo and *macque choux* are served with separately cooked rice.

Many Cajun dishes and serving styles reflect traditional practices. For example, red beans is thought of as a Monday evening supper because Sunday was usually a busy washing day; red beans could be allowed to slow cook on the oven through the day while the wash and other Sunday chores were tended to. Historically, Cajun women have done most of the cooking in the home, while men did most of the outdoor food preparation, such as barbecues or festive communal hog butcherings (known as *boucheries*).

Mardi Gras, while famous in all of Louisiana, is particularly distinctive in Cajun country. The *Courir de Mardi Gras* is the rural Cajun counterpart to the urban parades associated with New Orleans. Borrowing heavily from old world French traditions, the *courir* is a run through the countryside. The runners, either on horseback or on foot, wear colorful costumes and masks largely inspired by medieval French carnival wear.

Étouffée

Étouffée, which is sometimes spelled phonetically, "A-2-Fay," comes from the French word for "smothered." It is most commonly served with shellfish, either shrimp or crawfish. *Étouffée* begins with a *roux*, a technique central to many Cajun dishes. The *roux* can be cooked to either a light brown or blonde *roux*, for a buttery flavor, or a darker one for a deep, nutty flavor.

1 cup diced onions
1 cup diced celery
1 cup diced bell peppers
1 cup diced tomatoes
1 tablespoon garlic

1 tablespoon tomato paste
1 stick of butter
¾ cup flour (all-purpose)
1 cup green onions
2 pounds of shrimp
1 teaspoon dried basil
½ teaspoon white pepper
½ teaspoon black pepper
½ teaspoon cayenne
1 teaspoon Louisiana style hot sauce (Tabasco, Crystal, or similar)
1 teaspoon Worcestershire sauce
shrimp stock, as needed (about 3 cups)

To make a *roux*, melt a stick of butter in a large skillet on high heat. Add the flour and whisk until blended. Continue to stir the *roux* until it turns a light brown. Add the onions, garlic, celery, bell peppers, tomatoes, and half of the green onions (reserve the other half to garnish the finished dish). Add the tomato paste and all of the dry seasonings and cook until the vegetables are soft (about 15 minutes). Add the shrimp or crawfish, folding them into the mixture. Add the Worcestershire and hot sauce. Incorporate the shrimp stock slowly, adding a small amount at a time and stirring carefully. Simmer until mixture is smooth and the shrimp are cooked.

Serve over white rice and with a few green onions on top.

Maque Choux

Although *maque choux* is sometimes served as side dish or an accompaniment, this preparation is intended to be served as a main course, and it could even be served over rice.

1 stick of butter
1 cup sugar
1 cup diced onions
2 pounds of corn kernels (7 to 8 cups)
1 cup diced tomatoes
1 cup diced red bell peppers
2 cups of half and half or heavy cream
2 cups diced bacon or diced *andouille* sausage (browned and set aside)
½ teaspoon white pepper
½ teaspoon black pepper
½ teaspoon red pepper flakes
½ cayenne pepper
2½ cups of chicken stock
parsley
green onions

Cut the kernels off of an ear of corn, then run the back of a knife along the cob to extract the juices. Melt the butter. Add sugar and whisk until light brown. Next, add the onions and corn with juice from the cobs. Cook on high heat until soft. After about 15 minutes, when the corn begins to soften, you will start to see a white film on the bottom of the pan. Add red bell peppers, tomatoes and spices. Add the stock and simmer (be sure to scrape the bottom of the pan). Cook for another 5 minutes. Add cream and reduce. Add in the bacon or sausage. Serve topped with some fresh parsley and green onions.

Place in American Culture

Cajun cooking has also been greatly influenced by its own commercial renaissance. With the popularity of iconic Cajun chefs, such as Paul Prudhomme, as well as the immense popularity of Cajun or Cajun-influenced products, such as Zatarain's and Tabasco sauce, Cajun flavors have spread beyond their traditional boundaries. In the 1980s Paul Prudhomme (b. 1940 Opelousas, Louisiana) brought Cajun cuisine to national attention with his series of cookbooks, television appearances, and packaged spice blends. Prudhomme helmed New Orleans's legendary eatery, Commander's Palace, where he blended Cajun flavors and traditions with New Orleans's creole cuisine. In the years since Prudhomme's tenure at Commander's Palace, the two cuisines have become increasingly blended. It is not uncommon to now see the phrasing *Cajun/Creole* on menus and in restaurants.

Prudhomme's successor at Commander's Palace was a young New Englander with Portuguese and French-Canadian roots named Emeril Lagasse. Using the ubiquity of his shows on the cable TV Food Network, Lagasse brought continued national attention to the cooking styles of southern Louisiana. Lagasse's show *Emeril Live!* ran for a decade and provided cable entertainment with one of its first culinary superstars.

Some dishes and cooking techniques have entered into American mainstream culture. Alabama-born country superstar Hank Williams introduced many Americans to some of the staple dishes of Cajun cuisine, such as *filé* gumbo, crawfish pie, and the eponymous jambalaya, through his recording, "Jambalaya (On the Bayou)," released in 1952. Also, Paul Prudhomme's many prominent television appearances brought phenomenal popularity to blackened redfish in the 1980s, leading to Prudomme and many others packaging and selling "Cajun" seasonings and spice mixtures internationally.

Noted Restaurants and Chefs
Southern Louisiana is replete with examples of Cajun and Cajun-influenced cuisine. Some chefs and restaurants of note include:

John Folse. Born in St. James Parish, Louisiana, Folse opened his flagship restaurant, Lafitte's Landing, in 1978. Its success afforded him the opportunity to introduce his style of Cajun cooking to many visiting heads of state. In 1989 he became the first foreign chef to prepare a state dinner at the Vatican. Folse has also raised the profile of his cooking through his widely broadcast public television show, *A Taste of Louisiana*. His evangelism for the cuisine of his home state was recognized in 1994 with the opening of Nicholls State University's Chef John Folse Culinary Institute, an academic college dedicated to the research and preparation of Louisiana's foodways.

Donald Link. Listing his Cajun grandparents as his primary influence, Link rose to prominence with his New Orleans restaurant Herbsaint. His second restaurant, Cochon, strongly features influences from his childhood in Cajun country. Link has won numerous accolades, including several James Beard Foundation awards. He emerged as one of the guiding forces in the rebuilding of the Gulf Coast culinary landscape after Hurricane Katrina.

Marcelle Bienvenu. Known as "The Queen of Cajun Cooking," Bienvenu has made it her mission to document and share the history, techniques, and recipes of the Cajun kitchen with the rest of the world. As a columnist for the *New Orleans Times-Picayune*, Bienvenu has worked to preserve family recipes, community favorites and localized traditions endangered by hurricanes Katrina and Rita. Bienvenu is a frequent collaborator with both historians and renowned Louisiana chefs and has written or cowritten some of the most significant works on the region's cuisine.

Further Reading
Beinvenu, Marcelle, Carl A. Brasseaux, and Ryan A. Brasseaux. *Stir The Pot: The History of Cajun Cuisine.* New York: Hippocrene Books, 2005.
Folse, John D. *The Encyclopedia of Cajun and Creole Cuisine.* Gonzales, LA: Chef John Folse and Company, 2004.
Gutierrez, C. Paige. *Cajun Foodways.* Jackson, MS: University Press of Mississippi, 1992.
Link, Donald. *Real Cajun.* New York: Clarkson Potter, 2009.
Prudhomme, Paul. *Chef Paul Prudhomme's Louisiana Kitchen.* New York: William Morrow, 1984.

Graham Hoppe with recipes by Joseph Vuskovich

CAMBODIA
(Southeastern Asia) Cambodian American Foodways, Khmer American Foodways
See also: Thailand, Laos, Vietnam.

Background

Bordered by Thailand, Laos, and Vietnam, Cambodia (also known as Kamboja or Kampuchea) dominated Southeast Asia from the ninth to thirteenth centuries. Trade with India, Portugal, and Spain; years as part of either Siam or Vietnam; and then French colonial rule all influenced Khmer foodways.

Cambodian, also called Khmer, people first came to the United States in significant numbers after the official end of the Khmer Rouge regime (1975–1979). Approximately 150,000 refugee immigrants were dispersed around the country, thanks to a federal attempt to encourage assimilation. Despite this policy, Khmers, like other immigrants before them, eventually clustered in certain areas. Now just over 276,000 (2010 Census), Cambodian Americans live all over the United States, with the largest communities in Long Beach, California, and Lowell, Massachusetts, and smaller communities in Fresno and Stockton, California; Providence, Rhode Island; Cleveland, Ohio; Seattle, Washington; and Portland, Oregon. Even smaller numbers are found in Midwestern towns such as Des Moines, Iowa.

Foodways

Centuries of interaction with India, Thailand, and China as well as France have had their influences on Khmer foodways, evident in the curries, soups, dishes flavored with chilies and peanuts, sautéed and grilled fish dishes, spicy shellfish, banana-leaf-wrapped sticky rice, basil-infused stir fries, coconut-milk-based stews, rich coffee flavored with sweetened condensed milk, and the ubiquitous baguettes. A variety of rice (from sweet or sticky to fragrant jasmines as well as brown and black varieties) constitutes the staple food, grown in the rich fields of the Mekong Delta, which also supplies abundant fish. Rice is transformed into soups, noodles, snacks (fried rice cakes or banana-leaf-wrapped "puddings"), and desserts (coconut-milk-infused sticky rice with mango) and served at every meal. Spices such as pepper from Kompot, cardamom from the Cardamom Mountains, sour tamarind, *prahok* (a fermented fish paste), palm sugar, turmeric from Battambang, as well as *galangal*, star anise, ginger, lemongrass, *kaffir* lime leaves, and lime juice provide the essential flavors of traditional Khmer dishes.

Cambodian food in the United States has been transformed over time and place and has become more accurately Cambodian American food in this country. Already influenced by centuries of Chinese (Funan), Asian Indian, Thai (Siam), and French food traditions, the raw ingredients of rice, fish, pork, tofu, egg, duck, and Southeast Asian tropical fruits and vegetables have now acquired a bit of American flavor; in particular, beef and chicken are now more common in American-made dishes (cattle in Cambodia are work animals with consequently tough meat), and vegetables such as tomatoes and corn have made their appearance. Similarly, animal proteins are more predominant in this country, serving less as flavoring and more as main dish. Despite these differences, however, Khmer foodways, along with other Southeast Asian dishes, have broadened the American palate.

There are different ways to explore Khmer American foodways—through cooking techniques (grilling, steaming, frying, boiling), occasions (every day, festivals or holidays), or place (home, street, market, festivals, restaurants). Women are the cooks in Cambodian society and often come together to prepare foods, especially for family gatherings and Buddhist temple festivals, which revolve around the life cycle of Buddha. As American Cambodian communities move into second- and third-generation families, daughters and granddaughters who work outside the home also prepare American foods; when mothers and grandmothers visit, they often take on the role of providing traditional fare to their extended families. Cambodian men in this country are more often the gardeners, intensively cultivating small plots of suburban, rural, or even urban yards to produce varieties of familiar fresh vegetables and even fruits not always available in areas where Southeast Asian markets do not exist.

Street and festival foods include easily transported items such as spring rolls (smaller and crispier than egg rolls) or fresh rolls with shrimp, bean sprouts, basil, and mint leaves with savory dips; marinated, thinly sliced, and grilled meats (pork, chicken, and now beef); steamed banana-leaf-wrapped sticky rice with coconut milk or raw coconut wrapped around banana pieces; or seafood fritters. In Cambodia, street food also includes fried crickets—either sweet or savory, fresh lotus seeds, and tiny, spiced shellfish. For all home, holiday, and restaurant meals, melons and squash alike show up in savory dishes, and fruits such as mango and pineapple complement fish. Fruit "smoothies" or "shakes" are also popular at restaurants and festivals. Flavorful and colorful fruits such as durian, mangosteen, bananas, mango, papaya, dragon fruit, and more are featured at holidays and in restaurants.

The predominant key to Khmer foodways, whether in the United States or in Cambodia, is freshness—fresh fish, vegetables, fruits, and meats—as well as a strong aesthetic consciousness that dictates the arrangement of foods in markets, on the home table, and at festivals. Open air, covered markets are found throughout Cambodia, as are small convenience stores packed with a mixture of Southeast Asian, Western, and European prepackaged foods. These markets feature raw and cooked foods, as well as huge bags of rice, fabric, shoes, jewelry, cooking utensils, and more. In the United States, Southeast Asian food markets feature a similar range of items as well as DVDs and CDs with popular music, music videos, films, and television shows. Such shops, along with Buddhist temple complexes and nightclubs (in larger towns), serve as the community centers and meeting places where food, drink, and conversation are shared, facilitating sociability and affirming and reproducing community.

Rice is typically served at every meal in some form or another. Khmer home and (celebratory) meals feature three to four (everyday) to ten or more dishes as well, such as curries, soups, vegetable mixtures, fish, or duck plus condiments (similar to Asian Indian chutneys) served alongside. Meals at home or at holiday festivals are not divided into courses as they are at restaurants but are served all at once. Although Western hygiene practices have surfaced at community events (individual plastic baggies of sticky rice fill large, woven palm baskets instead of large mounds from which individuals helped themselves), the basic mode of service continues to be similar to a large buffet from which individuals or families fill a tray of small bowls from which those known to each other eat with spoons and chopsticks.

Khmer Chicken Curry
Serves 4

Ingredients:
curry paste—blend in food processor until a paste and add 2 tablespoons hot water
galangal (1 one-inch piece, peeled and sliced)
turmeric root (2 one-inch pieces, peeled and sliced OR 2 teaspoons powdered turmeric)
garlic (2 cloves, chopped)
lemongrass (1 stalk, sliced thin)
shallot (4 shallots peeled and chopped OR ½ onion, diced)
kaffir lime leaf (2 pieces, sliced) OR 2 lime leaves sliced
1 can coconut milk (not sweetened or coconut cream)
1 small tablet palm sugar OR 2 tablespoons brown sugar
1 sweet potato, cubed
1 onion, diced
1 carrot, sliced

4 to 6 long beans cut into one-inch pieces OR ½ to ⅔ cup green beans (one-inch pieces)
1 chicken breast, sliced or cubed (your taste)
Fish sauce to taste—maybe 1 tablespoon (it will not taste fishy!)
¼ teaspoon salt
4 star anise
½ cup water OR good-quality chicken broth

To cook:

In a large saucepan, heat coconut milk to a simmer on medium high heat, add curry paste, and cook for 10 minutes (simmering) with sugar, sweet potato, carrot, onion, and long beans or green beans.

Add cubed (raw) chicken and simmer for about 15 to 20 minutes.

Add salt, star anise, fish sauce, and water. Stir and cook until vegetables are tender and chicken is cooked through. Do not let vegetables get mushy.

Serve with steamed jasmine rice or baguette.

Rice:

Start rice cooking at the same time the coconut milk is heating. A traditional method of judging water/rice ratio: put desired amount of rice (1 cup dry is good for this recipe, which will make 2 cups cooked) in saucepan, add a pinch of salt, put the tip of your thumb touching top of rice and add water until water reaches first knuckle. Heat covered rice, water, and salt to boiling. Turn temperature down so that the rice simmers for about 10 minutes. Turn off and leave on heat until curry is ready.

Holiday Feasts

Cambodian American communities most commonly celebrate *Chaul Chhnam* (New Year, which is celebrated in mid-April), the ascension of the Buddha, the annual water festival, and weddings. For all of these events, food is varied and plentiful. Community members gather to prepare large quantities of sticky rice, fried rice, fish or chicken soups, roast and sliced pork, chicken-pork sausage, sour greens, spring rolls and fresh rolls, and various condiments. Desserts include brightly colored jelled coconut cups, fruit trays, and American-style cookies. Weddings also include traditional Western white wedding cakes, while *Chaul Chhnam* celebrations sometimes include large sheet cakes decorated with good wishes for the new year. Community members usually prepare these dishes in groups, often starting several days before the big event. Women gather to cook most of the food, while men are in charge of the roast pork, which is best prepared on a spit over an open fire.

While most Khmer are Buddhist, many of those who were once refugees celebrate Christmas with their sponsor families or host hot-pot potluck-style meals in their own homes. Holiday celebrations are generally community oriented, with women cooking together at someone's house or at the local *Wat* (temple). Buddhist calendar holidays include a formal service with chanting led by monks, and these services are always held before 11 a.m. so that the monks can observe their religious strictures of not eating after noon. Afterward, community members serve the monks, and then women prepare portable bamboo tables filled with a variety of dishes from which family members eat. Less traditional celebrations involve long buffet-style tables laden with the various dishes noted above from which individuals serve themselves.

Place in American Culture

Khmer food is not well known in the United States. For most Americans, it would be similar to Thai, but it does not incorporate chili and heat to the degree that the latter does.

Restaurants and Chefs

Not surprisingly, Cambodian restaurants tend to be in those parts of the United States where there are a critical mass of Cambodians, particularly Lowell, Massachusetts; Long Beach, California; and Seattle, Washington. Some also serve a range of Southeast Asian food, particularly Thai, which is more familiar to most non-Khmer patrons, as well as Chinese. Homemade noodle dishes, oxtail soup, *beef lok lak*, and fruit "shakes" are common. The most widely known restaurant is Chef Longteine de Monteiro's Elephant Walk in the Boston metropolitan area, which serves a rather upscale menu of French-inspired Khmer cuisine, including dishes such as *Crevette Kep Sur Mer* (shrimp with lemongrass, tamarind, coconut milk, wild lime, asparagus, and more with jasmine rice). The Elephant Walk also offers cooking classes. Lowell boasts at least twenty Khmer restaurants, including other French-influenced places such as Tepthida Khmer (serving a large range of reasonably priced traditional dishes including lemongrass-marinated crispy frog legs and *kruoch chean*, or fried quail, plus fusion dishes such as butternut catfish curry) as well as Denise Ban's more affordable Simply Khmer. Many reviewers have noted Simply Khmer for the excellence and variety of such dishes as *trey jein swai* (fried catfish with mango sauce) and *tuk kroeung khmer* (ground, smoked fish with *prahok*, garlic, chilis, fresh lime juice, and vegetables), among others. While there are too many restaurants to list, a few others to note are Senmonorom, which serves Cambodian hot pot; Peephup Tmei's *tum yum* (lemongrass/lime-flavored chicken soup); or Viet-Thai's *mee ka thang*, flat noodles with eggs, vegetables, fish cakes, meat, and gravy.

Most Khmer eating establishments in the United States are small, relatively inexpensive, family-friendly places. At this writing, Long Beach, California, leads the nation in the sheer number—twenty-two!—of Cambodian restaurants, including Phnom Penh Noodle House (traditional homemade noodle soups) and Siem Reap Asian Cuisine (oxtail soup, crispy quail), as well as those that also serve Thai, such as Little Lalune Cuisine (*beef lok lak*—beef over lettuce, cucumbers, tomatoes, and onion with a lime pepper sauce, fried pork intestines) and Crystal Thai-Cambodian (papaya salad, boat noodles), or Chinese, such as Hak Heang (*lok lak*, noodle bowls, or traditional breakfast porridge) or Golden Chinese Express (shrimp fried rice, *beef lok lak*)—just to name a few. In the Pacific Northwest, there are Portland's one-time food cart and now full-on restaurant, Sok Sab Bai (serving limited quantities of oxtail soup, Khmer sausage, or *prahok katee*, sautéed pork with coconut milk and fermented fish paste), and Seattle's Phnom Penh Noodle House (lots of traditional homemade noodle soups, curries, and fruit "smoothies") and Queen's Deli (connected to a small grocery and featuring chicken coconut curry, papaya salad, and beef skewers, among other traditional dishes). Cambodian restaurants can also be found in Denver, Providence, and the San Francisco Bay area.

Further Reading

Başan, Ghillie. 2007. *The Food & Cooking of Cambodia*. London: Southwater, 2007.

de Monteiro, Longteine, and Katherine Neustadt. *The Elephant Walk Cookbook: The Exciting World of Cambodian Cuisine from the Nationally Acclaimed Restaurant*. New York: Houghton Mifflin Harcourt, 1998.

Rivière, Joannès. *Cambodian Cooking: A Humanitarian Project in Collaboration with Act for Cambodia*. Singapore: Periplus Editions, 2005.

Rachelle H. Saltzman

CAMEROON

(Middle Africa) Cameroonian American Foodways

Background

With a population of 21.7 million, Cameroon is located in Central Africa on the Gulf of Guinea. Cameroonians represent 240 tribes and three major ethnic groups: Bantus, Semi-Bantus, and Sudanese. Diplomatic relations between the

United States and Cameroon were established in 1960 after the African nation gained independence from partial French rule. A Cameroonian American woman now living in Santa Fe, New Mexico, Ceci Tadfor, describes her native country:

> Cameroon is referred to as Africa in miniature, which means it encompasses a bit of every part of Africa: culture, climate, religion, etc. There is the rain forest, the desert, savannah, grassland and everything in between. There are over two hundred and fifty dialects spoken in Cameroon. As these dialects differ so are the different foods that come from it.

According to the 2000 US Census, approximately 7,908 Cameroonians reside in the United States. However, in 2012 the Chia Report reported that there were over thirty-three thousand Cameroonians in the United States, with the largest population pockets in the Washington DC, area. Most of these immigrants arrived after 2000.

There are a number of associations for Cameroonians and Cameroonian Americans spread out across the country from Los Angeles to Pittsburgh. These groups seem to offer a variety of events meant to bring those of Cameroonian descent together. Given the small number of groups and the small number of Cameroonians in the United States, it would be difficult to make statements about assimilation or retention of ethnic character. In part this is due to the low numbers and in part due to the French colonization of Cameroon until 1960, which brought Western influences to the African nation well before immigration.

Foodways

The traditional foods of Cameroon are much like its neighbor nations in Africa, indigenous foods with colonial influences. According to *Food in Every Country* in 1472, the Portuguese came to Cameroon with New World foods such as maize, cassava, tomatoes, and peppers. The Cameroonians mixed this with indigenous food such as millet and peanuts. As with food in most cultures, foods in Cameroon are regionally based dependent on climate and geography. A staple dish is *fufu*, made out of starchy ingredients such as yams. Cassava is also used and is sometimes fermented before being cooked. One method is for it to be wrapped in banana leaves and steamed or fried.

One can also find French influence in dishes such as prunes stewed in tomatoes. Cameroonian food culture also includes a very hot pepper, usually ground into a paste. Cameroonian American Ceci Tadfor pointed out that when she came to the United States, she felt more at home foodwise in New Mexico, where very hot peppers were commonly used, than in the Southeast where she attended college. She describes the difficulty of defining Cameroonian food:

> No one can ever really write a "Cameroonian cook book" because it will be almost impossible to come up with all the different foods that is prepared in the different areas, it will probably be an encyclopedia. People from different areas eat differently. They might use the same base foods such as cocoyams, plantain cassava, beans or yams, but the preparation is very different from area, to area.

A national dish is "bitter leaves" stewed with smoked fish and ground peanut paste. Spinach is oftentimes substituted for the bitter leaves in the United States, partly because of the bitterness but also because of availability. Also, it is common in Cameroon to stew fish and beef (and other available meats, such as pork or chicken, and shrimp) together, a taste that does not always fit the American palate. Peanut-based dishes, such as chicken in peanut sauce, tend to be popular among Americans, but many Cameroonians find chicken in the

United States to be soft and "mushy" since they are used to older, laying hens.

Many of the ingredients for Cameroonian food are unavailable in the United States, so individuals traveling back home frequently bring ingredients with them, freezing them to save for special occasions. Some ingredients can be obtained from African and other ethnic groceries as well as health food stores, but substitutions are common. Ceci Tadfor's recipes below give the ideal ingredients, but she oftentimes adapts them for American contexts, using whatever is available. She also makes the fish and seafood optional, according to American tastes (which oftentimes do not relish a "fishy" flavor).

Ndole

Ingredients:

    2 pounds stew beef (optional)
    1 large dry (smoked) fish (optional)
    1 pound shrimp (optional)
    2 cups raw groundnut paste (can use peanut butter)
    1 cup fresh bitter leaves (or dry bitter leaves—soak overnight)
    2 packs fresh spinach (washed and chopped)
    1 tablespoon fresh ground garlic
    2 medium onions
    ½ cup crayfish (crushed) (optional)
    1½ cups vegetable oil
    2 cups water
    2 fresh ground habanero peppers (optional)
    salt to taste
    4 boullion cubes

Preparation:

Wash, season, and cook beef until tender. Wash, cut, and steam fish, or cook until tender. Wash, clean, and prepare shrimp. In a large pot, heat one cup of oil. Add one of the chopped onions, salt, and garlic. Stir well. Reduce heat, and add groundnut paste. Cook for about 45 minutes, stirring occasionally to keep the groundnut paste from burning. Add water and beef. Stir well, and cook for about thirty minutes. Add bitter leaves, spinach, crayfish, and pepper. Add dry fish, shrimp, and boullion cubes. Reduce heat, and cook for about another twenty-five minutes.

In a frying pan, pour in the remaining oil. Add remaining onions, lightly sauté, and add to stew.

Serve with *miondor*, *bobolor*, boiled rice, fried plantains, boiled plantains, or food of choice.

Steamed Fish

Ingredients:

    2 whole fish (in Cameroon, red snapper, sole, or mackerel would be fish of choice, but salmon is a popular alternative in the United States)
    4 medium tomatoes (diced)
    1 medium onion (chopped)
    2 tablespoons ground *njangsang* (native spice)
    2 tablespoons fresh ground ginger
    2 tablespoons fresh ground garlic
    1 teaspoon ground *jowe*
    1 teaspoon ground country onion (native spice)
    1 teaspoon ground *beh beh* (native spice)
    2 fresh ground habanero peppers
    ¼ cup olive oil
    2 bouillon cubes
    salt to taste
    banana leaves for wrapping

Preparation:

Wash and cut fish to desired sizes. Mix all ingredients together. Marinate fish in mixture.

Wrap in leaves and steam for about an hour and a half.

Serve with fried plantains, rice, boiled plantains, and other items.

Cameroonians eat three meals a day, with breakfast often consisting of porridges, fried eggs, fried plantains or chips (potatoes), or bread and tomato, usually washed down with tea, which is produced locally. Coffee is also grown there and drunk either black or with milk. Coffee and tea plantations historically were significant in the economy, and they continue to contribute to exports.

Lunch and dinner might be *fufu* or rice (a native-grown variety substituted in the United States with basmati or jasmine) with a stew or sauce. Boiled peanuts are commonly served as an appetizer, and the meal might be accompanied with "ginger brew" or wine. A typical meal would begin with hand washing because foods like *fufu* and stews are eaten with the fingers. Fish is usually eaten by hand so that the bones can be taken out easily, but forks and spoons are also available.

There is a gender- and age-related aspect to meals in Cameroonian culture: men eat first, then women and children last. Food preparation is primarily the responsibility of women and is an important aspect of their identity. As Tadfor explains:

> In Cameroon cooking is an integral part of a woman's life. As a young girl you grow up watching your mother, grandmother, aunt, sister or some other woman in your life cook. There are no recipes, you learn by watching and helping in the kitchen. If you have questions, you ask as you go along, or at a later time.
>
> By age ten most young girls are trusted with the responsibilities of cooking for a family of up to ten to fifteen people. Sometimes these could be immediate family and other times it could be extended family. Besides cooking, the young girls are also expected to take care of their siblings and other house chores. These are usually carried out without complaints or resentment, because this is part of the culture as well as a part growing up.
>
> In the old days young girls had to be trained to be good cooks, because it will help them catch a good husband and it will also help them be a good wife. They will be able to prepare nutritious foods for their children.

This is all changing in most of the big towns and even in smaller villages. Young girls are going to school to pursue an education just like the young men, and so they do not spend most of their time at home with their mothers learning to cook or helping them at the farms.

It is always a pride to a mother to know that her daughter(s) can cook. She can talk about them with pride and know that she did her job well in bringing them up the way culture requires.

Hospitality and generosity are important aspects of Cameroonian food culture, and these have been carried over to the United States where Cameroonian Americans use food to bring people together. Ceci Tadfor describes the attitudes in her homeland:

> The smell of good food always draws men around the compound to come to where ever that good smell is coming from. In the African culture, you don't have to be invited to come in and share a meal. Thus, a compound that always lets out the smell of good food always attract people, mostly young men, and they always want to know who the cook is. When you cook you never limit the amount of food to the number of people in the house, because you never know who will come by to visit, and a visitor is not allowed to say no when he or she is offered food.

Place in American Culture

Cameroonian food is not well known in the United States and is generally categorized as simply African or central African. Many of the food staples, such as corn, millet, peanuts, and tomatoes, found in Cameroon are also readily available in the United States, but others are not. It is also important to note that Cameroon has had Western influences since the fifteenth century and that its metropolitan areas feature a wide variety of foods from around the globe, so that Cameroonian Americans tend to be cosmopolitan in their eating habits.

Restaurants and Chefs

There are a number of restaurants serving Cameroonian food in metropolitan areas with large African populations, but these usually advertise themselves as African or West African. The Washington, DC, area, in particular, has a number, including one in the Maryland suburbs named after the Cameroonian footballer (soccer player) Roger Milla. The Chowhound Internet site includes some entries about restaurants that either offer some Cameroon dishes or are run by a Cameroon chef (http://chowhound.chow.com/topics/360378).

Perhaps typical of other African cuisines is the catering business and cooking classes of Ceci Tadfor in Santa Fe. She advertises her menus as African and American, but she features Cameroonian dishes, adapting them to the tastes as well as the resources of her customers. She describes her own background and motivations for continuing her cooking. She is also completing a cookbook.

I grew up in Cameroon in a small town called Buea, which was the capital of former West Cameroon, ruled by the Germans and then later on the British and the French. Buea has a very refreshing climate with the beautiful Cameroon Mountain, which is 4070 feet high looking down on the city. Mami Ncha raised me; she is my grandmother. Whenever she was not at the farm or in the market she was in the kitchen cooking. I always enjoyed watching her cook. I would ask of her if there was anything I could do to help with the cooking. She would give me the chores of getting the spices and ingredients for the foods she was going to cook ready. I always enjoyed doing that. Sometimes by the time she returned from the farm or the market I would have the food ready, and she was always very impressed. By observing and helping Mami Ncha in the kitchen as much as I could I developed a passion for cooking. I would cook and have friends over, I would offer to cook when friends had a party or other occasions that required food. It is that passion for cooking and for food that has pushed me into introducing Cameroonian food here in Santa Fe. Most of the people who have tasted my cooking have always encouraged me to open a restaurant, but I don't think I am at the point in my life where I would like to be involved in a project that big. I continue to cook for events around town and I do enjoy doing it.

Further Reading

"Cameroon." Food in Every Country. Accessed July 29, 2014. http://www.foodbycountry.com/Algeria-to-France/Cameroon.html.

Cameroon Today. Accessed July 29, 2014. http://www.cameroon-today.com.

Njila, Hinsley. "A Guide to Understanding Cameroonian Immigrants in the US." The Chia Report. Last modified April 3, 2012. Accessed July 29, 2014. http://www.chiareport.com/2012/04/a-guide-to-understanding-cameroonian-immigrants-in-the-us.html.

U.S. Department of State. "Fact Sheet." Bureau of African Affairs. Accessed July 29, 2014. http://www.state.gov/r/pa/ei/bgn/26431.htm.

Elinor Levy and Ceci Tchakounte Tadfor

CANADA
(North America) Canadian American Food

Background

Canadian cuisine is as diverse is its people and geography. The coasts offer a variety of fresh seafood, the prairies supply the country with beef and bacon, and among the lush greenery there are berries, apples, and game meat galore. A commonality found in all Canadians is a sweet tooth for all things maple flavored, and a cold beer is never turned down, whether it is a warm summer's eve or a cold and snowy night at a neighbor's house watching the hockey game.

To understand the influences embedded in Canadian cuisine and foodways, one must understand the beginnings of Canada. Prior to colonization, Native Americans were the sole inhabitants of Canada, using a history of hunting, fishing, and gathering. Due to the immense size and geographical variation of Canada, Native Americans had a varied diet depending on the primary location of their lands. For example, in the north, blubber and seal is eaten, but inland prairie Native Americans would eat buffalo and deer.[1]

The French arrived, bringing with them a rich culinary history of buttery, sugary treats and laying down the framework for much of Canada's more iconic treats.[2]

Major immigration also included the English, Scottish, and Irish, although their culinary flavors did not have as large of an impact as did the French.[3]

As immigration to Canada continued, so did the growth of flavors, and more regional variation began, with Asian influences on the West Coast, Eastern and Western European influences on the prairies, and English, Irish, and Scottish influences continued on the East Coast.[4]

Canadians began immigrating to America as early as the eighteenth century with the expulsion of French Canadians from Acadia (Nova Scotia) when it was came under British rule.[5]

The French Canadians settled in Louisiana, under rule of the Spanish, and the Cajun culture was born. Between this period and until the US Civil War, immigration from Canada to America declined until the war created a boom and there was a need for industry workers, enticing many British Canadians to settle in states nearest the border, such as New England and Virginia. With the continuing promise of economic fortune, Canadians continued to migrate to border states, such as Massachusetts, New York, Michigan, Maine, Vermont, Wisconsin, and Illinois well into the nineteenth and twentieth centuries.[6] Migratory French Canadians formed communities once in America in order to preserve their traditions.

After World War II, Canadian immigration steadily declined. However, the draw of booming economies and higher wages was still enticing to many professionals.[7] People move for careers, love, family, and school, and they bring with them favorite Canadian delicacies and a keen interest in exploring their new environment.

Foodways

Canada and the United States are both transglobal, multicultural countries—countries grown out of immigration and colonization from other cultures. Thus, Canadians in America tend to eat primarily the same foods as Americans, with the some interesting exceptions, such as the high demand experienced by Canadian Sweets and Treats Catering, the only Canadian-themed catering company in all of American. The owner, Donna Marie Artuso, is well informed about the desire for Canadian foods in America, as she ships her foods to Canadians all across America. She finds that despite the similarities in most consumption habits of Canadians and Americans, Canadians in America still have a sweet tooth for butter tarts, Nanaimo squares, and *tarte au sucre*. Nanaimo bars are claimed by the city of Nanaimo in British Columbia, although the exact origin is unknown. Despite there being a variety of ways to make this sweet treat, it is most well known for its hard, dark chocolate topping, rich creamy middle, and a cookie crumble bottom. Other variations include coconut or different flavors in the middle, such as mint.

Donna Marie believes that the most notable Canadian delicacies are the desserts, but she also fills the demand for Canadian game meats, *tourtière*, and coastal seafood. Despite being in high demand all year round, she notes that her busiest days of the year are Canada Day on July 1 and Canadian Thanksgiving.

The following recipe comes from the author's grandmothers.

Tourtière
This recipe makes 3 double-crusted pies.

Ingredients for crust:
   5 cups flour
   1 tablespoon sugar
   1 teaspoon baking soda
   1 pound lard (Tenderflake) cut into small cubes
   1 beaten egg in a measuring cup filled with 2 tablespoons lemon juice or vinegar and topped to 1-cup mark with ice water

Directions:
1. Mix flour, sugar, and baking soda with a fork in a large bowl.
2. Then add lard, beaten egg, and lemon juice (or vinegar) water mixture and stir wet and dry ingredients together. Use a pastry cutter to mix the dough and then work the dough with your hands until you are able to form 6 patties.
3. Chill for an hour so before rolling out to fit in your 9-inch pie plates.

Ingredients for filling:
   1½ pounds ground beef
   1½ pounds ground pork
   1 large onion, finely chopped
   2 garlic cloves, finely chopped
   fine breadcrumbs
   1 teaspoon salt
   1 teaspoon savory
   ¼ teaspoon cloves (or to taste)
   ¼ teaspoon cinnamon (or to taste)

About 1 cup of water, add just enough slowly to mixture to get thick consistency.

Directions:
1. Brown the pork and beef slowly in a large pot. Drain and then rinse the fat off.
2. Add the onions, garlic, and salt. Add the remaining spices a little at a time and adjust to your taste.
3. Roll out pastry to fit your pie plate. Sprinkle about ¼ cup of fine breadcrumbs onto the bottom of the crust. Pour in the cooked meat mixture. Cover with a top crust. Be sure to cut small steam vent holes in the top crust.
4. Brush top crust with a beaten egg mixed with a little water.
5. Bake at 350°F for about 40 minutes.

Holiday Feasts
Holiday feasts generally resemble that of American holidays—a household of friends and family sitting around a table filled with spicy pumpkin pie and whipped cream, a succulent turkey, creamy mashed potatoes, and fresh cranberry sauce. The difference in the dates for Thanksgiving, Canadian Thanksgiving is on the second Monday of October and American Thanksgiving in late November, has led to some unique traditions. Canadian Americans tend to congregate with each other in October in order to share and give thanks together. But what they choose to eat does not always resemble a traditional holiday meal. For example, when a group of Canadians interning in Washington, DC, got together for Thanksgiving, it was an opportunity to treat themselves to a fancy restaurant with a diverse menu with options of seafood, Italian, or Southern. This speaks to an interesting notion of community: when maintaining Canadian culture, it is less about the tangible aspects and more about the action of being together.

Place in American Culture
Notable differences discovered by Canadians living in America between classically Canadian foods and American interpretations of classic

Canadian dishes might include poutine, vodka Caesars, and hamburgers. In Canada, deep-fried cuts of potatoes, cheese curds, and a thick coating of gravy define a *poutine*. In America, Canadians often find that even simply ordering gravy with your fries seems odd. A Caesar is a spiced vodka beverage, known as a Bloody Mary in America. The main difference is the type of mix; Canadians use Clamato juice, and Americans use pure tomato juice. Lastly, in Canada if you are served a hamburger that has "pink" in the middle, more often than not it will be sent it back to the kitchen, as Canadians fear that pink burgers could make one sick, whereas many Americans want to be able to choose and welcome some pink in their burger.

Notes

1. "Canadian Aboriginals," *Food in Every Country*, accessed November 12, 2014, http://www.foodbycountry.com/Algeria-to-France/Canada-Aboriginals.html.
2. Donna Marie Artuso, Canadian Sweets and Treats Catering and Event Planning, http://canadiansweetsandtreats.com/.
3. Artuso, Canadian Sweets and Treats.
4. Artuso, Canadian Sweets and Treats.
5. Elliott Robert Barkan, *Immigrants in American History: Arrival, Adaptation, and Integration* (Santa Barbara: ABC-CLIO, 2013).
6. Barkan, *Immigrants in American History*.
7. Barkan, *Immigrants in American History*.

Further Reading

Artuso, Donna Marie. Canadian Sweets and Treats Catering and Event Planning. Telephone, October 31, 2014.

Barkan, Elliot Robert. *Immigrants in American History: Arrival, Adaptation, and Integration*. Santa Barbara: ABC-Clio, 2013.

"Canadian Aboriginals." *Food in Every Country*. Accessed April 5, 2014. http://www.foodbycountry.com/Algeria-to-France/Canada-Aboriginals.html.

Zeidler, Maryse. "Dessert's Origins Unknown, Nanaimo Calls It Its Own." *The Globe and Mail*, December 31, 2013. http://www.theglobeandmail.com/news/british-columbia/origins-unknown-nanaimo-calls-it-its-own/article16143830/.

Bailey M. Cameron

CAPE VERDE

(Western Africa) Cape Verdean American Food

Background

Immigrants from the Cape Verdean islands off the western coast of Africa represent a mix of Portuguese and African cultures, heritage, and language, represented in Crioulo, the creole language still spoken in Cape Verde and among some immigrants and their descendants. Historian Marilyn Halter notes, "They are the only major community of Americans of African descent (albeit of mixed ancestry) to have voluntarily made the transatlantic voyage to the United States."[1] Halter and others also describe the difficulties in establishing population statistics for Cape Verdean immigrants and their descendants due to shifts in US policy, the tendency for Cape Verdeans themselves to identify themselves as Portuguese during some decades, racism, and questions about identity among Cape Verdeans up to present day.[2] The 2009 US Census listed ninety-one thousand Cape Verdeans, with 83 percent living in the Northeast,[3] but most researchers agree these numbers are likely to be low. Like immigrants from Portugal and the Azores, Cape Verdeans were first drawn to the United States as whalers, and they were later recruited as workers in the cranberry bogs of New England, especially Massachusetts and Rhode Island. The majority of Cape Verdeans remain in the New England area, with small groups also in California, Hawaii, and Florida. As with other immigrant groups, traditional foods are often showcased at festivals, particularly at celebrations of Cape Verde's independence from Portugal in 1975.

Foodways

Cape Verdean food traditions reflect the mixture of Portuguese and African cultures along with the environmental conditions of the islands, which were and are subject to drought. The national dish of Cape Verde, *cachupa* (also called *manchupa*), is a stew of dried corn (hominy), lima beans, greens (such as kale), and meat or fish, which can be found in two forms, *povera* (poor or everyday) and *rica*. *Rica* has additional ingredients, usually sausage (*linguica*) or richer cuts of meat. *Cachupa* is sometimes fried and served with an egg (typically this is the form found in Cape Verdean restaurants). Another everyday dish is *canja*, chicken soup made with onion and rice. Today this is also served at festivals. Basic foods include pork, beef, a variety of beans including lima and kidney, cabbage, carrots, corn (which was imported by the Portuguese to the islands), eggs, onions, rice, and fish. Seasonings include paprika, bay leaves, garlic, and onions. *Jagacita*, often abbreviated as *jag*, is rice made with onion, kidney beans, and paprika. *Gufong*, a fried dough made from flour, cornmeal, and bananas, is made for holidays and community festivals and has been a traditional breakfast food in some families. *Dulce de leche*, a candy made from milk, sugar, and white vinegar or lemon, is a treat for dessert. In New England, Cape Verdeans share a love of *linguica* (Portuguese sausage), codfish, scallops, tuna, and other fresh fish with Portuguese immigrants and their descendants along with grilled meat frequently served at Cape Verdean festivals.

Place in American Culture and Restaurants

As a minority among minorities, Cape Verdean culture has made some inroads in American hip-hop music but not yet food, except in restaurants and on Pinterest, the social media platform. There are Cape Verdean restaurants in Massachusetts and Rhode Island. Restaurant Laura in Dorchester, Massachusetts, in particular, features Cape Verdean dishes such as *cachupa* with eggs, *jagacita*, and other traditional dishes. An organization of Cape Verdeans of Southern California holds social events, including dinners.

Notes

1. Marilyn Halter, *Between Race and Ethnicity: Cape Verdean American Immigrants, 1860–1965*, excerpted on line 1993 (Chicago: University of Illinois Press, 1993), http://www.africanaheritage.com/haltercapeverdeansexcerpt.asp.
2. Marilyn Halter, *Between Race and Ethnicity*, 37, and Claire Andrade Watkins in *Some Funny Kind of Porto Rican*, PBS, written and produced by Claire Andrade Watkins, https://www.youtube.com/watch?v=rRl8KkICVAg.
3. US Census Bureau, Table 52, US Population by Selected Ancestry Group and Region: 2009, https://www.census.gov/compendia/statab/2012/tables/12s0052.pdf.

Further Reading

The Cool Cooks, "Auntie Laura's *Gufong*," thecoolcook.wordpress.com/2010/09/21/auntie-lauras-gufong-a-cape-verdean-favorite/.

Lima, Lucillia. "Lembranca: Crioulo Memories." In *Spinner, People and Culture in Southeastern Massachusetts*, volume 1. New Bedford, MA: Spinner, 1981.

Ramos, Lucy. "Black, White or Portuguese? A Cape Verdean Dilemma." In *Spinner: People and Culture in Southeastern Massachusetts*, volume 1. New Bedford, MA: Spinner, 1981.

Susan Eleuterio

CARIBBEAN (AMERICAS)

The islands in the Caribbean are grouped by the nationality of their colonizer or their primary and official language, since those factors have given commonalities in the food cultures. Some nationalities have entries of their own. These are marked with an asterisk (*).

British territories—Anguilla, British Virgin Islands, Cayman Islands, Grenada*, Turks and Caicos Islands, Montserrat.

English speaking but independent: Antigua and Barbuda, Bahamas*, Barbados*, Dominica, Jamaica*, Saint Kitts and Nevis, Saint Vincent and the Grenadines, Trinidad and Tobago*.

French territories: Guadeloupe, Martinique, Saint Barthélemy, Saint Martin.

French speaking but independent: Haiti*, Saint Lucia.

Dutch*: Aruba, Bonaire, Curaçao, Saint Eustatius, and Saint Maarten.

Caribbean, Dutch (also known as Dutch Antilles or Dutch West Indies): Aruba, Bonaire, Curaçao, Saba, Saint Eustatius and Saint Maarten.

CARIBBEAN, DUTCH (ALSO KNOWN AS DUTCH ANTILLES OR DUTCH WEST INDIES)

Aruba, Bonaire, Curaçao, Saba, Saint Eustatius, and Saint Maarten
(Americas—Caribbean) Antillean American, Caribbean American Food

Background

By the last quarter of the seventeenth century the Dutch possessed six Caribbean islands: Aruba, Bonaire, Curaçao, Saba, Saint Eustatius, and Saint Maarten. For much of its history, the territory was referred to as the Dutch West Indies. Within the Kingdom of the Netherlands, and from 1954 until 2010, the islands formed an autonomous country, the Netherlands Antilles. After 2010, the Leeward Islands—Aruba, Curaçao, and Saint Maarten—became separate countries within the kingdom, while the Windward Islands—Bonaire, Saint Eustatius, and Saba—are integrated into the Netherlands and are formally referred to as the Dutch Caribbean. The territory is 980 square kilometers, and most of the over three hundred thousand inhabitants live on Aruba, Bonaire, and Curaçao in the southern Caribbean; the rest of the population lives on the islands that are located southeast of the Virgin Islands.

Unlike Spain and Portugal, the Low Countries did not participate in the exploration of the Americas before 1580, when the Philip II of Spain (1527–1598) cut off the seventeen provinces from the salt and spice trade with Portugal in order to win the Eighty Years' War (1568–1648). Although the ships, men, and resources were lacking, the decision of the Spanish king forced the Dutch to look elsewhere for spices, particularly salt for the preservation of herring and cod. A year later, the northern part of the Low Countries became the Dutch Republic (1581–1795, officially: Republic of the Seven United Netherlands), and in 1585 the first Dutch ships crossed the Atlantic to find salt in Venezuela. Due to the Spanish monopoly in Latin America, the massive salt voyages were forcibly ended in 1609, and the Dutch state started encouraging attacks on Spanish ships. In order to exploit trading opportunities, in 1621 the Dutch West India Company (WIC) was established, and by the mid-1600s the Leeward Islands (Aruba, Curaçao, and Saint Maarten) were conquered from the Spanish, and the Windward Islands (Bonaire, Saint Eustatius, Saba, Anguilla, Saint Croix, Tobago, and the present-day British Virgin Islands) were in the possession of the WIC. Since the last quarter of the seventeenth century until 2010, the Dutch Antilles consisted of the same six islands: Aruba, Bonaire, Curaçao, Saba, Saint Eustatius, and Saint Maarten. The establishment of Dutch settlements on the islands was inspired by commerce.

Mistreatment by colonial forces, warfare, and imported diseases rapidly decimated the native peoples of the Caribbean substantially.

In order to supplement the workforce, already at the beginning of the sixteenth century, the Spanish started bringing African slaves to the Caribbean. The slaves were needed to work in the salt ponds and on the newly established plantations. After the WIC became active in the slave trade in 1665, the largest island, Curaçao, became the major trade center because it was unsuitable for the large-scale cultivation of sugar, cotton, and tobacco. Despite most slaves leaving the island, over 80 percent of its current population is of African derivation. The rest of the population derives from Dutch, Portuguese, North Americans, natives from other Caribbean islands, Latin Americans, Sephardic Jews, Lebanese, and Asians. Similarly, the majority of Aruba's ethnic groups constitute mixed black with a small population of Caribe Amerindians, white people, and East Asians. Most of the inhabitants of the Dutch Antilles are Roman Catholic; other religions include Anglican, Jewish, Muslim, Protestant, Mormon, and Baptist. Due to the Spanish Inquisition (1492), Sephardic Jews had to flee from Spain and its colonies. After the Spanish conquered Dutch Brazil (1581–1654), many migrated to the Dutch settlement in the Caribbean, and in 1634, on Curaçao they established the oldest Jewish community and synagogue in the Western Hemisphere.

While Curaçao became the center of slave trade, in Bonaire salt was harvested, and dyewood and corn (maize) plantations were established on the island. The WIC vessels also obtained meat, water, and wood. After Aruba was seized from the Spanish around 1630, the Dutch used the Amerindians to take care of the livestock, used as a source of meat for the Dutch Caribbean. Saint Martin served as a convenient halfway point between the Dutch colonies in New Amsterdam (New York) and Brazil and was used for salt-mining operations. The small island of Saba was a hideout for pirates and "undesirable" people. The population produced sugar and rum, and they engaged in (lobster) fishing. Saint Eustatius became a (duty) free port, known as the Golden Rock, and here commerce and the trade in arms and ammunition flourished. The American Revolutionary military bought nearly half of their military supplies via the island. It was also the first to internationally acknowledge and salute the independence of the United States. The "First Salute" in 1776 resulted in President Roosevelt paying the island an official visit in 1939.

Dutch Antillean Food Culture

The geography and history of the Dutch Antilles resulted in two distinct cuisines, with European, African, Asian, Jewish, and American influences. On Aruba, Bonaire, and Curaçao the Dutch introduced bread, potatoes, pulses, cheeses, and pork; the Indonesians *nasi* (fried rice), *bami* (fried noodles), and satay; and the Chinese brought their cabbages and *taro* (*dasheen*). All over the Caribbean, the leaves are widely used to prepare *callaloo*, a stew or soup. Brazilian Jews took with them their sweet and sour preserves (pickles), cooking styles, and ingredients such as capers, olives, citrus fruits, and almonds. During two centuries, the population of the Dutch Antilles largely consisted of African slaves. Their food was rationed and frugal and largely consisted of *funchi* (corn pudding) and starchy tubers such as yam, cassava, and sweet potatoes, supplemented with a little bit of salted mackerel or salted cod. Meat, chicken, and fresh fish were a luxury. The Africans introduced bananas and plantains to the Dutch Antilles, and apart from quickly incorporating New World starchy tubers such as cassava and sweet potatoes, ingredients such as peanuts, papaya, coconuts, and chili pepper also found their way into Creole cuisine. Following the abolition of slavery, leafy vegetables such as spinach, lettuce and chard, and potatoes and canned vegetables became more widely available. Apart from the development of a distinct Creole cuisine, the closeness to Venezuela resulted in many similarities between the cuisine of the Leeward Islands and South American cuisine. On the islands, the main afternoon meal usually consists of *funchi*, fried plantains, and rice with stewed or fried meat. Salted fish and meats are commonly used, and goat meat enjoys popularity on Aruba. Soup is the main Sunday and holiday meal. And on Curaçao, *keshi yená* is a specialty for which an Edam cheese is stuffed with a filling of meat or fish, capers, raisins, dried plums, and olives, prepared in a waterbath (*au bain marie*) or in the oven, and is served sliced in pieces.

The small Windward Islands share their culinary culture with the British Islands and enjoy dishes such as *johnny cakes* (flat, fried cakes made with flour, milk, and butter) and rice and peas with chicken, goat, or pork and starchy tubers such as the sweet potato, yam, and breadfruit. On most of the Dutch Antilles, breakfast usually consists of bread with coffee or tea, and most families eat a hot meal twice per day; the main meal is in the afternoon and they have a lighter evening meal. All over the Dutch Antilles, cakes known as *bolu* or *bolo* are popular. They can be prepared with coconut milk or are steeped in alcohol (brandy, rum, and liquor). The *bolu pretu* (black cake) served at weddings and on festive occasions is filled with dried fruits and is prepared months ahead. It is a cousin of the British Christmas cake. All over the islands, herbs, spices, lemons, and hot pepper are used abundantly. Food is frequently stewed, a technique locally known as *stobá*, or fried in oil, margarine, and butter.

Place in American Culture

After the World War II, an estimated 1.5 million people from the West Indies (or Caribbean) migrated to the United States, most settling in Florida and New York. Many Antilleans, however, preferred migration to the Netherlands, and only a handful of people migrated to the United States. These individuals frequently associate with other groups from the Caribbean region, sharing commonalities in food and culture.

Despite the former Dutch Antilles being a popular holiday destination among Americans, and the overall praise for the distinctive local cuisine, thus far, dishes from the small Dutch islands have not left a lasting mark on American cuisine. Internationally still best known is the eighteenth-century Dutch liquor Blue Curaçao. Due to its exotic appearance, it is widely used in cocktails and other mixed drinks popularized by Americans.

Karin Vaneker

CAYMAN ISLANDS
(Americas—Caribbean)

A British territory in the Caribbean along with Anguilla, the Bahamas, British Virgin Islands, Grenada, Turks and Caicos Islands, and Montserrat.

See entries for the Bahamas and Grenada.

CENTRAL AFRICAN REPUBLIC (REFERRED TO AS CAR)
(Middle Africa) Central African American Food

See also: Chad, Cameroon, Congo, Rwanda.

Background

Located literally in the center of the African continent, the Central African Republic (CAR) is landlocked and has been rocked with violence and political coups for a number of years. Also formerly known as Congo Free State and French Equatorial Africa, CAR was colonized by the French but gained independence in 1960.[1] While there have been a number of refugees fleeing the situation in CAR over the last few years, numbers of immigrants to the United States are difficult to ascertain. As is the case with other areas of Africa that were both colonized by Europeans and impacted by Arab slave traders, the cuisine of CAR reflects a mix of indigenous foods and cultures along with

Ethnic American Food Today 109

vegetables and fruits originally brought from the Americas such as corn, peanuts, sweet potatoes, tomatoes, chili, and cassava.[2]

Foodways

In addition to the crops and foods listed above, fish, wild game, insects, bananas, yams, okra, millet, onion, rice, and palm oil make up the food customs depending on the part of the country, tribe, environmental conditions (river, forest, grassland), or culture of origin. Dough (*gozo*) made from cassava or sorghum is a basic staple, along with vegetables, poultry, meat or fish when available.[3] *Fufu*, the doughy staple served with stews and dishes with sauces throughout west and central Africa, is made in CAR from cassava.[4]

Notes

1. EveryCulture.com, Countries and Their Countries, "Central African, Republic," http://www.everyculture.com/Bo-Co/Central-African-Republic.html, and Wikipedia, "Cuisine of the Central African Republic," http://en.wikipedia.org/wiki/Cuisine_of_the_Central_African_Republic.
2. EveryCulture.com, Countries and Their Countries, "Central African Republic"; Wikipedia, "Cuisine of the Central African Republic."
3. EveryCulture.com, Countries and Their Countries, "Central African Republic"; Wikipedia, "Cuisine of the Central African Republic."
4. EveryCulture.com, Countries and Their Countries, "Central African Republic"; Wikipedia, "Cuisine of the Central African Republic."

Further Reading

CongoCookbook.com. "Fufu." http://www.congocookbook.com/staple_dish_recipes/fufu.html.

EveryCulture.com, Countries and Their Cultures. "Central African Republic." http://www.everyculture.com/Bo-Co/Central-African-Republic.html.

McCann, James C. *Stirring the Pot: A History of African Cuisine*. Athens: Ohio University Press, 2009.

Osseo-Asare, Fran. *Food Culture in Sub-Sahara Africa*. New York: Greenwood Press, 2005.

U.S. Census Bureau. "The Foreign-Born Population from Africa: 2008–2012." http://www.census.gov/content/dam/Census/library/publications/2014/acs/acsbr12-16.pdf.

Susan Eleuterio and Lucy M. Long

CENTRAL ASIA

(Central Asia) Kazakhstan, Kyrgyzstan, Tajikistan, Turkmenistan, and Uzbekistan American Food

See also: China, India, Pakistan, Afghanistan, Iran.

Background

People from Central Asia (a historical and geographical area outlined below) have immigrated to the United States in several waves and with increasingly wider distribution in recent years. The first waves, including peoples of Afghanistan, the former Russian Empire, Iran, Turkey, and western China, would have arrived no longer ago than the late nineteenth and early twentieth centuries. Settlements mainly were on the East Coast, mainly New York and the surrounding areas. After the Russian Revolution of 1917, Central Asian peoples wishing to escape the imposition of a communist order arrived in greater numbers, and this is referred to as a diaspora population. These numbers reached only several thousand at most, and again, population centers were New York and some California-based communities.

Turks arrived in small numbers after the transformation of the Ottoman Empire into the modern Turkish republic after 1923, but most of these migrants came in small numbers steadily through the 1970s, and they followed the typical pattern of migrants seeking a better economic way of life. After the ouster of the Shah of Iran in 1979, Iranians arrived in the United States as refugees, fearing persecution from the new dictatorial, religious regime. Many Iranians settled in the Los Angeles area, often representing either wealthier or professional classes; they were also unofficially called the "shah's people."

In the 1970s, as a product of the Cold War and the result of negotiations between President Jimmy Carter and Soviet Premier Leonid Brezhnev, tens of thousands of Soviet Jews were allowed to emigrate from the USSR, with many of these people settling throughout the United States. New York City is home to significant numbers of Bukharan Jews, who are indigenous Central Asian people; more than ten thousand of these people call parts of Queens and Brooklyn, New York, their home today.

The most recent waves of immigrants mainly are younger people, some with skilled or professional backgrounds, but many without such backgrounds, too. They have left the new Central Asian republics for a number of reasons, including economic distress and political or religious oppression. Such groups of Uzbeks, Kyrgyz, Kazakhs, Tajiks, and Turkmen may be found throughout the United States, but they are mainly in the biggest cities, including New York, Los Angeles, Chicago, Phoenix, St. Louis, and Washington, DC, metro area.

Unfortunately, there are no reliable or accurate demographic data on these waves of migrants. Overall, people of Central Asian origin and of Central Asian heritage probably number somewhere in the one hundred thousand to two hundred thousand range.

While always risky in scholarship to claim what contemporary Central Asia is and is not, a discussion of ethnic foodways both clarifies and confuses that definition. The panoply of meats, dairy products, grains, fruits and vegetables, and herbs and spices that form the food items and dishes associated with Central Asia suggest specifying today's countries historically associated with all of these items. Moving from east to west, it is appropriate to include western China, especially Xinjiang, parts of northern India and Pakistan, northern Afghanistan, the five formerly Soviet republics of Central Asia, including Kyrgyzstan, Kazakhstan, Tajikistan, Uzbekistan, and Turkmenistan (independent countries since 1991), and northeastern Iran (known as Khurasan).

This geography embodies contiguous space, covering steppe, deserts, oases, and mountains. And along with such shared historical features as languages (notably Turkic and Iranic/Persian), religions, and cultural practices, the cultivation and raising of crops and animals for foods, to say nothing of the influences of foodstuffs and cookery, spread much further in today's world, and this incorporates Korea, Russia, and modern Turkey. Shared heritages and varying culinary influences are evident whenever we look at popular foods, how foods are arranged at the table, and how people consume particular types of dairy dishes or dishes based on making dough from wheat flour, and more. While the connections are not always easy to establish in an ironclad sense, the conjectures are also limited in how speculative they may be because of the proximity of cultural groups, and the kinds of dishes and methods of preparing foods that particular ethnic or national groups of people prefer preparing over others. In the information to follow, the spread of favored and indigenous Central Asian foods and dishes will be discussed in the context of far-flung American diets.

Foodways

From antiquity until the twentieth century, Central Asia featured a division of food-producing economies referred to as the steppe and the sown, associated with the dichotomy of pastoral nomads and farmers/peasant-farmers. Traditionally, pastoral nomads and seminomadic peoples produced and consumed many dairy products, such as heavy cream, yogurt, cheeses, and butter, and meat products, especially those that could be preserved through drying and smoking. Naturally, these were traded and bartered for all manner of grain-based products as well as all sorts of fruits and vegetables. For millennia, records show that Central Asian agriculture produced wheat, rice, millet, and sorghum along with musk melons, watermelons, pomegranates, onions, garlic, quinces, apples, pears, figs, and persimmons.

In the ancient world, what historians identify as Turko-Persian lands and cultures—most of modern Central Asia described above—experienced contentious and fractious trade relations with China and the Hellenistic and Roman worlds to lesser degrees; Central Asia always was connected to networks of international commerce that we conveniently refer to as the Silk Road—silk roads, really. There were many different trade networks flowing from various parts of China through Central Asia, the Middle East, the Near East, the Mediterranean, and western Europe. In addition to all manner of luxury and everyday trade items in goods and products, including the eponymous silk and gemstones such as carnelian, amber, and lapis lazuli, foodstuffs also factored in the trading networks. For Central Asians, this probably brought them increasing rice and its subsequent cultivation as well as millet and sorghum. And while it is still not determined conclusively, it is likely that the making and preparation of noodles (usually wheat based) came to Central Asia from the east. Today Central Asians are very fond of thick soup noodles and steamed dumplings that are prepared and consumed in similar ways throughout China. The word for steamed dumplings, for example, in many parts of Central Asia and Turkey are referred to as *manti* or *mantoo*. Koreans call steamed dumplings *mandu*, so a shared heritage can be discerned, even though the exact origins of these foods is uncertain.

The *tandir* or *tandoor* (as commonly known in South Asia—India, Pakistan, Bangladesh, and other countries) oven further illustrates this notion of a shared regional or neighboring heritage when considering Central Asian crops, foods, cookery, and means of food preparation. These special cylindrical ovens may be built on platforms above ground or dug below ground. Historically, they have been built mainly of clay and wool, but they also may be found of cement construction. While it is also traditional that the fuels used included dried-out cotton plant stalks or cattle dung, gas-fueled *tandir/tandoors* are also encountered. In Central Asia nearly every rural home and many urban homes have these (much as Americans have a kitchen stove and a barbecue grill) located in their courtyards or backyards. Typically, people bake round, flat breads and turnovers in these ovens simply by sticking raw dough and their associated fillings to the sides of the oven once the preferred high temperatures have been reached. Again, it is not easy to say authoritatively if this type of traditional clay oven has it origins in South or Central Asia, although it is a common and regionally shared way to bake.

Typical Meals and Special Dishes

Central Asians traditionally consume three daily meals, though, of course, there are probably as many regional variations as there are individual preferences. The major variations are not merely regional, ethnic, or national but also a matter of lifestyle and culture, including differences between urban residents and among people whose cultural background is pastoral nomadic (or seminomadic) and agricultural and sedentary. Also, much depends on the relative wealth and poverty of a given family.

At breakfast, Central Asians of the countryside often enjoy tea, bread, nuts (walnuts or almonds), fruits, eggs, heavy cream, yogurt, boiled milk, wild honey, and cold cuts, especially sliced sausage. Among the poorer families on most days, the meal often amounts to little more than tea, bread, and maybe odd clumps of grapes, a few nuts, and perhaps the leftovers from the previous evening's meal. Much the same applies to urbanites, with the major exception that they increasingly eat fewer homemade or homegrown items and now have greater access to processed juices, coffee, breakfast cereals, and canned items, whether produced domestically or imported. Among people whose ancestry includes the herders associated with the rearing of horses, camels, sheep and goats, and cattle, one may expect more dairy, animal fat, and meat in the diet at all meals.

Lunches and dinners have similar foods, save that more preparation time and perhaps lavishness is reserved for dinner. Central Asians consume many types of soup and stews, which have the advantage of being relatively easy to prepare and do not need constant monitoring. Typical ingredients—in no particular order—may include varying proportions of eggplant, tomatoes, corn, black-eyed peas, sweet peppers, chickpeas, carrots, potatoes, beef or mutton, cottonseed oil, animal fat, sunflower seed oil, cumin, basil, and occasional chili peppers. In addition to salt and black pepper, Central Asians flavor many dishes with vinegar, onions, and garlic. Many savory and hot dishes are prepared with eggs, noodles, rice, and in the form of steamed dumplings. Favorite dishes include *pilaf* (many variations constitute this dish of fried and later steamed meat, carrots, onions, garlic, and rice), broad noodles and beef or horsemeat, and steamed dumplings. Dumplings may be served with mutton and onions, eggs, and squash.

At mealtime, when families are all together, it is common practice for rural people in particular to sit on quilts or blankets in their homes and tents and serve their food on tablecloths, either covering the floor directly or tossed over low, rectangular tables. Often, many small dishes or bowls of snacking items are laid out before the main meal arrives. These dishes may include nuts, candies, yogurt, farmer's cheese, compotes, and seeds. During more special occasions, hearty soups usually precede the serving of the main dish, whether large platters of meat and steamed vegetables, sliced meats and noodles in sauce, or *pilaf*. And depending upon where one happens to be in Central Asia, it may be common for people to practice a kind of sex segregation at the table. Men and women do not always dine together. Sex segregation is most common even today among rural farming peoples. These patterns have been maintained in the United States as well.

With the significant exception of urbanites again, Central Asians are not big consumers of desserts, which is not to say they do not enjoy sweets, including candies, honey, and putting lots of sugar in tea. Ordinarily, before and after meals people may eat plenty of fruit, including apples, pears, peaches, apricots, figs, persimmons, pomegranates, and muskmelon and watermelon. On special occasions, including weddings and religious holidays, sweets may be served in the form of fried noodles with honey, simple cakes with or without icing, and special puddings of wheat grass (*sumalak*) and egg whites and sugar (a meringue-like dish called *nishola*) that accompany the spring equinox (*Nowruz*) and Ramadan, respectively.

In the United States, central Asian immigrants adapt to changing lifestyles and diets similarly to many other immigrant groups. Just as they may drive cabs, open small businesses, or train to be attorneys and medical doctors, so their diets and eating habits change, too. Nevertheless, while one may witness a group of Kyrgyz young men, for example, celebrating a birthday in Chicago at a sushi restaurant, one can be sure that these young men will also hold commemoration days wherein they may slaughter a lamb, roast it, and gather all of the necessary ingredients for the foods and dishes on which they were raised. Life in the United States may make this more challenging but not impossible.

Central Asians dine out with less frequency than Americans, but there is a growing idea of haute cuisine developing today in Central Asia as well as a long-standing tradition of street foods. It goes without saying that one finds many more dining-out choices in urban over rural environments, but eateries exist everywhere in Central Asia, including in small villages and towns. Basically, Central Asians enjoy eating out whenever they have varieties of meals to choose from that they either cannot or often would not try to prepare at home, and especially when they are tired from long hours of shopping in rural marketplaces.

As street foods and found in local eateries are several beloved dishes and snacks, which include specially prepared *pilafs*, *manti* (large, filled dumplings), *kabobs*, *samsa* (a variation on the *samosa*, famous in South Asia and also prepared in the *tandir/tandoor* oven), and a very famous noodle dish known as *laghmon*. What makes dining out special are the methods of preparation and the particular ingredients or spices used. *Kabobs*, commonly known as *shashlik* in Central Asia, are merely a variant on *kabobs* made and sold through the Middle and Near East as well. Because they are often marinated and cooked over braziers filled with wood charcoal or wood itself, ordinary people are unlikely to have these facilities at home—thus their special appeal. Although almost anyone above the age of sixteen has the basic ability to prepare *pilaf*, professional *pilaf* chefs are known throughout towns and cities because of their unique flavorings, ingredients, and more. Some may even use preferred and expensive short- or medium-grain rices that people discern as much as Americans may discern a particular bread flavor. People also enjoy *pilafs* made with fruits, such as quinces, currants, or pomegranates, and they may love the fact that a particular *pilaf* chef uses sheep tail fat instead of common vegetable oils, or that he simply loads his *pilaf* with lots of flavorful meat.

The *laghmon* is also very prized because of the labor intensity that goes into the making of the noodles. The especially thick noodles are pounded out and stretched on long counters by professionals (thus it is comparatively rare to make them at home) who even entertain customers while they wait. It is akin to watching your favorite pizza maker roll out the dough and flip it in the air! The noodles are then added to a rich tomato and vegetable broth, loaded with spices and finely cut pieces of beef. With the exception of the *pilaf*, almost all of the foods mentioned above as street foods or foods found in local eateries benefit from the frequent sprinkling of herb and garlic-infused vinegar that nearly all stands and eateries have. People occasionally make these vinegars at home, but not often.

In the region's large cities, such as Tashkent, Almaty, Ashgabat, and Bishkek, it is typical for Central Asians to enjoy Russian, Ukrainian, and Korean dishes, too, because of the significant historical presence of people whose ancestry ties them to those countries. Hence, Central Asians enjoy borscht, cabbage soup, *pelmeni* (small beef dumplings) in chicken broth, mayonnaise-based chopped salads, and spicy carrot and beet salads or marinated eggplant and varieties of fish.

Place in American Culture

Aficionados of Central Asian food and adventurous "foodies" usually have to do some searching to find Central Asian foods or eateries in the United States, with the exception of a few metropolises.

Overall, it is fair to say that most ingredients for cooking Central Asian dishes are readily available throughout the United States in large supermarkets. For example, nowadays it is relatively easy to find thick, whole milk yogurts or a sharp and briny sheep-milk cheese known as *brinza* typical in Central Asia. Americans also grill shish *kabob*, though not in the typical style found throughout Central Asia, which consists of skewers of meat only, or combinations of meat, fat, and liver served with vinegar and raw onions on the side. Also, owing to the Spaniards having been influenced historically by Middle and Near Easterners, many Americans have a passing familiarity with *paella*, a variation of *pilaf*—with non–Central Asian additions of shellfish and chicken. Genuine Central Asian dishes, however, are relatively unknown in the mainstream United States, and only a few Central Asian–themed cookbooks are available.

Noted Restaurants and Chefs

Restaurants and eateries specializing in Central Asian cuisine, whether Uzbek, Kyrgyz, or Afghani, are relatively rare in the United States, but they can most be found in New York City, which has the oldest Turkestani (Central Asian) community in the United States, including descendants who immigrated to areas of Manhattan, the Bronx, and Brooklyn during and shortly after the Bolshevik Revolution in 1917. Furthermore, since the collapse of the Soviet Union in 1991, tens of thousands of Central Asian immigrants call the greater New York area home, and one of the results is a profusion of wonderful restaurants preparing homemade dishes and *tandir*-baked flatbreads in Brooklyn and Queens. Rego Park and Forest Hills, Queens, are home to a sizable community of indigenous Central Asian Jews, known as the Bukharan Jews, whose cuisine represents a combination of mostly Uzbek and Tajik cookery. As almost all Central Asians are Muslims, the kosher and *halal* preparation of foodstuffs happily coincide.

There are also reports of a sort of fusion of Uzbek and Central Asian cuisines with other world cuisines because of the presence in New York of skilled chefs and creative cooks, including in fine dining restaurants in Manhattan and eclectic places in the Rockaways in Queens. The *New York Times*, in fact, is a good place to search for Central Asian eateries in that metropolitan area.

Outside of New York, the pickings are a little thinner, but reputable Central Asian dining as a result of smaller immigrant communities may be found in Baltimore, Philadelphia, Columbus, Chicago, St. Louis, Denver, Phoenix, and Los Angeles. Other cities may boast a Central Asian restaurant or, more commonly, restaurants offering hybrid combinations of Turkish and Central Asian dishes or Russian and Central Asian dishes. Again, those combined or hybridized cuisines reflect both centuries, even millennia, of cross-cultural interaction as well as the shaping of the contemporary world after the collapse of the Soviet Union and the large-scale movement of Central Asian peoples into Russia, Turkey, western Europe, and the United States.

Russell Zanca

CHAD

(Middle Africa) Chadian American Food
See also: Cameroon, Central African Republic Niger, Nigeria, Sudan.

Background

Few Chadians have sought opportunities in the United States even though their nation of ten million people has been challenged by extreme poverty (unabated by revenues from oil exports), droughts and unpredictable weather (which has instilled food insecurity and spread malnutrition and stunted growth in children), corruption, political upheavals, a cultural division between Christians (who predominate in the south) and Muslims (in the north), and influxes of refugees from violent conflicts in neighboring countries including the Central African Republic and Sudan. The Census Bureau counted only 275 Chadian immigrants to the United States between 1991 and 2005, and Chad and the rest of Middle Africa have accounted for just 5 percent of overall African immigration to America. Small Chadian communities have developed in the New York

City and Washington, DC, metropolitan areas, which are the largest enclaves for all African immigrants in the United States. The Chadian Community of New Jersey, Inc., which formed in 2011, runs an office in Jersey City, maintains a Facebook page with 110 "likes," and hosts annual gatherings at hotels as well as welcoming events for new immigrants, where clusters of men sit close together on cushions on an apartment floor and pour cups of tea. Another group, the Mid Atlantic Chadian Communities of America (MACCA), founded in 2004 in the Washington, DC, area, aspires to share and celebrate the Chadian traditional cultural heritage (including cuisine) through performances, events, conferences, and festivals.

Foodways

Chadian food culture varies greatly by region. In the nomadic desert areas of northern Chad, the people enjoy a diet rich in meat, especially lamb and goat. The meat can be grilled, stewed, dried, or boiled along with vegetables such as okra. Many dishes are prepared with yogurt, *ghee* (clarified butter), and milk and spiced with cardamom. Milk is also consumed as a beverage and blended with mango and papaya. In southern Chad, which is dominated by subsistence farming, people consume very little dairy, and protein typically comes from peanuts as well as dried fish from the lakes and rivers of the landlocked nation.

Millet is the basic Chadian staple. It is cooked into balls, pastes, and pancakes and eaten with stews such as *daraba*, a dish of eggplants and sweet potatoes simmered in tomato sauce and thickened with okra and peanut paste.

For Chadians, breakfast often consists of *boule* (a grainy porridge made from millet, sorghum, or maize) or fried dough balls. Popular drinks include green, black, and hibiscus teas. The main meal takes place in the evening, and meals are communal experiences where people sit on the floor around a shared plate set on a mat. Traditionally, men and women eat separately. Special occasions such as weddings and births are celebrated with as many as fourteen different dishes served on the communal platter.

Daraba

While recipes vary for this classic, here is a simple approach: Chop 20 fresh okra and three tomatoes. Cut a sweet potato and an eggplant into cubes. Finely shred a cup of spinach. Put these vegetables in a large pot, cover with water, bring to a boil, and then simmer until tender. Then mix in three-quarters of a cup of peanut butter and a cube of beef or chicken stock and simmer to thicken. Season with salt and cayenne pepper and serve with millet balls.

Place in American Culture

Because of the very small population of Chadian immigrants and the lack of specifically Chadian restaurants, food markets, or cookbooks, few Americans have experienced Chadian food. But the cuisine's obscurity has made it a source of bragging rights for some of the most adventurous and exploratory of American gourmands. Charles Biblios blogs on his website, *United Nations of Food*, about his quest to eat food from every one of the world's nations without leaving New York City. He discovered Chadian food at the United Nations African Mothers Association annual fund-raising buffet, where the wives of ambassadors prepared traditional foods from their countries. The Chadian main dish was "a delicious but mildly confusing whole salmon, baked with lemon, potatoes, and green beans," wrote Biblios. "Who knew that salmon was the national dish of landlocked Chad?"

The food writer Sasha Martin, a graduate of the Culinary Institute of America, blogged about Chadian recipes in 2010 on her website *Global Table Adventure* as part of her successful quest to cook 195 meals from 195 countries in 195 weeks.

Americans' lack of knowledge of Chadian cuisine is also the result of the paucity of Western tourism to Chad, which the *Lonely Planet* guide calls "Africa for the hardcore." And the American economist Tyler Cowan from George Mason University, writing in his 2013 essay "The Cookbook Theory of Economics" in *Foreign Policy*, asked his American readers, "When was the last time you came home hungry after a long day of work and reached for that Chadian cookbook? Could you even name a dish from Chad? It's not that Chadian food is lousy. Anyone who has had its dish of gently stewed beef with ground peanuts atop rice would agree it's delicious." Cowan speculated that the vibrant cuisines of less developed countries such as Chad are "largely unknown" because of the lack of commercialization in their traditional cultures.

Noted Restaurants and Chefs

While the immigrant community remains too small to support specifically Chadian restaurants or markets, Chadian cuisine has been promoted in America by an entrepreneurial West African chef, Yollande Deacon, from rural Cameron, which borders Chad. Deacon settled in Milwaukee, Wisconsin, after receiving her MBA from Marquette University. She launched Afro Fusion Brands, which produces African spices and sauces for the American market. On her Facebook page, Afro Fusion Cuisine, Deacon has endorsed the work of Belgium-based Chadian female chef Timike, who publishes recipes on the web and Facebook in French as *La Cuisine Tchadienne Moderne*.

Chadian Americans can also watch *Bonne Cuisine Tchadienne*, a series of lengthy cooking videos in French by female African chefs on tchadonline.com.

Further Reading

Biblios, Charles. *United Nations of Food*. "#91-99 The African Motherlode: Angola, Benin, Chad, Equatorial Guinea, Madagascar, Mali, Somalia, Sudan, and Tanzania." Posted on December 7, 2011. http://www.unitednationsoffood.com/2011/12/african-food-nyc-at-united-nations-african-mothers-association-fundraiser/.

Cowan, Tyler. "The Cookbook Theory of Economics." *Foreign Policy*, June 24, 2013. http://www.foreignpolicy.com/articles/2013/06/24/the_cookbook_theory_of_economics.

Fredrich, Lori. "Afro Fusion Brings African Flair to Milwaukee." OnMilwaukee.com, posted August 2, 2012. http://onmilwaukee.com/dining/articles/afrofusion.html.

Martin, Sasha. "About the Food of Chad (Tchad)." September 21, 2010. *Global Table Adventure*, http://globaltableadventure.com/2010/09/21/about-the-food-of-chad-tchad/.

McCann, James C. *Stirring the Pot: A History of African Cuisine*. Athens: Ohio University Press, 2009.

Osseo-Asare, Fran. *Food Culture in Sub-Saharan Africa*. Westport, CT: Greenwood, 2005.

Zuchora-Walske, Christine. *Chad in Pictures*. Minneapolis: Lerner, 2009.

Alan Deutschman and Sarah Tekle

CHILE

(South America) Chilean American Food

Background

Because of its long coastline and strategic location, Chile historically developed important ports and extensive maritime trade with other countries. Even after the Spanish conquest, European immigrants, including Germans, Italians, English, and other nationalities, continued to immigrate to Chile. These immigrants shaped Chilean culture, social practices, and political organization. Thus, Chilean cuisine, and that of its immigrants to the United States, has been shaped by its geography and immigrant diversity.

The earliest wave of Chilean American immigration occurred in the mid-1800s, in response to the California gold rush. From the Chilean port city of Valaparaíso, Chilean miners sailed to San Francisco where they concentrated in the neighborhood of Chilecito (Little Chile), a ravine located near current-day Telegraph Hill. The experienced Chilean miners brought technical skills and vast mining knowledge, in turn applied to placer mining in the California Sierra. Following the gold rush, many of the Chileans returned to Chile. Those who remained mixed with American society and, over generations, lost their Chilean identity.

The second wave of Chilean immigration to the United States did not occur until the 1960s. With the overthrow of Salvador Allende in 1973, many Chilean professionals, intellectuals, and students fled into exile, primarily to Europe and other parts of Latin America, although some sought political refugee status in the United States. Following the restoration of democracy in 1990, the Chilean government encouraged Chilean émigrés to return, offering financial incentives and other benefits. Many Chilean Americans and those residing in Europe returned to Chile during this period.

In general, Chileans have immigrated to other countries, such as Europe, Argentina, and Brazil, rather than the United States. Of these Chilean expatriates, only 13.3 percent reside in the United States. Since 1990, Chilean immigrants to the United States come for economic reasons, settling predominantly in the urban zones of California, New York City, and Florida. In the 2010 US Census, the Chilean American population was still estimated at only 125,000 people. More recent Chilean Americans tend to have less education and professional skills than the earlier political exiles. However, Chilean immigrants incur greater costs and face challenges to immigrate from the southern cone, in comparison to other Latin Americans whose countries are situated closer to the United States. In general, Chilean Americans make up a small percentage of the Latino population in the United States and do not identify with Mesoamerican or Caribbean culture or traditions. Instead, they tend to assimilate and exhibit a high rate of intermarriage with US citizens.

Foodways

Chile's long coastline provides a wide range of seafood and different kinds of fish, all incorporated into the national cuisine. The waters off the coastline are home to fish familiar to US residents, such as codfish, albacore, tuna, and salmon, but also to other varieties found primarily in Chile, such as corvine, congrio, and lubina. Common seafood items include scallops, lobster, sea urchins, clams, and mussels, and the conger eel is a national delicacy. Chileans commonly prepare fish and seafood in a wide variety of soups and stews.

Common foods also reflect Chile's indigenous heritage, particularly dishes that include beans or corn. The most common type of bean consumed is cranberry beans, known as *porotos*. Corn remains an important ingredient in many Chilean dishes, but Chilean cuisine relies on fresh corn, not the dried processed *masa* that characterizes Mesoamerican food delicacies, such as enchiladas or tamales. Together, beans and corn comprise major ingredients in *porotos Granados*, a stew of beans, corn, squash, garlic, and onion. Common in Chile are *humitas*, tamales made of grated fresh corn that is then mixed with onions, basil, salt, and pepper into a paste. This paste, or fresh *masa*, is wrapped in cornhusks and cooked in boiling water. Embellishing the indigenous staples, tropical fruits, such as *cherimoya*, *lúcuma*, and avocado, are consumed fresh or in sweet desserts and ice creams. In northern Chile, the Andean cuisines more heavily influence Chilean foodways, as demonstrated in tubers, such as *oca*, or the consumption of llama or alpaca meat.

Europeans have introduced new foods through Chile's long history of immigration. With the conquest and subsequent occupation, the Spaniards brought rice, wheat, sugar, among other crops, along with domesticated animals such as chicken, sheep, cattle, and pigs. *Empanadas*, a common Chilean food, are the result of Spanish influence and are traditionally filled with historically Spanish ingredients, such as meat, cheese, olives, raisins, and/or hard-boiled eggs. Other national dishes, such as *pastel de choclo*, or corn pie, represent a blending of indigenous and Spanish ingredients in new ways.

Pastel de Choclo (Corn Pie)

    3½ pounds chicken, cut in serving pieces
    2 cups chicken stock
    ¼ cup seedless raisins
    3 tablespoons olive oil
    2 medium onions, chopped
    3 medium tomatoes, peeled and chopped
    salt
    1 or 2 pinches ground cinnamon
    2 hard-boiled eggs, chopped
    12 small pimiento-stuffed olives, rinsed and halved
    ½ cup butter
    4 cups corn kernels
    1 tablespoon sugar
    2 teaspoons salt, or to taste
    4 eggs
    sweet paprika

Put chicken and stock in large casserole. Bring to boil, cover, and simmer over low heat until chicken is tender, about 45 minutes.

Cool chicken in stock. When cool, remove skin and bones. Chop chicken into 1-inch pieces.

Put raisins to soak in cold water for 10 minutes.

Heat oil in pan. Sauté onions until soft. Add tomatoes and cook 5 minutes longer.

Season with salt and drain.

Add raisins, cinnamon, chopped eggs, olives, and chicken. Set aside.

Make topping. Melt butter in saucepan.

Blend corn kernels to puree. Pour into saucepan and mix in melted butter.

Stir in sugar and salt.

Cook over very low heat, beating in eggs one by one. Cook, stirring with spoon until mixture has thickened. Let mixture cool slightly.

Butter a 2-quart soufflé dish and spoon in ⅓ of corn mixture, patting up to cover the sides of dish. Spoon in the chicken mixture. Cover with the rest of the corn.

Sprinkle with sweet paprika.

Bake in preheated 350°F oven for 1 hour, until topping is set and lightly browned. Serve hot.

Subsequent waves of immigration integrated new foods into the Chilean cuisine. In the nineteenth century, German immigrants brought baking traditions, along with cakes and other pastries. As a result, Chileans are second only to the Germans in worldwide bread consumption, incorporating a wide variety of different kinds of bread, such as *pan de huevo* (egg bread), *marraqueta* (a Chilean French bread), and *coliza* (a layered bread that is rectangular or diamond shaped with a flat top). Arab immigrants carried certain spices and herbs that were integrated into Chilean seasonings, while British entrepreneurs in the late nineteenth century brought the tradition of teatime and tea. Italian immigrants brought pasta and preserved meats, and French cuisine has influenced Chilean foods during the twentieth century. As a result, Chile displays a rich and diverse gastronomy, constructed by blending native foodways with these immigrant influences. This diversity is brought to the United States, enabling Chilean Americans to easily maintain and present many of their culinary traditions.

In addition, Chileans enjoy wine from the vineyards introduced by the Spaniards during the colonial period. Drawing on European contacts and technology, the Chilean industry developed a wide range of sophisticated and reasonably priced vintages, enabling Chilean Americans to continue enjoying Chilean vintages after immigration. Chileans also enjoy *pisco*, a grape-based alcoholic drink that serves as the base for the renowned *pisco sour*, made of *pisco*, lemon juice, sugar, beaten egg whites, and ice, that has become popular in American culinary culture.

In more isolated Chilean regions, such as Easter Island, the cuisine integrates Chilean and Polynesian foodways. Rapa Nui cuisine is characterized by the use of coconut milk in seafood dishes, such as ceviche, and the use of bananas or cassava in breads and cakes. The influence of this cuisine has not been carried to the United States by Chilean immigrants, reflecting the low numbers of Rapa Nui immigrants to the United States.

In Chile, Chileans would commonly eat four meals a day: breakfast, late lunch, tea, and later dinner. Breakfast is usually light, consisting often of little more than toast and milk. For Chileans working in business or an urban environment, adjusting to the US workday has not been difficult. As throughout Latin America, lunch was traditionally the main daily meal. For late afternoon tea, Chileans consume sandwiches or pastries, along with tea, a practice reflecting the long history of British influence. Dinners are usually taken in late evening, around 9:00 to 10:00 p.m.

Holiday Feasts
Food and traditional Chilean dishes play an important role in preserving Chilean identity and heritage during holidays and feast days. Chileans celebrate Christmas on December 25, as is practiced in the United States, but Chileans also celebrate Christmas Eve with a large family dinner following midnight mass. Chileans traditionally consume a Christmas cake with fruits and nuts, reflecting the historic influence of German baking traditions in Chile. Throughout the holiday season, Chileans also drink *cola de mono*, a Chilean eggnog that is often flavored with coffee. Chilean Americans celebrate New Year's Eve with parties, often large family affairs. In Chile, since the holidays fall during the summer months in the southern cone, families often hold picnics or travel to the beach for New Year's Eve. On September 18, Chileans celebrate Independence Day from Spain, and during this week, fairs are held throughout Chile. In the United States, Chilean Americans continue to organize the fairs on that day, constructing booths, selling traditional crafts, listening to Chilean folk music, and consuming different Chilean dishes, particularly *empanadas*.

Further Reading
Allende, Isabel. *Aphrodite: a Memoir of the Senses*. New York: Harper Perennial, 1999.

Baez Kijac, María. *The South American Table: The Flavor and Soul of Authentic Home Cooking from Patagonia to Río de Janeiro, with 450 Recipes*. Cambridge: Harvard Common Press, 2003.

Carnegie Library of Pittsburgh. "Latin American Food & Cooking." http://www.carnegielibrary.org/subject/food/latin.html.

Hernández, Alejandro. *Origins of Chilean Wine*. Bilingual Edition. Wine Appreciation Guild, 2011.

Janer, Zilkia. *Latino Food Culture*. Westport, CT: Greenwood Press, 2008.

Joelson, Daniel. *Tasting Chile: A Celebration of Authentic Chilean Foods and Wines*. Hippocrene Cookbook Library. New York: Hippocrene Books, 2004.

Lovera, José Rafael. *Food Culture in South America*. Westport, CT: Greenwood Press, 2005.

Marín, Robert. *Secretos de la Cocina Chilena/Secrets of Chilean Cuisine* (Bilingual Edition). Santiago: Origo Ediciones, 2006.

Marín, Robert. *Chilean Wine and Food Pairing*. Santiago: Origo Ediciones, 2007.

Ortiz, Elizabeth Lambert. *The Book of Latin American Cooking*. New York: Alfred A. Knopf, 1979.

Presilla, Maricel. *Gran Cocina Latina: The Food of Latin America*. New York: W. W. Norton, 2012.

Umana-Murray, Mirtha. *Three Generations of Chilean Cuisine*. New York: Lowell House, 1996.

Van Waerebeek-González, Ruth. *The Chilean Kitchen*. New York: Penguin, 1999.

Lois Stanford

CHINA

(East Asia) Chinese American Food
See also: Hong Kong, Macao, Taiwan.

Chinese American food is a diverse and complex subject. There are different variations and types, ranging from Chinese food that has been Americanized to adaptations of American ingredients through Chinese cooking methods and flavor profiles. There is a growing interest in the United States in regional Chinese fare, which represents changes in migration from China as well as the increasing demand for a wider range of Chinese foodstuffs and flavors. In summation, Chinese food has become a significant part of wider American foodways, and its ubiquity and popularity will continue to impact the way Americans eat.

Background

Immigrants of Chinese heritage have introduced and adapted their foodways to the United States, leading to the creation of Chinese-American ethnic food. These immigrants come from the People's Republic of China, Hong Kong, Macau, Taiwan, Southeast Asia, and other parts of the global Chinese diaspora. There are now an estimated four million individuals who claim Chinese heritage in the United States, representing the largest Asian American ethnic group.

The first Chinese came in the United States in 1785 when three seamen were reported in Baltimore but did not settle in the country. The first presence of a Chinese community dates to the nineteenth century when the 1849 California gold rush brought them to the central valley of California. Primarily young men with limited education, these migrants came from an area known as modern-day Guangdong Province. They came in search of gold, but their fortunes quickly ran out, and they shifted to other forms of work, primarily domestic and manual labor. By 1851 an estimated twenty-five thousand Chinese were in California. The 1860s drew another spike in immigration as workers were recruited by the Central Pacific Railroad to build the western portion of the Transcontinental Railroad. Known as coolies, these individuals were contracted to provide physical labor with the aim of earning enough money to send remittances back to family members in China. They also intended to eventually return to China. Those who stayed established small communities, some of which were known later as Chinatowns.

The Chinese Exclusion Act of 1882 restricted Chinese immigration to the United States and prevented immigrants from becoming American citizens. Further acts such as the Geary Act of 1892 required all Chinese to carry a residence permit at all times and limited civil liberties, such as bearing witness in court and receiving bail in habeas corpus proceedings. Other acts instituted throughout the early twentieth century further limited the civil rights of Chinese and shrunk their population size in the United States. It was not until the 1965 Immigration and Naturalization Act eliminated immigration quotas based on nationality that there was a significant rise in the Chinese American population, and during the 1960s and 1970s it nearly doubled in size. This wave of immigration came from other regions and provinces of the People's Republic of China and from Taiwan, Hong Kong, and Southeast Asia.

Although California and New York were the prime destinations of Chinese immigration, other parts of the country also host large enclaves, including Hawaii, Seattle, Chicago, Boston, Houston, and Philadelphia. Furthermore, contemporary Chinese immigrants to the United States now come from different regions and provinces across China. While the Cantonese-influenced foodways of early migrants dominated until the 1960s, today there is a wide range of regional cooking styles represented alongside Chinese American adaptations of traditional fare.

Foodways

The foodways of Chinese Americans are diverse and are based on the region of China from which they claim their heritage. Also, if Chinese Americans arrived in the United States from a secondary point, such as Taiwan or Hong Kong, their foodways will also reflect those influences.

Trade networks between China and America emerged in the nineteenth century, mirroring Chinese migration patterns into the United States and bringing foodstuffs across the Pacific from Mainland China. Seafaring vessels transported items such as rice, soy sauce, seasonings, preserved vegetables, meats, and fruit. These products came primarily from southern China and reflected the tastes of the early migrants, who came from modern-day Guangdong Province and ate variations of Cantonese cuisine. Early Chinese migrants came to the United States with their own supplies of food, and they replenished their supplies when depleted with these items imported from China. Some also grew small plots of vegetables and fruits in their new locales to supplement their diets.

The food of the "Celestials," an outdated term for the Chinese, was written about with great fanfare in nineteenth-century American newspapers. However, this enthusiasm quickly faded, and xenophobia against the Chinese was rampant during the late 1880s. Newspapers ran disparaging stories and editorials on the living habits of the Chinese, suspecting them of adulterating food and eating "strange" meats such as rats, cats, and dogs. These negative characterizations of the cuisine still linger today.

The overwhelming majority of Chinese immigrants are of Han descent, the dominant ethnic group comprising approximately 95 percent of the Chinese population. Han Chinese regional cooking centers around the dominant flavoring profiles of soy sauce, garlic, ginger, and scallions. Non-Han Chinese, such ethnic Hui, Dai, Tibetan, Korean, or one of the other fifty-five ethnic minority groups, have different foodways informed by their ecological, cultural, and environmental preferences and needs.

Chinese cuisine itself is highly regionalized. Depending on the methodology and systems of classification used, there are four, six, eight, ten, twelve, or more major regional cuisines. Many identify eight major regional cuisines: Cantonese (*Yue Cai*), Sichuanese (*Chuan Cai*), Anhui (*Hui Cai*), Shandong (*Lu Cai*), Fujianese (*Min Cai*), Jiangsu or Huaiyang (*Su Cai*), Hunan (*Xiang Cai*), and Zhejiang (*Zhe Cai*). These eight major regional cuisines correspond with the major cardinal points in China.

Dishes are separated between staple foods (*fan*) and supplementary foods (*cai*). Literally, *fan* and *cai* translate to mean "rice" and "vegetable," respectively. But in wider understanding, they refer to staple items such as rice, millet, or wheat and accompanying dishes such as meat, vegetables, seafood, and tofu. Meals, whether informal family meals or lavish celebration banquets, aim to achieve some balance between *fan* and *cai*.

Foodstuffs

While rice is commonly associated with Chinese and other East Asian dining, it is not the only staple grain. White rice is commonly eaten in the southern regions, although migrants who trace their roots to northern China eat millet, maize, or wheat as their main starch. Wheat, in particular, is common to the cuisines of northeastern China. It is transformed into noodles, dumplings, or steamed breads. Southern China has large agricultural diversity that translates to a variety fish and seafood, fowl, fruits, and vegetables in the foodways. The primary everyday protein is pork, which can be transformed many ways. Soy sauce, garlic, ginger, and scallions form the basis of Chinese seasonings. Other seasonings are added based on regional preferences. Sichuanese cuisine is celebrated for its distinctive "numbing hot" (*mala*) combination of chili peppers and Sichuan peppercorns, Hunan cuisine for its fiery fermented chili peppers, and fermented black beans (*douchi*) are beloved in southern Chinese cooking. Pickled vegetables (*suan cai*) are another common addition to the table in northern China.

Chinese American cooking has been transformed for a variety of socioeconomic reasons, as well as the need to adapt to product availability and the ecologies of the area of settlement. The foodways of those who settled in the south reflect adaptations borne out of necessity. Large groups of Chinese migrants moved to the Mississippi River Delta during the Reconstruction era. Stir-fried collard greens are a prime example of how this group localized to their environment. Because common Chinese greens like bok choy (*Brassica rapa chinensis*) or Chinese broccoli (*Brassica oleracea alboglabra*) were unavailable, collards (*Brassica oleracea acephala*), another member of the brassica family, were substituted for their similarities in flavor. Stir-fried crayfish, which transforms a local ingredient through ethnic cooking methods, is another example of the unique foodways that have risen among this community.

Preparation

Classical home cooking prioritizes the use of stir-frying, steaming, and boiling as culinary techniques. These methods are fuel efficient and help retain nutrients. The majority of Chinese in America trace their culinary roots to Cantonese cuisine, where rice is the common staple grain, pork is the preferred meat protein, and many greens, particularly those of the brassica genus, are featured. This culinary style also makes heavy use of fermented sauces, and when available, roasted meats such as goose and duck and lots of seafood and shellfish. In China, it was common for families to shop twice daily at their neighborhood "wet market" (*cai shichang*), a type of fresh meat and produce market, for their provisions to get the freshest ingredients. Many now shop as most Americans do, once a week at the local supermarket and, if available, local Chinese grocer.

Chinese American meals can be made in small kitchens with relatively few pieces of equipment. The most important cooking vessel is the wok. This concave pan is used to stir-fry, steam, boil, braise, stew, poach, sear, deep fry, pan fry, and smoke. Long-handled spatulas and ladles are used to manipulate foods in the vessel. Most Chinese kitchens rely on one knife, a *dao*, that is similar to a cleaver, but is multifunctional, used to slice, chop, dice, and mince as well as for transferring ingredients. The handle can also be used as a pestle to grind ingredients. Most ingredients in Chinese cooking are cut into bite-sized pieces since knives are not found at the dining table. Therefore the *dao* is one of the most important tools not only for preparing food but also for aiding the consumption of food. Many families have additional pieces of equipment such as a bamboo steamer, sand pot, and Chinese herbal medicine pot, but the *dao* and wok are essential.

In many Chinese American households, women do much of the domestic work. This extends to include shopping for food, planning for meals, and cooking. A Tang dynasty poem by Wang Jian documents how a new daughter-in-law was responsible for taking up culinary duties three days after her marriage:

> Three days after the wedding she enters the kitchen
> Hands rinsed she makes the stews and soups
> Not sure what delights mother-in-law's palate
> Maiden sister-in-law she sends for to taste

Other literary examples help support the distinction in gender division in household cooking. Mencius (372–289 BCE), a contemporary of the Chinese philosopher Confucius, wrote, "Gentleman keep their distance from the kitchen." Originally used to discuss morality, this quote has been misinterpreted to explain why it is unfitting for men to participate in domestic provisioning. However, expectations in gender roles have become more flexible in subsequent centuries, and it is not uncommon today to see men cooking for their families. Men may also be more involved in specific types of cooking, such as wrapping dumplings, which is often a communal act shared by multiple family members, or in the making of soup. Many Chinese American men have also adopted the hobby of barbecuing, another case of a gender-specific form of cooking.

Everyday Meals and Holiday Feasts

Everyday family meals tend to be simple affairs, including a mixture of protein, starch, and vegetables and using basic preparation methods, such as steaming, braising, or boiling. A typical Cantonese-style family meal might start off with a slowly simmered soup made of chicken, carrots, and corn on the cob. Main dishes would be served family style: steamed pork patty topped with a preserved mustard stem called *zhacai*; a steamed whole fish topped with shredded scallions, julienned ginger, and a drizzle of light soy sauce; boiled bok choy topped with oyster sauce; and a dish of stir-fried pressed tofu strips with vegetables. These dishes would be accompanied by steamed white rice. Seasonal fruits such as apples, oranges, or watermelon finish off the meal. Depending on the regional and family preference, soup may also feature as an important part of the meal. For those who trace their origins to Guangdong Province, soup making is elevated to an art and is considered essential to family meals. Not only do they stretch out a meal, but many soups are also considered medicinal. Applying elements of traditional Chinese medicine and humoral theory, they are used to prevent or alleviate minor medical conditions or are consumed as a general restorative.

Food plays an important part of many Chinese and Chinese American holidays. While many second-, third-, or subsequent generation Chinese Americans no longer observe all of the traditional Chinese feast days, there are several important cultural holidays that are still celebrated widely. The most important and popular among them is Chinese New Year, also known as Lunar New Year, and it is frequently shared with other Asian American groups. This holiday falls somewhere between mid-January and early March on the Western Gregorian calendar. While each day of celebration involves different activities, the most important of all is the dinner held on New Year's Eve when families reunite, much as they would for a Thanksgiving or Christmas dinner. This meal often features a whole chicken served with its head and feet, suggesting the wholeness of a family; a whole fish, representing prosperity and abundance; dumplings to encourage wealth and prosperity; noodles, symbolic of longevity; and other festive dishes. Sweets such as *niangao*, a sticky rice cake whose name sounds like the phrase *year high*, symbolize a more prosperous year than the last. Fruits such as mandarins and pomelo are eaten for their sweetness and festive coloring, which resemble the color of gold and money. The Lantern Festival, held on the fifteenth day of the lunar year, marks the end of the holiday season. Families commemorate by admiring the full moon, lighting decorative lanterns, and eating sweet, glutinous rice dumplings (*tangyuan* or *yuanxiao*) to commemorate family unity, happiness, and good luck.

Other important holidays that include food rituals include the Qingming Festival, or the Tomb Sweeping Festival, in which families bring food offerings to departed ancestors, and the Dragon Boat Festival, held in summer, where individuals celebrate by having dragon boat races and eating *zongzi*, a dish of stuffed, glutinous rice filled and wrapped in bamboo or reed leaves. Sometimes *zongzi* are affectionately called "Chinese tamales." The Mid-Autumn Festival commemorates the harvest and the gathering of friends and family. This occasion is celebrated with tea and mooncakes (*yuebing*), sweet or savory pastries that are decorated and often served only at this holiday. The most recognized are Cantonese-style sweet mooncakes, which are decorated with inscriptions and filled with a preserved duck egg yolk and sweet lotus paste.

The Winter Solstice, or Dongzhi Festival, is another important occasion for family reunion. Northern Chinese celebrate by eating dumplings (*jiaozi*), while others observe by eating glutinous rice balls. One popular version served at this holiday involves cooking the balls in sweet syrup of unfiltered glutinous rice wine and osmanthus flowers.

Glutinous Rice Balls in Glutinous Rice Wine and Osmanthus Honey Syrup

Ingredients:
- 2 cups glutinous rice flour
- 2 tablespoons regular rice flour or tapioca starch
- ¾ cup water, room temperature
- 1 jar fermented glutinous rice wine (*jiu niang*)
- 1 jar osmanthus flower honey (*tang gui hua*)
- optional ingredients: red, yellow, and blue food coloring

Directions:
1. Mix the flours together in a large mixing bow. Add water slowly, stirring with a spoon to make a soft dough. Be careful not to add too much water. The dough should not be sticky and should have the consistency of modeling clay. Gently knead the dough a few times to help bind the flours.
2. Optional: If desired, divide dough into portions and add a few drops of food coloring for festive-colored rice balls. Red, yellow, or green are popular color combinations. Knead dough to blend in coloring.
3. Divide dough into portions (if not already done in the previous step). Take a marble-sized chunk of dough and roll into a ball. Repeat and continue until done. Place shaped balls on a tray or sheet pan dusted with rice flower, and cover with a dry tea towel dusted with rice flour or plastic wrap until ready for use.
4. To make the glutinous rice wine and osmanthus honey syrup: Fill a pot with 3 cups of water, half a jar of glutinous rice wine, and osmanthus honey to taste. Bring to a boil and lower heat to a simmer.
5. To cook the dumplings: Using a separate pot, fill with water and bring to boil on high heat. Add dumplings, and gently stir to prevent sticking. Remove dumplings using a slotted spoon or a Chinese spider when they float to the top. If not serving immediately, put dumplings into a bowl filled with warm water.
6. To serve: Transfer dumplings into individual soup bowls. Add ladle of syrup into each soup bowl and serve.

While Chinese holidays are important to maintaining cultural continuity, many Chinese American families have also adopted American celebrations, frequently fusing foodways traditions. Contemporary Chinese American dishes such as turkey *congee* reflect the adaptation to American holidays and the availability of local produce. It is cooked by many Chinese American households the day after Thanksgiving as a way to deal with the remains of a turkey. The carcass is boiled into a stock. Then it is turned into congee, a type of soft rice porridge that is commonly served as breakfast food throughout China and as a snack in southern China. Shredded leftover turkey is added alongside garnishes such as scallions and finely julienned ginger.

Turkey *Congee*

- turkey bones (approximately half of the carcass)
- 2 scallions, tied into a knot
- 1-inch slice of ginger
- 14 cups water
- 1 cup raw white rice (ideally long grain)
- 2 cups cooked shredded turkey meat
- optional garnishes: whole dry-roasted unsalted peanuts, chopped cilantro, sliced scallions, finely julienned ginger, soy sauce, sesame oil, salt

Directions:

1. Place turkey bones, ginger, and scallions in a large stockpot and add water to pot. Turn to high and bring to a boil.
2. Once boiling, lower heat to medium and skim foam from the stock. Let simmer for one hour, after which remove and discard bones, scallions, and ginger.
3. Put rice into stock and bring to boil. Add shredded turkey. Reduce to low and cook until desired consistency.
4. To serve, ladle *congee* into bowls. Garnish with preferred toppings and season to taste with soy sauce, sesame oil, and/or salt.

Place in American Culture

Chinese American food has a unique place in American culture. While it is widely available, it is still perceived as distinct and separate from mainstream cuisine and suffers from the stereotypes of being fast and inexpensive. Soy sauce packets, fortune cookies, and the Chinese takeout box are the most enduring symbols of Chinese American cuisine; they reflect low-end fare. A *New Yorker Magazine* cover from November 1991 depicted these items amid a backdrop of Chinese takeout menus, reflecting their ubiquity in New York City and American life. Some restaurants and many food writers have sought to challenge these stereotypes. The defunct Mandarin in San Francisco and contemporary Michelin-starred Hakkasan in New York, for example, served high-end Chinese food. However, the majority of American exposure to Chinese cuisine comes from its less expensive counterparts.

Large American supermarket chains often carry ingredients for Chinese cooking, so that items such as soy sauce, rice, tofu, and sweet and sour sauce are easily attainable, and brands such as La Choy, Kari-Out, and Soy Vey have adapted Chinese flavors to a mass American market through their condiments for domestic cooks. Outside of major metropolitan areas with large Chinese American enclaves, however, it is often difficult to obtain ingredients for "homestyle" food or regional fare.

There is a long history starting in the mid-1800s of small "mom-and-pop" Chinese restaurants throughout the country, and these have spread a particular type of Chinese cooking, perpetuating stereotypes of the food culture. These also tend to feature Americanized Cantonese-style cuisine, and it can be difficult to find restaurants that serve regional Chinese dishes, such as Hunan, Sichuan, Dongbei, and Shanghainese. Americanized Cantonese fare remains the most popular type of Chinese restaurant cuisine, as its distinct lack of "exotic" spices and chilies makes it palatable to a wider range of eaters, particularly those accustomed to "bland" Anglo-American food. While most are run by enterprising Chinese migrants, individuals from other Asian ethnicities also own or work in Chinese restaurants wherever their own cuisine is less familiar. They frequently include one or more dishes from their own or other Asian cuisines, so that "Chinese" restaurants are now oftentimes pan-Asian. Many also offer "all-you-can-eat" buffets, and these may include mainstream American dishes as well. National restaurant chains like P. F. Chang's and Panda Express have also expanded the presence of Chinese food, although they tend to tone down the spices, leave out ingredients not familiar to European Americans, and generally cater to more mainstream, middle-class tastes.

Chinese American cuisine has been disseminated through restaurants, though cookbooks and television programs have also played a strong role in popularization. Some of the earliest accounts of Chinese food written for American audiences were in *The Chinese-Japanese Cook Book* (1914) by Sara Bosse and Onoto Watanna, the pseudonym of Winnifred Eaton, a woman of Chinese-British ancestry.

Past Chinese cookbooks in America were written as form of education and gastro-diplomacy. Bu-Wei Yang Chao's book *How to Eat and Cook in Chinese* (1945) aimed to have Americans appreciate the diversity of Chinese food and the richness of its cultural history. Other writers such as Irene Kuo, Florence Lim, and Gloria Bley Miller compiled encyclopedic tomes on how to master the cuisine. Contemporary food writers such as Grace Young and Eileen Yin-Fei Lo have written with a decidedly Chinese American voice. These cookbooks are crafted to sell audiences the art of Chinese gastronomy translated to an American readership while sharing intimate, personal reflections on Chinese life in America.

Chinese American food was also mainstreamed through specific restaurant dishes. *Chop suey*, meaning "odds and ends," is a classic Chinese American dish made of a mixture of meat and vegetables. It became fashionable in the early twentieth century among bohemian urbanites in locales such as San Francisco and New York. Its popularity can be seen through Edward Hopper's 1920 painting, *Chop Suey*, in which two young women are depicted dining at a *chop suey* establishment. Army cookbooks dating to the early 1940s featured recipes for *chow mein* and *chop suey*.

Aside from *chop suey*, other popular Chinese American dishes include *egg foo young*, an egg omelette filled with vegetables and meat; *moo goo gai pan*, an Americanized adaptation of a Cantonese mushroom and chicken dish; General Tso's chicken, made of spicy-sweet deep-fried chicken; *ya ka mein*, a beef noodle soup popular in New Orleans; and the *chow mein* sandwich, made of two slices of white sandwich bread filled with fried Chinese noodles and smothered in a celery and onion gravy. This is found in southeastern Massachusetts and Rhode Island.

The 1940s and 1950s saw the rise of a hybrid "Polynesian" cuisine in the United States, which incorporated elements of Chinese and other East and Southeast Asian flavors. Restaurants like Trader Vic's and Don the Beachcomber also spread Chinese flavors to a mass market. *Pu pu platters* entered mainstream American foodways through Hawaiian entrepreneurs. These platters featured Americanized Cantonese-Chinese items such as egg rolls, barbecued spare ribs, fried wontons, crab rangoon, and other finger foods.

Perhaps the most enduring symbol of Chinese American food is the fortune cookie. They have become a common feature of Chinese American restaurants, often presented at the end of a meal. While they are strongly associated with Chinese American restaurants in the United States, they have no presence in China except as the odd "American" treat. These yellow, crispy cookies are folded into a half-crescent shape with a slip of paper containing a message. They began as fortunes or inspirational messages, but they have evolved to include lottery numbers, jokes, Bible passages, adult-themed messages, or even insults. The origins of this cookie are unclear, but they were popular in California by the 1940s, when they were used in political campaigns, notably in that of Senator Stuart Symington and Adlai Stevenson at the 1960 Democratic convention. Today approximately three billion fortune cookies are made each year, most of which are destined for American consumption.

Chinese food has touched the cultural zeitgeist in other ways. Countless television shows and films mention or depict characters dining at Chinese restaurants or on takeout. The musical number "Chop Suey" featured in Rodgers and Hammerstein's 1958 Broadway musical and 1961 film adaptation *Flower Drum Song* uses the name of this dish to discuss immigrant life in America. The character who performs this song, an elderly Chinese woman, states that "living here is very much like *chop suey*," referring to the mixture of old and new, American and Chinese values. Popular holiday film *A Christmas Story* (1983) depicts a Christmas gone wrong. Instead of celebrating the holiday at home with a turkey and all the trimmings, the family eats at a Chinese restaurant instead when their neighbor's dogs destroy their Christmas feast. The protagonist, a young boy named Ralphie, describes their comical meal of roast Peking duck served with a head on and calls it "Chinese turkey." Chinese food has also been used as a vehicle for storytelling in the lives of Chinese Americans. Director Wayne Wang's films *Dim Sum: A Little Bit of Heart* (1985), *Eat a Bowl of Tea* (1989), and *The Joy Luck Club* (1993) all feature food prominently in the lives of Chinese American migrants as they gather to eat, discuss life, and struggle to adapt to a new culture.

Other ethnic groups have also adopted Chinese food. For example, many Jewish Americans observe "Jewish Christmas" by eating Chinese food and going to the movie theater. Both Chinese and Jewish cultural groups tend not to observe the Christian holiday, and many Chinese restaurants remain open for business on the day.

Diversity of Chinese America

In the twenty-first century, the already loose constructs of "Chinese American" cuisine have become even more clouded. This has been due to several major trends. First, the influx of immigrants from different regions of China has increased the availability of regional Chinese flavors in the United States and has allowed for a wider of diversity of Chinese cuisines to be represented. There has also been a reshaping of Chinatowns and Chinese communities. Immigrants from Guangdong Province dominated Chinatown in Manhattan until the late twentieth century, when waves of newcomers from Fujian overtook their numbers. Flushing, located in the borough of Queens in New York, is a Taiwanese American enclave. It has been renowned for the variety of regional Chinese cuisines represented, including but not limited to Shanghainese, Sichuanese, Hunan, Xinjiang and foods from the Hui minority, Cantonese, Fujianese, and more. However, linguistic differences still reveal much about different Chinese migrants, as groups tend to cluster along linguistic lines or village or provincial origins.

Chinese American cuisines have also adopted food products and novelties from greater Asia. For example, a common Chinese American beverage is bubble tea, also known as *boba*. Originating in Taiwan, this drink later spread throughout greater Asia. In the 1980s it began appearing on the West Coast, primarily in Taiwanese American enclaves. Now it has spread, and it is served in independent beverage shops as well as a drink option in some Chinese restaurants.

Noted Restaurants and Chefs

Chinese American food has moved beyond the simplistic stereotypes of *chow mein* and *chop suey* and is also being reinterpreted and invented by young chefs. Some are of Chinese heritage and have modernized it to take into account elements of American culture. Ming Tsai, celebrity chef who owns Blue Ginger restaurant in Wellesley, Massachusetts, is noted for operating one of the first restaurants to have full allergy labeling and has striven to make his restaurant allergy friendly. Chinese-born American celebrity chef Martin Yan has hosted his award-winning show *Yan Can Cook* on the Public Broadcasting Station (PBS) since 1978.

Ken Hom, a Chinese American born in Tucson, Arizona, has gone on to have a global career teaching Chinese and Asian cooking.

Some of the earliest prominent Chinese American restaurateurs were women. Joyce Chen (1917–1994) was an early educator, restaurateur, and food writer born in Beijing. She popularized northern Chinese food in the Boston, Massachusetts, area and coined the term *Peking ravioli* as a moniker for her famed dumplings. Today her name is associated with Chinese kitchen equipment, bottled Chinese condiments, and a line of frozen dumplings. On the West Coast, restaurateur, chef, and food writer Cecilia Chiang is credited with bringing northern Chinese flavors to San Francisco, which was already familiar with Cantonese fare. Her restaurant, The Mandarin, was a landmark in San Francisco. Her contributions to wider American cuisine were recognized in 2013 when she was awarded the James Beard Foundation Lifetime Achievement Award.

Individuals of non-mainland Chinese heritage have also made their impact on Chinese American foodways. The late Barbara Tropp was a food writer and restaurateur whose work influenced many to try regional Chinese cuisines. Mission Chinese Food in San Francisco, run by Danny Bowien, has gained recognition for its Americanized adaptations of Chinese classics such as Kung Pao Pastrami. "Bad boy" celebrity chef Eddie Huang, whose family originates from Taiwan, has popularized street food in Manhattan. His aesthetic blends American hip-hop and elements of African American street culture with Chinese flavors.

Chinese American cuisine continues to evolve through continued immigration and the increasing recognition of Chinese restaurants and noted chefs. While traditional Americanized Cantonese fare is still popular, American diners are developing tastes for regional specialties such as Shanghai soup dumplings (*xiaolong bao*), spices such as Sichuan peppercorn, or novel creations such as Kung Pao Pastrami, further broadening the complexity of Chinese American cuisine.

Further Reading

Anderson, Eugene N. *The Food of China*. New Haven, CT: Yale University Press, 1988.

Chao, Buwei Yang. *How to Cook and Eat in Chinese*. New York: John Day, 1945.

Chen, Teresa M. *A Tradition of Soup: Flavors from China's Pearl River Delta*. Berkeley, CA: North Atlantic Books, 2009.

Coe, Andrew. *Chop Suey: A Cultural History of Chinese Food in the United States*. New York: Oxford University Press, 2009.

Jung, John. *Chopsticks in the Land of Cotton: Lives of Mississippi Delta Chinese Grocers*. California: Ying & Yang Press, 2008.

Lee, Jennifer 8. *The Fortune Cookie Chronicles: Adventures in the World of Chinese Food*. New York: Twelve, 2008.

Lin, Hsiang Ju, and Tsuifeng Lin. *Chinese Gastronomy*. New York: Hastings House, 1969.

Roberts, J. A. G. *China to Chinatown: Chinese Food in the West*. London: Reaktion, 2002.

Willa Zhen

COLOMBIA

(South America) Colombian American Food

Background

The 2010 US Census estimated the population of Colombian Americans to be close to one million. This number is likely higher due to undercounting, but it still represents the largest population in the United States from any South American country and accounts for around 1.9 percent of the US Hispanic population as of 2011. The earliest Colombian immigrants arrived around 1940, with additional waves after 1960 and 1990. The majority of the Colombian American population (49 percent) has settled in urban areas in southern states such as Florida and in the Northeast in places such as New York and New Jersey (34 percent), with the Midwest and Western states, particularly Texas and California, slightly increasing their share. These immigrants have brought with them their love for traditional music and dance, patriotic and religious festivals, food and drink characteristic of their regional ancestry (both coastal and inland states), high respect for family elders, and high value placed on their children's education.

Foodways

Colombian American cuisine is highly diverse and retraces either the coastal or inland origin of the people. Coastal food is based on a diet rich in fish, rice (like coconut rice), fried plantain (*patacones fritos*), and all kinds of beans, but especially garbanzos, *frijoles*, and *gandules*. Soups (*sopas de pollo*—chicken, or *carne*—meat) figure prominently, especially the more traditional *sancocho costeño*, which is a rich soup made with a mixture of more than one kind of meat or fish, as well as potatoes, corn, yucca, plantain, sweet potatoes (*batatas*), and squash (especially *ahuyamas*, a kind of pumpkin), and garnished with herbs and spices such as cilantro, oregano, thyme, cumin, and *achiote*, among others. Generally, these foods are eaten accompanied by a variety of sauces such as *salsa de aji* or *sofrito* (tomatoes, onions, green and red peppers, and garlic, cooked in olive oil or lard) and also *bollos* (a very savory wheat- or corn-based long, steamed roll, usually wrapped in cornhusk leaves).

All Colombian Americans (coastal or interior descendants) thrive on eating *empanadas* (very popular meat or cheese fried patties), as well as *arepas* (fried or baked precooked cornmeal patties) filled on occasion with eggs or cheese. A more highly valued staple are the *hallacas*, similar to Mexican tamales, but larger and richer in meats and vegetables and cooked in banana leaves, and *pasteles*, which are larger rice-based patties wrapped in *bijáo* leaves grown by the river banks (found in some specialty markets in the United States) or in banana leaves. Some other selected dishes favored by Colombian Americans are *ajiaco bogotano* (a rich, thick, potato-based soup with chicken and corn), *bandeja paisa* (a combination of rice, beans, meat, eggs, and plantain) hailing from the state of Antioquia, *parrillada* (grilled meats), and several seafood specialties such as *ceviche de pescado* (fish marinated and "cooked" in lemon and spices) and *arroz de atún* or *arroz de camarones* (tuna or shrimp rice). The central place of seafood in the food culture perhaps reflects Colombia's geography as the only country in South America with coastlines along both the Atlantic and Pacific oceans.

Popular fruit juices are abundant and easily found in canned versions (which never compare with the real, fresh treat); including mango, *guanábana*, *melón*, *lulo*, *maracuyá*, *patilla*, and *níspero*. The sweet tooth of the community is satisfied with a large variety of *postres* (pastries and cakes) such as *arroz dulce* (milky sweet rice), *flan*, *cocadas* (coconut-based sweets), and *mazamorras de plátano* or *maiz* (thick, slow-cooked concoctions of ripe plantain or corn and milk). The national alcoholic drink, *aguardiente* (fermented sugarcane spiced with anise), is easily available ordered on the Internet, as are *rones* (rums) imported from any one of the states of Colombia. These are usually very high in alcohol content. The world famous *café Colombiano* (coffee), as either a *café tinto* (black) or *café con leche* or *cortadito* (coffee and milk), cannot be surpassed as the best way to close a great meal. Another popular drink, especially for weekend brunches, is a savory hot chocolate and milk spiced with vanilla or cinnamon.

Traditionally, women have taken the responsibility for food preparation at home, but men are sharing more and more of the burden, especially in the more time-constrained culture of the United States. Private catering businesses frequently fulfill the cravings of the Colombian American population.

Sancocho de Pescado
(from Carmen S. Dence's Kitchen)
Serves 8 to 10 people.

Sofrito

- 3 tablespoons olive oil
- 1 large onion
- 6 large garlic cloves peeled and chopped
- 1 each large bell green, red, yellow peppers, remove seeds and chop coarsely
- 1 large bunch cilantro, clean and remove the harder stems
- 1 12-ounce can of diced tomatoes and green chilies

- 8 cups of water
- ½ cup coconut milk (optional)
- 2 to 3 tablespoons of condensed skim milk (optional)
- 2 large ears of corn peeled and cut into 1-inch pieces
- 1 firm, yellow plantain peeled and cut into 1-inch pieces
- 4 medium-size potatoes, peeled, sliced or chopped into 1-inch pieces
- 3 celery stems, cut diagonally into 1-inch pieces
- 3 medium-size carrots, peeled, sliced diagonally
- 1 medium-size yellow squash, seeds removed and cut into 1-inch pieces
- 1 large sweet potato, peeled, cut into 1-inch pieces
- 1 cup of frozen green peas
- 1 to 2 pounds of fish (grouper, red snapper, tilapia, salmon) cut into medium-size pieces and seasoned with salt, black pepper, turmeric, and cumin as desired. A dash of hot sauce is optional, as it is the addition of *camarones* (shrimp) or any other shellfish.

Preparation:

Add the olive oil to skillet at medium heat, add all the *sofrito* ingredients in the given order and cook gently while stirring, for 5 minutes. Have the water simmering in a separate stockpot. Add the *sofrito* to the water and stir. Start adding all the vegetables, season, and cook gently at low heat for 1 to 2 hours or until all the ingredients are tender. Add fish and the milk if desired and cook for additional 10 to 15 minutes, stir well, adjust seasoning, and serve accompanied by white rice.

Holiday Feasts and Other Celebrations

Colombian Americans are ready to party informally any time, as part of birthdays, first communions, and *quinceañeras* (sweet fifteen) fiestas. However, more formal gatherings happen during Christmas and New Year festivities. On any of these occasions, food is the great unifier, and *cenas típicas* ("traditional suppers") are organized in which families bring a dish from their particular region of origin to be shared.

The most celebrated occasion is National Independence Day on July 20. Besides food and drinks, music, dance, and parades may be all part of the day, depending on the level of formal organization of the particular community. The Colombian consulates and embassy usually lead the efforts in geographical areas with larger populations, but there are private parties as well. Another popular celebration is the reenactment of the famous Barranquilla carnival, similar to the Brazilian festival and Mardi Gras.

Place in American Culture

Colombian American cuisine has had a limited influence in American culture. Most of the time it is presented to the public as part of the Hispanic or Latin flavors in which other countries, such as Mexico, Cuba, Argentina, Brazil, and the Caribbean region, are likely to be leading the trends. More recently, dishes from other regions, such as Perú and some Central American countries, are being noted for their special culinary richness. Since many of the Colombian restaurants have Facebook pages and are starting to use other social media such as Twitter, Colombian food may become better known outside of the current areas of Colombian American concentrations.

Restaurants

Colombian restaurants are found in areas with the highest population of immigrants. Cities with larger Colombian populations such as Houston, New York, and Miami and areas such as northern New Jersey are likely to be places to find the flavors and taste of authentic or adapted Colombian dishes. Many of the restaurants are family run, and several include a bakery as well. Some of these specialize in Colombian cuisine, but others serve authentic dishes as part of a larger Hispanic menu. Some also offer hamburgers, pasta, and other standard "American" casual dining fare, although these might be given a Colombian twist or be accompanied by items such as fried green plantains.

Further Reading

Brightwell, Eric. "Colombian-Americans: Happy Hispanic Heritage Month!" September 29, 2010. http://www.amoeba.com/blog/2010/09/eric-s-blog/colombian-americans-happy-hispanic-heritage-month-.html.

"Is the American Dream Possible for Colombian Americans?" http://colombiansandtheamericandream.weebly.com/.

Osorio, Jennifer. "Colombians and Colombian Americans, 1940–Present." In *Immigrants in American History: Arrival, Adaptation, and Integration*. By Elliott Robert Barkan. Santa Barbara: ABC-CLIO, 2013.

Pew Research Hispanic Trends Project. "Hispanics of Colombian Origin in the United States." http://www.pewhispanic.org/2013/06/19/hispanics-of-colombian-origin-in-the-united-states-2011.

Sturner, Pamela. "Colombian Americans." In EveryCulture.com, Countries and Their Cultures. http://www.everyculture.com/multi/Bu-Dr/Colombian-Americans.html.

Wu, Sen-Yuan. "People from Many Nations Form New Jersey's Hispanic Population." 2011. New Jersey Department of Labor and Work Force Development. http://lwd.dol.state.nj.us/labor/lpa/pub/lmv/lmv_14.pdf.

Carmen Sofia Dence with Susan Eleuterio

COMOROS (UNION OF THE COMOROS)

(East Africa) Comorian American Food
See also: Madagascar, Mayotte, and Mozambique.

Background

An archipelago of islands between Mozambique and Madagascar, Comoros was on Bantu (from continental Africa), Persian, Arab, and Portuguese trade routes, and many of its residents were taken away as slaves as well. The Portuguese "discovered" it in 1505, and it was a French colony from 1841 to 1975. Comorians today are Arab-African and predominantly Sunni Muslim. French, Arabic, and Comoran are official languages.

The country today is very poor, with half of the population below poverty level; however, an Internet website refers to it as a culinary paradise, partly because of the variety of cultural influences that can be found there, particularly in urban centers. Vanilla is a major agricultural export.

Foodways

Rice and meat form the basic meal, with seafood being abundant and the primary source of protein. A variety of spices are typical, including cardamom, cinnamon, cloves, coriander, nutmeg, and vanilla. A local specialty is *langouste a la vanilla*, lobster boiled in vanilla sauce. Vegetables include corn, tomatoes, peppers, and chilies, probably all introduced originally by the Portuguese, and tropical fruits are abundant—bananas, pineapples, limes, and oranges. Indian influence is significant and can be seen in the popularity of various pickled vegetables and fruits, *chapattis* (flat bread), and lentil soups.

Comorians are more likely to immigrate to France and other French-speaking island nations than to the United States. There are no statistics available for Comoronian Americans. The nation has also had long ties and territorial conflicts with Mayotte.

Lucy M. Long

CONGO
(Middle Africa) Congolese American Food
See Democratic Republic of Congo

COOK ISLANDS
(Polynesia, Oceania)
See entry on Polynesia. See also: Melanesia, Micronesia, Hawaii.

CORNWALL
(Northern Europe) Cornish American Food
See also: Wales, England.

While there is not much that remains distinctive Cornish fare in contemporary US food culture, there are a few key dishes that still stand out as uniquely Cornish dishes, especially in specific geographic regions of the country.

Background
Cornwall, the southwestern-most county of the United Kingdom, is geographically unique in that it is a peninsula surrounded by water on three sides. Geographic isolation and provincialism fostered a strong sense of Cornish identity that was brought to the United States. The Cornish had, by the nineteenth century, established a reputation as excellent miners and were in great demand as mining became a profitable industry in the United States. The earliest record of Cornish miners in the United States is a 1771 expedition to what is now the Upper Peninsula of Michigan. Within seventy-five years there were Cornish miners working across the United States from Pennsylvania, through the upper Midwest, and throughout the far West. Economic hardship and food scarcity fueled a massive wave of immigration during the nineteenth and early twentieth centuries. Today, two million Americans claim some degree of Cornish heritage, but it is generally not considered a distinctive ethnic group.

Traditionally the food of the Cornish includes fish, dairy products, pies, pastries, and a combination of these elements. Specific dishes often attributed to Cornwall include clotted cream, pasties, and stargazy pie—a fish pie in which the fish heads are placed to sick out from the pie crust, mimicking a star-gazing posture. While fish continued to be a part of the transplanted fare of Cornish families in the United States, other elements of the traditional cuisine were harder to come by or harder to replicate exactly. For example, clotted cream was a regional specialty of Cornwall because of *terroir*—or the effect of the soil on the taste of the food. The soil of the Cornwall and nearby Devon produced a particularly rich grass ideal for producing the thick cream apt for making the dish. Therefore, while clotted cream was theoretically reproducible anywhere that cow's milk is available, the taste and quality of the product was arguably not the same. The Cornish foods that most persistently endured in the United States were pies and pastries.

By far the most famous and distinctive Cornish food still consumed today is the Cornish pasty. While there are pasty shops in Wisconsin, California, and even Florida, the pasty has a significant role as the regional food of the Upper Peninsula of Michigan. Every town in the UP (as it is called by locals) has at least one pasty shop, and the drive across the Mackinac Bridge and through the town of St. Ignace is notoriously littered with pasty shops all claiming to have the UP's very best pasties.

The pasty is a hand-held, stuffed pastry ideal for miners to take into the mines. The local lore of the UP is that the miners would leave home with a hot pasty in the morning and could, throughout the morning, use it to keep their hands warm; they would then reheat their pasty by placing it on a shovel and holding it up to a lantern. The thick, hand-crimped dough crust was disposed of when the miner was done with his lunch—both dirty hands and the threat of arsenic poisoning made this an important safety option.

The UP offers an interesting study in ethnic foodways because, relatively isolated from lower Michigan until the Mackinac Bridge was constructed in 1957, there has been a careful and limited blending of the Finish, Cornish, Italian, French, and Native American food practices. The pasty, while widely acknowledged to be Cornish in origin, has several iterations in the UP. The "traditional"/Cornish dish is made with beef, potato, and rutabaga, while the Finnish version is beef, potato, and carrot. Historically, many other variations on the traditional pasty have been a part of the UP food vernacular, including the Cornish-attributed star-gazing pasty (a fish-filled tribute to stargazy pie). In the contemporary pasty shop, there are many more variations on the traditional pasty, including breakfast pasties, dessert pasties, pizza pasties, *empanadas*, and even chicken pot pie pasties.

When ordering a pasty in a UP pasty shop, the question asked is "with or without?" The item in question is rutabaga. The next question is "catsup or gravy?"

Traditional Cornish Pasty

Crust:
   3 cups flour
   1½ sticks butter (cold and cut into bits)
   1½ teaspoons salt
   6 tablespoons water

In a large bowl, combine flour and salt. Use your hands to mix in the cold butter; mix until the consistency of a course meal. Add water one tablespoon at a time to form dough. Toss mixture until it forms a ball. Kneed dough lightly against a smooth surface. Form into a ball, dust with flour, wrap in wax paper, and chill for 30 minutes.

Mix together:
   2 cups rutabaga, diced (note: the rutabaga should be diced slightly larger than the potatoes)
   3 pounds potatoes, diced
   2 cups onion, diced
   2 pounds ground beef

Preparing the pasty:

Divide the dough into a dozen (4-ounce) balls. Allow to warm to room temperature, and then roll each ball into a 10-inch oval. Put about ¾ of a cup of filling in the middle of each piece of dough. Use the edges of your hands to seal the pasty. Then crimp the edge. Bake for one hour at 350°F.

Restaurants

There are English/Cornish teashops and bakeries around the country that sell scones, pastries, and even clotted cream. There are a few pasty shops scattered across the country. However, the majority of these shops are located in the Upper Peninsula of Michigan, where there are several shops in most towns. Notable pasty shops include Lehto's in St. Ignace and Colonel K's in Menominee, Michigan.

Further Reading

Harben, Philip. *Traditional Dishes of Britain*. London: The Bodley Head, 1953.

Lockwood, Yvonne R., and William G. Lockwood. "Pasties in Michigan's Upper Peninsula: Foodways, Interethnic Relations, and Regionalism." In *The Taste of American Place*, edited by Barbara G. Shortridge and James R. Shortridge, 21–35. Lanham, MD: Rowman & Littlefield, 1999.

Roberts, W. R. *Cornish Recipes*. St. Ives, Cornwall: James Pike, 1977.

Amy Reddinger

COSTA RICA

(Central America) Costa Rican Food
See also: Mexico, Caribbean.

Background

Costa Rica was initially settled around AD 500 by a number of cultures, including the Chorotegas, Chibchas, Corobicis, and the Cabecar and Guaymi, who developed the staple food crops of beans, corn, fruits, and cocoa. Beginning in the 1500s, Spanish colonizers developed what is known today as Costa Rican food, using the indigenous crops but introducing rice, new spices, and meats, particularly pork, and new cooking techniques. This traditional Costa Rican cuisine remains today largely unaltered by outside ethnicities and influences even though the country has become a tourism hotspot.

The cuisine has sometimes been called bland, basic, and repetitive since beans and rice are heavily incorporated into every meal, but the food varies regionally. The Caribbean region incorporates more coconut into their cooking, while the San Jose side of the country is known for their *tico-tacos*, or Costa Rican–style tacos. San Jose is also currently regarded as producing the most innovative, tasteful, and creative Costa Rican cuisine, frequently incorporating new ingredients, such as the *pejibaye* fruit, similar to a yam, which can be eaten plain or incorporated in dishes.

Costa Ricans have immigrated to the United States for various reasons, including job opportunities, attending an American university or school, or marrying an American. They typically end up in California, Texas, New York, or New Jersey. The largest population resides in Los Angeles, with around twenty-four thousand immigrants; next is the New York City, area with around thirteen thousand.

Foodways

Costa Ricans seem to easily adapt their traditional customs to the United States, as exhibited in the many restaurants throughout the United States where Costa Rican natives prepare and serve their traditional foods as chefs in Central American restaurants. Everything is prepared the same way as in Costa Rica, and thanks to international food markets, Costa Rican ingredients are easier to come by.

Costa Ricans use a wide variety of spices in their foods, such as fresh cilantro, onion, oregano, garlic, and thyme. These spices are important ingredients within almost all Costa Rican cuisine, especially meats and soups. Natural, fresh, and mild flavors are preferred, and, in contrast to other Central American cuisines, hot sauces are generally not used. Beans and rice are the main entrees or staple foods in most meals; meats such as chicken, beef, pork, and fish are highly used, along with vegetables such as potatoes, corn, lettuce, and plantains, and fruits including bananas, guava, passion fruit, pineapple, and mango usually follow a meal. Corn is one of the most used vegetables, usually prepared in the form of tortillas. These foods are eaten daily, in various ways. Some popular main dishes include *gallo pinto*, which is made with beans, rice, onions, and Worcestershire sauce; *casodo*, made with beans, rice, meat, lettuce, tomato, and plantains mixed together; and *frito*, a pork stew. Soups are one of the most served entrees, and beans, fish, and beef are the main ingredients used in these.

Gallo pinto is known as Costa Rican's national food but was not recognized as such until the twentieth century when the Costa Rican government passed laws to promote more beans and rice to be grown than corn. Now the dish is not only widely available and inexpensive but also the preferred meal. Festivals also played a significant role in *gallo pinto* becoming a national food. Free plates began being served at festivals like the annual festival of San Jose and *Internacional de Arte*. The government did not expect all residents to want this free dish—only the lower socioeconomic class—but it appealed across all classes. This cultural experience has continued ever since and has become embraced by the people themselves as an authentic representation of their culture and cuisine.

Desserts are notable, including *pan de maiz*, similar to American pound cake but made from corn, and *flan*, a sweet caramel pudding. As for drinks, the most famous and favorite is coffee. Coffee is one of the two main exports of Costa Rica, the other being bananas. Costa Rican coffee is very strong, drunk black or with milk, and served hot no matter the local temperature. Another drink is *chan*, made from *chan* seeds, considered excellent for digestive health and added to sodas, milk, and water. *Pipa fria*, or cold coconut water, is widely consumed, as is *horchata*, made with rice flour, cold milk, cinnamon, and sugar.

Generally, Costa Ricans do not eat large meals. Lunch is the main meal of the day, and many employers provide an extra hour off for people to rest and save energy for later in the day. In the United States this is uncommon, so Costa Rican Americans have adapted somewhat to the American system of shorter lunches. Traditionally, women have been responsible for cooking and other domestic work, and even with changing times and women joining the workforce, they still often maintain their duties in the home, both in the United States as well as in Costa Rica.

Costa Rican Americans celebrate and gather for many traditional festivities, particularly holidays associated with Catholicism. During Rosario del Niño, families set up a nativity scene in December for Christmas. Holiday meals always include tamales, which are large banana leaves stuffed with meat, cheese, rice, and many other ingredients if desired. Chicken, rice, vegetables, and raisins are also prepared as main entrées, along with a "Russian salad," which consists of diced potatoes, beets, and peas mixed with mayonnaise. During religious holidays, such as Holy Week, Costa Ricans typically eat a vegetarian diet.

Place in American Culture

Costa Rican food is little known in the United States and is oftentimes conflated with Mexican or other Central American cuisines, partly due to the shared language of Spanish, but also because of similarities between these food cultures. At the same time, contemporary Costa Rican food culture has adopted and adapted American processed foods and fast-food establishments. Doritos, the American snack food adapted from the Mexican corn tortilla, have particularly been incorporated in Costa Rican food culture, and many unique flavors are sold there that are not in the United States. Taco Bell in Costa Rico actually featured the Doritos Locos Nachos before the Taco Bell chain in the United States.

Noted Restaurants and Chefs

Since Costa Ricans share many similarities with other Latino and Hispanic cultures, there are many restaurants that serve food easily conflated with Costa Rican cuisine. Most restaurant owners throughout the United States classify their restaurants under the general category of Latino, Spanish, or Hispanic cuisine anyway because all countries within the Central American location use similar ingredients (some even have the same meals). Three states that boast restaurants serving specifically Costa Rican food are Florida, California, and New York.

Some well-reviewed Costa Rican restaurants in the United States include: Antojitos in New Jersey, Irazu Costa Rican Restaurant and Catering in Chicago, Illinois, Las Delicias in Syracuse, New York, and Costa Rica Restaurante in Anaheim, California. Many of these restaurants have a family-oriented setting, provide enormous amounts of food, and have traditional music and sometimes dance for entertainment. The food tends to be less costly than some other cuisines because of the simplicity and inexpensive ingredients used. Also, the characteristically large portions means that food is oftentimes shared by many people.

Simply Delicioso on the Cooking Channel is an example of contemporary Costa Rican American cuisine. Chef Ingrid Hoffmann creates favorite American entrees while incorporating fresh Latino and Hispanic ingredients that are typically used in Costa Rican cuisine, like cilantro, onions, beans, and rice. She blends traditional *flan* and enchilada recipes with American recipes such as cheesecake and by making meals more time efficient. Chef Hoffmann is a Central American native who now lives and films her show in Miami.

Doris Goldgewicht is another well-known chef from Costa Rico and is an author and host of the show *Sabores*, which is shown worldwide. In February 2014, Chef Goldgewicht cooked traditional Costa Rican cuisine for the *New York Times Travel Show* in New York. This show is also known as *The Taste of the World Stage*, where chefs from all over the world come together to teach viewers their traditional ethnic dishes.

Further Reading

Chase, Cida S. "Costa Rican Americans." Every-Culture.com, Countries and Their Cultures. Accessed June 9, 2014. http://www.everyculture.com/multi/Bu-Dr/Costa-Rican-Americans.html.

"Costa Rican Cuisine." The Road Forks. Accessed June 22, 2014. https://www.theroadforks.com/worldtrip/costa_rica/costa_rican_cuisine.

"Costa Rica: Food Dining and Drinks." Safari the Globe. Accessed June 9, 2014. http://www.safaritheglobe.com/food_costa_rica.aspx.

"Food and Drink." Viva Costa Rica! Accessed June 9, 2014. http://www.vivacostarica.com/costa-rica-information/costa-rica-food.html.

"Ingrid Hoffmann." Cooking Channel. Accessed June 9, 2014. http://www.cookingchanneltv.com/chefs/ingrid-hoffmann/bio.html.

Morris, Erin. *Costa Rican Food: Typical and Traditional Cuisine*. Last modified 2013. http://gobackpacking.com/travel-guides/costa-rica/costa-rican-food-typical-traditional-cuisine/.

Preston-Werner, Theresa. "Defending National Foodways: Laying Claim to Tradition in Costa Rica." In *Rice and Beans: A Unique Dish in a Hundred Places*, edited by Richard Wilk and Livia Barbosa, 181–203. New York: Berg, 2012.

Melissa McGovern

CÔTE D'IVOIRE

(Western Africa) Ivoirian American Food
See also: Senegal, Sierra Leone.

Background

The first Ivoirian Americans arrived in the United States as slaves; however, voluntary immigration occurred mostly in the 1980s and 1990s after the Côte d'Ivoire's independence from French colonial rule, when Ivoirians saw the United States as a country rife with economic opportunity. Côte d'Ivoire remains a francophone country despite its independence, and the French influence continues to permeate foodways in both Ivoirian and Ivoran American cuisine. During the First Civil War of Côte d'Ivoire in the early 2000s, the United States experienced an influx of Ivoirian immigrants as many Ivoirians sought to escape the war. Most settled in New York City and Washington, DC, but there are populations of Ivoirian Americans in Baltimore, Atlanta, Seattle, and Los Angeles as well. As of 2013 there were roughly three thousand Ivoirian Americans in the United States, most of whom call New York City home.

Foodways

Cassava (also known as manioc) is a shrub plant found in tropical and subtropical regions. Its root, which takes its form as an edible tuber, serves as the main carbohydrate for Ivoirians. In the United States, where cassava is less readily available, it can be replaced with rice or maize. Various Ivoirian dishes are paired with *attieke*, a side dish of cassava *couscous* with onion, tomato, and pepper sauce. At a few Ivoirian restaurants in New York City, such as Ivoire

Restaurant, white rice and *couscous* are added to the menu as additional side dish options.

Fish are a staple in Côte d'Ivoire, and the tradition of grilled or braised fish as a main course continues in Ivoirian restaurants in the United States. Most dishes are titled with their French and Ivoirian names, so grilled fish are listed as *poisson braise* and fried fish are *poisson grille*. Lamb and chicken are also grilled or fried and added to the menus of Ivoirian-American restaurants, although it is important to note that chicken is also a staple meat in Côte d'Ivoire. The type of fish that is used in these dishes varies from region to region, although Nile perch is preferred. The entire fish sans scales is served, often posing the challenge of a maze of tiny bones that need to be picked out or around. It is most commonly grilled or fried.

Plantains are a popular food in Côte d'Ivoire, and they continue to be prepared and served in the United States. *Aloco* is fried sweet plantains (plantains tend to be sweet or bitter, but bitter ones are easier to grow because they are not as attractive to bugs) with onion and tomato sauce. Plantains are usually fried. The cassava is often processed into a *couscous*.

As one of the few glimpses of Ivoirian American food is that produced by restaurants in New York City, the issue of who prepares the food is usually invisible. Some Ivoirian restaurants outside the United States have a "Mama," a woman who runs the restaurant, and that practice does seem to carry over to the United States.

Place in American Culture

Côte d'Ivoire and its food is little known in the United States, particularly outside of New York and Washington, DC. This is partly because of the small number of immigrants.

Noted Restaurants and Chefs

The restaurants dedicated solely to Ivoirian cuisine are mostly found in New York City. Brooklyn, Manhattan, East Harlem, and the Bronx are the easiest areas in which to find Ivoirian American food. The New Ivoire, an Ivoirian restaurant in East Harlem, is only one of a handful of Ivoirian American restaurants in New York City.

Further Reading

"Abidjan." Yelp. Accessed September 4, 2014. http://www.yelp.com/biz/abidjan-brooklyn.

Central Intelligence Agency. "Côte d'Ivoire." Accessed September 3, 2014. https://www.cia.gov/library/publications/the-world-factbook/geos/iv.html.

Cruz, Earlene. "The Taste of Côte d'Ivoire in New York." New York in French. Accessed September 4, 2014. http://www.newyorkinfrench.net/profiles/blogs/the-taste-of-c-te-d-ivoire-in-new-york#.VAe5CkgbpAY.

Harris, Jessica B. *The Africa Cookbook: Tastes of a Continent*. New York: Simon & Schuster, 1998.

"New Ivoire." Yelp. Accessed September 4, 2014. http://www.yelp.com/biz/new-ivoire-new-york.

"Poisson Braise, Recipe for Côte d'Ivoire's Famous Grilled Fish." Global Grazers. Accessed September 4, 2014. http://globalgrazers.wordpress.com/2012/11/26/poisson-braise-recipe-for-cote-divoires-famous-grilled-fish/.

Sarah Wyer

CREOLE

(North America) Creole American Food
See also: Cajun, French, Haiti.

Background

Creole American food is both the food of an ethnic group and the food of a particular place. The group is closely associated with the place, New Orleans, and the surrounding region. Defining Creole food requires a fairly flexible definition of the group itself. The term was originally used in colonial Louisiana and in the Caribbean to refer to people born in the colonies of parents of foreign origin. Both European- and African-descended people were thus Creoles. In New Orleans and south Louisiana, the Creole ethnic category was linked to the complex system of racial categorization distinct from the system used in the rest of the United States. While most of the United States followed a strict binary system of racial classification, in Louisiana, as in much of the rest of the Caribbean, there were gradations between black and white. As Americanization proceeded after the Louisiana Purchase, the two systems often generated tensions, pushing white Creoles to assert the supposed purity of their European heritage and attempting to distance themselves from black Creoles. The latter found themselves caught between the two racial ideologies as well, often seeking to distinguish themselves from the American population of African descent through language and through ties to France, Haiti, and other parts of the French empire, but often suffering from the same racial restrictions that limited the freedom of black Americans. The distinction between white and black Creoles in New Orleans developed in a complex way through the twentieth century rise and fall of Jim Crow, the civil rights movement, and the development of black political power in New Orleans. The arrival of many other ethnic groups in New Orleans over the last two centuries means that Creoles are far from the majority. Yet their presence still deeply marks the city's identity, through music (many of the city's leading musical families are Creoles), architecture (from the grand mansions of the Garden District, to the shotgun houses that define many of the city's historic neighborhoods, Creole architecture defines how the city looks), and food, as well as through elements of language and style. New Orleans remains a Creole city.

Foodways

Creole foods remain central to the cuisine of New Orleans. There is a clear link between home cooking in the region and the foods prepared and served in restaurants ranging from neighborhood sandwich shops to the most expensive fine dining establishments.

Creole food is defined by both ingredients and techniques. The former include extensive use of seafood from the area's lakes, rivers, and the Gulf of Mexico. Crabs, shrimp, oysters, and crawfish are seasonally available in grocery stores, farmer's markets, and directly from fishers and, unlike much of the rest of the United States, most of the shellfish consumed in New Orleans is locally sourced. A wide range of local fin fish also contribute substantially to Creole cuisine. Popular species include black drum, redfish, sheepshead, flounder, catfish, and pompano. In addition to seafood, New Orleans Creole cuisine features extensive use of pork, beef, chicken, and even rabbit, which is often seen on restaurant menus. Creole cuisine is also characterized by the use of what is known locally as the "holy trinity," a *mirepoix* made of bell peppers, celery, and onion. Garlic, scallions, peppers (sometimes in the form of pepper sauces such as Tabasco or Crystal, two popular local brands), *filé*, bay leaf, cayenne, thyme, various kinds of "creole seasoning" mixes (home cooks often rely on local mixes available in grocery stores, chefs often mix their own), and considerable amounts of salt are also central to the cuisine. Rice, which is a major crop in Louisiana, accompanies many meals. Okra, beans, *mirlitons* (the local term for chayote squash), citrus (a local crop), and tomatoes (especially a locally grown variety called "Creole tomatoes") all contribute to the traditional local diet. Because New Orleans has long been defined by its port, the local Creole cuisine historically includes imported foods, including coffee, bananas, and imported wines and liquor (cocktails play a central role in Creole dining).

Although racial conflict has historically divided white and black, food in some ways unites them. One common local story suggests that in wealthier white Creole households, black Creole servants (or slaves, prior to the Civil War) prepared the food. Whether or not this is sufficient to explain the link, it is clear that the kinds of food historically prepared in Creole homes across the city included many of the same dishes. Mondays, for instance, are reserved for red beans and rice, often served with sausages or pork chops. The dish is served in homes, is often the staff meal in restaurants, and is usually found in school cafeterias and other institutional settings as well. Home meals have historically been prepared by women in Creole homes, although it is common for men to cook as well. Thus, while restaurant chefs in other cities will often cite their mothers or grandmothers as the source of their original inspiration, male New Orleans chefs often cite their fathers, uncles, or grandfathers, who taught them techniques and recipes, often while at the family "fishing camp" (where extensive and storied meals are often prepared, again, by both men and women).

Traditional Creole dishes are often time-consuming to prepare, with extensive prep work and long cooking times. A local joke suggests that every recipe starts with "first, you make a *roux*," referring to the combination of fat (usually oil) and flour, cooked until an appropriate level of darkness, then joined by the holy trinity and garlic, followed by whatever other ingredients are necessary. Gumbos, of which there is an endless variety, start in this manner. Other traditional dishes, including shrimp creole, crawfish or shrimp étouffée, and most kinds of stew, start with a *roux*. Red beans and rice does not, although it does include the Creole *mirepoix* and can take three to four hours to prepare. Other well-known local dishes, prepared in homes or restaurants, include boiled seafood, stuffed *mirliton*, trout *amandine*, shrimp *remoulade*, and desserts such as bread pudding and bananas foster. Perhaps one of the more striking aspects of Creole cuisine is that it has been extensively documented since the end of the nineteenth century, in cookbooks, magazines, and other media, creating a kind of Creole canon of ingredients, techniques, and recipes. In addition, Creoles (along with everyone else in New Orleans) of all backgrounds and genders consider themselves experts in local cuisine, and many discussions focus on the best places to acquire ingredients and the best techniques for preparing dishes. The local culinary culture is kept alive not only because people eat the dishes but also because they keep up a lively discourse about them in both the media and in everyday talk.

There are many holiday dishes in the Creole culinary canon. Like other Americans, Thanksgiving and Christmas are often celebrated with turkey, but in New Orleans, the bird is usually "dressed" with seafood, including most often oysters or shrimp. One of the more celebrated local holiday foods is "king cake." In New Orleans, king cakes are generally available from Twelfth Night until Mardi Gras day. There are a variety of styles, but they usually consist of a brioche-type cake with some kind of very sweet and colorful frosting (often in the green, gold, and purple colors associated with Mardi Gras). The cakes often contain a plastic baby. When brought to the workplace, the tradition is that the person who gets the piece with the baby is responsible for bringing the next cake to the office. Holiday meals might also include *café brulot*, which is a flaming alcoholic coffee drink.

Creole Food in American Culture

New Orleans has been a major tourist destination for Americans since the end of the nineteenth century. The local food has been a central attraction for tourists since then. As early as the 1920s, the city advertised itself as a tourist destination where Americans could find unusual and distinct kinds of foods. This reputation was enhanced by books, beginning, perhaps, with the writings of Lafcadio Hearn, who published one of the first Creole cookbooks in 1885. Travel guides often touted the city's reputation as a place for fine dining starting in the early twentieth century, contrasting with the reputation of most other American cities at the time. In the 1940s, the novelist Frances Parkinson Keyes contributed to the city's reputation as a destination for sophisticated diners with popular novels like *Dinner at Antoine's* and *Crescent Carnival*. The literature, guidebooks, reviews, and studies of Creole cooking, in particular, and New Orleans food in general, are too numerous to cite here.

Creoles and Creole food has also been featured in many movies and television series. It has often been misrepresented, confusing, for instance, Cajun food with Creole cooking. However, in New Orleans, people often cite the accuracy of local foodways represented on the short-lived series *Frank's Place*, about a restaurant in New Orleans owned by a black Creole that may have been based on the famous Creole restaurant Chez Helène. More recently, the HBO series *Tremé*, named for an historic Creole neighborhood in New Orleans, devoted many of its episodes and plot details to Creole foods, chefs, and restaurants.

There are restaurants in many American cities (and sometimes outside of the United States as well) that purport to serve New Orleans Creole food. New Orleanians tend to be skeptical of Creole food sold in other cities, claiming that the ingredients cannot match those found in or near New Orleans. However, it is likely that many Americans have a distinct sense of how to define Creole food.

Noted Restaurants and Chefs

It is possible that the original American "celebrity chef" was Madame Bégué, who ran a restaurant in New Orleans in the latter half of the nineteenth century and who published a popular cookbook, *Madame Bégué's Recipes of Old New Orleans Creole Cookery*, in 1900. The city is famous for some of the oldest restaurants in America, including Antoine's (1840), Tujague's (1856), Galatoire's (1905), and Broussard's (1920), all of which continue to serve variants on the Creole canon. Commander's Palace (1880) is famous not only for its Creole food but also for launching the careers of some of the more well-known celebrity chefs in the United States, including Paul Prudhomme and Emeril Lagasse. The restaurant is owned by members of the Brennan family, who may not be ethnically Creole, but who own many of the most famous Creole restaurants in the city. It is worth noting that many famous local chefs are not themselves Creoles, but most local restaurants develop their menus in ways that explicitly draw on Creole traditions and local ingredients. Thus, current celebrity chefs such as John Besh or Donald Link have developed local empires (and national media coverage) with a combination of their own creativity and devotion to Creole cookery.

Further Reading

Beriss, David. "Red Beans and Rebuilding: An Iconic Dish, Memory and Culture in New Orleans." In *Rice and Beans: A Unique Dish in a Hundred Places*, edited by Richard Wilk and Livia Barbosa, 241–63. Oxford: Berg, 2012.

Bienvenu, Marcelle and Judy Walker. *Cooking up a Storm: Recipes Lost and Found from the Times-Picayune of New Orleans*. San Francisco: Chronicle Books, 2008.

Collin, Rima and Richard Collin. *The New Orleans Cookbook*. New York: Alfred A. Knopf, 1987.

Fitzmorris, Tom. *Hungry Town: A Culinary History of New Orleans, The City Where Food Is Almost Everything*. New York: Stewart, Tabori and Chang, 2010.

Hearn, Lafcadio. *Lafcadio Hearn's Creole Cook Book*. Gretna, LA: Pelican, 1967.

Roahen, Sara. *Gumbo Tales: Finding My Place at the New Orleans Table*. New York: W. W. Norton, 2008.

Tucker, Susan, ed. *New Orleans Cuisine: Fourteen Signature Dishes and Their Histories*. Jackson: University of Mississippi Press, 2009.

Williams, Elizabeth. *New Orleans: A Food Biography*. Lanham, MD: AltaMira Press, 2013.

David Beriss

CROATIA

(Southern Europe) Croatian American
See also: Bosnia, Hungary, Italy, Serbia, Slovenia.

Background

Croatia's complicated history and geography created distinct regional cultures within the nation. The foods of these regions draw from significantly different cuisines: Mediterranean foods in the coastal section and in inland regions, Central European and Turkish dishes. Croatian cuisine overlaps extensively with Serbian, Slovenian, Hungarian, northern Italian, and Bosnian foods.

During the past 150 years there have been discrete waves of Croatian immigration to the United States. The earliest mid-nineteenth-century arrivals were from seafaring communities on the Adriatic coast, and they settled mainly in coastal cities such as San Francisco and New Orleans. The largest wave of immigrants came from the 1890s until World War I. These were mostly poor peasants coming both from inland sections of Croatia and from the coast. They settled mainly in industrial and mining centers: Western Pennsylvania, the Great Lakes industrial cities, and in remote Western mining towns. Immigration restrictions enacted in 1924 put a virtual halt to new arrivals for two decades. Croatian refugees arrived in the wake of World War II, and again during and after the 1990s Balkan wars. In between those times, from the 1960s to the 1980s, only a trickle of new arrivals came from Yugoslavia. The more recent arrivals settled widely across the country.

Foodways

Typical staples in a Croatian American kitchen include: meats—beef, pork, lamb, chicken, all types of seafood; starches—potatoes, rice, noodles, polenta (corn meal), crusty white breads; vegetables—cabbage, onions, green peppers, carrots, lettuce, tomatoes; fruits—apples, pears, peaches, oranges, lemons, grapes; spices—salt, garlic, black pepper, paprika, basil, and oregano. The cast of the cuisine is very straightforward, garlicky but not very hot (peppery).

Salads are another food category that may be served in a Croatian American–nuanced manner scarcely noticeable to outsiders. Croatians favor a simple dressing of wine vinegar with olive oil and a dash of salt and sugar. The salads themselves contain fewer ingredients than American mixed salads—perhaps only one or two ingredients such as sliced tomatoes with but a few diced onions mixed in, lettuce only, or *blitva* (Swiss chard) with boiled potatoes seasoned with garlic and olive oil. This can be served hot as a side dish or cold as a salad.

Wine is an important beverage in Croatian foodways, but inland Croatians often like to top off a glass of white wine with a splash of mineral water. The drink is called *gemišt*, a German loan word for "mixed." Coastal Croatians turn red wine into a refreshing drink called *bevanda* by mixing it with ordinary water, up to a 50-50 wine-water blend, according to one's taste and thirst.

In the United States, Croatians from all Old Country regions frequently come together in fraternal lodges and churches and have become familiar with each other's characteristic foods. Coastal Croatians have adopted many dishes of inland Croatians such as *sarma* (stuffed cabbage rolls) and *burek* (phyllo dough meat or vegetable pies). Inland Croatians, however, have been less disposed to learn to prepare the coastal seafood dishes or to use polenta (boiled corn meal) as the typical carbohydrate dish.

Sarma—stuffed cabbage and sauerkraut, a characteristic inland Croatian dish of Central European origin. A recipe by Stephanie Vuljanić-Lemke.

2 large heads of cabbage, fresh or brine-pickled
1 can (48 ounces) of sauerkraut

Filling:
- 1½ cups chopped onion
- 1 tablespoon butter
- 1 pound ground pork
- 1 cup ham or smoked pork loin, chopped
- 1 pound ground beef
- 2 eggs, beaten
- 4 cloves garlic, minced
- 3 tablespoons chopped parsley
- 1 tablespoon salt
- ½ cup long-grained rice, uncooked

Sauce:
- 4 tablespoons butter
- ¼ cup flour
- ½ cup chopped onions
- 1 tablespoon paprika
- 1 can (6-ounce) tomato paste
- 3 cups broth (beef, chicken, or vegetable), or water

Preparing the cabbage leaves:

Fill a large pot ⅓ full of water and bring to a boil. As you're waiting for the water to boil, remove the cores of two large heads of cabbage. Place cabbage in the water for five minutes to blanch. Remove from water and let cool.

Filling:

Sauté chopped onion in butter until brown. Let cool. In a large bowl combine with meats, eggs, garlic, parsley, salt, and rice. Mix well with hands. Set aside.

Open and drain canned sauerkraut. Spread ⅓ of the sauerkraut evenly on the bottom of a large pot. Carefully remove blanched leaves from cabbage heads (about 20 leaves). Using about ⅓ of meat mixture, form a sausage and place on the core end of the cabbage leaf. Tuck in sides of leaves and roll up cigarlike toward the edge of leaf. Place roll on sauerkraut, seam side down. Once you have formed one layer of cabbage rolls, cover with more sauerkraut. Form another layer of cabbage rolls, and cover with sauerkraut. Continue layering until all cabbage rolls are in the pot. Finish with a layer of sauerkraut.

Sauce:

In a pot melt butter and add flour, stirring constantly over low heat until flour is golden brown. Add chopped onion, paprika, and tomato paste. Stir well. Slowly pour in broth or water, stirring until mixture is smooth. Pour sauce over cabbage rolls. Cover pot and simmer over low heat for three hours. Let stand for 15 minutes before serving. Top with sour cream and garnish with freshly chopped parsley.

Čevapčiči—spiced meat rolls, a dish of Turkish origin, in this variant including pork, a Balkan Christian influence. A recipe by Stephanie Vuljanić-Lemke.

- 1 pound ground pork
- 1 pound ground beef
- 1 slice bread, soaked in milk and drained
- 1 egg
- 1 cup finely chopped onions
- 3 large cloves of garlic
- 2 teaspoons salt
- 1 teaspoon pepper
- 1 tablespoon chopped red pickled peppers (hot banana peppers are good as well)
- 2 tablespoons chopped pickled jalapeño peppers (depending on how spicy you like it)
- 1 tablespoon finely chopped parsley
- 1 teaspoon baking soda
- vegetable oil for frying

Mix and knead together all ingredients for five minutes. Taking about 1 to 2 tablespoons of meat mixture, form little finger shapes about 2 inches long and ¾ inches in diameter. You may grill, broil, or fry the čevapčiči, until they are well browned and thoroughly done.

Brudet—a coastal Croatian seafood stew. A recipe by Robert March.

This is the northern Adriatic version of the ubiquitous Mediterranean fish soup (*bouilla-*

baisse, *cioppino*, etc.). The saffron is a French or Spanish borrowing, but I feel it adds a lot to the flavor.

> 1 pound cod fillet (or other flaky fish), cut in ½-inch slices
> ½ pound cleaned squid, cut as above
> ½ pound shell-on shrimp
> 1 28-ounce can whole peeled tomatoes
> 2 medium onions, coarsely cut
> 5 cloves garlic, sliced
> ¼ cup olive oil
> 4 cups seafood stock
> 2 cups dry white wine
> 3 bay leaves
> ½ cup chopped parsley
> oregano, thyme, or marjoram to taste
> (optional) saffron threads to taste
> 1 cup polenta, cooked as per instructions on package, or 3 cups cooked polenta

Shell the shrimp, reserving the shells. Add these to fish stock and boil gently in a covered saucepan for 40 minutes. Discard the shells and reserve the stock.

Sauté the onions and garlic in olive oil in a soup pot on medium heat for about 5 minutes. Add the tomatoes and their liquid, breaking the tomatoes as they heat. Add the reserved stock, wine, and bay leaves and boil for one hour. Add the fish and herb seasonings and boil for 20 minutes. Add the squid and shrimp and continue boiling for 10 minutes. Serve in bowls over polenta.

It is traditional for women to take major responsibility for purchasing or raising food in gardens and for preparing daily meals. Most of the ingredients for traditional Croatian dishes are available at American supermarkets. The few exceptions, which are becoming rarer as American groceries widen their array of products, may need to be purchased in ethnic groceries (for example, coarsely ground corn meal for polenta, squid, whole unshredded heads of pickled cabbage, dried sheets of phyllo dough, *kajmak* and similar forms of fresh cheese, and the red pepper relish *ajvar*).

Men typically take the lead role in preparing food for public festive occasions. During the summer, lodges or churches sponsor lamb roasts, ordering several whole lambs from a wholesale butcher. Men take responsibility for putting the lambs on spits, inserting garlic slices in the meat, rubbing the lambs with garlic and salt, and tending the lambs (and sometimes suckling pigs) while they roast over a charcoal fire. The men rise well before dawn to begin the hours-long process so that roasted lamb will be ready to eat by midday. Lamb roasting is a time for male bonding, with shots of plum brandy and glasses of wine. Men also frequently prepare *bakalar*, a seafood dish served on holiday eves (traditionally meatless fast days). It is made from reconstituted dried and salted cod, typically prepared in a mixture with potatoes.

Place in American Culture

There are no foods ordinarily identified as "Croatian" that have entered mainstream American foodways, although many coastal Croatian foods are well known by their Italian names: Croatian *rižot* and *njoki* are *risotto* and *gnocchi* in Italian. Typical inland Croatian dishes such as *pečenje* (roast pork) are not that different from familiar American cuisine, although distinctive Croatian touches would be to rub the meat with plenty of salt and garlic and to roast potatoes in the pan with the meat.

Noted Restaurants and Chefs

In the United States there are no widely known Croatian celebrity chefs and very few Croatian restaurants. Few Americans have any idea of what Croatian cuisine is. The most famous Croatian restaurant is the Tadich Grill in San Francisco, which traces its origins to 1849, during the gold rush when it opened as a coffee stand. Since 1887 it has been a full-service restaurant specializing in grilled seafood in the

Dalmatian manner. In New York City, especially the Astoria section of Queens, there are a few Croatian eateries, some of them little advertised as they are dining rooms for private clubs such as the Rudar Social Club and the Istria Sport Club, but they are open to the public. In Chicago, Croatian Americans seeking their native cuisine usually frequent restaurants operated by Bosnians, Serbians, or Albanians. There are many in the North Lincoln Avenue neighborhood—Restaurant Sarajevo, Bosanski Okusi, Balkan Restaurant and Simplon Orient Express, for example.

Further Reading

Evenden, Karen. *A Taste of Croatia: Savoring the Food, People, and Traditions of Croatia's Adriatic Coast.* Ojai, CA: New Oak Press, 2007.

Pavicic, Liliana, and Gordana Pirker-Mosher. *The Best of Croatian Cooking.* New York: Hippocrene Books, 2007.

Wilson, Jennifer. *Running Away to Home: Our Family's Journey to Croatia in Search of Who We Are, Where We Came From, and What Really Matters.* New York: St. Martin's Griffin, 2012.

Richard March

CUBA

(Americas—Caribbean) Cuban American Food

Cuba's proximity to Florida has impacted its history and culture, and the reverse is also true. The Tainos, a subgroup of the Arawaks, were the indigenous majority in Cuba when the Spanish arrived in 1512. They traded with others in the region and with the newcomers, laying the foundation for a distinct national but heavily Spanish-influenced cuisine: Cuban Creole cooking, or *cocina criolla*. During the Spanish colonial period (1513 to 1821), Cuba was Spain's governmental and religious holdings in the New World. Florida was under this rule until its annexation by the United States in 1821, and trade with Cuba was constant so that some US foods were integrated into the cuisine years before the 1959 revolution. Today, Cuban cooking is commercially available in the United States in restaurants of all categories—from kiosks to upscale dining establishments. Large US supermarket chains as well as large Hispanic supermarkets—Sedano's and Bravo Supermarket, for example—carry Cuban foods. They prevail in urban areas, particularly South Florida, Tampa Bay, Orlando, Union City, New Jersey, and New York City and Los Angeles. Also, countless smaller Cuban cafeterias and Latin American grocery stores carrying Cuban foods are in small US towns.

Background

Today, there are two million people in the United States who are Cuban or of Cuban descent, the fourth-largest population of Hispanic origin. Seventy percent of the Cuban population lives in Florida; however, the Northeast also holds large populations. Union City, New Jersey, is referred to "Havana on the Hudson," and the state is home to seventy-eight thousand. New York State has seventy-seven thousand. The Midwestern United States has fifty-eight thousand, while the South has 1,492,000, with Florida and Texas the largest enclaves. The West has 147,000, with California home to 86,000. Cuban culinary traditions are vibrant through much of Florida, particularly in Key West, home of what has become known as the Cuban sandwich.

Fifty-eight percent of Cuban Americans are foreign born. "Classic Cuban" exiles left soon after Fidel Castro's toppling of the Fulgencio Batista regime in 1959, and by 1990, some 517,000 Cubans arrived. Fifty-two percent of today's Cuban population in the United States arrived after 1990. Cuban traditions are oftentimes reinforced in the United States by new immigration. The years 1959–1961 are considered the first wave of Cuban immigrants. This included the more the fourteen thousand unaccompanied children who came with Operation Pedro Pan. A second wave is from 1962 to 1977, with almost three hundred thousand leaving between 1965 and 1973. About eight thousand Cuban Chinese left the island during this time. From May to September of 1980, the Mariel Boatlift brought 125,000 to South Florida. The 1990s saw the *balseros* or rafters. The apex was in 1993, with 3,600 Cubans crossing the Florida Straits on makeshift rafts and arriving alive.

Foodways

Cuban cuisine has retained its identity with distinct marinades, seasonings, and cooking methods. The *adobo* or marinade can be a dry rub for meat and fish, mixing mashed garlic cloves, salt, pepper, and often, smaller parts of cumin and oregano. When the dry rub includes lime and/or sour orange and olive oil, the marinade is referred to as *mojo*. Depending on the meat or fish, *adobo* can be applied the day before or up to two days before cooking, especially when used as a marinade. The *sofrito*, which means "sauté" in Spanish, is a seasoning created alone—olive oil, garlic cloves, green pepper, and yellow onion and sometimes tomato sauce. *Sofrito* is then added to soups, stews, beans, rice, meats, fish, and sauces. After more than fifty years in exile for some and regular new arrivals, some Cuban Americans in the food and restaurant industries are keeping to the past while others further the Creole fusion by including more US foodstuffs—as noted in some recipes by Three Guys from Miami. They are also developing Cuban "Nuevo Latino Cuisine" first seen at Yuca Restaurant when it opened in Coral Gables in 1989.

Cuban American eating habits run the gamut: some prefer traditional foods. Traditionalists are not just older, classic exiles, though they might be included. Since 52 percent of Cubans in the United States arrived after 1990, their eating habits are closer to what was eaten in the homeland. Cuban Americans, particularly those in large cities, choose from the cuisines of other Latin American nationals as well as those of other US ethnic groups. Vegetarian Cuban Americans and those reducing meat appreciate the cultural reliance on varied rice and bean dishes, corn meal, plantains, tropical fruits, along with choices in root vegetables—cassava, *taro* root, white sweet potatoes, and tropical yams.

Traditional Cuban cuisine is a fusion of the foods and ways of many people including the Tainos, the Spanish, West Africans, Chinese, and those from the United States. The Tainos, a subgroup of the Arawaks, are credited with developing barbecue, both the word and techniques. The Tainos used a meat-drying method involving a wooden frame over a fire, which was later adapted to grilling meat. They also shared root vegetables and cooking methods, including the tropical yam, *taro*, and cassava. The annatto seeds used for body paint were adapted to bring a deep yellow orange to the Spanish rice dishes that call for a more costly saffron.

West Africans began arriving in Cuba in 1522, serving as slaves until Spain abolished slavery in 1879, and they made various culinary contributions. For one, they prepared various types of fruit and vegetable fritters, which continue to be popular in Cuban American cuisine. Their "one-pot cooking method" features rice with additional ingredients. Two popular rice and bean one-pot dishes traveled to the United States with Cuban exiles. Both are known as *congi*. The word *congo* is Haitian Creole meaning "red beans"; *riz* means "rice." One-pot red beans and rice or *congri oriental* is one of the stars of Cuba's eastern provinces. That is where French and French Creoles and West Africans established coffee plantations during the nineteenth century.

During the late 1850s, Chinese contract workers came to Cuba as sugarcane workers. About 150,000 came. The Chinese and Cubans share the love of two staples: pork and rice. Fried rice and other Chinese dishes are eaten in Cuban homes on both sides of the Florida

Straits. Cuban Chinese restaurants are in Miami and New York City. The *caja china* or Chinese box grilling method, has been credited to the Chinese. The grilling method reduces the time for roasting a whole pig. In the 1980s, a modern version of this box was developed in Miami by Roberto Guerra and his father, and the Chinese Box is today popular with grill masters across the country. Cuban Americans often use it to avoid the work required by the traditional method of roasting a holiday pig.

The Spanish contribution to Cuban cuisine is the largest. Christopher Columbus brought sherry, a by-product of Spanish wine. Diego de Velazquez brought sugarcane when he landed in Baracoa, Cuba, in 1512. By 1783, the main supplier of sugar to the United States was Cuba. Paprika, saffron, chick peas, various beans, *chorizo*, salted dried codfish, cheeses, olives, rice, olive oil, a variety of nuts—walnuts and hazelnuts in particular—dates, and raisins were a few other imports. In early November, a variety of Spanish nougat candies arrive on US supermarket shelves. They will be cut and served during the holiday season, as dessert or to serve with an afternoon glass of dry Spanish sherry or Cuban espresso.

Sofrito, a basic seasoning, means "sauté" in Spanish. It is part of countless Cuban recipes. Pigs and cattle were also brought. Pigs arrived in the southeastern United States in 1539 with Hernando de Soto and his expedition. They stayed for four years. The pig's descendants, known as wild boar or feral pigs, are called *jabali* in Spanish. Many Florida outfitters provide opportunities for hunting wild boar today. Spanish cattle descendants are known as Florida Cracker, Florida Scrub, or Cracker cows—they are recognized as one of the rarest and oldest breeds in the United States today.

Many US foodstuffs were in Cuban recipes as seen in the 1950s Cuban cookbooks and in the cuisine today. Cuban exiles brought Nitza Villapol's *Cocina Criolla* (Creole Cooking) and *Cocina al Minuto* (Cooking to Order), both popular cookbooks in 1950s Cuba. In Miami, they were reprinted and also translated into English, printed, and then distributed—without Villapol's permission. She remained in Cuba. Villapol was and remains the Julia Child of Cuban cooking. Her recipes include ingredients such as Vienna sausages, deviled ham, hot dogs, mustard, Accent, canned sweet peas, ketchup, Worcestershire sauce, hamburgers, and pasta dishes, to name a few. Coca Cola was introduced in 1900.

Before the 1959 revolution, fish and shellfish were bountiful in the waters off the island's coasts. Stone crabs were abundant off the northern coasts from Matanzas to Camaguey provinces. Rice was grown for national consumption in the southern parts of many of the provinces, stopping when the terrain became more mountainous as one traveled east. The eastern provinces were where coffee was grown due to cooler temperatures. Cattle were big in the province of Camaguey and further east. At the time, Cuba boasted a head of cattle for each Cuban, six million at the time. The eastern provinces are also known for the high quality of tropical fruits. Sugar was king and grown throughout the island, although there were few mills east of Havana. Pineapple plantations and citrus groves were also important.

Ropa Vieja, or Old Clothes

2½ pounds flank steak, cut in half

2 bay leaves

¼ cup Spanish olive oil

1 large onion, cut in half and thinly sliced

1 large green bell pepper, cut in strips

2 to 3 garlic cloves, finely chopped

2 cups drained and chopped canned whole tomatoes or prepared tomato sauce

½ cup cooking sherry

Salt and freshly ground black pepper to taste

½ cup drained, canned early sweet peas for garnish, optional

½ cup chopped, drained pimentos for garnish

1. Place the beef and a bay leaf in large saucepan, cover with salted water. Bring to a boil and then lower the temperature to low heat, covered, until the meat is tender, 1 to 1½ hours. Remove the meat to a plate and let it cool. Cut it into 2-inch chunks. Save the stock if you'd like.
2. Heat the oil in a large skillet over low heat and add the vegetables until the onions are tender, 6 to 8 minutes. Add the tomatoes, sherry, and the other bay leaf. Cook uncovered another 15 minutes.
3. Shred the meat and season with salt and pepper. Add to the tomato mixture and simmer on low for 30 minutes. Remove the bay leaves, and garnish with pimentos and peas.
4. Serves 6 to 8.

You can make this a day or two in advance. Let it cool before putting it in the refrigerator. When you are ready to serve it, heat it slowly in a skillet, about 30 minutes.

Yucca with Lime *Mojo* (Serves 6)
3 pounds fresh or frozen yucca
3 tablespoons salt (I would use 1 tablespoon)

For the *mojo*:
½ cup lime juice
4 garlic cloves, chopped (or 6 to 8)
½ cup olive oil
1 teaspoon salt
½ teaspoon black pepper

1. Peel the yucca, cut it in half lengthwise, and then again into 3-inch chunks.
2. Put the yucca in a soup pot. Cover with cold water and add the salt. Boil. Reduce heat to medium and cook, covered, about 30 minutes or until the yucca is pierced easily with a knife.
3. Combine the lime juice, garlic, salt, and pepper in a bowl or mortar. Let it sit for ½ hour.
4. When the yucca is done, drain and put in a serving bowl. Heat the oil and carefully toss the lime and garlic mixture into it—beware of splatter! Let the garlic cook a little; some of it may turn a bluish green at the edges. Do not brown the garlic! Take it off the burner and pour over the yucca.

Easy Guava and Cheese Dessert
guava paste
cream cheese spread or bar
Cuban crackers

Assemble in this order: cracker, cheese, guava

Or, in an exile modification, wrap a piece of American cheese single around a slice of guava paste.

Traditional Cuban American families follow a meal pattern present in Cuba today, in which children are served first, without seated adults. This way, the adult can ensure that the children eat the meal as well as serve, teach, and wipe up spills. The table is cleared, reset, and the adults gather for their meal. This guarantees a more pleasant meal, enhanced by adult conversation and few interruptions. Men are served first by their wives. During holiday celebrations or parties, adults and children eat at the same time, though a children's table is designated, and adult monitoring continues.

Most of the household cooking is done by women, especially grandmothers, aunts, or cousins who may share the household. Or they may live nearby and send cooked dishes to a working relative's home. Traditionally, men contribute to the cause by cleaning the fish they caught, harvesting and cutting fruit, or turning a heavy, whole pig on the grill. There are men who enjoy cooking, and there are women who do not. The collective nature of the Cuban family, with three generations often present or nearby and cousins part of the extended family, does not lead to encouraging cooking for all women. Instead, they pursue studies or professional training—higher earnings will eventually benefit the family.

Fresh Cuban bread with butter and eggs and ham or bacon and maybe French fries is a traditional breakfast available at Cuban restaurants throughout the United States; however, many Cuban Americans are now opting for healthier cereal and fruit. The hot meal at lunchtime, which persists in Cuba today, has been modified. Depending on the school or workplace, Cuban Americans may carry lunchboxes with contents familiar to their US counterparts. However, if a microwave is nearby, many bring dinner leftovers to enjoy a hot lunch.

Dinner is typically at home, although the meal has been fragmented by US work and school schedules. Because of the long cooking time involved for traditional meals, the evening meal might be made by another family member who doesn't work outside the home. If there is no such person, the woman will usually, but not always, provide the labor. With two adults working and coming home to prepare traditional foods, even with shortcuts, dinner may be served at 7 or 8 p.m. The pressure cooker has a big place in the Cuban kitchen, both in the United States and on the island. Those who do not want to cook may opt for *cantina*. This is affordable catering service delivers hot, cooked Cuban meals to people's doorsteps on a daily basis. Another option is takeout from *comida por la libra*, or food by the pound establishments.

Holiday Feasts

Cuban Americans use food to celebrate lifecycle, religious, and national holidays.

While it was not a holiday in Cuba, Thanksgiving Day has become an important celebration for Cuban Americans. Christmas Eve and New Year's Eve remain the most important ones. For these major holidays, traditional Cuban dishes are served while the main meat dish may change.

For Thanksgiving Day, Cuban Americans have incorporated the turkey—even though many consider it too dry and use a *mojo* marinade to adjust it to their tastes. Ham might also be served. Following is a Thanksgiving Day turkey recipe by Carmen Ballesteros de Echevarria, a Spanish immigrant to Cuba in 1917 who later became an exile in 1960 to the United States. It was translated from Spanish.

Thanksgiving Day Turkey

A fresh turkey, one that has never been frozen, is vital. Its weight is determined by the number of guests; keep the packaging and cooking instructions.

On Tuesday, day 1, you will need the turkey, a large bottle of white vinegar, a piece of cheesecloth or thin kitchen towel, and a large, nonreactive platter or pan. Rinse the turkey and its cavity under cool water and pat dry with paper towels. Place the bird on a platter and douse it (inside and out) with vinegar. Make sure to saturate the cheesecloth, too. Cover the turkey with the cheesecloth, put plastic wrap around it, and refrigerate for 24 hours.

On Wednesday, day 2, extract juice from 3 to 4 Persian limes and mince 4 to 6 garlic cloves. Measure ½ to ¾ cups of olive oil and mix with the garlic, lime juice, and salt and pepper to taste. Then, take the turkey out of the refrigerator and rinse the vinegar off and pat dry with paper towels. Put the turkey back on the platter and pour the marinade over it and inside the cavity, too. Cover the turkey again with the vinegary cheesecloth and plastic. Refrigerate another 24 hours. Consult package directions for pounds and cooking time.

On Thursday, Thanksgiving Day, preheat the over to 450°F. Transfer the bird to a roasting pan and bake, uncovered, for 15 to 20 minutes. This will sear the skin and lock in the juices to avoid dryness. Cover the turkey loosely with aluminum foil. You may foil the ends of the drumsticks, too. Then lower the heat and follow package directions for weight and time.

Every 20 minutes or so, uncover the turkey and baste it with the juices at the pan's bottom. This also prevents drying. About 15 minutes before cooking time ends, insert a meat thermometer to check the internal temperature, which should be indicated on package instructions. When it is ready, remove it from the oven and allow it to rest for 15 minutes before carving. That is the time to make the accompanying gravy.

Gravy:

Melt about ½ stick of butter in a skillet, then sprinkle about a tablespoon of flour on it and stir with a fork. The flour will cook a little and make a paste. Add a generous amount of pan drippings to the paste, along with some sherry or white wine. If you like, add a can of B&B mushrooms. If the gravy is too salty or thick, add water until it has the consistency and flavor you prefer.

Cubans may or may not stuff their turkeys. Depending on their level of assimilation, Cuban Americans will serve side dishes associated with an Anglo-Saxon version of Thanksgiving—sweet potatoes or cranberry sauce, for example. Most also serve traditional Cuban dishes as well. Depending on which side of the island the family originates, there are red beans and rice or *congri oriental,* or black beans and rice called *moros y cristianos,* or a pot of white rice and a pot of black beans. Boiled cassava with *mojo* sauce are present. Fried plantains—green, very ripe, or medium ripe—are a staple. A green lettuce salad with sliced tomatoes and avocado and a vinaigrette dressing is also typical. Loaves of freshly baked Cuban bread are sliced. It is worth noting that some historians say the first Thanksgiving was a Spanish and Timucuan native event, held in St. Augustine, Florida, which was settled in 1565 by Pedro Menendez de Aviles, and annually celebrated today by historical re-enactors.

Christmas Eve, or *Nochebuena,* and New Year's Eve remain the biggest celebrations. While not all Cuban American households will roast a whole pig on these two eves, roast pork, even if it is only a leg, will be served. Some will have a cooked roast pig delivered. Others will do it themselves, as the process is as important as the meal. A hole must be dug, the pig placed inside, and covered by palm or banana leaves and roasted for hours, depending on its size. In Cuba and wherever traditionalists are roasting a pig, guava bush branches are used to flavor it. The men know the outdoor roasting hours are made pleasant by a winter tropical day, rum, beer, and domino playing. The women will be inside making the side dishes and enjoying conversation, music, and perhaps a little sherry or rum as well. Traditional dishes will also be served on Christmas Eve and New Year's Eve.

Place in American Culture

Because of their many years in the United States, Cubans have made some adaptations to their eating habits and meal preparations, but some Cuban foods have also been adopted by mainstream American food culture. Espresso coffee is a traditional staple whose use has remained stable. Breakfast may include a traditional *café con leche,* hot milk with sugared Cuban coffee. A *café con leche* is a morning beverage, though some use it as a late-night snack. The Cuban coffee served throughout the day in demitasses is black and sugary, or it is a *cortadito,* a black, sugared coffee with a little milk cut in. Those watching their sugar levels use artificial sweeteners. Many non-Cubans enjoy Cuban coffee; however, Cuban Americans are astounded when an American orders a *colada* for his or her own consumption. The *colada* is a Styrofoam cup full of Cuban coffee and is meant to be shared. It comes with a little stack of paper cups. Ground coffee comes in many forms: instant, one-pound vacuum packs or larger cans. Even a cold can of *café con leche* to be poured on ice or reheated can be bought off the shelves. Cuban coffee is in large commercial supermarkets as well as small grocery stores. Cafe Bustelo, Café Pilon, and Café Llave are a few brands.

Three Cuban rum drinks are popular among Americans: the cuba libre, the daiquiri, and the mojito. Originally, the cuba libre refers to the Cuban War of Independence from Spain. It also applies to Cuban exiles' desire for a democratic Cuba today. Coca-Cola was introduced in Cuba in 1900. To it, rum and a slice of lime were added. The late-nineteenth-century daiquiri—a mix of rum, lime, and sugar—was given its birthplace's name. The drink was later refined and eventually introduced to the Army Navy Club in Washington, DC, in 1909 by Admiral Lucius Johnson. The mojito's origin is also debated, though the Africans' word *mojo* means "to cast a spell." US author Ernest Hemingway helped popularize the mint, lime, sugar, rum, and club soda drink.

One of the most iconic Cuban American foods owes its existence to early immigration history. During Cuba's war for independence from Spain (1868–1898), about one-tenth of the population left, the majority to Key West, Tampa, and New York City. In Florida, by the mid-1890s, about ten thousand Cubans resided, composing 2.3 percent of the population. Key West was a center for immigration and, as early as 1831, Cubans worked there rolling cigars. By 1883, more than eighty cigar factories employed about three thousand workers there, transforming Key West into a major cigar center. By the mid-1880s, the Cuban population was almost eighteen thousand. Key West Conchs, as they now refer to themselves, have adapted American recipes to include Cuban seasonings, but they also modified traditional Cuban dishes. The Cuban sandwich is one example. In Key West it is a *mixta*, adding tomato, mayonnaise, and lettuce to the classic ingredients in the Miami version—Cuban bread, mustard, pickle, ham, roast pork, and Swiss cheese.

In 1886, a Key West fire took Vicente Martinez Ybor's cigar factory. He had bought forty-nine acres of swampland two miles northeast of Tampa to create a company town, Ybor City. Operations were moved, and many Italian immigrants were hired, too. There, a piece of salami was included in the Cuban sandwich. Recently, the Tampa Cuban sandwich has sparked great debate in Florida as Miamians claimed their version as the original.

Noted Cuban American Restaurants and Chefs

Across the United States, countless Cuban American restaurants serve traditional Cuban Creole cuisine or use it as a departure point for fusion dishes. These are usually family run and tend toward casual dining. One well-known establishment is the Columbia Restaurant in 1905 in Ybor City, in the Tampa area. Today it has six locations in Florida. Another popular community gathering place is La Carreta. It was founded in 1976 in Miami and has nine Florida locations. These, as well as the well-known Versailles Restaurant, have maintained a role as community centers, not only for the local and out-of-town ethnic community but also for politicians, reporters, tourists, and families. Also, late-night clubbers might stop there for a heavy meal or hot breakfast until 3:30 a.m. on their way home.

Cuban American chefs have made huge contributions to American culinary culture. Chef Bernie Matz, of Cuban-Jewish descent, was and remains a key force in the enlivening of the restaurant scene in South Beach, on Miami Beach. His culinary contributions and entrepreneurial spirit are evident. Chef Jorge Castillo is one of "Three Guys from Miami," and he promotes Cuban culture and cuisine. He is also a TV personality and cookbook author. Chef Douglas Rodriguez is a key figure in "Nuevo Latino Cuisine," having opened the upscale Yuca in 1989 in Coral Gables and Patria in New York City in 1994. He has received many prestigious awards and nominations. In New York City, Chef Victor del Corral opened the original Victor's Café in 1963. He served traditional foods that evolved with the times. In 1980, the restaurant moved and became Victor's Café 52. He died in Miami in 2006 at age eighty-four. Chef Alex Garcia worked to popularize Cuban cuisine and Nuevo Latino cuisine in New York City and on the Food Network. He is a cookbook author, an executive chef, and an entrepreneur. In California, Chef Rolando Gonzalez worked with actress Jennifer Lopez to open Madre's restaurant in Pasadena. He went on to open Casa Don Rolando in Los Angeles. Chef Lourdes Castro has made a name with three popular cookbooks, teaching at New York University and founding two cooking schools.

Further Reading

Allman, T. D. *Miami: City of the Future.* New York: Atlantic Monthly Press, 1987.

Anton, Alex, and Roger E. Hernandez. *Cubans in America: A Vibrant History of a People in Exile.* New York: Kensington Books, 2002.

Bucuvalas, Tina, Peggy A. Bulger, and Stetson Kennedy. *South Florida Folklife.* Jackson: University Press of Mississippi, 1994.

Machado, Eduardo, and Michael Domitrovich. *Tastes Like Cuba: An Exile's Hunger for Home.* New York: Gotham Books, 2007.

Mann, Charles C. *1491: New Revelations of the Americas before Columbus.* New York: Vintage Books, 2006.

Mitchell, Patricia B. *Plantation Row Slave Cabin Cooking: The Roots of Soul Food.* Chatham, VA: Mitchells, 1998.

Pew Hispanic Trends Project. www.pewhispanic.org/2013/06/19.

Santiago, Fabiola. "Nitza Villapol, 74, Cuban Cooking Advisor." *Miami Herald*, October 21, 1998. www.latinamericanstudies.org/cuba/nitza.htm.

Tebeau, Charlton W. *A History of Florida.* Coral Gables: University of Miami Press, 1971.

Villapol, Nitza. *Cocina Criolla.* No date. New York: Studium Corporation.

Marisella Veiga

CURAÇAO
(America—Caribbean)
See Caribbean, Dutch.

CYPRUS
(Western Asia) Cypriot American Food, Greek American Food
Included in entry on Greece.

CZECHOSLOVAKIA
(Eastern Europe) Czech American, Czechoslovakian American, Bohemian American Food
See also: Poland, Austria, Germany, Hungary.

Czechoslovakian (also referred to as Bohemian) food was brought to America by several waves of immigration. While individuals came to the United States as early as the 1600s, the largest groups relocated as the result of specific religious and political events. The first large group came during the first half of the eighteenth century, the second followed the 1848 revolution, a third after the outbreak of World War II, a fourth following the 1948 communist takeover, and another after the Soviet-led invasions in 1968. The Czech (Bohemian) diaspora reflects people's desire not only for economic opportunities in America but also to escape political and religious persecution. Today there are approximately 1.7 million individuals of Czechoslovakian origin living in the United States and nearly 275,000 in Canada.

Background

My father said that when my grandmother was angry with someone who was German, she identified as Polish, when mad at someone Polish she identified as German, but 100 percent of the time she was Bohemian. To be Bohemian means many things, but, unlike the Americanized idea of it being a fashion trend or an unconventional artistic lifestyle, to individuals in the Czech Republic it means belonging to a specific ethnic group.

The history of this region of Eastern Europe comprises a series of empires and dominations. Perhaps more than almost any other country, what is today considered the Czech Republic has also been known by many other names, depending on who rules it, who won the last battle, or who deposed a regime. Originally the Czech Republic consisted of two regions: Bohemia and Moravia. Prior to 1918, it was known as the Moravian, Holy Roman, and Austro-Hungarian empires, after which was the formation for the Republic of Czechoslovakia. The Nazis occupied the western part of the nation during World War II. The nation was fully communist by 1948. This was followed by revolutions in 1968 and 1989. In 1992, Slovakia became independent, and the Czech Republic was formed. Each stage in the volatile and violent past resulted in immigration to the United States (and other countries). Today, Bohemian Americans are a population as diverse as their origins, and their foodways reflect the multitude of influences.

Foodways

The geographic and ideological complexity of Bohemia contributes to foodways that are equally entangled. Because of the plethora of political takeovers and slippery geographic boundaries, the food and culture represent the infusion of dominating nations as well as those endemic to the region. Both the language and food are richly seasoned with Polish, Austrian, German, and Hungarian flavors as well as Czech. Signature imported Bohemian dishes are inspired by the integration of the European sensibility about using everything, wasting nothing, and the American emphasis on quantity. Schnitzels, sausages, strudels, and goulashes are all borrowed from neighboring countries; yet Bohemian cooks add a distinctive twist. For example, Czech dumplings include farina and sometimes stale bread, whereas those of other nations might be made purely from potatoes. Meals typically begin with soup, focus on a main course, and end with a sweet dessert.

It is widely written, and affirmed in a recent visit home, that the mainstay of the Bohemian diet is pork and dumplings (*knedliky*). Traditionally meats are roasted, often breaded and fried, sausage (*klobásy*) is boiled or grilled, and potatoes mostly mashed or fried. Sauces, some made of a rather curious combination of meat and whipped cream, commonly accompany entrees. *Cmunda* is a favorite dish consisting of a hot potato pancake topped with sweet, boiled red cabbage and spicy, smoked pork. Garlic is widely used, as is dill. Particular food favorites include *kishka* (a sausage), as well as boiled cabbage, wild mushrooms, *ková polévka* (garlic soup), *bramborák* (potato pancakes), roast duck, and wild game. Bohemians use all parts of the animal. For example, from cows, meals are made from tongues, hearts, feet, brains, and kidneys.

Grandma (Stepanek) Merskin's Dumplings

Ingredients:
    4 medium-large potatoes (Idaho)
    2 cups flour
    ½ cup farina (Cream of Wheat)
    2 eggs
    salt

Directions:
    Boil potatoes with peel on. Drain when done. Flour a board and take skins off potatoes. Put the potatoes through a ricer on top of flour. Salt according to taste. Sprinkle farina over potatoes, put eggs on top of the mix. Knead together and roll into a long roll. Cut off into pieces and let sit for a half hour or so. Then put pieces in to boiling water for 20 minutes.

Very important in Czech identity is beer. The first brewery is traced as far back as 993 in Brevnov Monastery. The most traditional is a pale lager, pilsner type. This wheat-based beer, *světlé pivo*, is light. Since the thirteenth century, the city of Budweis has produced beer, which eventually led to a trademark dispute when the American company Anheuser-Busch began marketing Budweiser. In Europe one finds the beer marketed as *Budějovický Budvar* and in the United States as *Czechvar*.

Sweets are popular ways to conclude meals and to celebrate holidays: *roski* (almond horns); *palacinka*, crepe-like pancakes filled with fruit, jam, and chocolate and topped with whipped cream; *ovocné knedliky*, buttered, powdered-sugar-coated dumplings filled with fruit such as cherries, apricots, or strawberries, are examples. A sweet that is finding its way outside of the ethnic kitchen and in to mainstream American bakeries is the *kolache*. For Bohemian Americans, purchasing store-bought, brand-name jams, such as Smuckers, for the centers of *kolaches* was a true sign of success.

My grandmother's *kolache* recipe
Ingredients:
- ½ pound butter
- 2 egg yolks (don't beat, will drop in whole)
- 1 whole egg
- ½ pint sweet cream or ½ pint canned milk
- ¼ teaspoons salt
- 3 tablespoons sugar
- 1 ounce fresh yeast or 2 dry packages
- 1 teaspoon vanilla
- 3¼ cups flour
- filling for center of cookie (typically jam or preserves)

Directions:
Cream butter, add sugar, and cream again. Add eggs and sweet cream or milk and mix. Crumble/drop in the yeast and add the vanilla. Sift flour and salt and add to butter and egg mixture and mix until dough is well combined. Let freeze (or refrigerate) in a flour-dusted bowl overnight. The next day, take out half of the dough at a time. Roll out ¼-inch thick on a floured board. Cut in to rounds (using a small glass). Put on ungreased cookie sheet. Make a dent in the center of each circle and put in the filling. Let rise for 10 minutes. Put in a moderate oven; bake until golden brown. Sift powdered sugar over the top when cool.

Holiday Feasts

Bohemians run the gamut from devoted Catholic to avowed atheists, reflecting traditions of both conformity and resistance. Regardless, Christmas is one of the most important holidays. The night before is a meatless evening of semifasting for the following day's excesses. Typically fish, traditionally fried carp or fish soup, is served with salad. Christmas day (*vánoce*) is a time for pulling out all the stops. While no single dish defines the day for everyone, a typical meal would include roasted duck, dumplings (cooked with the duck), mashed potatoes, and gravy. Bohemian Christmas cake, *vánocka*, is a sweet bread dough flavored with nutmeg, lemon, raisins, and almonds, often braided. *Kolaches* and almond horns are favorites on this day, too.

New Year's Eve (*Silvestr*) is another important holiday in Bohemia. While in European Bohemian homes, boiled pig's head might be the main course, served with horseradish, the Bohemian Americans are likely to serve ham, potato pancakes, or small sandwiches.

Restaurants

Because of its heavy nature, based in meat, white potatoes, salt, and fats, the Bohemian diet has not been incorporated into mainstream American restaurants. Nevertheless, particularly in ethnic enclaves, Czech restaurants have survived despite the dietary health consciousness of the times. The largest Czech restaurant in the United States is Klas, established in 1922, just outside Chicago in the suburb of Cicero. Vesecky's Bakery, in nearby Berwyn, Illinois, is one of the oldest traditional bakeries. The Washington, DC–based Embassy of the Czech Republic maintains a state-by-state listing on the Web of Czech restaurants, as do many Czech societies. The presence of Czech restaurants in a wide number of states reflects immigration patterns, so that states with the greatest number include Illinois, Texas, Georgia, California, and New York.

Further Reading

Brizova, Joza. *The Czechoslovak Cookbook: Czechoslovakia's Best-Selling Cookbook Adapted for American Kitchens.* New York: Crown, 1965.

First Ladies Catholic American Society. *Slovak American Cookbook.* 26th edition. Beachwood, OH: First Catholic Slovak Ladies Association, 2010.

Sayer, Derek. *The Coasts of Bohemia: A Czech History.* Princeton, NJ: Princeton University Press, 2000.

Debra Merskin

D

DEMOCRATIC REPUBLIC OF CONGO
(Middle Africa) Congolese American Food
See also: Congo, Central African Republic.

Background
The Democratic Republic of the Congo (formerly the Republic of Zaire) was claimed by King Leopold II of Belgium in 1885, who declared it the "Congo Free State." In 1908, the Belgian government took over the territory from King Leopold and annexed it as a Belgian colony, which had control over the land until 1960, when a nationalist movement won the parliamentary elections. The Belgian influence continues to be present in the country's cuisine, although its traditional foodways are distinctly Central African. The DRC is the second largest country in Africa, and the official language is French, although four national languages are commonly used and recognized: Swahili, Lingala, Kikongo, and Tshiluba.

Due to over fifteen years of armed conflict and complex political unrest in their home country, the Congolese refugee population—composed of both government-recognized refugees as well as asylum seekers—has spiked in recent years. A September 2013 report from the United Nations noted that in the 2012 to 2013 fiscal year, 27 percent of the total number of refugees resettled in the United States originated from the Democratic Republic of Congo. The American Community Survey of 2010 estimated that a total number of eleven thousand people of Congolese descent resided in the United States, and Fronteras reported that an additional three thousand settled in this country in 2010. Immigrants and Americans with heritage from both the Democratic Republic of Congo and the Republic of Congo call themselves Congolese.

Many Congolese refugees make their home in upper New England—Maine, Massachusetts, New Hampshire, and Vermont—where many African refugees are placed through the United States Office of Refugee Resettlement. In 2012, the *Portland Phoenix* reported that 150 to 200 Congolese families resided in the Portland, Maine, area. In that region, infrastructure has been developed to support the Congolese community, including the Congolese Development Center in Lynn, Massachusetts, and the Congolese Women's Association of New England. By 2012 a Congolese immigrant had even established a farm there specializing in African produce, such as eggplants, amaranth, and pumpkins, supplying ethnic markets and an African restaurant. There are also significant populations in Charlotte and Raleigh, North Carolina, Iowa, and North Texas. Congolese Americans tend to speak English, French, and a number of Bantu languages and are over 95 percent Christian.

Foodways
Cassava, corn, rice, beans, and palm oil are essential ingredients in Congolese cuisine. Along with rice, *fufu* (also called *ugali*), a starchy food made from cassava flour, often accompanying stews, is extremely common. *Moambé*, a chicken entrée, is the national dish, and it consists of cassava leaves, hot pepper sauce, bananas, rice, peanuts, fish, chicken, and palm nuts. Other popular dishes include *pondu*—made from processed cassava leaves slow-cooked with green onions,

157

palm oil, and smoked fish and served with rice or *fufu*; and *madeso*—a bean dish of red sauce and fresh nutmeg. In general, fish is more frequently consumed than poultry, and beef, goat, and lamb meat are also common. *Mandazi*—a fried bread, similar to a doughnut—is popular for breakfast. *Gaufres*, a small waffle cookie, an example of the Belgian influence on Congolese cuisine, is a popular dessert.

Many of the traditional ingredients basic to the Congolese diet are not available in the United States, and immigrants have had to either find substitutions or emphasize those ingredients that are available. Rice, corn, and beans, therefore, are highlighted, and *fufu* might be made out of corn meal or even cream of wheat. In urban centers and in areas with a high concentration of African immigrants, many Congolese Americans source specialty ingredients at African markets, and they purchase more readily acquired ingredients, such as meat and veggies, from mainstream grocery stores.

Madeso Beans (Adapted from ImmigrantKitchens.com)

1 pound dried red beans
small red onion, sliced thinly
½ cup green pepper, sliced thinly
½ cup olive oil
1 tablespoon tomato paste
1 nutmeg nut
3 bay leaves
1 teaspoon salt

In a large bowl, cover dried beans with water and soak for 8 hours or overnight. Place beans in a large stockpot, cover with water, and simmer until soft, about 40 minutes. Strain and cool, then return to the large stockpot.

In a skillet, fry onions in ¼ cup olive oil on medium-high heat. When onions are translucent, add green pepper. After another minute, add tomato paste, stir until the oil becomes red in color. Add enough water to make a sauce out of the thick paste, and cook for about five minutes.

Grate about ⅓ of the nutmeg nut (about 1 teaspoon) into the sauce. Add 1 teaspoon of salt. At this point, you may need to add additional water so the sauce is neither watery nor too thick. Cook for about 15 minutes more on low heat, then pour sauce over the cooked beans. Add bay leaves, and cook beans with sauce, covered, for approximately 15 minutes on medium-low heat, stirring occasionally.

Serve with rice and hot sauce.

Place in American Culture

There are a number of Congolese and pan-African restaurants scattered around the United States, though often restaurants owned and operated by Congolese Americans bill their food as "African" rather than specifically Congolese, likely to better appeal to American customers. Because of the concentration of the US Congolese population in New England and other pockets around the country, Congolese communities have been for the most part able to retain their food traditions. While there is not much assimilation of Congolese cuisine, it has also not had a substantial impact on mainstream American foodways, to date.

Note

1. Mary Pols, "Farmer Grows Familiar Foods for Maine's African Refugees," *Portland Press Herald*, August 31, 2014, http://www.pressherald.com/2014/08/31/farmer-grows-familiar-foods-for-maines-african-refugees/.

Further Reading

Congolese Americans: Finding a Home in New England. http://congoleseamericans.wordpress.com/.

Congolese Development Center. http://www.cd-c.org/.

Elikia Restaurant in Coralville. http://elikia.weebly.com/.

McCann, James C. *Stirring the Pot: A History of African Cuisine*. Athens: Ohio University Press, 2009.

Osseo-Asare, Fran. *Food Culture in Sub-Saharan Africa*. Westport, CT: Greenwood, 2005.

Emily Hilliard

DENMARK

(Northern Europe) Danish American Food

Background

Americans of Danish descent are a small population. The 2010 census enumerates approximately 1,500,000 Americans with Danish ancestry. The majority of Danish Americans emigrated during the second half of the nineteenth century up to World War I. The size of this population, however, is a remarkable number because Denmark, itself, is a small nation whose current population numbers 5.6 million. Relatively large numbers of Danes came to America, and Denmark continues to maintain strong ties to America. Danes emigrated for numerous reasons, including dislocation following military conflicts, lack of economic opportunity, and a combined sense of adventurousness and entrepreneurism.

The Midwestern states of Minnesota, Wisconsin, Iowa, and Nebraska are often regarded as the heartland of Danish settlement, but Utah, Washington State, and New York have sizable populations, and California boasts the highest number of Americans of Danish ancestry and one of the most well-known Danish American towns, Solvang. Although Danish American communities are popularly associated with Lutheran settlements in the rural Midwest, the majority of Danes first settled in the Northeast in an urban area, and Danish immigrant history includes a strong presence of religious diversity including strong connections to the Mormon, Catholic, and Methodist churches. Overall, the Danish immigrant experience is one of rapid assimilation. The Danish language was often lost in families within one generation, and there are few distinctively Danish communities in the United States. Despite the rapid assimilation and relatively low profile of Danes in America, there is a subtle, yet oftentimes vibrant, presence of Danish traditions in America.

Foodways

Danish American foodways reflect this ethnic history. Some foodways traditions are surprisingly prominent, as most American have eaten a Danish pastry or butter cookie during the holidays. The foodways traditions that are more reflective of the immigration experience, however, are much more obscure to most Americans. Americans of Danish descent maintain food traditions from Denmark. The importance of pork, dairy products, baked goods, and various soups may continue to influence the culinary tastes of Danish Americans. The ethnic group may preserve ethnic food traditions in their families, such as open-faced sandwiches, yet they have also established their own culinary traditions that are distinctly Danish American (Hoobler and Hoobler, 1997). A closer look at this tradition reveals a richer and more vital heritage than what even many Danish Americans may imagine (Paulsen, 1967).

The pastry known generally as a *Danish* is the most mainstream expression of this tension between exoteric ideas about Danish cuisine. It is also an excellent example of the depth of the subtle tension between what people may envision as Danish food in America versus the reality of what actually has been preserved and adapted from Denmark. An actual Danish pastry typically is a lighter and flakier variant of the doughy version found in coffee shops, fast-food restaurants, convenience stores, and supermarkets. Danes in the United States and in Denmark do prepare and consume the pastry, but in Denmark it's known as *Wienerbrød*, or "Viennese bread." The Danes associate the pastry with Vienna, but its incorporation into Danish foodways is characteristic of the cosmo-

Ethnic American Food Today 159

politan aspects of Danish cuisine. This eclectic quality is also an important feature of Danish American foodways.

Those interested in moving beyond the franchise version of Danish pastries will undoubtedly encounter the handful of Danish bakeries in America. Although Danes have immigrated to the Americas for centuries, Danish immigration peaked during the decades before and after the turn into the twentieth century (Larsen and Bender, 1982). Most Danish immigrants quickly assimilated into the population within a generation or two. Consequently, Danish American communities are difficult to find in the United States. Although Solvang, California, is the West Coast's most visible Danish ethnic community, there are also Danish settlements in Oregon and Washington that host Danish bakeries.

Settlements in the Midwestern states of Iowa, Nebraska, Minnesota, South Dakota, and Wisconsin also support Danish food traditions, and the most famous Danish bakeries are in Racine, Wisconsin. Rather than the small, square-shaped pastry, Danish American pastry chefs are known for a round or oval-shaped doughy confection called a *kringle*. These pastries vary in size. Some can fit easily on a dinner plate, whereas others are about the size of a small pizza and shaped like a pretzel or a large loop of pastry dough that is covered with icing. *Kringler* (plural) include fruit filling, and flavors such as almond, cherry, or raspberry. A *kringle* often is ordered directly from a bakery, but Racine has been known for its active mail-order *kringler* for decades. Shipments are especially popular at Christmas time, and a Danish *kringle* is often prominently featured along with other Christmas cookies and baked goods at Danish tables during *jultid*.

These treats may include the store-bought Danish Christmas cookies commonly displayed in grocery stores. They may also include homemade cookies made from recipes brought from Denmark. The small, round cookies called *pebernødder* often feature ginger or cardamom as prominent spices. These popular cookies are most often served at Christmas time, and they are related to the *Pfeffernüsse*, or "pepper nuts," that are more widely known in other northern European traditions. Danish Americans may also take great pride in preparing another Christmas cookie called *klejner*. A *klejner* is a deep-fried baked good made from a diamond-shaped layout of pressed dough about the size of a playing card. It typically is cut out with a unique pastry knife that often is passed down as a family heirloom. A small slot is cut into the center, and the tip of the pastry is looped through the cut to form a unique half-knot that gives the *klejner* a distinctive shape when fried. There are other Danish Christmas cookies, and many Danish tables will display pan-Scandinavian influences as bakers are likely to make Swedish spritz cookies and serve other pastries and goodies during the holiday season—especially during morning or afternoon coffee breaks.

Holiday Feasts

Along with the prevalence of baked goods, other Danish foods are important elements of a Danish Christmas dinner. Most Danish Americans will eat American fare during the season, but numerous families use the holidays to celebrate their ethnic heritage through the preparation, consumption, and sharing of Danish recipes, many of them brought over by their immigrant forebearers (Kaplan, Hoover, and Moore, 1986). If appetizers are served prior to the meal, cheese and sausage will top crackers, but pickled herring may also be prominently featured. The meal, itself, may be initiated with servings of fruit soup. A Danish fruit soup may be eaten hot or cold throughout the year. Historically, a steaming fruit soup was a Christmas treat as it was made from dried fruits that were seen as special treats for the holidays. The centerpiece of a Danish American Christmas will likely be either roast pork or goose. Both meats may be served on the same table, and they will include a dressing made of prunes, apples, and raisins. It is likely that cinnamon and cloves will be included in the spices that enhance this fruit dressing that is stuffed into the goose before it is roasted. The entre will be served with generous helpings of vegetables, and Danish tables are apt to feature lavishly buttered beets and cooked red cabbage that have been part of family's recipes from Denmark, along with the sweet potatoes and other foodstuffs common to mainstream American dinner tables. The dinner will likely include cake, pie, and often a treat made of applesauce called *æblekage* for dessert. When planning a Danish Christmas dinner, however, cooks will include a special rice pudding called *ris à l'amande*. This porridge is flavored with sliced almonds and vanilla extract. Its presentation often includes a Christmas game that involves hiding an almond in one portion. The host cook will surreptitiously place a whole almond into a dessert cup filled with the pudding. When a family member or guest finds the almond in this pudding cup, he or she is honored with a prize. Usually it is a small gift, and suspicions are raised as it almost always is the youngest participant in the dinner party who wins the game. The tradition of playing games with rice pudding at *jultiden* also is evident on Christmas Eve. Rather than centering on a Santa Claus figure who would be left milk and cookies, the Danes honor the Christmas elves or *julenisser* with a gift of rice porridge. Its disappearance in the morning is often ascribed to the elves, but Danish oral tradition will usually attribute its consumption to a housecat.

It is clear that traditional Danish recipes are most likely to be used during the Christmas season. Along with the baked goods, Danes have also preserved a variety of foodways traditions that are still practiced around American dinner tables throughout the year. Alcoholic beverages, including a Danish cherry liquer called Peter Heering, may be served at special occasions throughout the year, but they are especially likely to be shared during the Christmas season. The skoal toast follows highly formalized patterns that make it a special ritual for Akvavit drinkers, but a strain of pietistic theology in Danish Lutheranism may continue to dampen the interests in consuming alcoholic beverages in some Danish American families and communities. Throughout the year, however, coffee is a staple beverage for many Danish Americans, and coffee breaks are still prominent elements of small town life. It is not uncommon, for example, to see restaurants and cafes crowded in midafternoon in many midwestern towns. The coffee break is not necessarily unique to Denmark, but "having coffee" is prominently associated with Danish ethnicity in these communities (Fink, 1980).

How do Danish American foodways connect to the actual foods consumed by the ancestors of Danes who settled in America? Danish foods served at Christmastime were not the everyday fare of most Danes in the nineteenth and early twentieth century. Immigrants and children of immigrants may have memories of *øllebrød* soup. This porridge was a staple of Danish meals, and it was often made of rye bread that was boiled in beer. It is largely no longer made in Danish American kitchens, but it exists in the memories of older Danish Americans—and on-screen in Gabriel Axel's 1987 film *Babette's Feast*. Danes in America may have substituted oatmeal, often served with prunes or raisins, for *øllebrød*, and this type of modification is characteristic of other adaptations of Old World tastes to fit New World cuisine.

A more common carryover is the Danish meatball known as *frikadeller*. These can be made of pork and/or ground beef, and these meatballs remain part of the everyday foodways of many families. Visitors to Denmark often remark on the sandwiches that are such prominent features of many menus—and even displayed in café and restaurant windows. Known as *smørrebrød* in Danish, these open-faced sandwiches exemplify the subtle, yet elegant, aesthetics evident in numerous Danish arts. There are elaborate rules for matching the appropriate bread with the right toppings, and even rigid constraints that determine how the bread is to be buttered. The sandwiches can constitute elements within the *haute cuisine* of fine restaurants. They also may be served at special occasions and festivals in Danish American communities (Christensen, 1987). It is not a stretch to suggest that a taste for pork, horseradish, and sandwich toppings among Danes in America has been influenced by this food tradition. One way to understand how sandwich toppings are chosen is to consider how their preparers create them by negotiating a tension between more fancy foods versus the everyday fare (Hansen, 1980). Everyday sandwiches might consist of ham and cheese, whereas the more elaborate sandwiches may be made from foods that take considerable time and effort to prepare, such as *rullepølse*, a rolled pork loaf, elaborately prepared from humble head cheese. The prevalence of soups and sandwiches in Danish American food patterns along with the common presence of pork and cheese are complicit with older eating patterns of Danish immigrants.

Within American communities where Danish ethnicity is highly visible, one of the most common traditional foods is the seemingly humble *æbleskiver*. The name translates as "apple slices," and this spherical, pancake-like food sometimes includes apple slices in the batter. It is made in a special pan, that usually of cast iron, and often contains seven to nine holes. These resemble muffin tins, and they are sometimes sold by the noninitiated under that rubric. A useful way to understand the importance of *æbleskiver* as a marker of Danish identity is to compare it to a rhubarb pudding that also is common within Danish foodways. There are accounts that *rød grød med fløde* (red pudding with whipped cream) was purportedly a shibboleth used as a code word among Danes in World War II because the /ø/ vowel is so challenging for a non-Dane to pronounce. In a similar manner, *æbleskiver* often serves as a shibboleth into Danish culture. "I'll bet you don't know what that pan is used for?" a Danish American may ask. The wrong answer will be followed by an attempt to teach one of the variant pronunciations of *æbleskiver*. More than likely, this lesson in Danish heritage will be followed by an invitation to an æbleskiver supper. In the Midwest, they are sometimes held like community-based fish fries or barbecues, but it's rare to find *æbleskiver* outside of Danish American homes—unless one travels to Denmark. There, *æbleskiver* may be sold from vendor carts throughout the day, but it has been adapted to American patterns of eating. In America, *æbleskiver* sometimes is eaten as a breakfast food, but more typically it is served with pancake syrup and other American condiments. Occasionally, when cooked at communal dinners, it is even made from packaged pancake/waffle mixes. An *æbleskiver* dinner may be used as a fund-raiser for churches and civic organizations. It may be accompanied by *medisterpølse*, a Danish pork sausage. Coffee will always be available as a beverage at one of these dinners.

Place in American Culture

Danish foodways is not overtly prominent in American culture. Although the Danish pastry has gone mainstream as part of a continental breakfast, it is difficult to identify many typically Danish foods that are part of American culture, other than butter cookies and Akvavit. Nevertheless, it is possible to find Danish cultural enclaves in a few communities scattered across the nation.

A small number of communities—notably Elk Horn and Kimballton, Iowa—support Danish ethnic festivals. People living in these communities will identify themselves as Americans, yet the Danish identity is a prominent, yet oftentimes subtle, element of their lives (Paulsen,

1967). Danes from Denmark attending these festivals may be quick to critique events such as an *æbleskiver* pan toss as "not Danish." The Americans engaging in this competition at Elk Horn, Iowa's, "Tivoli Fest" would be quick to agree. Some may assert that it's a Danish American version of the older American game of holding a "frying pan toss." As does making *æbleskiver* out of Bisquick, this competition, as well as Danish American foodways in general, reflects a cultural mixture. These foodways traditions are both Danish and American. Nevertheless, visiting Danes are also oftentimes quick to note that the foods they encounter in these American communities are surprisingly connected to their homeland's cuisine, even if their commemorative celebration makes them "more Danish than what's done in Denmark"— a remark that international visitors may make that can be interpreted ambiguously as a critique or a compliment.

Along with the specific recipes that are rooted in Danish food traditions, Danish foodways also include characteristic customs associated with holidays and ritual. A pastry called *fastelavnsboller* is a sweet roll that is coated with icing and often filled with whipped cream. They're made during *festelavn*, or "Fat Tuesday," to mark the shift into Lent during the calendar year. The sweet rolls may resemble cream puffs, and they're connected with related traditions of preparing and serving pastries and doughnuts during Mardi Gras. Other common foodways customs are associated with the everyday ritual of sharing a family meal. If the family offers a prayer to bless a meal, following the blessing, the host may exclaim *vær så god*, as a wish that the meal will do the diners well. At the conclusion of a dinner, it's an expected custom to reciprocate by thanking the cook with *tak fa mad*. Honored, the cook will usually smile and say *velbekomme*. Only after this exchange could the children leave the table.

The custom of thanking the host is subtle, but it is complicit with an important element of the ethnic culture. The ritual recognizes the value of *hygge*—a term with no exact English translation. Creating an experience that can be affirmed as *hyggelig* means that those participating in a mealtime connect the experience of sharing a meal with warm fellowship and deep social connections. A *hyggelig* house is a comfortable, cozy home, and traditional foodways provide important resources for creating this sense of deep hospitality.

Æbleskiver

By Sara Andersen, Danish immigrant to Audubon, Iowa, from Nykøbing Falster.

 2 cups buttermilk (evaporated milk can also be used)
 2 cups sifted flour
 2 teaspoons baking powder
 ½ teaspoon salt
 2 tablespoons sugar
 3 eggs

Beat egg yolks.
Sift baking powder with the flour.
Add sugar, salt, milk, flour, and baking powder.
Add stiffly beaten egg whites.
Place ¼ teaspoon shortening in each hole in the æbleskiver pan after it is heated.
Fill each hole approximately ⅔ or ¾ full.
Bake over a low heat on the stovetop.
When ½ baked, turn the æbleskiver with a hatpin or knitting needle. (Look for the browning around the edges and the breaking of bubbles in the mixture.)
Cooked when browned on both sides.
Served with jelly, applesauce, powdered sugar, or syrup

Noted Restaurants and Chefs

Although Danish foodways remain important components within some Danish families and even fewer communities, there are only a few Danish restaurants in America. The best-known restaurants, in fact, are bakeries located in Racine, Wisconsin. A number of bakeries there are prominent for their *kringles*, and they commonly ship these pastries across the nation during the Christmas season. The "Racine *kringle*" is well known to many American of Danish heritage, and its popularity has influenced the opening of similar bakeries in various communities where Danes have settled.

Danish American tourist sites also feature bakeries and gift shops that stock Danish foods. These may include imported treats from Denmark, and some stock locally made sausage or baked goods. There are few Danish restaurants in America. They are in towns that are promoted as Danish American communities, and visitors to Solvang, California, can enjoy Danish cuisine that is developed mainly from the immigrant culture of the early twentieth century. Entrees at the Danish Inn in Elk Horn, for example, may reflect some of the food commonly associated with holidays and festival occasions rather than the everyday foodways of Danish immigrants. The Elk Horn restaurant, however, also prominently features American fare as local residents are more apt to eat fried chicken or pork tenderloin rather than partaking of a diet of Danish foods when eating out in these communities. Because of the extremely limited number of Danish restaurants in America, no Danish American *haute cuisine* has developed from the immigrant experience. It remains to be seen, however, if American cuisine will be influenced from contemporary high cuisine in Denmark.

Further Reading

Christensen, Palle Ove. "Peasant Adaptation to Bourgeois Culture: Class Formation and Cultural Redefinition in the Danish Countryside." *Ethnological Scandinavica* (1987): 98–152.

Fink, Deborah Ruth. "Women's Work and Change in a Danish Community." PhD dissertation at the University of Minnesota, 1980.

Hansen, Judith Friedman. *We Are a Little Land: Cultural Assumption in Danish Everyday Life.* New York: Arno Press, 1980.

Hoobler, Dorothy, and Thomas Hoobler. *The Scandinavian American Family Album.* New York: Oxford University Press, 1997.

Kaplan, Anne R., Marjorie A. Hoover, and Willard B. Moore, ed. *The Minnesota Ethnic Food Book.* St. Paul: Minnesota Historical Society Press, 1986.

Larsen, Birgit Flemming, and Henning Bender. *Danish Emigration to the U.S.A.* Aalborg, Denmark: Danes Worldwide Archives, 1982.

Paulsen, Frank Martin. "Danish American Folk Traditions: A Study in Fading Survivals." PhD dissertation, Indiana University, 1967.

Gregory Hansen

DJIBOUTI

(East Africa) Djiboutian American
See also: Somalia, Ethiopia, Eritrea, and Yemen.

Background

Located in the "Horn of Africa," on the southeastern part of the continent, Djibouti borders the Red Sea (with Yemen across the sea), Eritrea on the north, Ethiopia south and west, and Somalia to the south. It has an extensive coastline and long history of trade and providing ports on major trade routes. Islam was established there in the mid-800s, but it was under French control since 1862 and was a colony from 1888 to 1977 (as part of French Somaliland). It is considered strategically important today, and it now holds military bases for France. US English, French, and Arabic are the official languages.

Harbors are Djibouti's only source of income. The land is barren desert, and other than what they can obtain from the sea, they depend on trade for food. They also experience severe droughts and have been given international aid. Although many Djiboutis leave as refugees, sources claim that there are less than three hundred individuals in the United States, and they are usually included with Somalians. There does not appear to be a large Djiboutian American community, nor a distinguishable Djiboutian presence in the United States, although a number of individuals have settled in Lewiston, Maine, close to a growing African community in Portland.

Foodways

The two main ethnic groups living in Djibouti are the Issa (from Somalia) and Afar (from Ethiopia). Islam is the dominant religion and shapes the food culture, which also displays influences from French and Indian cuisines and is similar to that of its neighboring countries. Djiboutians make a flatbread similar to but smaller and flatter than Ethiopian *injera*, called *lahoh* (Yemini name) or *canjeero*, but it is also made with *teff* flour. The bread is eaten with stews (*maroq*), and for breakfast it might be served with butter (or Indian *ghee*) and honey. The cuisine relies heavily on seafood, but it also includes beef, camel, and goat. A signature dish is a spicy beef soup called *fah-fah*, and vegetables are also stewed and spiced to make *yetakelt wet*. Meals can include rice or pasta with meat or rice and lentils. These are usually served with sauces, *berbere* or *niter kibbeh*, and a banana—the latter is a custom continued in east African restaurants in the United States. Indian influence on the cuisine is seen in the preference for tea over coffee, the popularity of small triangular pastries, *sambusas*, and the use of cumin to flavor a common oat porridge called *garoobey*.

Place in American Culture

Djiboutians in the United States are able to find foods similar to their own in Somalian and Ethiopian restaurants. African groceries carry some of the native ingredients of their cuisine, although mainstream supermarkets and health food stores now carry *teff* flour, much of which is actually being grown in the United States. Djiboutian Americans also shop at Indian groceries.

Further Reading

BBCNews.com. "Djibouti Profile." October 20, 2014. http://www.bbc.com/news/world-africa-13231761.

Infoplease. "Djibouti." http://www.infoplease.com/country/djibouti.html.

Lonely Planet. "Introducing Djibouti." http://www.lonelyplanet.com/Djibouti.

Wikipedia. "Djiboutian American." http://en.wikipedia.org/wiki/Djiboutian_American.

Wikipedia. "Djiboutian Cuisine.http://en.wikipedia.org/wiki/Djiboutian_cuisine.

Lucy M. Long

DOMINICA

(Americas–Caribbean)

See also: Barbados, Bahamas, Jamaica, and Trinidad and Tobago.

An English-speaking independent nation in the Caribbean along with Antigua and Barbuda, Bahamas, Barbados, Dominica, Jamaica, Saint Kitts and Nevis, Saint Lucia, Saint Vincent and The Grenadines, and Trinidad and Tobago.

For similar food cultures, also see British territories in the Caribbean.

DOMINICAN REPUBLIC

(Americas—Caribbean) Dominican American Foodways

See also: Cuba, Puerto Rico.

Background

After colonization, occupation, and encroachment by Spain, France, and Haiti, respectively, the Dominican Republic gained independence in 1844; however, it was occupied by the United States soon after due to political instability. During the United States' second occupation of the Dominican Republic in 1965, Dominicans immigrated in large numbers to the United

States. Immigration reached an all-time high in the 1980s when hundreds of thousands settled in the Northeastern United States. There are now approximately 1.5 million self-identified Dominicans residing in the United States. The states with the largest Dominican populations are New Jersey, New York, Massachusetts, Florida, Pennsylvania, and Rhode Island, while the Washington Heights neighborhood in New York City has the largest population of any city. Nonetheless, because 63 percent of the current Dominican American foreign-born population arrived after 1990, Dominicans are one of the least assimilated cultures in the United States, for they hold on to their culture, traditions, and cuisine with great force. Many Dominican families keep their cooking parallel to that of the Dominican Republic without much influence or inclusion from North American culture and cuisine.

Foodways

Similar to many other Latin American countries, the cuisine in the Dominican Republic reflects its diverse population. It commonly includes beans, rice, and the popular staple, yucca. These three food items are prepared in many different ways for various meals and occasions. Dominican dishes include traces of Taino (the native people who made up the original population of the Dominican Republic and other nearby Latin American countries), Spanish, and African food cultures.

In the Dominican Republic, dishes differ according to location and social class. While those who live in the mountains and farms eat more meat than those who live on the seaside, upper-class citizens also consume more meat and seafood than those in the lower classes. After immigrating, many Dominican Americans continue to maintain their household traditions in regard to how much chicken, pork, or fish they prepare and consume. Also, many Dominican Americans are of low socioeconomic status, with 26 percent actually at poverty level. This has a result similar to that of those in the Dominican Republic living in poverty, which means that their native dishes are usually made with less meat and use whatever is on hand. Despite often living in situations where there is little access to quality food, Dominican Americans have clung to their native cuisine with less Western adaptation and assimilation than any other Latin American population in the United States. Fortunately, it is easy for them to maintain native flavors in their cuisine because of the availability of Latin American spices and seasonings at major grocery stores due largely to the presence of the Goya food company.

Many of the most popular dishes in the Dominican Republic remain popular in the United States for Dominicans. *La Bandera*, which translates to The Flag, is considered the national dish of the Dominican Republic. It consists of meat, red beans, and white rice. A heartier version also contains fried plantains and a salad. The meat, which ranges from beef to chicken to pork, is most commonly marinated in a mixture containing such ingredients as oregano, parsley, pepper, adobo seasoning, Worcestershire sauce, garlic, and onion. The beans contain similar seasonings and other classic Dominican spices: chicken stock, tomato paste, oregano, adobo seasoning, parsley, garlic, apple cider vinegar, onion, and celery.

Another popular dish is called *sancocho*, which translates to "stew." Found in many other Latin American cultures but called by different names, this dish is most commonly made with approximately five different kinds of meat. However, many Dominicans, especially those of a low socioeconomic status, make *sancocho* with simply whatever meat and vegetables they have on hand. *Sancocho* is often paired with rice, as most Dominican dishes are, and a few slices of avocado. This dish is most commonly made on special occasions because it takes so much time to make. Below is a simplified recipe for *sancocho*.

Sancocho

Ingredients:
- 3 pounds chicken
- 2 pounds bone-in pork shoulder
- 2 pounds bone-in beef
- 1 pound goat meat
- 2 pounds of *longaniza* (a mildly spiced Dominican pork sausage usually only found at Dominican or Latin American grocery stores) or Italian sausage
- 4 large *platanos* (plantains) unripe and cut into medium-sized pieces
- 1 pound of potatoes
- 2 pounds of peeled and washed yucca cut into small pieces
- 2 pounds of *malanga* cut into very small pieces
- 2 pounds of pumpkin (preferably a Spanish pumpkin)
- 3 ears of corn on the cob cut into 6 pieces each
- 1 pound of yams cut into medium-sized pieces
- 6 liters of water
- 5 tablespoons of vegetable oil
- 1¼ tablespoons of oregano
- 4½ teaspoons of salt
- pepper
- 3 medium sour oranges (or 4 lemons)
- 2 tablespoons of chopped celery
- 2 green bell peppers cut into large pieces
- 3 medium-size onions
- 2 tablespoons of minced garlic
- oregano to taste
- thyme to taste
- parsley to taste
- 2 chicken bouillon cubes
- 2 teaspoons of vinegar
- 2 tablespoons Worcestershire sauce

Directions:
1. Cut the three pounds of chicken into pieces (the size does not matter).
2. Wash all of the meat, besides the sausages.
3. Take the three sour oranges and rub them on all of the meat, including the sausages. (This is a popular marinating technique among Dominicans in the Dominican Republic and in the United States.)
4. Add the oil, herbs, onion, garlic, Worcestershire sauce, salt, and pepper to a large stew pot. Once the seasonings begin to simmer, and the garlic begins to roast, add the beef and brown. This should take approximately 20 minutes.
5. Add the pork to the stew pot and allow it to simmer for 15 minutes.
6. Add a very small amount of water but only enough so it does not stick.
7. Add the chicken and the chicken stock to the pot, and allow it to simmer for approximately 10 minutes.
8. While the chicken and stock is simmering, boil the water in a separate pot, and then add the vegetables. Simmer the vegetables for approximately 10 minutes.
9. Add the vegetables and the water to the meat and allow it to simmer until the vegetables are soft.
10. When the vegetables are soft, remove about half of them from the pot with a slotted spoon or strainer and place in a small, heatproof bowl and mash.
11. Once the vegetables are mashed, return them to the pot and allow the stew to thicken.
12. Once thickened, the stew is finished. Serve in a bowl with a side of white rice and a side of sliced avocado.

Casabe, also known as *cassava bread*, is another popular Dominican dish. *Casabe* is a type of flatbread that is made from yucca flour. The native Taino people of the Dominican Republic invented this bread. It is a long-argued tale that this bread is what drove the people of Spain to conquer the land of the Dominican Republic. Nowadays, *casabe* is most often bought at local Dominican or Latin American grocery stores. Nonetheless, a sample recipe of this famous bread is as follows:

Casabe (Cassava Bread)

Ingredients:

1 pound of peeled, washed, and salted yucca

Directions:

1. Using the finest section of a grater, grate the yucca.
2. Squeeze the yucca with a cheesecloth or wet paper towel until as much liquid as possible has been drained from the yucca.
3. Break up any lumps, spread on a baking sheet, and place in a refrigerator (for no more than an hour) to dehumidify the yucca.
4. Heat a cast iron skillet to medium heat until very hot, but do not add any butter or oil.
5. When ready, place some of the grated yucca in the pan and flatten out using the back of a spatula.
6. When the bottom is golden (about 1 minute), flip and cook the other side until golden as well.
7. Serve warm, or cool it first to create the appearance and texture of a cracker.

Casabe is a plain-flavored bread, and thus it is often made by mixing in different seasonings to the yucca before refrigeration, such as cheese, garlic, and onion.

While in the United States, many Dominican families adapt to a smaller nuclear family that resembles Western culture, with a couple and their dependent children. In the Dominican Republic, like many other Latin American countries, family life is mostly nonnuclear and large, including people outside of the immediate family circle, such as cousins, nieces and nephews, aunts and uncles, grandparents, and family friends. These nonnuclear families are also often led by a single parent, or other family members. Food brings every member together three times a day. The food is cooked by an older female in the household, and other members of the family are expected to participate in the meal times. In the Dominican Republic, lunch is the most important meal, a trait adapted from their Spanish culture and heritage. While Dominican Americans have shifted the large meal to the evening, they continue to use food to bring their families together.

Holiday Feasts

The use of food to bring people together is also present in their national holidays. The Dominican Republic celebrates many holidays, having origins from both religion and the government. For most families, the two biggest holidays are Carnival and Christmas. The Carnival is usually celebrated throughout the month of February with parades, music, food, art, and various parties. This celebration most often climaxes on Dominican Independence Day, on February 27. Christmas is the largest religious holiday in the Dominican Republic and is celebrated for an extended period of time lasting around three months and ending after *Los Tres Reyes Magos* (The Day of the Kings or Three Kings Day). Throughout the Christmas season, Dominicans celebrate at private and community parties, but the most holy and special parts of the holiday are spent with family and paired with food and/or church. The importance of food when celebrating for Dominicans can be seen in the United States as well, where its role in maintaining community is emphasized. For example, the annual Dominican Day parade in New York City, which began in 1982, always consists of music, parties, food, and most importantly, community.

Place in American Culture

Dominican Americans consider "authentic" Dominican food to be food made by one's mother, grandmother, aunt, or other female relative. This food brings people together and is a way to reminisce and connect with their home country and culture. Dominican food sold in American restaurants, however, is oftentimes advertised as generic Latin American, Spanish, or Caribbean cuisine, and might be offered along with Cuban or Puerto Rican dishes. The restaurants that do carry true Dominican cuisine are most commonly small, Dominican-family owned and operated.

With the ever-growing Dominican American population, there are now several cookbooks containing Dominican dishes published in the United States; however, the majority of these cookbooks are labeled as Spanish, Latin American, or ethnic cuisine.

Noted Restaurants and Chefs

Dominican food has its own identity, and there are several authentic Dominican restaurants around the United States, but particularly in the Northeast. For example, one of the most popular is Paraiso Restaurant in Boston. Its popularity represents Dominican culture in that they hold food that tastes like home-cooked meals at a higher level. Nonetheless, there are several restaurants that feature modernized Dominican cuisine. For example, Merengue, owned by Chef Hector Piña, is an extremely popular restaurant in Boston that features Dominican cuisine but adds flavors from other Latin American and Caribbean countries. The success of Dominican restaurants and chefs in the United States speaks to the rise of the male Dominican cook in Western society.

Further Reading

Janer, Zilkia. *Latino Food Culture*. Westport, CT: Greenwood Press, 2008.

Matthews, Robert S. *The Heart and Soul of the Dominican Republic: An American's View of His New Country*. Bloomington, IN: Author House, 2007.

Torres-Saillant, Silvio, and Ramona Hernández. *The Dominican Americans*. Westport, CT: Greenwood Press, 1998.

Alexandria Ayala

E

ECUADOR
(South America) Ecuadorian American Food

Background
Despite its small size, about the size of the state of Colorado, Ecuador is marked by geographical variations that create culinary diversity. Ecuadorian food culture is divided into two subcuisines, that of the coast and that of the mountains. Given the relatively small numbers of immigrants to the United States, Ecuadorian Americans face great challenges in maintaining these regional culinary identities, struggling to maintain national identity in the face of broader Latino cultural influences.

Before the 1960s, few Ecuadorians immigrated to the United States. In 1964 Ecuador passed major land reform that redistributed land to small landholders yet also established private ownership and responsibility. As many new small farmers lost their private plots, peasants abandoned rural communities, and rural peoples from all geographic regions emigrated, primarily to Venezuela and the United States. Although the early immigration period was dominated by highland residents in the Quito area, by the mid-1990s, Ecuadorians were coming to the United States from all parts of Ecuador. Many Ecuadorian immigrants are undocumented, but it is estimated that there are five hundred thousand Ecuadorians residing in the United States, of which three hundred thousand, or 60 percent, reside in New York and New Jersey. Ecuadorian immigrants concentrate in neighborhoods where other South American immigrants reside, such as the borough of Queens.

The relatively small number of Ecuadorian immigrants, in contrast to other Latino populations, results in pressures faced by Ecuadorians to maintain their own national identity and culinary traditions. That is, not only do they face the influences of the dominant American culture, but they are also exposed to the cultural traditions of other Latino immigrant communities, such as Mexican, Puerto Rican, and Dominican, whose populations overshadow those of the Ecuadorian immigrants.

Foodways
Dishes characterizing national Ecuadorian cuisine reflect different regional culinary styles. In coastal Ecuador, fish, shrimp, crab, and clams represent key staples in the coastal diet. A popular dish is *encebollado*, a marinade of chopped fish, onions, and regional spices, while *ceviche*, raw seafood and/or fish marinated in the juice of citrus fruits (lemon, lime, or orange) and served cold, might be considered a national dish, although it characterizes coastal cuisine. In Ecuador, shrimp is most commonly used, but different kinds of fish are also added. Vegetables, such as onions or peppers, may also be added, and roasted peanuts are sprinkled on top. Ecuadorian Americans in New York City have made *ceviche* a widely available dish in local restaurants and local street vendors.

Another staple in coastal cuisine is bananas, and the region produces a wide range of varieties, including the yellow bananas most familiar to US consumers, short red bananas, *oritas* (tiny bananas), and green plantains, used in cooking. Green plantains are cooked like other starchy vegetables, and they are used as a side dish or to thicken stews or doughs. Ecuadorians prepare these in a myriad of different dishes, preparing them whole, sliced, raw, boiled, fried, and baked.

In highland Ecuador, potatoes represent an important staple, and they are prepared in many ways. First domesticated in the Andes, indigenous farmers bred a wide variety of kinds, reflecting both adaptations to different ecological niches as well as preferences for different dishes. In the United States, Ecuadorian immigrants can find unique potatoes in Latino specialty groceries. Potatoes are an important food item, whether as the principle ingredient in the main dish or as a side dish. Cheese is often combined with potatoes, as in the favorite dish below, *llapingachos*, a cheese and mashed potato patty. In addition to potatoes, highland Ecuadorians traditionally consume corn, either on the cob or in tamales.

Llapingachos (Potato Balls)

2 pounds potatoes
1 onion, finely chopped
½ pound white cheese, crumbled
2 tablespoons butter
vegetable oil
1 teaspoon salt
sauce
½ pound peanuts, roasted and ground
½ cup milk
3 tablespoons onion, finely chopped
3 tablespoons butter

1. Wash, peel, and boil potatoes until tender. Mash them and mix with 1 tablespoon butter and salt to taste.
2. Sauté the onion. Add the cheese to the onion.
3. Shape the mashed potatoes into small balls and stuff them with the cheese-based mixture.
4. Seal and fry them in hot vegetable oil until brown.
5. Sauce: Sauté the onions in 1 tablespoon butter. Add peanuts and milk. Cook over medium heat until the sauce thickens.
6. Serve the fried potato balls with the sauce in individual bowls.

Many Ecuadorian dishes are soups or stews, reflecting the colonial introduction of the Spanish *puchero*, or stew. Ecuadorian stews contain a variety of potatoes, other vegetables, and small amounts of meat. Fish and shrimp soups are more common in the coastal regions, while meat stew, such as *seco de chivo*, a stew made from goat, is more common in the highlands. These savory stews are slowly cooked in a sauce comprising onion, garlic, tomatoes, and chile peppers, to which seasonings, such as cumin, cloves, or unrefined sugar, may be added.

In general, the traditional Ecuadorian diet contained very little meat. One traditional meat, the guinea pig, or *cuy*, was one of the few domesticated animals in prehistoric times. In highland Ecuador, guinea pigs were raised at home in villages, whereas in the United States, Ecuadorian Americans face challenges in obtaining guinea pig meat and substitute pork or chicken in those recipes calling for guinea pig. In other cases, Ecuadorian American restaurants can special-order, frozen *cuy* in order to offer this delicacy to Ecuadorian American consumers.

Ecuadorian Americans may start their day with more American fare, such as cereal or pancakes, but equally common is a traditional meal of *chifles*, green plantain chips, toasted maize, *ají* chile sauce, and bread. The Ecuadorian midday meal is fairly simple, comprising three courses: first, a soup, often with fish or shrimp, followed by a main dish, which includes a starch such as potato, rice, or yucca, accompanied by beef, poultry, pork or fish. Heavier soups, such as *locros*, are potato based; cream-style soups are also popular among Ecuadorians. Following the main meal, dessert and coffee are common. The evening meal, dinner, is usually light, comprised often of coffee or tea accompanied by some sort of bread.

Holiday Feasts

Most Ecuadorian Americans are Catholic, and the persistence of traditional feast foods plays an important role in maintaining Ecuadorian identity. Throughout South America, Catholics carry out common folk practices, including the construction of the Nativity scene, the singing of Christmas carols, and attending midnight mass on Christmas Eve, the *Misa de Gallo*, after which families gather for a late evening meal. For Ecuadorian Americans, common Christmas dishes include *buñuelos*, fritters of cornmeal, lard, salt, and eggs, covered with sugar syrup, and *pristinos*, pieces of wheat dough in star shapes, spread with an egg wash, fried, and covered with more sugar syrup. In the months after Christmas, the abstinence and fasting of the Lenten season prepares the devout Catholic for the festivities of Holy Week and the resurrection of Christ on Easter Sunday. In respect for the sacrifices of the Lenten season, on Holy Thursday, Ecuadorians traditionally eat *juanesca* or *fanesco*, a dish comprising dried fish, grains, legumes, milk, and cheese. *Fanesco* may also include winter squash, beans, lentils, peas, fresh corn, rice, and slices of hard-boiled eggs. On Easter Sunday, Ecuadorians would eat *chigüiles*, tamales made of cornmeal, eggs, and cheese, wrapped in corn husks and boiled in water.

Place in American Culture

The concentration of Ecuadorian American in certain urban neighborhoods has supported restaurants and food vendors featuring Ecuadorian food and catering to the ethnic community. These typically sell *ceviche* with different fixings, a popular food among all Latino immigrant populations.

Further Reading

Buchanan, Christina. *The Ecuador Cookbook: Traditional Vegetarian and Seafood Recipes*. English and Spanish Edition. New York: Flying Fish Publications, 1998.

Carnegie Library of Pittsburgh. "Latin American Food & Cooking." http://www.carnegielibrary.org/subject/food/latin.html.

Garces, José. *The Latin Road Home: Savoring the Foods of Ecuador, Spain, Cuba, Mexico, and Peru*. New York: Lake Isle Press, 2012.

Janer, Zilkia. *Latino Food Culture*. Westport, CT: Greenwood Press, 2008.

Lovera, José Rafael. *Food Culture in South America*. Westport, CT: Greenwood Press, 2005.

Ortiz, Elisabeth Lambert. *The Book of Latin American Cooking*. New York: Alfred A. Knopf, 1979.

Presilla, Maricel. *Gran Cocina Latina: The Food of Latin America*. New York: W. W. Norton, 2012.

Weismantal, Mary J. *Food, Gender, and Poverty in the Ecuadorian Andes*. Prospect Heights, IL: Waveland Press, 1988.

Lois Stanford

EGYPT

(North Africa) Egyptian American Food, Mediterranean Foods
See also: Lebanon, Syria.

Background

Egyptian immigration to the United States is a relatively recent phenomenon, at least in any significant numbers. Unlike the Lebanese, who have an immigration history dating back to the nineteenth century, most Egyptian Americans arrived in the United States after 1952. It is also important to distinguish among Egyptian Muslims, who are usually Arabs; Egyptian Christians, who trace their Coptic ancestry back to the Phoenicians; and the much smaller number of Egyptian Jews, whose Semitic origins are related to, but not identical with, the Arabs.

Each group has had its own reasons for immigration, as well as its own distinctive culinary culture. According to the Arab American Institute, about 11 percent of Arabs living in the United States are of Egyptian ancestry. Estimates of the number of Egyptian Americans range from about eight hundred thousand to two million (the lower figure usually quoted by the US government, the higher number sometimes claimed by the diasporic community).

Contrary to what one might expect, most Egyptian Americans are Coptic Christians, not Muslims. As simply one example of this, the Islamic Center of Greater Toledo (one of the most significant mosques in the United States, and not far from Dearborn, Michigan, the largest Arab American population in the country) counts only one Egyptian member, but in the same metropolitan area, the Coptic Church of St. George numbers more than one hundred families. It is ironic that the Coptic religion, which shares its name with the country (from ancient Greek *Aigyptos*), has felt or actually been persecuted in modern Egypt; fears of persecution following Egypt's defeat in its 1967 war with Israel led many Copts to flee to the United States. Most Egyptian Americans are highly educated, and most reside on the East Coast, in particular New York and New Jersey, with a Coptic Archdiocese in Cedar Grove, New Jersey.

Foodways

Given the recent immigration history, no distinctive Egyptian American cuisine has developed. Many Egyptians would claim as their own a variety of well-known Middle Eastern dishes—such as *falafel*, *baklava*, pita bread, *kofta*, and *fattah* or *fattoush*—which, however, were brought to this country by earlier immigrants from the region. The Egyptian staples are rice and beans; *ful medames*, a bean dish similar to Mexican *refritos*, is often eaten for breakfast, while "Egyptian rice" is usually short-grain rice, often served with lightly fried orzo or similar small pieces of pasta added. Meat (aside from poultry) is either lamb or beef. Since Muslims do not eat pork, there is no tradition (even among Egyptian Christians) of raising or eating pigs, which are considered unclean. Muslim communities in the United States generally have a *halal* butcher; in the absence of *halal* meat, kosher meat is considered acceptable, since the method of butchering is the same and Muslims consider the God of Abraham as their own.

Some Egyptians would consider *koshari* to be the national dish, and it is one that translates well to the American context, since all the ingredients are readily available. Here is a basic recipe that can be adapted in countless variations:

Koshari

1 pound smallish pasta (elbow macaroni is suitable, as are *ditales*)
2 cups (dry) short-grained rice
2 cups garbanzo beans (canned, drained; or prepared from dried)
2 cups lentils (green or red) (canned, drained; or prepared from dried)
2 14-ounce cans crushed tomatoes
chili flakes or other hot peppers
2 onions, thinly sliced
7–10 segments garlic
vinegar, salt and pepper to taste

To prepare: First, fry the sliced onions until they are light brown and crunchy (do not burn). Set aside. Then, prepare a tomato sauce from the garlic and crushed tomatoes; additional spices may be desired, such as cilantro or parsley (*kusbara w bagdonis*). Take about a quarter of the sauce and add chili flakes or other hot pepper, along with some vinegar, to create a very hot sauce. Finally, cook and drain all of the starches and set aside in separate bowls.

To serve, each individual ingredient is placed on a buffet or simply on the dining table, and each person helps himself or herself to a portion of each, topping it all off with the fried onions and a quantity of hot sauce commensurate with the individual's courage and heat tolerance!

Holiday Feasts

Major holidays, of course, vary according to faith; but one holiday with a distinctive culinary tradition is celebrated by all Egyptians: *Sham el-Nissim*, which translates literally as "smelling the air," is a pre-Christian spring and fertility festival that has come to be celebrated on the Monday after Easter (Orthodox calendar). In Egypt, people of all faiths gather on this day to swim in the Nile and eat a special salted fish dish, hard-boiled and colored eggs, and other traditional dishes including *molokhiyya* (also spelled *mullukhia*), a broth made of dried mallow plant or jute; its consistency, often described as "slimy," can be compared to an okra stew. In the United States, where Easter Monday is a workday (and Orthodox Easter is not widely celebrated), some Egyptian Americans have taken to celebrating this holiday on Orthodox Easter, while others have given it up.

Place in American Culture and Restaurants

There are very few Egyptian restaurants in the United States; the major ones are located near concentrations of Egyptian American populations. They cater both to American exoticism—often incorporating elements of ancient Egypt in their decor or even menu—as well as the expat community. King Tut in Fort Worth, Texas, is a clear example; they serve not only Egyptian *shawarma*, *koshari*, and *kofta* but also other Mediterranean dishes such as gyros. Al-Masri in San Francisco is actually run by an American chef with extensive experience in Egypt, who finds it necessary to include the disclaimer "independently owned and operated by a native born and raised United States female citizen and military veteran"; apparently, in the post-9/11 world, even San Francisco is not free of the threat of ethnic profiling. Casa La Femme in New York is a high-end restaurant that offers a four-course, prix fixe menu based on the northern Egyptian cuisine of Alexandria, including *tagines*, *mahshi*, *goulash* (the Egyptian name for a phyllo dough stuffed with different fillings), and stuffed grape leaves.

Further Reading

Abdennour, Samia. *Egyptian Cooking: And Other Middle Eastern Recipes*. Cairo: American University Press, 2010.

Mehdawy, Magda. *My Egyptian Grandmother's Kitchen: Traditional Dishes Sweet and Savory*. Cairo: American University Press, 2006.

Riolo, Amy. *Nile Style: Egyptian Cuisine and Culture*. Expanded Edition. New York: Hippocrene Books, 2013.

Kristie Foell

EL SALVADOR

(Central America) Salvadoran American Food

Background

As of 2012, Salvadorans were the fifth-largest immigrant group in the United States. Significant emigration from El Salvador began in the 1980s as hundreds of thousands of Salvadorans (along with other Central Americans) fled civil war and political unrest. Between 1980 and 1990, the Salvadoran immigrant population in the United States increased from 94,000 to 465,000. From 1990 through present day, natural disasters, poverty, and continued political instability have continued to force migration out of El Salvador and into neighboring countries, Mexico and the United States. By 2010, there were about 1.6 million Salvadoran immigrants in the United States, with the largest concentrations residing in large cities, particularly Los Angeles, New York, and the Washington, DC, area.

Foodways

As is frequently the case, the second generation displays more cultural assimilation within their adopted home. The children of Salvadoran-born immigrants are in the American school system and are often beneficiaries of low-income food programs, generally eating non-Salvadoran foods outside of the homes. Adults also partake in nontraditional foods outside of the home, particularly for breakfast and lunch.

In the home, dinner is usually a traditional Salvadoran meal, with occasional ingredient substitutions, often from Mexican and American cuisine—such as wheat flour tortillas (instead of corn tortillas), sour cream (instead of Salvadoran *crema*), or American cheeses (instead of Salvadoran cheese).

Salvadoran cuisine is a blend of indigenous and Spanish influences, with corn as its main staple. Basic foods also include rice; bread; red, black, and white beans; beef, pork, fish, poultry, and eggs; dairy in the form of milk, cheese, sweet cream, and sour cream; fruits and vegetables such as mango, papaya, citrus, banana, jicama, avocado, plantain, yucca, potato, squash, tomato, tamarind, sweet and hot peppers, and onion; seeds, such as *achiote* (ground annatto seeds), pumpkin seeds, and sesame seeds; herbs such as laurel leaves, mint, cilantro, and parsley; and spices, including garlic, ginger, cumin, and oregano. Some ingredients unique to Central America used in Salvadoran cuisine include *loroco*, an edible flower often used in cheese *pupusas*; *pacaya*, tender palm flowers usually stuffed with cheese, battered, and deep fried; *chipilín*, a green herb used in tamales, *pupusas*, and soups; and *flor de izote*, the flower of yucca often cooked with eggs.

Coffee, fruit juices, sweet sodas, drinks made from corn (*atole de elote*) and rice (*horchata*), and beer (typically pilsner) are all common beverages.

Beans and corn (in the form of tortillas or *masa*) or beans and rice form the basis for many dishes, with a meat and vegetable sides rounding out the typical Salvadoran American plate. Soups and stews of meat, vegetables, and beans are also common. Proteins are often stewed or sautéed with aromatics, vegetables, and spices, roasted or fried. Tomato and chili-based sauces and pickled, raw, and fried vegetables are regular accompaniments to meals.

Sweet and savory baked goods are part of the repertoire for breakfast, lunch, dinner, dessert, special occasions, or snacks. Pastries include the sweet-savory and rich Salvadoran *quesadilla*, a dense cake made with rice flour, cheese, sour cream, and milk; *semita*, a sweet, often jam-filled tart; assorted intricately made cookies; *pastelitos de carne*, *masa* dough filled with meat and vegetables; and Salvadoran *empanadas*, plantain dough filled with sweet cream. Bread is also consumed as part of a sandwich (*panes rellenos* or filled bread) or a French-toast-like preparation.

The *pupusa* is the national dish of El Salvador and the most recognized Salvadoran dish in the United States. It involves making a dough from *masa* and water, preparing a filling (some combination of beans, cheese, pork, and/or vegetables), forming a small ball of dough into a bowl shape, stuffing it with the filling, pinching the dough closed over the filling, then patting the *pupusa* into a thick, flat round. It is then cooked on a griddle and served with *curtido* (a pickled cabbage and vegetable side) and a thin tomato salsa. Preparing more involved dishes such as *pupusas* or Salvadoran tamales (corn dumplings wrapped in banana or plantain leaves and steamed) are often reserved for days off or special occasions.

Salvadoran ingredients can be purchased in ethnic markets carrying food products from Central and South American and Caribbean countries. The Internet and *viajeros* (Salvadorans who bring products from El Salvador to sell to immigrant communities in the United States) are other sources for special ingredients and products from El Salvador. Salvadoran cheese, in particular, represents a taste of home, and Salvadoran Americans go to great lengths to get it.

Salvadoran American kitchens are typically the domain of women, adhering to the standard gender roles of a patriarchal culture. Many female Salvadoran American immigrants have full-time jobs while also holding down responsibility for the home and food preparation.

Most meals in the traditional Salvadoran American home are based on beans, corn tortillas, and/or rice. Fruit juices are also consumed regularly with every meal. Breakfast (*desayuno*) is a morning meal. A typical full breakfast can be black refried beans, tortillas, eggs, and fried plantains; a plate of *casamiento*, cooked rice mixed with cooked beans; or eggs and *chorizo* (spicy pork sausage) with tortillas. Black coffee or *café con leche* (coffee with milk) and a *pan dulce* (sweet bread), like Salvadoran *quesadilla*, is also a typical casual breakfast. American breakfast cereals with cold milk, egg sandwiches, and Mexican sweet breads might be eaten as well.

The midday meal, lunch (*almuerzo*), in El Salvador is often built around a hearty soup. In the United States, soup is less common, and lunch varies from rice with vegetables and a meat to beans topped with *crema salvadoreña* (Salvadoran sour cream) with tortillas, to a hamburger and French fries. Dinner (*cena*), more often than breakfast or lunch, will be a traditional Salvadoran meal. Rice, beans, vegetables, a meat, tortillas, cheese, and fruit juice make up a typical dinner plate.

Snacks, street food, and meal sides include *pupusas*, *yucca con chicharron* (yucca, a starchy root, with pork rinds), tamales, fried ripe or unripe plantains, and fruit. Many dessert dishes are made with bananas, often stewed or fried.

Pupusa de Frijoles y Queso (Beans and Cheese *Pupusa*)

2 cups *masa harina* (corn flour)
1 cup water (more or less as needed)
1 can refried black beans
1 cup grated cheese: *queso fresco*, mozzarella, Monterey jack, or manchego
vegetable oil
salt and pepper

Combine *masa harina* with salt and pepper in a bowl. Add water gradually until you form a moist dough that will not crumble. Mix the beans and cheese together in a separate bowl. With lightly oiled hands, divide the dough into 8 equal portions and roll each portion into a ball. Push your thumb into the center of one ball and form a well or bowl shape. Place about a tablespoon of bean and cheese filling in the dough bowl. Form the dough around the filling, pinching it closed, making sure to seal the filling in. Lightly pat the dough ball back and forth between your hands to make a thick, round disk (about ¼ inch). Repeat with remaining dough balls.

Heat a lightly oiled skillet to medium-high heat. Cook each *pupusa* a few minutes on each side until golden-brown. Place on a plate with a paper towel to drain. Cover with tin foil as you cook the rest of the *pupusas*. Serve with tomato salsa and *curtido*.

Curtido (Pickled Cabbage Slaw)

½ head of cabbage, shredded
1 carrot, grated
½ large onion, thinly sliced
1 jalapeño or other chili pepper, minced
¼ cup white vinegar
2 tablespoons sugar
salt

In a bowl, cover cabbage and carrots with boiling water. Let sit for 10 minutes and drain, pressing to release liquid. Dissolve sugar and salt in vinegar. Combine all ingredients in one bowl; stir to combine. Let sit for a few hours or overnight.

Holiday Feasts

The major religion of El Salvador is Catholicism, followed by other types of Christianity, mixed with native folk spirit beliefs. Holidays celebrated by Salvadoran Americans, therefore, include the major Catholic and Christian holidays (Christmas, Easter, etc.) as well as the

New Year (January 1), Central American Independence Day (September 15), and sometimes American Thanksgiving. Many of these holidays have specific dishes associated with them and are a time for Salvadoran immigrants to remember home.

Roast turkey (*pavo Salvadoreño*) cooked with vegetables and spices that are then pureed into a sauce is a popular meal on Christmas Day and Thanksgiving Day. *Mango en miel* (mango in honey) is a holiday dish prepared to celebrate Holy Week, the week before Easter. *Sopa de pescado*, a soup of fish, tomatoes, green peppers, cumin, and *achiote* thickened with corn flour is also a popular dish for Easter. On New Year's Day, *yucca con chicharron* is a common celebratory dish. Tamales are a special occasion food and made as gifts. Another general special occasion dish is *gallo en chicha*, a rooster stewed in fermented pineapple juice or fermented maize liquid, onions, tomatoes, sugar, raisins, and prunes.

In the first week of August, Salvadoran Americans celebrate the *Fiestas Agostinas* (August Feasts), a week-long affair honoring El Salvador's patron saint and namesake, *Salvador del Mundo* (Savior of the World), with street fairs, parades, and parties with all the Salvadoran street food specialties including *pupusas*, tamales, *elotes locos* (grilled corn with mayonnaise, ketchup, hot sauce, cheese, and mustard), and fried plantains.

Holiday and special occasion feasts are time for community and are often held at churches, homes, or community centers. Salvadoran restaurants can be gathering places for special occasions as well.

Place in American Culture

Salvadoran cuisine is not well known in the United States outside of cities with a large Salvadoran population. Even then, it is frequently grouped with other Latino/Hispanic food cultures. The *pupusa* is the iconic Salvadoran food item recognized by Americans, and while Salvadoran Americans might express some frustration that it is often the only thing people know of Salvadoran cuisine, it is the pioneer dish that is bringing Salvadoran food to greater popularity in the United States.

A handful of Salvadoran American food blogs and one cookbook written by a Salvadoran American (*Delicious El Salvador*) also are educating the public on Salvadoran culinary traditions. A Salvadoran American also wrote a food-centric children's book that weaves the author's food memories of El Salvador into the fantastical story.

The Food Network website provides a recipe for pork *pupusas* with pickled cabbage (*curtido*), and several Salvadoran restaurants have been featured on the Food Network television show *Diners, Drive-Ins, and Dives*.

Noted Restaurants and Chefs

The first Salvadoran restaurants opened in the United States were advertised as Mexican restaurants, some serving only Mexican dishes, some pan–Latin American fare, some with Salvadoran and Mexican dishes on the same menu, and some with a separate Salvadoran menu that had to be requested. Emblematic of this phenomenon and the dramatic increase in Salvadoran population in the United States, Gloria's Café in Los Angeles, which has the largest Salvadoran population in the United States, opened in 1981 as a Mexican restaurant run by a Salvadoran but did not serve Salvadoran food until 1995. Also scattered about Salvadoran immigrant neighborhoods and beyond are innumerable *pupuserias*, generally counter service establishments with a limited menu, and street vendors selling Salvadoran street food, drinks, and snacks.

Further Reading

Argueta, Jorge. *The Fiesta of the Tortillas/La Fiesta De Las Tortillas*. Translated by Joe Hayes and Sharon Franco. Spain: Alfaguara, 2006.

Bertera, Elizabeth M., Robert L. Bertera, and Sharada Shankar. "Acculturation, Socioeconomic Factors and Obesity Among Immigrants from El Salvador Living in the Washington, DC Area." *Journal of Ethnic and Cultural Diversity in Social Work* 12, no. 2 (2003): 43–59.

Janer, Zilkia. *Latino Food Culture: Food Cultures in America*. Westport, CT: Greenwood, 2008.

Maher, Alicia. *Delicious El Salvador: 75 Authentic Recipes for Traditional Salvadoran Cooking*. Los Angeles, Pacific Apicius Corporation, 2013.

Rivas, Maria Dolores de. *Cocina Salvadoreña*. La Libertad, El Salvador: Grupo Imprecen, 2005.

Romero-Gwynn, E., D. Gwynn, M. De Lourdes Lopez, B. Turner, J. Asarian-Anderson, and M. Daud. "Dietary Patterns and Acculturation among Immigrants from El Salvador." *Nutrition Today* 35, no. 6 (2000): 233–40.

Stowers, Sharon. "Gastronomic Nostalgia: Salvadoran Immigrants' Cravings for Their Ideal Meal." *Ecology of Food and Nutrition*, 51, no. 5 (2012): 374–93.

Stowers, Sharon. *Hungry for the Taste of El Salvador: Gastronomic Nostalgia, Identity, and Resistance to Nutrithink in an Immigrant Community*. PhD diss., University of Massachusetts, Amherst, 2003.

Annu Ross

ENGLAND

(Northern Europe) English American, Anglo-American, British American Food
See also: Cornwall, Ireland, Wales, Scotland.

Background

England is the primary political state within the United Kingdom (also known as Great Britain), which includes Northern Ireland, Scotland, Cornwall, Wales, Guernsey, Isle of Man, and Jersey. The term *British* as used in the United States can refer to all of these groups, but most commonly it is specific to the English. According to the 2009 census, 13 percent of Americans report British ancestry (second largest, next to German), with English heritage being strongest in pockets along the East Coast, throughout the South, the Appalachian mountain region, and scattered throughout the West, but is frequently mixed with other British Isles ethnicities, particularly Ulster-Scots (also known as Scots-Irish or Scotch-Irish). The largest communities reporting specifically English heritage are in Utah and Maine. Some smaller enclaves trace their genealogical lines several centuries back to England, but they do not necessarily think of themselves now as English Americans. A group on the Eastern shore of Maryland is an example. Their recipe for Smith Island cake is given here.

While England provided one of the primary foundations of American culture and foodways, contemporary English food is just as ethnic as any other cultural or national group existing within the mainstream food culture it helped to create. Oftentimes referred to as "expats," contemporary English Americans have access to British food products through online stores as well as teashops and British specialty stores. British products are also sold in Canada and are frequently available in the bordering American states.

Foodways

Some English foods seem the same as American, but they are prepared or used differently; for example, baked beans on toast for breakfast or a quick comfort meal, broiled tomatoes for breakfast, "mushy peas" (dried marrowfat peas cooked into a mush and frequently used similarly to mashed potatoes), and "crisps"—what Americans call "potato chips," while English "chips" refers to American "French fries." Cider in England generally refers to alcoholic "hard cider" rather than the juice of pressed apples as in the United States. Similarly, tea is a type of meal as well as a liquid to drink. "High tea" refers to dinner (usually more formally served and with an extensive menu), while "low tea" tends to be an afternoon snack of cakes, scones, biscuits, small sandwiches, fruit, and cheese served with tea and other drinks. English scones are more of a sweet baking-powder biscuit than the cakelike cookie common in the United States, and "biscuits" in England refer to what Americans call cookies. Standard English biscuits are not frequently available in the United States—McVitie's brand, digestive biscuits, and tea biscuits. Also, crisps come in different flavors, such as cheese and onion, prawn (shrimp) cocktail, salt and vinegar, and bacon.

Dishes thought of as English include roast beef and Yorkshire pudding, beef Wellington, dessert trifles (layers of sponge cake, gelatin, whipped cream, and other ingredients, such as brandy or rum and fruit), bangers and mash (sausages and mashed potatoes), and fish and chips (battered, deep-fried fish fillets and thick French fries). Also considered distinctively English are Weetabix breakfast cereal (although American-invented cornflakes are a standard for breakfast in England), Marmite (yeast extract) to spread on toast, marmalade, Nutella (chocolate hazelnut spread), clotted cream, treacle (molasses), and Cadbury's chocolate. Both Cadbury's hot chocolate and Horlicks Malted (basic English drinks) are sold as international foods in the United States.

Some English holiday traditions have been adopted and adapted by Americans. Charles Dickens's *A Christmas Carol* is a favorite book, movie, and theatrical production for the Christmas season and includes food—roasted goose (replaced by turkey in the United States) and plum or Christmas pudding for Christmas dinner, as well as the custom of wassailing or Christmas caroling with Christmas punch, and spiced wine or cider. The holiday is also celebrated with fruitcake and mincemeat pies and tarts, usually associated with English food culture. Christmas "crackers" are sometimes misunderstood in the United States as a food, rather than a British holiday item containing a trinket, paper hat, and a saying (similar to Chinese fortune cookies).

Place in American Culture

Americans tend to romanticize English culture—the accent, in particular—and they are fascinated by English royalty and the class system, as seen in shows such as *Upstairs, Downstairs* and *Downton Abbey*. They also follow the country's literature, popular music, and other film and television productions. The last is considered both "highbrow," as in PBS productions of Masterpiece Theater, and displaying a slightly odd, frequently irreverent sense of humor, as represented by Monty Python, Mr. Bean, and other English characters.

English food, on the other hand, is generally not thought of in the United States as being an interesting or gourmet cuisine. It is common to compare it unfavorably with French food and to characterize it as dull, plain, fattening, and very meat-and-potatoes oriented (similar to the stereotypes of the American Midwestern food culture). It is also lumped in with other food cultures of the British Isles, particularly Scots and Irish.

Restaurants and Chefs

Although some foods, such as scones, tea, and fish and chips that could be considered English are sold throughout the United States, these are not usually identified as "English." English food, per se, is generally sold in tearooms that proclaim their "Englishness" through their décor and dishes (tea cups), menu (scones, clotted cream, etc.), and the emphasis on tea itself. To be authentic, the tea is usually loose leaf rather than in bags, brewed in ceramic teapots, and served with milk or cream and sugar (rather than the more common lemon slices or lemon juice).

Perhaps the English chef best known to Americans is Jamie Oliver, who, in order to promote healthier eating, visited a school lunchroom in West Virginia and on national television expressed his dismay and disgust at what commonly passes in the United States as appropriate food for children. While he brought attention to the poor eating habits and the resulting problems with obesity of this particular town, he also played into the stereotype some Americans hold of the English as "snooty" and condescending. Be that as it may, Oliver's televised cooking show, along with shows by Nigella Lawson and others, is very popular among American viewers.

Further Reading

Berthoff, Rowland Tappan. *British Immigrants in Industrial America, 1790–1950.* Cambridge, MA: Harvard University Press, 1953.

Fischer, David Hackett. *Albion's Seed: Four British Folkways in America.* New York: Oxford University Press, 1989.

Lucy M. Long

RECIPE FOR SMITH ISLAND CAKE, BY ELAINE EFF

During the first half of the seventeenth century, a group of stalwart yeoman farmers left Cornwall and Dorset on the southern coast of Britain for a new life in America. They settled on the eastern shore of Virginia, specifically Accomack County, part of a long spit of land separated from the mainland by the "protein factory" of the Chesapeake Bay to the west and the Atlantic Ocean to the east. In short time, their need for more farmland and less authority pushed them northward to a group of islands in the Bay's Tangier Sound at what is now the Virginia-Maryland line. Originally known as the Russell Isles for a doctor on an early expedition, the cluster of high spots were renamed Smith Island.

The new arrivals lived in numerous scattered, small communities on the high lands or hammocks throughout the three main islands, eventually consolidating as three more populous communities—Rhodes (formerly Rogues) Point, Tylerton, and Ewell, "the capital." The Methodist Church gained a stronghold in the 1850s and ultimately functioned as the local governing body because of the islands' situation in Somerset County, twelve miles off the nearest landfall in Crisfield, Maryland, and the only inhabited offshore island in the state.

Farmers with grazing animals eventually watched their lands succumb to saltwater intrusion as their edges disappeared over time, thus taking a toll on the pastures and crops and the residents' self-sufficiency. For generations, families ate from their own or relations' gardens and herds.

Oddly enough, fig and pomegranate bushes still thrive there in defiance of low winter temperatures and increasingly reliable winds. Mainland communication and commerce was limited until regular private ferry and mail service was instituted in the twentieth century. Electricity did not arrive until the 1950s.

The island economy after the mid-1900s was primarily water based—hard and later soft crabs in summer and shoulder months and oysters in winter. Game and fish in season defined the men's work as well as the local diet.

Layer cakes have been show-off pieces on island dessert tables for centuries. It would not be difficult to find multilayer cakes in Europe as tortes, in the American South or elsewhere, often surrounded by much fanfare. But on Smith Island, ten layer cakes have been appearing on dinner tables, in watermen's "bails" or lunch boxes, and as a welcome offering to guests throughout living memory. However, here it is simply known as "cake."

The search for its roots began when a visitor pointed out that the festive repetition of yellow cake with layers of chocolate "icing" appeared to be more than just cake. The secret of making it "from the stump" or from scratch was embedded in the memory of every Smith Island woman. Variations included moist layers of fig, banana, and coconut cake with generous frosting. More recently chocolate peanut butter or "Reeses's" have found their way into marketable versions. Finding the bakers has always been easy, but discovering the cake's origins has been far less evident. Everyone remembered them always being there. And when pressed, one out of twenty women might even take credit for its invention. Many incorrectly credited the late island hostess, innkeeper, and cookbook author Frances Kitching with the cake's appearance. She helped popularize it with the thousands of guests she served at her home and boarding house over the years. More recently, sixth-generation islander Janice Marshall, who typically learned from her mother and grandmother, remembers that her great-grandmother, Rachel Marsh, in lean years sold or bartered cakes for food or services.

Marshall, who, like her neighbors and kin, turns out a finished cake in less than twenty minutes, recalled the presence of a now-long-forgotten kitchen appliance that likely accounts for the cake's curious form. The kitchen stove was fueled with wood and lacked an oven. Atop the burners was an optional tin-box-like, single-shelved "baker." The likelihood was minimal that a two-inch layer could rise within the device. But a series of quarter-inch pancake-thin layers were almost guaranteed and could be baked within minutes, then iced (or frosted) and voila! A stack of ten (or more) luscious round tiers shared the height of a normal two-layer cake, but with the extra bonus of frosting between each one. The sweet was a tremendous energy boost to the working waterman as he lifted oyster scrapes or crab pots on the Bay, particularly during the long winter outings spent away from home.

A fresh cake was made each weekend or as needed, so there was always a slice for a welcome home or greeting to whomever came by.

In 2008, a group of islanders, proud county and regional spokespersons and aficionados, tirelessly shared the still unknown delicacy statewide with lawmakers and a whole new fan base.* By the end of the legislative session, its virtues were widely praised, and it was designated the "official state dessert of Maryland." Today it is found in diners and four-star restaurants throughout the state and region and is still prepared in island kitchens and commissaries for widespread distribution and enjoyment.

*Senate Bill 315 was stewarded by the leadership and staff of Lower Eastern Shore Heritage Council and Somerset County Tourism along with a cast of hundreds of bakers, letter writers, lobbyists, and committed fans.

"Lill's from the Stump (from Scratch) Cake" by Lill Smith Marshall, from United Methodist Women of Tylerton Methodist Church's *Cooking Up a Storm on Tylerton*, 1991.

Cake

2 cups sugar
2 blocks soft butter
5 eggs
½ cup evaporated milk (an island staple)
½ cup water
2¼ cups sifted flour
1 teaspoon baking powder
1 tablespoon vanilla

Preheat oven to 350 degrees.

Grease and flour baking pans. (Five is ideal number depending on how many fit in your oven. Cakes may result in differing number of layers depending on batter distribution.)

Cream butter and sugar well.

Beat eggs separately and add to creamed mixture.

Add vanilla.

Mix evaporated milk and water together.

Alternately mix in flour and evaporated milk.

Add baking powder in last cup of flour.

Use large spoon or ladle to distribute batter to cake pans.

Place as many layers as your oven accommodates in a preheated oven. Bake for 6 to 8 minutes, until you can touch the top of each layer without it sticking to your fingertip or edges begin to turn golden. Mrs. Kitching suggests you "listen for the szzzz. If you hear it, it is not done."

Remove layers from oven and let cool in pans. Use knife to loosen edges.

Spread your favorite frosting on each layer and on the top and sides.

Clean emptied pans with paper towel, then regrease (and flour), add batter and bake.

Repeat, cook, and ice until completed. (Number of layers will vary.)

Using Packaged Cake Mix
One box Duncan Hines Classic Yellow Cake mix. Prepare as directed.

Grease and flour (if using spray oil, do not flour) at least 5 baking pans.

Place a large spoonful or ladle of cake batter in each pan. Bake at 350 degrees for about 8 minutes, until you can touch the top of each layer without it sticking to your fingertip.

Remove from oven and let cool in pans. Use knife to loosen edges.

Spread your favorite frosting on each layer and on the top and sides.

Chocolate Icing
    2 cups sugar
    1 cup evaporated milk
    5 ounces unsweetened chocolate
    1 stick unsalted butter
    ½ teaspoon vanilla

Put sugar and evaporated milk in a medium saucepan. Cook and stir over medium-low heat until warm. Add chocolate and cook to melt. Cook over medium heat at a slow boil for 10 to 15 minutes, stirring occasionally. Add vanilla. Icing will be thin but thickens as it cools. Add evaporated milk to thin as it thickens while spreading on each layer, top and sides.

Further Reading
Gulledge, Judy H., and Christine A. Gulledge. *Pennywinkle: Oral Histories from Tylerton, Smith Island in the Chesapeake Bay*. Norfolk, VA: Northeast Middle School, 1999.

Horton, Tom. *An Island Out of Time*. New York: W. W. Norton, 1996.

Kitching, Frances, and Susan Stiles Dowell. *Mrs. Kitching's Smith Island Cookbook*. Centerville, MD: Tidewater Press, 1981, 2011. (First edition did not even bother to include Smith Island cake, being such a commonplace, but the 2011 edition featured it.)

Documentary film: *Land & Water, People & Time: Smith Island*, 1996.

Elaine Eff

EQUATORIAL GUINEA

(Middle Africa) Equatorial Guinean or Equatoguinean American
See also: Cameroon, Gabon, São Tomé and Príncipe.

Background
Equatorial Guinea is a relatively small country (smaller than the state of Maryland) on the coast of West Africa. Bordering the Atlantic Ocean, Cameroon, and Gabon, it is tropical, hot, and humid with coastal plains rising to hills. It also includes several volcanic islands, one of which was colonized by the Portuguese in 1474, but other European powers used the region as a base for the slave trade. The area was colonized by the Spanish for 190 years until 1979 and was formerly known as Spanish Guinea, one of Spain's few colonies in Africa. It is the only African nation to have Spanish as its official language. Portuguese and Bantu are also used both officially and vernacularly.

The original natives of Equatorial Guinea were primarily Bantu and Fang as well as pygmies, but numerous slaves from elsewhere in Africa were brought in, both for work and to be traded elsewhere. The population is now primarily Roman Catholic. The country's natural resources include timber, diamonds, and oil. Because of the last, it is now considered one of the wealthiest nations in Africa, but most of the population lives in poverty with little education and poor health care.

There is no information on immigration to the United States, possibly because the numbers are too small to be listed.

Foodways

Equatorial Guinea has very little arable or irrigated land and only few permanent crops, including coffee and cocoa for export. Most farming, however, is at a subsistence level and focuses on raising plantains, yams, and cassava, which serve as staples for every meal. Groundnuts, known as peanuts in the United States, are the basis for sauces and desserts. Fish and seafood is featured, along with "bush meat" (rodents, snakes, monkeys), wild game, goat, and chicken, and they might be wrapped in leaves and grilled or stewed, oftentimes with peanuts into a creamy sauce served over boiled plantains.

These ingredients and preparations methods are typical of the Bantu-based food culture found throughout central Africa, but Equatorial Guinea is unique among African nations in the Spanish influence on the food. Dishes are known by their Spanish names—rice is made into *paella*—and fresh fruit, such as papayas, pineapples, or bananas, is a part of meals and snacks, which is unusual in much of Africa. They also drink palm wine, an alcoholic drink made from sugarcane called *malamba*, and an African tea, *Osang*, as well as locally brewed and imported beer.

Chocolate is also used in cooking, as in one of the unique dishes of the country, *lomandoha*, made from fish. Peanut sauce is very common and is usually made from a combination of onion and garlic simmered with tomato paste and peanut paste, and flavored with oregano, lemon juice, cayenne pepper, bay leaves, salt, pepper, and chili paste. Maggi cubes are frequently added as well. The sauce is used by itself or as the basis for stews, as in the national favorite, *pollo con salsa de cacahuetes* (chicken in peanut sauce). For this dish, a chicken, either whole or cut into pieces, is simmered in peanut sauce. If the sauce is unavailable, the dish is made in a similar manner, with the chicken boiled in water with chopped tomatoes, garlic, and onion (parsley is optional) and seasonings (chili paste, salt, black pepper) for about fifteen minutes. More water and peanut butter is added, and the stew is simmered for forty-five minutes, then served over boiled plantains or rice. Peanut butter is oftentimes used as a substitute or as a shortcut for cooking among middle Africans in urban areas, or in the United States.

Further Reading

BBCNews. Equatorial Guinea Profile. http://www.bbc.com/news/world-africa-13317174.

CeltnetRecipes.com. Equatorial Guinea Peanut Sauce. http://www.celtnet.org.uk/recipes/miscellaneous/fetch-recipe.php?rid=misc-equatorial-guinean-peanut-sauce.

Celtnet.com. Equatorial Guinea Recipes and Home Cookery. http://www.celtnet.org.uk/recipes/equatorial-guinea.php.

CIA World Factbook. Equatorial Guinea. https://www.cia.gov/library/publications/the-world-factbook/geos/ek.html.

iExplore. Equatorial Guinea Study Guide. http://www.iexplore.com/travel-guides/africa/equatorial-guinea/food-and-restaurants.

Migration Policy Institute. African Immigrants in the United States. http://www.migrationpolicy.org/article/african-immigrants-united-states-0.

Wikipedia. Cuisine of Equatorial Guinea. http://en.wikipedia.org/wiki/Cuisine_of_Equatorial_Guinea.

Wikipedia. Equatorial Guinea. http://en.wikipedia.org/wiki/Equatorial_Guinea.

World Travel Guide. Equatorial Guinea Food and Drink. http://www.worldtravelguide.net/equatorial-guinea/food-and-drink.

Lucy M. Long

ERITREA

(East Africa) Eritrean American food
See also: Ethiopia.

Background

Eritrea emerged as its own country only after a century of being ruled by others. It was colonized by Italy in 1890, then administered by Britain beginning in 1941, and then annexed by Ethiopia in 1952. After three decades of violent rebellion, Eritreans achieved their independence in 1991, but since then, their country has been ruled autocratically by a single president (Isaias Afwerkl) and a single political party. As a result of the repressive political environment—no elections, no free press, arbitrary arrests, and no limits on the duration of military service—Eritrea has ranked among the largest sources of African refugees immigrating to the United States in recent years. The United States admitted 1,824 Eritrean refugees in 2013; 1,346 in 2012; and 2,032 in 2011. Other motivations for immigration include extreme poverty and the ravages of droughts on a rural population that depends on subsistence agriculture. The Census Bureau's American Community Survey, conducted from 2008 to 2012, estimated the number of Eritreans residing in the United States as 27,148. Also, many Eritreans hold passports from other countries in Africa where they lived previously as refugees, so that these numbers may actually be higher than officially reported.

Eritreans have settled in metropolitan areas throughout America, and have started restaurants and other businesses clustered in the same enclaves—including Telegraph Avenue in Oakland, U Street in Washington, DC, and Fairfax Avenue in Los Angeles—as the Ethiopian immigrants who share so much of their heritage.

Foodways

Traditional Eritrean foodways are similar to those of the Ethiopians (described in fuller detail in the Ethiopia entry). At the center of both food traditions is *injera*, the spongy, sour, fermented, oversized pancake made from *teff*, a grain similar to millet. *Injera* is placed at the center of the communal table, where diners will tear it apart with their right hands and use it for scooping up spicy stews, sautéed greens, and sauces. *Injera* can be eaten at any meal of the day as well as for snacks and for special occasions. The laborious and skillful art of preparing *injera* is traditionally the woman's role.

While Eritrean and Ethiopian foodways are similar, some significant differences can be traced to history and geography: Eritrea's location on the Red Sea, abundant with fish, ensured a more prominent place for seafood. Eritreans are more likely to cook with tomatoes, a legacy of their country's decades as an Italian colony and also of the somewhat warmer climates created by lower elevations. The Italian influence has also made pasta dishes, such as spaghetti and lasagnas, an enduring part of the Eritrean diet.

In 2009 Tim Carman of the *Washington [DC] City Paper* asked local Eritrean restaurateurs Daniel Mesifeni and Ruth Berhe (the chefs at Dahlak) and Hiyoba Sebhatu (a manager of Enjera Eritrean Restaurant and Bar) about the differences between Eritrean and Ethiopian cuisine. They told him that Eritrean food was "lighter" and somewhat less spicy: Eritreans used less seasoned butter, and their version of seasoned butter wasn't as heavily perfumed with cinnamon and nutmeg. These cooks believed that the Eritreans' use of tomatoes would somewhat reduce the heat created by *berbere*, the spice mixture that's popular in both cuisines (which includes chili peppers, garlic, and ginger as well as many other ingredients). Also, the reporter discovered that Eritreans rely more on Middle Eastern spices (cumin, curry powders) introduced to their homeland during the period of Ottoman Empire rule.

Restaurants and Chefs

The food journalist and historian Harry Kloman, who teaches at the University of Pittsburgh, maintains a list on his website of more than three hundred Ethiopian and/or Eritrean restaurants in America, which can be found in all but ten states. While most of these establishments promote themselves either as

"Ethiopian" or as a combination of both national cuisines, a small but significant minority identify themselves specifically as Eritrean or use Eritrean place names: examples include the New Eritrea Restaurant & Bar in San Francisco and Café Eritrea d'Afrique in Oakland. In 2011 the San Francisco Bay Area, known for its fusion cuisine, also spawned an Irish-Eritrean food truck called Eire Trea. The venture was launched by an Eritrean immigrant, Absulam Abdai, together with Alan Hyland, an Irish immigrant who lived in the same apartment building in San Francisco. Their menu included separate Eritrean and Irish dishes (such as an Eritrean slow-cooked, free-range chicken stew with a tomato-based curry and *berbere*, served on *injera*) as well as several attempts at culinary fusion, which included corned beef cooked with Eritrean spices. The venture received local media attention and showed the beginning of an Eritrean influence on diverse strands of American food culture.

Further Reading

Carman, Tim. "Mild Frontier." *Washington City Paper*, January 9, 2009. http://www.washingtoncitypaper.com/articles/36663/mild-frontier.

Fetini, Alyssa, and Laura Hautala. "East Africans Share Community Values, Plates of Food." *Oakland North*, October 18, 2010. https://oaklandnorth.net/2010/10/18/east-africans-share-community-values-plates-of-food/.

Kauffman, Jonathan. "Eire Trea May Be the World's First Irish-Eritrean Food Truck." *San Francisco Weekly*, February 2, 2012. http://www.sfweekly.com/foodie/2012/02/02/eire-trea-may-be-the-worlds-first-irish-eritrean-food-truck.

Kloman, Harry. *Mesob Across America: Ethiopian Food in the U.S.A.* New York: iUniverse, 2010.

Alan Deutschman

ESTONIA

(Northern Europe) Estonian American Food
See also: Germany, Russia.

Estonian food in the United States shares many traits with the culinary traditions of Germany, Scandinavian, and Baltic Europe due to those regions' large influence on Estonian culture. While it is largely contained within the Estonian diaspora population, Estonian Americans strive to carry on the culinary traditions of their homeland in various ways.

Background

According to Census 2010, there are a total of 28,312 Americans of Estonian descent, most of whom immigrated to the United States after the late 1800s. The failed 1905 revolution in Russia brought the first major wave of Estonians to the United States, but emigration slowed down between 1920, when Estonia became independent from the Soviet Union, and World War II, when a large population of Estonians fled the country in light of Soviet invasion. Most Estonians made their way to Sweden, Germany, or Canada, but fifteen thousand of them came to America, mostly settling in urban areas such as New York and Chicago. These cities continue to serve as cultural hubs for the Estonian American community. Though many immigrants assimilated into American life, many longed to return to their native land, and they did their best to balance the two worlds through a network of Estonian schools, Estonian-language churches, and organizations such as the Estonian World Council, which were dedicated to maintaining the cultural heritage and language that was threatened by the Soviet occupation in the motherland.

Foodways

Estonian cuisine blends local traditions with the influences of Nordic, Russian, and German cooking. In regard to meat, pork is the most common choice, in addition to two of the most common dishes served—*seapraad* (roast beef) and *verivorst* (blood sausage, also called black pudding). Much of Estonian cooking also incorporates fish, most notably salmon and herring. Potatoes, cabbage, carrots, and beets are common vegetables; beets and potatoes are used to make a salad called *rosolje*, while cabbage and carrots are frequently stuffed into *pirukad*, which are small pastries filled with vegetables, meat, or fruit. *Kama*, a mixture of roasted and ground barley, rye, oat, and pea flour then mixed with sour or curdled milk and baked, is a traditional food that is often served as a dessert; it is one of the most distinctive foods in Estonian cuisine. *Kringel*, a braided pastry often featuring cardamom, is a common baked good as well.

Holiday Feasts

A Christmas (*Jõulud*) meal frequently features fresh pork, sauerkraut (*hapukapsad*), roasted potatoes, and *verivorstid* (which were often made in the autumn and saved for the holiday). At the New York Estonian House, many members of the diaspora, along with families, gather to make *verivorstid*, continuing the tradition across the ocean. In addition, *piparkoogid*—thin ginger cookies—are often paired with a pink fluffy dessert called *roosamanna*; the mixture is created by vigorously whipping cranberry juice, farina, and sugar together.

Roosamanna

Ingredients:

    1 cup cranberry or cherry juice, concentrated
    4 cups water
    ¾ cup farina flour (or cream of wheat)
    ½ cup sugar (less if preferred)

Directions:

1. Dilute the juice with water until you have 4 cups of liquid.
2. Add sugar to taste and bring to a boil.
3. Once mixture boils, pour farina flour in quickly, making sure to stir vigorously to avoid clumping.
4. Simmer at low heat for 15 minutes, stirring regularly until the farina has expanded and the mixture is thick and sweet.
5. Add more sugar, if necessary.
6. Pour into a bowl and let cool.
7. Whisk the mixture until the color lightens, and the texture is light and fluffy.
8. Serve with cold milk.

Place in American Culture

As Estonian cuisine is a blend of multiple cultures, many of its items, such as sauerkraut, can be found within larger and more well-known food traditions, such as German and Russian American cooking.

Noted Chefs and Restaurants

As the Estonian American community is a smaller community than most, there are very few restaurants that focus on its cuisine; more often than not, Estonian food is found within the various Estonian cultural centers around the country. New York Estonian House, for example, has served this function since 1947, offering Estonian dishes as well as beverages such as Saku beer, one of the most popular brews in Estonia. The House has attracted attention outside of the local Estonian community, having been featured in the *New York Times* and various food blogs throughout the city; one of its members, Karin Annus Kärner, published one of the major Estonian cookbooks, *Estonian Tastes and Traditions*, in 2005.

Further Reading

Kärner, Karin Annus. *Estonian Tastes and Traditions*. New York: Hippocrene, 2005.

Piiri, R. "The Estonian Food from the Time Past." In *Estonian National Cuisine*, ed. S. Siim, 8–27. Tallinn: Maaleht Ltd., 2006.

Nicholas Hartman

ETHIOPIA

(Eastern Africa) Ethiopian American Food
See also: Eritrea.

Background

Located in the Horn of Africa, Ethiopia is the continent's second-most populous country, with over ninety million people,[1] and the only one that was never a colony, with the exception of the 1936–1941 Italian occupation. Rich in cultural diversity, ecological resources, and political history, Ethiopia is home to more than eighty ethnic groups and languages, the largest being the Oromo (34 percent), followed by Amhara (27 percent), Somali (6.2 percent), and Tigray (6.1 percent).[2] The majority of the population is Ethiopian Orthodox (43.5 percent) or Muslim (33.9 percent), followed by Protestant Christians (18.5 percent). Amharic is the official working language, and English is the language used for secondary and postsecondary education.

The vast majority of Ethiopians live in rural areas, with less than 20 percent in urban areas, and more than 60 percent of the population is under age twenty-four. Ethiopia is one of the poorest countries in the world, ranking 173 of 187 on the United Nations Development Programme's Human Development Index.[3] Agriculture accounts for 46 percent of the nation's Gross Domestic Product and 85 percent of total employment,[4] reflecting the region's long heritage of ecological diversity. Russian botanist Nikolay Vavilov identified it as one of the twelve centers of the world for the domestication of plants, with unique varieties indigenous to Ethiopia of wheat, emmer, barley, sorghum, millet, cowpeas, flax, *teff*, sesame, garden cress, coffee, and okra.[5]

Migration Patterns

Ethiopia's internal and external migration flows have been driven by war, political instability, ethnic conflict, drought, food insecurity, lack of employment, and population pressures.[6,7,8] The outflow of immigrants since the late twentieth century, called the "Ethiopian Diaspora," unfolded in four stages: the first (before 1974) primarily consisted of educated elites; the second (1974–1982) included people fleeing the Derg's "Red Terror," while the third (1982 and 1991) largely comprised family members reuniting with their loved ones; a fourth stage occurred after 1991 when people fled violence and political repression.[9] The Ethiopian Diaspora has found refuge in countries around the world, with the greatest concentrations in the United States, Canada, Italy, Sweden, the United Kingdom, and the Netherlands, and smaller concentrations in the Middle East and other African countries.[10] Two notable characteristics of Ethiopian Diaspora immigrants are their continued engagement in the home country through formal organizations, and remittances back to their families and communities.[11,12,13]

Ethiopian Diaspora in the United States

Approximately 255,000 Ethiopian immigrants and their children live in the United States and account for 0.5 percent of the total US foreign-born population, as of 2014.[14] The majority (60 percent) arrived during or after 2000, making it one of the newest immigrant groups. Ethiopian immigrants in the United States have a median age of thirty-seven years, their average household size is 2.8 members, and 62 percent of those in the second generation have both a mother and a father born in Ethiopia. Despite having similar educational attainment as the general US population, the Ethiopian Diaspora has a lower median annual household income ($36,000 versus $50,000). The share of Ethiopian Diaspora households with high incomes (over $90,000 per year) is 11 percent compared to 25 percent of the general US population. The largest concentrations live in California, Virginia, Maryland, Minnesota, and Texas, and the most densely populated metropolitan areas are Washington, DC, Minneapolis, Seattle, and Atlanta.

Foodways

There is no single "Ethiopian" cuisine; rather, food diversity results from geographic, ethnic, class, socioeconomic status, education, seasonality, changes in land use, and migration patterns.[15] Food traditions in Ethiopia are as numerous as the cultural identities, linguistic traditions, and agro-ecological zones they come from.[16,17] Among the Sidama people from the Southern Nations, Nationalities, and People's Region, one of the staple plants grown by farmers is *ensete*, which the Sidama people use to make foods including *kocho* (a fermented flatbread) and *bula* (a thin drink served to people when they are feeling ill), and they also use the plant for other utilitarian and agricultural functions. Among the Gurage people from the Oromia region, *kitfo* (finely minced raw beef), flavored with *kibbeh* (fermented butter) and various spices, is an important dish, perhaps reflecting the tribe's great value placed on cattle. And among the Tigray people who live in northern Ethiopia, a fertile grain-growing area important for national and regional food security, *ga'at* (also known as *ganfo*, a porridge), made with cooked barley, sorghum, or wheat, is a comfort food often prepared for breakfast and distinguished by the crater filled with butter and spices.

Foodstuffs

Because Ethiopian cuisine is composed of numerous regional and ethnic variations, it is difficult if not impossible to identify a single set of common Ethiopian foods. Yet when asked to describe their food traditions, Ethiopians in diaspora inevitably agree about one food: *injera*. The foundation of an Ethiopian meal—whether in Addis Ababa, Stockholm, or Chicago—is *injera*. The flat, slightly sour, fermented pancake is usually eaten with other foods such as *wats* (stews made with spices and meat, often lamb, chicken, or beef), *shiro* (a stew of spices and beans, which might include lentils, chickpeas, or split peas), and *gomen* (sautéed greens, usually turnip greens, collard greens, or kale). Even if money is short and a household cannot afford sauces, vegetables, or lesser-quality flours like maize or barley, immigrants will sacrifice with lesser-quality *injera* in order to have it. *Injera* is eaten using one's right hand, tearing small pieces of the bread and using them to grasp the meat, beans, and vegetables for eating. The *injera* on which the stews are placed soak up the sauces, and these pieces (messy and soaked in oil as they may be) are consumed so that no food is left on the plate. Thus, *injera* functions as a food, eating utensil, and plate. When the entire "plate" of *injera* is gone, the meal is over. *Injera* is a food that can be—and often is—eaten in different forms for breakfast, lunch, dinner, and snacks. It is both a common, everyday food as well as a food consumed at holidays and festivals.

Injera is a food that reflects not only the cultural and culinary influences of Ethiopia but also its landscape. It can be made from the flour of barley, wheat, rye, or corn, but the traditional cereal crop is *teff* (*Eragrostis tef*). *Teff* is a tiny, round grain closely resembling millet. It requires certain climate conditions for growth, and it does best in high altitudes, with moderate rainfall, mild temperatures, and plenty of sunlight. Ethiopia provides one of the few climates in the world where *teff* can flourish. *Teff* can be red, white, or brown. It is a nutritious grain, high in protein, iron, fiber, calcium, potassium, and essential amino acids. Despite its nutritional density, the availability of *teff* is limited by its high cost, difficulty to harvest, and low availability. It is highly labor intensive to process, limiting its appeal to most of the general public except to the Ethiopian Diaspora and those familiar with it.

In Ethiopia, cooking and making *injera* are women's roles. Rural homes still rely on cooking with wood or charcoal as fuel, requiring skill and a learned practice in order not to waste fuel, injure oneself, or burn the food. Because of their cooking responsibilities, women chiefly manage household resources and ensure all family members get enough to eat. Ethiopians from the diaspora living in the United States often maintain this traditional gender role in the kitchen, particularly for making *injera*.

However, if this food tradition is to continue in diaspora, it will survive only with adaptation and innovation.

Procurement/Preparation

Injera is a time- and knowledge-intensive food to make, both in Ethiopia and in the United States, and thus it is not prepared daily. In rural Ethiopia, a household's mother or an aunt may make it a couple of times a week, cooking a large batch to last a few days and keeping it in a *mesob*, a large container handcrafted with grass and often colorfully painted. In urban areas of Ethiopia, households increasingly buy *injera* from a grocery store or market vendor. For Ethiopians in diaspora in the United States, most women can describe the steps for making *injera*, but they may or may not produce it themselves. The quality and grind size of *teff* flour, temperature, altitude, cooking implements, and water quality for making *injera* are different in the United States from the resources that would be used in Ethiopia, and most Ethiopian American recipes have been adapted to adjust to the altitude, climate, availability, quality of *teff* flour, and different cooking surfaces. But when a family yearns for the taste of their home in the Highlands of Ethiopia, or when a mother wants her children to remember where they come from when she describes her extended family back in Hawassa, these are times when adaptation and innovation are employed to create a recipe for *injera* that reflects traditional values and processes, combined with New World ingredients and utensils.

Injera Recipe Adaptation for the United States

The following adapted recipe for preparing *injera* in a low-altitude region of the United States includes New World ingredients and resources.

Prior to cooking, assemble the following ingredients and supplies:

mitad (pan on which to cook the *injera*)
lid for the *mitad*
sourdough starter
blender
large mixing bowl
sifter
teff flour (2 kinds, white and brown)
self-rising whole-wheat flour and barley flour
lukewarm water
something large and flat on which to place the *injera* when it is removed
coarse sea salt
paper towels and cloth towel

1. Obtain and prepare the starter 2 to 3 days in advance.

Some recipes use yeast as a starter, but it is ideal to obtain an *injera* starter from an experienced *injera* maker willing to share some. It is important to have a healthy, active starter or the *injera* will neither act nor taste right. Not "acting right" means it will not bake properly on the *mitad* by either sticking or not forming bubbles on top. [Note: There are *injera* recipes that use yeast rather than a starter, which may be easier to follow.]

2. The night before cooking the *injera*, mix 2 cups *teff* flour (1 white, 1 brown) with 2 cups of starter. Knead for about 10 minutes until a stiff dough forms. Slowly add water, a little at a time, until the mixture is the consistency of thin pancake batter. Cover batter with a towel and let rest overnight near a stove or warm place.

3. In the morning, the batter should have separated, with a layer of liquid on top. Drain the liquid. Reserve 2 cups of starter for the current batch and store the remainder in a container in the refrigerator. Blend the 2 cups starter, 2 cups of self-rising flour, and 1 cup of barley flour in a blender, adding enough filtered water to get it to a thin consistency. Next, combine the *teff* starter mixture with the wheat/barley flours in a large bowl. Once thoroughly mixed, cover with a towel and set it in a warm spot to rise for a few hours. Once

the batter has risen, place in the refrigerator until ready to use.

4. Prepare the *mitad* for cooking. A *lefse* grill can be used in place of a *mitad*. Once heated to medium-high heat (maybe 450 degrees), sprinkle coarse sea salt on the *mitad*. With a slightly damp paper towel, wipe the salt in a circular motion on the pan, which removes dirt or debris and helps prevent the *injera* from sticking. Never use oil or metal utensils on the pan or they may scratch and ruin the surface.

5. Remove batter from the refrigerator and organize utensils for pouring and removing the *injera*. Scoop the batter into a creamer or similar container with a little spout for easier pouring. The batter should be a little thinner than pancake batter, with an earthy smell reminiscent of toasted rye or barley. To make the *injera*, pour the batter, starting at the outer edge, making concentric circles toward the center until the batter covers the pan. Immediately place the lid on the *mitad* and wait about 30 seconds for it to cook. When you remove the lid, the *injera* should have formed thousands of small bubbles like a pancake. The bread should have just begun to peel along the edges, making it easier to peel the *injera* from the pan with your fingers than a utensil that may rip it. With one hand, gently lift half of the *injera* onto a flat tray or straw mat while the other hand holds the tray. Quickly pull the entire *injera* onto the tray without tearing it. Wipe the surface of the *mitad* with another paper towel and sea salt, and start the procedure over. Each time you remove the *injera*, place it onto a "cooling" tray before stacking it onto the pile of cooked *injera*. It is important to keep layers separate until cool or they will stick together.

Watching Ethiopian cooks gracefully and quickly produce *injera* proves how food production can be both science and art. Making *injera* requires both scientific and culinary knowledge in order to be perfect, and practice improves the final product. Because it is made from relatively few ingredients, quality ingredients and careful attention to every step in the process make sure it will come out right.

Meal System

While the foods themselves vary across Ethiopia's regions, consistency in the roles and social contracts these foods convey emphasize sharing with others and treating others as family. One example is the way in which Ethiopian meals are served, reflecting relational ties: traditionally, a family eats a meal together from a single, large piece of *injera* one to two feet in diameter, with the main stew placed in the middle and side dishes around it. Everyone tears off a piece of *injera* to use as a utensil to grab a bite from this common plate. A tradition among cherished friends is called *gursha*, a sign of friendship, generosity, and kindness, where one feeds the other a bite of *injera*, carefully grabbing a morsel of meat with a piece of bread and putting it into the friend's mouth. Whenever an Ethiopian household has a visitor, they are expected to serve coffee with a light snack, such as *injera* or popcorn.

For a variety of reasons, including Western schedules, changing personal food preferences, health/dietary restrictions, time constraints for making homemade *injera*, affordability, and convenience, most Ethiopian immigrant families in the United States no longer eat *injera* at every meal or from a common dish, and seldom outside of celebrations and holidays do they feed each other. While the daily food habits of Ethiopians in diaspora increasingly reflect Western ways, markets, local foods, and flavors, a traditional meal served to guests or for special occasions will still adhere to tradition in featuring key Ethiopian ingredients that emphasize freshness, spices, abundance in vegetables, lack of refined flours, and lack of sweeteners.

Because it is very difficult to find or obtain the large *mitad* required to make communal-meal-sized *injera* in the United States, an adaptation is to serve meal components in a buffet style, with food arranged at the center of a table or along a counter to take full advantage of the fragrant colors and abundant smells. No forks are necessary because the *injera* still serves as a utensil. Plates and napkins can be placed at the head of the buffet line. Each guest receives a plate on which to place a piece of *injera* followed by the *wats* and vegetables spooned on top. To eat, the guest rips a piece of *injera* with the right hand and uses it to scoop food into the mouth. Some may add extra *mitmita* alongside the *kitfo*. A meal is over when the final person finishes the last bite of *injera*.

Place in American Culture

Perhaps because Ethiopian dishes are time-consuming to prepare, or because Ethiopian immigrants are still a relatively new population in the United States, knowledge and familiarity with this cuisine is limited chiefly to urban areas with high concentrations of the new immigrants. Americans may associate coffee with Ethiopia, but most remain unfamiliar with the traditional way to make it by washing and roasting green coffee beans, grinding them, and then letting them steep in a traditional pot made out of clay called a *jebena*. When served, Ethiopian coffee is thick, rich, and poured in small proportions (like espresso), often in a traditional coffee ceremony that serves as a social event to honor social ties.

Because of its gluten-free characteristics, *teff* flour is increasingly available in natural and organic food stores in the United States as an alternative to wheat, and there are even a few producers growing *teff* as a specialty crop (such as the Teff Company in Idaho[18]). Yet most Americans may not be aware of the role the grain plays in Ethiopian and immigrant foodways, nor of Ethiopian cooks' preference for organically grown *teff* to guarantee good flavor and quality in *injera*. The different *teff* types, best identified by color (white, red, and brown), have different flavor profiles and nutritional value: lighter *teff* has a mild, nutty flavor, while darker *teff* is earthier and reminiscent of roasted grains.

In Amharic, *teff* comes from the word *teffa*, which means "lost," perhaps a reference to the grain's very small size, which makes it difficult to grind. The irony of its name is that what makes it unique and gives it a competitive edge also makes it difficult to sustain by farmers, processors, and consumers. What factors will work to sustain this food tradition, in the face of internal and external forces in Ethiopia and the United States, where those who customarily eat *injera* seldom make it and instead rely upon markets, restaurants, and women elders in their families to make it? If new generations of Ethiopians and Ethiopians in diaspora are not learning the art of *injera* making, will market demand for *injera* be enough to sustain this art and tradition?

Ethiopian Restaurants, Markets, and Chefs

Ethiopian foodstuffs may be found in the United States in specialty markets, especially in urban areas with high concentrations of Ethiopian immigrants. Besides *teff*, typical foodstuffs may include *berbere* (spice mixture of chilies, garlic, salt, cardamom, black pepper, and other spices[19]), *bulla* (powdered enset leaves that can be reconstituted with water to make a traditional drink), *koseret* and *beso bela* (spices used to make *niter kibbeh*, the Ethiopian spiced butter), *nech azmud* (white cumin seeds), *shiro* (mixture of ground chickpeas with spices that is reconstituted with water, garlic, and onions to make the popular sauce, *shiro wat*), and *tikur azmud* (black cumin seeds). Some businesses offer online sales of foodstuffs, traditional cooking utensils, and cookbooks.

Besides markets that have emerged to cater to Ethiopian immigrant food traditions, Ethiopian restaurants have flourished, appealing to diverse communities in the urban ethnic neighborhoods with the highest densities of Ethiopians in diaspora. Writer and Ethiopian food historian Harry Kloman, who regularly updates an extensive list of Ethiopian markets and restaurants, estimates that over three hundred Ethiopian restaurants now exist in the United States, in all but ten states.[20] The price points may vary, but seldom is there a really high-end, high-priced Ethiopian meal. It would defy the communal spirit of Ethiopian meals. Most restaurants emphasize traditional Ethiopian dishes with minimal "fusion" across cuisines, but broaden their offerings to help appeal to varying preferences (e.g., offering rice rather than *injera*). As well, many restaurants show transitions in gender roles, where male and female cooks may be found, as well as cooks and restaurant workers from varied ethnic backgrounds. In addition to restaurants, Ethiopian food carts, a convenient way to enjoy Ethiopian food on the run, have emerged, especially in settings adjacent to college campuses.[21]

The Ethiopian-born, Swedish-raised celebrity chef, restaurateur, and cookbook writer Marcus Samuelsson has brought international attention to Ethiopian cuisine through Restaurant Aquavit in New York City, Nordic-African fusion cuisine, TV performances, and as guest chef for an Obama state dinner at the White House. Recipes for selected Ethiopian food classics, adapted for Western cooks, may be found in his *The Soul of a New Cuisine: A Discovery of the Foods and Flavors of Africa*.

NOTES

1. Central Intelligence Agency, *The World Fact Book: Ethiopia*, accessed on October 31, 2014, https://www.cia.gov/library/publications/the-world-factbook/geos/et.html#.
2. CIA, *The World Fact Book: Ethiopia*.
3. United Nations Development Programme, *Human Development Report 2014: Sustaining Human Progress: Reducing Vulnerabilities and Building Resilience* (New York, 2014), accessed on 10/31/2014, http://hdr.undp.org/sites/default/files/hdr14-report-en-1.pdf.
4. World Bank, *World Development Indicators: Ethiopia* (Washington, DC, 2013), accessed on October 31, 2014, http://data.worldbank.org/country/ethiopia#cp_wdi.
5. Gary Nabhan, *Where Our Food Comes From: Retracing Nikolay Vavilov's Quest to End Famine* (Washington, DC: Island Press, 2008).
6. B. Berhanu, and M. White, "War, Famine, and Female Migration in Ethiopia, 1960–1989," in *Economic Development and Cultural Change* 49, no. 1 (2000): 91–113.
7. A. Bariagaber, "States, International Organizations and the Refugee: Reflections on the Complexity of Managing the Refugee Crisis in the Horn of Africa," *Journal of Modern African Studies* 37, no. 4 (1999): 597–619.
8. A. De Waal, *Evil Days: Thirty Years of War and Famine in Ethiopia* (Human Rights Watch, 1991).
9. Tassé Abye, *Parcours d'Éthiopiens en France et aux Etats-Unis: De Nouvelles Formes de Migrations* (Paris: L'Harmattan, 2004), as represented in A. Terrazas, "Beyond Regional Circularity: The Emergence of an Ethiopian Diaspora," *Migration Policy Institute*, June 1, 2007, http://www.migrationpolicy.org/article/beyond-regional-circularity-emergence-ethiopian-diaspora.
10. S. Fransen and K. Kuschminder, *Migration in Ethiopia: History, Current Trends and Future Prospects* (Migration and Development Country Profiles: Maastricht Graduate School of Government, 2009).
11. D. Aredo, *Migrant Remittances, Shocks and Poverty in Urban Ethiopia: An Analysis of Micro Level Panel Data* (Addis Ababa, Ethiopia: Addis Ababa University, 2005).
12. Migration Policy Institute, "The Ethiopian Diaspora in the United States," Rockefeller Foundation-Aspen Institute Diaspora Program (RAD), July 2014.

13. K. G. Giorgis and M. Molla, "The Impact of International Remittance on Poverty, Household Consumption and Investment in Urban Ethiopia: Evidence from Cross-Sectional Measures," in *International Migration and Development in Eastern and Southern Africa*, edited by Assefaw Bariagaber (Addis Ababa: Organization for Social Science Research in Eastern and Southern Africa, 2014).
14. Migration Policy Institute, "The Ethiopian Diaspora."
15. Paul Winters et al., "Sowing the Seeds of Social Relations: The Role of Social Capital in Crop Diversity," Food and Agriculture Organization of the United Nations, Agricultural and Development Economics Division, December 2006.
16. M. Worede et al., "Keeping Diversity Alive: An Ethiopian Perspective," in *Genes in the Field*, edited by S. Brush (Ottawa, Canada: International Development Research Center, 2000).
17. M. A. Altieri and L. C. Merrick, "In Situ Conservation of Crop Genetic Resources through Maintenance of Traditional Farming Systems," *Economic Botany* 41 (1987): 86–96.
18. http://www.teffco.com/.
19. *Saveur Magazine* has a nice recipe for homemade *berbere*: http://www.saveur.com/article/Recipes/Ethiopian-Spice-Mix.
20. See Mesob Across America, http://ethiopianfood.wordpress.com/shopping/; restaurants such as Alem Ethiopian Village in Milwaukee, Wisconsin; Ethiopian Diamond (http://www.ethiopiandiamondcuisine.com/), Chicago, Illinois; and Fasika (http://www.fasika.com/menu.html), St. Paul, Minnesota.
21. Food carts such as Dalo's Kitchen (http://www.dalos-kitchen.com/), Portland, Oregon; Fojol Brothers (http://fojol.com/), Washington, DC; and Mesob at the Curb (https://www.facebook.com/Mesobatthecurb), Seattle, Washington.

Further Reading

Cookbooks

Campbell, Hirut. *Traditional Ethiopian Cuisine*. Bloomington, IN: XLibris, 2014.

Deresse, Lena. *Cooking with Imaye: Ethiopian Cuisine Straight from Mom's Kitchen*. CreateSpace Independent Publishing Platform, 2014.

Ketsela Belayneh, Aster. *The Recipe of Love: An Ethiopian Cookbook*. Toronto: A. K. Belayneh, 2006.

Mesfin, Daniel J., comp. and ed. *Exotic Ethiopian Cooking: Society, Culture, Hospitality, and Traditions*. Rev. ed. Falls Church, VA: Ethiopian Cookbook Enterprises, 2006.

Samuelsson, Marcus. *The Soul of a New Cuisine: A Discovery of the Foods and Flavors of Africa*. Hoboken, NJ: John Wiley & Sons, 2006.

Sillan, Donna. *Sidama Sustenance: Foodways of the Sidama Tribe*. Mill Valley, CA: Blurb, 2012.

Solomon, Lydia. *How to Cook Delicious Food: Simple, Delicious, and Easy Recipes*. CreateSpace Independent Publishing Platform, 2013.

Yayehyirad, Mulusew. *Ethiopian Kitchen: You Can Make Injera*. Madison, WI: 2011.

Other References

Food and Agriculture Organization. *The State of the World's Genetic Resources for Food and Agriculture*. Rome, Italy: Food and Agriculture Organization, 1998.

Larsen, Hanne Pico, and Suzanne Österlund-Pötzsch. "'Ubuntu in Your Heart': Ethnicity, Innovation and Playful Nostalgia in Three 'New Cuisines' by Chef Marcus Samuelsson." *Food, Culture and Society* 15, no. 4 (December 2012): 623–42.

McCann, James C. *Stirring the Pot: A History of African Cuisine*. London and Athens: Hurst & Company and Ohio University Press, 2010.

Heidi Busse, Mulusew Yayehirad, Almaz Yimam, Janet C. Gilmore

F

FALKLAND ISLANDS/MALVINAS

(South America) Falkland Islander American Food

See also: England, Wales, Scotland, Argentina.

The Falkland Islands are an archipelago in the South Atlantic Ocean, east of Argentina. It is a British overseas territory and is perhaps most familiar to Americans because of the 1982 invasion by Argentina, in which Britain's rule was affirmed.

Many of the almost three thousand residents of the Falkland Islands are descended from settlers from Wales and Scotland who came to the islands as early as 1833. They are British citizens and frequently attend universities in the United Kingdom. There is no indication of Islanders immigrating to the United States.

Culturally, Falkland Islanders are for the most part British, and their food reflects that. Sheep are raised on the island, supplying lamb and mutton. Beef and fish are also common, along with the tea and cakes or biscuits (cookies) typical of British snacks and meals. Spanish is also spoken by many of the residents since those are the official languages of the closest countries, Chile and Argentina, and some traditions, such as the drinking of tea from the leaves of *yerba mate*, from those cultures may have been borrowed.

Further Reading

Bernhardson, Wayne. *Moon Patagonia: Including the Falkland Islands*. Altona, Manitoba: Friesens, 2011.

Cawkell, Mary. *The History of the Falkland Islands*. Oswestry, England: Anthony Nelson Ltd., 2001.

Wagstaff, William. *Falkland Islands: The Bradt Travel Guide*. Buckinghamshire, England: Bradt Travel Guides, Ltd., 2001.

Lucy M. Long

FEDERATED STATES OF MICRONESIA

(Micronesia, Oceania)

See entry on Micronesia (Micronesian American).

Micronesia includes: Guam, Marshall Islands, Palau, Kiribati, Federated States of Micronesia, Nauru, Northern Mariana Islands.

FIJI

(Melanesia, Oceana) Pacific Islander American Food, Fijian American Food, Soloman Islander Food, Papuan American Food

See entry for Melanesia (includes Fiji, New Caledonia, Papua New Guinea, Solomon Islands, Vanuatu, West Papua).

See also: Micronesia, Polynesia.

FINLAND

(Northern Europe) Finnish American Food

Background

Finns began to arrive in the United States in large numbers in the late nineteenth and early twentieth centuries. These immigrants did not represent a cross-section of Finland's population but were drawn from some regions and social strata more than others. Each had a discrete subculture, including foodways, and some regions, social groups, and classes were more influential in shaping the new Finnish American culture than others. This developing ethnic culture also drew from mainstream America and the cultures of other ethnic groups. Finnish American foodways and culture today are the result of multiple generations of development.

The majority of this first generation of immigrants came from western Finland. Finnish America today also includes Finland Swedes, Sami, Karelians, and Finnish Indians, each subculture with its own variation of Finnish American foodways. Since the last decades of the twentieth century, there has been an influx of Finnish nationals settling in the United States.

Michigan's Upper Peninsula is home to the largest, most dense Finnish American population; Minnesota is a close second. This region is the center of Finnish America, where communities maintain close contact, traditions are strong and viable, many cultural activists are located, and cultural activities are initiated. Other pockets of Finnish Americans are located in New England and upper New York, in zones extending from western Pennsylvania across northeast Ohio to Detroit and Chicago, from the Dakotas to Wyoming, Montana, and Idaho, from Washington and Oregon to northern California, and from southern California to Arizona, and in Florida.

Foodways

The process of immigrant Finns becoming ethnic Finnish Americans can be seen in their foodways. Some immigrant foods from Finland now exist only as memories; some dishes were abandoned and others preserved; other dishes nearly forgotten have been revived. Changes in the function, significance, and symbolism of foods took place. Dishes in Finland considered everyday have special meaning in the United States in expressing Finnish American ethnic identity.

Some Finnish Americans claim that the virtues of thrift and simplicity guided the development of their traditional style of cooking. *Mojakka*, for example, is made from readily available local ingredients; it is simple, quick to prepare, and inexpensive. This thin stew of meat or fish resembles a dish in Finland, but the term, *mojakka*, is of unknown origin. Some versions are clearly poor food: chunks of ring bologna, potatoes, and onion cooked in water and flavored with allspice. More commonly, it is made with beef or fish. It is the kind of dish that can be expanded to feed many, and it is often served at large community gatherings and work parties.

Fish, game, and wild berries are important items in the diets of Finnish Americans living in regions where these foods are plentiful. Especially noteworthy are the "caviar" from eggs of freshly caught lake trout, pickled herring, salted salmon, smoked fish, venison jerky and sausage, and berry soups. Salted salmon and smoked fish may be eaten with dilled boiled potatoes. Salted salmon is a favorite in scalloped potatoes, and fresh salmon and trout are favorites in fish stew (*kalamojakka*). *Lutefisk*, a dried, salted ocean cod, is eaten by some Finns at Christmas; however, it is not a widely shared tradition. *Burbot*, known locally as lawyer, is a freshwater cod known only in the deep, cold waters of the north country. Traditionally, Finns trap them as they swim up streams to spawn in December and January. However, commercial fishermen also catch them inadvertently in their nets and on lines, which they used to stack on piers for people to take for fertilizer. It is still considered junk fish by most, and only Finns in the Upper Peninsula were known to eat this ugly fish, which they say is the poor man's lobster. Commonly, they fry it and make a fish stew (*kalamojakka*). In recent years, however, *burbot* has become something of a delicacy and is served seasonally in a few lakeside restaurants in Wisconsin and Minnesota. In Finland *burbot* is considered a delicacy, and its caviar is especially savored.

A dish of historic importance in northern Europe is pea soup. Finnish Americans, like the Finns, make it with split green peas and some cook it with a ham bone or pieces of ham.

This soup is traditionally served in Finland on Thursday with crepelike pancakes and jam for dessert; some families in the United States have maintained this tradition, but many eat pea soup on any day. Pea soup and pancakes are traditional in Palo, Minnesota, on *Laskiainen* (Shrove Tuesday), a winter day on which there is a sliding festival.

Finns have a reputation as coffee drinkers, and the coffee pot is always on. When entering a Finnish home, you are always served coffee, either initially or before leaving, and coffee should never be served without pastry or food of some kind. A favorite with coffee is *pulla* or *nisu*. Nothing is more symbolic of Finnishness than this ubiquitous cardamom sweet bread always present at Finnish American functions and in homes. In addition, the coffee table may hold a variety of pastries, cakes, and open-faced sandwiches. Women are highly competitive about their pastries, and the coffee table is their display case.

Dairy products—milk, cream, buttermilk, and butter—are important staples in the Finnish American diet. Milk, for example, is the preferred drink by many at meals. Two iconic, traditional milk products are *viili*, similar to yogurt, and *juusto* or *leipajuusto*, a fresh, baked cheese. Immigrants brought their starters for *viili* from Finland. *Viili* is made with a spoonful of the previous batch. Traditionally, *viili* is made with nonhomogenized whole milk, which when clabbered forms a thin layer or crust of cream on the top. When nonhomogenized milk is unavailable, Finns resort to using homogenized milk. *Viili* should have a ropey, gelatinous consistency and a pleasantly mild taste from the lactic acid. When a spoonful is lifted out of the bowl, it should stretch. It is this stringy, slippery texture that repulses non-Finns and some Finnish Americans. Despite some negative opinions about *viili*, those who love it eat it as a snack or as a light meal with, for example, buttered rye bread and salt salmon. Some eat it with sugar and cinnamon.

Juusto or *leipajuusto*, known as "squeaky cheese" because it squeaks when one bites into it, is a fresh cheese, baked in the oven or broiler until lightly browned. Made with raw milk, it is at its best slightly warm from the oven. However, selling raw milk in many states is illegal and, by law, cheese from raw milk must be aged sixty days; consequently, traditional *juusto* is illegal. Nevertheless, Finns with friends or family with cows still make traditional cheese with raw milk. Some entrepreneurs make the cheese with pasteurized milk, which produces a rubbery consistency and a cooked milk flavor. There is, however, a steady decline of families with cows, and fewer individuals are making *juusto*. In desperation, some individuals without access to *juusto* have begun to make it using a combination of powdered milk and heavy cream. This demonstrates the centrality of *juusto* to Finnish American life. It is a treat and eaten on special occasions, offered on coffee tables along with pastries, and it plays an important role in ceremonial and ritual traditions.

Karelian *piirakka* is a "pie" traditional to eastern Finland but now served all over the country and known to most Finnish Americans. It is made with a thin rye, oblong crust about five inches in length. It is open at the top and filled with mashed potatoes or rice pudding and eaten with egg butter, chopped hard-boiled eggs mixed with butter, which is placed on top of the pie while it is still warm.

Finns love their bread, and it is present at every meal. Finnish rye bread is unlike most rye breads available in the United States. It and rye hardtack (also called crispy bread) are favorites, as is *rieska*—a flat, unleavened bread of oat, barley, or potato flour. Finnish bakeries on the East Coast and in Florida mail their highly valued *hapanleipa* (sour rye bread) all over the United States; enterprising home bakers in some locales are also offering Finnish rye bread.

Two typical Finnish American salads are sliced cucumbers and dill, dressed with a sweet and sour dressing, and beet salad: cooked sliced beets and carrots, plus any combination of cooked potatoes, boiled eggs, and pickles, raw onion, and pickled herring, dressed with sour cream or sour cream and mayonnaise.

Other vegetables include rutabaga and carrot casseroles, eaten everyday and a must on holiday tables. Potatoes are an all-time favorite eaten in many homes daily. It is said that without potatoes, one hasn't eaten. They can be baked, boiled with or without skins, cooked in milk and butter and eaten as a soup, or mashed.

Although eaten year round, rice pudding served with fruit soup is a tradition at Christmas. Rice is parboiled in water and then slowly cooked in whole milk. Fruit soup is often of dried fruits (prunes, raisins, etc.), but fresh or frozen berries and rhubarb sauce are also favorites. Prune tarts, made with a doughlike puff pastry and shaped into stars with a dab of prune butter in the center, are another traditional food at Christmas. Whipped "air" pudding is made from the juice of cranberries, a substitute for lingonberries, and farina; while still warm, it is whipped until it expands. It is eaten with cream.

A discussion about Finnish American foodways is not complete without mentioning two regional dishes: pasty, a dough-encased meat, potato, onion, rutabaga, and carrot baked turnover, and potato sausage. Pasty arrived in the Upper Peninsula, Michigan, in the mid-1800s with Cornish miners and was disseminated by workers in the woods and mines of the region. Finnish workers picked it up quickly, and soon Finnish women were making it, adding carrots and butter and claiming it as their own. As pasty spread, this monoethnic food (Cornish) became a multiethnic, Upper Peninsula regional dish. It became so engrained in Finnish culture that second- and third-generation children grew up thinking it was a Finnish dish. This belief was strengthened and perpetuated by Finnish ethnic church dinners that served pasty. It had become a Finnish dish in the Upper Peninsula.

Potato sausage is a specialty of Värmland, Sweden, and a favorite of Finns in the north country around Lake Superior. It is available in stores catering to Swedes and Finns and is also made at home, often by a male member of the family. The sausage is made of potatoes, pork and beef, onions, salt and pepper. It is cooked in salted water; some also fry it in butter afterward.

Everyday Meals

An everyday meal in a Finnish American household might include one Finnish dish to enhance the meal, or it might not include any identifiable Finnish dishes. Yet this meal could be Finnish because of the way it is prepared. For example, allspice is often added in beef stews and with pot roasts. Dill is more than a garnish; it is generously used with fish, in some salads, and on sandwiches.

A popular breakfast is oatmeal cooked in milk or water, often eaten with a glob of butter, some brown sugar and cold milk on top, rye bread with butter or toast with jam, fruit juice, coffee, and milk.

Pannukakku or *kropsu*, an oven pancake, is one of the Finnish American comfort foods. It can be eaten as a snack, light supper, breakfast, or dessert.

3 eggs
2 cups of milk
1 cup of all-purpose flour
a dash of salt and sugar

Slowly whip the flour into the egg and milk mixture until all has been absorbed and the mixture is smooth. Add salt and sugar. Let this mixture sit for about an hour. Heat the oven to 400 degrees. Place 4 glass pie pans in the oven and melt a generous heaping tablespoon of butter in each. Divide the above mixture between the pans. Bake until the mixture puffs up and becomes golden. When you remove them from the oven, the *kropsu* will deflate. Remove from pans and serve one *kropsu* per person with jams; lingonberry and cloudberry jams are favorites.

Supper might be potato sausage, beet salad, rye bread, and beer. Sunday dinner is often special. It might be a pot roast with potatoes, carrots, and onions, seasoned with whole allspice. There would be bread and butter and a lettuce salad, possibly with other vegetables if in the summer, without if winter. Milk would be the beverage. Dessert might be a fruit pie.

Festive Meals

Dinner on Christmas Eve is a festive meal. Depending on the region, it might include salted salmon or smoked lake trout and pickled herring of various kinds (in wine, in sour cream, etc.), dips and a vegetable tray, a baked ham (or goose, leg of lamb, roast beef, venison), beet salad, fruit or gelatin salad, rutabaga and carrot casseroles, a variety of breads and butter, pickles, prune tarts, rice pudding with fruit soup, variety of cookies, pies, and fruitcake. The meal could include all or some of these foods. It could also include other ethnic or mainstream dishes representing other members of the family.

Place in American Culture and Restaurants

The outsider's perception of Finnish American food depends on locality and degree of familiarity. In places with a high density of Finns, the food is more familiar to the general population, and some restaurants offer a couple of Finnish dishes on their menus, and in a few towns in the north country there are one or two Finnish American cafes. Here Finns have a reputation as bakers and coffee drinkers. Without contact with Finnish Americans, however, the mainstream does not know this cuisine or generalizes the foodways as the same as that of modern Finland. This notion is perpetuated by upscale Nordic restaurants in Minneapolis and New York City, where one or two Finnish dishes, often only slightly resembling the original, are on the menus.

Traditional Finnish American foodways, a legacy of immigrant ancestors, have endured for over one hundred years. However, these ethnic foods are not static. Finnish American foodways are constantly in flux as an amalgamation of regional and social differences in food and foodways, and the influences from Finland, American mainstream, and other ethnic cooking are still taking place. Women refer to cookbooks to refresh their memories about Finnish recipes and to learn new ones. Finns have greater access to raw materials today, and many travel to Finland, where they learn about the food there. Increasingly, Finns are cooking pan-Finnish, adopting dishes from different regions of Finland not known to their immediate families. The culinary legacy is ever changing.

Further Reading

Hannu, Mary Jo, and Robert Craig. "Rye and Roots: A Study Exploring Finnish-American Foodways and Ethnic Identity." *McNair Scholarly Review*, 19–44. Duluth, MN: The College of St. Scholastica, 1997.

Kaplan, Anne R., Marjorie A. Hoover, and Willard B. Moore. "The Finns." In *The Minnesota Ethnic Food Book*, 145–62. St. Paul: Minnesota Historical Society Press, 1986.

Lockwood, William G. "United States: Ethnic Cuisines." In *Encyclopedia of Food and Culture*, vol. 3, 442–46. Edited by Solomon H. Katz and William W. Weaver. New York: Charles Scribner and Sons, 2005.

Lockwood, William G., and Yvonne R. Lockwood. "Pasties in Michigan: Foodways, Interethnic Relations and Cultural Dynamics." In *Creative Ethnicity*, eds. Stephen Stern and John Allan Cicala, 3–20. Logan: Utah State University Press, 1991.

Lockwood, William G., and Yvonne R. Lockwood. "Finnish American Milk Products in the

Northwoods." In *Milk: Beyond Dairy*. Proceedings of the Oxford Symposium on Food and Cookery, ed. Harlan Walker. Totnes, England: Prospect Books, 2000, 232–39.

Lockwood, Yvonne R. "'Put the Coffee Pot On': Coffee Table and Visiting Traditions in Finnish America." In *Time for Food: Everyday Food and Changing Meal Habits in a Global Perspective*, ed. Patricia Lysaght, 157–69. Proceedings of the 18th International Commission for Ethnological Food Research, Turku, Finland, 2012.

Ojakangas, B. A. *The Finnish Cookbook*. New York: Crown, 1964.

Yvonne R. Lockwood

FRANCE

(Western Europe) French American Food
See also: Cajun, Creole, Canada.

Background

The French first began exploring North America in 1524; in 1541, the first French colony was established in Cap-Rouge, in present-day Quebec. It would be the first of numerous failed attempts at establishing colonies on the part of the French, who had to contend with cold winters, disease (mainly scurvy), and attacks by native residents and British colonists.

At its height, around 1750, New France territories spread from Hudson Bay and the Hudson Strait to the Gulf of Mexico and from Terre-Neuve to the Great Plains. This territory was greatly reduced—ceded to British forces—during the Seven Years' War (1756–1763), and the French gave up any claim to North American territory with the Louisiana Purchase of 1803.

Starting early in the seventeenth century and until the beginning of the eighteenth century, French immigrants (mostly from the Vienne region of France) settled in the colony of Acadia, a territory that covered modern-day eastern Quebec, New Brunswick, Nova Scotia, Prince Edward Island, and northern Maine. Following a series of conflicts, in 1713 Acadia fell to the British, and between 1755 and 1764 Acadians were forcibly removed in *le Grand Dérangement* (The Great Upheaval). While most Acadians were deported to France, many eventually resettled in Louisiana, in some cases after first moving to Saint-Domingue and escaping the Haitian revolution. The word *Acadien* evolved to become *Cajun* over the years.

The term *Creole*, conversely, refers specifically to French-speaking people of French, Spanish, or African descent who were born in the French territories. Immigrants to the territory were generally second sons of nobility with no hope of inheritance, indentured servants, and former convicts, as well as the descendants of slaves. While the region settled by Creoles spans a large swath of the southern United States, dipping into Florida to the east and Texas to the west, New Orleans is widely considered the cultural center of Creole culture.

While there have been other waves of French immigration to the Northeast of the United States, namely of Huguenots fleeing religious persecution, they were completely assimilated into the Dutch community, with whom they shared a faith, and no cultural traces remain. French immigrants to the United States are unique in that they did not come in waves, like their Irish and Italian counterparts, but at a steady and relatively low rate.

Today about 11.8 million Americans claim French descent, but their origins vary widely. Some have their roots in the Acadian diaspora; others are descended from fur traders and trappers. French American populations are particularly high in the Northeast (especially New England), the northern part of the Midwest, and Louisiana. Today, the United States is the second most popular destination for French nationals who choose to leave France: almost 170,000 French nationals live in the United States. They are generally highly educated, and most live in New York City, San Francisco, Los Angeles, and other large cities. While these cities do not have a French neighborhood, they do have an active French community; some have French language schools.

French immigrants in the United States are generally highly qualified and highly educated; their primary reason for moving to the United States is greater job opportunities. For these reasons, French immigrants tend to retain a strong cultural identity and little inclination to assimilate into mainstream American culture. The facts that French cuisine is highly regarded in the United States, and that previously hard-to-find products are now more available, has resulted in little to no adaptation of French cuisine to American tastes. Rather, the reverse seems to have occurred, particularly in more affluent and more highly educated circles.

Foodways

While there is no such thing as French cuisine, each region having its own distinct dishes and cooking methods, there are general principles that can be applied to all French cooking. Vegetables are generally as important, if not more important, than meat. Typical French dishes such as *ratatouille* and *gratin dauphinois* contain no meat. Cooked vegetables are not considered done until they have lost their crunch. A green salad, made of lettuce (generally butter or oak leaf) and vinaigrette, is served with lunch and dinner. Depending on the region, the salad is served either before or after the main course or with the cheese course. Bread (generally *baguette* or *bâtard*) is purchased fresh every day and consumed at every meal. Meats and vegetables are prepared separately, with some notable exceptions (such as quiche) and in stews. Bread is typically the only starch.

A staple to any French meal is *baguette* or *bâtard*. However, these breads being rather hard to find in the United States, and quite expensive where they are available, the habit of serving bread with every meal is less common in French American homes.

Salade verte—butter or oak leaf lettuce with a vinaigrette—is also served at some point during the meal at lunch and dinner. In spite of the wide availability of bottled salad dressings, the French prefer to make their own vinaigrette at home. This tradition has remained and has been incorporated into American culture, where vinaigrette is now a commonly offered dressing option in restaurants.

Typical meals generally include a serving of meat (chicken, lamb, pork, or beef) or fish (traditionally eaten on Fridays); one or two vegetables; and a starch. Cheese, fruit, or yogurt is commonly consumed for dessert.

Typical starches/carbohydrates are bread and potatoes and pasta.

Proteins such as meat are generally consumed just once a day. In more traditional homes, fish is eaten every Friday.

Vegetables are served at every meal and are central to French and French American cuisine. They are served in wide variety, and cooked using many different techniques: steamed with a sauce, baked au gratin, *mijoté* (slow cooked over low heat) in butter, oil, or stock, sautéed, cooked à *l'étouffée* (part steamed, part sautéed) on a bed of *lardons* (chopped-up bacon), or coarsely chopped and made into a *potage* (vegetable soup). Vegetables generally make up the largest part of what French people eat on a daily basis. Seasonal fruit is a common dessert after a French meal.

Coffee is consumed in very large quantities, to the point that establishments where coffee is served have been named after the drink: *cafés*. Coffee is typically served with milk in the morning, and as a shot of espresso with sugar after or between meals. Wine is also commonplace with dinner, and sometimes with lunch.

French foods are generally flavored with herbs, such as thyme, marjoram, tarragon, bay leaf, savory, and oregano. In the United States, lavender has been incorporated as a culinary herb. In addition, spicier foods (a result of North African influence) are made hot with *harissa* (such as in *merguez*, or spicy lamb sausage).

In France, the saying goes that when the best French chefs go home after work, they sit down to a meal their wives cooked for them. Indeed, both men and women cook, but men tend to do it professionally and women do it in the domestic sphere. Traditionally, in French American homes the kitchen, as the heart of the domestic realm, was rarely visited by men; all the cooking and meal preparation was done by women. However, as values have changed and gender lines have blurred, it is now common for men to participate in meal preparation.

Historically, French women have done their shopping on a daily basis: getting their meat, vegetables, and cheese at the biweekly *marché* and buying bread every morning. However, French immigrants to the United States were compelled to modify this tradition, either because of the absence of a biweekly farmer's market, because of distance (towns in the United States are spread out and require transportation), or because some stores were unavailable. Nonetheless, the recent popularization of farmer's markets all over the United States, and the growth in popularity of specialty items (such as freshly baked bread), have engendered a return to these traditions.

Boeuf Bourguignon (Beef Burgundy)

This hearty beef stew is a favorite at Sunday meals. It gets its name because two of its main ingredients—beef and red wine—are central in traditional Bourguignon cooking. This dish is traditionally served with garlic toast; fresh *tagliatelle* macaroni noodles, or steamed potatoes can be substituted.

This recipe can also be done in a crockpot. Serves four.

Ingredients:
- 1 pound beef (shoulder or other stewing meat), cubed
- 4 onions, chopped
- 1 *bouquet garni* (if none is available, make your own by tying together thyme, parsley, and bay leaf with cooking twine)
- 1 bottle red wine (pinot noir); or ½ bottle of red wine and 1.5 cup broth (vegetable, chicken, or beef)
- 2 tablespoons flour
- butter and olive oil
- salt, pepper
- 1 bunch carrots, chopped
- ½ pound crimini or button mushrooms, quartered
- parsley (for garnish)

In a large, heavy pot, thoroughly pat dry the cubed beef and brown in olive oil. Set aside. Use the olive oil, butter, and flour to make a *roux*; once the *roux* is golden (in about 2 minutes), add the onions and allow them to melt. Add the beef, mushrooms, carrots, *bouquet garni*, salt, and pepper; pour in the red wine and broth combinations until covered. Simmer over low heat for at least 3 hours. Serve with flat noodles, steamed potatoes, or garlic toast.

Sole Meunière (Miller Sole)

Hailing from Rouen, in Normandy, this method for cooking fish requires a dredging in flour, which is where it gets its name. This dish is an old French classic, having been around at least since the sixteenth century, when it was quite popular. The simple preparation allows sole, a delicate, light fish, to showcase its flavors, which it could not do under heavier sauces. *Sole meunière* is typically served with steamed and buttered new potatoes (*pommes de terre vapeur*). Serves two.

Ingredients:
- 2 sole fillets
- 3 tablespoons butter
- ½ cup flour
- salt and pepper
- lemon
- parsley

Clarifying the butter:

Place butter in a small saucepan and melt over moderate heat. Stirring occasionally to avoid browning, bring the butter to a light boil. Allow the white parts to cook off—this process is complete once the crackling sound ceases. Remove from heat and strain through a cheesecloth. When refrigerated, clarified butter will keep for several months.

Preparing the sole:

Pat the sole fillets dry with a kitchen towel or a paper towel.

Place flour, salt, and pepper on a soup plate. Dredge each fillet in the flour, making sure to shake off the excess. Place clarified butter in a large frying pan and place over moderate heat. Once the butter is hot, place sole fillets and cook quickly, 3 to 4 minutes per side, until the fish is firm. Remove from heat and add lemon juice and a small pat of butter. Garnish with parsley and serve.

Everyday Meals

Meal structures are rather rigid. There are four set meals—breakfast, lunch, *goûter* (afternoon snack), and dinner—and no eating occurs between meals. Eating is done while seated around a table. Family members eat lunch and dinner together, at the same time.

At the table, it is polite to have both hands above the table. Rather than cutting up food with the side of the fork, as is common in the United States, the knife is wielded in the right hand while the fork is held in the left hand. Bread is served with every meal and is often used to push food onto the fork, especially in working-class and rural homes.

Holiday Feasts

Food is central to any French holiday; meals can easily last several hours and include many dishes. The most important holidays, food-wise, are:

Christmas & New Year's Eve: The main Christmas meal, or *Réveillon de Noël* (Christmas Eve), is consumed on December 24, after returning from midnight mass. It is generally shared with families. A roast turkey is typically eaten at this meal, accompanied with potatoes and vegetables. For dessert, the *bûche de Noël* (a rolled *ganache* with buttercream icing and decorations made of meringue, confectioner's sugar, and candies) is found in Quebec and other former French colonies as well as France. At New Year's Eve, which is shared with friends, people sit down for a feast as well, but there is no set menu. People prefer to consume many small, delicate dishes. Oysters on the half shell, *foie gras*, lox, and caviar are frequent features at this meal.

La fête des Rois, celebrated on January 6—Twelfth Night—in France and during Mardi Gras in Acadiana, is a cake (the type of cake varies greatly by region) in which a token is hidden; whoever wins the token becomes king or queen for the day.

Mardi Gras, or the last day before Ash Wednesday, is the largest holiday in Acadiana. While there are no typical Mardi Gras dishes, with the exception of king's cake, in France Mardi Gras is celebrated by wearing a disguise and eating *crêpes*.

Easter is celebrated by eating lamb, asparagus, and chocolate.

Sunday Lunch: The biggest meal of the week takes place after Sunday Mass. It is generally shared with friends and family and can last several hours. While there is no set menu, it generally includes several courses, salad, a cheese tray, and an elaborate dessert such as *moëlleux au chocolat* (flourless chocolate cake) or *tarte tatin* (upside-down apple tart).

Place in American Culture

The term *French cuisine* is a misnomer, since the regional cuisines of France are many and varied; in addition, some foods—such as French fries—are not French in actuality. *Crêpes* come from the Bretagne region; *fondue* (and, indeed, most cheese- and potato-based dishes) come from the Alps; and *ratatouille* is a Provençal dish.

French cooking has historically been portrayed as fancy and gourmet, thus inaccessible to most Americans. It wasn't until Julia Child and *The French Chef* TV series, which first aired on WGBH in Boston in 1962, that Americans tried French cooking in their own kitchens. While the popularization of French cuisine in the United States can be attributed to Child, her success was bolstered by the fact that Jacqueline Kennedy had hired a French chef for the White House. Child's first cookbook, *Mastering the Art of French Cooking* (1961), which she cowrote with Louisette Bertholle and Simone Beck, provides technical guidance as well as instruction. Famously, the recipe for a plain omelet is eight pages long.

Soon after, in 1965, Henri Gault, a prominent French food critic, coined the term *nouvelle cuisine*, which referred to a departure from traditional French haute cuisine. Namely, freshness and quality of ingredients was emphasized; heavy, rich sauces were eschewed in favor of herbs or butter; and dish presentation was central. Chefs Jean and Pierre Troisgros are largely credited for this movement. While *nouvelle cuisine* eventually went out of fashion, its influence is still felt today, especially on French American food, where the movement's philosophy matched the values of the contemporaneous California cuisine phenomenon.

In the late 1990s and early 2000s, previously hard-to-find, high-quality items became available in grocery stores. Grocery stores, nudged by luxury-for-all gurus such as Martha Stewart, began to carry foods such as *fleur de sel*, *baguettes*, and *Morbier*, which were previously only available abroad. In addition, people grew more comfortable trying new foods and exotic cuisines and cooking techniques; for instance, during that period sushi saw its popularity grow exponentially.

As with all other ethnic foods, French American food is now viewed with less suspicion than previously, while remaining decidedly in the gourmet end of the spectrum. French American food has largely shed its image of being inaccessible to all but the very rich. There are more French restaurants, but they are more accessible; chefs and home cooks are more comfortable using ingredients and techniques (such as Roquefort and clarifying butter, for example) previously unseen outside of the kitchens of the most famous French chefs.

French habits around food have long been held as the pinnacle of healthfulness in the eyes of many Americans. Mireille Guiliano, who authored *French Women Don't Get Fat* (2004), is partly responsible for this belief, by claiming that the French, rather than dieting, maintain healthy eating habits, combined with moderate but regular exercise, throughout their lives. This, of course, is not unique to the French, but to all societies that predate cars, thereby relying on walking and cycling for transportation, and where there is little sprawl.

For a time it was believed that red wine, when consumed in moderation, helped in reducing the risk of heart disease. However, that belief has recently been challenged by the scientific community.

While both the Belgians and the French claim them as their own, French fries have undeniably become an integral part of American culture, to the point that Congress voted to have them renamed "Freedom Fries" after France declined to participate in Operation Desert Storm in 2003. French fries were popularized in the United States when soldiers returned from the north of France and Belgium at the end of World War I. The popularization of fast-food restaurants in the 1950s cemented the place of French fries in the American culinary cannon.

Interestingly, in recent years—with the popularization of gourmet, high-end foods—French ways have permeated American culture rather than the other way around. Culinary schools teach French cooking techniques, and many French sauces (such as *hollandaise*, *béchamel*, and *roux*) are prepared to accompany dishes.

In addition, the French art of wine making has exported itself to California, Oregon, and Washington State. Finally, many small dairies are eschewing American classics such as cheddar and American in favor of crafting cheeses using French techniques; goat cheese, a French mainstay, has also seen a recent spike in popularity in the United States. In some cases, such as *Les Trois Petits Cochons*, a US food distributor of French food, French nationals are creating French foods, such as *pâté* and ham, in the United States.

The influence of French culture in American cuisine can also be found in unexpected places, namely in the cuisines of ethnicities with previous colonial ties to France. For instance, Vietnamese *bánh mì* uses the French *baguette* introduced to Indochina during French colonial rule of Southeast Asia; Thai iced tea is sweetened with *lait concentré sucré* (sweetened condensed milk), which was introduced to the region through colonization.

Noted Restaurants and Chefs

Born to a well-to-do American family in Southern California in 1912, Julia Child did not develop an interest in cooking until 1948, when she and her husband, Paul, moved to Paris. At that time Child attended cooking classes at the Cordon Bleu, where she met Simone Beck and Louisette Bertholle, with whom she would eventually coauthor *Mastering the Art of French Cooking* and open a cooking school, *L'école des trois gourmandes*. Upon her and Paul's return to the United States, Child filmed *The French Chef* series, which would be the first of a number of cooking shows. Through her cookbooks and cooking shows, Child demystified French cuisine, making it accessible to home cooks, by focusing on technique. Child's impact on how Americans eat continues to be felt to this day.

Born and raised in Bourg-en-Bresse, then in Lyon, with a short but influential stint in a farming village in the Alps during World War II, Jacques Pépin first began working in a restaurant at the age of ten, when he helped his parents with the newly purchased business. At fourteen he apprenticed at a restaurant in Bourg-en-Bresse, where he eventually became chief apprentice, responsible for the entire kitchen. After a brief traineeship in Aix-les-Bains, at the age of seventeen Pépin was put in charge of his own kitchen, in a restaurant near Geneva. After a series of jobs all over France, he went to work at the exclusive Plaza Athénée in Paris. He was then drafted as a military chef during the Algerian War, where he served as chef to three different French prime ministers. After the war and a brief return to the Plaza Athénée, Pépin decided to immigrate to the United States. Soon after he met Julia Child; the two would collaborate for many years to come. After a brief stint working with the Howard Johnson chain of restaurants, Pépin opened his first restaurant: *La Potagerie* (*the kitchen garden*) in New York City. Soon after he started giving personal cooking lessons, which led to a long and fruitful teaching career. Like Julia Child, his cookbooks place emphasis on technique using simple and approachable language. *Jacques Pépin's Complete Techniques* (2001) continues to be a standard textbook in culinary schools the world over.

French restaurants in the United States are generally fine dining establishments; simple fare is more commonly found in private households. Several are notable for setting high standards. Le Bernardin, rated three stars in the Michelin guide, has been serving in New York City since 1986. Unique in that it serves almost exclusively seafood, Le Bernardin emphasizes freshness, presentation, and clean flavors. Per Se, also with three stars in the Michelin guide, has been serving New York City since 2004. The American owner, Thomas Keller, serves French American food; emphasis is on fresh ingredients and unusual flavor combinations. Per Se is also famous for its very high prices—the prix fixe menus start at $310. Mélisse, which has two stars in the Michelin guide, is located in

Santa Monica, California, and is owned by chef Josiah Citrin, a French-trained American. The menu emphasizes "luxury" ingredients, such as caviar, steak, and fish.

Further Reading

Child, Julia, Louisette Bertholle, and Simone Beck. *Mastering the Art of French Cooking*. New York: Knopf, 1983.

Pépin, Jacques. *Fast Food My Way*. New York: Houghton Mifflin, 2004.

Troisgros, Jean and Pierre Troisgros. *The Nouvelle Cuisine of Jean & Pierre Troisgros*. (ew York: Morrow, 1978.

Alexandra Gouirand

FRENCH GUIANA

(South America) French Guianese American Food
See also: Belize, Brazil, Caribbean (French), Guyana, Suriname, Haiti.

Background

French Guiana is on the northern coast of South America, bordering Suriname and Brazil. Now an "overseas department" of France, it has a very high GNP (Gross National Product) with a stable economy driven by exports from industries based on agriculture, forestry, and fishing. As a part of France, it participates in the French education, health, and social security systems, so citizens enjoy a high degree of stability and have little motivation to emigrate. Those who do are more likely to immigrate to France than to the United States or other English-speaking countries.

The region was "discovered" by Christopher Columbus, and by 1503 Spanish began settling on the coast around what is today the capital, Cayenne. They, along with the English, Dutch, Portuguese, and French, looked for gold there and tried to settle in the inland areas, but the tropical jungles were not to be domesticated. Slaves were brought from Africa and the Caribbean, and the slave trade thrived there. In 1624, the French opened a trading center on the coast, and from 1664 to 1676, the Dutch occupied the settlement of Cayenne. In 1667, the territory was awarded to France, who, in 1852, established it as a penal colony. The notorious Devil's Island was closed in 1939, but it is most likely the only reference to the country for many Americans. It was also host, like many other European colonies on the northern coast of South America, to utopian communities, such as that of St. Joseph of Cluny at Mana, established for freed blacks, and lasting from 1827 to 1846. In 1877 French Guiana was given representation in the French Parliament, and in 1946, it was given Overseas Department status.

French is the official national language, and the majority of the population is Creole, but the people of French Guiana are very diverse, including a number of Amerindian groups (the Arawaks were the first in the region), Maroons descended from African slaves, and, more recently, immigrant populations from Southeast Asia, Lebanon, Haiti, and the French Caribbean. French language and culture was an attraction for many, but some, such as the Hmong, from Laos, have been able to find there a similar climate and landscape as their homeland, along with space to re-create settlements based on their own culture.

Foodways

Although French Guiana has a great deal of biodiversity, its soil is poor, and many of its residents are involved in subsistence farming of cassava, *dasheen* (*taro*), sweet potatoes, manioc (tapioca), rice, corn (maize), bananas, and plantains. They also raise cattle, pigs, and poultry. Larger farms also produce for export sugarcane, limes, bananas, and tropical fruits.

The food culture is similarly diverse, but rice and shrimp and other seafood are basic staples throughout.

Further Reading

Encyclopedia Brittanica. French Guiana. http://www.britannica.com/EBchecked/topic/219071/French-Guiana.

EveryCulture.com, Countries and Their Cultures. French Guiana. http://www.everyculture.com/Cr-Ga/French-Guiana.html.

Gimlette, John. *Wild Coast: Travels on South America's Untamed Edge*. London: Profile Books, 2011.

Lonely Planet. Introducing French Guiana. http://www.lonelyplanet.com/the-guianas/french-guiana.

NationsOnline. French Guiana. http://www.nationsonline.org/oneworld/french_guiana.htm.

Redfield, Peter. *Space in the Tropics: From Convicts to Rockets in French Guiana*. Berkeley: University of California Press, 2000.

World Atlas. French Guiana. http://www.worldatlas.com/webimage/countrys/samerica/gf.htm.

Lucy M. Long

FRENCH POLYNESIA
(Polynesia, Oceania)
See entry on Polynesia.

G

GABON
(Middle Africa) Gabonese American Foodways
See also: Cameroon, Equatorial Guinea, Congo, Chad, Central African Republic.

Background
The Gabonese Republic is located on the west coast of Africa at the equator and is slightly smaller than the US state of Colorado. The country is almost completely covered with dense, tropical rain forest, and most of the over 1.5 million inhabitants live in cities in the low-lying Coastal Plain region; about a third of the population lives in the capital and largest city, Libreville. The remainder of the population consists of Baka or Pygmy people that are scattered across the inland region characterized by granite plateaus, mountains, and dense rain forest. Traditionally a nomadic people and considered the oldest inhabitants of Gabon, they speak the Baka language. The rest of the about forty Gabonese peoples speak Bantu languages and belong to the Fang, Ogooué, Sira, Myene, Nzebi, Mbete, and less numerous groups such as the Kota, Teke, and Vili. The official language, however, is French.

After Portuguese navigators arrived in 1472, a lucrative trade in hardwood, ivory, and slaves developed in the late 1500s followed by competition between the Dutch, Spanish, English, and French. From 1885 until 1960, Gabon was a French colony, and due to extensive efforts, nearly all Gabonese speak French. During the colonial period, a large majority of the population was converted to Christianity and is Roman Catholic or Protestant. A small part of the population consists of African Muslims and followers of traditional belief systems.

For many years, hardwood from Gabon's forests was a principal source of income, but since the late 1960s oil has provided Gabon with an unprecedented income and a rural exodus to cities. About a third of the workforce engages in subsistence farming, and the country cannot produce enough food to satisfy its needs. Due to the economic boom, 20 percent of the population currently consists of laborers from other African nations, while the majority of the around twenty-five thousand foreigners living in Gabon are French nationals.

Only a few Gabonese slaves were exported to the United States during the trans-Atlantic slave trade from the fifteen to the nineteenth century. As a result of wars and conflicts after independence from France in 1960, a number of Gabonese sought political asylum in the United States, and many young Gabonese study abroad in pursuit of higher education. There are about 250 Gabonese students across colleges in the United States, and there is currently a clustering at campuses in Oregon. In general, though, there is currently little to no permanent immigration of Gabonese to other countries.

Foodways
Gabon's main staple foods are rice, cassava, plantains, and yams. These starchy staples are usually boiled and pounded into a mash. A typical meal with plantains or *bâton de manioc* (cassava paste wrapped in plantain leaves) is usually served with a sauce, soup, or stew with some smoked fish, goat, beef, or chicken, but

also bush meat. Cooked, dried, or smoked meat from deer, monkeys, river rats, crocodiles, and bats is widely available at markets and street corners, and, in rural areas, it is often life sustaining. In the rain forest, food gathering is an important activity, and in some seasons the harvest of wild yams, fruit, and mushrooms is supplemented with termites and caterpillars. Gabonese are the largest fish eaters in Africa, and the coastal waters are rich in tuna, sardines, bass, barracuda, snapper, mollusks, and crustaceans. Plantains are eaten as a staple, but also as popular side dishes and snacks such as fritters.

Meals are often accompanied by a cooked green, leafy vegetable. Cassava leaves (*iporo*) with smoked fish are eaten nationwide, as is *andock* or *odika,* a sauce from the seeds of the indigenous Dika tree (*Irvingia gabonensis*), nicknamed wild mango. Natively grown Gabonese cocoa oftentimes gives food a chocolate flavor. The fruit is processed into a thick, solid paste that is then used to season dishes and in sauces. The oil-rich purple fruits from the butter fruit or African pear tree (*Dacryodes edulis*), locally known as *atanga*, can be eaten raw, roasted, and boiled, but they are usually used to create "bush butter," as the cooked fruit flesh has a texture similar to butter.

Many of these ingredients are not available in the United States, and Gabonese students have to frequent African or other ethnic markets or find substitutes for them. Also, like many Africans in the United States, Gabonese tend to shop at Indian groceries since they carry similar spices.

Most cooking is done over an open fire by women, and local and foreign cooking styles and preparation techniques are mixed. In rural areas, food is eaten from a bowl and often eaten with the right hand or a spoon. The use of coconut, palm, and peanut oil is common, and rice and sauces from peanuts or tomatoes are commonly flavored with *piment*, a hot chili pepper, or *berbere*, a (hot) spice mixture with cinnamon, fenugreek, ginger, and cayenne or chili pepper. In many dishes, fruits (mangos, guavas, and passion fruit) and vegetables (okra, cassava leaf, and eggplant) add taste and color, which is very important in Gabonese cuisine.

Throughout Gabon the French have left strong imprints on the cuisine, which is reflected via common dishes and ingredients such as *beignets* and *brochettes* (skewers), the widespread use of mustard and mayonnaise, and the many local *boulangeries* (bakeries) selling French-style baguettes and croissants. A favorite breakfast is a baguette with black-eyed beans and mayonnaise. In Libreville and larger cities, stores sell French delicacies such as olives, *pâte de fois gras*, and small cornichons (gherkins), and all sorts of cheeses. In rural areas, breakfast can consist of leftovers, but also of bread with coffee or hot chocolate. In cities, the breakfast is more sophisticated and includes a combination of bread, croissants, marmalade, eggs, and yogurt. With meals, water is the most common drink, but the national beer *Régab* is popular, too.

Nyembwe (Chicken with Nuts)

3-pound chicken, cooked and cut into pieces
3 onions, thinly sliced
½ cup palm or macadamia nuts
1 teaspoon cayenne pepper
1 teaspoon black pepper
2 teaspoons salt
2 teaspoons garlic, crushed

Boil the palm or macadamia nuts with ample water in a large saucepan. Cover and boil for a few minutes until the nut skins are soft, discard the skins, and crush or press the nuts with a mortar and pestle or potato masher. Put the mashed nuts in a pot; add 2 cups of water, the cayenne and black pepper, salt, garlic, and onions. Stir well. Simmer on a low heat until the sauce thickens, stirring frequently. Add the chicken pieces to the sauce. Heat through.

Place in American Culture

Gabon is not well known to most Americans, and its cuisine even less so. Because of the shared history of French colonialism, Gabonese living in the United States are able to find similar ingredients and dishes in Senegalese and other West African restaurants and grocery stores.

Further Reading

The Congo Cookbook. http://www.congocookbook.com/rare_recipes/barbara_krauss.html.

Katz, Solomon H., and William Woys Weaver, eds. *Encyclopedia of Food and Culture*, volume 1. New York: Scribner, 2003.

Karin Vaneker

GAMBIA

(Western Africa) Gambian American Food
See also: Senegal, Guinea.

Bordering Senegal and the Atlantic Ocean, Gambia was part of the Senegambia region that was colonized in the mid-1800s and split between France and Britain. Britain took Gambia, and English is the national language, which has made it easier for contemporary Gambians to assimilate into American culture.

As with most other African nations on the west coast, Gambia's people were first brought to the United States as slaves. The American historian Alex Haley made Gambia famous through his story of Kunta Kinte in *Roots*. In the 1970s, Gambians began coming to the United States for educational opportunities, and many have done well in professional fields, settling throughout the country but also establishing small communities and Gambian American Associations to maintain ties.

The cuisine of Gambia is similar to Senegal's, with *jollof* rice and chicken *yassa* (fried in onions), but it lacks the French influence. The basic staple is rice, as well as millet (steamed), couscous, cassava, peanuts frequently made into a paste (*domoda*), palm oil, greens (spinach or cassava leaves), and okra (called ladies fingers, reflecting British influence). Common proteins are fish, oysters, shrimp, chicken, and beef. Pork is not eaten since the majority of Gambians are Muslim, although the country boasts much ethnic diversity and peaceful interrelations. Dried fish is a staple seasoning, although European-processed seasonings, Jumbo and Maggi cubes, are now popular.

Further Reading

AccessGambia.com. Cooking Recipes in Gambia. http://www.accessgambia.com/information/food-recipes.html.

Wikipedia. Gambian American. http://en.wikipedia.org/wiki/Gambian_American.

Lucy M. Long

GEORGIA

(Western Asia) Georgian American Food
See also: Russia.

Background

To compare Georgian food to any other international food would not fully describe this unique culinary delight. Like its language—linked to Aramaic, the Georgian language is formed from one of fourteen unique alphabets in the world—Georgian food is truly unique.[1] It has Mediterranean characteristics, but it also has Asian along with European tastes, too.[2] Their food generally mirrors the geographical and social conundrum of Georgia. Prior to the fourth century, this country was linked more closely with Iran and Persia than the Roman Empire, but when Christianity was introduced with the arrival of Saint Nino, the connection to the west and Europe was solidified.[3] Today, Georgia is perceived as a European country rather than as western Asian.

It is difficult to assess the number of Georgians who have immigrated to the United States since they frequently were categorized as other nationalities.[4] There are communities of Georgian Americans in major cities such as New York and Chicago.

Foodways

Georgians and Georgian Americans recognize the uniqueness of their food and also make it the center of their cultural heritage, as demonstrated in two myths. In a creation story, the Georgians tell that when God was dividing up the world into countries, the Georgians were so engrossed in their meal that the world is divided up without them. On his way home God comes across the Georgian feast and is at first very cross with them. But the *tamada*, toastmaster of the *supra* or large supper, tells God that they have spent their time well praising God for his beautiful creation. God is so pleased with the Georgians that he gives them the last place left in the world, the one he has been saving for himself. Thus, the Georgians were given paradise.[5]

The other story tells of God creating the world. During this project he takes a break for a meal. While he is eating, he trips over the high peaks of the Caucasus Mountains, and parts of his entire meal fall onto the ground. Thus, the Georgians were blessed with their own manna from heaven, table scraps from the plate of God. This attests to the exceptional nature of Georgian food.[6]

The typical meal consists of small plates of different foods with distinctive tastes. A meat plate of pork, chicken, beef, or lamb will have been marinated in yogurt—*matsoni* in the Georgian language—and unique Georgian spices, then cooked over an open flame on a skewer. It is kabob-like in its appearance—but tastier! When served, this plate of meat will have onions littered along with the meat. Other plates might have eggplant cooked in the unique Georgian spices and decorated with seeds from pomegranates. Another plate will have bread or *lavash*, while another will have a dumpling called *khinkali*, which is filled with ground meat mixed with Georgian spices. Yet another plate will have tomatoes, cucumbers, cilantro, and walnuts mixed together with Georgian spices. A bowl on the table will usually be filled with *lobio*, a bean and cilantro creation that also uses the Georgian spices. No table would be complete, though, without the cheese-infused bread called *khachapuri*. This bread, which looks like a pizza, or, if made in the traditional manner, a two-handled tool with an egg in the middle, is loved by all.[7] A proper *supra* will have a table filled with these wonderful foods—all very fresh—and liters upon liters of wine, which is consumed in conspicuous manner.[8]

Key to all of these dishes are the unique Georgian spices. Describing the spices or even classifying them is very difficult. Tbilisi, the capital of Georgia, has been conquered at least twenty-nine times by Huns, Persians, Russians, and various other world powers who found Georgia filled with lovers, not fighters. These outside influences, along with the traditional spice route, brought a variety of spices and flavors that the Georgians made their own.[9] And like their language, no outside conqueror was ever able to take away their recipes. Spices commonly used include coriander, fenugreek (both ground and seeds), dried wild *berberis* (better known as barberry) berries, dried marigold flower petals, caraway seeds, garlic, basil, savory, bay leaves, parsley, and chili peppers. Mint, cloves, nutmeg, mace, and cinnamon are also used, particularly for sweet pastries. A unique spice mixture is *khmeli suneli*.[10]

Place in American Culture

Georgian food is not well known in the United States as a distinctive cuisine, and it is frequently confused with Russian or other eastern European food cultures. It seems difficult to Americanize Georgian food and, for the most part, purveyors of food from the Caucuses region keep it Georgian. In trying to replicate the unique spices, however, cooks usually look to India for similar tastes. Although close and still tasty, this is how American chefs seem to alter Georgian food. This change in spice is evident in the following recipe.

Khinkali (Georgian Dumplings)

4 cups flour
1¼ teaspoons kosher salt, plus more to taste
4 ounces ground beef
12 ounces ground pork
2 tablespoons finely chopped cilantro
1 teaspoon *muchi curry*
½ teaspoon crushed red pepper flakes
3 small yellow onions, minced
freshly ground black pepper, to taste

1. Stir together flour, salt, and 1¼ cups warm water in a bowl until dough forms; transfer to a work surface and knead until smooth, about 6 minutes. Wrap in plastic wrap and refrigerate dough for 40 minutes. Meanwhile, combine beef, pork, cilantro, *muchi curry*, crushed red pepper flakes, and onions in a bowl until evenly mixed; season generously with salt and pepper, and set filling aside.
2. Divide dough into 25 equal pieces, and shape each piece into a ball. Using a rolling pin, roll a ball into a 6-inch round. Place about 2 tablespoons of filling in center of round, and fold edges of dough over filling, creating pleats in dough as you go, until filling is covered. Holding dumpling in the palm of one hand, grasp top of dumpling where pleats meet and twist to seal pleats and form a knot at top of dumpling. Repeat with remaining dough rounds and filling. Bring a large pot of salted water to a boil. Working in batches, boil dumplings until they float and dough is tender, about 8 minutes. Drain and serve hot. Season with black pepper.

Restaurants

In the United States, Georgian restaurants seem to proliferate where Russians live. This is due primarily to the fact that Russians for over two hundred years have traveled to Georgia for the warm weather, beautiful mountains, clear rivers, and great food. Great Georgian food, therefore, can be found in Chicago—with a large Russian population—at Argo Bakery (argobakery.com), and in many areas of Brooklyn, New York, which also has a large Russian population. Brighton Beach, the largest enclave of Russians in Brooklyn, has several Georgian restaurants, including the Georgian House and Primorski. New to the restaurant business but located nicely in Manhattan is the Old Tbilisi Garden restaurant (174 Bleeker Street, New York).

Notes

1. Roger Rosen, *Georgia: A Sovereign Country of the Caucasus* (Hong Kong: Odyssey, 2004), 89.
2. Rosen, *Georgia: A Sovereign Country of the Caucasus*.
3. Ronald Grigor Suny, *The Making of the Georgian Nation*, second ed. (Bloomington: Indiana University Press, 1994).
4. For a discussion of the complexity of identifying Georgian immigrants, see Elene Medzmariashvili, *Third Wave Georgian Immigrant Women in the USA: Problems of Americanization*. Available online at http://www.spekali.tsu.ge/index.php/en/article/viewArticle/1/6.
5. Darra Goldstein, *The Georgian Feast* (Berkeley: University of California Press, 1999), xiv, introduction.
6. Goldstein, *The Georgian Feast*.
7. Rosen, *Georgia: A Sovereign Country of the Caucasus*, 91–95.
8. Rosen, *Georgia: A Sovereign Country of the Caucasus*, 95.
9. Goldstein, *The Georgian Feast*.
10. The Kitchn, Georgian Spice Mix, http://www.thekitchn.com/georgian-spice-mix-khmeli-sune-152742.

Further Reading

Georgian Recipes. Spices and Herbs Used in Georgian Cuisine. http://georgianrecipes.net/2013/07/28/spices-and-herbs-used-in-georgian-cuisine/.

Goldstein, Darra. *The Georgian Feast*. Berkeley: University of California Press, 1999.

The Kitchn. Georgian Spice Mix. http://www.thekitchn.com/georgian-spice-mix-khmeli-sune-152742.

Rosen, Roger. *Georgia: A Sovereign Country of the Caucasus*. Hong Kong: Odyssey, 2004.

Suny, Ronald Grigor. *The Making of the Georgian Nation*, second edition. Bloomington: Indiana University Press, 1994.

Matthew Reger

GERMAN-RUSSIAN

(Eastern European) German-Russian American Food
See also: Russia, Germany.

Background

Russlanddeutsche (German-Russian) foodways are quite diverse due to the different German-speaking groups who settled in various parts of the Old Russian Empire. Many of these colonists traced their origins to special manifestoes issued by Catherine the Great (1762–1796) and her grandson Czar Alexander I (1801–1825). When Russification measures later were introduced in the 1870s by less sympathetic rulers, growing numbers of Germans from Russia began looking westward and immigrating to North and South America.

Precise population numbers for German-Russian Americans today are extremely difficult to determine, but it is estimated that about 1.5 to 2 million citizens trace their ancestry to one or more of the major groups of Germans from Russia. The main German-Russian groups include: (1) Volga Germans, many of whom later settled in Kansas, Nebraska, Colorado, California, and the Pacific Northwest; (2) Black Sea Germans, who went to "Dakota Territory" and claimed prairie homesteads in what is now North and South Dakota; (3) Volhynian Germans, who principally settled in Michigan and Wisconsin; (4) Caucasus Germans, who settled in lesser numbers in the Midwest and California; (5) German-Russian Mennonites, who founded communities in Kansas, the Dakotas, Minnesota, and Oklahoma; and (6) Hutterites (the Hutterian Brethren), who established colonies in southeastern South Dakota and later branched out to other states and also the prairie provinces of western Canada. The least assimilated of all these immigrant groups are the Hutterites. They still live in agricultural colonies, speak and worship in German, and prepare traditional German-Russian foods on a daily basis.

Foodways

Despite having lived in the Russian Empire for generations, the German colonists retained many basic elements of German peasant cuisine: a preference for *Roggenbrot* (rye bread), *Wurst* (pork and beef sausages), egg and flour dumplings, sauerkraut, and *Kuchen* (a cake-like pastry). Yet the long sojourn in Russia did influence the foodways of even the most isolated German colonists, and the settlers eventually adopted a number of Russian and Ukrainian ethnic dishes, making them their own: *Bliny* (thin, crepelike pancakes with sweet or savory fillings), *Borscht* (a hearty vegetable soup, often made without red beets), *Halupsy* (a ground beef and rice mixture encased in cooked cabbage leaves), and *Kvass* (a thirst-quenching summer drink made from raisins and fermented rye bread).

Some Russian foods have become so synonymous with German-Russian ethnic identity that the early settlers gave these dishes German names. For this reason, later generations often refuse to believe that these foods are anything but *rein deutsch* (pure German) in origin. Many present-day Volga German Americans faithfully prepare *Gadofel un' Glees* (cooked potatoes with large, hand-pulled dumplings). Family members tell stories about this food and even sing German songs about its soulful quality and symbolic importance. Yet the dish is undoubtedly a borrowing from the Ukrainian *Halushky* (cooked potatoes and dumplings—drenched in oil and sautéed onions). Traditionally, this food was prepared in iron kettles "out in the open," while family members labored in the surrounding fields.

German-Russian American families still prepare ethnic dishes, especially on weekends when family members and friends congregate at one location. In Fresno, California, a typical Sunday dinner might consist of *Gummersalat* (cucumber and cream salad), chicken noodle soup with *Butter-Glees* (walnut-size butterball dumplings seasoned with allspice), and *Riwwelkuchen* (a coffee cake with a rich *streusel* topping). On festive holidays, square pieces of twisted sweet dough are deep fried in oil and then generously sprinkled with powdered sugar. This popular pastry goes by many names: *Grebbel*, *Kreppel*, *Fastnachtskiechla*, *Schlitzkiechla*, and *Rollkoka*.

For the Volga Germans especially, *Grebbel* serves as an important culinary bridge between the holiday traditions of one year and the next. Large amounts of *Grebbel* are made on *Silwesterabend* (December 31) and then shared and eaten on *Neujahrstag* (January 1). If Volga German elders are present, the "*Grebbel-Liedja*" (a humorous song about a parsimonious cook and her personal stash of *Grebbel*) will be sung to the accompaniment of clinking glasses and much laughter.

Among the colony-dwelling Hutterites, German-Russian foods are served daily in their large communal kitchens and "mess halls." The dishes include traditional specialties like *Rescha Zwieback* (toasted double buns), *Wuchdich* (steamed bread dumplings), *Shooten Kroffeln* (cottage cheese dumplings), *Dampffleisch* (stewed beef and vegetables), *Klopps* (ground beef and goose meatballs), and *Mohn Stritzel* (a cakelike dessert with a poppy seed and sour cream filling).

Homegrown watermelons are highly prized by the German-Russians. Traditionally, small watermelons are placed in large crocks and slowly turned into *Saure Arbuse*, with the addition of vinegar, salt, dill, and other spices. Or, the red flesh and juice of the watermelons are slowly boiled down to produce a molasses-like syrup that is used on bread, pancakes, and pastries.

Some German-Russian dishes are considered distasteful by those outside the group. These foods include *Blutwurst* (blood sausage) and *Schwartenmagen* (stuffed hog stomach). In the Dakotas, outsiders may mistakenly hear *placenta* for *Plachinta*, a vegetarian dish of crescent-shaped turnovers filled with a ginger and cooked pumpkin mixture. In Colorado, Kansas, and Nebraska, dumplings and pastries are made with a type of black nightshade berry (*Schwarzbeere*) that is still viewed by non-German Russians as being deadly poisonous. The seed for this "exotic" plant was brought to America by early Volga German immigrants who sewed the seeds in the hems of their dresses and other garments. "None of us have croaked from eating these berries—well, not yet anyway," joke many grizzled German-Russian Americans.

Place in American Culture

The influence of German-Russian foodways is most noticeable in the American heartland, where the majority of the early Germans from Russia first settled. This region lies primarily within the Great Plains, extending from the Canadian border south into Texas, and from central Kansas west to the Rocky Mountains.

The regional presence of two large German-Russian ethnic organizations has done much to cultivate a wider appreciation of *Russlanddeutsche* history, culture, and foodways. These organizations include the American Historical Society of Germans from Russia (AHSGR, founded in Lincoln, Nebraska, in 1968), and the Germans from Russia Heritage Society (GRHS, founded in Bismarck, North Dakota, in 1971).

The two societies have published German-Russian cookbooks, and the groups frequently feature speakers and workshops dealing with ethnic foodways at chapter meetings and annual conventions.

North Dakota has a large and diverse German-Russian population, and one out of every five North Dakotans is of German-Russian descent. College dormitories often serve German-Russian "comfort food" so that students get an occasional taste of home. In several of the state's larger cities (Bismarck, Fargo, Mandan, Minot), there are "Kroll's Diners," where German-Russian food is prominently and proudly featured. The daily menu items include *Fleischkiechla* (deep-fried meat turnovers), *Knoephla-Supp* (dumplings in a thick cream and potato broth), and Black Sea German *Kuchen* (a pie-shaped cake filled with custard and cut-up prunes, apples, peaches, or other fruit). Local TV commercials in North Dakota regularly remind viewers to go to the German-Russian diner, where they can feel at home and "*set down unt eat!*"

In 2000, Prairie Public Broadcasting produced an hour-long TV documentary, *Schmeckfest: Food Traditions of the Germans from Russia*. The program featured a variety of German-Russian foods and cooks from Colorado, North Dakota, South Dakota, and Minnesota. The documentary created considerable public interest in and renewed appreciation for German-Russian foodways in many parts of the United States.

Noted Restaurants and Chefs

The ethnic cuisine of the Germans from Russia still appears to be "terra incognita" for most chefs and culinary experts. Yet in 2011, Guy Fieri and the Food Network did a program that briefly featured a small German-Russian family restaurant in Brighton, Colorado. The place was Lauer-Krauts and one of the foods discussed was the German-Russian "krautburger," a baked turnover filled with seasoned ground beef, cabbage, and onions. Despite its very German-sounding name, the "krautburger" actually was inspired by the Russian *Pirog*. Perhaps for this reason, "krautburgers" also are known by the German-Russian names *Bierock* and *Beerock*. (Still other names include cabbage burgers, cabbage pockets, *Kraut-Gefilte*, *Krautbrot*, *Kraut-Strudel*, and *Runza*.)

"Krautburgers" have become widely accepted in the central and southern portions of the Great Plains region. In the late 1940s, an enterprising German-Russian family in Nebraska began making and selling Volga German-style "krautburgers" or *Runzas* on a regular basis. By 1979, the family started a franchise known as "*Runza* Restaurants." Today, these German-Russian *Runza* restaurants number more than eighty, and they can be found throughout Nebraska and also in the neighboring states of Iowa, Kansas, and Colorado. The *Runza* story is a true American success story and illustrates what can happen when a small group of people believe in themselves, their ethnic heritage, and grandma's recipes.

Further Reading

American Historical Society of Germans from Russia. *Kueche Kochen* [Kitchen Cooking]. Lincoln, NE: AHSGR, 1973.

Brungardt, Sam, ed. *Sei Unser Gast* [Be Our Guest]. Bloomington, MN: North Star Chapter of AHSGR, 1998.

Daes, Nelly. *Cookbook for Germans from Russia*. Fargo, ND: Germans from Russia Heritage Collection, 2003.

Hofer, Samuel. *The Hutterite Community Cookbook*. Saskatoon, Saskatchewan, Canada: Hofer, 1992.

Kloberdanz, Timothy J., and Rosalinda Kloberdanz. *Thunder on the Steppe: Volga German Folklife in a Changing Russia*. Lincoln, NE: AHSGR, 1993. [Chapters 10 and 11 are devoted to German-Russian foodways and recipes.]

Mertz, Beata (comp.). *Food & Folklore*. Bismarck, ND: Germans from Russia Heritage Society, n.d.

Prairie Public Broadcasting. *Schmeckfest: Food Traditions of the Germans from Russia.* Television documentary. Fargo, ND, 2000.

Timothy J. Kloberdanz

GERMANY

(Western Europe) German American Food
See also: Mennonite, Amish, Pennsylvania Dutch, Austria.

Background

Germans first arrived in the United States rather late when compared to other Europeans, which reflects their relative lack of colonial ambitions prior to the nineteenth century. While some might trace the first "Germans" in the New World back to Leif Eriksson's voyage, most scholars date the beginnings of a significant "German" presence to the foundation of the first permanent German settlement in the United States—Germantown, Pennsylvania—in 1683. Between 1840 and 1880, Germans were the largest group of immigrants to the United States. It is important to point out the wide variety among people classified as "German": prior to German unification in 1871, "German" was an ethnolinguistic designation only, not a nationality, and most German-speaking immigrants would have identified as Bavarian, Swabian, Prussian, or even Czech, Hungarian, or possibly Austrian (see separate entries).

The Early German immigrants were often motivated by religious persecution or evangelistic zeal; the infamous Hessians were the exception rather than the rule. Some German religious groups—Mennonites, Moravians, Hutterites, Amish, and Pennsylvania "Dutch" (from *deutsch*, the German word for "German")—have remained relatively unassimilated, not only in regard to their foodways but also in terms of language; many still speak German as it was spoken at the time of their arrival, which is why they often refer to the surrounding community as "the English." Large-scale immigration occurred in several waves in the nineteenth century: hunger, poverty, overpopulation, or general lack of opportunity in the "old country" drove many to the "New World," while the failed revolution of 1848 sent wave after wave of political refugees. It could be said that these nineteenth-century immigrants identified either with their religion (Lutheran or Catholic) or else with socialism and other progressive schools of thought.

In the twentieth century, the World War I effectively mandated assimilation. The US government maintained so-called "sedition maps," which were little more than demographic surveys indicating where most of the German Americans lived. Automatically suspected of sympathy with Kaiser Wilhelm, many German Americans found it expedient to give up their language almost overnight, even if they had resisted doing so for several generations. World War II sent only a small number of refugees, with relatively greater numbers arriving as POWs, as "economic refugees" of a devastated postwar Germany, and a trickle of people persecuted in communist Europe; among these were the Donauschwaben, who maintain a cultural presence to this day. After about 1960, as West Germany experienced its "economic miracle" and East Germany disappeared behind the Berlin Wall, immigration to the United States slowed to a trickle of individuals with their own motivations. German unification in 1990 did not result in a large influx of displaced East Germans, who were able to seek new opportunities in a reunified Germany or in a resurgent Europe that provided easy internal mobility following the implementation of the Schengen Treaty in 1995. At the present time, German immigrants to the United States are very much like other immigrants from Western Europe: usually highly educated, they come as students, as sought-after professionals, or for personal reasons. German Americans are spread throughout the United States, with greater numbers across the

Midwest and Northeast, as well as a significant number in Texas.

Foodways

Well into the twentieth century, German peasant fare was based mostly on starches and vegetables, with meat reserved for holidays. The main starches were potatoes (still a preferred side dish in the form of *Petersilienkartoffeln* or parsleyed potatoes) and a wide range of breads; with a "waste not, want not" mentality, leftover bread was reused in everything from gruel to dumplings (*Semmelknoedel* and *Kloesse*). Noodles are a feature of southern German cuisine from Swabia to Austria; the traditional *Spaetzle* survives in many German American homes, as well as in packaged version in supermarkets. *Spaetzle* can be made either with egg or in a "poor man's" version composed of nothing more than flour, water, and a bit of salt. The German dark breads, such as rye and pumpernickel, overlap with Jewish and Eastern European cuisine; they have been incorporated into American food culture without much continuing sense of their German-ness. Of course, the most identifiably German "bread" is the pretzel, which has a firm place in American culture. Interestingly, the most authentically German version, the soft pretzel (*Laugengebaeck*), has experienced a renaissance as mall food (Auntie Anne's pretzels). Of the packaged, shelf-stable pretzels, there a few brands, like Snyder's, that retain some German reference, while most brands have been thoroughly Americanized ("Rold Gold," "for example, is not exactly a German name)!

The quintessential German vegetable is the cabbage, although root vegetables also have a strong presence; both of these foodstuffs grow well in Germany's colder climate and mountainous regions and can be successfully stored or preserved for winter. So central is the cabbage that many German families told their children that babies were left "under the cabbage leaves" (the origin of the "Cabbage Patch Kids" dolls that were so popular in the 1970s to 1980s). (The other German myth about where babies come from—that they are brought by the stork—at least has some basis in reality: storks preferred to nest on warmer rooftops, such as those where a baby was being delivered or kept warm.) Aside from sauerkraut, cabbage is also popular in the form of stuffed cabbage leaves.

"Meat" in German and German American culture has usually meant pork and chicken; of course, there are also beef dishes, but these were often consumed by nobility and the wealthy. The schnitzel is a good example: an everyday schnitzel is *Schweinsschnitzel*, while veal or *Kalbsschnitzel* is a higher-priced, more luxurious menu item. It was typical of peasant food to use every part of the animal and to preserve as much as possible: pickled pigs' feet, head cheese, and, of course, sausage are all typical German dishes. Chicken is most often served as roasted chicken or *Brathendl*; a fair approximation of the popular German franchise *Wienerwald* (which specializes in whole- and half-roast chickens) can be found in Frankenmuth, Michigan.

German sausage culture was and is highly localized, with each region and even individual town boasting its own combination of ingredients, spices, and casings. Thus "Frankfurter" and "Wiener" originally designated specific styles of sausage made in Frankfurt and Vienna (Wien), respectively; as frankfurters, wieners, or simply hot dogs, they have been thoroughly incorporated into American culture (especially "America's pastime," baseball, where getting a hotdog to eat in the stands is part of the experience). But some variety persists: the bratwurst is a perennial favorite at cookouts, and German American sausage companies such as the Koegel Meat Company (founded in 1916 by a German immigrant in Flint, Michigan) or Usingers still turn out an impressive variety of authentic regional sausages, from Thueringer and Weisswurst to Bockwurst, Jaegerwurst, and headcheese. Usinger's boasts thirty-one varieties of link sausages alone!

Beer became the province of German Americans beginning in the 1850s, with Milwaukee as the focal point of the industry until late in the twentieth century. Here brands such as Pabst, Schlitz, Blatz, Miller, and Old Milwaukee created reputations, fortunes, and dynasties; the smell of yeast hung over the downtown area until well into the 1980s. This industry has mostly relocated to the warmer climate of St. Louis, where the Anheuser-Busch family already had a strong presence. By some accounts nearly half of all current beer sales can be attributed to the companies founded by German Americans. Arguably the resurgence of microbrewing, beginning in the 1980s, can also be traced back to their influence and to the German ethos of beer making expressed in the Beer Purity Law (*Reinheitsgebot*) of 1516.

There are two major German American festivals in the United States, one of which may be on the wane, while the other is firmly ensconced in American culture. These are Oktoberfest and Christmas! Oktoberfest and the beer-hall tradition in general continue either as identifiably German American events, often organized by civic groups with ethnic ties, or else as assimilated outdoor "Fest" events such as Milwaukee's Summerfest, which now incorporates a wide variety of ethnicities but is identified more with beer and live music performances than with any particular ethnic group.

It may sound presumptuous to call the American Christmas celebration a German tradition, but the fact is that many of America's most cherished and widely practiced traditions, from the Advent wreath to the decoration of a live tree, originated in Germany. The German influence on the foods of Christmas is seen most clearly in the frenzy of cookie baking that afflicts many American households at this time of year. Gingerbread is derived from the German *Lebkuchen*, of which the very German gingerbread house, a seasonal favorite, was made. Most grocery stores stock *Pfeffernuesse*, and specialty stores usually have *Stollen*, whether simple *Butterstollen* or the more luxurious marzipan variety.

These two dishes have had tremendous staying power in the United States and are still prepared in German American families that may otherwise have little connection to the "old country." One reason for their popularity is that they use common, inexpensive ingredients. At holidays these dishes may appear as sidekicks to an American pot roast or a German-inspired *Sauerbraten*, but as everyday fare, they may occupy a much larger share of the plate.

Spaetzle: In Germany, *Spaetzle* is prepared in two main ways: as a side dish/accompaniment, usually with browned bread crumbs as garnish; or as a main dish related to macaroni and cheese, called *Kas'spatzen* in southern Germany. In German American cuisine, *Spaetzle* are used almost exclusively as a side dish or a substitute for noodles; sometimes they are fried after boiling, but they are usually served without any additional garnish. The basic recipe is extremely simple: flour, water, and salt, with an egg or two added in if times are good. There are two ways to form the noodles: using a *Spaetzlepresse* (a potato ricer will do) or *vom Brett* (rolling a slightly firmer dough and chopping it directly from the chopping board into boiling water).

For a smallish batch, start with a cup of flour and ½ teaspoon of salt in a mixing bowl; stir in water (and egg, if using) until it forms a gooey batter. The batter should be firm, not runny, but it should also be "sticky." If you plan to use the cutting board method, you will want a slightly firmer batter, closer to dough.

Preparation: Bring a large pot of water to a rolling boil. Taking care not to burn yourself from the steam, put your batter into a potato ricer (*Spaetzlepresse*) and press it into the water. It will come out as multiple "snakes."

Or, if using a cutting board, place your dough on the cutting board and chop it into the water in narrow slices. This will yield a heartier noodle.

Regardless of method, watch the pot carefully and skim the noodles off into a bowl as they rise to the top (this means they are done). Drain and serve as you would any pasta, or briefly fry in butter or lard before serving.

Everyday sauerkraut: "Real," traditional German sauerkraut is pickled or fermented in a process that can take days or weeks (this is true of most dishes with *Sauer* in their name, like *Sauerbraten*). This is an everyday variety that can be quickly prepared on the stovetop:

Ingredients:
    ½ to 1 head cabbage, white or red
    1 to 2 tart apples
    shortening (lard, butter, or margarine)
    vinegar (a red wine or apple cider variety is
        best, but white will work)
    sugar
    2 to 4 juniper berries
    salt and pepper to taste
    optional: 1 onion; caraway seeds

Slice the onion (if using) into thin slivers. Heat oil or shortening over medium heat in a large, heavy-bottomed pan and "sweat" the onion.

Slice the cabbage: this can be done by hand, for a more rustic dish, or using a meat slicer for thin, even strips. Add sliced cabbage to the pan in batches (as room allows); allow each batch to cook down to make room for the next.

Core and slice the apple (you may wish to peel it first); add to cabbage and simmer briefly.

Add seasonings and adjust to taste. Start out with 2 tablespoons of vinegar and 1 tablespoon of sugar (adjust proportions to your taste). Then lower heat, cover, and simmer until the kraut reaches desired consistency: about 20 minutes for a still-crisp version, or up to an hour for a version with well-combined flavors.

Place in American Culture

The role of Germans in American culture has ranged from "underdog" to "bearer of high culture" in the nineteenth century, and from "vilified enemy" to "invisible and assimilated" in the twentieth. Willa Cather provides memorable portraits of the hardships endured by an immigrant group that did not speak the common language. The sense that Germans were somehow "backward" survives in the description of unfashionable clothing as "duchy" or "dutchy," while the nickname *Dutch* (again as a misappropriation of *deutsch*) was used not only for baseball stars but for many a school child as well. At the other end of the spectrum, Germans and German Americans played a leading role in establishing American cultural institutions, particularly in the musical world, but also in the establishment of higher education (with American PhD programs largely based on the German model). The "German as intellectual" is portrayed in in Louisa May Alcott's *Little Women*, as the man Jo marries, referred to as "the professor," is a German with whom she establishes a school for boys.

Restaurants

A current (2014) listing of all "German" restaurants in the United States, prepared by *German World* magazine, runs to several hundred entries. German American restaurants generally fall into four categories: First, highly authentic German-style restaurants that reproduce German (or Austrian or Swiss) cuisine for high-end consumers in the United States. These generally maintain their authenticity through ongoing contact with Germany or through the occasional infusion of "fresh blood." One of the most historic is Mader's Restaurant in Milwaukee. Founded by immigrant Charles Mader in 1906, the restaurant is now run by his grandson, Victor, and hosts a $3 million collection of medieval armor and other Germanic treasures, including the "World's Largest Hummel Store." A second "authentically German" category appeals to a mass market; the "Hofbräuhaus" franchise exemplifies a German American business partnership that has plunked down "a perfect re-creation of the Munich Hofbräuhaus" right next to the Hard Rock Cafe in Las Vegas. Although the Hofbräuhaus brand of beer has only been importing to the United States since 1997, the market was prepared by more than a century of German American brewing tradition, as well as Americans' familiarity with the Oktoberfest and beer garden concepts. Third, there are "mom-and-pop"–type restaurants that advertise themselves as German—usually with some form of the word *Haus*, often in an ungrammatical neologism such as *Essenhaus*, but whose menus may bear little resemblance to anything found in Germany, aside from hot dogs and sauerkraut. Finally, there are restaurants owned or run by recent German and Austrian immigrants such as Wolfgang Puck, whose cuisine may or may not have "German" elements, but who undeniably come from the German cultural sphere. (Puck apparently learned that most Austrian branch of cuisine, pastry making, at his mother's knee, but his own ouevre has been most influenced by classic French cooking and by nouvelle cuisine.)

Writing in the July 2011 edition of *Bon Appetit*, Andrew Knowlton listed the following seven restaurants as "the Foodist's favorite Germanic restaurants": Gruner, Portland; Bar Tartine and Leopold's, San Francisco; Frankford Hall, Philadelphia; Prime Meats, Brooklyn; Cafe Katja and Seäsonal, New York City. Of these, only "Gruner" has an identifiably German name; Leopold's, Katja, and Frankford might connote German-ness to someone already familiar with the culture, while the remaining three appear thoroughly mainstream Anglo-American establishments (apart from the umlaut in Seäsonal). On closer inspection, all but Bar Tartine, in fact, reveal themselves as German, Austrian, or at least central European. This small sampling of one food writer's favorite "Germanic" restaurants attests to the broad acceptance of a Germanic food aesthetic, as well as the vital ongoing cross-pollination between German cuisine(s) and the US restaurant market.

As this brief overview indicates, the German American food landscape is multilayered, comprising many different waves of immigration, generations of German Americans in the United States, and an ongoing contact with the home country.

Further Reading

Bavarian Inn of Frankenmuth. http://bavarianinn.com/.
Berghoff Catering and Restaurant Group. http://www.theberghoff.com/.
German World. "German Restaurants in the US." http://www.germanworldonline.com/index.php/directory/german-restaurants-in-the-us/.
Hofbrauhaus. http://www.hofbrauhauschicago.com/.
Koegel's. http://www.koegelmeats.com/.
Mader's. http://www.madersrestaurant.com/.
Rippley, La Vern J. *The German-Americans*. Lanham, MD: University Press of America, 1983.
Rockenwagner, Hans. *Das Cookbook: German Cooking . . . California Style*. Pasadena: Prospect Park Books, 2012.
Schmidt, Linn, and Birgit Hamm. *Grandma's German Cookbook*. New York: DK Press, 2012.
Sheraton, Mimi. *The German Cookbook: A Complete Guide to Mastering Authentic German Cooking*. New York: Random House, 1965/1993.
Tolzmann, Don Heinrich. *The German-American Experience*. New York: Humanity Books, 2000.
Usinger's. http://www.usinger.com/.

Kristie Foell

GHANA

(Western Africa) Ghanaian American Food
See also Gambia, Nigeria, Liberia.

Background

In 1957 and after fifty-seven years of British colonial rule, Ghana became the first independent African nation. The country is situated on the Gulf of Guinea in western Africa. It is home to over twenty-five million people and is one of the world's poorest countries. More than half of the population lives in cities; along the Atlantic coast its capital, Accra, has over 2.2 million inhabitants. The city is located in the Greater Accra Region, the smallest administrative region and the country's largest metropolitan area. Kumasi, in the center of the former African kingdom Ashanti, is the second largest city; it is located in the middle belt of Ghana, it is and a most important producer of cocoa—Ghana's major cash crop. The Ghanaian population is almost exclusive Ghanaian and consists of over seventy ethnic groups. The coastal Fanti and the Ashanti belong to the Akan. Other major ethnicities include the Ewe of the basin of the river Volta which covers about 45 percent of Ghana; the Mole-Dagbani is in the upper and northern regions; the Guan is distributed all over Ghana; and the Ga-Adangbe is in the Greater Accra and Eastern region. English is the country's national language, but over 80 percent of the population speaks the Akan language or one of the many distinct tribal languages.

Agriculture is the major occupation in the country; it is predominantly practiced on small and medium farms up to ten hectares, with a variety of farming systems in six ecological zones with different climates and soil types. Ghanaians prefer fish over meat, and over two million people engage in the small domestic fishing industry. Most rural households raise a few sheep, small goats, and poultry for meat, milk, and eggs. Keeping pigs is prevalent in the Accra and Ashanti region, and cattle ownership is more common in the north where over half of the population is Muslim. Since the mid-1980s, most Ghanaians are Christians (Catholic or Protestant), and a quarter of the population is Muslim; a little over 10 percent of the population belongs to other faiths.

Present-day Ghana derives its name from the legendary ancient Kingdom of Ghana (c. 830–c. 1235), one of the earliest and most powerful African empires in the Sahel. The kingdom grew rich from the trans-Saharan trade route through which gold, salt, ivory, slaves, and other goods moved to the Mediterranean or Arabia. But contemporary Ghana is the core of the Ashanti Empire (1701–1957). Before colonial rule, it was one of the most sophisticated kingdoms in south Ghana. Apart from a military force, the land was rich in gold and kola nuts (L. *Cola*), which the Ashanti traded for beads, copper, and salt from the Niger River.

Of the over forty-two million African Americans today, there are many that trace their roots back to the about five hundred thousand Ghanaians shipped to the United States during the African slave trade (c. 1517–c. 1850). Their ancestors most often landed on plantations in the southern states, but a number of Ghanaian sailors also went to live in US ports. The second major influx followed after Ghana's independence in 1957. In the 1960s and 1970s, Ghanaian immigrants were mostly students, but in the following decades, a military regime and economic instability, in conjunction with better and more specialized education, became major reasons for immigration. Of the over one hundred thousand Ghanaians currently living in the United States, most can be found in communities in and around cities. The largest Ghanaian community resides in the New York Bronx. The borough has an estimated population of twenty thousand Ghanaians and includes several enclaves with vibrant communities. Just north, over 2 percent of the predominantly African American population of Mount Vernon (New York) comes from Ghana. Also, due to its manageability, cosmopolitan character, racial diversity, and standing as capital city, over ten thousand Ghanaians settled in the Washington metropolitan area. Since the early 1990s there have developed substantial Ghanaian communities in Prince George's and Montgomery county (Maryland), Arlington and Alexandria (Virginia), as well as in central and northeastern neighborhoods of the District of Columbia. The inner cities and suburbs of Chicago, Boston, Atlanta, and Los Angeles also host communities.

Social and professional networks are considered important for support and success among Ghanaians, but they also help to preserve, construct, and sustain a Ghanaian lifestyle. This strong commitment to ethnic heritage and community, as well as deep religious roots within the Ghanaian community, has resulted in the establishment of numerous Christian churches, organizations, and events that support Ghanaians and their culture in the United States.

Numerous Ghanaians work in health care, most often as home health aides, and because of the substantial size of the communities, more Ghanaians have started to cater to in-group needs, setting up local businesses like barbershops, hair salons, eateries, groceries, and convenience stores.

Foodways

The indigenous palm tree (L. *Elaeis guineensis*) was historically an indispensable part of the Ashanti diet; its fruits were used for palm oil and the sap was tapped and fermented for palm wine. Grains (millet and sorghum) were less important staple crops than plantain, yam, and cocoyam (taro). Yams (L. *Dioscorea*) play an especially important role in the history and culture of Ghana. It is generally believed that the earliest inhabitants were hunters and gatherers that settled in the Volta basin many thousands of years ago, harvested wild yams, and gradually incorporated these in their farming systems. The foragers processed the bitter-tasting tubers into food through a lengthy process involving opening the root, pulverizing it, and washing it in water. The tubers were probably also cooked and pounded into a soft, thick paste similar to Ghana's beloved staple *fufu*. Nowadays *fufu* is usually made from yams, sometimes combined with plantains, but in several regions, cassava and cocoyam tubers or corms are preferred. The use of a mortar and pestle is among the most ancient piece of cooking equipment and it is not restricted to the preparation of *fufu*. Ghanaians use different types of mortar and pestles for grinding or pounding ingredients into one of the country's great variety of pastes, purees, and sauces.

Around 4000 BCE the foragers probably started keeping livestock such as goat and sheep. During the same period, cowpeas (black-eyed peas, L. *Vigna unguiculata*) were first cultivated and became a major source of protein in the Sub-Saharan region. Traditionally they are intercropped with millet and sorghum and consumed in a variety of ways: the roasted or boiled seeds are eaten or ground into flour for breads. The green pods are eaten fresh, and the leaves serve as a potherb. Dishes such as *moin-moin*, a savory pudding or cake, and *akara balls*, fried cowpea paste, enjoy great popularity in Ghana. In addition, tropical forest plants such as okra (L. *Hibiscus esculentus*), melegueta pepper (L. *Aframomum melegueta*), and akee (L. *Blighia sapida*) were domesticated. Okra is among the most famous and popular ingredients in the many souplike stews Ghanaians like to eat with their starchy staples. During the intensification of agriculture, around 1000 CE, chicken, rice, and cocoyam from Asia were probably introduced. Rice is a common staple, but it is also used in more special dishes such as *dirty rice* with "stinky fish" and distinctive red (from tomato paste) *jollof* rice, usually considered the signature dish for West Africa and for which almost every cook prepares his or her own version. *Kontomire* is both Ghana's equivalent of spinach and a popular stew from cocoyam (taro) leaves of which many varieties exist. It is also used in *palava sauce*, a staple stew that can contain a variety of ingredients, with meat, fish, or shrimp, but it always contains palm oil and greens.

Fishing was always an important occupation in Ghana. From the coast, dried, smoked, and salted fish was exported to Ashanti and elsewhere. Meat is expensive and often a food of the affluent. Therefore, in Ghanaian cuisine it became the custom to mix fish such as sardines, anchovies, sea breams, groupers, croakers, and tunalike species with meat in traditional dishes. Mollusks, octopus, and shrimps that are dried and smoked, and often grounded into a powder, are commonplace. Due to fish being a major source of animal protein for most people, nowadays tilapia cultivation and consumption is steadily increasing. This mixing of fish and meat, however, is perhaps one reason Ghanaian dishes have not been widely accepted in the United States, since that flavor combination is not part of mainstream American food culture.

In the last part of the fifteenth century, Portuguese explorers started settling on the coast of Ghana, then known as the Gold Coast. In the decades after 1471, several European powers (the Dutch, Swedes, Danish, Germans, and British) started competing for a dominant position in the profitable trade from the Gold Coast, where they built forts that often were attacked, sold, and captured. The Europeans, especially the Portuguese, brought an array of new crops from the Americas, Asia, and other parts of Africa, such as corn, plantains (L. *Musa*), peanuts, cassava, and sweet potatoes. Corn was referred to as *manputo* (Portuguese grain), and by 1800, it was a common crop and prepared in novel ways such as the now traditional dishes *kenkey*—a fermented ground maize, boiled into a thick porridge, and steamed in a corn husks or plantain leaf; and *banku* or *akple*, a cooked and fermented dough from corn flour with or without cassava.

For centuries, the native bambara groundnut (L. *Vigna subterranea*) was as appreciated as the cowpea, but since the 1960s it has largely been replaced by South American peanuts, said to be introduced by the Portuguese, which had been used for centuries and are the basis for Ghana's famous peanut soup. The Portuguese probably also introduced wheat, breads, and marmalade, and although colonial foods were viewed with skepticism and labeled as "white man's food," bakeries specializing in butter bread, sugar bread, tea bread, buns, and more are commonplace throughout Ghana and the diaspora. Pound cake with and without raisins or currants, ice cream, hot, sweet, milk tea, butter, *akpeteshie* (white sugarcane rum), beer, sweet custard, porridge oats, evaporated milk, condensed milk, and sausage rolls were brought to the country during the British colonial rule. The British habit of eating porridge for breakfast resulted in *Tom Brown*, a common Ghanaian breakfast porridge from toasted corn flour.

In the beginning of 1896, the British also introduced cash crops and plantations for oil palm, rubber, and eventually cocoa. Today, Ghanaian cuisine reflects great regional diversity and the influence of colonial powers and modernity. The popular hot black pepper sauce, *shito*, is widely used with a variety of traditional dishes but also on white bread and spring rolls.

Most Ghanaian food takes a long time to prepare, and cooking most often starts with acquiring fresh ingredients. A trip to open air markets and grocery stores can take several hours; therefore, commodities like instant coffee and margarine are widely appreciated. Traditionally, girls learn to cook from relatives at a young age, and cooking from a book shows inadequacy, but Ghanaian newspapers frequently publish traditional and modern recipes. To a certain extent the Ghanaian meal pattern of two heavy and one light meal per day reflects the ongoing modernization in its cuisine. Especially in cities, the traditional breakfast of *ampesi*, starchy tubers boiled with fish and onions and then pounded, is replaced by a light or street breakfast with an omelet and tea. The urban elite might skip the preparation of traditional food on weekdays, but as traditional life is extremely important for Ghanaians and Ghanaian Americans, traditional food remains an intrinsic part of special occasions and sometimes weeklong celebrations. Whereas regular meals are seldom accompanied by beverages, alcoholic beverages are ubiquitous even among Muslim Ghanaian Americans on these occasions.

Place in American Culture

Despite the large number of Ghanaian Americans, Ghanaian cuisine is little known in mainstream American culture. This may be due to textures, flavors, and ingredients that fall outside the typical American palate. Many traditional Ghanaian ingredients cannot be easily purchased in the United States, so Ghanaian Americans frequently shop at ethnic groceries—Indian, Southeast Asian, and Hispanic ones as well as African. Also, there seems to be a movement among some Ghanaian (and other African immigrants) to start farms specializing in traditional West African produce.

Restaurants

In Ghana "chop bars," street vendors and catering businesses are ubiquitous, but the country has no restaurant tradition. Restaurants as they exist in the Western world are limited to larger cities such as Accra and Kumasi and often located in luxury hotels. Ghanaian immigrants to the United States have opened modest restaurants in cities hosting Ghanaian communities, such as New York and the Washington metropolitan area. These usually advertise themselves as simply "African" or "West African," but they differ from the more French-influenced cuisines being served in many West African restaurants and frequently offer typical one-course Ghanaian meals. In addition, a number of Ghanaian restaurants participate in the biannual New York African Restaurant Week.

There also are dozens of casual eateries oftentimes located in grocery stores and even the barbershops and hair salons that are commonly frequented by Ghanaians and West Africans.

Further Reading

Konczacki, J. M., and Z. A. Konczacki. *An Economic History of Tropical Africa: Volume One: The Pre-Colonial Period.* New York: Routledge, 1977.

La Fleur, J. D. *Fusion Foodways of Africa's Gold Coast in the Atlantic Era.* Leiden, the Netherlands: Brill, 2012.

Ministry of Food and Agriculture, Republic of Guana. Average Yield for Major Crops in Ghana, 2011–2012. http://mofa.gov.gh/site/?page_id=5883.

New York African Restaurant Week (NYARW), http://nyarw.com/.

Karin Vaneker

GIBRALTAR

(Southern Europe) Gibraltarian Food
See also: Spain, Italy, Algeria, England.

Gibraltar is a two-thirds-square-mile British Overseas Territory on the tip of southern Spain. It is famous for its landmark Rock of Gibraltar. Its official language is English, but many residents also speak Spanish. Gibraltarians are unlikely to immigrant to the United States.

Gibraltar's culture and food is a mixture of British and southern Mediterranean, displaying influences particularly from Spain and Italy, but a number of other cultures as well. Internet sources describe its national dish as a type of bread make of chickpea flour, water, olive oil, salt, and pepper called *calentita*.

GREECE

(Southern Europe) Greek American Foodways

Background

Eating is more than a necessity in Greek culture—it is one of the great pleasures of life and an essential component of social activity. "If the pot boils, friendship lives" is a Greek proverb that lays a foundation for food, friendship, and hospitality traditions—all of which are highly regarded among Greek Americans.

According to the 2010 census, over 1,315,775 Americans claim Greek heritage. The first to arrive was Teodoro in the Spanish expedition to

Florida led by Alvar Nunez Cabeza de Vaca in 1528. From the eighteenth to the late nineteenth centuries, a limited number of Greek sailors and merchants settled throughout the country. In 1768, about five hundred Greeks were among the indentured colonists brought to work on a British plantation in New Smyrna, Florida. Many of their descendants remain in nearby St. Augustine, where their history is commemorated at the St. Photios National Shrine. Greek residents of New Orleans founded the first Greek Orthodox Church in the Americas in 1864. But this is only the prelude.

Almost half a million Greeks immigrated to the United States from 1891 to 1921 due to agricultural failures and an economy overburdened with refugees from Turkey and the Balkan Wars. By 1920 the largest Greek communities were in New York (Queens) and Massachusetts (Boston/Lowell), with significant ones in Chicago, San Francisco, Utah, Detroit, and several New England states. In Tarpon Springs, Florida, the sponge industry created a large Greek community drawn primarily from the Dodecanese Islands. Although many immigrants intended to return, the majority stayed and established new businesses and families. Immigration slowed in the mid-twentieth century, but a smaller wave arrived shortly after World War II, and a steady stream continues into the present.

Despite extensive intermarriage and assimilation, many Greek Americans preserve their cultural heritage and cohesive communities through strong ties to family and other social institutions. The Greek Orthodox Church historically played a pivotal role in preserving Greek culture, and it continues to flourish. It welcomes non-Greeks entering the church through marriage or from other Orthodox communities, and it provides opportunities for children and adults to learn the language through Greek school and to absorb the culture through participation in church-sponsored events.

Today Greek heritage is reinforced through a diasporic nationalism facilitated by media and transportation. Newspapers, magazines, and newsletters are published in the larger communities or by regional organizations, and some, like New York's *National Herald* or Boston's *Hellenic Voice*, circulate nationally. Many households also enjoy Greek television or radio via satellite or the Internet. Another element reinforcing cultural ties is the easy access to Greece provided by the airlines. It is not uncommon for a sizeable portion of Greek American communities to spend summers or other vacations in their ancestral villages. Food plays a significant role in maintaining Greek ethnic identity in the United States and is a focus of social gatherings and family life.

Foodways

Greek Americans prepare the general array of foods in the American diet, but there is still a strong emphasis on and appreciation of Greek cuisine. Family cooks take their work seriously, and Greek Americans often dine out—frequently at Greek restaurants. Certain dishes are widely known to mainstream Americans because they are made publicly available through special events or restaurants, but many Greek regional, sacred, holiday, and community foodways remain relatively obscure. Over time and throughout the diaspora, there is also an ongoing process in which some foodways are preserved while others are replaced or altered in response to new conditions.

Foodstuffs

In Greek American kitchens, some of the most important staples are lemons, olives, olive oil, garlic, onions, feta, grape leaves, rice, orzo, cucumbers, tomatoes, *filo* (a paper-thin dough), and Greek yogurt. Pantries usually include Greek pastas, coffee, honey, and lentils as well as dill, oregano, basil, mint, anise, bay leaves, cumin, cardamom, mastic, coriander, cinnamon, cloves, and nutmeg.

In towns with a sizable ethnic population, Greek markets sell imported staples, canned goods, and even frozen foods. If there are no Greek stores, Italian or Arabic markets frequently sell Greek products or offer comparable items. Today it is also possible to order necessities from Internet companies. Live Easter lambs and kids are purchased from local farms or whole prepared lambs are ordered from Greek butchers. Vacations in Greece provide an opportunity to stock up on essential foodstuffs or kitchen supplies.

Preparation

As in Greece, there continues to be a strong emphasis on women creating large home-cooked Greek meals, especially among the older generation. Many men also pride themselves on their culinary skills, and in a few households they are the primary cooks.

Households often possess a *briki* (small, long-handled pot used to make Greek coffee), as well as the tiny cups in which it is served. Many Greek American homes also boast a substantial supply of restaurant-quality baking sheets suitable for large quantities of cookies and pastries. Other important kitchen supplies include a mortar and pestle, spice grater, olive oil can, and straight wood rolling pin. In Tarpon Springs, some residents of Dodecanese heritage buy large, clay pots in the garden departments of home supply stores in which they bake lamb for Easter.

Everyday Meals

Greek American cuisine relies heavily on fresh, seasonal vegetables, meat, seafood, and assorted imported supplies. Many meat and poultry dishes are widely known favorites: lamb *yiouvetsi* (lamb with tomatoes and orzo), chicken roasted with garlic and lemon, *pastitsio* (a noodle and meat casserole topped with *krema*, white sauce), *mousaka* (layered eggplant and ground beef topped with white sauce), *keftedes* (Greek meatballs), *dolmades* (stuffed grape leaves; called *fila* by Dodecanese Islanders), rice pilaf, and roasted potatoes. Often meats are braised and then cooked *kokkinisto*, or in a tomato-based sauce with onions, garlic, and spices. Many vegetables are simply sautéed in oil with very little added water. Popular seafood dishes include grilled octopus, baked fish (*psito psari*), and stuffed or fried squid. Lemons are squeezed liberally over seafood. Greek bread (similar to Italian) is served at lunch and dinner, but it is usually consumed plain. A wide array of pastries, such as *baklava*, *koulourakia* (twisted butter cookies), *kourambiedes* (crescent-shaped butter cookies with nuts), *galaktoboureko* (custard in *filo*), rice pudding, and *loukoumades* (fried honey puffs), are made for special occasions or daily hospitality. In the United States, sugar or a sugar-based syrup is often substituted for honey in pastries.

Some dishes have been adapted to locally available ingredients, American tastes, or convenience. For example, Greek Americans in the pecan-growing region of north Florida and south Georgia sometimes use pecans rather than walnuts or pistachios in *baklava*. Many women, taking price and convenience into consideration, use frozen spinach and domestic feta in their *spanakopita* (spinach pies). Others use sugar syrup rather than honey to sweeten pastries, either because of taste or price. Kalymnians in Tarpon Springs cook with *thrivi*, an herb that grows wild on island hills, but in its absence they substitute thyme.

Greek Americans generally follow American meal patterns. This has been modified from Greece, where the largest meal of the day is in the early afternoon and is followed by a nap. For many, however, breakfasts still frequently consist of cursory cups of coffee and toast, while the quantity of food served at other meals is larger than in American households. Families often unite for a weekly Sunday meal.

Unfortunately, despite the relatively healthy qualities of the Greek diet, the enormous quantity of food served at meals has established Greeks as the most overweight population in Europe. There also is a cultural tendency to perceive a chubby child as a healthy child—an attitude probably correlated to the mass starvation that occurred in occupied Greece during World War II. Although many Greek Americans have changed their eating patterns, obesity is still a problem.

In larger Greek American communities, the *kafeneion* (coffee house) is still an important institution. As in Greece, it provides an environment in which men gather to imbibe coffee and spirits and to play cards, smoke, snack, and discuss politics, sports, or local people and events. Greek coffee is stronger than espresso; it is prepared in a *briki*, and the grounds settle to the bottom of the cup. Although frowned upon by the church, some people practice the tradition of *kafemandeia*, or reading fortunes from shapes made by the thick coffee grounds left in the cup.

Holiday Feasts—Secular Celebrations

Greek Americans celebrate many types of festive secular occasions. They frequently socialize and share their cultural heritage at events organized by regional clubs, fraternal organizations, Greek schools, and sometimes churches. For American holidays such as Fourth of July, communities may organize picnics or parties replete with Greek food, music, and dance. Thanksgiving usually acquires an ethnic flavor, with turkey stuffed with rice pilaf accompanied by Greek side dishes. Increasingly popular are celebratory dinner-dances, semiformal events with catered dinners and a Greek band or deejay.

During the early to mid-twentieth century, Greek churches sponsored annual picnics at pleasant outdoor venues. In the last few decades these have been displaced by the ubiquitous Greek festivals. While their primary function is church fund-raising, festivals offer the public a chance to sample a limited range of food, music, dance, and imported artifacts. Festivals generally feature a narrow, stereotypical representation of Greek American foodways rather than the wider range shared within the community. Nevertheless, they provide a formal opportunity for elders to teach young community members. Older women supervise younger women in baking quantities of pastries or entrees to sell—and the time together allows them to share vital knowledge about those traditions, as well as other significant cultural information and community history. In recent years festivals have offered new items, such as excellent wines produced by the burgeoning Greek wine industry.

Life Cycle Events

Greek Americans observe selected lifecycle events with elaborate rituals. At wedding receptions, guests receive *boubounieres* (small packets or boxes usually containing five *koufeta*, or sugar-coated almonds). Some believe that the almonds symbolize the sweetness and bitterness of married life, and that the odd number signifies the indivisibility of marriage. Another belief is that if an unmarried woman puts the *koufeta* under her pillow, she will dream of her future husband. *Koufeta* are also served at baptism parties.

There are strong food traditions surrounding death. On the night before the funeral the *Trisagion*, a prayer service led by the priest, is held at the funeral home. Afterward, close friends and relatives visit the grieving family to bring foods, such as *paximadia* (dry cookies similar to biscotti) that are associated with mourning. Following the burial, mourners share a meal (*makaria*) to celebrate the life of the deceased. Upon arrival guests are offered brandy, then a meal. Fish with *skordalia* (a thick sauce or dip made from garlic, olive oil, potatoes, salt, and vinegar) is usually the main entrée since Christ shared a meal of fish with his disciples after the resurrection. Greek coffee and *paximadia* are served before or after the entree.

Women make *kolliva* for funerals or memorial services. *Kolliva* is assembled in a mound-like shape from boiled wheat, powdered sugar, raisins, ground walnuts, slivered almonds, parsley, sesame, anise, and cinnamon, then covered with graham cracker crumbs or breadcrumbs and powdered sugar. Sugarcoated almonds and confectioners' candies form a cross and the initials of the deceased. *Kolliva* is highly symbolic: the mound signifies the grave, wheat connotes rebirth, powdered sugar reflects the soul's purity, and candies embody the sweetness of eternal life. The family presents *kolliva* to the church, where it is placed on a table with candles and blessed by the priest during the service. Afterward it is distributed to the congregation.

Holiday Feasts—
Religious Food Traditions

The Greek Orthodox faith encourages fasting on almost half the days of the year. Depending on the holy day, there may be a prohibition against consuming meat (including poultry), fish with backbones, dairy products, olive oil, and/or wine—though vegetables, fruits, grains, and shellfish are always permitted. For example, some of the dishes associated with Lent are *fasolada* (white bean soup); *revithada* (chickpea stew); *kalamarakia tiganita* (fried squid); *gemista me rizi* (tomatoes, peppers, or other vegetables stuffed with rice); octopus *stifado* (stew); *horta* (boiled greens dressed with lemon and olive oil); grape leaves stuffed with rice, herbs, and pine nuts; *fakes me rizi* (lentil and rice pilaf); *briam* (roasted vegetable casserole); *fasolakia* (green bean and tomato casserole); *taramosalata* (creamy dip with salty carp roe); and *melitzanosalata* (eggplant dip). People bake *lazarakia*, small spice breads in the form of Lazarus, on the Saturday before Holy Week to commemorate Christ raising Lazarus from the dead. In compliance with Lenten restrictions, they lack eggs or dairy.

Easter is the most important day in the Greek Orthodox calendar. Preparations start well in advance with baked goods such as *tsoureki*, an Easter bread usually spiced with anise or mastic, braided, and decorated with a red egg on top. On Holy Thursday, families dye boiled eggs red in reference to Christ's blood. The resurrection is celebrated with a late Saturday night service. Afterward, worshippers return home, where they play a game with the red Easter eggs by tapping their eggs against those of other family members. Whoever cracks the others' eggs without harming their own wins. They break the Lenten fast with *magiritsa* soup, traditionally made of lamb neck, head, and innards as well as rice, dill, butter, vegetables and *avgolemono* (egg lemon sauce). Easter Day is celebrated among families, friends, church, or community organizations with a feast of roasted lamb and many other dishes that have been avoided during the strict Lenten fast.

Vasilopita is a cake or sweetened bread associated with St. Basil's Day, January 1. According to legend, citizens of Caesarea raised a ransom of gold and jewelry to stop a siege of the city. When the siege was suspended without the ransom, St. Basil was unsure who had donated the items, so he baked them into loaves of bread and distributed them randomly. Miraculously, everyone received what they had donated. Thus, like the king cakes of western European tradition, *vasilopita* contains a hidden coin that confers good luck on the receiver in the coming year. Today the cake may be served at any convenient time between New Year's Day and the beginning of Lent. The sign of the cross is usually cut into the cake before serving.

Prosforo is the bread used in Greek Orthodox services. Like the bread of earlier times, it is made with the simplest ingredients: flour, yeast, water, and salt. Each loaf is stamped with a *sfragida*, a wooden seal carved with religious symbols. Community women periodically bake and contribute *prosforo* to the church as an offering along with wine, oil, and lists of the living and deceased for whom they wish to have prayers said.

Greek American Innovations

There have been some substantive innovations in Greek American cuisine over the last several decades—some of which were prompted by technology. For example, *filo* (also spelled *phyllo*) is the dough used in sweet and savory Greek pastries. Until the mid-twentieth century, it was handmade in a long process that required great skill to repeatedly roll and stretch it into paper-thin sheets. Although the first *filo* machine was patented in 1946, it was not until the 1970s that *filo* machines were perfected in Cleveland by George Pappas and his uncle, Jim Kantzios. As a result, commercially produced *filo* became widely available, and Pappas's company, Athens Foods, became the largest world producer. The ready availability of *filo* and the introduction of premade *filo* cups have also led to their use in a vast number of fusion recipes.

Gyros seem omnipresent not only in Greek American eateries but also in American food courts and diners. The Greek original consists of strips of pork or chicken roasted on a vertical spit near a heat source. As the meat cooks, it is sliced off and served in a pita with tomato, onion, various sauces, and sometimes French fries. In the United States, *gyros* may have been first served during the 1960s. In the 1970s, Chicago Greeks developed the modern vertical rotisserie cooker and the recipe for processed gyro meat. The latter consists of finely ground beef and lamb mixed with seasonings and breadcrumbs, which is then fused by hydraulic pressure to metal cylinders, flash frozen, and shipped to customers. American *gyros* are usually served on pita with tomatoes, onions, and *tzatziki* (a sauce or dip of yogurt with grated cucumbers, garlic, olive oil, and mint or dill).

Although Cincinnati chili was originally developed by Macedonian immigrants in 1922, its ingredients are similar to those in some regional Greek recipes. A Greek employee who worked as a chef in the original chili parlor modified the recipe and started Skyline Chili, which now has franchises and loyal followings in several states. Characterized by seasonings such as cinnamon, clove, and allspice, Cincinnati chili is considered a regional dish—and many Greek Ohioans consider it their own. It is ordered in a variety of ways based on the addition of components: chili sauce, spaghetti, cheddar, onions, and kidney beans. In addition, the chili is served on hot dogs and covered with grated cheddar.

In recent years, *baklava* ice cream has become a mainstay at Greek festivals and restaurants. It is currently produced by numerous small ice cream shops as well as larger commercial manufacturers.

Place in American Culture

Early waves of Greek immigrants to the United States often established food-related businesses such as restaurants, grocery stores, or sweet shops offering ice cream and candies. More than a century later, Greek-owned restaurants and diners have become a staple in almost every town, though the sweet shops have virtually disappeared. While some eateries serve exclusively Greek cuisine, many specialize in local fare, but add a Greek salad and a few other well-known dishes. In this way, a vast number of Americans have become acquainted with a limited range of Greek food. Moreover, the massive number of Greek festivals draws in enormous crowds who inhale their culinary offerings. Overall, Greek American restaurant cuisine, while retaining its character as an ethnic food experience, has become relatively familiar to non-Greeks. Cookbooks (commercial or church produced) and Internet recipes abound, allowing easy access to all who wish to integrate Greek dishes into meals.

Small Greek restaurants and diners usually offer a fairly standard menu that includes *gyros*, *souvlaki* (shish kabob), *mousaka*, roasted chicken, lamb, fried squid, stuffed peppers, *spanakopita*, Greek salads, and *baklava*. Some restaurants offer regional specialties associated with the origin of the owner's family.

Many restaurants owned by non-Greeks offer a Greek salad. In truth it bears little resemblance to traditional salads, which frequently omit lettuce. Most often a Greek salad served in a non-Greek restaurant resembles an ordinary American side salad with a sprinkling of domestic feta and an olive. In Greek-owned restaurants, the salad contains slabs of feta (again usually domestic) and there are more olives, but it is still similar to the side salad. However, customers usually have the option to order a *horiatiki salata* (literally village-style salad) containing tomatoes, cucumbers, onions, imported olives, large slices of feta—and no lettuce. In addition, the salad dressing is more frequently to contain olive oil than in non-Greek establishments.

Numerous Greek American foods have been assimilated into mainstream American cuisine. Feta cheese is commonly found in grocery stores and restaurants. Unfortunately, it is usually domestic, which is vastly different from the original. Greek feta is a brined cheese made from sheep or goat's milk that comes in varying degrees of saltiness and hardness. It also possesses a mellow, nuanced flavor, whereas salt is the only distinctive flavor of the cows' milk American version. Thus, Greek Americans often buy their table or salad feta from specialty stores, reserving the domestic type for baking. Similarly, Greek olives, pita, olive oil, and frozen *filo* dough have become grocery store staples, though the selection of olives is quite limited compared to the possibilities. Pita has been so assimilated by American culture that it now comes in trendy whole wheat or multigrain versions. All of these items are now commonly seen in fusion cooking.

Greek American food has had a starring role in several icons of popular culture. At the Olympia Restaurant in the "Cheezborger Cheezborger" skits during the early 1970s on *Saturday Night Live*, John Belushi played Pete Dionasopolis. His staff, consisting entirely of cousins and siblings, took orders from diners who could order only cheeseburgers, chips, and Pepsi (not Coke). Dan Aykroyd grilled with a cigarette dangling from his mouth. When things got tough, they danced "because we are Greeks!" It was truly stereotyping at its best.

More recently, *My Big Fat Greek Wedding* was a massive hit with not only American but also Greek American audiences. While it portrayed and reinforced many stereotypical views of the ethnic group, most found the many inside jokes very amusing. Food was a big component of the movie—from the heroine's job in the family restaurant to the enormous quantities of food generated for any event, incredulity that anyone would not eat meat, foisting ouzo on unsuspecting WASPs, and the lamb roasting on a spit in the yard. One tragic scene portrayed the despair of the heroine when she brought her ethnic food to elementary school and was ridiculed by the other children.

Currently, as the Mediterranean diet is touted as one of the world's healthiest, Greek food is again taking center stage. Among the virtues of the Mediterranean diet is a reliance on olive oil, which is also gaining adherents among beauty devotees for its beneficial attributes for hair and skin. Greek yogurt has also become a national craze, produced by myriad companies (including Turkish) and in numerous forms—including ice cream. Its success is due to the fact that thick, creamy yogurt tastes infinitely better than the watery, sweetened substitute long inflicted upon Americans.

Noted Restaurants and Chefs

There have always been fine Greek restaurants, but today a growing number of upscale restaurants serve nouveau Greek cuisine, traditional dishes not found elsewhere, or fusion cooking. This has coincided with the emergence of a few widely respected Greek American chefs. Perhaps the best known is Michael Psilakis, who learned to cook traditional Greek food from his family. He owns several restaurants in the New York City area, including FISHTAG, Kefi, and three MP Tavernas, which serve variations of Greek and fusion cuisine. He and his restaurants have received numerous prestigious awards.

Cat Cora (Katerina Karagiozi) grew up in a Greek family in Jackson, Mississippi, that combined the flavors and ingredients from their native island of Skopelos with southern cuisine. She is the only female Iron Chef and was awarded the 2006 *Bon Appetit* magazine teacher of the year award. Cora has opened several restaurants, including Cat Cora's Kitchen in several airports, Kouzzina (Greek), and Cat Cora's Q (barbecue).

Although not a professional chef herself, Diane Kochilas has had a notable influence on national and international appreciation of Greek food. A Greek American from New York, Kochilas has written several cookbooks that combine amazing traditional and new recipes with narratives that combine ethnography and food history. She also has written about Greek cooking for the *New York Times* and *Saveur*, has a regular column in the Greek newspaper *Ta Nea*, and conducts a cooking school on her family's home island, Ikaria.

Recipes and Case Study: Tarpon Springs

One of the most widely known Greek American communities is Tarpon Springs. Nestled around the bayous and Anclote River on the central coast of the Gulf of Mexico, it has a unique heritage based on its maritime history and Dodecanese Island (especially Kalymnos, Halki, and Symi) culture. Beginning in 1905, Greek men were recruited to practice their traditional occupation when natural sponges were discovered in the waters near Tarpon Springs. Those who did not dive staffed or maintained the boats, sold sponges, or practiced related maritime occupations.

Today, the sponge industry endures, and Tarpon Springs preserves a strong Greek character and maritime heritage. In recent years, many Greek Americans from throughout the United States and Greece have relocated to the area because of its cultural infrastructure. Among its twenty-four thousand residents, the percentage of Greek descent has shrunk to about 20 percent, as many have resettled in nearby communities for work or larger homes. Yet the city remains the epicenter of such a large ethnic population that the Greek government established a consulate in Tampa. While some major US cities have a larger Greek population, no other has a larger percentage with Greek heritage than Tarpon Springs.

Along the sponge docks on Dodecanese Boulevard, a plethora of Greek eateries, tourist stores, nightclubs, and community events are frequented by locals and tourists. Some businesses cater primarily to the ethnic community, including two small Greek markets, a Greek butcher shop, a wholesale Greek food business, several bakeries, and three traditional *kafeneia*. Greek American identity is reflected in the built environment (cemetery, sponge docks, Greek Town, churches, and chapels), boats, occupations, music and dance in clubs, or embedded in community events, organizations, beliefs, family values, foodways, sacred and secular events, and religious practices. Tarpon Springs also provides important cultural resources to the region, such as the annual Epiphany celebration, musical groups, and a megabakery that supplies numerous church festivals and Greek events in the southeast.

Local Foodways

Tarponites maintain many Dodecanese food traditions that are rarely found outside private homes or regional organizations. For instance, in the early twentieth century, spongers went to sea for several months. Although the men often ate fresh fish, they broke the monotony with a preserved meat dish called *kavourmas*. Before sailing, the crew prepared enough to last an entire trip. Outside over a wood fire, they filled a washtub with beef or lamb, stirring it with a small paddle as it simmered in fat for hours before being sealed into containers. The preparation of *kavourmas* became a social occasion as well as a necessity. Sponge boats no longer needed to prepare it, but some still make it for special occasions or to teach others about the tradition.

For Easter, many women prepare the Dodecanese Easter bread called *eftazimo*. Made in observance of God's command to Moses to prepare unleavened bread for the flight to Israel, the name refers to kneading the dough seven times. Although it does not contain yeast, the juice of fermented garbanzo beans provides enough leavening to raise the dough. The juice is mixed with flour, salt, sugar, anise, mastic, and nigella seeds to produce loaves with a delicious and unusual flavor.

Hidden in backyards throughout Tarpon Springs, families may fatten lambs and kids in the weeks before Easter. When they are slaughtered by a local Kalymnian butcher, ritual practices include the orientation of the lamb's head to the east, cutting a cross-shaped incision on the animal's throat, and using a fresh sponge soaked with lamb's blood to make the sign of the cross over the doorway. The cross refers back to the sign used to protect the Jewish households during their persecution by the Egyptians before Passover.

A few families build the traditional Dodecanese oven, or *fournos*, to cook breads, meats, and other regional specialties in their back yards. On Holy Saturday, they assemble to light the oven and prepare food for the Easter feast. One delicious Kalymnian dish is *mououri*, lamb stuffed with rice, red sauce, and spices, then sealed in a clay pot. When the oven is white hot, they insert the pot, seal the oven with clay, and cook the lamb overnight. This is often an occasion of merriment, as family members playfully smear each other with leftover clay.

When people first dine at a Greek restaurant in Tarpon Springs, many are shocked to find potato salad in the middle of the Greek salad. In the Tarpon Springs and Tampa areas, most non-Greeks expect to find potato salad due to the influence of successful local restaurateur Louis Pappas. Pappas, who had emigrated from Sparta, served as a cook in the American army during World War I. To fortify the troops, he added potato salad to the regular salad—and continued the practice after opening a family restaurant in Tarpon Springs in 1925. Today his descendants operate multiple restaurants of various types, but all serve the signature salad—as do most area Greek restaurants.

Fila (Kalymnian Stuffed Grape Leaves) with *Avgolemono* Sauce, by Katerina Zaronias

Filling:
    2 pounds ground beef
    1 cup rice
    1 medium onion, chopped
    1 8-ounce can tomato sauce
    1 tablespoon salt
    1 teaspoon pepper
    1 cup water

Pot:
    1 jar grape leaves, rinsed
    1 large tomato
    1 stick butter
    beef or pork bones

Mix together ground beef, rice, onion, tomato sauce, salt, pepper, and water. In the bottom of the pot, lay one layer of unfilled grape leaves or beef or pork bones. Then roll about 2 tablespoons of filling into each grape leaf (put in middle, fold sides in, and roll away from you) and roll them up. Layer them tightly in the pot. On top of the rolled grape leaves layer sliced fresh tomato and sliced butter. Add water to the top layer of grape leaves. Cook covered on medium for one hour.

Avgolemono (Egg-Lemon) Sauce

    1 large or 2 small fresh lemons
    2 eggs

Squeeze lemons in blender and add eggs. Blend for 30 seconds, and then gradually add about ½ of the juice from the pot. Pour mixture over the grape leaves. Shake the pot to make sure the sauce distributes evenly.

Sponge Boat One-Pot Dinner: Grouper Souper, by Captain Taso Karistinos

- 4- to 5-pound whole grouper (preferred), or fillets
- 2 medium potatoes, diced
- 2 medium onions, diced
- ½ head of celery, chopped
- 1 carrot, sliced (optional)
- 1 teaspoon salt or to taste
- 1 cup olive oil
- 5 to 6 lemons

Put vegetables into a large pot with just enough water to cover them, and boil until potatoes and carrots are soft.

If you use a whole grouper, scrape off the scales, take off the gills, and clean out the throat. On the boat the grouper is cut into steaks and cooked with the head and bones. Add the fish to the pot and simmer until the meat is soft, about 25 minutes. If you use fillets, the fish takes less time to cook. If you have used the whole fish, carefully lift out the pieces so that the bones do not disperse. Remove the bones and skin, then return the rest to the pot. Squeeze 5 to 6 lemons into the soup, and let it boil 1 minute to incorporate the lemon juice into the soup. Cool the soup slightly, then serve. Feeds 4.

Conclusion

Greek American foodways represent an ongoing interchange between original ethnic recipes, adaption to American conditions, adoption of individually generated recipes, technological innovations, and the international evolution of foodways. They also reflect an unchanging appreciation for flavor, family, friendship, and life in general that underlies the culture.

Further Reading

Rouvelas, Marilyn. *A Guide to Greek Traditions and Customs in America.* Bethesda, MD: Nea Attiki Press, 1993.

Sutton, David. *Remembrance of Repasts: An Anthropology of Food and Memory.* New York: Berg, 2001.

Tina Bucuvalas

GREENLAND

(America—North) Greenlandic American Food
See Denmark.

Greenland, a large island between the Arctic and Atlantic oceans, is an autonomous country within the Kingdom of Denmark. Culturally, it is Scandinavian since Norway and Denmark colonized it, although the native Inuit people have maintained their distinctive lifestyle.

Covered with glaciers, Greenland has no agriculture to speak of, and Greenlanders historically depended on the sea for food (sea mammals and fish) as well as birds and some land mammals, such as reindeer, musk-oxen, foxes, hares, and polar bear. The Norse introduced sheep and cattle. Wild berries, such as blueberries and crowberries, along with seaweed and seasonal wild greens, historically were the primary vegetables or fruits. Potatoes, rice, and onions are now common staples, as they are in much of Scandinavia.

Inuits traditionally used the blubber, hide, and innards of seals and whales (primarily narwhal or bowhead), consuming it raw, smoked, boiled, dried, frozen, or fermented. Fish and mammals are similarly "prepared" in those ways. A basic staple is *mattak*, rawhide and blubber, which is extremely high in vitamin C. The "national dish" is *suaasat*, a soup consisting of whatever meats or fish are available, and onions, potatoes, rice, or barley for starch. Salt and pepper or a bay leaf would be the only seasonings.

There is little information on Greenlanders in the United States; the 2000 census gives the population of Americans claiming that ancestry as 312.[1] Greenlanders who immigrated to the United States are categorized as either

Greenlandic American with Danish descent or Greenlandic American with Inuit descent. They would be referred to in the United States as Scandinavian American, but, by citizenship, they would be Danish. Traditional Greenlandic Inuit food would not be accepted by mainstream American food culture.

Note

1. US Census Bureau, "Table 1. First, Second, and Total Responses to the Ancestry Question by Detailed Ancestry Code: 2000."

Further Reading

BBC News. Greenland Profile. http://www.bbc.com/news/world-europe-18249474.

Geographia.com. Greenland. http://www.geographia.com/denmark/greenland.html.

Greenland.com. http://www.greenland.com/en/.

Hannah M. Santino

GRENADA

(Americas—Caribbean) Grenadian American Foodways

Background

Since Grenada's discovery, it has been controlled by the French and British, respectively. In 1974, Grenada gained its independence, but there was much civil distress, so in 1983, the United States invaded in order to restore order on the island and assist in the removal of the Cuban military presence. However, it was in the 1950s after World War II that Grenadians began migrating to the United States in large numbers. Favoring the Northeast, the majority of Grenadians settled in New York, Boston, and Washington, DC. Due to 82 percent of Grenadians considered as black, many of the people who migrated to the United States settled in neighborhoods that were dominated by African Americans. The result was a large assimilation of Grenadians into African American culture and cuisine.

Foodways

The majority of the people living in Grenada are descendants of African slaves, European settlers, and East Indian settlers. This results in Grenadian cuisine having traces of all of the aforementioned cultures. Fruits, vegetables, rice, and spices such as nutmeg are common staples in Grenadian cuisine. They are used in drinks, desserts, and in various dishes both every day and on special occasions. Grenada is known as "the spice island," which can be seen in the popularity of nutmeg ice cream in Grenada. In the United States, the Grenadian love of spice did not fade. They use hot peppers, nutmeg, cinnamon, curries, and various other spices in their cooking. Sugarcane is another popular food item in Grenada, and it is also a large product of export. This results in rum being a popular beverage for Grenadians due to its being made from sugarcane juice.

Meat and seafood are also incorporated into the majority of meals. In the United States, Grenadians tend to use more meat than seafood due to cost and accessibility. In Grenada, common drinks and snacks from North America are sold, but meals resemble more of the typical Caribbean cuisine with variations of stews, rice, and meats, and fresh fruit and vegetables. One of the most popular dishes in Grenada, and also the national dish, is called *Oil Down*, a type of stew with a broth made from coconut milk (straight from the coconut shell).

Oil Down

Ingredients:

- approximately 9 young *Dasheen* leaves (a leafy green vegetable that can be substituted with water spinach)
- 1 sprig (or small stem) of celery
- 1 sprig (or small stem) of chive
- 1 sprig (or small stem) of thyme
- 2 medium, chopped carrots
- 2 chopped green peppers
- 1 pound of dumplings (made from kneading together flour, salt, and water)

1½ teaspoons of turmeric

1 large, peeled breadfruit (a popular starchy vegetable that can be found in some Asian and Latin American grocery stores)

1 thinly chopped medium onion

3 cloves of minced garlic

1½ teaspoons of sugar

3 cups of coconut milk (preferably from the shell, but powdered or canned is suitable)

½ to ¾ pounds of meat of choice salted overnight (preferably fish)

lime juice

Directions:

1. Take peeled breadfruit and cut into eight separate pieces, and then cut in half.
2. Wash the salted meat, and then rinse with lime juice and water.
3. Remove the skin, rinse, and cut the onion into small pieces.
4. Remove the seeds from the green peppers and cut into thin wedges.
5. Cut sliced peppers into small pieces.
6. Add cold water to a large saucepan and place rinsed meat in water. Bring to a boil and then drain saucepan. (Repeat this step three times in order to thoroughly remove salt.)
7. Cook meat until tender and drain.
8. Sauté onion and garlic in hot oil until garlic is roasted and onions are translucent.
9. Stir in meat, chive, thyme, celery, and salt to taste.
10. Add the two cups of coconut milk and stir.
11. Add the breadfruit, sugar, and pepper. Stir.
12. Cook until the breadfruit has absorbed most of the liquid.
13. Add 1 remaining cup of coconut milk and take out the sliced green peppers.
14. Stir and cook on a medium-low heat until there is no liquid remaining.
15. Serve hot.

Grenadian Americans still make *Oil Down* in the United States, but the recipes vary; most commonly they exclude breadfruit and *dasheen.* Many Grenadian spice techniques derive from Africa and thus are shared with the African American population. Upon migrating to the United States, Grenadian American cuisine is seen as African American due to the large amount of assimilation that occurs within their culture. For the majority of Americans today, this translates to soul food or southern cuisine and is labeled as such in restaurants.

Holiday Feasts

In Grenada, the majority of holidays are affiliated with religion. Therefore, these holidays are spent equally between church and at home with family. For other holidays, such as Independence Day, February 7, which celebrates Grenada's independence from the United Kingdom, it is celebrated with parades, festivals, and lots of food. The people of Grenada also have several social gatherings outside of governmental and religious holidays. A *cook-up* is a common gathering of people in Grenada where food preparation followed by consumption takes place. Females and young children complete the food preparation for both holidays and everyday meals.

Place in American Culture

After settling into mostly African American communities in the United States, most Grenadians have assimilated to that culture and cuisine and are thus seen marginally as African Americans. Now, Grenadian American cuisine resembles what is typically viewed as "soul food," or modernized African American cuisine. Modernized "soul food" consists of dishes such as chicken fried steak, collard greens, grits, and sweet potato pie. In the Grenadian American community, recipes are passed down between family members, most commonly the females. However, the outside community sees Grenadian and Grenadian

American cuisine as African American or occasionally Caribbean. Coincidentally, this is also how it represented in the few cookbooks published in the United States that contain Grenadian cuisine.

Noted Restaurants and Chefs
Although there are not many famous chefs known to be Grenadian American, there are a few. For example, Yvette LaCrette is considered the "go to" chef for Caribbean food and events. Many Grenadians migrated to the United States illegally, and the majority of those who came legally assimilated to African American culture. Therefore, Grenadian American cuisine, restaurants, and chefs are seen as African American or Caribbean instead of Grenadian.

Further Reading
Eisenberg, Joyce. *Grenada*. New York: Chelsea House, 1988.
Henry-Banthorpe, Dayliah, and Alleyne Gunston. *Tastes of Spice*. Grenada: AllyDay Creative Projects, 2006.
Pang, Guek-Cheng. *Grenada*. New York: Marshall Cavendish Benchmark, 2011.

Alexandria Ayala

GUADELOUPE
(Americas—Caribbean)

A French territory in the Caribbean, along with Martinique, Saint Barthélemy, and Saint Martin.

For similar food cultures, see other Caribbean ethnic groups, particularly Haiti.

GUAM
(Micronesia, Oceania)
See entry on Micronesia (Micronesian American).
Micronesia includes: Guam, Marshall Islands, Palau, Kiribati, Federated States of Micronesia, Nauru, Northern Mariana Islands.

GUATEMALA
(Central America) Guatemalan American Food

Guatemalan food is relatively new in the United States, brought by Guatemalan immigrants fleeing political unrest in Guatemala during the 1980s. While Guatemalans retain a distinct cuisine and traditional dishes, Guatemalan restaurants in the United States often serve a mixture of Guatemalan and Mexican food on menus, appealing to broader tastes. Ingredients for these dishes can be found in groceries that cater to all Central Americans.

Background
There were few Central American immigrants recorded during the early 1900s, and until 1960, US immigration records did not distinguish among immigrants from different Central American countries. During the 1970s, economic challenges, an earthquake in 1976, and growing political unrest drove more Guatemalans to leave their country. Prior to 1980, the Guatemalans who immigrated to the United States tended to identify as white, middle class, and urban. During the 1980s, the Guatemalan government embarked on counterinsurgency campaigns in the western highlands of Guatemala, forcing many indigenous peoples and peasants to flee. Since 1980, an estimated three hundred thousand Guatemalans have entered the United States as undocumented immigrants. These immigrants, predominantly Mayan Indians from rural highland communities, faced deportation if caught by the Immigration and Naturalization Service. The United States did not recognize the Guatemalans as political refugees seeking asylum but rather identified them as economic immigrants.

By 1990, the US Census recorded over 225,000 foreign born from Guatemala as residing in the United States, although those numbers underestimated the total number of immigrants since many were undocumented. Unofficial estimates were that there were over five hundred thousand Guatemalans residing in the United States at that time. Guatemalan immigrants comprise the second-largest group of Central American immigrants in the United States, second after those from El Salvador.

Guatemalan immigrants have concentrated in certain cities throughout the United States, both along the West and East Coast. Ladinos, that is those of mestizo ancestry, tended to concentrate in Chicago, New York, and the San Francisco Bay Area. Wealthier Guatemalan Americans have also settled in Miami, Florida. The Mayans who migrated to the United States during the political unrest of the 1980s reestablished their indigenous communities and maintained their ethnic ties by settling in specific US cities. Historically a Mexican/Chicano neighborhood, the Pico-Union district of Central Los Angeles became the destination site for Guatemalan Mayan immigrants, including Mayan Chujes, Quichés, and Kanjobals. In contrast, the Mayans from Quiché and Totonicapán in Guatemala's southwestern highlands tended to immigrate to Houston, Texas. Other Kanjobal Maya, working as migrant workers, sought settlement in the rural farming community of Indiantown, Florida. These indigenous immigrants spoke their respective Maya language as their primary tongues; while the men were often bilingual Maya/Spanish speakers, the women were predominately monolingual. By settling together with others from their home communities, retaining their indigenous languages, and bringing along many traditions, such as the marimba, the Guatemalan Maya immigrants have often drawn on their ethnic ties to maintain cultural traditions.

Foodways

Guatemalan cuisine is grounded in the prehistoric foodways of ancient Maya civilizations. The prehispanic Maya cuisine was based on the staple foods of maize, beans, chile peppers, squash, and tomatoes, all foods that remain at the core of the modern Guatemalan cuisine.

With the Spanish Conquest in the sixteenth century, the Columbian exchange brought Old World foods, such as rice, pork, chicken, and wheat, among other foods, that were incorporated into Guatemalan foodways. Despite its relatively small land area (approximately 42,042 square miles), Guatemala is marked by great ecological and cultural diversity, which are reflected in its food culture. Guatemala's cuisine is divided into three subtypes: indigenous, Spanish, and Livingston. The Maya Indians of Highland Guatemala retained their traditional dishes and culinary practices, integrating European foods over time. The Ladinos, those who identified with their European ancestry, reproduced the Spanish colonial culinary style established during the colonial period. Finally, in a small strip of eastern Guatemala that borders the Caribbean, the indentured workers from India and Africa reproduced a tropical cuisine that shares more in common with Belize or the Circum-Caribbean nations than with the rest of Guatemala. Among Guatemalan American immigrants, the indigenous and Spanish colonial cooking styles dominate.

Both indigenous and Spanish styles use many of the fruits and vegetables native to the New World. These foods include *chayote*, a pale green, pear-shaped vegetable that can be boiled, fried, mashed, or baked; cilantro; and chocolate. Corn tortillas are a staple to all meals. In the highland Guatemalan villages, Maya women spent hours preparing the maize kernels through the nixtamalization process of soaking them in a lime solution, grinding the prepared kernel to prepare the *masa*, and shaping the tortillas by hand to cook on the *comal*, a flat, clay platter, over the open fire. In the United States, Latino groceries sell corn tortillas processed at industrial tortilla factories, and Guatemalan Maya women no longer have to make tortillas by hand. Beans are another Guatemalan staple, specifically black beans, which historically have been harder to find in US groceries, but Latino groceries have generally provided both canned and dried. In indigenous communities, black beans are prepared in soups or pureed to be eaten with corn tortillas, while in the cities, they are consumed with rice.

The most important food among Guatemalans is the tamale, first developed in prehistoric times by the ancient Mayan civilizations. Tamales are made of a maize paste or dough wrapped around a meat or vegetable filling. In contrast with Mexicans, Central Americans often cook the *masa* in chicken stock that results in a softer-textured tamale. Other kinds of tamales can also be made with dough from flour, potatoes, or green bananas. In Guatemala, tamales are traditionally wrapped in banana leaves or fresh cornhusks and then steamed to cook the ingredients. A special Guatemalan delicacy, *chuchitos*, are corn *masa* tamales filled with chicken, pork, or turkey, combined with tomatoes and chiles. These tamales may also include other ingredients in the *masa*, such as tomato sauce, mashed potatoes, annatto, or allspice. Also popular are *chilaquiles*, not to be confused with the Mexican dish of the same name, that are tortillas stuffed with cheese or other ingredients, dipped in a batter, and then fried or baked. Often tortillas, combined with seeds of different kinds, are used to thicken Guatemalan stews, as in the well-known chicken dish, *jocón*, replicated below.

Guatemalan *Jocón* Recipe

2½ to 3 pounds chicken, cut into serving pieces
4 cups of water
2 teaspoons of salt
¼ cup pumpkin seeds
¼ cup sesame seeds
2 corn tortillas, chopped, soaked in water and drained
1 cup tomatillos, husked and chopped
1 bunch cilantro
1 bunch scallions
1 to 5 jalapeño or serrano chile peppers, chopped (depending on spiciness preferred)

1. Place chicken, water, and salt in large pot over medium-high flame. Bring to a boil, immediately reducing heat to medium low and simmering for 1 hour.
2. Remove chicken from pot, cool, shred with fingers, remove skin, and set aside. Strain and set aside broth.
3. Heat dry skillet over medium flame. Add pumpkin and sesame seeds and toast, stirring occasionally, until lightly browned. Grind toasted seeds in coffee grinder into fine powder.
4. Add ground seeds, tortillas, tomatillo, cilantro, scallions, and chile peppers to blender. Add 1 cup of reserved chicken broth and blend until smooth.
5. Return cooked chicken to pot. Add pureed sauce. Add 1 to 1½ cups of reserved broth to make thick sauce.
6. Heat at medium hot and then reduce to simmer for 15 to 25 minutes. Adjust seasonings and serve.

Since many Guatemalan immigrants historically came from small rural villages, they also brought with them traditional uses of different foods as medicine. In Guatemala, traditional curers use teas, herbs, and other natural remedies to heal the sick. In the United States, Guatemalan immigrants seek out herbs, such as chamomile or *hierba buena*, a mixture from Mexico, at Latino *botánicas*, or medicine shops, to cure mild ailments, such as upset stomachs or headaches.

The daily pattern of meals varies between urban and rural areas. In urban areas, where many Guatemalan immigrants have settled, people normally eat three meals a day. For breakfast, Guatemalans generally consume coffee, eggs, beans, or toast. The eggs may be dressed with *chirmol*, a red chile and tomato salsa. In Guatemala, the midday meal was the main, largest meal of the day, consisting of soup, meat, rice, vegetables, and salad. In the United States, lunch is often a simpler fare, such as beans, tortillas, and eggs. Dinner was later in the evening, a lighter meal that might consist of bread, rice, or beans. Living and working in the United States has forced Guatemalan urban immigrants to adjust their meals to follow the American pattern of eating a lighter lunch and consuming the main meal as dinner in the evening. In rural areas, immigrants would begin the day with coffee, black beans, and tortillas. Midday meals were traditionally larger, although often not as varied as urban meals. Late in the evening, dinner might often be little more than black beans and tortillas, perhaps accompanied by eggs and some vegetables.

Holiday Feasts

For Guatemalan immigrants, religious and holiday feast days can play important roles in maintaining cultural identity and heritage. Here food also plays important roles. Most Guatemalans are Catholic, approximately 60 percent, although evangelical Protestantism has spread widely throughout Guatemala. For Catholics and Mayan who continue to practice indigenous beliefs through popular Catholicism, the liturgical calendar provides a series of feast days through which Guatemalans reinforce family and cultural bonds. Christmas marks the beginning of the Catholic calendar, and Guatemalans celebrate Christmas through parties, processions, and various festivities. Homes are decorated with small, yellow fruits, called *manzanillas*, and tamales and punch are always served on Christmas Eve. Following the abstention and fasting of Lent, Guatemalans celebrate Holy Week, known as *Semana Santa*, with festivities, processions, and special foods. *Torrejas*, pastries, *encurtidos*, spicy vegetables with vinegar, and candied fruits are popular foods. Those of Mayan descent prepare *tobic*, a vegetable, beef, and cabbage soup; *kilim*, chicken in a seasoned sauce; and *joch*, a hot drink made with *masa*, barley, cinnamon, and brown sugar. To close the Catholic calendar, on All Saint's Day in November, also known as the "Day of the Dead," Guatemalans follow the Mexican practice of constructing altars on the gravesites of their ancestors, offering food and drink to their spirits when they return to share in the food and communion with their families.

Place in American Culture

The earliest Guatemalan immigrants to the United States faced challenges maintaining traditional foodways and adapted recipes from ingredients available in Mexican groceries. With the influx of Central American immigrants, Latino food companies, in particular Goya, expanded their Caribbean product line to include more Central American offerings. Both Latino groceries and supermarkets with Latino food sections now include a wide range of Latino foods, including fresh, processed, and frozen. Having these foods more readily available makes it easier to maintain traditional foodways.

At the same time, many Guatemalan immigrants, particular indigenous families in both urban and rural settings, are faced with budgetary and time constraints. Their daily fare may much more closely approximate working-class US cooking, while the traditional foods may be reserved for special feast days and community celebrations.

Restaurants

In neighborhoods of Central American immigrants, local restaurants often reproduce the traditional foods that are more difficult to reconstruct in household kitchens. Outside of Salvadorean restaurants, or *pupuserías*, many Central American restaurants may serve a variety of different fare, including Mexican, Guatemalan, and Nicaraguan, adapting their menus to serve a broader Latino clientele.

Further Reading

Anderson, Lynne Christy. "Why Not Teach Them to Cook? Beatriz's Guatemalan Tortillas con Frijoles y Queso." In *Breaking Bread: Recipes and Stories from Immigrant Kitchens*, by Lynne Anderson. Berkeley, University of California Press, 2010.

Janer, Zilkia. *Latino Food Culture*. Westport, CT: Greenwood Press, 2008.

McDonald, Michael R. *Food Culture in Central America*. Santa Barbara: Greenwood Press, 2009.

Moreno-Damgaard, Amalia. *Amalia's Guatemalan Kitchen: Gourmet Cuisine with a Cultural Flair*. Beaver's Pond Press, 2012.

Presilla, Maricel. *Gran Cocina Latina: the Food of Latin America*. W. W. Norton, 2012.

Lois Stanford

GUERNSEY

(United Kingdom, Northern Europe) British American Food
See: England.

GUINEA

(West Africa) Guinean American Food
See also: Sierre Leone, Niger, Gambia, Senegal, Côte d'Ivoire, formerly French Guinea (1890–1960).

Background

Guinea stretches from the coast of the Atlantic Ocean inland to highlands and the sources of major rivers, the Niger, Gambia, and Senegal. A colony of France from 1890 to 1960, it has abundant natural resources, and agriculture and mineral production (iron, diamonds, gold, uranium) now drive the economy. It holds twenty-four ethnic groups and is primarily Muslim, and French is the national language.

Like other West Africans, many Guineans were brought to the United States as slaves, particularly to the southern coastal areas that grew rice because of their traditional knowledge of that crop. In the later 1900s, human rights issues and poverty forced many Guineans to leave. The 2000 census showed slightly over three thousand immigrants in the United States, but by 2010, that had increased to over ten thousand in New York alone. Rhode Island and Washington, DC, have other large communities, but they can also be found in Atlanta, Boston, Chicago, and Columbus, Ohio. Many Guinean Americans work as taxi drivers and hairbraiders.

Foodways

Guinean American food culture is similar to that of other West Africans in the United States and also reflects French influence in traditions of baking and pastries. It is not well known in the United States, and, if available, it is usually found with other West African cuisines.

An example is a restaurant in Columbus, Ohio, which has one of the highest populations of African immigrants in the country. The restaurant, Medina: A Taste of World Cuisine, specializes in Guinean food, but it advertises itself as Mediterranean, African, Asian, and American soul food. On their website, they offer dishes from Guinea on special order, although they do not identify what those are. Their menu is typical of other West African restaurants that offer the "signature dishes" of a number of African countries.

Among the dishes featured on their menu are *thiebou djeun* (considered the national dish of Senegal and described as "fish stewed in a rich sauce with eggplant, carrots, cassava, and cabbage over exotic rice and tomatoes"), marinated lamb or chicken spiced with curry powder and served over steamed white rice, *maffeh* (lamb cooked in a creamy peanut butter and tomato sauce with yams, carrots, and cabbage), *thiebou yap* (lamb served with brown rice and fresh mixed vegetables), *thiouh* (meat, fish or meatball stewed in tasty tomato sauce with fresh vegetables served over steamed white rice), *athieke* (couscous cassava from the Ivory Coast made with fish or chicken or lamb seasoned in onion and tomato sauce), *dibi* (grilled lamb served with spaghetti, couscous, or salad, and tomato, eggs, and onions), *brochette* (grilled beef chops, chicken chops, or shrimp marinated with special spices), and *fataya* (beef or chicken in flour).

Further Reading

JourneyMart. Guinea. http://www.journeymart.com/de/guinea/food.aspx.

Medina Restaurant. http://medinacolumbus.com/index.php.

Lucy M. Long

GUINEA-BISSAU

(Western Africa) Guinea-Bissauan American Food

See also: Cape Verde, Guinea, Senegal.

Background

With the Atlantic Ocean on its west and Senegal and Guinea on its other borders, Guinea-Bissau was occupied by the Portuguese from late 1400s to 1974. Although it achieved independence as the Republic of Guinea-Bissau in 1974, it currently has high rates of poverty and food insecurity. Numerous slaves were taken from there, but very few immigrants came to the United States afterward. At the same time, some African Americans have discovered they are descendants of Guinea-Bissauan slaves.[1] The 2000 census lists only three hundred Guinea-Bissauans in the United States. As with other descendants of West Africans in the United States, there is still much to explore in terms of foodways.

Foodways

Guinea-Bissauan food culture is similar to those of other West African countries—*fufu*, rice, palm wine and palm oil, millet, couscous, lemons, tomatoes, mangoes, papaya, bananas, plantains, corn, peanuts, sweet potatoes, dried fish, and techniques such as frying in oil. Basic dishes focus on soups and stews, including soups thickened with the ground seeds of melons and squash (*egusi*). The Guinea pepper and chiles are particular to Guinea-Bissau cuisine. Also influenced by Arabic and Portuguese culinary traditions, "Guinea-Bissauans often say that if they haven't eaten rice at a meal, they haven't eaten at all."[2] The nation currently grows cashews for export, along with coconuts, palm nut, and olives.[3] Portuguese pastries such as *pastel de nata* (a custard tart) and white flour bread[4] can be found in Guinea-Bissau. One place to learn about Guinea-Bissau culture in the United States is the Philadelphia Portuguese Heritage Festival, which features the cultures of many former Portuguese colonies.

Notes

1. Wikipedia, Guinea-Bissauan American, http://en.wikipedia.org/wiki/Guinea-Bissauan_American.
2. Global Table Adventure, About the Food of Guinea and Guinea-Bissau, http://globaltableadventure.com/2011/05/31/about-the-food-of-guinea-and-guinea-bissau/; CultureGrams 2009, "Republic of Guinea-Bissau."
3. Wikipedia, Cuisine of Guinea-Bissau, http://en.wikipedia.org/wiki/Cuisine_of_Guinea-Bissau.
4. Global Table Adventure, About the Food of Guinea and Guinea-Bissau; Wikipedia, Pastel de Nata, http://en.wikipedia.org/wiki/Pastel_de_nata.

Further Reading

Celtnet Recipes. Guinea Bissau Recipes and Cookery. http://www.celtnet.org.uk/recipes/guinea-bissau.php.

Culture Grams World Edition. "Republic of Guinea-Bissau." UN Development Programme, Human Development Report 2007/2008. New York: Palgrave Macmillan, 2009.

Martin, Sasha. About the Food of Guinea and Guinea-Bissau. http://globaltableadventure.com/2011/05/31/about-the-food-of-guinea-and-guinea-bissau.

Our Food Recipes. Guinea Bissauan Food Recipes. http://www.our-food-recipes.com/guinea-bissauan-food-recipes.html.

Philadelphia Portuguese Heritage Commission. http://www.portugalinphilly.com/history-culture/1987---philly-s-portuguese-connection.

Philadelphia Portuguese Heritage Festival 2013. http://www.last.fm/festival/3615282+The+Philadelphia+Portuguese+Heritage+Festival+2013.

Slow Food Foundation. Wild Palm Oil. Guinea Bissau. http://www.slowfoodfoundation.com/presidia/details/4433/wild-palm-oil#.VGUix4dlSAA.

Wikipedia. Cuisine of Guinea-Bissau. http://en.wikipedia.org/wiki/Cuisine_of_Guinea-Bissau.

Wikipedia. Guinea-Bissauan American. http://en.wikipedia.org/wiki/Guinea-Bissauan_American.

Lucy M. Long and Susan Eleuterio

GUYANA

(South America) Guyanese American Food
See also: Belize.

Background

Guyana (formerly British Guiana) is located in the northeasterly region of South America and is an ethnically diverse country with a population of approximately eight hundred thousand. The "six races" that comprise Guyana's population include Amerindians (the first Guyanese), Africans (former slaves), Chinese (indentured laborers), East Indians (indentured laborers), Europeans (colonialists and indentured laborers), and mixed-race individuals, often referred to as Douglas. Due to race-based political strife, economic depression, and other factors, many Guyanese emigrated from Guyana. In fact, more Guyanese reside abroad than in Guyana. Most Guyanese who migrate live in large urban centers such as New York City and Atlanta, Georgia.

While Guyana's ethnic diversity is demonstrated through various cultural expressions, Guyanese food constitutes one of the most crucial and enduring articulations of race, gender, nationhood, and other identities in the Guyanese community. It is not surprising, then, that "Guyanese food" serves as an important gustatory symbol of Guyaneseness for Guyanese Americans and other expatriate Guyanese. As anthropologist Sidney Mintz argued: "What we like, what we eat, how we eat it, and how we feel about it are phenomenologically interrelated matters; together, they speak eloquently to the question of how we perceive ourselves in relation to others." Guyanese Americans use "Guyanese food" as a unique symbol of identity through which they articulate notions of "home," distinguish themselves from other ethnic groups, and in the process, construct an "imagined community" with other Guyanese through acts of cooking and eating.

Guyanese use the term *Guyanese food* to encompass plethora of cuisines, which reflect the heritages of the Guyanese people, creolization in the New World, and key socioeconomic and political developments in Guyana. Thus, for example, Guyanese food includes Amerindian *pepperpot*, African *fufu*, Chinese *chow mein*, East Indian curry and *roti* (a flat bread), and European souse—all of which were brought with the Guyanese from their ancestral homes and modified in Guyana.[1] On the other hand, foods like *Cassava lick-down*, and *rice flour bakes* are relatively new constructions, which emerged in Guyana in the 1980s during a harsh economic and political period.[2] President L. F. S. Burnham had banned the importation of wheat flour and other food items, forcing the Guyanese people to improvise new cuisines in order to survive. Thus, the manners in which the cuisines are integrated into the corpus of "Guyanese food" are crucial to understanding the important role that food plays in the Guyanese community.

Foodways

The foodstuffs that Guyanese use to prepare their cuisines include starchy staples, essential proteins, and a vast assortment of vegetables. The main starchy staples are rice, flour, and "ground provisions" (plantains, cassava, eddoes, and other tubers), while proteins include fish, beans, and peas, and various kinds of meats, such as beef, pork, deer, *labba* (agouti), and turtle. Vegetables include squashes, such as pumpkin and zucchini; legumes, such as *bora* (a long green bean) and same (a flat green bean); and green leafy vegetables such as cabbage, bok choy, and *eddo* leaves (leaves of the *eddo* root); and an assortment of other vegetables, including *corilla* (also known as bitter melon), eggplant, and okra. The food items listed previously are used in a variety of Guyanese dishes, but they are often determined by financial means, religious values, and personal tastes of individuals preparing and consuming the meals.

In order to obtain the food items needed to prepare their cuisines, Guyanese in Guyana use fresh fruits and vegetables from their kitchen gardens, or purchase them from locally owned farms, open markets, and itinerant venders who sell their produce on large trucks. However, in the United States, Guyanese purchase foodstuffs from international markets and "Chinese stores," which are open markets that sell fresh fruits and vegetables and various ethnic foods. In many instances, Guyanese who live in areas where they cannot obtain the foodstuff to prepare their cuisines would travel to New York City; Atlanta, Georgia; and other areas with large Asian and Caribbean populations to purchase the items. When they cannot travel to purchase food items, they would have friends, relatives, or storekeepers ship the items to them. Many Guyanese also use substitutes, particularly canned foods, when they are unable to obtain authentic foodstuffs. Thus, for example, when they cannot obtain dried coconuts to make buns or cook stews they use prepackaged shredded coconut or canned coconut milk or cream, respectively.

Regardless of how they obtain the foodstuffs, the average Guyanese home uses them to prepare three square meals (breakfast, lunch, and dinner) and a variety of pastries, sweets, and other snacks. Some of the typical foods that Guyanese prepare for breakfast include hot cereals (porridges), bakes (fried bread), and salt-fish or stews, roti and stews, ground provisions and stews, bread and tea, and, less frequently, rice and stews.[3] Guyanese also consume "breakfast foods" such as roti and stews during other meal times. However, Guyanese lunches are generally heavier meals with prepared rice, such as cabbage and chicken with rice; *bora* (long green bean) and rice with fried fish; and curried chicken and rice. While the possibilities for rice and stew meals are endless, lunch cuisines often also include *pepperpot* and bread, *chow mein*, fried rice with vegetables and meats, and one-pot meals such as cookup rice (rice, peas or beans, and meats cooked in coconut milk), and *metemgee* or *metem* (ground provisions and meats boiled in coconut milk).[4] Guyanese often consume lunch cuisines for dinner, but more often than not, their dinners include lighter breakfastlike dishes with teas or other hot beverages. Between meals, Guyanese often consume a variety of snacks, such as fudges, plantain chips, *salara* (red-dyed coconut bread), buns, cakes, and foods from other ethnic groups.

The foods Guyanese prepare and consume are not only influenced by the time of day but also by the time of year; that is, cultural (race-based) celebrations, holidays, and holy days. Thus, for example, African Guyanese prepare *fufu* and one-pot meals like cookup rice and *metemgee* during Emancipation Day celebrations and *kweh-kweh* rituals, while East Indians prepare curries, *bara* (a type of flat bread with split peas), and *mittai* (a sweet) during Diwali and Phagwah.[5] Also, many Christians, particularly Anglicans and Catholics, forego eating meats during the Lenten season but bake cross buns and other pastries on Good Friday.

Additionally, Guyanese prepare specific cuisines during Christmas, such as *pepperpot* and bread, black cake (dark fruit cake), ginger beer, and *mauby* (beverage made with a type of tree bark), while on Old Year's Night (New Year's Eve) they make cookup rice, particularly black-eyed peas cookup. By continuing to cook the foods they ate back home in Guyana, Guyanese are able to reconstruct a sense of belonging through memory, to maintain tradition, and to create an imagined culinary community, to cite Benedict Anderson, with other Guyanese in the United States and around the world.

Pepperpot is one such dish that occupies a crucial place on the Guyanese foodscape, as it is a uniquely Guyanese cuisine as well as the Guyana's national dish.[6] Made with cassereep, a thick, brown sauce that is extracted from the bitter cassava, and many different kinds of meat, *pepperpot* is quintessential Christmas morning breakfast for Guyanese of all religious faiths (see recipe below).[7] Once *pepperpot* is cooked, it does not need to be refrigerated, but rather is brought to a boil each day to keep it fresh. Thus, Guyanese would consume *pepperpot* for breakfast, lunch, and dinner by varying only the starchy staple (bread, rice, roti) with which they consume it. As Guyana's national dish and an American construct, *pepperpot* is one of the few cuisines that have the ability to conflate culinary ethnic divisions and unite Guyanese. The aroma and the taste are two features of *pepperpot* that keep Guyanese singing its praises and reciting the "*Pepperpot*" poem in its honor.

"*Pepperpot,*" by A. J. Seymore

I love to eat some *pepperpot*
Especially when it's very hot
It's made of every kind of meat
Boiled in cassava cassereep
It's such a tasty, dainty dish
but seldom ever made of fish.

While cooking and eating Guyanese foods enable Guyanese to construct racial and national identities, gendered values are particularly articulated through food preparation and consumption. While "proper women" are expected to be skillful cooks, "real men" are expected to eat healthy, energy-giving foods, such as broths, *metemgee*, porridges, and soups. In most households women are the principal cooks who feed other members of the family. Thus, from a young age, girls are taught how to skillfully prepare a variety of dishes in anticipation of romantic relationships and impending marriages. Food is such a crucial aspect of marriage, and the Guyanese community at large, that men often cite poor cooking or bad food as a reason for infidelity and physical abuse of their wives; women, on the other hand, use *obeah* (witchcraft) in food to control men or poisons to kill them. Thus, it is through food that boys and girls become properly socialized men and women in the Guyanese community or push the boundaries of established gendered roles.

Place in American Culture

Because "Guyanese food" constitutes such a diverse body of cuisines with equally diverse origins, it is not surprising that many of these foods are also prepared and consumed in one way or another by Asian Americans, Caribbean nationals (West Indians), and many other ethnic groups in the United States. However, Guyanese often argue that while they may cook the same cuisines as these other ethnic groups, the unique combination of spices and cooking methods they use distinguish their curries, for example, from those of Indians from India and other West Indians. In order to maintain the "Guyaneseness" in their cooking, they spend countless hours teaching the youths (particularly young women) to properly hone the craft of cooking "Guyanese food" and harshly critiquing each other's cuisines. Thus, for example, Guyanese often refer to someone's cookup as "cookup's friend" or "cookup's cousin," to highlight what they regard as the food's inauthentic appearance, smell, or taste. To maintain the distinctive tastes of their foods, Guyanese also turn to Guyanese cookbooks such as *What's Cooking in Guyana*, which was produced in 2004 by the Carnegie School of Home Economics in Guyana.

Noted Restaurants and Chefs

While Guyanese prepare meals in their individual homes, on a daily basis they also frequent Guyanese restaurants to supplement their meals or simply to get a taste of home without going through the drudgery of cooking. At these restaurants they may purchase relatively small quantities of breads, *roti*, pastries, snacks, and entire meals, or they may cater for larger events such as weddings. For example, restaurants such as Salt 'n Pepper and Sybil's in Brooklyn and Bamboo Garden and Brown Betty's in Queens cater to a large and vibrant Guyanese community in New York City. Additionally, restaurants like Lynmine International Cuisine in Plainfield, New Jersey, and Timehri Restaurant in Orlando, Florida, sell Guyanese foods but also highlight specific place names in Guyana and, thus, add another layer of complexity Guyanese identity negotiations through food. Moreover, Jamaican, Trinidadian, and other Caribbean restaurants also serve as pan-Caribbean establishments where West Indians could eat familiar cuisines or try new ones. Also, an increasing number of Caribbean restaurants also sell a conglomeration of cuisines from all over the Caribbean in order to accommodate the larger Caribbean and increase their marketability. While Guyanese and other West Indians may frequent particular restaurants because of the taste of the cuisines, more often than not, it is the nationality associated with the restaurant—such as a Guyana-based name on the restaurant, a Guyanese owner, or a large body of Guyanese employees—that keeps customers committed to that establishment. Thus, for many of the Guyanese patrons, food is, to quote Ferrero, "a symbolic and cultural connection with the homeland."[8]

Conclusion

Food is a crucial marker of identity in the Guyanese American community. Through food production, preparation, and consumption, Guyanese negotiate racial, gendered, and national identities. As each cuisine is generally linked to a specific ethnic group and geographic origin, "Guyanese food" simultaneously facilitates national unity and ethnic divisions in the said community. It is also through cooking and eating that Guyanese embrace gendered values by adhering to preexisting parameters of maleness and femaleness or transcending those boundaries. However, while they continue to cook the same foods in the United States, time constraints, lack of ingredients, and changing tastes often compel Guyanese to modify the ways they prepare "Guyanese food." Ultimately, through acts of cooking and eating the same cuisines, Guyanese symbolically bind themselves to each other, creating a larger imagined culinary community.

Pepperpot
Ingredients:
    1½ pounds beef
    1 pound pork
    ½ pound trotters (tripe) or cow's heels
    ½ pound pigtail
    1½ cup cassava cassareep (or to taste)
    1 red hot pepper
    1½ sticks of cinnamon stick
    2 ounces brown sugar (or to taste)
    1 pinch of salt (or to taste)
    2 stalks basil (marri'd man poke)
    1 bunch fine-leaf thyme
    1 large onion (finely chopped)
    2 garlic cloves (finely chopped)
    6 cloves

Directions:
1. Parboil pigtails, then scrape to remove hair and dirt.
2. Pressure cow heel.
3. Boil tripe.
4. Combine all meats into a large saucepan once they are tender.
5. Add cassareep and other ingredients to meats.
6. Cook on low fire for approximately one hour or until meats are fully cooked.
7. Add salt and sugar to attain desired flavor.

Note: Bring *pepperpot* to a boil every day to prevent spoiling. Refrigeration not needed.

Eat with cassava bread, dense homemade bread, rice, or starchy staple of your choice.

Black-Eyed Peas Cookup Rice

Ingredients:
- 2 small dried coconuts (grated)
- 1½ cans of coconut milk
- 1½ pints of long grain parboiled rice
- 2 pounds meat (1 chicken, 1 beef)
- 1 pint of dried black-eyed peas
- 1 small onion (finely chopped)
- 1 small tomato (diced)
- 2 green onions/scallions (finely chopped)
- 3 cloves of garlic (finely chopped)
- finely chopped fresh seasonings (fine leaf thyme, thick leaf thyme, and celery)
- 1 lemons/1 cup of lemon juice
- 2 bouillon cubes
- 1 tablespoon butter/margarine (optional)
- 1 tablespoon browning/soy sauce (for color)
- all-purpose seasoning or salt, black pepper, cumin, basil, red pepper (crushed or finely chopped)

Directions:
1. Wash peas; boil or pressure with light salt until parboiled.
2. Clean meats (chicken and beef) with lemon or lemon juice.
3. Season meats with all-purpose seasoning, black pepper, red pepper, cumin, and basil. Add browning or soy sauce. For best results, season meat overnight and refrigerate.
4. Sauté onion, tomato, garlic, and a portion of fresh seasonings.
5. Add seasoned meats to sautéed seasonings; stew together until meats are half cooked.
6. Combine parboiled peas, half-cooked meats, coconut milk, bouillon cubes, and butter/margarine.
7. Bring to boil for about 20 minutes; add seasonings to taste.
8. Lower heat, cover pot, and let cook for another 30 minutes or until rice is moist.
9. Serve with vegetable salad, fried yellow plantains, fried fish, or achar.

Notes
1. *Pepperpot* is a spicy brown spice souplike meal made with *cassareep* (a thick brown sauce) and different kinds of meats; *fufu* is a doughlike staple made from pounded cassava, yams, or other tubers; and *chow mein* is a type of noodle.
2. *Cassava lick-down* is made from boiled and pounded cassava; rice flour bakes are a type of fried bread, made from pounded rice.
3. Guyanese often argue that country folks, such as Berbicians (people from the county of Berbice in Guyana), are notorious for eating rice meals for breakfast.
4. See Richard-Greaves 2012 and 2013.
5. Emancipation Day is a commemoration of the end of slavery; *kweh-kweh* is an African Guyanese prewedding ritual; Diwali is a Hindu festival of lights; Phagwah is a Hindu festival that involves the throwing of dyes and powders.
6. Jamaicans prepare a dish called *pepperpot*, but it is markedly different from the Guyanese *pepperpot*.
7. Cassereep gives the *pepperpot* its unique color and taste. It is sold in many international markets, but many times Guyanese would have

it shipped from Guyana because they argue that it is more authentic. However, when it is unfeasible to obtain cassereep, some Guyanese use burned sugar as a substitute.

8. Abarca 2002, 9.

Further Reading

Abarca, Meredith E. "Authentic or Not, It's Original." *Food and Foodways* 12, no. 1 (2002): 1–26.

Albala, Ken. *Beans: A History*. New York: Berg, 2007.

Carnegie School of Home Economics. *What's Cooking in Guyana*, 2nd ed. Oxford: Macmillan, 2004.

Counihan, Carole M. *The Anthropology of Food and Body: Gender, Meaning, and Power*. New York: Routledge, 1999.

Knight, Franklin W., and Colin A. Palmer, eds. *The Modern Caribbean*. Chapel Hill and London: University of North Carolina Press, 1989.

Mintz, Sidney. *Sweetness and Power: The Place of Sugar in Modern History*. New York: Penguin Group, 1989.

Momsen, Janet H., ed. *Women and Change in the Caribbean: A Pan-Caribbean Perspective*. Bloomington: Indiana University Press, 1993.

Rabe, Stephen G. *U.S. Intervention in British Guiana: A Cold War Story*. Chapel Hill: University of Carolina Press, 2005.

Ray, Krishnendu. *The Migrant Table: Meals and Memories in Bengali-American Households*. Philadelphia: Temple University Press, 2004.

Richards-Greaves, Gillian. "Cookup Rice: Guyana's Culinary 'Dougla' and Ethnic Identity Negotiations." In *Rice and Beans: A Unique Dish in a Hundred Places*, 192–225. Edited by Richard Wilk and Livia Barbosa. Oxford: Berg, 2012.

Richards-Greaves, Gillian. "The Intersections of 'Guyanese Food' and Constructions of Gender, Race and Nationhood." In *Food and Identity in the Caribbean*, 75–94. Edited by Hanna Garth. Oxford: Berg, 2013.

Gillian Richards-Greaves

GYPSY

(North America) American Gypsy, Roma American Food

Background

There is no such thing as a Gypsy American cuisine. Even more than for other ethnic groups, there is not one but many Gypsy American cuisines. Following their departure from India sometime around AD 1000, they dispersed throughout Europe, the Middle East, and beyond. In the process, they were fragmented into a great number of national and tribal groups lacking sustained contact with one another and consequent cultural exchange. Only a few of these groups came to America in sufficient numbers to establish real communities. These came at different times from different places and had considerable cultural differences even prior to arrival in America. It is not surprising, therefore, that there are major differences in the cuisine of these American Gypsy communities.

The very name by which Gypsies call themselves is a good example of this cultural heterogeneity. The majority of Romani speakers are properly called by the name they use for themselves, *Roma* (singular, *Rom*, masculine, or *Romni*, feminine). With the development of greater political consciousness, this has gained wider usage, both among other Romani groups and among the general public. But a number of other groups, including those who speak one of the several creolized Romani languages, prefer other terms. Most Anglo-Romani speakers prefer to be called Romnichals, Romanies, or simply Travellers. Many do not object to being called Gypsies. Most Sinti and Manouche, the majority located in Germany and France, respectively, strongly object to being called *Roma*. There is no term in Romani that denotes all these people despite their common history. Hence, we are stuck with a term, *Gypsy*, which many consider pejorative.

Despite the general misconception that Gypsies are nomadic, only a minority are. Ever since their arrival in Europe, the majority have been settled, sometimes in cities and towns, sometimes on the periphery of peasant villages or in separate hamlets. Of those that were nomadic, some traveled more or less fixed annual routes; others wandered internationally to the extent they were allowed. Therefore, some American Gypsy communities led a settled life even prior to their emigration. Those who were nomadic prior to coming here continued nomadic life here, continuing or developing new peripatetic occupations. Gradually these groups were sedentarized, though possibly moving their domicile often or men maintaining a seasonal nomadic lifestyle related to their occupation.

The major American Gypsy communities are Rom (including Kalderash, Machwaya, and Lovara), Ludar, Romanichal, and Bashalde. Each community developed its own distinct foods and foodways, as well as other cultural attributes in isolation from other Gypsy communities.

The first Gypsies to come to America were deportees from England in the seventeenth century, but the Romanichals of present-day America descended from immigrants beginning around 1850. Around 1880 Gypsies began to come from Eastern Europe, along with waves of non-Gypsies from these same countries. Roma came especially from Russia, Serbia, and the Austro-Hungarian Empire. The Kalderash predominated among these and dispersed throughout North America. The largest community today is in New York. Machwaya came from the village of Mačva, Serbia, and after a period of nomadism, most settled in California. The first Bashalde, or musician Gypsies, came from two Slovak villages in what was then Hungary. They settled first near Pittsburg, then dispersed to other northern industrial cities—Detroit, Cleveland, Chicago—to settle in Hungarian American communities. Ludar, speaking a creolized dialect of Romanian, were also a part of the massive East European immigration beginning around 1880. Until 1865 they had suffered as slaves in what is now Romania. In America, some are still peripatetic, traveling with carnivals, black topping and roofing, or selling rustic furniture door to door. Others are settled in widely scattered trailer park communities.

By far the most important and far-reaching factor shaping what Gypsies eat and how they prepare their food is a complex of beliefs concerning pollution and ritual purity that originated in India. These are more stringently held in some groups than others, and specific practice varies from one group to another, but all Gypsy life has been shaped to some degree by these beliefs, and this is particularly true of food and food preparation. American Roma are particularly strong adherents and serve as a good example.

Roma believe in a bifurcated world divided into Gypsy and non-Gypsy, men and women, ritually clean (*wuzho*) and unclean (*marime*). The body above the beltline, especially the head, is considered sacred; that below, especially the genital area, is *marime*. A woman is *marime* during and six months after childbirth and during menstruation. A *marime* woman cannot cook or serve food to men. She cannot step over anything belonging to a man or allow her skirt to touch his things. For a woman to throw her skirt at a man or to lift her skirt at him is a defiling act. Women's and men's clothing must be washed separately. Upper garments must be washed separately from lower garments. A tablecloth would never be washed with underwear. Dishes could never be washed in the same sink or wash pan as clothing. All food is prepared, served, and eaten with the greatest concern for ritual quality. Anything brought into the home from outside is considered possibly polluted and is, therefore, scrutinized with care. Only freshly grown foods are considered safe, but everything, including meat, is cleansed thoroughly before use. People who, for some infraction, have been declared *marime* cannot eat with others. Roma do not eat with strangers or with those they don't trust. To refuse to eat with a Rom is a sign of distrust, implying that he is not ritually clean.

Non-Gypsies follow none of these proscriptions and are, therefore, considered *marime*. Many Romani households will keep a separate coffee cup and other tableware that they reserve for the use of non-Gypsy guests. Some will destroy or discard a cup that a non-Gypsy guest has used.

There are also certain qualities of lifestyle that are emphasized in most Gypsy communities, though not necessarily true of all groups or for all members of any group. These include spontaneity, adaptation, improvisation, and extravagance even in the face of poverty. These can be seen as adaptive strategies that have allowed Gypsies to cope more easily with problems such as discrimination, poverty, and pariah status. These qualities are present throughout Romani culture, including food and foodways.

Spontaneity in Gypsy cultures is such that dishes are never exactly the same. One uses what is available or what comes to mind. No one uses a cookbook or written recipe, so recipes are never standardized. Moreover, the common practice of not storing foodstuffs ahead, either because of not having money to build up stores or through lack of facilities to store them, means fewer options when cooking. One must think creatively.

Foodways
Each Gypsy community developed its own distinct foods and foodways, often completely in isolation from one another. Nevertheless, a few generalizations can be made. Those groups most recently nomadic emphasize stewing and frying, rather than baking, steaming, or roasting, other than whole animals on a spit. Traditionally, wild foodstuffs, both vegetable and animal, were incorporated into their diet. Now settled, they have less need or access to these, but a few still play a role. Nettles are still prepared by some women, and hunting and fishing are popular pastimes, especially among Machwaya. Vegetables are not particularly important in most Gypsy diets, though some groups or individuals greatly appreciate them. Lettuce is an exception, considered lucky because it is the same color as money.

Roma have the most distinctive cuisine and also have been the most studied. Romanichals and Bashalde are the most acculturated, and nothing has been reported on Ludara diet. Roma generally prefer fatty meat to lean and there is widespread preference for pork. Black pepper, red pepper, salt, vinegar, garlic, and onions are considered lucky (*baxt*) foods and all are made much use of. Most American Roma like spicy food. Celery is believed to promote virility. At feasts, a stalk of celery is laid at every place setting. Bread is essential at every meal, and there is a general appreciation of quality bread. There are several home-baked traditional breads, including some that were made by nomads without the benefit of an oven.

Whenever possible, Roma purchase the best quality available, butter not margarine, and free-range eggs. As fat they usually use lard, drippings, bacon grease, or butter. There is a widespread taboo among Gypsies against eating horsemeat due to their reliance and close association with horses during the period of nomadism.

Roma tend not to eat in restaurants unless they have to, though this restriction has lessened in recent years. Meals prepared by non-Roma (*Gadje*) are avoided because of presumed impurity. They will not usually eat food prepared by non-Gypsies and brought to them. If forced to purchase cooked food while traveling, the preference is for food wrapped in plastic or paper rather than food on plates. If forced to eat in a restaurant, many will avoid eating utensils, preferring to eat with their fingers. Often they will ask for paper or plastic cups, which they can be sure have not been previously used by a non-Gypsy. If food is suspect for any reason, it will be rejected. They prefer well-lit restaurants where food preparation can be observed.

In an extended family household, the most recently arrived daughter-in-law is usually expected to do the cooking under the supervision of her mother-in-law. Roma marry young, and this is how most Romani women learn to cook, specifically in the style of their husbands' families. Although cooking is generally considered women's work, men frequently cook, as when the usual female cook is forbidden to do so because of *marime* conventions. Some men take great pride in their cooking abilities. A demonstration of this can be seen viewing Rusty Mark's regular entries on YouTube. Among American Roma, men cook all festival food, thereby ensuring that the food is ritually safe.

Holiday Feasts

Feasting is important among Gypsies everywhere but seems to have reached its highest expression among American Roma. Of special importance is the *slava*, a saint's day feast most often fixed according to the Orthodox calendar. A *slava* feast brings good luck, good health, and prestige to the family that gives it. Over time, some *slavas* have become traditional for some families or groups of related families. In other cases, a *slava* is given because of a promise to a saint for curing a person in ill health. Food for a *slava*, which must be of the utmost ritual purity, is prepared the night before by the family giving the slava. Each *slava* features a specific meat: roast pig for Saint John's Day; fish for Saint Nicholas; roast lamb for Saint George, Saint Mary, Saint Anne, and Easter. A *slava* feast should also include certain auspicious foods: *gushvada* (cheese strudel), *pirogo* (noodle cake), and especially *sarmi* (stuffed cabbage). An excess of food is very important, and great attention is paid to its display.

A *slava* held by a Machwaya family in Santa Rosa, California, in 1965 serves as an example. Folding tables had been put together to form a single table 8 feet wide by 120 feet long. On the table at one end was a three-fourth lifesize statue of a saint with an offering of a half-full gallon jug of wine and banks of flowers. At the center of the table was a tower constructed of two brass trays on legs, one on top of the other. A whole roasted pig lay on the top tray, and both trays were heaped with fresh fruit—apples, oranges, bananas, pineapples, and grapes dangling around the edges. Elsewhere on the table were three five-foot-tall candles, each presented by a different member of the host family. Each sat in a brass pot and was decorated with ribbons and flowers. Several large pots of flowers completed the table decorations. The remainder of the table was covered with paper plates set rim-to-rim, 2,100 in all according to the hosts. Down the center were larger plates with roasted chickens, roasted turkeys, pigs' heads, and whole roasted suckling pigs. Each place setting consisted of a china plate with either half a roasted chicken or an equivalent chunk of roasted pig. Beside the plate was a knife and fork, a paper napkin, one-sixth of a head of celery, a couple of green onions, three large slabs of bread, and a smaller paper plate with blobs of catsup and mustard (used as dips for the celery). The smaller paper plates covering the remainder of the table held an array of side dishes, including *sarmi*, chopped offal in brown gravy; rice; green beans cooked with peppers, oil, and lots of garlic; potato salad; macaroni salad; green salad; pickled beets; hot peppers; pickled green tomatoes; and an apple pastry. There was an open bar, kegs of beer, and punchbowls of vodka and orange juice. Twenty pigs had been roasted for the affair. Eating the food is no more important than its conspicuous presentation for everyone to see.

Lavish feasts are also obligatory at weddings, funerals (*pomana*), baptisms, *pakiv* (a feast honoring some important individual), and *kris pomana* (the trials at which laws governing social behavior are resolved). Newly arrived Romani immigrants were also quick to adopt Thanksgiving and New Year's celebrations. Some Romani families like feasting so much they will celebrate both Catholic and Orthodox Christmas and Easter. Photographs from special occasion feasts, especially weddings, are commonly displayed on YouTube.

Feasts have great social significance. Guests number in the hundreds and may come from across North America. The sharing of food at a feast table expresses mutual respect, friendship, and acceptance of one another's ritual cleanliness.

Over the last several decades there has been a steady conversion to Evangelical Protestantism. The majority of American Roma are now members of Evangelical churches with Romani pastors. Since saints are not recognized in these churches, those who have converted no longer celebrate *slava*, though other feasts may still be held.

A traditional dish prepared both for feasts and everyday is *pirogo*.

Pirogo

    16 ounces egg noodles
    2 pounds large curd cottage cheese
    5 cubes butter
    4 cups granulated sugar
    2 cans evaporated milk
    1 cup heavy whipping cream
    8 ounces cream cheese
    6 eggs
    1½ cups raisins (optional)

Boil egg noodles according to directions on package. Strain and put in bowl with butter and cream cheese. Mix until melted. In separate bowl, mix cottage cheese, eggs, canned milk, cream, sugar, and raisins (if used). Combine contents of the two bowls and mix well. Place in baking dish and bake in a 350-degree oven until firm and golden brown, approximately 1½ hours.

Place in American Culture

Many, perhaps most, Americans are ignorant that some of their fellow Americans are Gypsy. It is not surprising, then, that they know nothing of Gypsy food and foodways. Despite the abundance of attention given in recent years to culinary concerns in America, virtually none of this concerns Gypsy food. There is one notable exception: the appearance in 2005 of the first Romani-American cookbook, *Gypsy Open-Fire Cookbook*, by "Jacey." She is Romani, born and raised in America. The book is short on contextual information, but the recipes are authentic. Also, one must note the appearance on YouTube of the many Gypsies presenting recipes. These have obviously been modeled after television food programs. Presenters are usually women (sometimes with a man in the background adding comments), but occasionally they are by men. Judging by the presentations, and often by viewers' comments, these are directed at fellow Roma.

Noted Restaurants and Chefs

Although there are many American restaurants bearing some form of "Gypsy" in their names, there are no Gypsy restaurants in the United States, in the sense of a Romani-owned restaurant serving Romani food: The Little Gypsy; Gypsy Camp Restaurant and Cocktail Lounge; Mr. Juian's Gypsy Pub; Gypsy Inn; Gypsy Room; Zingaro Bar; the Zingaro (a gourmet food truck); Zingaro Bar and Grill; Zingari Italian Restaurant; Zingaro Restaurant; and more.

Further Reading

Gropper, Rena. *Gypsies in the City: Culture Patterns and Survival*. Princeton, NJ: The Darwin Press, 1975.

Hancock, Ian. "Romani Foodways: The Indian Roots of Gypsy Culinary Culture." *Roma* 35 (1991): 5–19.

Jacey. *Gypsy Open-Fire Cookbook*. Baltimore: Publish America, 2005.

Miller, Carol. "Macwaya Gypsy *Marimé*." MA Thesis, University of Washington, 1968.

Miller, Carol. "American Rom and the Ideology of Defilement." In Farnham Rehfisch, ed., *Gypsies, Tinkers and Other Travellers*. London: Academic Press, 1975.

Miller, Carol. *The Church of Cheese: Gypsy Ritual in the American Heyday*. Boston: GemmaMedia, 2010.

Pickett, David. "The Gypsies of Mexico, Part 2." *Journal of Gypsy Lore Society, Third Series* 45 (1966): 6–16.

Salo, Matt, and Sheil Salo. *The Kalderas in Eastern Canada*. Canadian Centre for Folk Culture Studies Paper 21. Ottawa: National Museums of Canada, 1977.

Sutherland, Anne. *Gypsies: The Hidden Americans*. New York: The Free Press, 1975.

Thomas, James. "Disease, Lifestyle, and Consanguinity in 58 American Gypsies." *Lancet* 2 (1985): 377–70.

Thomas, James. "Health Care of American Gypsies: Social and Medical Aspects." In *Papers from the Eighth and Ninth Annual Meetings*. Edited by Cara DeSilva et al., 128–38. New York: Gypsy Lore Society, North American Chapter (1988).

William G. Lockwood

H

HAITI
(Americas—Caribbean) Haitian American Food

Background

The Haitian community in the United States shares many cultural and gastronomic similarities with other Caribbean immigrant groups, particularly in its close cultural ties to West Africa. Nevertheless, the history of Haitian immigration to the United States has unique elements and is reflective of not only US immigration policies but also how those policies relate to immigrants' race and how negative media portrayal of a particular ethnic group can affect the group's reception and assimilation into mainstream American society.

The Republic of Haiti was officially founded in 1804 after it achieved independence from France in a violent slave rebellion, making the country the first free black republic in history and the second independent state in the Americas after the United States. However, records of migration to the United States occurred long before the colony of Saint-Domingue became present-day Haiti. Jean Baptiste Point du Sable, a mixed-race African and white man from Saint-Domingue, became the first nonindigenous settler in the city of Chicago, Illinois, and in 1968 the city declared him the founder of modern-day Chicago. During the Haitian revolution, as well as its aftermath, many of the white French landowners and mixed-race free people of color (*Gens de Couleur Libres*) also resettled in Louisiana.

Postrevolution, migration out of Haiti was based mostly on linguistic and cultural ties to their former colonizer, France, as well as other former colonies such as Quebec. Additionally, many Haitians also crossed the border into neighboring Dominican Republic to work in agriculture. Haitian immigration to the United States was minimal until the late 1950s, with an estimated five hundred Haitians immigrating permanently to the United States a year. After 1957, when dictator François "Papa Doc" Duvalier came into power, this number increased exponentially to nearly seven thousand immigrants per year, mostly to New York City, Boston, and Chicago.

The first case of Haitian refugees arriving by boat to South Florida is reported to have occurred in 1963, followed by another one in 1973. Starting in 1977, Haitian refugees began to arrive by boat to the United States with regularity, and by 1990 the US Census counted nearly three hundred thousand Haitians residing in the United States. The most recent figures from the US Census's 2012 American Community Survey put the total ethnic Haitian population in the United States at 927,038.

Following the rise to power of Duvalier in 1957, as well as throughout subsequent regimes in Haiti, the reception of Haitians in the United States has been fraught with controversy over their status as political refugees versus economic immigrants. In spite of personal accounts of atrocities in their homeland and threats to their lives if they return, the stance of the Immigration and Naturalization Service (INS) has leaned heavily toward the latter view, with few Haitians being granted political asylum. The attitudes of the INS toward the overwhelmingly black Haitian immigrants (over 96 percent according to 2012 American Community Survey data) have consequently made the government organization the target of accusations of racism and prejudicial policies.

Few immigrant groups to the United States have been as maligned as Haitians have over the past forty years. The Centers for Disease Control (CDC) has repeatedly identified the population as a health threat starting with tuberculosis in the 1970s and then AIDS in the 1980s, with the Food and Drug Administration (FDA) refusing to accept blood donations from anyone of Haitian descent at that time. The CDC and FDA decisions influenced the general population's attitudes toward Haitians, and subsequently many were discriminated against. American popular culture's misrepresentations of *Vodou* (also popularly spelled as *Voodoo*) religious practices and their association with Haiti also led to further alienation of the Haitian community in the United States. Furthermore, many Haitians find themselves linguistically isolated, speaking a language, Haitian Creole, which is unique to their homeland. As a result, many Haitians have attempted to mask their identity and assimilate into mainstream African American culture—Anglicizing their names, refusing to speak their native tongue, eliminating their accent, and eschewing all aspects of Haitian culture, including the cuisine. There have even been cases of youths committing suicide after having been outed as Haitian.

While vestiges of this attitude continue to persist, many Haitians are beginning to feel more comfortable publicly expressing their ethnic identity and culture. Recently, there have been more efforts to develop Haitian enclaves in such places as Miami, Florida, where a Haitian Cultural Arts Center as well as a Haitian market inspired by the iron market in Port au Prince, the capital of Haiti, have been established.

The largest population of Haitians in the United States is in New York City, particularly in Brooklyn where there is a concentration of Haitian-owned businesses. There is a smaller population of Haitians living in Queens who are generally considered to be from the middle to upper-middle classes of Haitian society. In South Florida, which has the second-largest population of Haitians, the community has established an enclave in the Little River/Lemon City area of Miami, which has been deemed Little Haiti and is the heart of the Haitian community in Florida and arguably the United States. Haitians have also settled in North Miami, North Miami Beach, Fort Lauderdale, and Delray Beach. Boston, Massachusetts, also has a significant population of Haitian Americans. The community is most prominent in the Mattapan area, particularly along Blue Hill Avenue, which is considered the "Haitian Downtown." There is also a smaller population of Haitians that established themselves in Cambridge in the 1960s and 1970s.

Foodways

Haitian cuisine shares many characteristics with other Caribbean cuisines, particularly in its use of tropical vegetables. Its culinary influences primarily come from West Africa and the Arawak people who originally inhabited the island, as well as some influences from France and the Middle East. The cuisine favors spicy, bold flavors. Many dishes are seasoned with cloves and scotch bonnet peppers, as well as garlic, scallions, green peppers, and thyme. Tomato paste is a staple in preparing most sauces, and monosodium glutamate (MSG) is present as a flavor enhancer in either its pure form or in bouillon cubes. A seasoning unique to Haiti is *djon djon*, commonly referred to as Haitian black mushrooms, which are dried and soaked in water to procure a black liquid that is used to flavor rice and other dishes. *Tri tri*, tiny dried shrimp, are also used to flavor rice dishes, and raw cashews are used as a luxurious embellishment to many foods.

Long grain rice is the most popular grain and accompanies most meals, with a preference for jasmine rice and occasional use of *basmati* rice in the United States. Cornmeal porridge, called *mayi moulen*, bulgur wheat, and millet are also popular and provide variety. Rice, in particular, is typically either cooked with seasoned red or black beans in a dish called *diri kole* or served with pureed beans known as *sòs pwa*. Grains are often supplemented with other starches such as plantains, malanga, white yams, potatoes, and breadfruit. Popular vegetables include eggplant, watercress, cabbage, spinach, okra, chayote squash, carrots, peas, beets, celery, and bell peppers. Most Haitian meals include at least one animal protein, such as pork, beef, chicken, hen, goat, turkey, guinea hen, fish, blue crab, conch, salted cod, smoked herring, canned sardines, or spiny lobster. Oxtails are a delicacy, as are beef trotters, which are used in a dish called *ragou*.

Haitians have a particular multistep method of preparing meat to season, tenderize, and preserve it. It begins with washing the meat several times to remove excess blood, scrubbing it with salt and citrus juice, and then scalding it with boiling water. It is then rubbed with a wet spice mixture called *epis*, which typically contains parsley, scallions, citrus juice, garlic, cloves, thyme, salt, and scotch bonnet chiles. Traditionally, *epis* is made in a large, wooden mortar and pestle, but most cooks in the United States use a blender. The majority of the cooking in both the private and public spheres is done by women, and each has her own particular method of preparing meat, as well as her own recipe for *epis*. After the meat is prepared, it is left to marinade and can either become part of a stew or braised and then deep fried in what is collectively classified as *fritay*. Most cooking is typically done in cast aluminum pots called *chodye*.

The most popular *fritay*, called *griyo*, is made of pork and is considered by many to be the national dish of Haiti. *Fritay* of other meats such as goat, beef, or turkey is typically know as *taso*. *Fritay* also includes fried chicken and fried root vegetables and fritters. All *fritay* is typically accompanied by a fiery slaw called *pikliz* made of shredded cabbage, carrots, and other vegetables preserved in vinegar and seasoned with scotch bonnet chiles. Stewed dishes, which are typically called *nan sòs* (in sauce), are cooked in a tomato-based sauce seasoned with many of the spices used in the *epis*. A particularly significant stew is called *legim* and consists of a medley of vegetables that include most, if not all, of those mentioned above with any meat that is available.

Breakfast is an important meal for many Haitians and is very hearty. Cornmeal porridge and a plantain porridge made with evaporated milk called *labouyi bannann* are popular. Salted cod or beef liver in a spicy tomato sauce are also common breakfast dishes, as well as a dish of spaghetti with chopped hot dogs that came about during the US occupation of Haiti and remains a beloved breakfast staple. Creole bread, which is denser and softer than a French baguette, is also popular with breakfast along with sweetened coffee and milk. Puff pastries stuffed with spiced beef, chicken, salted cod, or smoked herring are very common snack foods and are known as *pate*.

Haitian Spaghetti and Hot Dogs
This is an adaptation of a typical Haitian breakfast dish. You can omit the hot dogs or replace them with smoked herring or shrimp.

Ingredients:
    1 teaspoon fresh minced garlic
    ½ cup finely diced onion
    4 whole cloves, crushed
    1 small bay leaf
    ½ teaspoon fresh thyme
    1 tablespoon tomato paste
    1 tablespoon ketchup
    2 teaspoons hot sauce
    2 tablespoons vegetable oil
    4 hot dogs, sliced

½ pound spaghetti (around half a package)
1 cup pasta water
optional: bouillon cube

1. Boil pasta in salted water and cook until al dente; drain and set aside, reserving at least 1 cup of the pasta water.
2. Add oil to a frying pan and set heat to medium.
3. Add cloves and bay leaf and fry until fragrant.
4. Add sliced hot dogs and cook until they turn crispy and begin to brown.
5. Add onions, garlic, and thyme and fry until the garlic just starts to turn golden, being careful to constantly stir the ingredients so that they do not burn.
6. Now add tomato paste, ketchup, and hot sauce along with ½ cup of pasta water and stir to create a sauce.
7. Add salt and pepper to taste. You can also crumble in about a ¼ teaspoon of bouillon cube or more to taste, if you prefer.
8. Add the al dente pasta and stir until all the pasta is coated in sauce.
9. Simmer for a few minutes until the pasta absorbs most of the sauce.

Haitian confectionary is typically very sweet. *Tablette*, a ginger-laced brittle made with peanuts, cashews, or coconut, is found at most Haitian bakeries in the United States along with *pate* and creole bread. Desserts such as *pen patat*, *dous*, and *blan manje* use tropical products such as yams and coconut. Yellow cake scented with almond essence and covered in buttercream is another popular dessert, as are tropical fruit ice creams.

Nonalcoholic drinks feature prominently with Haitian meals. Lime, grapefruit, passion fruit, soursop, or other tropical juices are typically mixed with water, a generous amount of sugar, and either vanilla or almond extract to make a refreshing drink. *Akasan*, a hot beverage made with corn flour and milk and seasoned with spices and vanilla, is a favorite at breakfast time. Haitians are particularly proud of their national rum, Barbancourt, and will drink it straight or in mixed drinks. *Kleren*, a type of moonshine that can be flavored with tropical fruit, is popular especially during the pre-Lent carnival season. Prestige is the national lager and features at parties and other events.

Festival Meals

The majority of Haitians practice Christianity, and many of the holidays observed revolve around the Christian liturgical calendar. Christmas is celebrated with *diri djon djon*, a rice dish made with *djon djon*, cashews, *tri tri*, and lima beans or peas. *Kremas*, a thick rum punch made from condensed and coconut milks, is a necessity at Christmas. A potato salad made with mayonnaise and chopped beats, as well a macaroni gratin and stewed guinea hen, also feature at important occasions. New Year's Day, which is also Haitian Independence Day, is celebrated with *soup joumou*, a soup containing beef, noodles, *calabaza* pumpkin, and other vegetables that was reportedly prohibited to the slaves. Many Haitian rites of passage, such as birthdays, christenings, and weddings, typically feature Haitian-style yellow cake. *Vodou* (*Voodoo*) practitioners observe the feast days of particular deities, or *lwa*, with lavish food offerings that vary across deities and are dictated by oral tradition.

Because many of the fresh ingredients required in Haitian cuisine are also used in other Caribbean cuisines, most Haitian communities have easy access to their foodstuffs in larger cosmopolitan cities. In places like South Florida, many Haitian immigrants also grow produce in their home gardens, including medicinal herbs. *Djon djon* is readily found in most groceries where there is a significant Haitian population and is regularly imported from Haiti, although some Haitians use *djon djon*–flavored bouillon cubes made by the German company, Maggi.

Few adaptations have been made in the United States to the cuisine, except perhaps the use of some processed foods to supplement fresh products, such as lemonade powder instead of fresh lemon juice. Additionally, Haitian cooks in the United States will add their own seasonings to American dishes to make them more palatable.

Place in American Culture

Haiti has had an indirect influence on American cuisine for the past several hundred years. Peychaud's bitters, for instance, which is a cocktail mainstay in New Orleans, was invented by a Creole from the colony of Saint-Domingue who resettled in Louisiana. It has also been argued that the method for American barbecue, as well as the word, derived from the Haitian Creole *boukanen*, although this claim has not yet been authenticated. For much of the mainstream American population, however, Haitian cuisine still remains relatively unknown, even in cities with significant Haitian populations. The previously mentioned health risks attributed to Haitians have made many outsiders ambivalent toward sampling the cuisine. Media portrayal of the poverty experienced in Haiti and the pathetic state of refugees arriving by boat, as well as the association with *voodoo*, have added to the popular imagination that Haitian food is unsafe to eat or not worth eating. In the 1980s and 1990s, and persisting to a lesser extent today, there was even a rumor in Miami that Haitians ate stray cats.

Because of the negative portrayal of Haitians and their subsequent desire for invisibility, many Haitian restaurants and food purveyors have refrained from overtly branding themselves as Haitian, preferring to use words such as *island*, *Caribbean*, or *tropical* instead. Additionally, many business names are given in French or English to further deflect any negative attention. Nevertheless, attitudes toward Haitians and Haitian cuisine are changing in cities with significant enclaves. This can be especially seen in Miami-Dade County, Florida, as many of the neighborhoods that abut Haitian communities begin to gentrify and more non-Haitian residents move in. Their curiosity leads them to sample Haitian cuisine and become fluent in Haitian culinary terminology. Additionally, with the increased self-pride in many Haitian communities, young Haitian American entrepreneurs are beginning to start small food businesses doing upscale catering that combines Haitian flavors with American fine dining presentations or marketing their own line of seasonings such as *epis* to non-Haitians. There recently have been food festivals in cities such as North Miami, Florida, and Somerville, Massachusetts, that not only feature local Haitian restaurants but also promote Haitian agricultural exports such as fair trade coffee. Furthermore, culinary travel show hosts such as Anthony Bourdain, Andrew Zimmern, and Guy Fieri have showcased Haitian restaurants and even done entire shows in Haiti, bringing mainstream American attention to Haitian cuisine.

Restaurants

South Florida has a high concentration of Haitian restaurants. Perhaps the most famous and accessible to non-Haitians is Tap Tap in Miami Beach, which is owned by a white American couple who became enamored with Haitian culture. It features toned-down renditions of Haitian classics in a colorful, touristic style restaurant that is often host to cultural presentations and live music, and the restaurant also features tropical cocktails made with Barbancourt rum. Other Haitian restaurants include Chez Le Bebe in Little Haiti, which was featured on Andrew Zimmern's *Bizarre Eats*, as well as Chez Madame Johns Restaurant in North Miami. There is also the popular chain of restaurants specializing in seafood called Chef Creole. Popular bakeries include New Florida Bakery and Cayard's Bakery.

In New York, restaurants such as YoYo Fritaille in Brooklyn and Creole Bagelry are favorites, as well as Kombit Bar and Restaurant and Le Soleil Restaurant, among many others. La Caye Restaurant and Bar is unique as it offers more elegant presentations of Haitian cuisine in a fine dining atmosphere and is a favorite among non-Haitians, serving as an introduction to the cuisine. Many of Boston's Haitian restaurants are located in Mattapan, like the popular bakery Au Beurre Chaud. Other restaurants are located in Somerville, such as Highland Creole Cuisine and Sunrise Cuisine. Camie's Bakery and Restaurant in Cambridge is one of the older Haitian restaurants in Boston and provides the Haitian community with creole bread, *pate*, and *tablette*, as well as a concise menu of *fritay* and stews.

Further Reading

Jonah, Janty Louis. *Haiti Cherie Cooking Recipes*. Bloomington, IN: Booktango, 2013.

Ménager, Mona Cassion. *Fine Haitian Cuisine*. Pompano Beach: Educa Vision, 2005.

Stepick, Alex. *Pride against Prejudice: Haitians in the United States*. Boston: Allyn and Bacon, 1998.

Yurnet-Thomas, Mirta. *A Taste of Haiti*. New York: Hippocrene Books, 2003.

Carlos C. Olaechea

HAWAIIAN

(USA, North America) Hawaiian Foodways
See also: Polynesia.

Background

The importance of food in the Hawaiian belief system can be seen in the following proverb, *I ola no ke kino i ka māʻona o ka ʻōpū* (The body enjoys health when the stomach is well filled).

In 1959, the Hawaiian Archipelago consisting of eight major islands (Niʻihau, Kauaʻi, Oʻahu, Molokaʻi, Lanaʻi, Kahoʻolawe, Mauʻi, and the island of Hawaiʻi) and hundreds of little isles was officially designated as part of the United States of America. Located more than two thousand miles away from any continental landmass, the Hawaiian Islands are the most geographically remote archipelago on earth.

There are over one million people living in Hawaii, with the majority in Honolulu. The biggest island, Hawaii Island, also known as the Big Island, has a population of over 180,000 people. There are also large Hawaiian communities in California, Washington, Texas, Florida, and Nevada. In the 2010 US Census, about 1.2 million people identified themselves as Native Hawaiian and Other Pacific Islander. Most of the residents of Hawaii are people from various ethnicities such as Japanese, Chinese, Filipino, Portuguese, Korean, Samoan, Marshallese, and other groups.

Foodways

Pre-Contact foods included traditional Hawaiian foods that are eaten raw or steamed such as *poi* (from steamed taro corms that have been smashed and diluted with water), *ʻulu* (breadfruit), *ʻuala* (sweet potato), *limu* (seaweed), *kalo* (taro) leaves, *hoio* edible ferns, and meat including seafood, chicken, and pork. Post-Contact, when venereal diseases and other afflictions resulted in the devastating loss of countless Native Hawaiians, agricultural production of such staples as taro and sweet potatoes also decreased as there were fewer people left to till it.

Whaling ships and early sailors introduced salted fish, which resulted in the dish, *lomi lomi* salmon (raw salmon marinated in tomatoes, green onions, chili peppers, and salt). The arrival of the Japanese, Chinese, Portuguese, Puerto Ricans, and later Filipinos to work in the formerly taro-producing plantations and the rise of the sugar industry in the 1850s led to the establishment of plantation camps, where workers of all ethnicities lived and mingled with one another. Sugar continued until it was supplanted by rice, which was phased out in the 1950s. Once again, some fields were converted back to growing taro as *loʻi*. For example, in the 1980s, taro was once again dominant in places such as Hanalei, Kauai and Waipio Valley, Hawaii.

Preparation

When Captain Cook, the first European credited with discovering the islands, arrived in 1778, the traditional diet of the Hawaiians included taro, fish, pork, dog, and coconuts. There were strict *kapu*, or taboos, that forbade women to consume bananas, pork, coconuts, certain species of fish, and turtle, with death as the penalty for breaking the restriction. The preparation of food was left to men, who had their own eating house separate from women. Women and men could not eat together, and the only place they were allowed to mingle was in the sleeping house, where no eating took place.

The fall of the *kapu* system occurred in 1819, after the death of Kamehameha I, during the ʻAi Noa, which translates as "to eat freely, without observance of taboos." Kamehameha's son, Liholiho, broke tradition by permitting women and men to mingle and eat together during a feast, as witnessed by foreigners and high-ranking *aliʻi* (chiefs).

After the arrival of Cook, missionaries, and other Westerners, it can be said that the composition of what is today known as Hawaiian cuisine can be tied to the historical, political-economy processes and immigration waves to Hawaii of Europeans, New England missionaries, Puerto Ricans, Japanese, Chinese, Portuguese, Filipinos, and Polynesians from other islands, resulting in a Creole mix of language, culture, and food.

Everyday Meals

These days, traditional Hawaiian foods include *poi*, pork, and fish. These staples are enjoyed along with a plethora of popular dishes that were brought by Hawaii's diverse immigrants as represented in a typical lunch plate: two scoops of white rice, a heaping serving of macaroni salad, and a choice of grilled meat marinated in Japanese *teriyaki* or Korean *bulgogi*-inspired sauce, or *huli huli* chicken (grilled chicken basted with a sweet sauce that includes pineapple juice). Such a lunch would sometimes be followed by a favorite island treat, shaved ice with various fruit flavors and sprinkled with *li hing mui* (salty plum powder from China).

Plate lunches, *bento* boxes (take-out Japanese lunch box with rice, meat, pickled vegetables), and *manapua* (steam buns filled with pork or chicken) brought by Chinese immigrants make up everyday informal Hawaiian cuisine. The mix of Asian, Polynesian, and Western influences can also be seen in the more formal Hawaii regional cuisine dishes, which chefs such as Sam Choy, Roy Yamaguchi, Peter Merriman, Alan Wong, and George Mavrothalassitis have promoted by using fresh local ingredients including wild-caught fish from the sea, grass-fed Big Island beef, and organic greens as well as fruits grown in the islands. This movement to sustainable food is offset by Hawaii's continuing reliance on goods shipped in from the mainland available at a lower price, compared to the high-priced organic and local ingredients.

However, the future for a more locally based Hawaiian cuisine remains promising, with more individuals growing their own food. Coffee, cacao for chocolate production, and macadamia nuts flourish in the Big Island, taro is grown in Kauai, and vegetables harvested from Oahu and Hawaii are some of the premium exports as well as favorite sources of food for island residents. On Hawaii Island, a thriving aquaculture near the Kona airport includes lobsters that are fed by water pumped in from two thousand feet below sea level.

Plantation foods that were commonly eaten and shared among different ethnic groups include the Filipino *pinakbet* (a stew of bitter melon, string beans, tomato, onion, pork, shrimp, and garlic flavored with *bagoong* [fermented shrimp paste] and *adobo* [pork or chicken cooked with garlic, vinegar and soy sauce]); Okinawan favorites such as homemade fermented *miso*, *rafute* (pork flavored with *shoyu* or soy sauce), and *nishime* (vegetable stew); Portuguese sweet bread and bean stew, *linguica* or *chorizo* (Portuguese sausage), and, on special occasions, *malassadas* (also spelled *malasadas*), which consist of fried dough with yeast sprinkled with sugar. Other plantation favorites that remain popular include chicken papaya, a dish from the Philippines made with chicken, green papaya, ginger, and *malunggay* (morinda leaves), and *chicken hekka* (chicken cooked *sukiyaki* style with long rice noodles, ginger, mushrooms, bamboo, and *mirin* vinegar). For treats, there was *buchi-buchi*, a Filipino dessert of sweet *mochi* rice flavored with coconut and sugar for dessert. Pickled green mangoes, guava jelly, and jam and passionfruit juice were also regular treats, and like the above dishes, are still widely consumed in Hawaii and elsewhere in areas with large populations of Asian and Pacific Islander Americans.

Other dishes that remain in the Hawaiian everyday repertoire come from the ocean, such as *poke* (raw fish, typically yellowfin or ahi tuna marinated with sea salt, seaweed, Maui onions, chili pepper, crushed roasted *kukui* or candlenut called *inamona* and soy sauce). Salted, sun-dried *'ōpelu* (mackerel scad) and other fish, various kinds of seaweed both dried and fresh, squid, mullet, *'opihi* (limpets), and both reef and deep-sea fish of all varieties are caught and enjoyed. From rivers and other freshwater sources, shrimp, bass, crayfish and *'o'opu* (goby) are gathered.

The gathering of plant resources is typical of local life, including foraging in the spring for tender young bamboo shoots known as *takenoko* by the Japanese, and finding edible jelly fungus known as *pepeiao*, which is used in *chop suey* and other dishes. Fruits such as avocadoes and mangoes can be found in the wild. Hunting for wild boar yields a number of dishes, including *laulau* (pork wrapped in taro leaves) and *kalua* pig (roast pork). From cattle, there is *pipikaula* (dried marinated beef), which is eaten anytime, popularized by *paniolo* (Hawaiian cowboys).

Pork *Laulau*
Ingredients:
   1 pound salted codfish (rinsed), or butterfish, sliced into pieces
   1 pound pork butt, sliced into 1½ inch cubes
   Hawaiian sea salt to taste (pepper optional)
   taro leaves for wrapping, without stem
   banana leaves for outer layer wrap

Method:
Season fish and pork with sea salt. If using salted cod fish, rinse fish several times to remove extra salt. Place a handful of meat onto the middle of several taro leaves. Wrap securely and place each bundle into a banana leaf (or foil) and secure with a string. If using foil, wrap tightly. Place in steamer to cook for four hours or more, until meat is tender.

Holiday Feasts
In Hawaii, get-togethers or parties are called *pā'ina*, and this is a term also applied to feasts, although now the word *lū'au* is instead used by many, especially those in the tourism industry. A traditional *lū'au* is typically held to celebrate a one-year-old's birthday and is attended usually by three hundred to five hundred people, and it is a fairly recent term introduced in 1856 by the Pacific Commercial Advertiser. Holidays, birthdays, anniversaries, weddings, and graduations are now celebrated as a *lū'au*, which has become a synonym for party. Dishes served at a *lū'au* typically include raw *'opihi*, *kalua* pig, *teriyaki* beef, chicken long rice, *poi*, and *laulau* along with baked and fried fish. Dessert includes traditional Hawaiian sweets such as *haupia* (coconut milk mixed with arrowroot) and *kulolo* (mashed taro with coconut cream).

Place in American Culture
Each year, an estimated eight million visitors land in Hawaii and bring back experiences of

the tourist version of the *lū'au*, which, along with popularized hula, have taken root in countless imaginations around the world as the quintessential Hawaiian or Polynesian experience. The popularity of tiki bars with their trademark décor of fruity cocktails, lit torches, and tiki masks in the 1930s, such as Trader Vic's and Don the Beachcomber, further exoticized the idea of Polynesian culture.

The advent of World War II brought canned goods into Hawaii and elsewhere, resulting in snacks such as the well-loved *Spam musubi* (Spam and rice wrapped in *nori* seaweed) available early morning on grocery counters and at the checkout in gasoline stations throughout Hawaii.

The appeal of the *lū'au*, with its buffet-style offering of multiple dishes in an atmosphere of relaxed environment accompanied by music and dance entertainment, has led to the rise of *lū'au*-themed parties where the attire is casual Aloha shirts and dresses, with guests wearing leis and enjoying food to the accompaniment of ukulele and drums.

The appeal of Hawaiian food and its accompanying colorful images of Hawaii has led to more Hawaiian-style casual eateries such as L & L Hawaiian Barbecue and King's Hawaiian Bakery and Restaurant. Along with the exposure of local foods in such hit television shows like *Hawaii-Five O*, such eateries have shined the spotlight on dishes like the *loco moco*, ground beef patties served with rice and over-easy eggs all smothered in gravy; *mochiko* chicken (chicken fried in *mochi* flour); *Spam musubi*; and *teriyaki* bowls. Hawaiian snacks and lunch plates can be found wherever there is a sizeable Hawaiian and Pacific Islander population.

A present trend in Hawaii that is on its way to becoming embedded in American popular culture is for local Kahuku shrimp prepared all ways and served in food trucks such as Giovanni's Shrimp Truck along Oahu's North Shore, which is now a mecca for both locals and visitors alike.

Noted Restaurants and Chefs

Cooking shows such as *Sam Choy's Kitchen* exposed viewers to Pacific Rim cuisine, also known as Hawaiian regional cuisine. Roy's Restaurant is a chain of fine dining restaurants with locations around the United States that feature Hawaiian fusion dishes.

Began in 1991, Hawaiian regional cuisine is drawing attention from around the world for the dedicated use of local ingredients in both ethnic-inspired dishes and continental favorites. For example, a dish at Merriman's restaurant in Waimea, Hawaii Island, features "fish and chips" made with fresh local fish and sweet potato grown from Molokai and served with avocado and sea asparagus grown in Oahu.

Further Reading

Fujita, Ruth, Kathryn L. Braun, and Claire K. Hughes. "The Traditional Hawaiian Diet: A Review of the Literature." *Pacific Health Dialogue* 11, no. 2 (2004): 250–59.

Laudan, Rachel. *The Food of Paradise: Exploring Hawaii's Culinary Heritage*. Honolulu: University of Hawaii Press, 1996.

Namkoong, Joan. *Food Lover's Guide to Honolulu*. Bess Press: Honolulu, 2006.

Margaret Magat

HMONG

(Laos, Southeastern Asia) Hmong American
See also: Laos, Thailand.

Background

The Hmong are an ethnic minority with ancient roots and a complex modern history. Written accounts refer to Hmong in central China more than four thousand years ago, and for centuries Hmong have consistently maintained their independence from ruling governments. When China's Tang dynasty began to persecute minorities in the seventh century, Hmong migrated south—eventually settling in the highlands of Laos, Vietnam, Burma, and Thailand.

Their practice of slash-and-burn agriculture required a migrant lifestyle, and the historical persistence of Hmong cultural identity can be attributed to this mobile self-sufficiency and strong community support. The family unit is very important to Hmong, and Hmong Americans continue to honor eighteen patrilineal clans in the United States.

Hmong began to migrate from Southeast Asia in large numbers following the 1975 takeover of Laos by the communist Pathet Lao Party. In what has become known as the "Secret War," the United States covertly enlisted Hmong in the fight against the spread of communism during the conflict in Vietnam—beginning with the Kennedy administration and continuing through 1973. The Hmong, sensing an impending takeover by the Pathet Lao, fought in order to maintain their independence from any government. Following the communist victory, Hmong began to escape—primarily to refugee camps in northern Thailand. From there, asylum was granted by countries around the world. In 1980 alone, the United States admitted close to twenty-five thousand refugees.

According to the 2010 census, there are approximately 260,000 people of Hmong descent living in the United States—most of them first-generation immigrants. Between 2000 and 2010 the Hmong community grew by 40 percent and continues to grow today—though new trends are taking shape. The states with the largest Hmong populations include California, Minnesota, and Wisconsin, while populations in Alaska and southern states such as North and South Carolina, Florida, and Arkansas have seen significant growth in the last ten years. Poverty has declined overall, but the Hmong continue to be one of the poorest ethnic groups in the United States. In 2010, 29 percent of Hmong nationwide worked in manufacturing.

Bountiful vegetables are the basis for Hmong cuisine, and Hmong are masters of herbal seasonings. Hmong food balances salty, sweet, sour, bitter, and spicy flavors through the careful combination of fermented fish sauce, lime, and herbs. In Laos, Hmong made use of many vegetables unknown in the United States, including fragrant leaves without English names foraged from the surrounding forests. Mustard greens are a staple and can be stir-fried with meat or added to soups. Tender gourd and pumpkin vines are stripped of their rough skins and simmered in a simple broth. Green papaya salad is a favorite across Laos. Shredded papaya is pounded in a mortar and pestle with garlic, chili peppers, fish sauce, sugar, cherry tomatoes, and lime. Before green papaya was widely available in the United States, many Southeast Asian immigrants improvised with shredded carrot or cabbage. As in Lao cuisine, Hmong favor spicy dipping sauces—usually pounded chili, garlic, onions, and fish sauce, with additional herbs such as cilantro and lemongrass, or vegetables such as eggplant, added as desired. Many Hmong Americans maintain their own herb gardens, in which they grow lemongrass, cilantro, green onions, and regional plants such as *ntiv* (sweet fern), *pawj qaib* (sweet flag), or *koj liab* (duck feet herb).

Many Hmong dishes that feature meat use as much of the animal as possible, following a culinary heritage in which meat was sometimes scarce. For example, if a main dish uses a lean meat, an accompanying soup will be made from the bones. Chicken is often cited as a favorite, and chickens are also incorporated into many traditional practices, including divination and healing. *Nqaij qaib hua xyaw tshuaj* is a chicken soup prescribed for new mothers for a month after a baby is born, and it is regularly enjoyed by whole families. A whole chicken is cooked in water with lemongrass, black pepper, and a mix of herbs preferred by the chef. With a phonetic written-word system only adapted for the Hmong language in the twentieth century, recipes were—and continue to be—passed down through oral tradition. Variations on the most common dishes are endless. This includes *laab*, the national dish of Laos, and beloved by Hmong. This minced-meat salad combines finely chopped chicken, pork, fish, beef, or duck with fish sauce, herbs, chili, and toasted sticky rice powder. While sometimes made with raw fish or beef, *laab* is more often cooked.

Hmong who have settled in America have a plethora of new food options available. While beef is less common in traditional cuisine, modern cooks are incorporating it into simple stir-fries and soups. Dairy products and baked goods, while also not part of their culinary heritage, are embraced by Hmong Americans. For many, economic challenges have inhibited the continuation of healthy traditional foodways. Low-income populations are more likely to succumb to obesity and related chronic diseases due to little time for exercise or cooking, sedentary jobs, and the temptation to succumb to cheap and convenient fast foods. For the Hmong, who are historically farmers, the lack of garden space in America in which to cultivate fresh produce is cited as one reason for overall decreased vegetable consumption. Rice is present at every Hmong meal. While many in Laos enjoy sticky, or glutinous, rice as an everyday food, Hmong tend to reserve it for special-occasion sweets. At mealtime, a Hmong table is laid out with several dishes, such as a soup, simply prepared vegetables, one or more chili sauces, rice, and a meat dish. People will serve themselves small portions at a time from shared plates—sometimes dipping their soup spoon into a communal bowl. Sweets, many of which are based on sticky rice and sweet coconut milk, are typically enjoyed as snacks rather than at the end of a meal.

Hmong practice a version of animism in which the physical and the spiritual worlds are complexly interrelated—and food is often used in religious ceremonies. Believing that people have more than one soul, Hmong entrust the care of these souls to a shaman, or *twix neeb*. While Hmong Americans use Western medicine, many also continue to consult shaman. An illness can be cured through a ceremony, herbal remedies, or a combination of both. In the most traditional of rituals, animal sacrifice is sometimes called for, and the chicken, pig, or cow is then cooked for those in attendance. Such occasions include *hu plig* (the welcoming of a new baby) and *ua neeb ua yaig* (a healing ritual). The most important annual event is *xyoo tshiab*, or Hmong New Year. Communities across the United States organize public events that feature traditional foods, entertainment, and handicrafts. At New Year, men will sometimes replace women in the kitchen and prepare festive foods such as *ncuav*, or pounded sticky rice (called *mochi* in Japan).

While the foods of neighboring Thailand, China, and Vietnam are loved by Americans across the country, Hmong food—or for that matter, the Hmong in general—do not enjoy the same renown or understanding. Hmong are more likely to be known for their traditional arts, or perhaps their excellent produce (such as the flower sellers at Pike Place Market in Seattle), than their cuisine. Despite their role in the Vietnam War, and today's growing population, many Americans remain unfamiliar with the Hmong. Anne Fadiman's acclaimed ethnography *The Spirit Catches You and You Fall Down* (1997) chronicles the drastic chasms in cultural understanding present in California in the 1980s. Cultural friction still exists and has played out brutally on public hunting grounds in Wisconsin. In 2004, a Hmong man hunting deer killed six white men upon confrontation, and in 2007 a Hmong squirrel hunter was murdered.

Restaurants and Chefs

Not surprisingly, even in urban areas with large Hmong populations—such as Fresno, Sacramento, and Merced, California; Milwaukee, Wisconsin; and Minneapolis-St. Paul, Minnesota—restaurants marketing Hmong cuisine are scarce. Diners wishing to try Hmong fare may have better luck exploring area grocery stores or farmer's markets for homemade takeaway dishes. In north St. Paul, Hmong Village hosts a variety of smaller vendors, while the Hmong House, a more formal dining establishment, opened in 2013. Establishments featuring Thai and Lao cuisine are far more common across the country—there visitors will be able to sample the green papaya salad, *laab,* and sticky rice popular across Laos and northern Thailand.

Further Reading

Alford, Jeffrey, and Naomi Duguid. *Hot Sour Salty Sweet: A Culinary Journey through Southeast Asia.* New York: Artisan, 2000.

Breining, Greg, "On the Hunt." *Minnesota Monthly*, October 2011, accessed October 17, 2014. http://www.minnesotamonthly.com/media/Minnesota-Monthly/October-2011/On-the-Hunt/.

Du Pont De Bie, Natacha. *Ant Egg Soup: The Adventures of a Food Tourist in Laos.* London: Sceptre, 2004.

Fadiman, Anne. *The Spirit Catches You and You Fall Down.* New York: The Noonday Press, 1998.

Ikeda, Joanne P. *Hmong American Food Practices, Customs, and Holidays.* Chicago: Diabetes Care and Education Dietetic Practice Group of the American Dietetic Association, 1999.

Loan Pham, Kim, Gail G. Harrison, and Marjorie Kagawa-Singer. "Perceptions of Diet and Physical Activity Among California Hmong Adults and Youths." *Preventing Chronic Disease: Public Health Research, Practice, and Policy* 4, no. 4 (2007).

Pfeifer, M. E., and B. K. Thao, eds. *State of the Hmong American Community.* Washington, DC: Hmong National Development, 2013.

Quincy, Keith. *Hmong: History of a People.* Cheney: Eastern Washington University Press, 1988.

Scripter, Sami, and Sheng Yang. *Cooking from the Heart: The Hmong Kitchen in America.* Minneapolis: University of Minnesota, 2009.

Kathryn Clune

HONDURAS

(Central America) Honduran American Food

Background

Honduras, a country roughly the size of Tennessee, has maintained a Latino population in the United States since at least the 1800s, but Honduran Americans have historically struggled to gain recognition as an independent ethnic group and are typically categorized with other Central American populations. This shapes their food culture and its place in mainstream American society.

Honduras became independent from Spain in 1821, and after a brief period as part of the First Mexican Empire and various attempts in interim years trying to form part of a united Central American region, it declared its status as an independent republic in 1838. Some immigration occurred throughout this time, but the first substantial wave was a result of the business practices of the United Fruit Company. Run by US businessmen, the Boston company moved its headquarters to New Orleans in 1933, where it stayed until 1985. United Fruit grew a vast empire in the Central American tropics, and it quickly came to control over 650,000 acres of fruit plantations in Honduras alone. The company hired many Honduran nationals as part of its workforce, which offered opportunities for mobility between Honduras and the United States, whether directly via ships transporting bananas and fruit to New Orleans or in other venues such as personal service sectors. It was not uncommon for United Fruit representatives to bring families of foreign workers to the United States to serve as maids, cooks, and gardeners, or as inexpensive labor in other service sectors.

While a notable Honduran American population grew in New Orleans, there were also Hondurans immigrating to other Latino strongholds in the United States throughout the 1900s. In general, Hondurans tended to settle in metropolitan areas where other Spanish-speaking groups were prevalent, blending in with Spanish-speaking groups in New York, Los Angeles, Houston, Miami, and other major US cities. For the most part, Honduran immigration was overshadowed by larger migration waves of other Latino groups, particularly during the 1980s when many countries in Central America were caught up in violent civil wars. Although Honduras managed to avoid most of the extreme political and social upheaval that affected its neighbors, subsequent natural disasters, including Hurricane Mitch in 1998 and flooding in 2008, prompted new and increased waves of Honduran immigrants to the United States. Census Bureau data indicate that over 75 percent of Honduran immigrants currently residing in the United States immigrated post 1990. It is also important to note that while major metropolitan centers still have the largest concentrations of Honduran Americans, 2010 Census data reveal Honduran settlements throughout the United States, including throughout many states in the south and in the US heartland.

There can be considerable ethnic diversity among Honduran immigrants. Over three hundred years of Spanish colonization and control contributed to a largely *mestizo*, mixed European and indigenous, population throughout Honduras and much of Latin America, in general. However, pre-Colombian indigenous groups native to the Mesoamerican region include the Maya, Miskito, Lenca, Pech, and others, and some Hondurans retain significant influence and ancestry related to an indigenous heritage. Additionally, the northern Central American coastline is home to the Garifuna, a mixed Carib, Arawak, and African population. There are estimates of close to one hundred thousand Garifuna in Honduras, and additional Garifuna populations are found throughout Belize, Guatemala, and other Central American countries. Many Garifuna have immigrated to the United States, with current totals of around ninety thousand Garifuna living in diaspora communities in the larger US metropolitan areas, though not all of these immigrants are Honduran. These various Honduran ethnicities all shape the nature and character of the Honduran American population in the United States.

Foodways

Honduran American food uses fresh ingredients and shares some similarities with recognized foods from other Latino groups. Staple ingredients include rice, beans, corn and flour tortillas, plantains, green bananas, proteins such as chicken, pork, fish, and beef, tropical fruits, and fresh dairy products such as cheese and table creams. Garifuna populations also incorporate cassava as a primary staple ingredient. Unlike Mexican foods, Honduran food is generally not spicy, though a spicy condiment sauce can be added individually to one's plate depending on personal preference. Pickled vegetables, known as *encurtido*, are also available as a condiment to meals. Foods are typically well seasoned with garlic and other herbs and spices, and they tend to be savory rather than sweet. Dishes are usually cooked in quantities that can feed a number of people or can be eaten over several meals.

Most traditional Honduran American foods are homemade and include few preprocessed ingredients. Tortillas are generally handmade and tend to be thicker than the Mexican-style ones found in US grocery stores. Honduran markets that carry a wide selection of Honduran foods exist in large cities such as New York and Los Angeles, but outside of major metropolitan areas imported Honduran products are difficult to find. Selected Honduran foods, particularly popular snacks or carbonated drinks, can sometimes be obtained in smaller cities in Mexican or other Latino markets aiming to appeal to a wider Latino clientele. Substitution for ingredients is common when Honduran products cannot be found.

Honduran American women are usually responsible for preparing daily meals. This can sometimes change with the style of cooking; for instance, men are more likely to participate with meal preparation when grilling is involved. Gender roles are not set in stone, however, and demands due to work schedules in multi-income families often dictate who shares the responsibilities for a given meal. Schedules also influence the meal systems in families, but, in general, Honduran Americans do not snack throughout the day. Lunch and dinner tend to be more substantial, and families try to eat together when they can. Beans can play a part in every meal. One of the most typical Honduran foods consumed is a *baleada*, a folded flour tortilla filled with mashed beans and cheese or a Honduran cream called *mantequilla*. Baleadas can also contain other ingredients as desired, leading to a variation in names: *baleadas sencillas*, or simple *baleadas*, contain mostly the base ingredients of beans and cheese, while *baleadas preparadas*, prepared *baleadas*, incorporate one's choice of other ingredients such as sliced avocado, scrambled eggs, pickled vegetables, *chorizo* sausage, or thin fajita-style meat, among others. The tortillas are warmed on both sides, and fillings are added to taste. This food is very adaptable to any given meal, and it can be portable if one needs to eat quickly on the go.

Other meal preparations are more complex, but generally they do not rely on specialized kitchen equipment. Most Honduran American kitchens have a heavy cast-iron griddle, called a *comal*, that is used for making tortillas, and some have a tortilla press, though many pat or roll out tortillas by hand. Two notable foods require specialized techniques using plantain leaves. Honduran tamales are ground corn dough, filled with a variety of fillings and wrapped in plantain leaves for steaming. The leaves not only act as a package for the contents of the tamales, they also impart additional flavor to the dish. Plantain leaves are also used on *sopa tapado*, covered soup, which is a traditional dish that is found in many Honduran American homes. The dish varies substantially throughout Honduras; interior regions tend to include beef and pork while coastal regions incorporate seafood as the protein. The recipe below comes from Olancha, the largest of the eighteen departments of Honduras.

Sopa de Tapado Olanchano (serves six)
Ingredients:
 1 onion
 2 medium tomatoes
 1 green bell pepper
 2 cloves garlic
 4 tablespoons chopped cilantro
 1 tablespoon oil
 3 cups water
 2 cubes of chicken broth
 2 pounds of dried, salted beef (2½ pounds stew meat can be substituted)
 1½ pound pork butt cut in 1-inch pieces
 1 pound of cassava
 3 green plantains
 2 green bananas
 3 ripe plantains
 2 cans coconut milk
 plantain leaves to cover pot

Instructions:

Chop the onion, tomato, bell pepper, and garlic. In a large pot, cook the chopped vegetables in oil. When vegetables are softened, add the beef and pork pieces and brown lightly. Stir in the cilantro and cook briefly. Add water and chicken broth cubes and gently simmer, covered, until meat is almost tender, approximately 1 to 1½ hours.

While meats are simmering, peel the bananas, plantains, and cassava and cut into bite-sized pieces. Keep these ingredients separate, as they will be layered individually later. When meats have reached desired tenderness, remove the stewed meat mixture and save the remaining broth in a separate bowl. In the pot, layer the cassava first, followed by a layer of green plantain. Next, place a layer of the cooked meats, using about half of the meat mixture. A green banana layer comes next, followed by the remaining meats. Spread the final layer of ripe plantains on top.

Pour the coconut milk in with the reserved broth and stir together. Pour the liquid mixture carefully over the layered dish. Tuck plantain leaves down into the pot to cover the soup, lid the pot, and simmer gently until the plantains are tender, approximately 20 to 30 minutes. If plantain leaves cannot be found, parchment paper can be tucked over the soup to keep in the moisture, but some flavor will be lost. Serve warm.

Honduran American food includes a variety of soups that are eaten throughout the year. These types of one-pot meals can be prepared in large quantities and, though somewhat time-consuming, are not overly difficult to prepare. Holiday fare varies. Christmas and New Year's Day are celebrated with family feasts that can include roasted poultry or pork and an impressive variety of other dishes. For the Lenten season leading up to Easter, seafood soup, *sopa de mariscos*, is ubiquitous due to the Catholic tradition of giving up meat as a personal sacrifice during Lent. Nonreligious holidays such as celebrating Honduran independence are sometimes observed in areas where there are large populations of Honduran Americans. These celebrations tend to be acted out in social groups.

Place in American Culture

Honduran American food is largely undiscovered in mainstream US society. In places that it is found, such as in some cookbooks and restaurants, it is still very much treated as ethnic fare. Part of the reason for its relative unfamiliarity is likely due to the historical tendency to lump Honduran Americans in with other Latino groups, and therefore assume that Honduran food is equivalent to Mexican food; although there are certainly similarities, there are also differences. In more recent years, greater awareness of Honduran Americans as a distinct group has helped to improve the visibility of Honduran American foodways, and there seems to be a growing niche for Honduran food in US culture, particularly in the food truck industry. Food trucks offer relatively low start-up costs and can be strategically located for owners to gain the maximum clientele and profits at given times and seasons. Additionally, consumers who frequent food trucks are often looking for a taste of the exotic and are willing to experiment with ethnic options. Honduran food trucks can be found in locations such as Houston, Texas; Alexandria, Virginia; Columbus, Ohio; Denver, Colorado; Baltimore, Maryland; and other major metropolitan areas where Honduran Americans have a greater population density.

Noted Restaurants and Chefs

Honduran restaurants can be found in large cities, and if one looks carefully, they can even be discovered in smaller towns and cities across the United States. Notable restaurants include Adelita's Café in Miami, La Perla de Ulua in New York, and Lempira Restaurant in Los Angeles. Start-up restaurants are common, but it often proves difficult to achieve a measure of staying power in cities with high overhead costs and fierce competition. While one might expect to find Honduran restaurants in these bustling cities, it might come as more of a surprise to find successful Honduran eateries such as Rosalinda Restaurant Hondureño in Little Rock, Arkansas, or three locations of Lempira Restaurant in Charlotte, North Carolina, a business unrelated to the similarly named restaurant in Los Angeles and which offers a combination of Honduran, Salvadoran, and Mexican fare.

Honduran Americans are an active force in the US restaurant scene as chefs and cooks, at times specializing in the flavors and tastes of their own heritage and at other times becoming proficient in preparing diverse ethnic cuisines. It is not uncommon to find Honduran Americans cooking in the kitchens of Mexican, Asian, Italian, or other restaurants. Conversely there are some, such as Chef Jesus (Jay) Bonilla, who build careers with their Honduran culture in the spotlight. Bonilla has become a sensation in the Los Angeles area, sharing his love for cooking and traditional Honduran flavors both through the recipes that he creates as a chef and restaurateur and by helping others experience cooking on a media program produced by the Multi-Cultural Cooking Network.

The impact of Honduran Americans and their foodways in contemporary society will continue to grow. Once rather isolated in large cities, the Honduran American influence can now be seen throughout the United States, and exposure to these new tastes and preparations leaves many US consumers hungry for more.

Further Reading

Bertelsen, Cynthia D. "Honduras." In *Food Cultures of the World Encyclopedia*, edited by Ken Albala, 183–90. ABC-CLIO: Santa Barbara, 2011.

Brown, Anna, and Eileen Patten. "Hispanics of Honduran Origin in the United States, 2011." *Pew Research: Hispanic Trends Project*, June 19, 2013. Accessed March 19, 2014. http://www.pewhispanic.org/2013/06/19/hispanics-of-honduran-origin-in-the-united-states-2011/.

Chinchilla, Norma Stoltz, and Nora Hamilton. "Central American Immigrants: Diverse Populations, Changing Communities." In *The Columbia History of Latinos in the United States Since 1960*, edited by David G. Gutierrez, 187–228. Columbia: New York, 2004.

England, Sarah, and Walter L. Krochmal. "Hondurans." In *American Immigrant Cultures: Builders of a Nation*, edited by David Levinson and Melvin Ember, 395–400. Macmillan: New York, 1997.

Janer, Zilkia. *Latino Food Culture*. Greenwood: Westport, 2008.

Neu, Denese. "Honduran Identity within South Louisiana Culture." *Folklife in Louisiana: Louisiana's Living Traditions*. Accessed March 28. 2014. http://www.louisianafolklife.org/LT/Articles_Essays/Hondurans1.html.

M. Dustin Knepp

HONG KONG
(East Asia) Chinese American
See also: China, Singapore, Taiwan.

Background

Between 1966 and 1987, approximately three thousand to seven thousand Hong Kong Chinese immigrated annually to the United States, with the first large wave occurring after passage of the 1965 Immigration and Naturalization Act. The majority of these immigrants settled in urban Chinatowns located in San Francisco and Manhattan. A second wave transpired in the late 1990s when the US Immigration Act of 1990 increased Hong Kong's annual quota to twenty thousand as concerns over the potential impact of Hong Kong's 1997 reversion back to Communist Chinese rule led many of its citizens to relocate abroad. This second wave of Hong Kong immigrants favored suburban residential areas over densely populated urban settings, leading to the establishment of new suburban Chinatowns. Over time, as Hong Kong settled into being a Special Administrative Region of China, many expatriates returned home, and overall immigration to the United States declined. Today, there are over three hundred thousand Hong Kong immigrants residing in the United States, with concentrations in San Francisco, Los Angeles, Seattle, Honolulu, and New York, among others. In the United States, Hong Kong immigrants generally fall under the broader category of "Chinese" and are often distinguished by their fluency of Cantonese, though it's also the prevalent language in southern Guangdong. "Hong Kongers" or "Hong Kong people" have also been used as popular terms to distinguish those with ties to Hong Kong, as opposed to mainland China.

Foodways

Since Hong Kong's establishment as a British crown colony in the mid-nineteenth century, Cantonese-speaking migrants from Canton/Guangdong have played a central role in shaping Hong Kong foodways. Therefore, despite exposure to international influences as a port city and a substantial population of residents reflecting Hakka, Chiu Chow, and Shanghai descent, Hong Kong cuisine still remains characterized as primarily Cantonese, both in restaurants and the home. In this entry, "Cantonese" will be used synonymously with "Hong Kong" cuisine. However, in the broader scheme of discussions covering regional Chinese foodways, Cantonese cuisine generally refers to foodways associated with Guangdong province and formally recognized as one of China's Eight Culinary Traditions.

Within Cantonese cooking, the freshness of ingredients is emphasized, along with balanced flavors. The goal is to enhance the texture of the ingredients, as opposed to disguising it with strong sauces or spices. Therefore, Cantonese food is considered milder than other types of regional Chinese food, such as Sichuan or Hunan dishes. Plain, white rice is a staple served alongside Cantonese dishes.

All types and aspects of meats are used in Cantonese cooking, including offal, snake, and goose. However, fresh seafood tends to be favored due to Guangdong and Hong Kong's proximity to the coast. Vegetarian Buddhist dishes also comprise a key aspect of Cantonese cuisine, with bean curd and wheat gluten ingredients used in place of meat and fish, and a variety of seasonal vegetables featured. At dinner banquets, Cantonese restaurants may serve fancier, complicated dishes, which include roasted suckling pig, braised abalone, jellyfish, and roasted goose.

Fresh herbs are rarely used, besides ginger, scallion, and garlic. Soy sauce, white pepper, cornstarch, rice wine, sesame oil, salt, oyster sauce, and cooking oil are the mainstays for Cantonese-style sauces. Occasionally, preserved ingredients, such as preserved pork, salted duck eggs, Chinese sausage, fermented black beans, and dried scallops, may be incorporated into dishes, reflecting the Hakka influence on Cantonese cuisine.

Other types of sweets and snacks popular in Hong Kong include egg tarts, sweetheart/wife cake, pineapple buns, sausage buns, sesame balls, and a variety of other Chinese pastries. Most of these can be found in the United States, though Hong Kong–style milk tea has not gained as much traction as Taiwanese pearl milk (*boba*) tea.

Dim sum is another central aspect of Cantonese cuisine (with hints of Shanghai influences), although it is rarely made at home. Rather, *yum cha*, as it is called in Cantonese, comprises the social practice of dining together with friends and family over small bites in a teahouse or restaurant setting. Hallmark dishes include *congee*, different types of dumplings, steamed buns, roasted meats, noodle dishes, deep-fried or pan-fried dumplings, and desserts such as mango pudding, steamed sponge cake, and egg tarts. Dim sum remains as popular as ever in both Hong Kong and the United States, particularly for weekend brunch gatherings with friends and family.

Alternatively, the *cha chaan teng* (tea restaurant) provides another venue for fast, casual dining in Hong Kong. Reflecting its history as a British colony and exposure to Western influences, *cha chaan tengs* offer Hong Kong's interpretation of Western fare and drinks. Hong Kong–style milk tea, instant noodles with stir-fried meat, macaroni, French toast, and sandwiches frequently appear on menus with a Cantonese twist. Most *cha chaan tengs* are open throughout the day in Hong Kong, though mid-morning and late afternoon are considered peak hours. In the United States, the *cha chaan tengs* would be considered similar to 1950s coffee shop diners and are sparsely found, even among areas with a high concentration of Hong Kong immigrants.

While Cantonese-style cuisine has historically dominated Hong Kong's culinary scene, the influence of large minority populations (Hakka, Chiu Chow, and Shanghainese) that have settled in Hong Kong can also be seen. The Hakka cooking style emerging in Hong Kong has largely been shaped by Guangdong and Fujian influences. Hakka-influenced dishes reflect strong flavors and are often described as salty, pickled, or fatty, with pork, pickled, or preserved ingredients and soy sauce being the most commonly used ingredients. Steamed eggs with dried scallops and braised chicken with black bean sauce are two examples of classic Cantonese dishes incorporating Hakka influences.

While Chiu Chow cuisine reflects Guangdong and Fujian influences, the cooking style and techniques used tend to be more Cantonese. Similar to Hakka dishes, Chiu Chow can be categorized as hearty and flavorful, with preserved foods heavily incorporated into dishes. Other key aspects include potent sauces, a preference for seafood and vegetable ingredients, and an extensive repertoire of desserts unique to Chiu Chow cuisine, such as the use of root vegetables. Chiu Chow–influenced dim sum include steamed chive dumplings and Chiu Chow *fun gor* (dumplings).

Shanghainese cuisine favors slow-cooking and braising ingredients for an extended period of time (also known as red cooking). Soy sauce, rice wine, and rice vinegar are used to create sauces and flavor dishes, with an emphasis on fresh meat and seasonal vegetables. Soy sauce chicken and *xiao long bao* (Shanghai dumpling) are two Shanghai-based dishes that frequently appear in Cantonese cuisine.

Preparation

Hong Kong's high population density, coupled with small living quarters, limited storage space, and Cantonese cooking's emphasis on fresh ingredients, has meant that food ingredients are often purchased in small quantities daily or every few days. Prior to the 1970s, supermarkets were not prevalent in Hong Kong, so wet markets, single commodity stores, and local ministores were the primary resources for food items. In the United States, whereas Chinese cooking ingredients used to only be sparsely available in Chinatowns and small Chinese grocery stores, they can now be readily found in farmer's markets as well as American and Chinese supermarkets such as 99 Ranch and Pacific Supermarket on the West Coast and Kam Man Food on the East Coast. This increased availability, along with more spacious homes and kitchens, has allowed Hong Kong American families to purchase groceries weekly, though residents in older urban Chinatown enclaves may still elect to shop more frequently. Traditionally, women have been responsible for the preparation and cooking of meals in Hong Kong, with assistance from domestic helpers. Within Hong Kong American families, this responsibility may shift between male and female household members, depending on commitments outside of the home and personal interests in cooking.

Steaming and stir-frying with a minimal amount of oil are often the preferred cooking techniques for making Cantonese dishes in the home and restaurants. These styles are also popular for their quick cooking time and ability to showcase the freshness of ingredients, though deep-frying, braising, and roasting are also techniques used in Cantonese-style cooking.

Everyday Meals

Dining in Hong Kong typically revolves around five mealtimes—breakfast, lunch, afternoon tea, dinner, and *siu yeh* (late night). For dining outside of the home, dim sum is available mainly during breakfast and lunch hours, while banquet dishes are reserved for dinner functions, with most restaurants also offering *tong sui* (usually a variation of a sweet soup) as a dessert. However, in the United States, eating is typically more aligned with the American practice of three core meals (breakfast, lunch, and dinner). Snacks may be consumed throughout the day. Dim sum is served during the lunch hour only, though specialty stores and fast-food eateries located inside Asian malls or markets may offer it throughout the day. While many Cantonese American restaurants offer multicourse banquet menus, *tong sui* may not be consistently offered as a dessert at the end of dinner.

A traditional Hong Kong American home-cooked dinner consists of soup, several meat and vegetable dishes, and sweets or fruit for dessert. All are served family style, with white rice accompanying the main dishes. Slow-cooked soup used to be a main staple of the dinner meal. However, most families nowadays can no longer afford the extended cooking time required to simmer the meat, bones, and other ingredients, often for six or more hours. So the soup course has been either eliminated or replaced by less time-intensive soups, such as a simple winter melon soup. Main dishes for home-cooked dinners frequently include a variety of steamed dishes (steamed scallion-ginger fish fillets, egg custard, steamed tofu with minced meat) or stir-fried meat and vegetable combinations (tomato and beef, *gai lan* with oyster sauce). Fully cooked roasted meats (barbecue pork, roast duck, soy sauce chicken) prepared by Cantonese delis may also be purchased to augment the meal.

Holiday Feasts

Key Chinese holidays celebrated in Hong Kong include Chinese Lunar New Year, Ching Ming, Tuen Ng, Mid-Autumn Festival, and Chung Yeung. Of these, Chinese New Year and the Mid-Autumn Festival are the most celebrated holidays by Hong Kong Americans in the United States today. Families typically gather for a multicourse dinner meal on Chinese New Year's eve. *Nian Gao* (Chinese New Year cake) and other auspicious foods are then eaten during the Chinese New Year celebratory period to bring in prosperity, happiness, and good luck. During the Mid-Autumn Festival, moon cakes are often gifted in honor of family unity and celebration of the autumn harvest.

Place in American Culture

Although Chinese cuisine was first introduced in the United States during the mid-eighteenth century, interest in Chinese food did not peak until after World War II. Initially, Chinese food was equated with the rustic dishes consumed by primarily Cantonese migrant workers who arrived to be laborers in the 1800s. Following World War II, Chinese food had become synonymous with Cantonese cuisine due to the new wave of Guangdong and Hong Kong immigrants. However, in response to racial attitudes and culinary preferences of the time, as well as efforts to make Chinese food appear less "exotic" and more appealing to the American palate, Chinese restaurants began incorporating familiar American ingredients into Chinese dishes, such as ketchup, leading to a new genre of "Chinese American" cuisine. Notable Chinese American dishes that remain popular today and reflect Hong Kong and/or Cantonese influences include "sweet and sour pork" and "beef and broccoli." These dishes appear predominantly on Americanized Chinese restaurant menus and may not be as readily available in upscale restaurants focused on serving traditional, authentic Hong Kong or Cantonese cuisine.

As overall Chinese cuisine gains traction in the American culinary landscape, a new tradition of blending dishes has emerged in both restaurants and home cooking. Using a variation of Cantonese sticky rice (*lo mai fan*) as stuffing in traditional American Thanksgiving dinner is one example. Conversely, airing TV documentaries such as *May Food Keep Us Together* in the United States helps keep Hong Kong American immigrants connected with the people and food comprising Hong Kong cuisine.

Noted Restaurants and Chefs

Martin Yan, a Hong Kong–trained chef, has played an instrumental role in introducing

Chinese and Asian cuisine to the public through his televised series *Yan Can Cook*, which has aired since the late 1970s. He also operates the M. Y. China and Yan Can restaurants in Northern California.

Further Reading

Bartlett, Frances, and Ivan Lai. *Hong Kong on a Plate*. Central, Hong Kong: Roundhouse Publications, 1997.

Coe, Andrew. *Chop Suey: A Cultural History of Chinese Food in the United States*. New York: Oxford University Press, 2009.

Lo, Eileen Yin-Fei. *The Dim Sum Book: Classic Recipes from the Chinese Teahouse*. New York: Crown, 1982.

Lo, Eileen Yin-Fei and Alexandra Grablewski. *The Chinese Kitchen: Recipes, Techniques and Ingredients, History, and Memories from America's Leading Authority on Chinese Cooking*. New York: William Morrow, 1999.

Wu, David. "Chinese Café in Hong Kong." In *Changing Chinese Foodways in Asia*, edited by David Wu and Tan Chee-beng, 71–80. Sha Tin, NT: Chinese University of Hong Kong, 2001.

Mary Gee

HUNGARY

(Eastern Europe) Hungarian American
See also: Austria.

Background

Individual immigration of Hungarians to the United States can be traced as far back as the American Revolutionary War. Perhaps the first historically notable émigré was Agoston Haraszthy, often referred to as the "Father of Californian Viticulture" for having imported more than one hundred thousand European vine cuttings and for having founded Buena Vista Winery, which is now the oldest commercial winery in the country.

Group emigration, for the most part, occurred in three distinct waves. Several thousand "Forty-Eighters" arrived between 1849 and 1850, having fled Hungary after Austrian defeat of the Hungarian Revolution of 1848. This group consisted primarily of men of the gentry (middle nobility) with strong educational backgrounds and sound upbringing, who very easily assimilated into American society and established good standing with their neighbors.

The reputation of Hungarian immigrants changed with the second major wave, the turn-of-the-century "Great Economic Immigration," which brought 650,000 to 700,000 ethnic Hungarians to the United States. These immigrants were mostly uneducated, unskilled workers, laborers from the rural areas of Hungary seeking temporary work in the industrial cities of the northeastern United States with every intention to return to Hungary after earning enough capital to become independent farmers back home. They congregated in ten major states in the northeast: New York, Ohio, Pennsylvania, New Jersey, Illinois, Michigan, Connecticut, Wisconsin, Indiana, and West Virginia. They were drawn to these places because of the accessibility of unskilled work in coalmines and steel and textile mills in these areas. It was this second wave of economic immigrants that were designated by their American neighbors as "Hunkies," an ethnic slur that referred to laborers from Central Europe.

The third wave of immigrants included refugee intellectuals fleeing the spread of nazism in the 1930s, post–World War II political immigrants in 1948 and 1950, and the Freedom Fighters who left Hungary after the failed Revolution of 1956. It was this last group of Hungarians who restored the reputation of Hungarians as a learned, polite people. They did so in part with significant contributions to the study of mathematics, sciences, and engineering, and with inventions that had lasting impacts on American society.

According to 2010 census data, the population of total Hungarian Americans in the United States is 1,511,926. Census data from the year 2000 shows that in this year they were dispersed mostly in Ohio (193,951), New York (137,029), California (133,988), Pennsylvania (132,184), New Jersey (115,615), Michigan (98,036), and Florida (96,885). This data is mostly in line with the original settlement patterns of the first two waves of Hungarian immigrants, except that California experienced significant immigration from the third major wave and individual immigration afterward. All seven cities with the highest population of Hungarians have seen the population decrease between 1990 and 2000. This might be because third-wave emigrants have died between 1990 and 2000, leaving behind descendants who have assimilated and no longer consider themselves to be Hungarian. The most significant drop in the population of Hungarian Americans occurred in New York (a change of 49,869 between 1990 and 2000). This explains the noted disappearance of many Hungarian restaurants and specialty stores in the state.

Foodways

To fully understand the contemporary cuisine of Hungarian Americans, it is first necessary to understand the history of Hungarian food as an ethnic cuisine, along with the many events and peoples that shaped it. Hungarian cuisine can be traced as far back as the eighth century AD, when the Magyar tribes first migrated from the steppes of the Ural Mountains to the Don River. During this time the Magyars learned agriculture and cattle breeding from the surrounding Bulgars and Alans. Meals were often one-pot stews or soups prepared in cast iron cauldrons over an open fire. This element of nomadic cuisine survives today; soup continues to play a crucial role in any proper Hungarian and Hungarian American meal.

Perhaps the oldest surviving relic of ancient Hungarian cuisine is *gulyásleves*, known in the United States as *goulash*. The stew was developed by the Magyar herdsmen who settled in the Carpathian Basin in the Middle Ages. Since that time the dish has evolved with each community that has adopted it. In the late nineteenth century, the peasants of the Great Plains added paprika powder, resulting in a spicier soup that later evolved into a stew named *pörkölt*. The gentry added sour cream, turning the broth into a sauce to pour over meat. This gave rise to *paprikás*. At one point, *gulyásleves* also served as a symbol of cohesion during the struggle to preserve national identity against the homogenizing effects of the Austro-Hungarian Empire. Since then it has been adapted as Hungary's national dish and is prepared by Hungarians all over the world.

Western flavors were first introduced to Hungarian cuisine in the fifteenth century, when King Matthias married the Italian princess Beatrice, who brought with her garlic, pasta, cheeses, and turkey, along with a team of Italian chefs and pastry chefs. Onions became very important in Hungarian cooking at this time, as did the serving of thick gravies and sauces poured over game. King Matthias was one of Hungary's first gourmands and is said to have spent much time in the palace kitchen in the company of his royal chefs. A dish that particularly recalls this influence is *nokedli*, a *spätzle*–type egg dumpling often served as a side dish to *pörkölt*. The dish is thought to have descended from Italian *gnocchi*, from which it also probably got its name.

Ottoman rule over Hungary (1541–1699) also had significant impacts on Hungarian culture and cuisine. Perhaps their most important contribution was paprika, which today is something like the mascot of Hungarian cuisine. The spice was originally used only in peasant kitchens; it dangled in the gardens of the upper classes solely for decorative purposes. In the late nineteenth century, however, paprika started replacing pepper in the kitchens of the gentry and nobility. Today it is used to season almost every typical Hungarian dish.

As the Ottomans raided Hungarian towns, they took all domestic animals except swine, since pork was forbidden by their religion. As a result, the use of pork lard as primary cooking fat became popular during this time. Pig slaughters are still a very important part of Hungarian village tradition: they give rise to sausages, *tepertő* (cracklings), smoked fat back *szalonna*, and innards from which many dishes are traditionally made. While these ingredients can be inexpensively purchased in any Hungarian market today, they are difficult to source in the United States. Innards, including the tripe, brain, liver, and lungs of pork, are traditionally made into a *pörkölt*, sautéed with onions or breaded and fried. Hungarian American home cooks often search for these ingredients in Portuguese or Chinese markets, where they are more commonly sold. In parts of the United States where such ethnic markets do not exist, these dishes are lost and forgotten.

The Ottomans also introduced new vegetables to Hungarian cuisine, including the *Capiscum annuum* pepper, eggplants, corn, and tomatoes. Along with the veggies themselves, they brought the method of stuffing them. Stuffed cabbage rolls are one of the most festive dishes in Hungarian cuisine, derived from an Ottoman dish called *lahana sarma*, which is essentially meat rolled in cabbage. Hungarians and Hungarian Americans often prepare stuffed cabbages for special occasions.

The rule of the Hapsburg monarchy of Austria during the seventeenth century brought Austrian and German cooking methods into Hungary as well as the French cuisine emulated by the upper classes. They brought *schnitzel* (thinly pounded, breaded and fried meats), sausages, and potatoes, along with a dish of cooked vegetables thickened with a roux of flour and lard called *főzelék*. The Hapsburgs also introduced to Budapest the coffeehouse culture, pairing with the coffee the Turks left behind a wide array of pastries both originally Austrian and borrowed from the French. The coffeehouse (*cukrászda*) continues to play an important role in the cuisine of Hungary. Since the monarchy era, a variety of pastries have been developed as specifically Hungarian, and they remain very popular dessert items at Sunday meals. As many of the more elaborate pastries and cakes are typically prepared by trained pastry chefs and purchased at a *cukrászda*, neither Hungarian nor Hungarian American home cooks prepare them at home. A handful of Hungarian bakeries in the United States, including Farkas Pastry Shoppe in Cleveland, Ohio, and Tulipán Hungarian Pastry and Coffee Shop in Wooster, Ohio, offer a wide range of these baked specialties.

From the early 1950s communist rule put an end to culinary advancement. Political oppression and nationalization in Hungary resulted in shortages of fresh produce, and the cost of dining out was prohibitive for most. During this time dishes such as soup and *főzelék* became everyday staples in school and institutional cafeterias. Some of these cheap but hearty dishes eventually came to be considered comfort foods in Hungary, and a few of the more trendy restaurants in Budapest have brought them back as ironic "retro" relics of the past. Nevertheless, they are not dishes that appear on Hungarian American restaurant menus, as the latter were designed by immigrants or descendants of immigrants who fled Hungary as a result of socialism and are thus maybe not quite so fond of dishes that recall this era.

In the last decade, Hungarian cuisine has seen a resurgence of pride and has made great strides to take back those traditional items that were forbidden or unavailable during the communist era. Hungarian Americans have brought to the United States their most integral culinary practices and traditions, although they have adapted recipes to their new environment.

Procurement and Preparation

It is rare to find Hungarian food specialty stores in most US cities. More often than not

Hungarian items are lumped together with Polish, Russian, and Czech products at Central European retailers. In New York the most well known of Hungarian food emporiums, Paprika Weiss, closed in the mid-1990s. The Hungarian Meat Market, with locations in Manhattan and Fairfield, Connecticut, remains one of the only specifically Hungarian food stores on the East Coast.

Based in Burbank, California, Otto's Import Store & Deli also offers a wide array of imported Hungarian products at wholesale and retail prices. Otto's is a favorite among Hungarian restaurant owners in the United States, but for Hungarian American home cooks who do not have such easy access to these stores, ingredients often have to be replaced with items found at American supermarkets.

Hungarian fat back *szalonna* is often replaced with bacon, cow's milk quark with cottage cheese, and strudel dough with *phyllo*. Cold smoked sausages (*lángolt kolbász*), which are cooked and not dried, are ingredients needed to prepare a weekday dish called *Rakott krumpli*, a casserole of thinly sliced potatoes, hard-boiled eggs, onion, sour cream, and bread crumbs. Along with paprika, the sausage gives the dish its unique smoky flavor. While dried and cured *gyulai* and *csabai* sausages can be purchased in many Central European specialty shops, cooked sausages from Hungary are rarely imported and thus are very difficult to find in the United States. As a result, other paprika-based cooked sausages, such as *chorizo*, are often used to replace them. Some ingredients, such as ewe's milk quark, poppy seed, and chestnut puree (eaten with whipped cream as dessert), are irreplaceable. Traditional dishes that call for them are no longer prepared in the United States.

Perhaps the largest obstacle Hungarian American home cooks face is the limited variety of paprika found in American supermarkets or even Hungarian import stores. In Hungary there are eight different grades and brandings of paprika varying in color and pungency. These are "special quality" (*különleges*), "delicate" (*csípősmentes csemege*), "exquisite delicate" (*csemege*), "pungent exquisite delicate" (*csípős csemege*), "noble sweet" (*édesnemes*), "half sweet" (*félédes*), "rose" (*rózsa*), and "hot" (*erős*). There are also two different terroirs producing the spice, Kalocsa and Szeged. None of these have anything to do with spicy chili varieties (e.g., cayenne) that can commonly be found in the United States. In fact, a spicy quality is an unwanted feature when it comes to Hungarian paprika, as it is believed to show neglect from the farmer and an inability to keep the peppers from getting too much sun. Certain dishes have only traditionally been made with certain specific types of paprika, and many Hungarian Americans choose to stop preparing the dish altogether rather than prepare it with the incorrect type.

One notable exception to the scarcity of Hungarian specialty shops in the United States are Cleveland, Toledo, and Columbus, Ohio, where Hungarian communities have formed over the course of one hundred years and remain active to this day. Although by 1990 these cities saw a drop in the number of residents who were Hungarian by birth, older organizations such as churches and folkdance groups were replaced with new ones by second- and third-generation Hungarian Americans in an effort to preserve cultural traditions and awareness of ethnic background by American-born Hungarians. To this day, Hungarian Americans from all over the United States visit Ohio to attend festivals and to visit the Hungarian Heritage Museum in Cleveland and the Hungarian Reformed Church of Columbus. Hungarian Americans also visit Ohio to buy specialty items in the multiple import stores offering Hungarian products. Takács Grocery and Meats in Toledo and Dohar Meats in Cleveland both carry a wide array of dry and cooked sausages as well as smoked fat back and various types of paprika.

Everyday Meals

A dish that both Hungarian American home cooks and restaurants tend to make often is *paprikás csirke nokedlivel*, a creamy paprika-flavored stew prepared with chicken. It is known commonly in the United States as *chicken paprikash*. *Nokedlivel* refers to the egg-based dumpling served with the stew. The dumplings are usually prepared with a kitchen utensil called a *nokedli szaggató*, which is specifically designed to grate the soft, moist dough into boiling water. The utensil is difficult to find in the United States and is thus usually brought directly from Hungary. Some Hungarian American home cooks who do not have the utensil prefer to leave the dumplings out of this recipe completely, replacing it with macaroni or some other small, store-bought pasta. The recipe follows.

Chicken Paprikash (*Nokedlivel*)
Ingredients:
   Paprikás csirke
   2 pounds chicken thighs and wings
   1 large white onion
   1 green bell pepper
   1 tomato
   2 tablespoons of lard
   1 teaspoon hot paprika
   10 ounces sour cream
   2 tablespoons flour
   Nokedli
   1 cup of flour
   1 large egg
   ¼ cup of water
   salt

1. Clean chicken thighs and wings. Divide thighs into upper thighs and drumsticks.
2. Mince onion finely. Wash and clean bell pepper; slice into quarters. Peel tomato and dice.
3. Into a pan, add lard and allow it to heat at a high temperature. When it's bubbling, add the minced onion and toast it for about 1 minute. It's important for the onion not to brown or caramelize.
4. Remove pan from heat and stir in paprika.
5. Toast paprika for about a minute, or until onion is well flavored with paprika.
6. Add pieces of chicken and flip until the surface browns.
7. Add a half-cup of water. Stir well.
8. Add sliced peppers and tomato, along with a pinch of salt.
9. Cover pan and cook on low heat until the chicken gets tender. If necessary, add only a small amount of water at a time. The sauce should be thick.
10. Remove pepper from the pan and cook on medium heat until some of the liquid evaporates and the sauce becomes thick.
11. In a small bowl combine sour cream, flour, and 3 tablespoons of the chicken's cooking liquid. Stir until it dissolves into a homogenous roux. Add roux to pan and shake it. Do not stir, as this might break the pieces of chicken.
12. Cook for an additional 4 or 5 minutes on low heat.

For *Nokedli*:
1. Set a pot of salted water to boil.
2. Combine ingredients in a bowl and stir into a homogenous mass of sticky dough.
3. Let dough rest for 10 minutes.
4. Grate the dough over a *nokedli* slicer, allowing the bits of dough to drop into boiling water. Repeat until all dough is used.
5. Cook dumplings until they float to the top of the water.
6. Dump dumplings into colander and rinse with cold water to remove excess starch.
7. Serve *nokedli* in a pile with *paprikás csirke* poured over the top.

Meal System

The traditional Hungarian breakfast generally consists of bread or toast with butter, cold cuts, and sliced vegetables. On rare occasions a *villás reggeli* (literally "breakfast with a fork") is prepared; this consists of eggs, cold steak, and *körözött* (Liptaur spread). Lunch (*ebéd*) is the largest meal of the day, and in Hungary it consists strictly of three courses: soup, entrée, and dessert. Hungarian soups can be divided into three or four different categories based on ingredients, preparation time, and whether or nor a roux is added. When it is followed by an entrée, the soup is generally a dilute *alapleves* made from a broth and only one other ingredient—for example, green bean soup, potato soup, or caraway seed soup. This type of light soup is consumed as it is believed to help build an appetite rather than to satisfy hunger in any way. The main dish can include meat and a salad of pickled cabbage, tomatoes, or cucumber whose acidity cuts the fat and paprika heat of the often lard-based entrees. A light snack called *uzsonna* is sometimes consumed in the afternoon, followed by a very light dinner (*vacsora*) that mimics lunch—an open-faced sandwich with vegetables.

In assimilating to the culture of the United States, the Hungarian American meal system has become pronouncedly different from that which is common in Hungary. This has to do with the fact that in the United States lunch breaks are usually an hour or less and people rarely go home to eat. The traditional tripartite lunch is a rarity among working Hungarian Americans, and the dilute soup is almost never brought to work. Typically only the entrée is brought to work, or homemade Hungarian food is replaced by whatever soup-salad-sandwich combination is available at the workplace. While some first-generation Hungarian Americans who are still accustomed to having a large lunch bring their warm lunches to work, those who have been in the States longer have adapted and now eat dishes traditionally served for lunch at dinnertime. Many Hungarian American families have, nevertheless, kept the custom of preparing a large lunch on weekends. Weekend dishes generally take several hours to prepare, allowing families to gather and socialize.

Holiday Feasts

Holidays mark significant culinary practices in Hungarian culture. On Christmas Eve, families gather for a dinner of either fish (e.g., breaded and fried local carp) or roasted turkey (drumsticks are most popular). Stuffed cabbage is prepared and eaten on Christmas Day, as well as during the week between Christmas Day and New Year's Eve; it is an easy dish to reheat and actually improves in flavor the longer it sits. This is also true for a dessert pastry called *beigli*, a roll of sweet yeast bread filled with a paste of walnuts or sweet poppy seeds. *Beigli* is also popularly prepared during this week. On New Year's Eve, a stew of lentils is made, and the stew is consumed for lunch on January 1, as it represents good luck and financial prosperity for the upcoming year.

On Good Friday families start a fast, eating no meat until Easter Sunday when a large meal is consumed for brunch. No Easter meal is complete without a ham, cured and smoked with special care and set aside on farms specifically for Easter. The meat is generally served with accompaniments such as mustard, radishes, and onions. Other traditional items include hard-boiled eggs or a mayonnaise-based egg salad and braided challah bread (*kalács*).

Some Hungarian Americans make a strong effort to maintain these culinary customs in an effort to preserve cultural heritage. Elder members of the family often considerate it their duty to embed these cultural values into younger generations of American-born Hungarians, and so they continue preparing holiday dishes year by year just as they did in Hungary. Other families choose parts of these culinary traditions that they personally enjoy most or those which are easiest to carry out using ingredients obtained in the United States. Fisherman's stew (*halászlé*), for example, has largely been abandoned as a traditional Christmas dish by Hungarian Americans because of the absence of freshwater fish that tastes like those found in Lake Balaton or Tisza River in Hungary. Similarly, some families only prepare walnut *beigli* as opposed to the classic walnut and poppy seed duo because of the difficulty of finding the right quantity and grade of poppy seeds necessary to make the filling. In some cases, Hungarian American families select dishes, which may not be associated with holidays in Hungary but which are nevertheless preferred by members of the family. These often replace traditional Hungarian holiday dishes on special occasions. More assimilated Hungarian Americans choose not to cook at all and celebrate instead by eating at a restaurant.

Apart from religious or national holidays, Hungarian families also gather for Sunday lunch, a tradition that many Hungarian Americans also follow. One of the most important Sunday meals is *húsleves* or "meat soup." The dish is intricate, complex, and takes several hours to prepare. It is made by stewing vegetables (celeriac, kohlrabi, onion, cabbage, carrot, parsley root) and beef (marrow bones, shank, rump). Fine egg noodles are sometimes also added. The broth is strained and eaten separately as the appetite-inducing dilute soup, while the stewed vegetables and beef are consumed as an entrée with condiments including horseradish and hot mustard. The greatest obstacle for Hungarian American cooks in preparing this very culturally important dish is the availability of vegetables such as kohlrabi and celeriac in American grocery stores. Parsley root is almost never available and is often substituted for parsnip, which, although it might resemble the ingredient closely in form, gives the dish a very different flavor.

Place in American Culture

Goulash was brought to the United States by the first wave of immigrants and started to appear in cookbooks by the 1860s. During the Great Depression, the dish emerged as one of the most popular dishes in the country, as it called for cheap, rough cuts of beef that were tenderized by hours of cooking and flavored with paprika powder alone. At this time *goulash* became a comfort food staple in the United States, assimilating into local cuisine. As *goulash* was adopted, its Hungarian roots faded, and today the dish is no longer recognized by Americans as a Hungarian dish specifically but is instead considered a pan-Eastern/Central European specialty. Its roots are often mistaken for Austrian or German.

A popular custom in Hungary that still survives among Hungarian American families is gathering to roast bacon on a stick held over an open campfire. This tradition holds cultural values similar to that of roasting marshmallows over the fireplace in the United States. In Hungary *szalonna*, a thick, smoked fat back, is used. Since *szalonna* is not commonly found in the United States, many Hungarian Americans use thick slabs of American bacon instead. As the bacon roasts, the fat dripping off is captured on slices of rye bread, which are then consumed with chopped tomatoes, peppers, onion, radish, and the crispy, roasted bacon itself. Second- and third-generation Hungarians named this tradition "hunky turkey," which was easier for both them and their non-Hungarian friends to pronounce than *szalonna sütés*. Interestingly, the term *hunky* was originally an offensive ethnic slur used to refer to second-wave Hungarian immigrants working in mines and factories on the East Coast and the Midwest. Naming this tradition "hunky" is a way of demonstrating pride or, at least, a sense of humor about the negative stereotypes once applied to the Hungarian people.

Restaurants

One of the most emblematic Hungarian establishments in the United States was Café Budapest once situated in the basement of the Copley Square Hotel in downtown Boston. The restaurant was owned by Jewish sisters Edith and Hedda Rev, who had fled Hungary during the revolution of 1956 after being interned in Auschwitz only twelve years earlier. When the sisters immigrated to Boston, Edith opened Café Budapest, which quickly became known as "the Russian Tea Room of Boston." The restaurant was lavishly decorated and romantic, the place to get dinner before attending a Pops concert at the Symphony Hall nearby. The menu featured a wide range of Hungarian dishes and helped put Hungarian cuisine on the map in the northeast United States. After thirty-seven years, Café Budapest shut its doors in 2000. Boston residents lamented the closing of the restaurant as a great tragedy.

One of the most noted surviving beacons of Hungarian cuisine in the United States today is the Hungarian Pastry Shop in the Morningside Heights neighborhood of Manhattan. The café is a favorite among Columbia University students who stop there to lounge and work while enjoying an old-world pastry. While the shop offers many international favorites, such as *tiramisu* and *baklava*, the pastry case is always stocked with Hungarian classics, such as *dobos torta*, *rigó Jancsi*, *lúdláb*, and *francia krémes*. The café also offers *rétes*, popular as "strudel" in the area of the former Austro-Hungarian Empire. The *rétes* fillings are those also popular in Hungary: poppy seed, sour cherry, quark cheese, and apple.

Recently, the famous Zingerman's Bakehouse in Ann Arbor, Michigan, has also started offering Hungarian foods. The team at Zingerman's traveled to Hungary in 2011, 2012, and 2013 to conduct research before designing Hungarian baking and cooking classes, along with a Hungarian food tour that will commence in May of 2015. The bakery currently offers a wide spectrum of Hungarian pasties, including *pogácsa* (a savory biscuit made with cheese or pork cracklings and sprinkled with caraway seeds), *beigli* (Christmastime pastry with sweet walnut or poppy seed filling), and *flódni* (a layered pastry with poppy seed, raisins, walnuts, and apples).

As the central hub of Hungarian culture within the United States, Ohio is known not only for specialty shops with imported products but also for Hungarian restaurants with decades of history. Balaton restaurant in Cleveland, for example, has been serving traditional Hungarian food since the 1960s. The kitchen is especially well known for its stuffed cabbage, *goulash*, and *lecsó*, a stew of yellow paprika and tomatoes.

One of the most iconic restaurants in Toledo is Tony Packo's located in the Hungarian neighborhood of Birmingham. Originally a sandwich and ice cream shop opened by Tony Packo, the son of Hungarian immigrants, in 1932 the restaurant became popular among locals for a dish called the Hungarian hot dog, made with Hungarian *kolbász* sausage and a spicy chili sauce poured over the top. The dish became famous in 1976 when Jamie Farr mentioned it on his television show *M*A*S*H*. Tony Packo's Hungarian hot dog is an example of fusion cuisine, as it is made with a Hungarian ingredient but prepared as a popular American dish. The restaurant's menu also features more traditional Hungarian foods such as chicken soup with dumplings, *chicken paprikash*, and stuffed cabbage.

A particularly strong trend among Hungarian American home cooks and Hungarian restaurants in the United States is the quotidian preparation of dishes that in Hungary are only prepared on festive occasions, when visitors come and, occasionally, for the Sunday meal. Examples include *pörkölt*, *paprikás*, *gulyás*, *bécsi szelet*, and *francia szelet*. Most of these dishes call for meat, which is less expensive in the United States than in Hungary. On the other hand, good-quality vegetables are significantly more expensive in the United States. This difference leads to the gradual disappearance of vegetable-based dishes that are commonly prepared as everyday meals in Hungary. One example is the *főzelék*, a hearty dish of steamed vegetables thickened with a flour roux or with sour cream. Varieties include cabbage, pepper, potato, sauerkraut, tomato, pea, kohlrabi, lentil, bean, squash, spinach, sorrel, green beans, or any combination of the latter. While *főzelék* is frequently prepared for lunch or dinner during the week in Hungary, Hungarian Americans rarely make it at home, and it rarely appears on Hungarian restaurant menus in the United States. In addition to the accessibility of inexpensive meat, this trend can also be attributed to a desire of Hungarian American home cooks and restaurant owners to show off their culture by offering what they think to be the highlights of their cuisine.

Many classic Hungarian dishes tend to appear on the menus of pan-Eastern/Central European restaurants, where iconized dishes from countries neighboring Hungary are also offered. It's not uncommon, for example, to see "Hungarian *goulash*" next to Polish *pierogies*, followed by Austrian *wienerschnitzel*.

Some specifically Polish, German, or Russian restaurants also sometimes offer a handful of Hungarian dishes. The latter tend to be only those celebratory foods that have been proudly offered in Hungary to guests from neighboring countries to show off what are considered to be the highlights of Hungarian cuisine. Recipes for these dishes were subsequently brought back by visitors as examples of Hungarian cuisine and published into their own cookbooks. They were eventually placed on menus of restaurants in those neighboring countries as well as on menus of ethnic restaurants in the United States. A common example of this is *goulash*, which was served frequently to German tourists visiting Hungary and brought back to Germany under the name *gulasch*. The dish became popular, and the recipe was culturally adopted, as *gulasch* was placed on menus in many restaurants around Germany. As German restaurant owners immigrated to the United States, they brought the dish with them and offered it as a German dish in their new German restaurant in the United States.

Further Reading

Beecher, J. Lucas. "Magyars in Toledo." *Toledo Daily Blade*, January 26, 1907.

Marks, Gil. *Encyclopedia of Jewish Food*. Boston: Houghton Mifflin Harcourt, 2010.

Várdy, Steven Béla. *The Hungarian Americans: The Hungarian Experience in North America*. New York and Philadelphia: Chelsea House, 1990.

Venesz, József. *Hungarian Cuisine*. Budapest: Corvina Press, 1977.

Wass de Czege, Albert. *Our Hungarian Heritage*. Florida: Danubian Press, 1975.

Lili Kocsis

ICELAND
(Northern Europe) Icelandic American
See also: Norway, Sweden.

Background
According to the 2010 census, just over fifty-one thousand Americans claim Icelandic heritage. There is speculation that the first group migrated to the United States in the 1700s after a devastating volcanic eruption; Icelandic Mormons followed them in the mid-1850s in pursuit of religious freedom. The greatest waves of immigration occurred in the late 1870s and after World War II. These immigrants tended to settle in existing Norwegian and Swedish settlements in the Dakotas, Minnesota, Wisconsin, and Utah.

It is likely that it is this original linkage with Scandinavia that has resulted in Icelanders being thought of as Scandinavians. Icelanders, however, consider themselves a distinct group, as evidenced by Icelandic American cultural groups established in the United States since the founding of the Icelandic National League in 1919. Although the last few years have propelled the country into US consciousness, in large part by aggressive marketing by the tourism industry, Icelandic cultural presence in the United States remains minimal.

Foodways
Traditional Icelandic food (*Þorramatur*) was about survival, using only ingredients that were available, especially during the harsh winters on the remote, isolated island nation. The diet consisted solely of fish, lamb, *rúgbrauð* (dark rye "geyser bread" that is cooked in the ground), potatoes, and dairy, such as butter and *skyr*, a fermented dairy product that is a cross between yogurt and cheese. Seasonings were limited to Icelandic mosses and arctic thyme, which covers much of the barren landscape.

Fish and lamb are eaten daily and prepared in various ways, but most commonly it is smoked and dried. The entire lamb, including the head (*svið*), organs, testicles (*súrsaðir hrútspungar*), and blood used to make blood sausage (*blóðmör*), is used. Fish, both fresh and dried (*harðfiskur*), remains a staple, while horse, whale, and fermented shark (*hákarl*) are considered delicacies. Today, many different foods are increasingly imported into the country, but people continue to enjoy traditional foods as a way to connect to their ancestors and historical roots. Although known as an egalitarian society, women, historically and presently, usually do food preparation.

During *Þorrablót* (midwinter feast), Christmas, and other cultural celebrations, *Þorramatur* is laid out buffet style. In general, Icelanders eat informally, with people helping themselves. Meals always include strong coffee; baked goods, such as *kleina* (fried dough); and Iceland's signature distilled schnapps, *Brennivín*, also known as "black death." Icelanders love sweets and sugar is widely used, even added to savory foods.

Fish soups are eaten regularly in Iceland, and no two soups taste the same since each family has its own recipe. Icelanders use whatever they have available at the time of preparation, with the only reliable ingredient being fish. Let this recipe serve as a guide and use any vegetables you have available for the soup.

Fish Soup

Serves 4 as a main dish or 6 as an appetizer

- 3 quarts homemade fish stock
- ¾ pound cod or similar, cut into ½-inch pieces
- ¾ pound arctic char or salmon, cut into ½-inch pieces
- ¾ pound shrimp, peeled (shells used for stock)
- 2 tablespoons butter
- ½ cup vermouth or white wine
- 1 tablespoon tomato paste
- 2 large leeks, minced
- 1 large onion, minced
- 6 cloves of garlic, minced
- 3 stalks of celery, finely chopped
- any other vegetables available, cut into small pieces
- 1 teaspoon each, dried parsley and thyme
- 3 bay leaves
- salt and pepper, to taste
- crème fraîche

Melt butter in a large pot. Add vegetables, cook until tender, about 10 minutes. Add vermouth and reduce the liquid by half; add the tomato paste, stir to combine. Add the stock, herbs, and bay leaves. Bring to a boil; reduce and simmer, 30 minutes to an hour. Add fish and cook until just done, no more than 5 minutes.

Ladle into bowls and to each bowl add fresh herbs (dill or parsley) and 1 teaspoon of crème fraîche. Serve with crusty bread and good butter.

Place in American Culture

Because of the limited traditional diet of Icelanders, Icelandic food is perceived as unusual to Americans. It is most widely known today for its outrageously smelly fermented shark, *Brennivín*, and hot dogs (*pylsur*), as this is what is written about in popular tourist guidebooks.

Icelandic food continues to remain relatively unavailable in the United States, though in tandem with the recent marketing of Iceland, certain Icelandic foods such as Icelandic butter (*Smjör*), *skyr*, and beer are now being carried by a national food chain. Restaurants that are opening are based predominantly on the concept of New Nordic Cuisine, which has been gaining in popularity in recent years, although the focus remains more on Scandinavia, in general, rather than on Iceland, in particular. The main concepts of New Nordic Cuisine are a reliance on locally sourced ingredients along with the use of traditional preparation methods. With the recent increased awareness of and interest in Iceland, the food culture is being explored and highlighted, framing it in terms of the locavore movement, which continues to gain popularity around the world.

Noted Restaurants and Chefs

Siggi Hall is an Icelandic celebrity chef famous for promoting Iceland's local ingredients internationally. Gunnar Karl Gíslason is a pioneer of Icelandic-specific cuisine under the umbrella of New Nordic Cuisine. While both chefs have attained status in their fields, they are best known to those with a specific interest in Iceland or Nordic cuisine. They have yet to gain international notoriety that is widespread in the general population. This is consistent with the limited infiltration of Icelandic culture into the US mainstream.

Noma in Copenhagen, Denmark, is a world-renowned restaurant that propelled the philosophy of New Nordic Cuisine into the international spotlight. Due to Icelanders' close association with Scandinavians, Noma must be mentioned as a major force in the world of Nordic cuisine.

In recent years, the annual Taste of Iceland food festival has been held in various US cities as a way to introduce Americans to Icelandic culture through food and to encourage tourism in Iceland. Thus far, it has been held in Denver, Colorado; Seattle, Washington; New York City; and Boston, Massachusetts.

In the early 1900s in New York City, there was a Scandinavian restaurant called Iceland Restaurant. Recently, an Icelandic restaurant, SKÁL (Icelandic for "cheers"), opened in New

York, continuing to embed Iceland further into mainstream food culture in the United States.

Further Reading

Barer-Stein, Thelma. "Iceland." In *You Eat What You Are: People, Culture and Food Traditions*, 196–200. Ontario: Firefly Books Ltd., 1999.

Gíslason, Gunnar Karl and Jody Eddy. *North: The New Nordic Cuisine of Iceland*. Berkeley: Ten Speed Press, 2014.

Presser, Brandon, Carolyn Bain, and Fran Parnell. *Lonely Planet: Iceland*. Oakland, CA: Lonely Planet, 2013.

Maggie Ornstein

INDIA

(Southern Asia) Indian American Foodways
See also: Pakistan, Bangladesh, Sri Lanka.

Background

Asian Indian immigrants arrived in the United States over three major time periods. The first group came between the 1890s and 1947, when India was still under British rule. The second immigrated between 1965 and 1994 after the passage of the US Immigration and Nationality Act. The third and largest wave came to the United States after India signed the General Agreement of Tariff and Trade (GATT) and the processes of globalization intensified in India, between 1995 and the present. Each of these time periods brought in a new class and caste of Indians from different geographic regions, which played a major role in diversifying Indian cuisine in the United States.

The First Wave of Indian Immigrants: 1700s–1947

The 1900 Census counted 2,031 Asian Indians residing in the United States. Most of the Indians who came to the United States prior to 1947 were uneducated men from rural areas of the state of Punjab. They tended to be single men from poor Sikh and Muslim families who had left India either to serve in British or other European armies, or to work as indentured laborers in British colonies of Suriname, Guyana, Trinidad, and Tobago. There were also a handful of servants who had accompanied their masters to England or other countries. Due to restrictive US immigration policies, a majority of them had entered the United States through Britain or one of their colonies in South America or the Caribbean. Fewer Hindus from working-class families left India during this time due to lack of financial resources and/or their complex religious beliefs, many of which were tied to foodways. Many upper castes would banish individuals and their families if they consumed food or drink prepared or served by a member of another (lower) caste in a manner different from what was stipulated by their community.

Although a small population of Indians settled on the East Coast, most immigrants made their base in California or Oregon. Since the majority of immigrants were from rural areas, they were naturally drawn toward agricultural work. In due course of time, they bought over eighty thousand acres of land in San Joaquin and Sacramento valleys and developed communal living and dining arrangements with other Asian Indian immigrants. Since Indian men were barred from marrying white or Caucasian women, they married Mexican or Mexican American women—many of whom who had come to work at their farms. Interestingly, even though most of these Indians were non-Hindus, they came to be known as the Mexican-Hindus. They taught their Mexican brides how to cook various vegetables and Indian breads. The preference for fresh vegetables and spicy foods in both cultures led to the fusion and development of Mexican-Indian cuisine in the West.

In 1907, Indians became victims of prejudice and discrimination. Racial riots broke out against Asian Indians, and hundreds of Indians were driven out of their homes in Bellingham, Washington. Beginning in 1917, several laws and regulations were passed restricting the rights and immigration of Asian Indians. In 1923, the US Supreme Court ruling in *US vs. Bhagat Singh Thind* disqualified Asian Indians from obtaining US citizenship and stripped naturalized Asian Indians of their citizenship. Over thirty-two thousand acres of land that Indians had acquired were claimed by the US government. This prompted a number of Indians to leave the United States, but many stayed behind. Over the years, it was this generation of Indians that consisted of approximately 80 percent Sikhs and 20 percent Muslims from the state of Punjab who determined the main characteristics of Indian cuisine in the United States. Today most of the food that is served in Indian and Nepalese restaurants and at Asian Indian parties, along with natural and organic foods developed by companies such as Amy's Kitchen, Saffron Road, and Patak's, have their origin in Punjabi cuisine.

The Second Wave of Indian Immigration: 1965–1994

Indians who immigrated to the United States between 1965 and 1994 were mostly English-speaking, educated professionals or students from financially prosperous families. They had grown up in larger cities and had some exposure to Western culture. These professionals were prized in the United States for their academic skills and talents and were regarded as an asset to the US economy and workforce. Because of expanded professional opportunities and their familiarity with a fast-paced urban lifestyle, most of these immigrants chose to settle in metropolitan cities such as New York City, Chicago, Los Angeles, or San Francisco. Over the decades, sizable Indian populations began to grow in suburban areas of Silver Springs (Maryland), Queens (New York), and San Jose and Fremont (California). Indian migrants of this time period began to pay more attention to American lifestyle and cultures, including food preferences of mainstream Americans. This knowledge proved invaluable for Indian restaurateurs and entrepreneurs who wanted to reach out to both Indian and American people through food. This period also saw the growth of Hindu philosophical movements in the United States. Several Indian spiritual leaders such as Maharishi Mahesh Yogi—the founder of Transcendental Meditation technique, and A. C. Bhaktivedanta, the founder of International Society of Krishna Consciousness—settled in the United States and promoted the message of nonviolence and vegetarianism. When celebrities such as musician and former Beatles member George Harrison started taking an interest in Indian cultural practices, their fans also began to explore various aspects of Indian culture, including cuisine. These years also saw a substantial increase in the number of Indian restaurants in the United States.

The Third Wave of Indians: 1995–present

In April 1994, India signed the GATT, which opened its doors to multinational companies. With increasing number of Indians arriving to the United States and more Americans traveling to India and developing a palate for Indian cuisine, a new and expanded market for Indian food emerged. The presence of busy Indian professionals wanting to consume Indian food in the relaxing atmosphere of their homes and more Americans wanting to have spicy Indian snacks for a beer treat has created a booming market for processed Indian food and drinks. In recent years, both Indians and American entrepreneurs have introduced new genres of Indian or India-inspired "fusion" foods. A whole line of instant meals, microwavable dishes, canned foods, and frozen dinners is being produced and distributed by individuals and corporations in India, Pakistan, Canada, England, and the United States for Western consumers. A new category of fast-food Indian cafés and restaurants has expanded in metropolitan towns throughout the United States, and Indian spices and drinks have made their way into mainstream grocery stores, with companies such as Lay's selling curry-flavored potato chips and Starbucks selling chai or chai latte. In larger metropolitan cities, such as Boston, Chicago, and New York, Indian entrepreneurs have started delivering home-cooked Indian meals to busy Indian families in the same way that many single professionals in Indian metropolitan towns subscribe to meal service. In this way, India-inspired cuisine is becoming a part of American households.

Foodways

In contemporary United States and India, Indian food encapsulates a multitude of histories and geographies. Indian cuisine is very dynamic, and the regional cuisine of every state in India has been influenced by the culinary traditions and religions of its conquerors and travelers. Persian, African, Arab, Portuguese, English, Dutch, Sinhalese, Chinese, Nepalese, Tibetan, Burmese, and several other South East Asian traditions have all had influence on traditional Indian cookery. In the United States, Indian cuisine has thrived with its interactions with Vietnamese Sriracha sauce, Thai chili peppers and lemongrass, Japanese teriyaki sauce, Mexican tortillas and salsa, and Italian seasonings and pasta sauce. For many Indians in the United States, it is not the food but the style of cooking, spicing, and modifying a dish with Indian ingredients that makes it "Indian." Similarly, in India we see a new generation of individuals cooking Indianized versions of "foreign foods" such as pizza, burgers, chop suey, and chow mein.

This intermingling of foreign foods with Indian spices, recipes, and cooking practices in everyday cooking in India makes defining authentic Indian food highly complex and controversial; however, there are certain terms for Indian food that are regarded as inauthentic by Indians both in India and in the United States. For instance, there is no such thing as "curry" in Indian cuisine. Scholars have speculated that perhaps the Indian dish *kadhi*, made from yogurt and chickpea flour, inspired the British to label all Indian vegetable and meat dishes as curry. It was used by the British colonial officers in India to refer to vegetable and meat dishes prepared in gravy of onion, garlic, ginger, chili peppers, and tomatoes and has become a generic term for certain spice mixtures as well as for sauces and stews using those spices. In the United States, ethnic Indians do not ordinarily use the term *curry* among themselves, and they use that word only to describe or explain their vegetable or meat dishes to fellow Americans. Ethnic Indians, especially those from South India, Maharashtra, and Gujarat, use fresh leaves called *curry-patta* in their cooking. These leaves release a delicate aroma and enhance color and flavor to almost any salty dish. Indians have a specific or a descriptive name for all of these recipes. For example, in Hindi, people use the word *sabzi* or *tarkari* for vegetables and *saag* for leafy greens. If they prepare a soupy dish with potatoes, peas, and tomatoes, they refer it by its key ingredients mentioned above—for example, *aloo-matar-tamatar ki rasedar sabzi*.

In the contemporary United States, many companies such as Natural Organics, McCormick spices, and Penzeys have started manufacturing curry powders and marketing it through major grocery stores. Interestingly, their consumption is largely limited to non-Indians. Ethnic Indians tend to view curry powder with skepticism. They use individual dried spices such as mustard, cumin, and sesame seeds with powdered turmeric, coriander, chili pepper, *garam masala*, and dried mango in their cooking. When they add a combination of these spices to hot *ghee* or oil in a designated order, sometimes along with a paste of freshly ground onion, chili, garlic, and ginger, each one of them releases an aroma that defines the flavor of their entrée.

In India, the cuisine of every region is directly or indirectly influenced by foodways of different castes, classes, and communities. At the same time, the foodways of every region is distinctive because of the vegetables, spices, and crops found in that area. Indian food is broadly categorized into North Indian and South Indian food.

Wheat is the staple crop of North India and is used in a variety of flours ranging from all-purpose and whole wheat, and along with other grains, such as maize, oats, sorghum, and millet, to make bread. The flour is first mixed with water and kneaded into dough, which is divided into small balls that are then rolled out generally into circular shape and cooked or deep fried in a skillet. Rice is the staple crop of South India; consequently, that cuisine features an array of rice-based dishes, such as lemon-rice, coconut-rice, *vangi bhat* (aubergine-rice), *bisibella bhat* (vegetable rice), and *idlis* (steamed rice cakes).

North Indian food is generally cooked in vegetable, peanut, or mustard oil and consists of a variety of wheat- or grain-based breads and entrées. Being heavily influenced by Persian and Arab cuisines, it is creamier and heavier than South Indian food. South Indian cuisine is higher in water content, which makes it lighter and less greasy. Many South Indian breads and cakes, such as *dosa*, *appa*, and *idli*, involve soaking, grinding, and fermenting rice or a combination of rice and lentil flour overnight and mixing them in a batter before cooking or steaming. While most of the nonvegetarian North Indian dishes include mutton, lamb, and chicken, South Indian recipes, reflecting its geography, includes a variety of seafoods.

The method and order of spicing food is also different in North and South India. In most North Indian dishes, onions, garlic, ginger, and green chilies are minced or ground to a paste and then deep fried along with a whole array of powdered spices such as turmeric, clove powder, chili, and coriander powder. In South Indian dishes, most of the above-mentioned spices are lightly sautéed and seldom deep fried. Because most of the South Indian states are bordered by the coastal regions of the Arabian Sea, Indian Ocean, and Bay of Bengal, there is extensive use of coconuts.

In ethnic Indian American homes, food preferences are rooted in the geography and traditions from the family's home region in India. For instance, immigrants from the state of Gujarat continue to favor slightly sweetened flavors to their meals, whereas people from the eastern states of Assam, West Bengal, Bihar, and Odisha find their meals incomplete without rice and *panch phoron* spice.

In ethnic Indian households, adaptation and Americanization of Indian foods have been primarily guided by the lifestyle of its residents. Much depends on whether immigrants are living by themselves, with their families, or with their Indian or non-Indian roommates. For instance, while chopped vegetables, sliced meats, and products that can stay refrigerated for an extended period of time are regarded as conveniences by all ethnic Indians, processed and canned foods have gained popularity particularly among busy students and professionals. If they are living with their parents, though, it is not uncommon to cook flatbreads such as *chapatis* and *parathas* on daily basis. Many families also substitute white flour and whole wheat tortillas for *chapatis* or *rotis* in their everyday meals. Sometimes Indians who have access to East Asian grocery stores also stock up on frozen Malaysian *parathas*—a North Indian layered bread that is native to India but has been developed for Indians in Malaysia. Ethnic Indians also like *pita*, *lavash*, and other types of Middle Eastern flatbreads. Many ethnic Indians prefer to eat freshly baked *naans* at Indian restaurants as opposed to more expensive and less flavorful frozen *naan* or *kulcha* sold in grocery stores.

Young Indian students and professionals who have greater opportunities to socially engage with American friends and colleagues also have more exposure to world cuisine. Consequently, several Mexican, Italian, Thai, Vietnamese, and Middle East foods and condiments such as tacos, salsa, refried beans, pastas, pasta sauces, *hummus*, *baba ghanoush*, sour cream, various types of cheeses, coconut milk, and tofu have become part of their kitchens. Certain high-calorie foods such as ice cream, big bags of potato chips, beer, wine, processed juices, and soda pop that Indians do not eat on a daily basis in India because of their higher cost have also become part of their regular snack foods in the United States.

Most ethnic Indians visit both American grocery stores and Indian markets to purchase their food supplies, and while most keep a limited amount of canned foods such as tomatoes, corn, garbanzo beans, and various types of soups in their pantry as convenience foods, they prefer fresh and frozen foods. Busy Indian professionals also like to stock up on microwavable frozen dinners that include other ethnic dishes and "American" foods as well as Indian.

In recent years, several reputable Indian food companies such as Swad, MTR, Deep, Udupi, and Ashoka have started making frozen or microwavable Indian snacks and gourmet entrées that are precooked and require reheating. They include but are not limited to vegetarian dishes such as *palak paneer* (spinach with milk curd), *matar paneer* (peas with milk curd), *bhindi-masala* (spicy okra), *dal-makkhani* (butter *dal*), *chana masala* (spicy chickpeas) and popular South Indian, Gujarati, and Maharashtrian appetizers such as *idli* (rice cakes), *vada* (fried dumplings made out of lentil), *dosa* (onion-and-potato-stuffed crepes made out of rice and *urad* lentil flour), *uttapam*, *upama*, and *dhokla*. Certain foods such as *samosas* and breads such as *paratha*, *roti*, *kulcha*, and *bhatura* are sold in frozen forms. Frozen *samosas* can either be deep fried or baked in the oven. In addition to these foods, Indian companies such as Gits manufacture a wide variety of instant food mixes that include both everyday and gourmet meals, such as *sambar* (lentil soup with vegetables), *idlis*, and labor-intensive dishes like *gulab jamun* (sweetened dumplings made out of milk curd), *ialebi* (Indian sweet made out of flour), and *kulfi* (Indian ice cream). These instant foods are ideal for busy Asian Indian households because they can significantly reduce preparation and cooking time.

Ethnic Indians rely on Indian grocery stores to stock up on some of the above-mentioned new types of food and to replenish their supplies of *basmati* rice; lentils including yellow split peas, pigeon peas, *urad*, and *moong* beans; *chapati* flour, chickpea flour, cracked wheat flour; farina; various types of Indian pickles; packaged sweet and salty snacks, including tea biscuits, and loose tea. They also carry vegetables and fruits, such as bitter gourd, green gourd, baby eggplants, okra, coconut, mangoes, papayas, and lychees, not easily found in American grocery stores. Many groceries contract with local Indians to prepare fresh *samosas* and *laddoos* (sweet balls made out roasted or chickpea flour or with *boondi*) to sell at their stores.

If there is no Indian grocery store in town, people can order a variety of specific Indian products through online stores in the United States. Other Asian and Mexican grocery stores frequently carry fresh fruits and vegetables, as well as packaged spices such as cumin, red chili pepper, whole mace, cinnamon, bay leaf, and others used in Indian cooking.

In ethnic Indian families, women, whether single or married, are expected to know how to cook, while men are not. Even though the advent of modern kitchen gadgets such as microwave ovens, rice cookers, milk boilers, electric kettles, mixers, and grinders has greatly simplified cooking for Indian men, most professionals end up eating out or consuming microwavable and instant foods. Men who cook or can cook on regular a basis are highly admired by their family and friends. Ironically, well-educated Indian men (sometimes women as well) who come to the United States from upper-middle-class families often have far less experience in cooking Indian food than the children of ethnic Indians born and raised in the United States.

Most Indians do not use any measures or maintain a recipe book for creating dishes. Estimating the amount of ingredients and spice to prepare meals continues to be the dominant way of cooking. Every cook brings their own style to the table according to their taste and/or preference of their families. The essence of Indian cooking lies in knowing various types of spices, flavors, and aromas they generate and an understanding of different types of cooking methods. Improvisation and a combination of cooking techniques are expected. In an Indian home-cooked meal, there is the opportunity and flexibility for experimentation and substitution. For example, if one does not like to deep fry the onions and garlic, they could either lightly sauté or roast them. Strictly speaking, no dish is "incorrect" unless it is a drastic deviation from its original version. If a mistake is made, it can be readily rectified and transformed into another dish by adding yogurt, buttermilk, tomatoes, or evaporating extra fluids.

This expectation of experimentation carries over to Indians in the United States, and many individuals enhance their food by incorporating American spices such as rosemary, Italian seasoning, garlic powder, or adding Indian spices such as red pepper, *garam masala*, and dried mango powder to American recipes that they like. Indians also like to invent new dishes by cooking nontraditional Indian vegetables such as broccoli, baby corn, American squashes, and meats, and breads in an Indian style. They like to use vegetable, canola, and sunflower oils for everyday cooking, but they prefer mustard, peanut, and sesame oils for stronger flavor. Most reserve olive oil for non-Indian foods. Many Indians make clarified butter or *ghee* by melting a regular stick of butter in a pan and separating the residue. Some purchase *ghee* from the store. Pure *ghee* is expensive and heavier than vegetable oils, so most Indians use just a small dollop in their main cuisine or gourmet foods to enhance the aroma of their dish.

Three cooking devices that are integral to Indian households are the pressure cooker, *belan* (rolling pin), and *kadhai* (wok). Although these utensils can be purchased in the United States, most prefer Indian products. For example, the Indian *kadhai* has a more rounded base, and the *belan* has firm handles and is smaller in size compared to the ones available in American markets. Most Indians regard Hawkins and Prestige brands of pressure cookers manufactured in India as superior to American pressure cookers. Indian pressure cookers let out a sharp whistle as they release steam, and users can calculate cooking times of specific dishes based on the number of whistles. The five-liter and larger-sized pressure cookers come with steamers, and it is not uncommon for Indians to prepare two dishes simultaneously using a pressure cooker. Ethnic Indians who like to prepare *idli*, *dhoklas*, and *momos* make sure that they have appropriate steamers or a combination steamer to make all of those foods. Ethnic Indian families also keep essential cookwares in their homes. For example, South Indian families may have a traditional coconut grater, a flat, nonstick *dosa* pan, and an Indian-style coffee percolator. Similarly, a North Indian family may not be able to do without a mortar and pestle and a pair of kitchen tongs called *chimta* that they need to flip the *chapatis*. All ethnic Indian households like to maintain traditional *masal-daan* (spice box) in their kitchens, which comes in very handy when they are rapidly adding essential spices while cooking salty meals.

Most ethnic Indians find electric stoves and flat burners installed in American kitchens ill suited for Indian cookery, since a number of Indian dishes are prepared on high heat and many require slightly rounded traditional cookware. Sometimes certain breads such as *chapatis*, snacks such as *papadam*, and vegetables such as eggplant have to be roasted on an open flame, but the coiled surface of the electric stove makes it difficult to do so. Many Indian companies have started manufacturing metal meshes and electric *chapati* makers that are compatible to American electrical outlets.

Everyday meals can range from a takeout pizza to a chipotle burrito, however many ethnic Indians derive true satisfaction from a sumptuous, home-cooked meal made from scratch. For North Indians a typical meal consists of *dal* (lentil soup) or *bhat* (plain cooked rice), *sabzi* (a vegetable dish), and *chapatis* or *parathas*. South Indian families substitute *sambar* (yellow split pea lentil soup with vegetables) or *rasam* (watery broth of lentil soup with tamarind flavor) for *dal*, and they may serve *dosa* or *idli* instead of *chapati*. Both North and South Indian foods are served with a variety of condiments such as *achar* (pickled vegetables), *raita* or another yogurt- or buttermilk-based dish, mint, coriander, or coconut *chutney* and fried or roasted *papad* or *papadam* (a very thin and crisp chip made of spicy lentil or potato dough). Sometimes individuals may add or experiment with some American spices or substitute tortillas or tortilla chips and condiments from other cultures, but very little modification is done to this menu.

It is not uncommon for most North Indians to start their day with chai, and South Indians to start theirs with coffee, but American black coffee is an acquired taste for most Indians. South Indians tend to prefer percolated coffee with milk and sugar. Oftentimes, ethnic Indians are satisfied with a Nescafe type of instant coffee, as that is commonly served in India. Indians like to have small, only slightly sweet cookies, which, in the British tradition, they call biscuits, with their morning drink. Children are encouraged to drink milk or a nutrition drink like Horlicks, Bournvita, or Boost before they leave for school. Many ethnic Indians prefer a heavy breakfast before they leave for work, with an emphasis on salt rather than sugar. It may consist of a continental breakfast with eggs, toast, bagels, or English muffin on the side, or perhaps a potato- or vegetable-stuffed sandwich called *hot dog*. More traditional breakfast dishes include *upma*, made out farina, *bread pakora* with sauce (bread fried in a spicy chickpea flour batter), *daliya* or cracked wheat porridge served with milk or cooked *daliya* fried in spice, *idli*, *dosa*, *uttapam*, or *parathas* stuffed with spicy potatoes, *mooli* radish, grated cauliflower served with pickle, or *puri-sabzi* (puffed whole wheat bread deep-fried like a *sopapilla*).

Indians are very particular about cleanliness and washing hands before dining. The dining table where prepared food is placed must be wiped clean with a damp cloth before meals. Although Indians use silverware, many Indians prefer to eat native dishes, like *dal*, *sambar*, or *rasam-chawal*, without utensils the traditional way, breaking off a piece of bread by hand, and scooping the vegetable or lentil dish with it. Indians are expected to eat with their right hand and serve food from their left hand, and it is improper to serve oneself with the same hand used for eating.

Traditionally, men and/or older people are served first, followed by children, then the women. Unleavened Indian breads such as *chapati* and *parathas* taste best when they are served hot off from the skillet, so sometimes an older woman relative who has already eaten relieves the person cooking breads so that they, too, can eat it while it is hot.

In Hindu families, rules connected with maintaining purity in preparing and serving meals can be quite intricate. All ethnic Indians, though, understand and enforce the concept of *jootha*, or contamination and impurity. For example, if someone has taken a bite from a dish, another person cannot use the same spoon without washing it with soapy water. If a cook wants to taste food while cooking, they must wash their hands before touching the cookware again. No food that is being prepared for religious services can be eaten until it has been offered as *Bhoga*, or offerings to the gods during rituals.

Holiday Feasts

When it comes to Indian holidays, there is a popular Hindi saying, *Saath vaar, solah vyavhar*, which means there are sixteen holidays in a week of seven days. In Hindu families, if people choose, they can observe a fast everyday. Each day of the week is dedicated to a different deity and comes with different food restrictions. For instance, those observing a fast for *Surya*, the Sun God, must eat food without salt on Sundays. Those who are observing fast on Wednesday—the day dedicated to *Ganesh*, the Remover of All Obstacles—must consume only yellow-colored foods that day. Many Hindus also observe fast on *Purnima* or the Full-Moon Day, and *Chaturthi* or the Fourth Day after the full moon. Hindu religion is highly ritualistic, and people observe fasts to commemorate *Navratri*—a nine-day festival devoted to the goddess Durga; they dedicate *Pitra Paksha*, a fortnight of ancestor rites, in which they prepare and offer the favorite dishes of the three previous generations of their deceased relatives to Brahmins or to the poor.

Indian Americans participate in holiday festivities and observe fasts according to their preferences. In cities where there is well-established population of Indians from the same linguistic region in India, festivals such as *Navratri*, *Durga Puja*, *Diwali*, and *Holi* are celebrated as large-scale community events. People visit each other's homes and share traditional snacks. In cities where Indians are scattered and each one of them might have a few acquaintances, potlucks are frequently organized to celebrate the holiday. Traditional Hindu families maintain an altar in their house. If they cannot do *puja* or ritual worship on daily basis, they perform it on their main holidays. As part of *puja*, *bhog* in the form of a sweet dish is offered to the deities and a *prasad* (portion from that *bhog* after it has been blessed by the gods) is redistributed among the family members and those attending the puja. No portion of the *bhog* must be consumed prior to the puja.

During certain fasts, Indians can consume only *phalahari*, or fruit-based foods that are prepared in rock salt. Many of these fruits and snacks are made and sold by US-based sweet shops such as Royal India, Sukhadia, and Bengali Sweets and may be purchased online. Shops such as Sukhadia, which cater to the needs of all Indians, list traditional food products specific to the festivals. Many of these businesses also offer catering service to Indian families hosting wedding celebrations and engagement ceremonies. Certain American celebrations such as baby showers, graduation parties, and Thanksgiving dinners have also become part of ethnic Indian holidays.

Place in American Culture

In the last decade, Indian food has gained popularity throughout the United States but has not assimilated to the extent of losing its identity as Indian food. In cookbooks, India-inspired recipes always retain their ethnic identity. Many Americans associate Indians with being vegetarians and their food as hot and spicy. American restaurants often sell "curry-flavored" entrées, but there is no exclusive Indian dish that has been assimilated in the US foodways. Chai tends to be viewed as a type of "tea-latte," and curry as a spice used in Indian cuisine.

Restaurants and Famous Chefs

Indian restaurants in the United States cater to both Indians and non-Indians. Most Indians like to go out for Indian buffet to savor an array of dishes that are special-occasion party foods served at weddings and formal luncheons and dinners. The restaurant foods are often labor-intensive and rich, which most families do not cook at home. Several Indian restaurants offer special event packages to help Indian families mark important celebrations. Occasionally, a restaurant might consider making traditional cuisine as requested by a family, but most stick to serving what has become a standard menu for Indian restaurants, offering typical dishes such as *naan, matar paneer, palak paneer, aloo gobhi, chicken tikka masala,* and *chana masala*. Most of these items are part of Punjabi cuisine, and in the last two decades they have become representative of Indian cuisine served at restaurants, formal dinner parties, and wedding feasts throughout the world. In contrast, South Indian cuisine remains more exotic and there are relatively few restaurants, although, with the popularity of frozen South Indian dinners, many North Indian restaurants have started serving South Indian snacks as appetizers. All Indian restaurants serve chai, but since most ethnic Indians prefer to drink homemade chai, it continues to be a popular drink among non-Indians dining at Indian restaurants. In general, the food served in Indian restaurants satisfies the palates of Indian Americans and non-Indians alike, but it does not fully represent the diversity of regional foods found in home cookery.

Further Reading

Achaya, K. T. *Indian Food: A Historical Companion*. Oxford: Oxford University Press, 1994.

AsianNation.org. "Indian Americans." Accessed July 28, 2014, http://www.asian-nation.org/indian.shtml.

"Difference between Southern Indian Food and North Indian Food." Accessed on July 27, 2014, www.differencebetween.info/difference-between-southern-indian-food-and-northern-indian-food.

Kirchner, Bharti. *The Indian Inspired Cookbook: A New Cuisine for the International Table*. Los Angeles: Lowell House, 1993.

Lai, Eric. "Instant Identity: The Emergence of Asian Indian America." In *The New Face of Asian Pacific America: Numbers, Diversity, and Change in the 21st Century*, ed. Eric Lai et al. Asian Week and UCLA Asian American Studies Center, 1998.

Pavri, Tinaz. "Asian Indian Americans." Accessed on July 28, 2014, www.everyculture.com/multi/A-Br/Asian-Indian-Americans.html.

Singer, Eliot A. "Conversion Through Foodways Enculturation: The Meaning of Eating in an American Hindu Sect." In *Ethnic and Regional Foodways in the United States: The Performance of Group Identity*, ed. Linda Keller Brown and Kay Mussell, 195–214. Knoxville: University of Tennessee Press, 1984.

Deeksha Nagar

INDONESIA

(Southeastern Asia) Indonesian American
See also: Malaysia.

Background

According to the Migration Policy Institute, Indonesian immigrants were recorded in the US census for the first time in 1990. They numbered 48,387. In 2011, this population doubled to 97,244. Anecdotal evidence, however, suggests that Indonesians have been migrating to this country since the 1950s—albeit in small numbers—due to political events in Indonesia. It was a Dutch colony from 1602 until World War II (1942). After independence from the Dutch in 1945, many migrated first to the Netherlands and then to the United States. During and after the massacres of 1965–1966, thousands of Indonesians of Chinese descent fled to escape an anticommunist purge following a failed coup.

The 1980s and 1990s saw an increasing influx of Indonesian nationals coming to the United States to attend community colleges and universities. This trend continues, and every year, some find jobs here, enabling them to stay on. The Immigration Act of 1990 established the Diversity Visa (DV) program, in which fifty-five thousand immigrant visas were made available in an annual lottery starting in fiscal year 1995, enabling Indonesians to attain legal immigration status. There was another surge after the May 1998 riots, a series of incidents of mass violence that occurred throughout Indonesia. Up to one hundred thousand ethnic Chinese

Indonesians escaped the country, many seeking asylum in the United States.

Indonesians living in the United States are predominantly from the larger cities on the island of Java—the capital Jakarta, Bandung, Solo, and also from Padang in West Sumatra. They settled mainly on the West Coast, in northern and southern California, in particular around Los Angeles and its suburbs, and Seattle, Washington. The main draws are the mild climate and an already existing large Asian population.

Foodways

Indonesian cuisine is made up of numerous distinct regional cuisines and is also shaped by the religious traditions of those regions—primarily Muslim, but also Hindu (Bali) and some Christian. It shares ingredients, flavors, and cooking techniques with other Southeast Asian cultures, but three-and-a-half centuries of Dutch colonization also left its mark, most notably in the adaptation of a native feast (*nasi Padang*) into *Rijsttafel* ("rice table" in Dutch), a formal presentation of numerous (up to forty) dishes representing the variety of spices, textures, and ingredients in Indonesia.

Foodstuffs

The most common ingredients in an Indonesian American pantry include condiments and sauces: sweet soy sauce (*kecap manis*), soy sauce (*kecap asin*), shrimp paste (*trassi/terasi*), and palm sugar (*gula jawa*). Herbs and spices are garlic (*bawang putih*), ginger (*jahe*), turmeric (*kunyit*), nutmeg (*pala*), white pepper (*lada putih*), galangal (*lengkuas*), lemongrass (*serai*), candlenut (*kemiri*), coriander (*ketumbar*), tamarind (*assem*), Indian bay leaves (*daun salam*), cutcherry (*kencur*), *kaffir* lime and its leaves (*jeruk purut*), panda leaf (*daun pandan*), and chilies (*cabe*). Other ingredients are tofu (*tahu*), *tempeh*, fried shallots (*bawang goreng*), and coconut milk (*santen*). Just a decade ago, it was hard to find many staple ingredients in the United States, and these items were smuggled in via suitcases. However, all these ingredients are now easily found in Asian markets.

Preparation

Indonesian dishes are well known for their complexity and labor-intensive cooking methods. For many dishes, the first step is to make a spice paste (*bumbu bumbu*). The mortar and pestle are the traditional implements used to grind herbs and spices into a paste, and ingredients are ground in order of texture and softness. Modern cooks often use a food processor, but connoisseurs agree that the taste and texture are inferior.

Ready-made spice pastes imported from Holland and Indonesia are also available at Asian markets, drastically cutting down on prep times. However, they lack the pungency and flavor of freshly made, from-scratch pastes.

The spice paste is first cooked in oil until fragrant before meat and/or vegetables are added and cooked accordingly. Cooking methods include braising, deep-frying, stir-frying, and other methods. Several dishes are twice cooked (usually braised first and then deep fried). Candlenut is often used to thicken sauces, and curries braised for hours with coconut milk are common.

Many cakes are steamed rather than baked, and rice flour, tapioca flour, and/or coconut milk are just as common ingredients as wheat flour. Popular cakes include the Dutch-influenced *kue lapis legit*, also called *Spekkoek* (a very rich, layered spice cake, although very few attempt this at home), *kue nagasari* (steamed banana cake), and *pisang goreng* (fried banana).

Women are the primary cooks in Indonesian households. However, modern Indonesians in the United States, especially ones born and raised here, tend to share kitchen responsibilities. Most, however, do not cook Indonesian cuisine every day.

Indonesian restaurants have sprouted up in cities with large Indonesian communities, and very often, one or two ladies within a community will cater Indonesian meals, making it easy to enjoy the cuisine without cooking it at home.

Everyday Meals

An everyday Indonesian meal usually comprises a meat dish, a vegetable side dish, and/or soup plus white rice. To name a few of the most popular dishes: *ayam goreng kuning* (fried turmeric chicken), *sate* (satay), *gado gado* (vegetables with peanut sauce), *sayur asem* (tamarind vegetable soup), *sup buntut* (oxtail soup), *opor ayam* (white chicken curry), *sayur lodeh* (vegetable coconut soup), *tahu/tempeh goreng* (fried tofu/*tempeh*). All-in-one meals include *nasi goreng* (fried rice), *soto ayam* (turmeric chicken soup with noodles), *bakmie/bihun goreng* (fried egg or rice noodles), and *bakmie ayam* (chicken noodles).

Rice dishes are traditionally eaten with hands or a fork and spoon, while noodle dishes are eaten with a fork or chopsticks.

***Gado Gado* Sauce**

From theasiangrandmotherscookbook.wordpress.com
Makes: about 1 cup of sauce
Time: 30 minutes

- ¼ cup oil (or just enough to coat the peanuts)
- 1 (12-ounce) package raw peanuts (about 2¼ cups)
- 2 to 3 *kaffir* lime leaves
- sliver of shrimp paste (*terasi*), toasted (optional)
- 1 tablespoon seedless wet tamarind, or lime juice
- 3 tablespoons Indonesian palm sugar or packed brown sugar
- 2 teaspoons salt
- 1 teaspoon chili paste such as *samba oelek* (vary amount according to taste)

Pour the oil into a wok or large skillet. Heat the oil over medium heat until it shimmers. Add the peanuts and stir-fry them until the skins turn a darker shade of reddish brown and the insides turn golden brown, about 4 to 5 minutes. Toss them continuously so they cook evenly and don't burn.

When the peanuts are done, scoop them up with a slotted spoon and leave to cool on a plate lined with paper towels. Remove any burnt peanuts, they will taste bitter.

When the peanuts are cool enough to handle, grind them until fine like sand in a food processor, or pulverize them with a mortar and pestle, in which case, grinding them until the texture of coarse sand will do.

In a small pot, combine 1½ cups water, the lime leaves, shrimp paste, tamarind, sugar, and salt. Bring to a boil over medium-high heat and then reduce the heat and simmer for about 5 minutes, breaking up the shrimp paste and tamarind pulp.

Using a strainer or slotted spoon, remove the leaves and any remaining tamarind pulp. Add 1 cup ground peanuts and bring to a boil. Save the remaining 1 cup for later. Simmer until thick and creamy, stirring often so that the sauce doesn't stick to the bottom of the pot—about 8 to 10 minutes.

Stir in the *sambal oelek*. Taste and adjust the seasonings.

Serve the peanut sauce with vegetables, over *soba* noodles, or as a dipping sauce with grilled meats like satay. Garnish with fried shallots, fried shrimp crackers, and *kecap manis*.

Note: The sauce will keep for up to a week in the fridge. To reheat, add a little water if it's too thick, and warm on the stove or in the microwave.

Yellow Coconut Rice

From *The Asian Grandmothers Cookbook: Home Cooking from Asian American Kitchens* by Patricia Tanumihardja
Time: 45 minutes
Makes: 6 to 8 servings as a as part of a multicourse, family-style meal

2½ teaspoons ground turmeric
1 teaspoon salt
1 cup warm water
1½ cups coconut milk
1 plump stalk lemongrass, bruised and tied into a knot
1 *salam* leaf
4 *kaffir* lime leaves, crumpled
2½ cups long-grain rice
2 cups water
Garnishes:
1 small red bell pepper, cut into strips
1 small cucumber, peeled and cut into coins
fried shallots

Dissolve the turmeric and salt in the warm water.

In a large pot, bring the coconut milk, lemongrass, *salam* leaf, and *kaffir* lime leaves to a gentle boil over medium-high heat. Reduce the heat to medium-low. Add the turmeric water. Tip the rice into the pot and add the water. Bring to a gentle boil, stirring occasionally.

Simmer uncovered until all the liquid has just been absorbed, about 10 minutes. Reduce the heat to low. Cover and cook for 15 to 20 minutes, or until the rice is tender but not mushy; the rice grains should still be separated. If the rice is still hard, make a well in the center of the pot, add a little water, and cook a few more minutes. Halfway through the estimated cooking time, gently fluff the rice with a fork or chopsticks.

Let the rice cool. Fish out the lemongrass, *salam* leaf, and lime leaves and discard.

On a large serving platter, mound the rice into the shape of an upturned cone. Garnish with red pepper strips, cucumber slices, and fried shallots.

Holiday Feasts

To celebrate special occasions like a birth or wedding, a typical Indonesian feast would feature *nasi tumpeng* (yellow coconut rice shaped into a cone) accompanied by an assortment of popular dishes such as *ayam goreng kuning*, *rendang daging*, or *empal* (sweet fried beef). Dutch-influenced dishes like *galantine* (pork and chicken roulade), *pastel tutup* (mashed potato casserole), and *macaroni schotel* (macaroni casserole) are relatively easy to make and feed many. Traditional snacks such as *frikadel* (meat sausage), *croket* (potato cutlet filled with meat and vegetables), and *risoles* (chicken and vegetables in béchamel sauce, wrapped in a pancake, breaded and deep fried) are also popular during festive occasions. *Hari Raya Idul-Fitri*, commonly called *Lebaran* (*Eid*), is the biggest annual celebration for Indonesian Muslims. Families will prepare weeks in advance for their special *Lebaran* meal. Dishes usually include *ketupat* (rice wrapped in bamboo leaves), *opor ayam*, gul*ai daging* (beef rib stew), *sambal goreng ati*, and *sayur lodeh*. Various types of sweets such as *kue lapis*, *kolak* (sweet potato and bananas cooked with coconut milk and palm sugar), and *dodol* (a sticky, chewy, toffee-like confection made with coconut milk, rice flour, and palm sugar) are also served.

Some Indonesian American families incorporate these dishes into American holidays such as Thanksgiving and Christmas.

Place in American Culture

Indonesian cuisine is not as well known as some of its Southeast Asian counterparts, and Indonesian restaurants are not widespread in the United States. This is perhaps due to the lack of familiarity among Americans with Indonesia in general, and it has not been considered a preferred holiday destination. However, Elizabeth Gilbert's 2006 best-selling memoir *Eat Pray Love* and the subsequent film starring Julia Roberts raised Indonesia's profile in the United States, even if only shining the spotlight on Bali, a lone Hindu enclave in the midst of a predominantly Muslim archipelago of 17,500 islands. A sharp spike in tourists was reported not long after the book's publication and film's release.

The best-known Indonesian dishes in the United States include *sate* (satay), *gado gado* (vegetables with peanut sauce), *nasi goreng* (fried rice), and beef *rendang* (spicy beef curry), most likely because of their similarity to more popular Southeast Asian dishes. *Rijsttafel* is offered at some restaurants, and it tends to refer to a buffet or a style of serving.

Noted Restaurants and Chefs

A few dozen Indonesian restaurants are interspersed throughout the United States, in Texas, Florida, Washington, DC, New York City, and other cities with an immigrant population. For example, Seattle, Washington, and Columbus, Ohio, each have a restaurant featuring Indonesian food, but the bulk of them are in California (San Francisco and Los Angeles and its suburbs). Southern California (LA area) has the best selection of Indonesian restaurants, including Indo Kitchen, Borneo Noodle House, Chicky BBQ & Grill, Bakmi Yanti, Bakmi Parahyangan, and Ramayani. Indonesian dishes are sometimes included on menus at pan-Asian restaurants or at restaurants featuring other Southeast Asian cuisines, particularly Malaysian. Also, *rijsttaffel* is served in some of these restaurants.

Even though Indonesian restaurants have not yet made a splash on the US culinary scene yet, there are two up-and-coming chefs who are making a name for themselves. Brothers Eric and Erwin Tjahyadi co-own Komodo Café and Food Truck (komodofood.com), specializing in East-West fusion cuisine and Indonesian dishes such as *nasi goreng* and *rendang*. Chef Erwin is considered one of LA's hottest rising culinary stars.

Yono's (yonos.com) is a fine dining restaurant in Albany, New York, featuring a menu inspired by global cuisines—Asian, Mediterranean, and French—and Chef Widjiono "Yono" Purnomo's interpretations of his native Indonesian cuisine. Chef Yono is the recipient of the National Restaurant Association's 2010 Faces of Diversity American Dream Award, has cooked at a number of James Beard House events in Manhattan, and has appeared on major network TV shows.

Further Reading

Oseland, James. *Cradle of Flavor: Home Cooking from the Spice Islands of Indonesia, Singapore, and Malaysia*. New York: W. W. Norton, 2006.

Owen, Sri. *Indonesian Regional Cooking*. New York: St. Martin's Press, 1995.

Owen, Sri. *The Indonesian Kitchen: Recipes and Stories*. Northampton, MA: Interlink, 2008.

Samuel-Hool, Leonie. *To All My Grandchildren: Lessons in Indonesian Cooking*. Berkeley, CA: Liplop Press, 1981.

Von Holzen, Heinz. *Authentic Recipes from Indonesia (Authentic Recipes Series)*. Hong Kong: Periplus Editions [HK] Ltd., 2006.

Yuen, Dina. *Indonesian Cooking: Satays, Sambals and more*. North Clarendon, VT: Tuttle, 2012.

Pat Tanumihardja

IRAN

(Western Asia) Iranian American Food, Persian American Food

Background

Before 1935, Iran was referred to as Persia. Iranians speak a native language called Persian or Farsi. Typical Persian households value education, and the culture pays attention to the healthfulness of food as well as to its artistry and presentation. It also emphasizes large spreads of fresh, homemade stews and rice and sumptuous tables composed of seasonal, highly aromatic *khoresht* stews, soups, yogurt-based side dishes such as *khiyar mast* (yogurt, cucumbers, and chopped fresh dill), and saffron-scented rice. Persians also like to grill, particularly lamb or beef (ground or cubed) and chicken breast (cubed) *kebobs*.

Foodways

In most Persian American homes, authentic Persian foods are prepared using traditional techniques. Long-grain, flavorful Persian rice with saffron is the basic signature dish in Persian cooking. Rice can be cooked plain or with vegetables, lentils, lima beans, or dried fruits such as cherries or raisins. Persians make rice in two ways. The simple, casual method is rice cooked in water with the ratio of approximately one to two and some butter or vegetable oil and salt to the taste, similar to *basmati* rice but with more flavor and aroma. The formal way involves more steps. To make the rice fluffy and keep each grain slender and separate, the rice must be washed several times to remove the starch, then cooked in boiling water with salt (sea salt recommended), drained when al dente, and, at last, steamed in a pot with melted butter drizzled on top. As a final touch, saffron water (saffron soaked and steeped in hot water for at least fifteen minutes) is added to the rice before the steaming process to add a splash of canary yellow to the rice. This type of rice is referred to as *polo*. Different types of vegetables are often added, especially when rice is paired with fish or a slow-cooked lamb shank stew with tomato-based sauce. *Sabzi polo* is rice with finely chopped chives, garlic chives, and cilantro, and *baghalie polo* is rice with lima beans and finely chopped garlic chives, cilantro and dill. These foods are well received by North Americans.

Traditionally, oil and flat bread (*lavash*) is placed under the rice before steaming. This creates a crunchy treat known as *tadique*, which literally translates to "the bottom of the pot." Rice is paired with *khoresht* stews, which include a type of animal source protein, mostly beef, lamb, chicken, or fish; legumes, mostly beans and lentils; and vegetables, such as Persian chives, parsley, cilantro, and carrots.

Examples of different types of *khoreshts* are *khoresht-eh bademjan* (sautéed eggplants, tomatoes, fresh lemon juice, and previously cooked chunks of beef or lamb); *ghormeh sabzi* (sautéed chopped parsley, Persian chives, dried lemons, finely chopped golden onions, and kidney beans or pinto beans slowly cooked with previously cooked chunks of beef or lamb); *khoresht-eh haveege* (sautéed thickly shredded carrots, finely chopped golden onions, sautéed tomatoes, slowly cooked with previously cooked chunks of lamb or beef); *khoresht-eh fesenjan* (pomegranate sauce, finely chopped walnuts [in a food processor], one to two tablespoons of sugar to neutralize the sourness of pomegranate juice and cooked chicken); *khoresht-eh gheyme* (cooked yellow lentils and previously cooked chunks of beef or lamb chicken); and *khoresht-eh karafs* (chopped sautéed celery and onions, tomatoes with beef or lamb). All of the above foods are cooked in a covered dish on a low heat until the vegetables are cooked in the meat broth. Many Persians prefer meat with bones to enhance the flavor and aroma of the *khoresht*.

Persian food is generally mild. The spices used in *khoreshts* vary from house to house but typically include black pepper, ground turmeric, and sometimes, ground cumin. Sour is a preferred flavor, so lemon juice or dried lemon is frequently added to *khoreshts*. There are usually more vegetables in *khoresht* than meat.

Kebobs are widely used in Persian cuisine, at both restaurants and home. Different types of meat are used, and it is usually marinated in chopped onions, salt, and pepper for several hours in the refrigerator. Ground beef *kebobs* are called *kabob koobideh*, whereas kabobs made with filet mignon are called *kebob bergh*. Persians also grill or saute liver along with vegetables such as onions, potatoes, and tomatoes and spices such as turmeric and black pepper.

Meat dishes such as *koofteh tabrizi* (Tabriz refers to a major city in the North West of Iran) are also available in most of the Persian homes and some restaurants. These are giant meatballs generally made with ground beef and are stuffed with a cooked egg; chopped walnuts; golden, thinly sliced onions; a sour currant called *zereshk*; and dried fruits, such as sautéed sour cherries and chopped apricots.

Persian Americans use the variety of seasonal vegetables found in North America in the many types of salads and soups in Persian cuisine. The traditional salad consists of chopped cucumbers, tomatoes, onions, and parsley with homemade dressing made from olive oil and lemon juice. One of the most popular soups is called *ash-eh reshteh* and is usually made with green vegetables such as Persian chives or regular chives, parsley, cilantro, spinach, sautéed onions, chicken or beef broth (made from scratch), lentils and legumes, and some flour noodles. *Ash-eh reshte* is typically garnished with *kashk* (a Persian dairy product often substituted with sour cream in Persian American homes). This food is usually garnished with sautéed thinly sliced golden onions and garlic, then garnished with dried mint, dramatically enhancing the flavor. Different types of *dolmeh* (stuffed vegetables such as grape leaves, sweet peppers, eggplants, and tomatoes) are also widely used in Persian homes and restaurants.

Vegetarian foods such as *kashk-eh bademjan* (sautéed eggplant, golden onions slowly cooked with some water) are usually well liked among North Americans.

Holiday Feasts

One of the most important Persian holiday feasts is *Nowruz* (translated as "new day"), the Persian New Year that takes place on the first day of spring according to the solar calendar. This day is celebrated by setting a beautifully decorated *Sofre-ye Haft Seen*, a table with seven Persian objects starting with the letter S. Most are food related: *sabzi* (a plate of fresh, deep-green vegetables), *somak* (a red spice sprinkled on foods such as kabobs), *seer* (garlic), *seeb-e sorkh* (red apples), and *serke* (vinegar). A plate of sweets, pastries, and dry-roasted nuts are usually also included. Among nonfood related items are a *samovar* (used to make tea in a traditional way). Foods eaten on this festive day usually include *dolmeh* (stuffed grape leaves) with garlic yogurt sauce and sautéed white fish with saffron accompanying *sabzi polo* or *bagalie polo* (rice dishes with chopped vegetables and saffron). *Khiyar mast* (yogurt with grated garlic) and chopped Persian cucumbers are consumed as a side dish. Persians sit around this table as a family at the time of the entrance of the new year.

Place in American Culture

Americans are generally not familiar with Persian cuisine, although they may know it as part of the larger categories of Middle Eastern or Mediterranean. Those who have tasted it typically find it appealing and palatable.

Restaurants and Chefs

There are many Persian restaurants in North America (United States and Canada), especially in larger cities, such as Los Angeles, New York, Washington, DC, and Chicago where large Persian populations reside. Almost all of them carry a Persian (or Farsi) name and are based on fine dining. Often, they also offer live Persian music and/or dancing. The majority of these restaurants serve Persian foods without modification, partly because they cater primarily to Persian customers. As has been practiced since ancient times, fresh ingredients are used to prepare the food. Rice with saffron is a popular dish, along with *dolmeh* (grape leaves with different stuffings) and eggplant prepared in a variety of ways. Another signature food is the Persian salad (chopped cucumber-tomato-onion with lemon juice/olive oil dressing based), commonly known as Greek salad in the United States, with added feta cheese oftentimes served in Greek and Middle Eastern restaurants and even mainstream American-style restaurants. Common desserts served in Persian restaurants are fresh fruits, traditional Persian pastries, and an authentic chilled desert called *ferny* (rice pudding made with rice four, milk, and flavored with vanilla or powdered green cardamom seeds that are added during the cooking process). Another unique, aromatic chilled dessert often served in restaurants is *shole zard* (a pudding with rice cooked in saffron water and slightly sweetened with sugar and decorated with a powder composed of dried Persian pink rose petals and cinnamon).

A yogurt-based beverage, *doogh*, with some herbs such as dried powdered mint or oregano is commonly served in Persian and Middle Eastern restaurants and can be found in Persian and Middle Eastern supermarkets as a bottled beverage.

Further Reading

Batmanglij, Najmieh. *Food of Life: Ancient Persian and Modern Iranian Cooking and Ceremonies.* Washington, DC: Mage, 2011.

Bundy, Ariana. *Pomegranates and Roses: My Persian Family Recipes.* New York: Simon and Schuster, 2012.

Shahla Ray

IRAQ

(Western Asia) Iraqi American Food, Chaldean American Food

Background

Immigration from the Middle East and North Africa has increased significantly in recent years: in 1920 there were approximately fifty thousand immigrants from the region living in the United States. In 2012 the population in the United States was approximately 961,000. Of all the immigrant groups from the Middle East and North Africa, Iraqis comprise the largest single-country immigrant group with 177,000 immigrants in 2012. Roughly 20 percent of Iraqis in America have come since 2000 as a result of violent political conflicts in Iraq during the reign of Saddam Hussein and the Iraq War. In the United States, these immigrants live predominantly in California, New York, Michigan, Texas, and New Jersey. The Iraqi population is particularly concentrated in the Detroit area, with about 150,000 residents as of 2014, and smaller populations in the cities of Chicago, Illinois; San Jose, El Cajon, San Diego, and Turlock, California; and Oaxaca, Mexico.

While sharing historical ties to Iraq, Iraqis in America are, in most cases, religiously, linguistically, and culturally distinct from residents of Iraq today. The majority of the population in Iraq is Muslim, while the majority of Iraqis in America are Chaldean, or Iraqi Christian, and prefer to be referred to as American Chaldeans versus Arab Americans. The Chaldeans were converted to Christianity by the Apostle Thomas and belong to the Eastern Rite of the Roman Catholic Church. As Catholics, they share beliefs and traditions of Catholics but are governed by their own leader and involve rituals unique to the Eastern Church. Services may be performed in English, Arabic, or the historic Chaldean (Aramaic) language.

While the majority of Iraqis in America are Chaldean, they comprise only 10 percent of the population in Iraq. Thus, many of the early Chaldeans came to the United States for religious as well as economic reasons. US immigration laws in the 1960s and Saddam Hussein's rise to power in the 1980s were causes for a second and third wave of immigration. Both early and subsequent immigrants settled in Detroit for three primary reasons: they were lured by the promise of jobs in the automobile industry; there was an existing community of Arabic-speaking Christian Lebanese immigrants; and the close proximity to Windsor, Ontario, which also had a significant community of Chaldean immigrants.

The majority of Chaldeans in the United States can trace their heritage to the village of Telkaif. As such, most are distantly related to one another, and ties to family are quite strong. As Catholics, families are typically large and include all extended family members. The strong sense of family and community connection has been, and continues to be, a key ingredient in the successful migration from Iraq to the United States. Typically, the first to migrate were males, and once they had become settled they would then arrange for the female members of the family to come as well. As more people came, they in turn would encourage their extended families and those of their in-laws to migrate. Once in the United States, Chaldeans often open their homes and places of business to help one another build a new life.

The primary occupation for Chaldeans in the United States is merchant. According to the Chaldean Chamber of Commerce, roughly nine out of ten grocery stores in Detroit are owned by Chaldeans. Specifically, "61% of Chaldean Americans own at least one business and 39% own two or more." Grocery store ownership dates back to 1923: there were only seven Chaldean men in Detroit and four Chaldean-owned stores. In the late 1960s, many of the large chain grocery stores pulled out of Detroit, and the Chaldean community was quick to fill this niche. By the 1980s there were over one thousand Chaldean-owned grocery stores in the region (Sengstock). As the grocery store market has become saturated in recent years, new Chaldean immigrants have turned to related occupations, such as party stores and gas stations. Children and grandchildren of long-established immigrants work in businesses that serve the grocery stores, such as wholesale food supply, store fixture and appliance maintenance, and commercial real estate. As a significant feature in Chaldean American life, the grocery store often determines the logistics of community and religious celebrations. As the stores are open late, widely attended events such as weddings and church gatherings are often held late at night to accommodate the work schedule of the employees and owners of the grocery, gas, and party stores.

Foodways
Common foods in the Iraqi diet include meats such as beef, chicken, lamb, and fish. Tropical fruits are popular as snacks and desserts or made into jams. Vegetables such as green beans, eggplants, and lentils may be featured as their own dish or cooked with meat for a stew.

The religious distinction between Iraqi Chaldeans and Iraqi Muslims is the greatest influence in the dietary choices and foodways of these two groups. For the Iraqi Muslim, foodways are determined by *adab*, which refers to Iraqi etiquette and the fourth of the five pillars of Islam, fasting during Ramadan. Ramadan lasts for twenty-nine to thirty days and is determined by the Islamic lunar calendar. Rules for etiquette include appropriate social greetings, health practices, and dietary laws. The dietary laws detail which foods are prohibited and the rules for animal slaughter. Prohibited foods include pork, blood, alcohol, and carrion (the dead and decaying flesh of an animal). Meat from herbivorous animals is allowed but must be slaughtered by a Muslim, Jew, or Christian. The term, *halal*, refers to food that is permissible for Muslims to consume.

For Iraqi Muslims, the absence of food (fasting) is in many ways more significant than the symbolic and material nature of the food itself. During *swam*, the fasting and self-control required by Islam, Muslims are required to give up three things: (1) all food and water during daylight, (2) smoking or other tobacco use, and (3) sexual activity. Chewing gum is also forbidden. Muslims are also taught to give up all impure, negative, and mean thoughts. The most immediate goal of *swam* is to get close to Allah, and Muslims believe that this can be achieved by controlling their desires through the abstention of food and sex. A secondary goal is to promote empathy with those less fortunate and without easy access to food. Done out of love for Allah, *swam* teaches the principle of love. Muslims begin each day of Ramadan with the predawn meal, *suhoor*, and end the day with *al-iftar*.

The seriousness and significance of fasting, *fard*, for Ramadan are illustrated in the consequences for breaking it. If one breaks it unintentionally but continues it for the remainder of the day, the fast stays valid. If one breaks the fast or has sexual relations, then they must do one of three acts. They may free a slave, but if that is not possible, they may fast for two consecutive lunar months (sixty consecutive days). If that is not possible either, then they may feed and or clothe sixty people in need.

There are, however, exceptions for the fasting requirement. People who are sick, have diabetes, or are traveling, and women who are pregnant, nursing, or menstruating, are exempt. The days missed, however, must be made up by the next month of Ramadan. Persons unable to fast due to illness may "make up" the *fard* by buying meals for those who are poor.

As Christians, the Iraqi Chaldeans are not bound by Islamic ideology and thus have very different dietary practices. They are not prohibited from consuming pork or alcohol, and they follow the foodways of their ancient ancestors. The Chaldeans trace their lineage to people living on the northern Tigris-Euphrates Valley, referred to as Mesopotamia (present-day Iraq). Mesopotamian civilizations date back to 3500 BCE and include the Sumerians (3500–2600 BCE), Babylonians (1792–539 BCE), and Assyrians (1115–612 BCE).

In the 1930s three clay cuneiform tablets were found south of Baghdad, on the site of ancient Babylonia. While one of the tablets was badly damaged, the other two revealed ancient recipes and cooking practices. These tablets, housed at Yale University, are significant in that they represent the earliest record of written recipes. The tablets include numerous recipes for stews and bird dishes including bird pies and bird bullion. The ancient Mesopotamians also ate a lot of bread: ancient records reveal approximately three hundred varieties of both leavened and unleavened bread. The Iraqi flatbread called *khubuz tannour* dates back to ancient Sumeria, and it gets its name from the domed clay oven, the *tannour*, in which it is baked. As bread was such an integral part of the diet, the tannour was essential and well cared for. The ingredients are simple and fat free—the bread contains only water, flour, yeast, and salt—it is also known as water bread, or *khubuz mei*.

The tablets indicate that the ancient Mesopotamians were skilled in pastry making as well. In addition to the ingredients of regular bread, honey, dates, raisins, and fats, such as butter, were added to make the earliest fruitcakes. Usually the cakes were made with higher-quality flour than regular bread and, since they called for specialized and expensive ingredients, they were beyond the means of most of the population and were enjoyed by the noble and elite. One can see the relationship between cakes, beauty, and luxury in that a beautiful woman is often called a *keka* and the word for cake is *ka'ak*.

Preparation

The large and extended structure of Chaldean families shapes food preparation and eating practices. Families often cook and eat together, and eating with one's cousins, grandparents, and in-laws several times a week is common. Families also help one another with childcare and cleaning tasks as well. While later generations of Chaldeans have become increasingly Americanized, the household primarily operates as a gendered one with women being responsible for meal preparation.

Everyday Meals

Many Iraqi dishes can be traced back to the Sumerians. These include the *kleicha* (cookie) and the national dish of Iraq, *masgouf* (seasoned and grilled carp). Omelet dishes, *ujja*, can be traced to medieval times. These and other signature foods are described below. Other common foods are nuts, specifically pistachios, dried fruits such as dates and raisins, pickled vegetables, jams, cheeses, breads, and sweets.

Similar to the Indian spice blend, *garam masala*, *baharat* is a general multipurpose spice blend. Although the ingredients are similar, different regions and even individual households will have their own blend. Typically baharat will contain the following ground spices: cumin, coriander, black pepper, cinnamon, cardamom, cloves, allspice, nutmeg, chili, turmeric, and perhaps rose petals.

The *kleicha* is to Iraqis what the chocolate chip cookie is to Americans. The term refers to a collection of cookies that are shaped and filled to the family members' individual tastes and preferences. Although some of the cooking methods have changed, the *kleicha* dates back to the ancient Sumerians, and it is featured at holiday celebrations and feasts. For Muslims, the cookie was traditionally made for two feasts: *Eid al-Fitr* and *Eid al-Adha*. *Eid al-Fitr* is a three-day feast to celebrate the end of the month-long Ramadan fast, which begins when the new moon appears. *Eid al-Adha* celebrates the end of the pilgrimage rites in Mecca and lasts four days. Iraqi Christians traditionally baked *kleicha* for Easter Sunday, and Iraqi Jews for Purim.

Making *kleicha* was traditionally a group event, and young and old helped out in the process. The dough is made from white flour, the spice blend *hawaij*, salt, water, yeast, and *dihin hurr* (rendered butter from cow's milk), and mixed in a large bowl called a *nigana*. Mixing the dough is somewhat akin to kneading. As the dough is left to rise, the ingredients for the filling are assembled. Common fillings are walnuts ground with sugar and cardamom and dates mashed with cinnamon, cardamom, rosewater, crushed coriander, and toasted sesame seeds. The nut-filled *kleicha* are then formed into half-moons, and the date-filled ones are made into balls and designed with delicate and intricate designs. The half-moon or crescent shape is symbolic of the end of Ramadan, which is recognized by the appearance of the new moon. Because of the skill required, the adults usually made the stuffed ones and the children made the *kleicha* thins, *khfefiyyat*, from the leftover dough. Using an *isikan*, a cookie cutter of sorts, or made free form, the thins are also carved with designs.

Once the cookies were designed and laid out on large trays, they were brought to the bakery. There they would be glazed with egg and baked in the *tannour*. Out of the oven, they were cooled and placed in large wicker baskets, covered in embroidered muslin cloth, and stored, often up high and away from children. In modern times, with the prevalence of gas ovens and smaller families, the cookies are baked at home and in smaller quantities. Because of the relative ease of preparation, they are no longer reserved for religious feasts but are enjoyed year-round for a variety of occasions.

The *makhlama* is the contemporary Iraqi omelet that can be eaten as a side dish and a sandwich. Traditionally, it is made with ground meat but can easily be adapted as vegetarian. The dish can be either baked in the oven or cooked on a stovetop in an iron skillet and is relatively simple in both ingredients and preparation. To start, potatoes are cut into small cubes and then cooked in a small amount of oil. Next, one sautés an onion, then adds the cooked potatoes along with tomato, curry powder, salt, pepper, dill, parsley, and mint and cooks for a few more minutes. The mixture is then pressed down into an even circle, and small dents are made to hold the eggs. Eggs are broken into the dents and can be cooked whole, sunny-side up, or broken to mix in with the potatoes. As a final step, chili powder is sprinkled on top, and the dish is cooked just until the eggs are done. *Makhlama* can be served with bread, parsley, and lemon.

Fish are an obvious staple in Iraqi cuisine given its location between the Tigres and Euphrates rivers. *Masgouf* is a simple dish of carp that is cut in half and then brushed with a mixture of olive oil, salt, tamarind, and turmeric. Traditionally, it is cooked over an open fire for two to three hours. Adaptations are often made when cooking this dish in other areas for the sake of time. In restaurants in the United States, catfish, salmon, and white fish are often substituted for carp.

Holiday Feasts

Muslims begin each day of Ramadan with *suhoor*, the Ramadan breakfast. As the pre-dawn meal, accompanied by the *fagr* (dawn) prayer, that will sustain people throughout the day, *suhoor* is typically a heavy meal. The Ramadan dinner, *iftar*, includes the *Maghrib* (evening) prayer. The fast is traditionally broken with three dates, as that is how the Prophet Mohammed broke his daily fast. *Iftar* is a social event and may be held at a mosque, a family home, or other large community venue and is often served buffet style. Both meals tend to include water, juices, dates and other dried fruits, pistachios, cheeses, breads, salads, main dishes, and sweets. At the conclusion of Ramadan, Muslims celebrate *Eid al-Fitr* for three days. As a celebration of the conclusion of *fard*, any sort of *halal* food may be served. Regional specialties, desserts, and other sweets are featured prominently.

As Catholics, Chaldeans celebrate the major holidays of Lent, Easter, and Christmas. During Lent, Christians abstain from most meat, although fish is allowed. Everyday recipes are often adapted to include fish instead of other meats, or one may simply eat a vegetarian diet during Lent. A signature Christmas meal includes *pacha*, cow intestines stuffed with rice and lamb. Leg of lamb is often served as an alternative for some of the younger Chaldeans.

Place in American Culture

Iraqi food has yet to gain popularity or even much familiarity within mainstream American culture, and it tends to be lumped along many distinct food cultures and cuisines from the Middle East into the large generic category of Mediterranean. While this food genre and the restaurants that serve it have become increasingly popular in the United States, knowledge of traditional Iraqi and Chaldean cuisine is largely absent.

Noted Restaurants and Chefs

As the majority of Iraqis in America have settled in Detroit, it is the home of some of the best Iraqi Chaldean food in the United States. These restaurants are owned and operated and supported by the large Chaldean community. As the Chaldean population continues to grow in San Diego, California, more restaurants are opening there as well.

As Iraqi and Chaldean restaurants, and by extension chefs, play a relatively small part in mainstream American culture, the cuisine is becoming recognized via two other culinary outlets: cookbooks and food trucks. *Ma Baseema*, meaning "how good it is," was published in 2011 by the Chaldean American Ladies of Charity. Alongside the history and the recipes for Chaldean cuisine, the book teaches about the culture as well. In 2012 Kay Karim published *The Iraqi Family Cookbook*, which won the 2012 Gourmand World Cookbook Award for the "Best Arab Cuisine Cookbook" in the United States. Nawal Nasrallah published the second edition of *Delights from the Garden of Eden: A Cookbook and History of the Iraqi Cuisine*, chosen by *Saveur* as one of the top ten cookbooks of 2013.

In 2004 Michael Rakowitz, along with his Iraqi-Jewish mother, began Enemy Kitchen. The goal was to use food as a mechanism for conversation about war, conflict, and culture. The project began by teaching students how to cook Iraqi food at the Hudson Guild Community Center in New York City. In 2012 the Enemy Kitchen food truck was part of Chicago's Smart Museum of Art exhibition, *Feast: Radical Hospitality in Contemporary Art*.

Further Reading

Auclair, G., and J. Batalova. *Middle Eastern and North African Immigrants in the United States*, September 26, 2013. http://www.migrationpol

icy.org/article/middle-eastern-and-north-afri can-immigrants-united-states.

Chaldean American Chamber of Commerce. *Chaldean American Chamber of Commerce*, 2013. http://chaldeanchamber.com/community -overview.

Chaldean American Ladies of Charity. *Ma Baseema: Middle Eastern Cooking with a Chaldean Flair*. Ann Arbor: Huron Rover Press, 2011.

Ciezadlo, Annia. *A Day of Honey: A Memoir of Food, Love & War*. New York: Free Press, 2012.

Civitello, Linda. *Cuisine & Culture: A History of Food and People*, 3rd ed. Hoboken: John Wiley & Sons, 2011.

Karim, Kay. *The Iraqi Family Cookbook (Hippocrene Cookbook Library)*. New York: Hippocrene Books, 2012.

Nasrallah, Nawal. *Delights from the Garden of Eden: A Cookbook and History of the Iraqi Cuisine*, 2nd edition. Shelfield: Equinox, 2013.

Schleifer, T. "Iraqi-Americans Watch Chaos in Alarm." *New York Times*, June 21, 2014, A7.

Sengstock, M. C. *Chaldean Americans*. EveryCulture.com, Countries and Their Cultures, http://www.everyculture.com/multi/Bu-Dr/ Chaldean-Americans.html.

Terraaas, Aaron. "Middle Eastern and North African Immigrants in the United States." *Migration Policy Institute*, September 26, 2013. http:// www.migrationpolicy.org/print 4190.

Laura K. Hahn

IRELAND
(Northern Europe) Irish American

Background

The Irish were among the first Europeans to settle in the New World. They first arrived in America not long after the first settlements at Jamestown (1607) and Plymouth (1620); however, the central and most essential early migration for Irish and Irish American foodways occurred in the late seventeenth century as the New World potato made its way to Ireland, ushering in centuries of nutrition and misery in equal measure.

Immigration from Ireland, which included the entirety of the Emerald Isle (the current Republic of Ireland and Northern Ireland), was a subset of British immigration during the early American colonial period and was generally small but steady until the late second decade of the eighteenth century, which saw a large spike. For fifty years until the American Revolution in 1775, when immigration stopped due to the war, there was a steady and substantial stream of Hibernian immigrants, primarily Protestant Scots-Irish, who came both to find a better life and as prisoners. These immigrants settled mainly in the Mid-Atlantic States.

The next major wave of Irish immigration to the United States occurred as a result of the Great Famine, also known as the Irish Potato Famine (1845–1852). While the famine occurred as a result of human intervention in the form of British political ineptitude and malfeasance, at the core of the famine was the biological plague of potato blight, which destroyed the majority of the potato crops, the core of the Irish diet, for almost a decade. While precise numbers are elusive, it's estimated that during this time more than a million Irish died from disease and starvation, and more than one and a half million migrated, with the majority of those coming to the United States and settling along the Eastern Seaboard. Cities such as Boston were between one-third and one-half Irish at this time.

Currently more than 10 percent of the American population claims Irish ancestry, and some pockets of the country, primarily north of the Mason-Dixon Line, claim even larger populations. Boston has over 20 percent Irish-ancestry population, and many towns in southeastern Massachusetts, which saw Irish American migration from South Boston in the 1950s and 1960s, claim more than 40 percent ancestry.

Foodways and Place in American Culture

As with Italian American food, actual Irish American food exists somewhere between a commercialized and stereotyped nostalgia for old-country foods (that often were created in America, e.g., spaghetti and meatballs) and a much more prosaic reality. Put another way, the vast majority of contemporary Irish Americans eat like "regular" Americans and typically enjoy Irish American food dining out and during holidays and other special occasions.

Irish American food in the United States revolves around two cultural touch points, the Irish pub and St. Patrick's Day.

The Irish pub is not just an American phenomenon, but also an international one, with an estimated seven thousand pubs worldwide. The prime attraction of an Irish pub is the traditional atmosphere and the alcohol, typically centered around imported Irish stout on tap (typically Guinness) and a selection of Irish whiskeys. The hallmarks of an American Irish pub also include a comfortable but somewhat upscale dining area with authentic or re-created classic Victorian woodwork, enough space for the occasional live band, and an ever-changing menu of international quick food, from actual Irish fare such as shepherd's pie to pizza and jalapeño poppers.

In many ways the Irish pub's continued success runs counter to many larger food and cultural trends, especially the desire among a large portion of the population to avoid foods rich in carbohydrates, such as beer and potatoes. However, it's a testament to cultural branding, of the belief in "Irishness" as welcoming, forgiving, and lilting, that the Irish pub remains successful in spite of few attempts to make it a more contemporary and healthy experience.

St. Patrick's Day is a beast of a different color: green. In parades and other annual celebrations on March 17, revelers dress up in green clothes and adorn shamrocks while eating green-colored food, rivers flow green, and many celebrants end the evening green at the gills. In the Northeast it's also traditionally the day to plant green peas.

The traditional Irish American St. Patrick's Day meal is corned beef and cabbage, the most American of Irish American dishes. Corned beef and cabbage is an oven-baked boiled meal that can also include potatoes, carrots, and other root vegetables. It is related to a New England boiled dinner, which substitutes pork shoulder (typically smoked) for corned beef and also is often eaten on St. Patrick's Day.

Although corned beef has a history in Britain and Ireland, corned beef and cabbage as a dish is an invention of the American Irish, and it is now sold in Ireland to American tourists looking for an "authentic" Irish experience. Most likely the dish arose in the close quarters of New York in the late nineteenth and early twentieth century as the Irish bought less-expensive beef brisket from Jewish merchants rather than the bacon they desired, and cheaper heads of cabbage rather than potatoes.

Related to boiled dinners and another excuse to get some mileage out of cheap cuts of meat, Irish stews are popular in both Ireland and the United States. Among the most popular on American menus are lamb (or Irish) stew and beef stewed in Guinness. Both rely on browning meat with some onions, adding a meat stock and additional vegetables, and simmering on the stove top or cooking in the oven for a few hours.

Beyond their place in stews, potatoes, the national dish of Ireland, loom large in Irish American cuisine. In fish and chips they take their place alongside a large slab of fried whitefish. In bangers and mash, they sit mashed along with Irish sausages.

Although not as common as some of the other dishes mentioned here, the Irish favorite *boxty* makes its way onto many Irish American pub menus, often taking the place of a tortilla or wrap. *Boxty* are pancakes made of grated potatoes, white flour, egg, milk, and baking soda. Like pancakes or crepes, they can be filled with sweets or savories.

In shepherd's pie, potatoes serve as a golden crown. Shepherd's pie is a variation of a traditional Irish cottage pie, although the Irish shepherd's pie traditionally includes minced lamb while the American version, catering to American tastes, typically includes ground beef. The dish consists of a seasoned mixture of sautéed beef with corn layered into a baking dish, topped with mashed or whipped potatoes, and baked in the oven until warmed through. It can also incorporate all manner of leftover chopped vegetables along with the corn.

Irish American Shepherd's Pie

Traditional Irish shepherd's pie includes ground lamb (and is often called cottage pie). However, American sensibilities dictate that this dish, an Irish pub favorite, include ground beef, making it a more dinner-worthy, sit-down-with-a-fork version of the American classic burger and fries.

Ingredients:
   2 pounds potatoes
   8 ounces sour cream or yogurt
   salt and pepper
   2 pounds ground beef
   one medium onion, chopped
   1 garlic clove, minced
   ¼ teaspoon mustard powder
   16 ounces fresh or thawed frozen corn
   ½ cup milk or yogurt
   4 tablespoons melted butter
   4 ounces grated Dubliner cheese (optional)
   smoked paprika (optional)

Directions:
1. Boil and peel potatoes; mash or rice with sour cream or yogurt and salt and pepper to taste.
2. Heat oven to 350 degrees.
3. In a large nonstick skillet, cook beef and onion. After about five minutes, drain excess fat, then add garlic and mustard power; cook until meat is no longer pink. Let cool slightly, and then incorporate corn and milk or yogurt.
4. Place meat mixture in ungreased 2 quart baking dish. Crown with mashed potatoes and top with butter.
5. Bake for 25 minutes, sprinkle with grated cheese, and then bake an additional 5 to 10 minutes.
6. Remove from oven and sprinkle with paprika.

Beyond main meals, the Irish breakfast is often seen on American restaurant menus, particularly at brunch, although less so in homes. While there are slight variations, the full Irish breakfast typically includes Irish sausage and bacon, black pudding and white pudding, eggs, tomatoes, baked beans, mushrooms, and, of course, some form of potato (typically leftover and reheated), alongside fruit juice, coffee, and, perhaps, Irish coffee.

Irish coffee is the stuff of legends and arguments. Most basically, Irish coffee is two parts brewed coffee to one part Irish whiskey heated with a teaspoon of brown sugar, and then topped with one-to-two parts heavy cream. While this exact combination of this recipe is up for debate, the real debate is with whether this is an Irish or Irish American creation. One story says that it was first served at the forerunner to Shannon Airport to American travelers, while another claims that it was first created in San Francisco. Either way, the drink involves Irish Americans and plays into cultural beliefs about the Irish and drinking on the sly.

And, of course, drinking alcohol is something that Irish Americans do enjoy. As in food, most Irish Americans are assimilated and tend to drink "American" drinks. However, the Irish pub caters to Irish alcoholic drinks. The drink most associated with Ireland is Guinness beer (brewed in Dublin or Canada, depending on the type), although there are numerous other imported Irish beers popular in the United

States, including Harp Lager, Smithwick's Irish Ale, Beamish Stout, and Murphy's Irish Stout.

Irish whiskeys are also popular in Irish American pubs and in other bars as an alternative to American (bourbon), British (scotch), and, increasingly, Japanese whiskies. Irish whiskeys gain their distinct flavor through strict adherence to the Irish Whiskey Act of 1980. According to the act, Irish whiskey must, most basically:

- be made in Ireland
- have an ABV of less than 94.8 percent
- derive its aroma/flavor naturally from a natural grain (typically peat)
- age at least three years in wooden casks

The most popular Irish whiskeys in the United States include Jameson, Bushmills, and Tullamore Dew.

In terms of commercial food products that find their way from the grocer to the table, the most popular items are both dairy oriented. The two most popular and available cheeses are Cashel Blue, a cow's milk cheese similar to Roquefort or gorgonzola and often crumbled on salads, and Dubliner, a cow's milk cheese that approximates traditional cheddar. Along with these cheeses, Kerrygold Pure Irish Butter has made inroads in the United States as a "real" butter due to its higher fat content than typical American butter.

Among sweets, desserts, and treats, the most popular is Irish soda bread. Irish soda bread is a quick bread made from a soft flour, baking soda and powder, butter, sugar, salt, buttermilk, and, raisins (typically) or some other candied fruit. A popular regional product are Irish potatoes, which are a candied specialty of the Philadelphia region made of cinnamon, sugar, and cream cheese and sold around St. Patrick's Day.

Noted Restaurants and Chefs

Irish American cuisine never enjoyed a fine-dining period in the United States. It is likely that this is, in part, due to both the quotidian nature of Irish cuisine (meat and potatoes) and the poor reputation of the quality of Irish food in Ireland prior to the food renaissance that accompanied the rise of the Celtic Tiger economy in the last decade of the twentieth century. Put another way, Ireland had a history of poverty, and the cuisine of the poor often isn't celebrated until it is clearly in the rearview mirror and looked back on nostalgically.

While there are no Irish American fast-food chains, Bennigan's is an Irish American casual-dining chain founded in 1976 by the Pillsbury firm. At its height the company had over three hundred restaurants worldwide, but a failure to keep current with rivals such as Chili's and Applebee's forced the company into bankruptcy, which ultimately resulted in its present American size, approximately two dozen locations. Bennigan's is apparently still trying to keep pace with the Mexican-themed Chili's, as its signature dish is the County Clare Sampler, which, counterintuitively for an Irish dish, features nachos and quesadillas. Alternately, the Columbus-based Claddagh Irish Pub is an expanding regional chain with thirteen locations in the upper Midwest that features a range of Irish and Irish American dishes among the occasional plate of nachos.

As noted above, Irish pubs are ubiquitous around the country, and there are seemingly as many "Top Ten Irish Pub" lists as there are food and travel publications. However, some pubs do pop up more often on best-of lists, some for their food, some for their alcohol selection, most for their atmosphere. These top pubs include the Irish Bank (San Francisco), Blackthorn Irish Pub (Boston), Doyle's Café (Jamaica Plain, Massachusetts), McSorley's Old Ale House (New York City), the Harp (Cleveland), the Black Sheep Pub and McGillin's Olde Ale House (both Philadelphia), and the Irish Oak (Chicago).

The most famous Irish American chef is fourth-generation American Bobby Flay. While television celebrity Flay is best known for barbecue and Southwestern style, and his Irish roots are not readily apparent in his preparations, perhaps his most heartfelt creation was 2011's *Bobby's Ireland*, a tour of his ancestral home. Irish-born and Washington, DC, based Cathal Armstrong, author of *My Irish Table: Recipes from the Homeland and Restaurant Eve*, is considered an up-and-coming star in the Irish American culinary world.

Further Reading

Armstrong, Cathal and David Hagedorn. *My Irish Table: Recipes from the Homeland and Restaurant Eve*. Berkeley, CA: Ten Speed Press, 2014.

Drymon, M. M. *Scotch-Irish Foodways in America: Recipes from History*. CreateSpace Independent Publishing Platform, 2009.

Irish Abroad. http://www.irishabroad.com/Culture/kitchen/recipes.asp.

Johnson, Margaret M. *The Irish Heritage Cookbook*. San Francisco: Chronicle Books, 1999.

Arthur Lizie

ISLE OF MAN

(Northern European) Manx American, English American, British American Food
See also: England, Wales.

Background

Settlers from the Isle of Man (a 221-square-mile island in the Irish Sea, currently part of the United Kingdom) began coming to the United States, specifically northeastern Ohio, in the early 1820s. They established farms on the outskirts of Cleveland, and they quickly adapted while retaining some of their traditions. Manx, a Gaelic language, was spoken at home, and seasonal and Christian holidays were celebrated. Manx also settled in other parts of the United States and Canada, and today there are Manx societies in Ohio, Illinois, Wisconsin, Minnesota, California, Washington, DC, and Vancouver. The North American Manx Association and smaller societies keep in touch via the Internet, and they proudly share recipes and news of their gatherings.

Foodstuffs and Preparation, Everyday Meals, and Common Foods

Food in the Isle of Man in the 1800s was relatively simple by necessity and geography, with barley and herring being prominent staples. Potatoes became prevalent at the beginning of the nineteenth century and quickly superseded barley and oats. They were cooked in their jackets and eaten with salt herring, mashed and made into potato cakes, and added to stews and hot pots. The common name for mashed potatoes was *tittlewhack*, a word derived from the sound made by the wooden pestle used to mash big tubs of potatoes. When the first new potato of the season was eaten, it was believed to be lucky to make a wish as it was sure to be granted.

When Manx immigrated to America in the nineteenth century, they adapted to what was locally available, although the recipes passed down through families still feature barley, oats, herring, and potatoes, prepared relatively simply. A favorite bread, which survives in many variations in Manx American families, *bonnag*, is explained further below.

Holiday Feasts

According to Alice Cannell from Cleveland, the harvest was one occasion for merriment and food:

> There was always great rejoicing when the last of the corn was reaped at harvest time, it was usual for the farmer to provide a supper for all the workers. The end of the reaping was known as the *Mheillea* (the Harvest Home), a name which is still applied to harvest suppers. A dish that was popularly served at the *Mheillea* was herring pie.

Jim Kneale, the current president of the North American Manx Association, reports, "As far as our own family, our traditions are fairly recent: Christmas *bonnag* on Christmas morning with a cup of coffee to open the presents. Baking fills the house with smells of cinnamon and nutmeg. Meanwhile, the kids can lick the bowl and spoon, as it doesn't have raw eggs."

The Association offers several recipes for *bonnag* on its website, including one from Mr. Kneale.

Christmas *Bonnag*

2½ cups white flour
1 cup sugar
1 teaspoon baking soda
1 teaspoon cream of tartar
½ tablespoon cinnamon
2 tablespoons butter
8 ounces candied fruit (fruit cake mix)
¼ teaspoon vanilla
1 cup buttermilk

Preheat oven to 350 degrees. Mix the dry ingredients well together in a bowl and cut in the butter with a pastry blender until it is the size of oatmeal. Mix in candied fruit. Add vanilla to buttermilk, then mix quickly for 1 scant minute. Place in a 9-inch cake pan. Bake about 35 minutes, or until a toothpick inserted in the center comes out dry.

Variations ("we've never made the same version twice"):

1. Substitute Chinese five spice or allspice for the cinnamon.
2. Substitute raisins, chopped maraschino cherries, dried cranberries, or other fruit for the candied fruit (which is difficult to find after Christmas).
3. Substitute 1 teaspoon almond extract for the cinnamon and 2 ounces of chopped dried cherries for the candied fruit.

Loosely adapted by Jim Kneale from Peggy Fargher's Fruit *Bonnag*, in Suzanne Daugherty's collction of recipes, available on http://www.isle-of-man.com/manxnotebook/history/diet/bonnag.htm.

The Washington, DC, Manx Society celebrates Twelfth Night. The notice for the Washington, DC, Manx Society's Twelfth Night celebration in January 2013 explains how this holiday is observed with fun and food:

> Here's to 2013 and another 12th Night. Remember how it goes? Once everyone has gathered, the "First Footer" arrives to drive out any bad spirits left from last year. He presents the traditional gifts of bread, coal, and money to make sure we have food, health, and wealth throughout the year. We then sit down to an all-you-can-eat feast of roast meats, vegetables, salads, *bonnag* (Manx bread), beverages, and desserts. Afterwards, we'll find the tail of the Manx cat, play the pass-the-parcel game, and sing "Auld Lang Syne."

Place in American Culture

Like many other American ethnic groups, the Manx, who were largely Methodist, established "relief societies" to aid their fellow Manxmen in need. An annual dinner organized by the Mona Relief Society in the Cleveland area was described by traveler H. Hanby Hay in 1897:

> In the evening I looked into the faces of four hundred Manx-American men, women, and children gathered for the love of the dear little Island. . . . After some hearty speeches, we all sang "Ellan Vannin." . . . sung by three hundred voices, with hearts at the back of them, was worth travelling hundreds of miles to hear. With tears in my eyes I was escorted to supper. I found myself seated at the head of a table covered with

delicacies, nor did I wonder at the dainties when I heard they were all prepared by fair Manx hands. Dancing followed, and a sort of informal reception.

Noted Restaurants and Chefs

There are no known Manx American restaurants or chefs; food preparation and celebration is on the family or society level.

Thanks to Jim Kneale and Alice Cannell for their personal memories and links to other sources.

Further Reading

"Interview with Mr. Henry Hanby Hay." *Isle of Man Examiner*, August 7, 1897. http://www.isle-of-man.com/manxnotebook/fulltext/mid1897/pt2.htm.

Betty J. Belanus

ISRAEL

(Western Asia) Israeli American Food
See also: Lebanon, Syria, Jordan, Jewish American Food.

Background

Israel was built by Jewish immigrants from all over the world. This is reflected in the makeup of the American Israeli community. Some are of European descent, while others are from Northern Africa and western Asia (particularly Morocco, Tunisia, Yemen, Iraq, and Iran). More recently, there has been emigration of Israelis from the former Soviet Union to the United States. Israelis distinguish themselves from the American Jewish community. They see their Jewish roots as an inherent part of their historical heritage and do not necessarily see the religious component as a defining feature of their ethnic identity.[1] According to the 2009 US Census, Israeli immigrants in the United States number around 140,000. Enclaves are located in the New York metropolitan area, Los Angeles, Miami, and Silicon Valley. Israelis living in America often describe their living situation as "temporary" and a means to improve their financial or educational status with eventual plans of returning to Israel. Among them one can find individuals with blue-collar occupations such as taxi cab drivers or movers and construction workers who came to ameliorate their economic situation. Others are students and professionals looking for education and employment opportunities. Personal reasons, such as marriage or unification with family members, also account for a portion of Israeli immigration to the United States.

Foodways

Food traditions in Israel reflect the multicultural makeup of its population. Thus, it is hard to identify foods that are uniquely Israeli. This also applies to Israeli foods available in the United States. Some studies suggest that there is an emerging Israeli cuisine, which is a mixture of Middle Eastern, Mediterranean, and European traditions;[2] yet most of the foods considered Israeli are borrowed from other cultures—for example, *burekas* from Turkey, North African *couscous*, and a wide range of European foods including chicken soup, *kreplach*, gefilte fish, and chopped liver. Still, distinctive foodways can be identified in the Israeli American diet. If possible, the main meal of the day is eaten at lunch, rather than dinner. Late afternoon social gatherings for coffee are common, and refreshments include *pitzuchim* (a selection of shelled nuts and sunflower seeds) followed by a hot beverage and cake. On weekends a typical Israeli breakfast might include Israeli salad (chopped tomatoes, cucumbers, onions, and parsley) dressed with olive oil and lemon juice, eggs, fresh bread, and soft, white cheese.

Many Israeli food items are exported to American supermarket chains and small groceries that serve areas with high concentrations of Israelis and for the kosher market. Common items are the snack foods Bamba, a peanut doodle, and Bissli, made of fried pasta covered in spices. Israeli milk products such as soft, white cheese and puddings are flown into New York and Los Angeles. Other Israeli items on the shelf include pickles and canned goods, chocolate spread, jam, and soup nuts. Frozen Yeminite *jachnun* and *malawach* along with *burekas* are also available. An Israeli company is one of the largest commercial producers and distributors of *hummus* (chickpea and sesame spread) in the United States.

Israelis value home-cooked meals. Home cooking is perceived as healthier and also signifies dedication to the family unit. Similar to American Jewish families, mealtime is important particularly on Friday nights and is an integral part of the family tradition. In most homes, there is a gender-based division of labor regarding food preparation. Women are generally responsible for cooking daily meals, while men barbecue and sometimes prepare special dishes for their family. These include homemade *hummus* and finely chopped Israeli salad, whose preparation is considered laborious.

Israeli breakfasts have gained a reputation for being both diverse and extravagant, with a wide assortment of cheeses, vegetables, breads, and condiments. However, in many families, where both parents work, only a light meal is eaten during the week. Easy-to-prepare items such as cold cereals, granola, yogurt, toast, and cottage cheese with coffee are common. Lunch is traditionally the heavy meal of the day, but this is not always practical in the United States. A typical lunch might include *schnitzel* (fried chicken cutlets) with either French fries, mashed potatoes, or rice along with a vegetable. Roast chicken, meatballs, or fish fillet are also commonly eaten. Israelis traditionally consume smaller amounts of beef, and pork consumption is rare. Dinner mostly consists of eggs and Israeli salad, with cheeses, spreads, and bread. Elaborate cooking is saved for weekends, holidays, and special occasions.

The most famous Israeli signature dish is *hummus*, a chickpea paste made with tahini sauce (sesame paste). *Hummus* is often considered an Israeli food, even though it originates from other Middle Eastern countries. Israeli *hummus* is sold across America in supermarkets under the brand name Sabra, which is owned by an Israeli-based company. Other possible Israeli signature dishes are *falafel*, *m'jadera*, *shakshuka*, *shawarma*, and Israeli salad, none of which can trace their roots to Israel. For example, *shakshuka*, poached eggs cooked in a thick, spicy tomato and pepper sauce, has its origins in Northern Africa. When looking for an authentic 100 percent Israeli food, there is consensus for only a single dish: liver-flavored eggplant salad.

Holiday Feasts

Most Israelis demarcate the Sabbath with a special Friday night family dinner. Some will start the meal with wine and challah, followed by a three-course meal that often consists of favorite dishes of family members. Soup or/and salads is followed by a meat or fish with starch and vegetable side dishes. The meal concludes with fruit and/or cakes.

The Israeli culinary tradition includes all the Jewish holiday foods: apples dipped in honey for the Jewish New Year, potato pancakes (*latkes*) and doughnuts on Hanukah, *matzo* for Passover, *hamentashen* on Purim, dairy food on Shavuot, and dried fruits and nuts on Arbor Day. On New Year's and Passover, lavish meals are prepared and include special dishes. One might find gefilte fish or *harimeh* (fish in a spicy tomato and pepper sauce) followed by roast beef, leg of lamb, or duck.

Israel Independence Day is celebrated as a social event with Israeli music and an Israeli-style *mangal* (cookout). Foods include grilled kebabs and chicken eaten with *pita* bread. Side dishes include *hummus*, *tehini*, olives, fresh cabbage salads, Israeli salad, and eggplant salads.

Place in American Culture

Israeli foods do not have a large impact on the American culinary landscape. However, the growing interest in the Mediterranean diet and healthy foods such as olive oil, vegetables, legumes, and whole grains is increasing the popularity of Israeli and other Middle Eastern dishes. *Falafel*, *hummus*, *tehini*, and *pita* can be bought in most cities across America. In contrast, Israeli supermarkets and restaurants can only be found in defined areas where Israelis and American Jews live in high concentrations.

Noted Restaurants and Chefs

Maoz Vegetarian is an international chain of *falafel* restaurants with franchises in six states. In the true Israeli style, Maoz Vegetarian serves its *falafel* stuffed into a *pita* with added salads and *tehini* sauce topped off with French fries.

Aroma Espresso Bar is a chain of Israeli coffee shops that has been exported to many locations in Europe and the United States. The American menu is similar to the original Israeli menu and offers a wide variety of salads, sandwiches, and pastries.

Another Israeli export to the American restaurant scene is the Max Brenner chain. With locations in New York, Boston, Philadelphia, and Las Vegas, this famous chocolatiere serves a variety of gourmet foods containing chocolate and markets a line of sweets.

In addition, several restaurants from New York, Miami and Los Angeles serve what is defined as typical Israeli cuisine. Menus include *falafel*, *hummus*, *couscous*, *shakshuka*, *tabouli*, fried cauliflower, and eggplant dishes. All of these foods can also be considered Middle Eastern.

There are several well-known Israeli-born chefs working in the United States. Interestingly, none are famous for their Israeli dishes. Each has their individual style of cooking, and all claim to add a personal Israeli flavor to their foods.

Notes

1. Cohen and Haberfeld 2007.
2. Gvion 2013, and Avieli 2013.

Further Reading

Avieli, Nir. "'Size Matters': Israeli Chefs Cooking Israeliness." *Studies in Contemporary Jewry* (2013).

Cohen, Yinon. "Israeli-Born Emigrants: Size, Destinations and Selectivity." *International Journal of Comparative Sociology* 52, no. 1/2 (2011): 45–62.

Cohen, Yinon, and Yitchak Haberfeld. "Self-Selection and Earnings Assimilation: Immigrants from the Former Soviet Union in Israel and the United States." *Demography* 44, no. 3 (2007): 649–68.

Gold, Steven J. "Israeli Jewish Immigrants." In *Multicultural America: An Encyclopedia of the Newest Americans*, volume 4, edited by Ronald H. Bayor, 1149–88. Santa Barbara: Greenwood/ABC-CLIO, 2011.

Gvion, Liora. "'We Are More of a Family Now': Food, Motherhood and Family in the Privatized Kibbutz." *Gilui Daat* 1, no. 1 (2012): 99–119. (in Hebrew)

Gvion, Liora. "Is There Jewish Food in Israel?" *Studies in Contemporary Jewry* (2013).

Morawska, Ewa. "Exploring Diversity in Immigrant Assimilation and Transnationalism: Poles and Russian Jews in Philadelphia." *International Migration Review* 38, no. 4 (2004): 1372–412.

Stark, Aliza, and Liora Gvion. "Food in Israel." In *Food Cultures of the World Encyclopedia: Volume 1, Africa and the Middle East*, edited by Ken Albala, 259–66. Santa Barbara: Greenwood/ABC-CLIO, 2011.

U.S. Census Bureau, 2009 American Community Survey, http://www.census.gov/compendia/statab/2012/tables/12s0053.pdf.

Liora Gvion and Aliza H. Stark

ITALY

(Southern Europe) Italian American Food

Though Italian immigrants formed a demographically significant part of the population of the United States, it must nonetheless be said that their cookery has had a disproportionately important influence on the culinary culture of the nation as a whole, an influence which has been manifested at various levels (restaurant, fast food, home cookery) and which has steadily increased from the first halting acceptance of Italian American foods by the American mainstream during the World War I on to the current period in which elements of Italian American and Italian cooking, very often moderated to the American mainstream by Italian Americans, have become a central part of current American food trends. The strength of that influence has largely been due to the remarkable degree to which Italian immigrants and their children resisted culinary assimilation, maintaining a wide range of traditional foodways from Italy, sufficiently so that Italian American cuisine—at least as practiced among culturally conservative families in the twentieth century—could reasonably be regarded as a regional (extrametropolitan) Italian cuisine as much as an American ethnic cuisine.

Background

The Italian presence in North America during the colonial period and on into the early decades of the nineteenth century was limited primarily to individuals and individual families; only in the mid-nineteenth century do we find the beginnings of small Italian communities in some cities, communities that in many cases were dominated by immigrants from the region of Liguria and its principal city, Genoa. Demographically significant immigration from Italy to the United States began to develop gradually only in the 1870s but expanded dramatically in the 1880s, when the need for labor in the United States aligned with socioeconomic and political pressures in Italy that gave rise to massive emigration from almost all parts of the newly formed Kingdom of Italy and coincided with large-scale emigration from other lands in southern and eastern Europe to the "New World." While immigrants from northern Italy favored northern Europe and South America, especially Argentina and Brazil, as their main destinations, immigration from southern Italy favored the United States: in the peak period from 1880 to 1920, more than four million Italians immigrated to the United States, and of these as many as 80 percent were from the south. The southern regions that contributed the most to this movement were Campania and Sicily, while Calabria and Basilicata also contributed particularly significant numbers; a southern region relatively less involved in immigration to the United States at this time was Puglia.

In the United States, Italian settlement was focused in the cities of two broad areas. The most important of these was a zone that comprised the north of the Mid-Atlantic region and southern New England. By far the greatest concentration of Italian settlement was in New York City and directly across the Hudson River in New Jersey; large urban communities of Italian immigrants developed also in Philadelphia, Trenton, Newark, New Haven, Providence, and Boston, with an outlier just to the south in Baltimore. The other broad zone of Italian settlement was in the Great Lakes region; here, as along the East Coast, important communities developed in a number of cities. The largest of these communities was in Chicago, but other concentrations of Italian immigrants formed in northern New York (Syracuse, Rochester, Buffalo), western Pennsylvania (Pittsburgh), Ohio (Cleveland, Youngstown), Michigan (Detroit), Wisconsin (Milwaukee), Indiana (Indianapolis), and Minnesota (Minneapolis-Saint Paul). Though many small communities of Italian immigrants arose throughout most of the rest of the United States, there were few major urban concentrations outside of the East Coast and

Great Lakes regions just mentioned. The most significant ones were in Saint Louis and New Orleans, which were relatively isolated, and in San Francisco, which served as the point of diffusion for Italians to other communities in the Bay Area and in agricultural and fishing centers in nearby counties of central and northern California.

Three basic stages can be seen in the social history of Italian Americans which have direct bearing on the development of their culinary culture: (1) the Early Community Stage, which began with the initial establishment of Italian communities in the United States in the nineteenth century and continued until late in that century, when Italian immigration involved relatively few women and primarily single young men, significant numbers of whom returned to Italy; (2) the "Little Italy" Stage, comprising roughly the first half of the twentieth century, during which time Italian communities grew considerably but also stabilized culturally, thanks in part to a greater presence of immigrant women, and developed a distinctively Italian American culture through the interactions between Italian Americans of different Italian regional origins and through the interaction with mainstream American culture and the cultures of other immigrant groups; (3) the Suburban Stage, beginning roughly in the 1950s and continuing today, which has been characterized by the gradual reduction and even complete dissolution of the urban "Little Italy" communities with dispersal of their populations especially to suburban settings and ever-increasing exogamy.

Foodways

Historical Development of Italian American Foodways. There are two misconceptions about Italian American cuisine that are widespread in both popular and scholarly writing about the subject. The first involves the well-known diversity of metropolitan Italian regional cuisines: it is assumed that such diversity gave rise to an immigrant cuisine that was to a significant degree a sort of jumble of regional dishes. The second is that Italian American cookery was rapidly Americanized to a significant degree.

With regard to the culinary background of Italian American cookery, it is certainly true that the encounters of Italians from various regions led to a certain degree of culinary *koineization* or leveling of regional culinary differences in the United States. Working against this natural process, however, were the effects of chain migration, by which immigrants from particular towns or subregions in Italy tended strongly to settle together in particular immigrant communities in the United States. In this way, parochial associations from the old country continued, and aspects of local Italian culture (religious, linguistic, culinary) could be preserved among extended families and circles of friends living in close proximity in their American neighborhoods. Marriage outside of such small groups was originally discouraged but increasingly took place, though Italian Americans of the second generation tended still to marry within the Italian community. Given that the vast majority of Italian immigrants were from southern Italy, however, there was still relatively little need to compromise or adapt, for all the regional and subregional cuisines of the Mezzogiorno share to a great degree the same culinary foundations—gustatory aesthetics, preferred basic ingredients, cooking methods, meal structures, culinary calendar—and, additionally, they share almost all basic styles of dishes (e.g., pasta with legumes, sautéed bitter greens, stuffed vegetables, dressed flatbreads, baked pastas, etc.), so that compromise and blending could easily occur without involving any major changes.

With regard to the question of Americanization, many food writers, particularly those not belonging to the Italian American community, have taken the easily observed Italian American restaurant cookery, in which Americanized elements clearly have long been present, as being representative of Italian American cuisine in general. In truth, Italian American domestic cookery, especially as practiced within culturally conservative families, was and to a considerable degree remains quite distinct from public cookery with only certain points of overlap.

That Italian Americans during the Early Community and Little Italy stages were, relative to other European immigrant groups in the United States, particularly resistant to cultural and especially culinary assimilation to mainstream American ways is well documented. It was widely believed by Americans before World War I that Italian foodways were not only uncivilized but also unhealthy, and even well-intentioned social workers active in Italian American communities felt that the adoption of American eating habits would be a key to helping cure the perceived shortcomings of this ethnic group. Indeed, mainstream America and some of the better-established immigrant ethnic groups considered southern Italians (but generally not northern Italians) exceptionally backward and commonly attributed to them a range of negative stereotypes: they were seen by many as inherently dirty, emotionally unstable, untrustworthy, and naturally inclined toward violence and criminality. They were so sufficiently marginalized that there were extended public debates about whether southern Italians could be considered "white," which, in the context of the even more virulent prejudices toward African Americans and Asians in the United States, is quite telling.

For the majority of Italian Americans such bigotry reinforced in-group social and economic ties that played an important role in strengthening the maintenance of traditional foodways. In this way, family and very local community relations became the center of Italian American life. The daily family meal and especially the Sunday feast were key institutions that fostered community and ethnic pride and served as a means by which traditional culinary knowledge was passed on to new generations, not just as recipes for individual dishes but as a full cuisine, including the aforementioned culinary foundation (gustatory aesthetics, etc.). Furthermore, mainstream prejudice, which excluded them from many aspects of the business world, also pushed Italian Americans to develop the culinary infrastructure necessary to maintain their traditional foodways.

Within the Little Italies themselves, shopkeepers were needed who could obtain or produce Italian foodstuffs: Italian-style breads and pastries, cured meats (*prosciutto*, *salami*, *capocollo*) and fresh sausages, fresh cheeses (*ricotta*, *mozzarella*, *tuma*), particular seafoods (eel, squid, snails, salt cod), and meat cut according to Italian preferences. To obtain necessary imported foodstuffs (e.g., olive oil, grating cheeses, tinned anchovies, etc.), community members also entered the fields of wholesale imports and shipping. Demand for other foodstuffs that could be produced in the United States gave rise to further entrepreneurial and manufacturing opportunities. Most notable among these was the rise of the American dried pasta industry, in which Italian Americans played a leading role (e.g., Ronzoni in New York, Prince in Boston, etc.). Examples of packaged goods companies selling both domestic and imported products that started within the Italian American community are Pastene (originally a pushcart business in Boston) and Progresso (originally founded in the New Orleans Sicilian community). The Italian American communities of central California also played an important role in the network supplying immigrant communities around the country, developing businesses specializing in vegetables (e.g., artichokes, *rapini*), fruits, and nuts favored by Italians, as well as being instrumental in the rise of the California wine and olive oil industries.

Italian American Domestic Cuisine. Poverty in southern Italy and parts of northern Italy during the period of the great wave of immigration to the United States was deep: hunger was a key motivation for many Italians to leave their homeland. In all parts of Italy, the diet of the poor at this time included little fresh meat and generally very little fresh fish and seafood. The staple was bread, commonly containing a little wheat flour supplemented with flour from other grains and even milled legumes under dire circumstances. Other starchy foods of the poor in both northern and southern Italy were potatoes and *polenta* (corn meal). Dried pasta was eaten by the urban poor, but, as a purchased item, it was uncommon for the rural poor, whereas fresh pasta, as a food specific to various holidays and special occasions, was well known. Of central importance in the diet were legumes, greens, and garden vegetables and fruits. In mountainous areas, chestnuts were important, with chestnut flour being used to make up shortages in other grain flours. Lard was universally used, and olive oil very widely used for cooking and flavoring, though they were in short supply for the destitute.

Key flavoring agents were onions, garlic, and in southern and central Italy also hot chilies, as well as cultivated and wild herbs (parsley, basil, oregano, fennel, rosemary, marjoram, mint, etc.); pine nuts and raisins were also included in certain sweet and savory dishes. To the degree they were available, small amounts of umami-bearing agents were essential to flavoring dishes: salted anchovies, cured pork products (*pancetta*, *prosciutto*, *guanciale*, etc.), and hard cheeses for grating (*pecorino*, *grana*, *ricotta salata*). Wine vinegar was a particularly important product for flavoring and food preservation. Where possible, foraging was also an important source of foodstuffs for the poor, yielding mushrooms, wild vegetables and greens, medicinal herbs, snails, frogs, and more.

Though most Italian American immigrants to the United States had been poor and a great many had long endured limited and monotonous diets in Italy, they did not arrive in America without good knowledge of the ingredients and dishes that their daily routine had been lacking. With the relative prosperity that even menial jobs in the United States offered—food prices in the United States were comparatively very low—they quickly were able to establish regimens very much akin to those of middling economic social strata in their home regions. The most obvious changes were the increases in Italian immigrants' consumption of meat and dried pasta, but these developments were in no sense elements of a process of Americanization; rather, they were simply instances of exploitation of improved economic circumstances that allowed the immigrants to enjoy dishes that were already part of their regional cuisines but unavailable to many for regular consumption on account of poverty. The inclusion of increased amounts of dried pasta and meat were still very much regulated by the culinary foundations brought over from Italy, and, indeed, with regard to meat, American observers in the early twentieth century were surprised by its measured role in the Italian American diet.

Though greater access to dried pasta and meat were noteworthy developments, an even more fundamental development was the greater access to high-quality bread, the true Italian staple food, made from all-wheat flour, and the bread bakery became without a doubt one of the most common and important of neighborhood institutions in Italian American communities.

Overlooked in discussions of the history of Italian American cuisine is the role of increased access to fresh fish and seafood, which constituted a more revolutionary development than the increased access to dried pasta and meat for the many immigrants who came from the mountainous interior regions of Italy, where fresh foods from the sea were all but unknown. Seafood was less important in the Italian American communities of the Midwest, but for those on the East, West, and Gulf coasts, it rapidly became an integral part of the diet, regardless of where in Italy their members hailed.

It should be noted that these culinary developments through greater prosperity—increased consumption of dried pasta, meat, seafood, and wheat bread—can all be observed occurring in parallel fashion in the regional cuisines of Italy during the twentieth century.

For many culturally conservative Italian American families, as in Italy, there was a pattern to the appearance of foods through the week that bore a certain relation to the yearly culinary calendar: Sunday was a minifeast day, Friday and for many also Wednesday were days of abstinence from meat, while the remaining days were the "ordinary" days. On the "ordinary days," meat could be consumed and often was, but meals could be composed primarily of pasta (or *polenta* or rice) and vegetable or fish dishes. On Fridays, fish or seafood was the norm as the main dish, and for many this was the case on Wednesdays as well, though on these days meals comprising vegetable dishes were also commonly enjoyed, including hearty pasta with legume preparations (pasta with beans, chickpeas, and others). On Sundays, a weekly holiday, more elaborate and abundant main meals were the norm, typically eaten in the early afternoon. For many Italian American families, this Sunday meal most often entailed a slow-cooked meat *ragù* prepared for pasta, with the pasta dressed with the sauce and the meat served separately after the pasta. In addition, a roasted meat dish with vegetable side dishes was common, though before roasted meats, the pasta dish could well be not with a *ragù* but rather some other special condiment, such as a mushroom sauce, or could entail a special form of pasta, such as ravioli or fresh noodles (*tagliatelle*, *fettucine*), fresh shaped forms of *maccheroni* (*cavatelli*, *fusilli*) or gnocchi, served with a simple sauce; baked pasta dishes (stuffed shells, *ziti* with meat sauce and cheeses) would also be appropriate. In any event, the Sunday meal had to be special and well differentiated from those of the ordinary days.

Meal structures in Italian American cuisine were generally as in Italy. Though some meals might feature pasta as the main dish, more often pasta would be a first course, followed by a main meat, fish, or vegetable dish and one or more accompanying side dishes. A simple salad was normally included, dressed with olive oil and either vinegar or lemon, and always served after the main course. Italian bread would necessarily be available throughout the meal. For adults, wine, especially red wine, was the traditional drink, alongside water. After dinner, fresh fruit was commonly set on the table while espresso was prepared for the adults. Desserts were generally reserved for Sundays or other special occasions.

Thus, in all general ways, the basic patterns of eating for culturally conservative Italian Americans were in accord with those in a large part of Italy and especially in the south of Italy. The tradition of having the main meal of the day in the afternoon on weekdays and Saturdays, as well as on Sundays, was, however, impossible to maintain for most Italian American families, given the constraints of work and school schedules in the United States. Consequently, Italian Americans' lunch habits began to resemble those of other Americans, as workers and students would often take along sandwiches made at home. But the constitution of the sandwiches often remained very ethnic—bakery-made bread filled with Italian cold cuts and cheeses, slices of leftover meats or sausages, omelets (*frittate*), tinned fish or prepared vegetables—and contrasted starkly with the mainstream's slices of American bread with simpler, less aromatic fillings of cooked ham or peanut butter and jelly; lunchtime in school or at the workplace became, then, a place of ethnoculinary encounters that made lasting impressions on many.

Preparation

Cooking among Italian Americans was primarily the work of the women, with mothers playing a key role in the passing on of culinary traditions to daughters and daughters-in-law; the figure of the grandmother (*nonna*), however, held an especially revered position in the culinary life of the family. Given the centrality of foodways in the culture, Italian American men have commonly taken an active interest in cooking, and many became well versed in the preparation of at least basic dishes; men also played key roles in activities such as winemaking, gardening, and more. For many Italian American families in the earliest period, living conditions were cramped and kitchen facilities limited; families lacking ovens would take prepared dishes to the local bakery for cooking. When able to purchase their own homes, Italian American families often had two kitchens: one on the main floor of the house, which was used minimally, and another in the basement, where all serious cooking took place.

Everyday Meals

The breadth of Italian American domestic cookery and its general fealty toward Italian regional cuisines can be seen through the dishes popular within the community but less well known to mainstream America until recently, as a result of the current trend of interest in Italian regional foods.

First-course dishes: Pasta: While pasta dishes with marinara sauce and tomato-based meat sauces are iconic elements of Italian American cuisine, these dishes, though frequently consumed, appeared alongside many other pasta preparations in the domestic regime. Particular noteworthy is a family of very simple dishes made with spaghetti and a condiment featuring olive oil and garlic as the base (*spaghetti aglio e olio*); variations include hot chiles (*aglio olio e peperoncino*), anchovy (*con alici*), fried breadcrumbs (*con mollica*), and so on; traditionally, such dishes are not served with grated cheese. A great many combinations of pasta with a specific vegetable, with or without tomatoes, were also frequently consumed—with potatoes, cauliflower, eggplant, zucchini, *rapini*, cabbage, and others. Some simple dishes were thought to have restorative qualities, such as pasta *cacio e uova* (with beaten eggs and grated cheese) or pasta with ricotta (pasta served just with some of its cooking water and fresh ricotta). Pasta dishes with seafood (clams, mussels, shrimp, periwinkle snails) have also had an important place in domestic cooking. A particularly beloved summer dish for many Italian Americans on the East Coast has long been spaghetti or linguine with a simple tomato sauce and blue crabs.

Polenta and rice: In communities and individual families of northern Italian origin, *polenta* and *risotto* dishes often played a greater role than dried pasta; among southern Italians, such dishes were known (especially *polenta*, served soupy with tomato sauce) but typically not consumed with great frequency.

Soups: In addition to vegetable soup (*minestrone*) and simple beef and chicken soups, a distinctive and popular Italian American preparation is Italian wedding soup, which features escarole and/or other leafy greens and very small meatballs in chicken stock.

Second-course dishes: Meat: The triumvirate of meatballs, Italian sausage, and *braciole* (rolls of thin beef slices, filled with seasonings such as garlic, parsley, *pecorino*, sometimes pine nuts and raisins) is important in Italian American cooking; each of the meats could be prepared alone and function as a main course or could appear alone or in combination, cooked in a tomato sauce used to dress pasta. Italian sausage can be fried, baked, or grilled; the combination of sausage and peppers is widely consumed and often appears in outdoor settings (street fairs, cookouts, etc.). Certain offal dishes, such as tripe, liver, *zuffritt'* (pig's pluck stew with a spicy sauce), and *capuzzelle* (cloven lamb's head, seasoned and baked), were part of the cuisine but have declined considerably in popularity in recent decades. Of more enduring popularity are many sautéed veal preparations (*alla Milanese*, veal and peppers). Noteworthy is chicken *alla cacciatore* ("hunter style"), in which chicken pieces are sautéed, then braised with herbs, wine, and vinegar, but also commonly included are tomatoes and peppers. An old dish that often formed part of the Sunday dinner was chicken cut in pieces with potato wedges, roasted in the oven with olive oil, garlic, rosemary, white wine (or lemon juice), and peas; lamb cut in pieces received similar treatment. Of pork dishes, sautéed pork chops with vinegar peppers accompanied by fried potatoes is an old and popular Italian American preparation. Similarly beloved is steak *alla pizzaiola* (pizza-makers style): thin slices of beef braised in an oregano-flavored tomato sauce.

Fish: A regional Italian American specialty of San Francisco is the fish and seafood stew *cioppino*, related to the Ligurian *ciupin*, brought to the Bay Area by Genoese immigrants. On the East Coast there appears a similar dish, *zuppa di pesce*. Fried squid was surely popularized by Italian Americans in the United States, where squid was formerly little consumed and very cheap; also popular among Italian Americans were stuffed squid. Salt cod (*baccalà*), a staple in Italy, remained popular in the United States, and was prepared in a variety of ways—fried or cooked in a tomato sauce with olives and potatoes. A typical seafood dish at least on the East Coast was conch (*scungilli*), often served boiled and sliced in a salad with celery, onions, etc.

Vegetable dishes: Aside from such well-known dishes as eggplant *alla parmigiana* and stuffed peppers, we call attention to *ciambotta*, a summer vegetable stew resembling *ratatouille*. With Sicilian families, the vegetable medley *caponata* made its way to the United States. Sliced zucchini (fried) and eggplant (fried or boiled) could be made *alla scapece*—that is, dressed with olive oil, garlic, vinegar, and mint. An example of a regional Italian American vegetable dish is "Utica greens," popular in Utica, New York, and the surrounding area, which augments basic sautéed greens (esp. escarole) with garlic and hot peppers with chicken stock, chopped *prosciutto*, grated *pecorino*, and breadcrumbs.

Sweets: Many of the most interesting traditional sweets made in the Italian American community are associated with major holidays and other feast days, but throughout the year some families produce a range of baked goods (e.g., lemon or almond cookies, *biscotti*, and various pies and torts). Neighborhood pastry shops (*pasticcerie*) were formerly very numerous, and those remaining still are important sources for specialties such as *cannoli*, *sfogliatelle*, and *pasticiotti*, as well as for rum cakes and *ricotta*-filled cheesecakes. *Spumoni*, a molded ice cream containing three bands of different colors and flavors (usually cherry, pistachio, and chocolate), is closely associated with Italian Americans.

Holiday Feasts

The vast majority of Italian immigrants were Roman Catholic, and their families have generally remained faithful to the church, or at least to the intimate cultural associations that grew out of the religion and marked the rhythm of weekly meals and the observations of major and minor holidays.

The most distinctive, and for many the most popular, holiday meal of the Italian American calendar is on Christmas Eve. What is particularly distinctive about this meal is that the occasion is one of the most joyous of Catholic holidays while also being anciently a day of strict abstinence from animal products (meat, cheese, and eggs). Though many families have long moved away from observing the abstinence rules, others maintain them directly, or, since traditional dishes all conform to the rules, indirectly. Consequently, the Christmas Eve feast centrally involves a variety of fish, seafood, and vegetable dishes, giving rise in recent decades to the term *the feast of the seven fishes*, although traditionally no such specific number was required. A typical meal might begin with some vegetable-filled fritters or bits of pizza dough stuffed with cooked cauliflower or anchovies and fried in olive oil, alongside some crudités and olives. Typical pasta dishes are simple and usually include fish or seafood: spaghetti with clam sauce, spaghetti with anchovies, with tuna, and more. The main course includes a range of different fishes, with some fish receiving multiple treatments (frying, baking, boiling); particularly common are salt cod, eel, whiting, smelt, squid, octopus, and shrimp. Vegetable side dishes are always included, and for many families broccoli or *rapini* are essential. To finish the meal, fresh fruits and nuts are on offer, as well as imported nougats (*torrone*) and fried, shaped dough bits dressed with powdered sugar or honey (e.g., *struffoli*).

Christmas day feasts are more variable in their composition but also follow the pattern of *antipasti*, a special pasta course (ravioli, a baked pasta, tortellini in broth, etc.) and then roasted and boiled meats, followed by fruits, nuts, sweets, and then a varied dessert course, usually including *panettone* (an enriched sweet bread).

The Easter day meal follows the same pattern, but the most traditional meat served is lamb. The most distinctive dishes of the Easter period are the various savory pies: on Good Friday (a fast day), *pizza di scarola* (filled with escarole, anchovies, olives, pine nuts, and raisins) used to be commonly eaten in families with ties to Campania. On Easter Saturday and Sunday, savory pies featuring pork products, cheeses, and eggs are traditional (e.g., *pizza rustica*, *pizza chena*, *scarcedda*, etc.). Elaborate special desserts include the Neapolitan *pastiera* (*ricotta* pie with wheat berries) and the Sicilian *cassata*.

Italian Americans have generally embraced the central elements of the American Thanksgiving meal but incorporated these dishes into the structure of an Italian festive meal. Thus, the first course would commonly be an elaborate set of *antipasti*, including sliced Italian cold cuts and fresh and aged cheeses, olives, and various vegetables (cooked, pickled, and raw), accompanied by Italian bread. The next course would be a substantial, festive pasta dish, such as lasagna, followed then by a full roast turkey dinner (sometimes with other meats served as well) with the appropriate side dishes and trimmings. The dessert course would often bring together both the traditional American pies and Italian sweets.

It is difficult to say to how widely Italian American cuisine as described above survives today. Without doubt, there are families that maintain the tradition largely intact, especially among those living in the remnants of urban Little Italies or in suburbs in which there are substantial Italian American populations and/or for whom family and old community networks have remained close. But the great diaspora from the urban communities to the suburbs starting in the 1950s has led to far-reaching Americanization: though many families maintain various particular Italian American dishes, their culinary foundation has shifted—often abruptly—from the old basis of Italian foodways to an essentially American set of aesthetics, rules, and attitudes about food. In other words, the trend is for Italian Americans to move from cooking Italian American cuisine to cooking American cuisine, albeit with some abiding traditional dishes included in their cookery and perhaps an ethnically inspired inclination to favor adoption of (more or less Americanized) dishes of Italian origin that were not part of the Italian American repertoire and have been learned not through family or community tradition but through visiting restaurants, reading cookbooks, or watching cooking shows on television. Many of the specific changes that this culinary shift entails are reflected in the public cookery of Italian restaurants and celebrity chefs in the United States.

Italian American Public Cookery

Contrary to general belief, Italian American restaurant food is not indicative of Italian American cuisine as a whole: rather, restaurateurs have focused on celebratory traditional dishes, eschewing most ordinary homey dishes, and have invented many new concoctions, such as veal

Ethnic American Food Today

parmigiana and *penne* with vodka sauce, which have come to be thought of as quintessentially Italian American. The iconic pairing of spaghetti and meatballs likely began in the simple "spaghetti houses" of the early twentieth century, meeting non-Italian expectations of meat and starch served together in one course. Particularly important, Italian American contributions are the informal or fast-food dishes: sandwiches of various types (subs, New Jersey's Italian hot dog, Chicago's Italian beef, Philadephia's cheesesteak, New Orleans's muffaletta) and pizza. Though pizzerias have existed since the late nineteenth century in Italian American neighborhoods, pizza's enormous mainstream popularity dates from the post–World War II years. Regional pizza differences have developed in the United States, though East Coast styles share the trait of no fat or only a little olive oil in the dough, while Chicago styles (thin crust, deep dish, and stuffed) use a short dough.

By the 1970s, a new trend of "northern Italian" restaurants began, scorning the older "red-sauce joints" and claiming to be authentically Italian. Ironically, most newer "Italian" restaurants make just as many concessions to American expectations—serving salad as an appetizer, compressing the primo and secondo into a pasta dish topped with meat, excessive use of butter, cream, and garlic, and streamlined versions of festive dishes such as lasagna. All of these deviations from traditional Italian and Italian American foodways can be found in the cookery of American families of Italian descent for whom the connection to the old tradition has been largely broken and a shift to an essentially mainstream American culinary foundation has occurred—in other words, this style of cooking is not really Italian American, but rather an American take on traditional Italian and Italian American foods.

Place in American Culture

While Italian American restaurants and adapted forms of Italian American dishes remain extremely popular with the broader American population, followers of gourmet or "foodie" trends tend to regard Italian American cookery simplistically and negatively, comparing it unfavorably to "authentic" metropolitan Italian regional cuisines and especially those of central and northern Italy. As a consequence, many traditional Italian American dishes of southern Italian origin are inappropriately compared to similar dishes from elsewhere in Italy, and names of southern Italian foods, preserved in correct dialect forms among Italian Americans, are absurdly disparaged as "corruptions" of the cognates in standard Italian. The image of Italian American cuisine has also been distorted through its appropriation by industrial food purveyors and the chain-restaurant industry (e.g., Olive Garden, Buco di Beppo, etc.), where Americanized versions of Italianate dishes that often bear no relation to traditional Italian American domestic cookery are offered while being marketed through stereotypical notions of Italian American ethnicity.

For culturally conservative Italian Americans, the recent explosion of interest in Italian regional foods in the United States is a mixed blessing: a far broader range of high-quality traditional (and new) ingredients are now more widely available than ever before, even in basic grocery chain stores, but this trend coincides with and is partly related to the continuing disappearance of the small, Italian American–owned food shops that were so much a part of the ethnic community's life. On the other hand, just as mainstream American cookery has benefited recently from the incorporation of Italian regional ingredients, dishes, and cooking methods, so, too, has Italian American cookery, in which the traditional culinary foundation makes it all the easier to adopt naturally elements from other related cuisines of Italy.

Images of Italian Americans in popular culture are heavily stereotypical and often negative, with an extreme focus on organized crime. As a consequence, the use of family and culinary tropes in films such as *The Godfather* and *Good-*

fellas and television series such as *The Sopranos* have reinforced long-standing misconceptions about Italian Americans in the United States. While some Italian Americans actively use these associations in marketing their restaurants and other food-related businesses, many within the ethnic community find this linking of family, foodways, and criminality in pop culture extremely offensive. Some works focusing on foodways without reference to crime do, however, exist: Particularly noteworthy in this regard is the film *Big Night*, in which the clash of American and Italian culinary cultures is explored.

Noted Restaurants and Chefs

There are many well-known Italian American chefs active in both the restaurant business and food media who have a deep knowledge of Italian American food traditions, though they may focus professionally on other culinary specialties; for example, Michael Lomonaco (New York), Tony Mantuano (Kenosha/Chicago), and Michael Chiarello (Napa Valley). More widely known Italian American food personalities are Rachael Ray and Giada De Laurentiis, but, while their cooking draws heavily on Italian ingredients and dishes, their cooking styles are purely American. The most famous Italian American celebrity chef today is Mario Batali, who, after spending three years in Italy, returned to the United States and marketed himself as an expert on Italian regional cuisines in his television career; his cooking draws heavily on Italian tradition, but he often presents traditional dishes adapted to American tastes and/or altered in accordance with his personal style. Among high-profile Italian American celebrity chefs, Lidia Bastianich stands out for having a deep knowledge of Italian and Italian American foodways and for treating both with respect for tradition.

Italian and Italian American restaurants in the United States number in the thousands and span the entire range of price, atmosphere, and quality. The vast majority of the higher-end restaurants offer or claim to offer Italian (as opposed to Italian American) cooking. Examples of critically acclaimed restaurants that unabashedly embrace their Italian American identity are vanishingly few; the best-known example is Rao's in East Harlem, New York.

Further Reading

Academia Italiana della Cucina. *La Cucina. The Regional Cooking of Italy.* Translated by Jay Hyams. New York: Rizzoli, 2009.

Barr, Nancy Verde. *We Called It Macaroni: An American Heritage of Southern Italian Cooking.* New York: Knopf, 1990.

Bastianich, Lidia Matticchio. *Lidia's Italy in America.* New York: Knopf, 2011.

Cinotto, Simone. *The Italian-American Table: Food, Family, and Community in New York City.* Urbana: University of Illinois Press, 2013.

Diner, Hasia R. *Italian, Irish, and Jewish Foodways in the Age of Migration.* Cambridge, MA: Harvard University Press, 2003.

Gentile, Maria. *The Italian Cookbook: The Art of Eating Well; Practical Recipes from the Italian Cuisine.* [n.p.]: Forgotten Books, 2012 [orig. 1919].

Levenstein, Harvey. "The American Response to Italian Food, 1880–1930." *Food and Foodways* 1 (1985): 1–24.

Malpezzi, Frances M., and William M. Clements. *Italian-American Folklore.* Little Rock: August House, 1992.

Ruggerio, David. *Little Italy Cookbook.* New York: Artisan, 1997.

Anthony F. Buccini

JAMAICA

(Americas—Caribbean) Jamaican American Food

Jamaican food is one of the more prominent Caribbean cuisines in America. American chefs often embrace its spicy flavors, and traditional Jamaican restaurants can be found in most large American cities. As Jamaican immigration to the United States continues to grow, it is likely that its lively cuisine will continue to gain in popularity.

Background

The first documented Jamaican immigrants arrived in America on a Dutch frigate in 1619. Twenty indentured workers from throughout the Caribbean settled in Jamestown and lived as free men despite the arrival of Jamestown's first slaves in 1629. After 1838, Jamaicans were enlisted to perform temporary agricultural work in the United States, filling an acute labor shortage caused by emancipation. The majority of these workers returned to Jamaica with their earnings, a practice that still exists to some degree today. The United States also recruited Jamaicans to help fill labor shortages during each World War and to help build the Panama Canal. The largest influx of Jamaican immigrants to the United States began after 1965, when new immigration policies limited Jamaican immigration to Great Britain. This trend accelerated further in 1976 as the United States relaxed its own immigration quotas. By the early twenty-first century, Jamaicans were the largest group of American immigrants from the English-speaking Caribbean, but because many have entered the country illegally, the total number of Jamaicans in the United States is impossible to determine. According to the US Census Bureau's American Community Survey, the official number of Jamaican-born Americans was approximately seven hundred thousand in 2009, but informal estimates put the actual number up to three times higher, with the majority of Jamaican Americans living in New York City and Miami.

Foodways

Jamaican cuisine reflects the influence of many different cultures. English, African, Arawak Indian, Spanish, Creole, East Indian, Middle Eastern, Mexican, and Chinese elements are each present in many Jamaican dishes. The prevalence of Caribbean grocery and specialty stores, along with frequent visits to family in Jamaica, allow many Jamaican Americans to remain connected to their traditional foodways.

Curried goat and rice, fried fish, pepperpot stew, turtle soup, rice and peas, and liver and green bananas are each common Jamaican American dishes. Tropical versions of traditionally English sweets are popular desserts, while coffee, tea, and carrot juice are favorite beverages. The scotch bonnet pepper figures prominently in many Jamaican recipes, including well-known jerk barbecue. About four times hotter than a jalapeño pepper, the scotch bonnet adds a sweet, fruity element to its fiery flavor that many recognize as distinctly Caribbean.

Women prepare most daily meals in a Jamaican American households. Shared meals are important to Jamaican Americans, in part because many families have undergone prolonged separation during the immigration process. Although women are responsible for day-to-day cooking, barbecue is a man's world. Outdoor jerk barbecue pits erected for special occasions are masculine spaces where neighbors and family gather together to roast chicken or pork with the spicy jerk seasoning first pioneered by Jamaican Maroons, a band of Spanish and British slaves who escaped into Jamaica's mountains and fought for their freedom. Barbecue pits can be constructed in a variety of shapes and sizes, with the fifty-gallon drum being one of the more popular configurations.

The national dish of Jamaica is *ackee* and saltfish. This simple stir-fry derives its uniqueness less from any complicated preparation than from its unique principal ingredients. Saltfish is salted cod packed tightly into a loaf. The cod must be rinsed multiple times before being added to the dish. Despite several rinses, it still retains a significantly salty flavor. *Ackee* is a fruit native to West Africa. Because it is toxic if prepared incorrectly, *ackee* can be difficult to find in the United States. *Ackee* trees are common in Jamaica, and the fruit is plentiful. When prepared correctly it has a soft consistency similar to scrambled eggs. Onions, peppers, and occasionally bacon round out the dish, which can be served at any meal of the day.

If *ackee* and saltfish are Jamaica's national dish, beef patties are its national snack. A flaky pastry filled with spicy ground beef, the patty is designed to eat on the go. Whereas some people trace its lineage back to Welsh pasties, others suggest the Central and South American *empanada* is a closer relative. Regardless of its origin, the Jamaican beef patty remains a popular early morning or late night snack in Jamaica, where patty stands, each with its own distinctive recipes for crust and filling, vie for dominance. In America, Jamaican patty stands are well established in New York and Miami and are popular with Jamaicans and others alike. While the traditional beef patty is well represented, variations are also common, ranging from healthier whole grain crusts to creative or vegetarian fillings involving vegetables, chicken, or *tofu*.

Traditional Jamaican Beef Patty

Ingredients for Pastry:
   1 pound flour
   ½ cup ice cold water
   ½ cup melted butter
   ½ cup shortening or beef suet
   1 teaspoon salt
   1 teaspoon of baking powder
   ½ teaspoon of curry powder, medium hot
   1 teaspoon of turmeric or 1 drop of *annatto*

Ingredients for Filling:
   4 tablespoons butter
   2 small white onions, finely chopped
   1 chopped scotch bonnet pepper
   1 pound ground beef
   1 teaspoon curry powder
   1 teaspoon crushed dried thyme
   1 teaspoon ground allspice
   1 teaspoon salt
   1 teaspoon black pepper
   ½ cup breadcrumbs
   ½ cup beef or chicken stock
   ½ cup water
   2 eggs, beaten

For the crust:

In large mixing bowl, sift flour. Add baking powder, curry powder, salt, and turmeric. Work in butter and shortening until mixture is crumbly. Slowly add water until mixture is a slightly sticky dough. Wrap dough in plastic wrap and chill for 1 hour.

For the filling:

Add chopped onions, chopped pepper, and butter to large skillet and fry until just beginning to brown. Add beef, curry powder, thyme, allspice, salt, and pepper and cook until meat is browned. Drain any excess fat if necessary. Add stock and breadcrumbs, cover and simmer for 10 minutes or until mixture is moist but not watery.

Preheat oven to 400°F. Remove dough from refrigerator and roll flat on a floured surface until dough is approximately ⅛-inch thick. Cut dough into 8-inch circles. Place approximately three tablespoons of filling in the center of each pastry circle. Moisten the edges of the pastry with water and close the circle around the filling, sealing the edges with the tines of a fork. Mix water and eggs; brush the top of the pastry with egg wash.

Place patties on greased baking sheet and cook for 30 to 40 minutes or until golden brown. Allow patties to cool 10 minutes before serving.

Christmas is the biggest holiday for Jamaicans, who add a tropical twist to many familiar European holidays. A Jamaican Christmas dinner traditionally involves chicken, oxtail, roast ham, curry goat, and rice and *gungo* peas. *Gungo* peas ripen in December, making them a symbol of the Christmas season for many Jamaicans. For dessert, Jamaican Christmas fruitcake is traditionally served, along with a cold beverage made from dried sorrel, cinnamon, cloves, ginger, orange, and rum.

Place in American Culture
Many Americans associate jerk seasoning with Jamaica, and jerk dry rubs and marinades are available in the majority of mainstream grocery stores. The prevalence of American tourism to Jamaica has introduced Americans to other Jamaican delicacies, including Blue Mountain coffee and spicy Jamaican ginger beer.

Some health-conscious Americans have embraced the Rastafarian cuisine known as *Ital*. *Ital* is a vegetarian cooking style that focuses on whole, unprocessed foods and avoids chemicals and pesticides. Simple meals prepared without animal products of any kind are seasoned with spices Rastas believe to be infused with healing properties.

Noted Restaurants and Chefs
Jamaican restaurants are common in New York and Miami and can also be found in most American metropolitan areas. They are generally casual and range from quick service patty stands and jerk shacks to more relaxed sit-down eateries that showcase a variety of traditional Jamaican delicacies. Jamaican music is often an important aspect of the Jamaican dining experience, and restaurants will frequently host live reggae musicians. Although Jamaican restaurants are enjoyed by people of all backgrounds, they often double as community gathering places for Jamaicans or immigrants from other parts of the Caribbean.

Further Reading
Alleyne, Mervyn C. *Roots of Jamaican Culture*. London: Pluto Press, 1988.
EveryCulture.com. Countries and Their Cultures. "Jamaican Americans." http://www.everyculture.com/multi/Ha-La/Jamaican-Americans.html#ixzz33i704Vn7.
Jones, Terry-Ann. "Jamaican Immigrants in the United States and Canada: Race, Transnationalism, and Social Capital." New York: LFB Scholarly Publishing, 2008.
Moskin, Julia, and Kim Severson. "Jamaican Passions." *New York Times*, July 20, 2005.
Sackett, Lou. "Jamaican Vegetarian Cuisine." *HealthQuest*, December 31, 2001, 41.
Scala Quinn, Lucinda, and Quentin Bacon. *Lucinda's Authentic Jamaican Kitchen*. Hoboken, NJ: John Wiley & Sons, 2006.

Amy B. Santos

JAPAN
(East Asia) Japanese American Food

As has been the case with most ethnic cuisines in America, that of Japan arrived with immigrants. Since the 1970s Japanese food has grown steadily in popularity in the United States, and by now a wide array of Japanese foods has entered American food culture. Sushi, the quintessential Japanese food, is ubiquitous: freshly made sushi can be enjoyed at high-class restaurants, while packaged sushi can be purchased in many supermarkets. *Teriyaki* has likewise become a mainstream sauce, enjoyed even by those who otherwise may not like Japanese food, and Japanese steakhouses featuring flamboyant *teppanyaki* chefs are increasingly common. On the other hand, certain Japanese foods are still regarded as exotic—perhaps even disgusting—by most Americans. Yet with so many of its foods appearing in so many venues within American food culture, Japanese cuisine has established a place in mainstream America.

Background

The end of Japan's Edo-period seclusion policy, which had expressly prohibited emigration, opened the gates for many Japanese to migrate overseas. In 1868—the first year of the ensuing Meiji period—approximately 150 Japanese men left for Hawaii to work on a sugar plantation, and a period of larger-scale government-sanctioned emigration followed between 1885 and 1924. During this time roughly two hundred thousand Japanese moved to Hawaii, mainly to work on sugar plantations, and another 180,000 relocated to the mainland (chiefly California, Utah, Oregon, and Alaska) to work on farms and in mining camps, sawmills, and salmon canneries. These first waves of emigrants consisted mostly of male laborers in search of work. But with the Gentlemen's Agreement of 1907, Japan and the United States took steps to curb the migration. Japan barred further emigration of male workers to the US mainland, while the United States consented to allow family members of those already in the country to immigrate. Hence, many Japanese women emigrated to join husbands to whom they had been wed through long-distance matchmaking. The establishment of families led to the formation of Japanese communities in settlements. Burgeoning Japantowns of the early twentieth century included those in San Francisco, San José, and Los Angeles.

US policy during World War II forced Japanese and Japanese Americans on the West Coast and Hawaii into internment camps, where the scarcity of Japanese ingredients—amid a general food shortage—posed great difficulties for the maintenance of Japanese foodways. After the war, the Japanese and Japanese American population dispersed across the mainland.

The postwar years brought many new immigrants (mostly agriculturalists and agribusiness specialists such as chick sexers), and the international expansion of Japanese firms in the 1980s allowed many professionals and their families to settle in America. According to the US Census Bureau, as of 2010 over 1.3 million people in America claimed Japanese as their ethnic background (including those who claimed Japanese among multiple racial and/or ethnic backgrounds). While a growing number of interracial and interethnic marriages has resulted in increased racial and ethnic diversity within the group of Japanese (*nikkei*) Americans, traditional Japanese food has continued to play an important role in shaping Japanese Americans' ethnic identity. In 2012 the cultural organization Discover Nikkei launched an online series called *Nikkei Chronicles*, one manifestation of which is *ITADAKIMASU! A Taste of Nikkei Culture*, a social network space that invites people of Japanese descent the world over to post food-related memories and experiences.

Foodways

Japanese cuisine revolves around a few key seasonings: soy sauce, rice vinegar, *sake* (salted cooking *sake*), *mirin* (sweet cooking *sake*), *dashi* (broth made from kelp, anchovies, sardines, or bonito), and *miso* (fermented soybean paste). These seasonings, sometimes combined with sugar and salt, are used for all manner of cooking preparations: marinating, sautéing, simmering, and more. Fish can be grilled with soy sauce and ginger (with a little sugar and *mirin*); vegetables can be marinated in vinegar, sugar, and salt; cubed pumpkin can be simmered in seaweed broth (with a little sugar, *mirin*, and soy sauce); and boiled spinach can be sprinkled with grated dried bonito and soy sauce.

Staples of Japanese meals include short-grain rice and noodles (*udon*, *soba*, and ramen). Rice or noodles usually accompany other dishes served on separate plates. However, they can easily be turned into the base of a single-bowl Japanese-style fast-food meal: either rice topped with cooked vegetables and meat or soup with noodles. Potatoes (e.g., *jaga-imo*, *satsuma-imo*), yams (e.g., *sato-imo*, *naga-imo*), dried vegetables (e.g., shiitake mushrooms, daikon), and seaweed (e.g., kelp, *wakame*, *hijiki*, *nori*) also appear frequently in Japanese cuisine.

Some foreign foods adopted by Japanese culture have become signature Japanese foods overseas. Tempura (a method of battering and deep-frying) was introduced into Japan in the sixteenth century by Jesuit missionaries from Portugal. Today "tempura"—in Japan and elsewhere—refers to vegetables and seafood dipped in a batter made from flour and eggs, then deep-fried in vegetable oil.

Ramen is a dish consisting of Chinese-style noodles—brought to Japan by Chinese immigrants—in soup. Ramen typically comes with one of four flavors of broth: soy sauce, *miso*, salt, or *tonkotsu* (a soup base made from pork bones); it is commonly garnished with chopped scallions, *menma* (processed bamboo shoots), seaweed, and sliced pork or hard-boiled egg. Ramen is most familiar in America in the form of instant noodles. These instant noodles were invented in the 1950s by a Japanese man named Momofuku Ando, and they have since spread worldwide. According to the World Instant Noodles Association, in 2012 the United States ranked fifth in the world in instant-noodle consumption—and first among Western nations, trailing only China/Hong Kong, Indonesia, Japan, and Vietnam. Despite warnings about their high calorie and sodium content, instant noodles are widely consumed due to their convenience.

A particularly curious example is what is known today as "Japanese curry." Eaten by British officials stationed in Japan near the end of the nineteenth century, curry was regarded as an exotic dish, suggesting to the Japanese the otherness of the West, notwithstanding that the British had "invented" curry in their colonization of India. From that time on the Japanese have cherished the tantalizingly spicy aroma of this thick, yellow sauce poured over short-grain rice. It actually attained the status of a national food in Japan. Japanese curry has entered American foodways through Japanese restaurants that serve dishes such as "curry rice" and "noodles in curry soup," and instant Japanese curry roux is available in the ethnic food aisles of American supermarkets alongside *miso*, soy sauce, rice, and ramen noodles.

Sushi, no doubt, sits at the head of the roster of famous Japanese foods. There are many different kinds of sushi: *nigiri-zushi* (a piece of fish atop a small rice ball), *maki-zushi* (rice and other ingredients wrapped in a sheet of *nori*), *temaki-zushi* (make-it-yourself *nori*-wrapped sushi), *nare-zushi* (partially fermented fish with rice), and *oshi-zushi* (rice and fish pressed in a mold). *Nigiri-zushi* and *maki-zushi* are the types most often found in restaurants and delis, both in Japan and in America. *Temaki-zushi* is a common type of sushi made in Japanese homes, which is often featured at parties. *Nori* wrappers, vinegary rice, pickles, fresh vegetables, *sashimi* (sliced raw fish), cured fish eggs, and other ingredients are placed on a table, and each person creates his or her own hand-wrapped sushi. Several varieties of *nare-zushi* and *oshi-zushi* exist, but they tend to be marketed as regional specialties in Japan and are not yet well known outside the country. The popularity of sushi has made *wasabi* conspicuous in today's American cuisine. *Wasabi* (*Was-*

abia japonica) is a Japanese horseradish whose root is grated as a condiment for sushi. *Wasabi* nowadays comes in plastic tubes (which may or may not contain real grated *wasabi*), and it is more common for American—and even Japanese—households to keep tubes of *wasabi* rather than fresh *wasabi* root.

The traditional gender roles associated with Japanese food preparation are becoming less rigidly defined. In Japan women have historically been in charge of cooking in the home, whereas the profession of chef has long been the exclusive preserve of men. Nowadays, though, it is still not difficult to find Japanese who cling to the notion that home cooking is exclusively woman's work, and that a woman's smaller hands and weaker grip make her unsuited to the job of professional chef—it has become modish for men to cook in the home, while at the same time the career path of chef (especially sushi chef) has opened to women. America is witnessing similar changes in the profession. Grill and sushi chefs in American restaurants are still predominantly male (even as the number of non-Japanese chefs has increased); yet female sushi chefs are increasingly visible behind American sushi counters. And their numbers will surely grow, as the California Sushi Academy (est. 1998) boasts multiple female graduates.

Everyday Meals

The diversity of regional cuisines in Japan makes it difficult to list everyday meals pertinent to the entire country. Nonetheless, two staples of Japanese cooking must be mentioned: steamed rice and *miso* soup. Rice is so central to Japanese cuisine that the word for *steamed rice* (*gohan*) doubles as the word for *meal*. *Miso* soup (*miso-shiru*) is also a central component of homemade Japanese meals. It can easily be prepared by making a broth with kelp (*kombu*) or dried fish such as anchovies (*iriko*) or bonito (*katsuo*), simmering some vegetables and other ingredients in the broth, then blending in *miso* paste at the end.

Ease of preparation does not indicate a lack of significance, however. The different flavors of *miso* result mainly from differences in the type of fermentation starter (the combination of grain, salt, and bacteria) that is mixed into the steamed soybeans, and in the duration of the fermentation process. Different regions in Japan are known for their own varieties of *miso*, and multiple types of *miso* may even be combined into a single paste. Each household has its own favorite *miso* and broth for *miso* soup. Hence *miso* soup is considered emblematic of *ofukuro-no-aji* (the taste of mom's home-cooked meals). An old Japanese bromide states that "*Kekkon suruto miso-shiru no aji ga kawaru* [*Miso* soup tastes different after marriage]," meaning that newlywed men soon discover that their wives cook *miso* soup differently from their mothers.

A typical contemporary Japanese-style meal consists of rice, soup (*miso* or clear), and a set of several small dishes (*okazus*) flavored differently. The *okazus* may include *hijiki-ni* (simmered seaweed and vegetables), *hiya-yakko* (tofu garnished with grated dried bonito, grated fresh ginger, or chopped scallions), *daikon-oroshi* (grated daikon), *kyuri-no-sunomono* (shredded cucumber and *wakame*, seasoned with vinegar), *kinpira-gobo* (simmered shredded burdock and carrots), *niku-jaga* (simmered potatoes with thinly sliced beef), grilled or simmered fish, deep-fried chicken bits, deep-fried pork chops— the list is endless. Together the different *okazus* should complement the steamed rice, with no two dishes in the meal flavored in exactly the same way. Ideally the *okazu* combination will change from one day to the next, offering the palate a kaleidoscope of sensations.

***Namasu* (Vinegar-Marinated Carrot and Daikon Strips)**

Ingredients:
　1 carrot
　½ small daikon (roughly equal in size to the carrot)

2–3 teaspoons salt
4 tablespoons rice vinegar or apple vinegar
1 tablespoon sugar

Cut carrot and daikon into thin strips; place in bowl. Rub salt into vegetable strips; let stand for about 10 minutes. Wring internal moisture from vegetable strips; place in separate bowl. Combine vinegar and sugar, then pour over vegetable strips to marinate.

Options: Add lemon juice or salt to taste.

For a more robust flavor, add chili sauce, chili oil, *wasabi*, or ginger.

This is a nice side dish to oily food. Also, the carrot and daikon make an auspicious reddish-white color combination.

Buta no kocha-ni (Tea-Boiled Pork)

Ingredients:

1–1½ pounds pork (boneless ribs or loins are recommended)
3–4 tea bags (unflavored black tea or oolong tea)
water
½ cup rice vinegar
½ cup soy sauce
½ cup *mirin* (if *mirin* is not available, use *sake*—or white cooking wine—and sugar; *mirin* can be approximated by combining *sake* and sugar in a 3:1 ratio)

In large saucepan or stockpot, boil enough water to cover pork; add tea bags. Add pork to boiling tea; reduce heat when pork's surface is cooked; simmer 1 hour. Combine rice vinegar, soy sauce, and *mirin* in different saucepan to make marinade; heat to boil. Place pork in container and add marinade; meat should be at least half-covered. Allow meat and marinade to cool; then cover container and refrigerate. After a few hours, turn meat over so as to marinate other side. Ready to serve after half a day, or the next day.

Holiday Feasts

Many important culinary customs in Japanese culture are connected to the New Year's celebration, during which various vegetables and seafoods are consumed because it has traditionally been considered auspicious to receive blessings from both land and ocean. On New Year's Eve, *soba* (buckwheat noodles) are eaten to mark the *toshikoshi* (year-crossing) and to wish for longevity (because the noodles are long). On January 1 people eat an assembly of foods (*osechi*), many of which carry positive associations that reflect social values and auspiciousness, sometimes enabled by the use of wordplay. For instance, black beans (*mame*) are served to wish for diligence because *mame* means both "beans" and "hardworking." *Kobumaki* is a simmered sardine-kelp roll; it symbolizes felicity, from the pun with *kobu* ("kelp") and *yorokobu* ("to be happy"). Other foods represent lingering traditions and values from olden times. *Tatsukuri* is a dish consisting of caramel-glazed dried sardines that wishes for an ample harvest (because in preindustrial Japan sardines were considered the most desirable of agricultural fertilizers). *Kazunoko* is herring roe, the plenitude of whose eggs symbolizes familial prosperity. Longevity is encoded in shrimp because their bent backs and long moustaches resemble those of old men.

People also eat *ozōni* (literally a "simmered mix of things"), a soup that contains rice cakes (*mochis*) and vegetables. The soup can be a simple *dashi* (with salt and *sake*), or *miso* can be added. Although the types of *mochi* and other ingredients for this soup vary regionally, the significance of the soup always resides in the rice cakes. Rice symbolizes bounty and fertility because rice has long been Japan's primary crop. Furthermore, a rice cake stretches, thus metaphorically connoting longevity. Consuming rice cakes celebrates the coming of the New Year and the beginning of a new seasonal cycle.

Moreover, rice cakes are the most important offerings made to the deities of the New Year, who are believed to visit homes to bestow good luck. Round, layered rice cakes—called *kagami-mochis* (mirror rice cakes)—are placed in the family room or kitchen, or before the household Shinto altar. Each *kagami-mochi* consists of two round rice cakes, the smaller one placed atop the larger and decorated with a *daidai* (a bitter citrus fruit) symbolizing familial succession, and sprigs from the *yuzuriha*, a type of evergreen tree emblematic of righteousness and familial prosperity. It is within the rice cakes that the deities are believed to nest temporarily during their visits to the household due to the cakes' resemblance to a mirror, one of the sacred objects in Shinto. On January 11, the day of *kagami biraki* (mirror-opening), the deities leave this temporary dwelling, which family members then eat—often in an adzuki bean soup called *zenzai*—in order to ingest their residual blessings.

Other occasional foods include *oseki-han* (red rice), which consists of dark red adzuki beans and sticky rice steamed together to create a combination of colors—*ko-haku* (red-white)—that is regarded as auspicious within Japanese culture. *Oseki-han* is customarily served at all manner of celebrations, especially those marking hallmark life events such as graduation and marriage. Red snapper (*tai*) also appears at festive affairs, for its *ko-haku* color combination (reddish skin and white flesh) and its rhyme with the word for *auspicious* (*mede-tai*).

For Japanese immigrants and their descendants who believe strongly in the power of symbolism and the significance of observing customs, it is important to maintain homeland traditions surrounding calendar and life events. The practice of ingesting such highly meaningful foods is one means through which to honor their ethnic heritage.

Place in American Culture

Japanese food has become all the more visible in American culture thanks to the Japanese television series *Iron Chef*, which featured cooking duels between veteran chefs and up-and-coming challengers. The series debuted in Japan in 1993 and was very popular during its original run there. Some years later the series aired on the Food Network in the United States, introducing many new ingredients to Americans hitherto unfamiliar with Japanese cuisine. The program became such a hit outside of Japan that spinoffs were produced not only in the United States (*The Next Iron Chef*, *Iron Chef USA*, and *Iron Chef America*) but also in Australia, Israel, Thailand, the United Kingdom, and Vietnam.

Yet, long before its surge onto the mainstream scene, everyday Japanese food had been kept alive among immigrants and their descendants in America. Memoirs by Japanese Americans like Linda Furiya and D. Mas Masumoto describe their families' daily eating habits, including intergenerational disputes over what is nutritious. Ethnographers such as Yano and Yoshimura have studied how Japanese American businesses like delicatessens and grocery stores allow Japanese and Japanese Americans to find comfort in familiar foods, and to help them to nurture a sense of ethnic identity and community.

Since the 1970s, American culture has witnessed the increasing popularity of Japanese food. Its emphasis on fish, vegetables, and soy products has made Japanese cuisine appealing as a healthy alternative to red meat and dairy products for a growing number of health-conscious Americans. *Edamame* (steamed or boiled immature soybeans) and *soba* are promoted on cooking shows as "healthy" foods, and they are sold in trendy grocery stores. Meanwhile, certain items continue to be portrayed on cooking- and travel-themed television programs as weird or grotesque foreign foods, despite their immense health benefits: for instance, *natto* (soybeans fermented with *Bacillus subtilis*, which results in slimy strings) and *yamaimo* (grated yams, often described as mucuslike).

Especially remarkable is the proliferation within the American culture of sushi. Initially sushi's high price and exotic nature helped to solidify its status as an epicurean delicacy. But gradually more economical sushi became accessible as a fast food at mall food courts and in grocery stores. Today, packaged sushi is readily available in seafood and deli sections of supermarkets, while tony sushi restaurants continue to promote the idea of sushi as culinary art.

The sushi cultures of America and Japan differ fundamentally. American sushi rice is made with less vinegar, to reduce its pungency, and the rice tends to be compressed more tightly for ease of grasping with inexpertly handled chopsticks. But the most salient difference is the relative importance of the sushi roll (*maki-zushi*). In Japan sushi rolls tend to be viewed more as side dishes to the main dish of hand-molded sushi (*nigiri-zushi*: a piece of fish atop a rectangular rice bed). Artistically varicolored sushi rolls with multiple fillings do appear on festive occasions in Japan, but the kinds of rolls common in American sushi restaurants are absent from Japanese sushi bars, where chefs take pride in the quality fish procured daily at fish markets. The placing of the fish atop the rice in *nigiri-zushi* enables the sushi chef to exhibit the fish proudly and the customer to examine its quality and to compliment the chef on it. Though simple, this mode of presentation is significant: high-quality fish is flavorful and costly, and those able to understand and afford it visit fancy sushi bars first and foremost to enjoy the fish. In this type of environment, where the quality of fish matters so, simple vegetable rolls containing sliced cucumber, pickled plum, or *kanpyo* (cooked dried calabash) act as appetizers or finishers, or to offer respite between courses of *nigiri-zushi*. Although nowadays in Japan sushi restaurants that offer less expensive sushi serve California rolls (with imitation crab, cucumber, and avocado), and supermarkets sell packaged sushi rolls with shrimp tempura and the like, other types of *maki-zushi* remain unique to America.

American sushi culture is characterized by its elaborate rolls, such that American restaurants often feature sushi rolls containing ingredients inimical to Japanese practice (for instance, "spider rolls" with deep-fried crabs, or "Philly rolls" with salmon and cream cheese). The *nori* wrappers are concealed (because Americans seem to find their blackish hue unappealing), and fillings are made colorful with fresh vegetables like sprouts, avocado, and shredded carrots. There are even extravagant rolls named "red dragon" and "caterpillar" that use—instead of the traditional *nori*—thinly sliced avocado and carrot as wrappers. Artful and colorful, American sushi rolls are rich in varieties of visual presentation.

Another American favorite is brown-rice sushi. Brown-rice sushi might seem sensible from an American perspective because, while sushi itself is regarded as "healthy," brown rice is considered healthier than white. But brown-rice sushi is a foreign concept in Japan. Sushi is not necessarily marked as a healthy food in Japan, it being just another quotidian meal. And brown rice's dryness makes it unsuitable for sushi rolls and beds. Those Japanese who enjoy brown rice add it to other meals, but find it impractical for sushi.

Moreover, American sushi is frequently served with sauces, oils, or gravies containing ingredients such as lemon juice, chili paste, olive oil, *teriyaki* sauce, or mayonnaise. Eyes and tongues trained in fancy Japanese sushi bars are apt to suspect that fish slathered with sauce must be of low quality—because in Japan the use of elaborate sauces on raw fish would be regarded as an attempt to camouflage tasteless fish. In American sushi culture, by contrast, the sauce frequently *defines* the fanciness of the sushi, as if in imitation of the importance of sauce in prestigious French cuisine. Mainstream American sushi—while it does not eschew quality fish—does not *rely* on the quality of the fish for its value; it operates on its own terms. Now that American sushi variations have become something that a native of Japan would consider "exotic," sushi can be said fully to have entered America's food culture. Indeed, America's establishment of an autonomous sushi culture is only one manifestation of a worldwide sushi boom, which has bolstered the international fish trade.

In addition to sushi, many other foods of Japanese origin have become part of mainstream culture in America, and some are favored even by those not in the habit of eating Japanese food. *Teriyaki* sauce is one such food. In Japanese food culture *teriyaki* is a term describing a method of cooking and flavoring, and *teriyaki* sauce is made by combining soy sauce, *mirin*, *sake*, and sugar in a pan as chicken or fish is being fried. But in America bottled *teriyaki* sauce is more common, since not all households have *mirin* and *sake* (or even soy sauce) in their cupboards. *Teriyaki* sauce is bottled by such companies as Annie Chun's, Kikkoman, and Yamasa. *Teriyaki* as a flavor is so common in today's America that meat products such as sausage, barbecued ribs, and beef jerky are sold with *teriyaki* flavoring.

Rice crackers have also become popular in America in recent decades. Often dubbed "Oriental mix," assorted rice crackers share space in snack aisles with chocolate-covered malt balls, yogurt-covered raisins, and gummy bears. Rice is free of harmful gluten and is thus safe for those with gluten intolerance. And rice crackers are usually baked rather than fried, which makes them low in fat. Hence, rice crackers are marketed as healthy alternatives to standard American snacks such as cookies and potato chips.

Lately, *wasabi* peas have been setting the American snack world on fire with their fierce, spicy flavor. Produced by the prominent Japanese company Kasugai, roasted dried green peas with *wasabi*-flavored coating have for decades been a standard snack in Japan. Today exported Kasugai snacks can be found in major grocery stores in America, and similar products are made by domestic companies as well.

In the United States, Japanese foods are distributed by major Japanese food traders such as the Nishimoto Trading Co. and JFC International, Inc., both of which were established in the early twentieth century. As refrigeration and freezing techniques for food importing and exporting developed, more and more Japanese food items became available in America.

Japanese grocery stores are found in numerous cities in the United States. Mitsuwa is a Japanese grocery chain that operates supermarkets in multiple states, and there are countless smaller-scale chains as well as family-run establishments. Japanese groceries are readily available at non-Japanese Asian grocery stores as well: major retailers include the Chinese grocery chain 99 Ranch Market and the Korean chain Han Ah Reum (known also as H-Mart or Super-H). One need not go to an Asian grocer to procure Japanese foods in America, however. It is not unusual to find rice, soy sauce, *mirin*, *sake*, *miso*, *tofu*, *nori*, *wasabi*, and Japanese curry sauce mix in the ethnic food sections— and daikon, nappa, and bean sprouts in the produce sections—of American supermarkets.

Noncomestible items from Japanese food culture are also popular among some Americans. One notable example is plastic food models. In Japan many restaurants have near their entrances display cases filled with plastic replicas of the dishes on their menus, to attract customers and to whet their appetites. Replicas exist of all kinds of foods, Japanese and non-Japanese: pizza, spaghetti, ramen, tempura, samosas, curry, crêpes, and ice cream. These food models have drawn the attention of many visitors to Japan, so much so that the Tokyo district home to the wholesalers that sell cooking supplies and food replicas to chefs and restaurateurs has become a tourist hotspot. Sushi replicas have even been fashioned into keychains and USB flash drives sold as kitschy souvenirs in Japan, and they are available to nontravelers through Internet vendors.

Japanese cooking utensils have also made their way onto the American market. Novelty rice molds (to create sushi beds or rice balls in the shapes of bears, cats, rabbits, hearts, cars) and vegetable cutters (to cut vegetables into the shapes of flowers, leaves, hearts, stars) were originally created for Japanese chefs, as well as for Japanese mothers who make boxed lunches (*bento*s) for their children. But these tools are now sold online—even by so visible a retailer as Amazon—to cooking enthusiasts in America.

The presence of Japanese food and food-related items in American culture is conspicuous, as many Japanese words (i.e., *miso*, *sake*, *tofu*)—along with the foods that they name—have entered the American lexicon and diet.

Noted Restaurants and Chefs

Nobu Matsuhisa is a Japanese celebrity chef known for his fusion cuisine that, due to his restaurant experience in Peru, combines Japanese and South American elements. His American notoriety derives from his first restaurant—Matsuhisa—in Beverly Hills, which opened in 1987. Partnering with the actor Robert De Niro, he later opened the restaurant Nobu. Both restaurants now have multiple locations nationwide. Masaharu Morimoto is a celebrity chef from Japan who became famous in America by appearing on *Iron Chef* (in both its Japanese and US versions). He now runs restaurants in Pennsylvania, New York, California, and Hawaii. Roy Yamaguchi is a Hawaii-based celebrity chef specializing in Hawaiian fusion cuisine. Founder of the restaurant chain Roy's (est. 1988), he remains in the public eye by publishing cookbooks and appearing on television programs.

Though not as widely known in America as the aforementioned male chefs, some women celebrated in Japan for their home cooking have published cookbooks in English. Katsuyo Kobayashi—Japan's analogue to Julia Child—was one of the first homemakers to become well-known for quick-and-easy home recipes, presented on such long-running television shows as *Kyo no ryori* [Today's Cooking]. She has published nearly two hundred food-related books in Japan, a few of which have been translated into English—such as the recent *The Quick & Easy Japanese Cookbook* (2012). In America Kobayashi may be best remembered for having defeated Iron Chef Chen Kenichi in the *Iron Chef* episode "Potato Battle."

Another notable example is Harumi Kurihara, a homemaker who became known throughout Japan in 1992 for a cookbook that targeted women who cook daily for their families. More than a million copies were sold, an enormous commercial success for a cookbook. Like Kobayashi's, Kurihara's rise to fame as a celebrity homemaker (someone without formal professional training in cooking) was empowering to many women. It was not until 2004 that she made her debut on the world culinary scene with her first cookbook in English, *Harumi's Japanese Cooking*. This book was named not only "Best World Asian Cuisine Book" but also "Best Cookbook of the Year" at the 10th Gourmand World Cookbook Awards in 2004. Kurihara was the first Japanese to receive these awards.

Also contributing to the popularity of Japanese food in America are well-known restaurant chains. Benihana is a company that franchises Japanese-cuisine restaurants—including Haru, Samurai, and RA Sushi—in the United States. Benihana (the name means "safflower") began in 1964 as a small New York restaurant founded by a Japanese immigrant named Hiroaki "Rocky" Aoki (1938–2008). It is he who deserves credit for popularizing in America steakhouses with *teppanyaki*-style grills (*teppan* means "iron griddle"; *yaki* means "grilled," "broiled," "pan-fried")—the familiar performance in which chefs grill meat and vegetables right in front of the guests, with acrobatic deployment of cooking knives evocative of sword-wielding samurai warriors (an ever-popular American image of Japanese culture). This mode of culinary entertainment has been copied by many other restaurants throughout America—to the extent that it today constitutes the dominant American idea of "Japanese" restaurants. This grilling style has subsequently been imported into Japan, and one can now find grill restaurants offering similarly ostentatious performances in the homeland of inventor Aoki.

Happi House is a fast-food chain known for its *teriyaki* and tempura dishes. Founded by Joe Ikeda, Richard Tanaka, and Carlo Besio, its first location opened in 1976 in San José's Japantown. "Happi" refers to the *happi* coat, a traditional Japanese garment worn for festivals. Reportedly, these three businessmen were inspired to start the restaurant upon seeing the food served during the annual Obon Festival in Japantown—thus the nominal tie to festivity.

Sarku Japan is a nationwide fast-food chain that specializes in *teppanyaki*-style stir-fry dishes and sushi. Established in 1987, the company now has over two hundred locations in thirty-seven states, many of them in the food courts of shopping malls.

In addition, there are numerous regional chains and local businesses. As of 2012 the Japanese Restaurant Info website listed 6,438 Japanese restaurants operating in the United States.

Conclusion

In December 2013, UNESCO certified Japanese food (*washoku*) as an "Intangible Cultural Heritage," responding to a petition filed by the Japanese government in March 2012. This designation will certainly elevate the international profile of Japanese cuisine and validate its artistic nature. Some foods that originated in Japan—such as sushi, *teriyaki* sauce, and *wasabi* peas—have already secured positions in everyday American culinary culture, and more will surely follow.

Further Reading

Aoki, Tamotsu. "The Domestication of Chinese Foodways in Contemporary Japan: Ramen and Peking Duck." In *Changing Chinese Foodways in Asia*, edited by David Y. H. Wu and Tan Chee-beng, 219–33. Hong Kong: Chinese University Press, 2001.

"The Benihana History." http://www.benihana.com/about/the-benihana-story.

Bestor, Theodore C. "How Sushi Went Global." *Foreign Policy* 121 (2000): 54–63.

Bestor, Theodore C. "Supply-Side Sushi: Commodity, Market, and the Global City." *American Anthropologist* 103, no. 1 (2001): 76–95, 2001.

Bestor, Theodore C. *Tsukiji: The Fish Market at the Center of the World*. Berkeley: University of California Press, 2004.

Cheung, Sidney C. H. "The Invention of Delicacy: Cantonese Food in Yokohama Chinatown." In *The Globalization of Chinese Food*, edited by David Y. H. Wu and Sidney C. H. Cheung, 170–82. Richmond, Surrey: Curzon, 2002.

Cwiertka, Katarzyna. "Eating the Homeland: Japanese Expatriates in the Netherlands." In *Asian Food: The Global and the Local*, edited by Katarzyna Cwiertka and Boudewijn Walraven, 133–52. Honolulu: University of Hawaii Press, 2001.

Cwiertka, Katarzyna. "From Ethnic to Hip: Circuits of Japanese Cuisine in Europe." *Food and Foodways* 13, no. 4 (2005): 241–72.

Cwiertka, Katarzyna. *Modern Japanese Cuisine: Food, Power and National Identity*. London: Reaktion, 2006.

Discover Nikkei. Nikkei Chronicles series, *ITADAKIMASU! A Taste of Nikkei Culture*. http://www.discovernikkei.org/en/journal/chronicles/.

Discover Nikkei. Nikkei Wiki, Food and Agriculture. http://www.discovernikkei.org/en/about/what-is-nikkei.

Dusselier, Jane. "Does Food Make Place?: Food Protests in Japanese American Concentration Camps." *Food and Foodways* 10, no. 3 (2002): 137–65.

Furiya, Linda. *Bento Box in the Heartland: My Japanese Girlhood in Whitebread America*. Emeryville: Seal Press, 2006.

Ishige, Naomichi. *The History and Culture of Japanese Food*. London: Kegan Paul, 2001.

Issenberg, Sasha. *The Sushi Economy: Globalization and the Making of a Modern Delicacy*. New York: Gotham, 2007.

"Japanese Americans." In *Encyclopedia of Japanese Descendants in the Americas: An Illustrated History of the Nikkei*, edited by Akemi Kikumura-Yano, 275–92. Walnut Creek: AltaMira, 2002.

Japanese Restaurant Info. http://www.japanese restaurantinfo.com/.

Laemmerhirt, Iris-Aya. "Imagining the Taste: Transnational Food Exchanges between Japan and the United States." *Japanese Journal of American Studies* 21 (2010): 231–50.

Louie, Elaine. "She Has a Knife and She Knows How to Use It." *New York Times*, June 5, 2002. http://www.nytimes.com/2002/06/05/dining/she-has-a-knife-and-she-knows-how-to-use-it.html?pagewanted=all&src=pm.

Masumoto, D. Mas. "Brown Rice Sushi." *Western Folklore* 42, no. 2 (1983): 140–44.

National Japanese American Historical Society. *The Rice Cooker's Companion: Japanese American Food and Stories*. San Francisco: The National Japanese American Historical Society, 2000.

Rath, Eric, and Stephanie Assmann, eds. *Japanese Foodways, Past and Present*. Urbana: University of Illinois Press, 2010.

Rathburn, Arthur C. *The American Japanese*. Fredonia: Brite, 2004.

Washoku, trational dietary culture of the Japanese, notably for the celebration of New Year. UNESCO.com. http://www.unesco.org/culture/ich/index.php?lg=en&pg=00011&RL=00869.

World Instant Noodles Association. "Expanding Market: National Trends in Instant Noodles Demands." http://instantnoodles.org/noodles/expanding-market.html.

Yano, Christine R. "Side-Dish Kitchen: Japanese American Delicatessens and the Culture of Nostalgia." In *The Restaurant Book: Ethnographies of Where We Eat*, edited by David Beriss and David Sutton, 47–63. Oxford: Berg, 2007.

Yoshimura, Ayako. "Oriental Shop: An Ethnography of Material Communication inside an Asian Grocery Store in Madison, Wisconsin." M.A. thesis, Memorial University of Newfoundland, 2009.

Ayako Yoshimura

JERSEY

(United Kingdom, northern Europe) British American Food

See: England.

JEWISH-ASHKENAZI

(North America) Jewish American, Ashkenazic American

See also: Jewish Sephardic.

Background

Ashkenazic Jews are historically characterized by use of the Yiddish language, a specific set of liturgical and cultural practices, and a distinct family of cuisines influenced by geography and coterritorial non-Jewish populations.

The name *Ashkenaz* comes from the name of one of the great-grandsons of Noah (Genesis 10:3), who became associated with Germanic-speaking lands. The Jewish communities that began populating the Rhine Valley, or Loter (Ashkenaz I), in the ninth century became the forerunners of Ashkenazic Jewry.[1] Their identity as a separate cultural and religious community was written into law in the year 1000 CE when Rabbi Gershon established a ban on polygamy for Ashkenazic Jews (other Jewish communities have de facto bans on polygamy).

The Yiddish language and a specific Ashkenazic identity developed together, and by the sixteenth century rabbis as far away as the Holy Land were debating whether one's religious observance should follow the practices of one's Ashkenazic ancestry or current location.

In the fourteenth large numbers of Ashkenazic Jews emigrated eastward from German-speaking lands, mostly to the kingdom of Poland-Lithuania, both to escape persecution in the west and at the encouragement of King Casimir the Great. The area of settlement stretching across Eastern and Central Europe (Ashkenaz II) became the largest area of Jewish settlement, and the Yiddish language was spoken in the largest contiguous language area in Europe (with the exception of Russian).

In the nineteenth century many Ashkenazic Jews seeking economic opportunity, fleeing oppression, or both emigrated to the Americas, Australia, South Africa, and Israel (then Palestine). This Ashkenazic diaspora became the majority of Ashkenazic Jews with the destruction of the Jewish communities of Europe during the Second World War.

The first Jewish immigrants to the Americas were Sephardic, and until the 1820s, Ashkenazic Jews were a tiny minority within a minority of American Jewry. They initially settled primarily in urban centers of the Mid-Atlantic and New England coast, but have since settled throughout the United States.

The oldest Ashkenazic synagogue in America, established 1795, is Congregation Rodeph Shalom in Philadelphia.[2] Ashkenazic Jews from Western Europe began coming to the United States in large numbers in the 1820s and in even larger numbers from Eastern Europe in the 1880s. Jews were somewhat more likely to emigrate as families than groups such as Italians, among whom a majority of immigrants were men, and the Irish, among whom a majority were women.

Foodways

Ashkenazic foodways in America are the practices of individuals and communities informed by *kashruth*, the Jewish dietary laws, whether honored in observance or in the breach, the foodways of the coterritorial peoples, and by the shared Jewish requirements involving the Jewish ritual calendar and the Sabbath. The flavors most characteristic of the cuisine of Ashkenazic Jews from Central and Eastern Europe are salty and sour—smoked fish, smoked sturgeon stomachs, pickled cucumbers and other vegetables, pickled apples, sauerkraut with or without cranberries—and such seasonings as parsley, dill, and garlic. Knishes or *knishkes*, baked pastries stuffed with potato, cheese, kasha, or meat, are a favorite, as are *pirogen*, boiled dumplings made with pasta dough and filled with potatoes, cheese, or sour cherries. Breads include dark sour rye, Kaiser rolls or hard rolls, salt sticks, bagels, bialys, *malai* (cornbread), and *challah* for the Sabbath.

Ashkenazic cuisine is paradoxically the best-known and least familiar of the Jewish cuisines in America. This cuisine is best known in that some preparations, such as bagels, blintzes, and pickled cucumbers, are so familiar to Jewish and non-Jewish New Yorkers that they have become in the United States regional foods associated with New York rather than ethnic foods associated with Eastern Europe.[3]

This cuisine is, however, also the least familiar in that many dishes, such as organ meats, anything jellied, and some complex festive pastries have vanished entirely from the repertoire of North American Jews. *Ptcha*, a garlicky aspic made from jellied calves' feet, was a familiar and beloved dish in Eastern and Central Europe that has fallen out of favor and almost entirely vanished in America. While many Ashkenazic foods are identical or similar to non-Jewish coterritorial foods, a few dishes are understood to be uniquely Jewish developments. These are gefilte fish (literally, stuffed fish), which is made from forcemeat of freshwater fish. The forcemeat may be stuffed into a fish skin or formed into quenelles and poached in fish broth, or *yoykh*. *Kugel*, a substantial savory pudding of noodles, potatoes, or other starchy foods, and knishes are also eaten.

Sabbath Foods

Traditional Sabbath foods are rich, celebratory foods that can be prepared without cooking on the Sabbath itself. *Cholent*, a stew of beans and barley that may include *flanken* (top ribs) or similar cuts of meat, potatoes, and whole eggs, is cooked overnight in a low oven. Other traditional Sabbath foods include chicken broth, or *goldene yoykh*, especially with noodles, gefilte fish, *kugel*, especially noodle *kugel*, and *farfl*, bits of dried and toasted pasta dough that are cooked in water.

The Ashkenazic kitchen is distinguished as well by remedies for the sick, most famously chicken broth and also *gogl-mogl*, a tonic made with hot milk, honey or sugar, and egg yolks.

Holiday Meals

During the eight-day holiday of Passover, Jewish law forbids the consumption of leavened products made with wheat, oats, rye, spelt, or barley. Ashkenazic tradition broadens this prohibition to include rice, corn, legumes, and many other seeds and grains. Ashkenazic cuisine, like all Jewish cuisines, has a rich tradition of ingenious recipes for the home cook to make do with the limited ingredients permitted during Passover. Beloved recipes of the season include *kneydlekh* or *matzo* balls, the fluffy dumpling made from eggs, schmaltz or other fat, *matzo* meal, and seasonings; sponge cakes; nut cakes; potato pancakes; and *matzo brei*, an analog to French toast made of *matzo* soaked in beaten eggs and fried. Beginning in the second half of the twentieth century, an enormous industry has emerged to provide kosher-for-Passover foods, including highly processed grain-free cereals, noodles, cake mixes, pizzas, and other products craved by the grain deprived. There are many strategies for simulating the flavors and textures of grain products, most using potato starch and vegetable gums. The difficulties of preparing foods for Passover have inspired many to leave home entirely for the week, creating an industry to provide Passover vacations, tours, and cruises.

Challah

¾ cup warm water
3 packets active dry yeast
4½ eggs (leave over part of one egg for the glaze)
4 yolks (so that you have about 10 ounces eggs and yolks, combined; you can make it more or less yolky depending on your plans for the whites)
¼ cup olive oil
¼ cup honey
6½ cups bread flour (30 to 32 ounces)
4 teaspoons kosher salt
sesame or poppy seeds

Dissolve the yeast in the water. Add eggs, oil, honey, flour, and salt and work into a stiff dough. Knead the dough for about fifteen minutes and allow it to rise, covered, in a warmish place until doubled. Punch down the dough. At this point you can begin shaping the loaves, or allow the dough to rise overnight in the refrigerator.

Divide into twelve pieces and roll each piece into a smooth, seamless sphere. Roll each dough lump slightly to elongate. Go back to dough lump number one and roll each one a little more. Continue until you have twelve ropes about 12 to 15 inches long. Braid into two *challahs* of six strands each. To braid six strands, fasten them at the top, then move the leftmost rope to the center, and the rightmost but one to the left. Then move the rightmost to the center, and the leftmost but one to the right. Continue to the bottom and pinch the ends together.

Allow the *challahs* to rest 40 minutes or so. Preheat oven to 400 degrees. Brush with remaining half egg beaten with a teaspoon of water and sprinkle with sesame or poppy seeds. Bake for 30 minutes or until brown.

Matzo Balls (*Kneydlekh*)

4 eggs, extra large or jumbo
1 cup Streit's white *matzo* meal
½ cup melted butter, coconut oil, or olive oil, or a combination (traditionally *matzo*

balls would be made with schmaltz, rendered chicken or goose fat)
¼ cup water
1 tablespoon salt
black pepper, cayenne pepper, sweet paprika

Break eggs into a bowl. Season lavishly with salt, pepper, cayenne, and paprika. Add water and olive oil or melted butter. Beat the egg mixture and while beating gradually sprinkle in enough Streit's *matzo* meal to make a loose, muddy mixture. You will think that it is too soft, and you will be tempted to add more *matzo*. Valiantly resist this temptation! It is just right when it looks like it is still too loose. Refrigerate the mixture overnight.

Bring one or two (or three) large pots of wildly salted water to a boil. Roll dough into balls the size of walnuts. Lower the flame under the water slightly so that it is simmering serenely. Gently lower the *matzo* balls into the water. Leave enough room for the balls to double in size. After a minute or two you may raise the heat to boiling and cook, covered, with no peeking for one hour. If you use all whole wheat *matzo* meal, cooking time is longer and you will want to add a bit more butter. If you use all white *matzo* meal, cooking time is shorter.

Place in American Culture

Some Ashkenazic foods have become familiar and beloved staples of American foodways. Bagels can be purchased in McDonald's and Dunkin' Donuts. Levi's Rye bread used the images of American Indians, Quakers, and others in their advertisements to assure consumers that "you don't have to be Jewish" to love their product. Both Jewish breads that enjoy widespread popularity in America such as bagels and those such as *bialis*, a dry onion roll with an indentation in the center, that have not achieved the same crossover success, are prepared with more fat and sweetener in the New World than in the Old.

Ashkenazic cooks reacted to unfamiliar ingredients with varying degrees of enthusiasm. Adaptations of traditional recipes with New World ingredients such as salmon gefilte fish in the Pacific Northwest and pumpkin knishes and *challah* began appearing in Jewish cookbooks published in America.

Restaurants and Chefs

Ashkenazic restaurants are either *milkhik* (dairy) or *fleyshik* (meat) in accordance with *kashruth*, the Jewish dietary laws. Many contemporary Ashkenazic restaurants are not kosher but nevertheless observe the separation of traditional meat and dairy cuisines in their menus even while flouting the laws of *kashruth* in their kitchens.

A traditional dairy restaurant will serve blintzes, *pirogen* (*pierogi*), noodles with cottage cheese, egg dishes, soups, and fresh, cured, and smoked fish dishes (fish and eggs are considered *pareve*, neither meat nor dairy by the Jewish dietary laws).

Delicatessens and appetizing stores are two types of Ashkenazic retail establishments that have flourished in the Americas. Ashkenazic delicatessens specialize in cured meats and the distinctive mustard and pickles that accompany them. The meats of the standard delicatessen menu include corned beef, pastrami, tongue, salami, *knoblewurst*, and hot dogs. Sour rye bread, usually with caraway seeds, is the preferred staple. Jewish rye, confusingly, is sometimes still called "cornbread" in Ashkenazic bakeries and delicatessens because the Yiddish word for *rye* is *korn*, pronounced "corn."

Appetizing stores are the dairy analog to delicatessens. These stores specialize in smoked and cured fish such as salmon, mackerel, whitefish, herring, and sable, as well as candied fruits and roasted nuts. Appetizing stores have not enjoyed the crossover success of the Jewish delicatessen, and, with few exceptions, they are no longer a prominent part of the Ashkenazic foodscape.

Bakeries make the Ashkenazic breads mentioned above and pastries such as *rugelach* (small corners), cream cheese pastry filled with chopped nuts, jams, or chocolate; strudels filled with fruit, cheese, or savory cabbage; and *babkas*, coffeecakes made of rich yeast dough filled with nuts and cinnamon or chocolate.

Kosher restaurants in contemporary America frequently serve no traditional Jewish foods at all (while some restaurants that do serve traditional Ashkenazic foods are not kosher). Ashkenazic communities support kosher restaurants serving American, Italian, Indian, Chinese, and other cuisines. Since the end of the World War II, pizza has become enormously popular. If a community has only one kosher eating establishment, it will almost always be a pizzeria. Since the 1990s, sushi has joined pizza and *falafel* among the default kosher fast foods.

Notes

1. Max Weinreich and Yivo Institute for Jewish Research, *History of the Yiddish Language*, 2 vols., Yale Language Series (New Haven, CT: Yale University Press, 2008).
2. Hasia R. Diner, *A Time for Gathering: The Second Migration, 1820–1880*, The Jewish People in America (Baltimore: Johns Hopkins University Press, 1992).
3. In this, they follow many ethnic foods on the move. See William G. Lockwood and Yvonne R. Lockwood, "Ethnic Roots of American Regional Foods," in *Current Research in Culinary History: Sources, Topics, and Methods*, ed. Jillian Strang, Bonnie Brown, and Patricia Kelly (Radcliffe College, Cambridge, MA: Culinary Historians of Boston, 1986).

Further Reading

Diner, Hasia R. *A Time for Gathering: The Second Migration, 1820–1880*. The Jewish People in America. Baltimore: Johns Hopkins University Press, 1992.

Joselit, Jenna Weissman. "Jewish in the Dishes: Kashrut in the New World." In *The Americanization of the Jews*, edited by Robert M. Seltzer and Norman J. Cohen, 247–64. New York and London: New York University Press, 1995.

Kirshenblatt-Gimblett, Barbara. "Kitchen Judaism." In *Getting Comfortable in New York the American Jewish Home, 1880–1950*, edited by Susan L. Braunstein and Jenna Weissman Joselit, 75–105. Bloomington: Indiana University Press, 1991.

Levy, Esther. *Jewish Cookery Book, on Principles of Economy, Adapted for Jewish Housekeepers, with the Addition of Many Useful Medicinal Recipes, and Other Valuable Information, Relative to Housekeeping and Domestic Management*. Philadelphia: W. S. Turner, 1871.

Sarna, Jonathan. "How Matzah Became Square: Manischewitz and the Developement of Machine-Made Matzah in the United States." In *Sixth Annual Lecture of the Victor J. Selmanowitz Chair of Jewish History*. Touro College, New York, 2005.

Sternberg, Robert. *Yiddish Cuisine: A Gourmet's Approach to Jewish Cooking*. Northvale, NJ: J. Aronson, 1993.

Weinreich, Max, and Yivo Institute for Jewish Research. *History of the Yiddish Language*. Yale Language Series. 2 vols. New Haven, CT: Yale University Press, 2008.

Eve Jochnowitz

JEWISH-SEPHARDIC

(USA, North America) Jewish American Food, Sephardic Food

See also: Jewish Ashkanazi, Spanish.

In common parlance, Americans distinguish between *Ashkenazim* who comprise the majority of Jews in the United States, whose ancestry derives from Germany and Eastern Europe, and *Sephardim* who originate in Spain and Portugal. But there are many more ethnic groups represented within Judaism. There are *Mizrahim* including Iraqi and Syrian Jews, Yemenites, *Maghrebi* of Northern Africa, Italian Jews, Greek Romaniotes, even Indian and

Chinese Jews. The term *Sephardic* is complicated by the fact that it also denotes a distinct liturgy, and thus many Middle Eastern Jews are sometimes considered Sephardic although their ancestry is not from the Iberian Peninsula.

This entry focuses solely on Spanish and Portuguese Jews since the culinary traditions of this group are unique and still strongly reflect Iberian roots. How Sephardic Jews got to Spain, stayed there for nearly two millennia, and went from there to the eastern Mediterranean and then to America is a long and complicated story but bears brief discussion since numerous ingredients and culinary techniques were influenced by the path this community followed.

Background

All Jews ultimately originated in the ancient kingdoms of Judea and Israel. After the destruction of the first temple in 586 BC, a community of Jews was said to have escaped to the Iberian Peninsula, identified by the prophet Obadiah as Sepharad. Following a revolt against their Roman overlords, the second temple was also destroyed in AD 70, and Jews were dispersed in every direction, a process called the diaspora. One large group resettled in the Roman province of Hispania. They remained there among the Roman population that eventually converted to Christianity, then stayed among the Germanic Visigoths who ruled after the collapse of Rome. They also remained and prospered materially and intellectually among the Moors who conquered most of the peninsula in AD 711. A number of newly introduced ingredients such as eggplants and spinach were used in both Moorish and Jewish cooking, and they also shared similar food prohibition, particularly against pork.

The Sephardic people remained during the period of the Reconquista, too, when Christians took over piecemeal in the course of the next seven centuries, finally conquering the remaining Kingdom of Granada in 1492. In the same year the Jews were expelled from Spain and in 1497 from Portugal. Some went to the Netherlands and its colonies; some secretly escaped to the New World beyond the reach of the Inquisition and remained there nominally as Catholics, although sometimes still observing remnants of Jewish customs. In Northern Mexico and the Southwest of the United States, many people are now rediscovering their Sephardic heritage. A large proportion of Jews also remained in Spain as Christian converts or *Conversos*. Their secret practice of Judaic rites and dietary laws was a major reason the Inquisition was so important in Spain in the early modern period, mainly to undercover crypto-Jews, or *marranos*.

The majority of Sephardic Jews, however, emigrated under the protection of the Muslim Sultan of the Ottoman Empire, settling in what is today Turkey and Greece. Some also joined other communities in Northern Africa. Here they retained their culture and language (Ladino—a dialect of fifteenth-century Spanish with words borrowed from Turkish and Greek, and written in Hebrew characters). Most importantly, they retained their cuisine as a mark of identity. They adopted many Ottoman dishes, too, most notably the use of flaky pastries such as phyllo. The largest Sephardic populations were found in the cities of Salonika, Smyrna, Istanbul, and Kastoria.

A large portion of this community immigrated to North America and, to some extent, South America between 1880 and 1920, mostly driven out by Turkish nationalism and a Balkan war in 1912 to 1913. The majority went to New York, at least initially. They still spoke Ladino after four hundred years outside of Spain. Those who remained in the Balkans were almost completely decimated by the Nazis in World War II. Those who managed to leave before the war, about twenty-five thousand people, brought with them to America a cuisine completely different from Ashkenazic cooking, redolent with spices and vegetables and flavors one would not hesitate to call medieval. In the nearly two millennia of separation, they also practiced holidays and food rituals differently, and although Sephardic Jews have always been a minority within American Judaism, their food culture was so sharply distinguished that it was easily recognized as a cuisine unto itself.

To give a sense of the size of this community, keeping in mind many people are left unclassified because of mixed background or lapsed faith, of all Jews who comprise about 2 percent of the US population, somewhere between five and six million, only about 8 to 10 percent claim Sephardic heritage, which is about six hundred thousand. The American Sephardi Federation recognizes 112 congregations or community centers in the United States (excluding Yemeni, Persian, and Bukharan groups), mostly in the New York area, but also in Los Angeles, increasingly Florida and with communities in Seattle, Montgomery, Alabama, Indianapolis, and even Alaska. Some official congregations appear to consist only of a minimum of thirteen regular members.

The oldest of these synagogues, Sherith Israel in New Amsterdam, dates back to 1654, and others in Philadelphia, Newport, and Charleston are also of colonial origin. Nonetheless, it is difficult to speak of a cohesive community today after a great deal of intermarriage both with Ashkenazim and with non-Jews. Ironically, it may be among the only well-defined ethnic cuisines in America without a well-defined community.

Foodways

Apart from kosher rules that specify the avoidance of pork, shellfish, or mixing meat and milk in the same meal, Sephardic cooking bears little relation to well-known Ashkenazic cuisine. Like the language Ladino, Sephardic cooking is in many ways a rudiment of fifteenth-century Spanish cooking with various borrowings from Ottoman and Middle Eastern cookery. The use of spices and especially sugar in savory dishes harkens directly back to the Middle Ages. So, too, do various sour sauces and others incorporating nuts, as well as pastries and signature bean stews that were prepared before sundown and eaten during the Sabbath when no cooking could take place.

There are also unique dishes that one finds in no other cuisine, such as *huevos haminados*, which are hard-boiled eggs, originally roasted but more commonly boiled or baked in a pot of water for many hours until brown inside and deeply fragrant. Onion skins might be added to hasten the browning as well. These are served along with other feta or *kashkaval* cheese and watermelon or grapes with bread, perhaps even a sweet loaf such as *pandericas* flavored with grated orange peel, and perhaps a salad to constitute an entire meatless meal. Good olives are also requisite.

Another set of recipes use an oil-based dough that is wrapped around various fillings. The dough may be yeast raised, yielding small pies, but it is also often unrisen and crunchy. These are variously called *boyos*, *borekas* and *bolemas*, or *pastel* when cooking in a tray and sliced. These filled rolls are served for breakfast (*desayuno*) or as snacks when company arrives or starters for a meal. The most common fillings are a combination of spinach and feta bound with egg, which makes these a cousin of the familiar *spanakopita*. Leeks, eggplant, or ground meat can also go inside, or just cooked onions and cheese, perhaps bound with mashed potato. Olive oil is absolutely central to this cuisine and is used in all these pastries rather than butter.

Fish also plays a prominent role, especially when fried and seasoned with a sour vinegar or lemon-based sauce—which is a descendant of the medieval Spanish *escabeche*. Among the most distinctive meat dishes are those stews incorporating beans (*avas*), which were cooked slowly on Friday night to be eaten the next day on the Sabbath when no cooking could take place. These go by various names such as *hamin* or *adafina* and are closely related to the *cocidos* of late medieval Spain and the modern *cocido*

Madrileno. Smoke rising from a chimney on a Friday night was a telltale sign for early modern Inquisitors to see if a Converso family was secretly practicing Judaism.

A number of biscuits and sweets are also directly descended from old Spanish recipes. A *pan d'Espagna* or sponge cake (*pan esponjado*) is found in Mexico and even Japan, brought there by the Portuguese (*kasutera*), but it is also Sephardic. Sweet *roscas* (rolls), *susam* (sesame candy), *marzipan*, and *soplados* (a meringue) all have roots in Iberia. Added to these are the Ottoman *baklava*, *kataif*, and *loukum* (Turkish delight). These are not only desserts but also snacks one might offer guests or nibble on while playing cards in a coffee house, sipping *raki* (an anise-flavored spirit). *Biscochos* are a ubiquitous snack with coffee, and are dry, hard rings or twists, only slightly sweet, brushed with egg and sprinkled with sesame seeds. They are also called *taraleekos* or *coraleekos*.

Four centuries under Ottoman rule profoundly influenced Sephardic cuisine, so one finds not only baklava and Turkish-flavored meatballs, but stuffed grape leaves (*yaprak*) and a whole variety of stuffed vegetables such as peppers, eggplants, onions, and tomatoes.

But there are also recipes from Spain that have scarcely changed at all after five hundred years since the expulsion. Rice pudding with cinnamon and rose water, or cooked fruit desserts called *composto*, can be found in medieval cookbooks. A sauce called *almadrote*, made of cheese, breadcrumbs, garlic, and olive oil, usually served on eggplant, is also found in medieval cookbooks such as the *Libre de Sent Sovi* and *Rupert of Nola*. Another medieval rudiment is the *pepitada*—a milk drawn from melon seeds, not unlike almond milk, often drunk to break the Yom Kippur fast.

Panezico de Asucare or *Boyos Dulces*

Apparently adapted from *Cooking the Sephardic Way*, Sephardic Sisterhood of Tifereth Israel (Kansas City: North American Press, 1971) by Julia Albala before 1977. Some punctuation and orthography retained from the original.

4 cups of flour
1 cake yeast
1 egg
¼ cup oil
½ cup sugar
½ teaspoon cinnamon
pinch salt

Warm 2 cups water or milk, dissolve yeast in center of flour with water. Add egg into hole. Add oil, sugar, cinnamon and salt, make dough, bring it all together work until smooth. (Do not knead.) Cover for 1 hour then knead. Cover for ½ hour knead well. Form small roll and knead each roll. Feather top and top with beaten egg. Let sit while oven warms. Bake 375° on flour pan until done (golden brown), approximately 15 minutes.

Holiday Meals

Holiday celebrations are also quite different among Sephardim compared to Ashkenazim. In Passover, for example, five grains that might be used for leavened bread (barley, spelt, rye, oats, and wheat) are forbidden in both traditions, unless made into *matzo*, but rice and beans are allowed for Sephardim. The *kitniyot* (bits), which also include seeds such as sunflower, sesame, and mustard, as well as corn, were declared permissible by Rabbi Joseph Caro in the sixteenth century, but another ruling among Ashkenazi authorities thought it safer to ban them since they can be used as leaveners. The *Charoset*, a kind of fruit compote used on the seder plate, also tends to be more based on dried fruits, spices, and nuts. A whole set of dishes using *matzo* as the base rather than pastry are also common for Passover, and may be filled with leeks, spinach, or ground lamb, and are also called *pastel* or *mina*. There is also a special sweet made with *matzo* meal, walnuts, honey, and lemon juice called *cupeta*, which is baked in a tray and sliced into diamonds. A related recipe, also going back to Roman times, still exists in Southern Italy as well.

Other dishes are associated with particular holidays, such as doughnut-like fritters called *bimuelos* eating during Hanukkah. Since they are fried in oil, they recall a day's worth of oil lasting eight days in the Temple while under siege. With the same logic, fried leek patties, *keftes* or *albondigas de prasa*, are eaten, much like potato pancakes among the Ashkenazi.

During the festival of trees holiday of Tu B'shevat (called *Las Frutas*), fruits are served as well as a whole wheat pudding with nuts and cinnamon. This is called *colva* and is also traditionally presented to a family when a baby cuts his first tooth.

Place in American Culture

Although there are synagogues and groups that claim Sephardic ancestry and observe a distinct liturgy, the term *Sephardic* is used loosely to mean any group not Ashkenzi, thus encompassing a wide array of cultural and culinary practices. In the latter half of the twentieth century, an influx of Jews from across the Arab world further muddled this picture. In general, it is still useful to make a distinction for Jews of Spanish origin, because at least culturally they are Hispanic. Interestingly, in the early twentieth century, due to linguistic and to some extent gastronomic sensibilities, Sephardic immigrants preferred to live among Hispanics in neighborhoods such as Harlem or among Puerto Ricans and Cubans, with whom they also often worked in the garment industry.

The place of Sephardic cuisine in the United States has little to do with the surviving communities, though. In a sense it is well known, as evidenced by many cookbooks and featured stories in food magazines, precisely because is exotic, unexpected, and very different from Eastern European Jewish cooking. Its fascinating history also makes this cuisine a fascinating time capsule that has retained distinct features after so many centuries precisely because it has always been a minority culture surrounded by people of different faiths. Sephardic foods have thus become a powerful statement of identity.

Noted Restaurants and Chefs

Strangely, the interest in Sephardic culture has led to a tourist trade, mostly not in the United States but in Spain, and here one can find Sephardic restaurants such as El Fogón Sefardi in Segovia or Casa Mazal-Juderia in Cordoba. Spaniards, too, take an active interest in these. In the same spirit, a restaurant in Brooklyn called La Vara (named for a Sephardic newspaper published from 1922 to 1948) caters to a fascination with this little-known culture.

Further Reading

Anavi, Yvette. *Sephardic Cuisine*. Beyond Borders Publishing, 2000.

Angel, Gilda. *Sephardic Holiday Cooking: Recipes and Traditions*. Mount Vernon, NY: Decalogue, 2004

Ben-Ur, Aviva. *Sephardic Jews in America*. New York: New York University Press, 2012.

Cohen, Stella, and Marc Hoberman. *Stella's Sephardic Table: Jewish Family Recipes from the Mediterranean Island of Rhodes*. Cape Town, South Africa: Hoberman Collection 2012.

Dobrinsky, Herbert C. *A Treasury of Sephardic Laws and Customs: The Ritual Practices of Syrian, Moroccan, Judeo-Spanish and Spanish and Portuguese Jews of North America,* rev. ed. Hoboken: Ktav; New York: Yeshiva University Press, 1988.

Gerber, Jane S. *Jews of Spain*. New York: Free Press, 1994.

Gitlitz, David, and Linda Kay Davidson. *A Drizzle of Honey*. New York: St. Martin's Press, 1999.

Goldstein, Joyce, and Beatriz da Costa. *Sephardic Flavors*. San Francisco: Chronicle, 2000.

Marks, Copeland. *Sephardic Cooking*. New York: Plume, 1995.

Marks, Gil. *Encyclopedia of Jewish Food*. Hoboken: John Wiley & Sons, 2000.

Miner, Viviane. *From My Grandmother's Kitchen: A Sephardic Cookbook.* Gainesville, FL: Triad, 1984.

Roden, Claudia. *The Book of Jewish Food: An Odyssey from Samarkand to New York.* New York: Knopf, 1996

Sternberg, Robert. *The Sephardic Kitchen: The Healthy Food and Rich Culture of the Mediterranean Jews.* New York: William Morrow, 1996.

Twena, Pamela Grau. *The Sephardic Table: The Vibrant Cooking of the Mediterranean Jews.* New York: Houghton Mifflin, 1998.

Ken Albala

JORDAN

(Western Asia) Jordanian American Food
See also: Israel, Palestine, Lebanon, Syria, and Turkey.

Background

Jordan is a country in an area in the eastern Mediterranean known as the Levant, a geographical and cultural region with an ancient and very rich history. The Levant is a term referring to the shared history, heritage, and modern culture connecting Cyprus, Israel, Palestine, Jordan, Lebanon, Syria, and Turkey. Jordan also shares physical borders with Israel and Palestine to the east, Syria to the north, Iraq to the northeast, and Saudi Arabia to the southeast. Ancient trade and pilgrimage routes, namely the King's Highway, crossed Jordan, and from a culinary perspective, they brought in new foodstuffs such as rice and spices.

Though Jordanian cuisine overlaps in many ways with its neighbors, it also has a distinct culinary tradition of its own, growing out of Bedouin culture. The Bedouin—nomadic and seminomadic herders living in the sprawling deserts of Jordan—developed ways of cooking that used the foods readily available to them: dairy and meat products from sheep and goats.

The climate and geography also heavily influences the cuisine of Jordan: it is one of the driest countries in the world and is made up of about 85 percent desert. To the north, the climate is ideal for growing huge expanses of olive trees. Despite (or perhaps due to) the dryness of the climate, parts of Jordan produce wheat and flavorful fruits and vegetables.

Jordanians began immigrating to the United States in earnest just after World War II. Post–World War II to the late 1980s mark periods characterized by conflict, revolution, and a struggling economy stemming from Palestinian resistance to Israeli occupation. These decades saw many Jordanians immigrating to the United States. US Census records show that as of 2011, an estimated 72,730 people reported Jordanian ancestry, with an estimated 63,334 claiming Jordanian birth. Since 1940, the number of Jordanians obtaining legal permanent resident status in the United States has increased from three during the period of 1940 to 1949 to 53,550 in the period of 2000 to 2009, with the most significant jump during the 1970s, a period of time marked by civil war in Jordan and its aftermath. The vast majority of Jordanians that have immigrated to the United States have historically been Eastern Orthodox Christian, while Jordan's population is over 90 percent Sunni Muslim.

Like many other recent immigrant groups, Jordanians tend to immigrate to places in the United States with established Jordanian and Arabic communities and also tend to retain many of their traditions from home. The first Jordanian American communities emerged in New York but now exist all over the United States. Within the context of the Arab American population, Jordanian Americans only make up about 3 percent of this demographic. Significant populations are difficult to nail down since most large Arab American communities reflect this nationwide average. Keeping this in mind, large communities of Jordanian Americans live in Illinois (Chicago), California (Los Angeles, Orange County), New York, and New Jersey (New York City metropolitan area).

Foodways

Much of Jordanian food shares ingredients and dishes with the surrounding region. Differences emerge in how a dish is prepared and served. Typical staple foods for Jordanian Americans are very much the same as they are in Jordan. Fats include olive oil and tahini; starches and carbohydrates are bulgur wheat, *freekeh* (roasted green wheat), rice, and various types of flatbreads (*pita*, or *khubz*, mostly due to its availability). Dairy products are significant parts of the diet—goat's milk or cow's milk yogurt, *labneh* (strained and salted yogurt), and *jameed* (dried and salted yogurt), as are legumes, especially chickpeas and lentils. Meat features lamb, beef, chicken, and fish, and typical fruits and vegetables are tomatoes, cucumbers, eggplant, cauliflower, onions, grape leaves, squash, arugula, and lemons. Typical spices and flavorings are mint, garlic, sumac, *za'atar* (an all-purpose spice mix of thyme, sumac, salt, and toasted sesame seeds, with many variations), cinnamon, clove, coriander, cumin, allspice, cardamom, orange flower water, and rosewater. Drinks are frequently lemonade blended with mint, wine (if Christian), Turkish and Arabic coffee, and sweetened black tea with mint.

Many Jordanian ingredients are commonly found in mainstream American supermarkets while, specialized ingredients and prepared foods are available in Middle Eastern or Mediterranean markets located in areas with a large Arabic, Greek, or Turkish populations. Though finding ingredients is relatively easy, the quality is not always the same. Foods such as *jameed*, sumac, *za'atar*, and olive oil are commonly brought back from trips to Jordan. The humidity in most areas of the United States makes it difficult to make their own *jameed* at home as done traditionally, but *labneh* is easily made: once the salted yogurt is strained of all its whey and is thick enough to form into balls, the balls are preserved in olive oil and sometimes herbs. Due to California's comparable climate to Jordan, some specialty, seasonal produce, particularly green almonds and green cherries, can be procured in farmer's markets.

As in Jordan, women still do most of the cooking in Jordanian American households, although this is changing. In Jordan, it is very common to cook more food than is needed by a single family on a daily basis as guests are always expected to stop by one's home and it is customary to offer them something to eat almost immediately. In the United States, guests do not drop by as often, but large quantities of food are still made out of habit, and sometimes shared with neighbors. Labor-intensive dishes are usually made by a group of women as a social activity in preparation for a special occasion or family gathering.

For Jordanian Americans, everyday meals vary from family to family but most likely incorporate some American elements due to convenience or changing tastes. Some Jordanian Americans may start their day with a typical Jordanian breakfast: *foul* (a dish of mashed fava beans with olive oil, lemon juice, onion, garlic, cumin, and parsley), *hummus* (a dip made with chickpeas, tahini, olive oil, lemon juice, and garlic), *labneh*, *pita* bread, and pickled vegetables. However, Jordanian Americans rely more on typically American breakfast fare, or a simplified version of a Jordanian breakfast consisting of kitchen staples: flatbread with *labneh* and olive oil.

These breakfast dishes are also part of a typical *mezze*—an array of small dishes meant to be shared as a meal or as appetizers to a main dish. Other *mezze* dishes include *moutabel* (roasted eggplant pureed with olive oil, tahini, and garlic); *wara' aynab* (also *dawali*), known by Americans as *dolma* (grape leaves stuffed with spiced ground beef or lamb, rice, minced vegetables, and herbs and served hot); *falafel* (deep-fried balls made with ground chickpeas, parsley, garlic, and spices); and *kubbeh* (deep-fried croquettes made from ground meat, bulgur wheat, herbs, and spices) and *kubbeh nayyeh* (a similar dish served raw). Some of these dishes are particularly time intensive, so they are either store bought when available or made in groups for special occasions.

Most everyday meals for Jordanian Americans forego *mezze* and follow a standard American format: a salad, perhaps an additional vegetable side, and a main dish. Coffee and black tea are taken continually throughout the day and are always offered to guests in abundance.

As in Jordan, salad is an integral part of any meal. A salad could be typically Jordanian: *tabouleh* (bulgur and finely chopped mint, parsley, tomatoes, and onion dressed with olive oil and lemon juice), arugula salad (arugula dressed with olive oil and lemon juice), or the ubiquitous *s'laata* (tomato, cucumber, onion, mint, parsley, olive oil, lemon juice, and sumac). A salad could also resemble something more typical to Americans: lettuce with whatever vegetables are handy, tossed in a familiar dressing of mint, lemon juice, olive oil, and garlic.

Commonly cooked main dishes include: *magloobeh* (a dish translated as "upside down," with meat, roasted eggplant, and cauliflower, rice and spices cooked in layers with chicken broth and spices and turned upside down before serving), *mujaddara* (lentils, rice, and onions fried until crisp in a large quantity of olive oil), *rashouf* (a soup made with lentils, yogurt, and rice), and *saniyat dajaj* (chicken baked with potatoes, tomatoes, onions, and spices).

Holiday Feasts

Depending on their religious background, major feasting holidays for Jordanian Americans are Easter, Christmas, *Eid al-Fitr*, and *Eid al-Adha*. Feasts can also be held to celebrate weddings, baptisms, and other big family gatherings. Holidays are spent either gathering at a family member's or friend's home or with Jordanian or Arabic community associations in a large gathering space.

In the United States, special occasion meals will typically include dishes that are normally too labor intensive to make on a regular basis. Feasts can start with *mezze*, leisurely eaten in the living room. Special main dishes may include *kousa mahshi* (summer squash stuffed with ground meat, rice, and spices and typically cooked and served with stuffed grape leaves) and *mansaf* (lamb cooked in a yogurt sauce made with *jameed*, topped with pine nuts, almonds, and more yogurt sauce and served on top of aromatic rice), known as the national dish of Jordan and the crowning glory of any feast. Some families choose to eat their first few bites of *mansaf* with their right hands to honor the way Jordanians have eaten for thousands of years.

Typical desserts include *knafe* (a cheese pastry made with shredded filo dough and flavored with orange blossom or rose water) and *hareesa* (a cake made from semolina flour and flavored with orange flower or rose water).

Place in American Culture

Americans are more likely to be familiar with Jordanian food when referred to as "Mediterranean" or "Middle Eastern" food. Though specific Jordanian variations on this cuisine may not be widely known, most major cities in the United States will have restaurants with dishes similar to those outlined above. In addition, foods such as *pita*, *hummus*, and *moutabel* (known in the United States as *baba ganoush*) can now be considered refrigerator staples for many Americans and are available in many major grocery stores around the country.

Notable Restaurants and Chefs

Restaurants owned by Jordanians do not often advertise as serving specifically Jordanian food, as the more general Mediterranean, Middle Eastern, or Arabic descriptors are far more familiar to most Americans. As such, it is very difficult to determine which restaurants are owned by Jordanians or serve Jordanian food. One can get a very good impression of Jordanian food by eating in Mediterranean, Middle Eastern, or Arabic establishments, but a specialty dish such as *mansaf* is served at only a limited number of restaurants and is a good indicator of additional Jordanian-tinged dishes on the menu.

Further Reading

Abu-Jaber, Diana. *The Language of Baklava.* New York City: Pantheon, 2005.

The Electronic Encyclopedia of Chicago. "Jordanians," by Stephen R. Porter. Accessed September 16, 2014. http://www.encyclopedia.chicagohistory.org/pages/677.html.

Hourani, Cecil. "Jordan." In *The Oxford Companion to Food*, 3rd ed. Edited by Tom Jaine. Oxford: Oxford University Press, 2014.

Hourani, Cecil. *Jordan: The Land and the Table*. London: Elliott & Thompson, 2006.

Cecilia Peterson

K

KAZAKHSTAN
See entry for Central Asia.

KENYA
(East Africa) Kenyan American Food

Background
There are 88,519 immigrants of Kenyan origin in the United States, according to the 2010 American Communities Survey. These immigrants come from diverse economic and ethnic backgrounds in Kenya, which has over forty ethnic groups. These ethnic groups have distinct traditional staples that shaped the migration history and cultural traditions of the group, and by the particular climatic conditions of the settled regions that have in turn determined the kinds of crops that can be grown. As an example, the Luo, who settled in western Kenya, consume fish and *ugali* (a hard mash cooked from milled or stone ground maize/sorghum and millet). In contrast, beans, maize, and potatoes are the staple foods for the Kikuyu in central Kenya.

In addition to specific staple foods consumed by particular ethnic groups, there is a national cuisine of sorts that has been shaped by Kenya's trading and settlement history stretching as far back as the eighth century. Arab and Persian traders reputed to have reached Kenya by the seventh century settled the coast and had a major influence on the coastal cuisine and culture. Once associated with a regional cuisine, coastal dishes with an Arab influence are now popular throughout Kenya. Another major influence of Arab and Persian culture on Kenyan cuisine is in the use of spices typically used in Middle Eastern cuisine, including cumin, cardamom, and cinnamon.

European culture also has had an impact on the country's cuisine. This is linked to the country's colonial history as part of the British East Africa protectorate established in 1895 and then becoming a Kenyan colony in 1920. A direct influence of British culture can be seen in the Kenyan love of sausages, fish and chips, and tea! Indirectly, starting in 1895, about thirty-two thousand Indian laborers were brought to the Kenyan colony to construct the Kenyan-Ugandan railway. Many of these laborers settled in Kenya after the railway completion in 1903 and were later joined by voluntary migrants and family from India.

Indian cuisine has had a particularly major influence on Kenya cuisine, with dishes such as *pilau* (rice with vegetables or meat), *chapati* (a flat wheat bread), and Indian-style curries being particularly popular in Kenya today for holidays, festivities, and special occasions. Similarly, the Indian *samosa*, a savory pastry filled with meat, is now a wildly popular snack as an accompaniment to 10 o'clock and 4 o'clock tea. Since independence in 1964, increased mobility and urbanization have also made some ethnic staples more widely consumed. This has included *ugali* and *githeri* (maize and beans cooked together) and *sukuma wiki* (collared greens fried with onions and tomatoes), which are now eaten as staples in many households regardless of ethnic group.

Foodways
Kenyan immigrants carry these influences with them when they migrate to the United States.

Kenyans are finicky eaters, and most households seek to re-create Kenyan dishes on a regular basis. Typical staples in Kenyan American homes include *ugali*, chicken or beef stew, *sukuma wiki*, *gatheri* rice, bean stew, fruits, and vegetables. Other signature dishes such as *pilau*, *biriani*, *samosa*, and *nyama choma* (meat, preferably goat, grilled over glowing charcoal) are prepared during special occasions and festivities. Festivities include public holidays in Kenya such as Independence Day, Christmas, and Ramadan. Kenyans also gather in each other's homes on weekends, at church, and as part of professional or business groups. At such occasions Kenyan food is cooked and eaten, and there is a celebration of Kenyan culture, including speaking Swahili and listening to Kenyan music.

Typically women cook these dishes in Kenya, with men specifically tasked with slaughtering animals and roasting meat. Many of these dishes take significant time to prepare, including regular trips to the market to purchase fresh ingredients, and they have long cooking times. In Kenya, homes may have more than one adult woman in the household, meaning grocery shopping, meal preparation, and cooking roles can be shared. In the United States, gendered roles are somewhat relaxed, with more Kenyan American men carrying out more domestic work including cooking, grocery shopping, and cleaning up.

Few grocery stores cater directly to East African consumers in the United States; however, most ingredients used in Kenyan cuisine can be found with ease. Spices can be found at large grocery stores even in smaller towns. Rarer spices are normally sold in Indian or Middle Eastern ethnic food stores in larger towns. Specialty meats such as goat can be bought directly from farmers or from ethnic stores that stock goat meat from New Zealand and Australia. Starchy foodstuffs including cooking bananas and milled cornflour are sold at ethnic stores selling Latino or West African food. Fruits and vegetables, which are preferred fresh, can be bought at large grocery stores, although most Kenyan Americans complain about the quality and taste of these foods. For example, although mangoes and bananas can be bought at almost any store in the United States, the taste is quite diminished compared to fresh fruit bought in a Kenyan market.

Although these ingredients are similar to ones used in Kenya, modifications in cooking techniques or length of cooking time are often necessary to accommodate different varieties or tastes. As an example, in Kenya, fresh goat meat is grilled over charcoal or an open fire and then consumed with *ugali* and *kachumbari* (a salsa-like accompaniment specifically made for meat, made of diced tomatoes, red pepper, cilantro, lemon, grated carrots, and red onion). In many places in the United States, however, goat meat can only be bought frozen. In addition, the taste of the meat from New Zealand and Australia is somewhat different since other goat breeds are raised in these countries. To retain a Kenyan flavor, the meat may be marinated before grilling or may also be cooked in a curry, therefore diminishing the difference in taste.

Because of the difference in the taste and in order to reduce time and labor spent cooking and searching for ingredients, most Kenyan American homes have incorporated American cuisine into their diet. Most Kenyan Americans consume significant amounts of American foods ranging from pasta to burgers to tacos. The cost of meats in the United States also has an influence on the diet. Although beef is consumed more often in Kenya, chicken is cheaper in the United States. As a result, more chicken is consumed in Kenyan American homes than would normally be consumed in Kenya.

A Kenyan Staple: Meat Stew and Rice
Meat Stew:

This requires two pounds of beef cut into small pieces. Grass-fed beef produces a flavor that is closest to Kenyan beef. Also, cuts that have a little marbling produce a better flavor than completely lean meat. If using beef with a little marbling, reduce the amount of vegetable or olive oil used.

> 1 cup beef stock
> 1 large yellow onion, peeled and diced
> about 2 tablespoons of cooking oil (vegetable oil or olive oil)
> 3 carrots, peeled and sliced
> 3 medium-sized red potatoes (or any potatoes really) peeled and cubed (red potatoes are preferred because they are firm and hold their shape in the stew better)
> salt to taste
> 1 teaspoon tomato paste
> 2 garlic cloves (skip if you don't like the taste or smell of garlic)
> Optional: 1 teaspoon curry powder

To prepare: Cook onions in oil over medium low heat until soft and just beginning to brown. Add meat, stir, and cover when juices begin to froth. Cook covered until meat juices have dried. Add diced carrots and cook, stirring often for one minute. Add potatoes and cook, stirring for one minute. If using curry powder, please add at this stage. Add tomato paste and stir for approximately one minute. Add beef stock to the pot and mix ingredients well until tomato paste is completely dissolved. Taste broth to determine whether additional salt is needed. Add more salt to the stew if desired. Simmer over low heat until vegetables are tender and meat is cooked to desired softness. Once meat is ready, add crushed garlic and cook for an additional minute.

Steamed Rice

> 1 cup basmati rice (preferably authentic basmati bought from an Indian food store)
> 2 tablespoons olive oil
> 2 cups water
> salt to taste, approximately ½ teaspoon
> optional: you can add chicken boullion to the water if a more savory taste is desired

To prepare: Boil water over high heat. While water is cooking, put rice in a strainer and rinse thoroughly under cold water. Once water boils, add olive oil and salt. Add rice and reduce heat to low. Cook covered over low heat until all the water is absorbed. Remove from heat and keep covered until ready to serve.

You can also add coconut milk to make coconut rice. If adding coconut milk, reduce cooking water by ½ cup. Follow the rest of the steps outlined above. When half of the water is absorbed, add ½ cup of coconut milk and fluff rice gently with fork. Reduce to very low heat. It is important to add the coconut milk later and cook over very low heat so as to prevent the rice from sticking to the bottom of the pan.

Serve meat stew and rice with steamed, green leafy vegetables (kale, spinach, or Swiss chard).

Place in American Culture

Kenyan food is not as well known as some other African cuisines, such as Ethiopian or Moroccan. East African food cultures generally have not been embraced by mainstream American food culture.

Noted Restaurants and Chefs

Kenyan restaurants exist in in larger cities with large African immigrant populations, such as New York City or Chicago, but they also appear occasionally in smaller but more cosmopolitan, "adventurous" cities such as Santa Fe, New Mexico, which hosts the Jambo Café, run by a chef from Kenya. Its menu is typical of many African restaurants trying to reach a broader clientele outside its specific ethnic group, and its website describes it as offering the flavors of Africa and the Caribbean (http://www.jambocafe.net/about/).

Further Reading

Goody, Jack. *Cooking, Cuisine, and Class: A Study in Comparative Sociology*. Cambridge: Cambridge University Press, 1982.

Harris, Jessica B. *The Africa Cookbook: Tastes of the Continent.* New York: Simon and Schuster, 1998.

McCann, James C. *Maize and Grace: Africa's Encounter with a New World Crop, 1500–2000.* Cambridge, MA: Harvard University Press, 2005.

McCann, James C. *Stirring the Pot: A History of African Cuisine.* Athens: Ohio University Press, 2009.

Osseo-Asare, Fran. *Food Culture in Sub-Saharan Africa.* Westport, CT: Greenwood, 2005.

Samuelsson, Marcus. *The Soul of a New Cuisine: A Discovery of the Foods and Flavors of Africa.* New York: Houghton Mifflin Harcourt, 2006.

Van der Post, Laurens. *African Cooking.* New York: Time-Life Books, 1970.

Sheila Navalia Onzere, with research assistance by Baily M. Cameron

KIRIBATI
(Micronesia, Oceania)
See entry on Micronesia (Micronesian American).
Micronesia includes Guam, Marshall Islands, Palau, Kiribati, Federated States of Micronesia, Nauru, Northern Mariana Islands.

KOREA, NORTH
(Eastern Asia) Korean American Food
Included in entry on Korea (Korea, South).

North Korea is officially the Democratic People's Republic of Korea. On the northern half of the peninsula of Korea, it split from the southern half, South Korea, in 1946 with a communist government backed by Soviet support. Soviet troops left in 1948, but it has continued under communist rule with Chinese support. Its citizens are not allowed to immigrate to the United States, although Koreans from both the northern and southern parts of the peninsula did come to the United States prior to the establishment of the two countries and consider themselves as belonging to one nation and culture. Both groups are referred to as Korean American.

KOREA, REPUBLIC OF (SOUTH KOREA)
(East Asia) Korean American Food
(Includes North Korea)

Background
The history of Korean American food is relatively short. The first wave of Korean immigrants were brought to Hawaii as contract laborers on sugar plantations in 1903 to 1905. In 1905 the Korean immigration to America abruptly halted because Japan took over Korea as its protectorate, thus usurping Korea's rights for diplomacy with other countries. In 1908, the Roosevelt administration entered into an agreement with Japan, known as the Gentlemen's Agreement, that allowed Japanese immigrant men in America to bring their wives to the United States. Thus, the so-called picture-bride program started. Consequently, when Japan made Korea its colony in 1910, Korean men residing in America were allowed to bring their wives or picture brides. Between 1910 and 1924, a total of eight hundred Korean women came to America to join their husbands. Young Korean students came to America either to study or to work in the hope of helping their countrymen to regain their freedom. Included among them was Syngman Rhee, first president of the Republic of Korea in 1948.

With immigration restrictions, after the Korean War, only women married to service men, their families, or adopted orphans were allowed into the United States. After the passage of the 1965 Immigration Act, when national origin quotas were removed, larger numbers of Koreans began to arrive. According to 2010 Census data, there are approximately 1.4 million Korean Americans, constituting nearly .4 percent of the total US population. Large Korean enclaves have been established in Los Angeles, New York, and New Jersey, with smaller K-towns in most major cities.

Foodways

Traditional Korean cuisine is centered around rice, which is often prepared with beans, barley, or other grains. Accompanying it is a form of soup or stew, grilled fish, or meat. These are often highly seasoned, including combinations of garlic, ginger, red or black pepper, scallions, soy sauce, sesame oil, and sesame seeds. Along with each meal is a variety of side dishes called *banchan*. These small dishes are often composed of blanched, boiled, pan-fried, or steamed vegetables, along with an assortment of pickled items called *kimchi*. With the traditional meal, all dishes are served at the same time, with the soups boiling hot and with everyone eating directly from the same receptacle. Meals are eaten with thin, metal chopsticks and a long spoon.

Kimchi is vital to both traditional and modern Korean and Korean American meals. Given the Korean peninsula's mountainous landscape and dramatically different climate differences, early Korean foodways relied heavily on methods of preserving foods with the use of salt. While salt preservation of a variety of foraged and farmed vegetables had been prevalent in early Korean foodways, with the introduction of the red pepper (*gochu*) in 1592, the taste and texture of *kimchi* changed dramatically. During the nineteenth century, nappa cabbage was cultivated specifically for the production of *kimchi*. This is the form most prevalent on tables today; however, even cabbage *kimchi* varies dramatically based on region. The most common seasonings include brine, scallions, ginger, garlic, fish sauce, and salted shrimp called *saeujeot*. In the southern areas where the winters are less harsh, *kimchi* contains high levels of salt, chili peppers, and brined fish. In the northern regions, *kimchi* is often more watery and replaces fresh for brined seafood. Other common varieties are made from daikon radishes, cucumbers, mustard greens, and scallions.

Traditionally, *kimchi* was buried in clay pots for a significant amount of time to produce fermentation. Today, the advent of technology such as the *kimchi* refrigerator and massive supermarkets has shortened the process to about a week from mixing to ready to serve and has obviated the need for *kimchi* production in strict accordance to the availability of seasonal produce.

The rise of *kimchi* as Korea's most quintessential food was neither accidental nor natural, however. Continued efforts of the Korean government have propelled *kimchi* into its status of a national food. The government has not only promoted the production of the dish through scientific research into *kimchi* making, packing, preservation, and nutrition but also actively works to educate the public. School textbooks at all levels include sections on Korean foods such as *kimchi* and *doenjang* (fermented bean paste), and all elementary school lunches are required to include *kimchi*. The government also has actively worked to commercialize and export *kimchi* to the international community. The 1984 LA Olympics, 1988 Seoul Olympics, and 2002 Korea-Japan World Cup were all arenas where the Korean government presented *kimchi* as a national food to the international market.

Alcohol also plays an important role in Korean culture. *Soju* is the most popular beverage. It was traditionally made from grains such as rice, wheat, or barely, but modern producers have replaced these with starches such as sweet potato. *Makgeolli*, a cloudy white, unfiltered rice wine served in bowls, has also made a resurgence in popularity. Korean's strict culture of etiquette extends to its drinking culture. One never pours his or her own drink; rather, two hands are used when receiving or pouring for an elder. It is also customary to turn away from the elder when drinking the beverage. Drinks must also not be refilled unless they are entirely empty. Drinking is also accompanied by foods designed to be eaten with alcohol called *anju*. While these may be simply nuts and fruit, they may also include more substantial, heavily flavored or fried foods. One example that has gained popularity both in Korea and in the United States is fried chicken. Unlike that typically found in America, Korean fried chicken is fried twice, usually seasoned with spices, sugar, and salt prior to and after each frying; some have garlicky, sticky sauces, while others focus on thin, crispy skin. Platters of fried chicken are served alongside beer or occasionally *soju* but are rarely eaten as a meal in Korea.

Modern Korean food has been heavily influenced by globalization. While grilled, marinated meats such as the thinly sliced *bulgogi* or sliced short ribs called *galbi* are still available, more and more Koreans are using foreign ingredients such as olive oil and cilantro in their daily meals. In fact, Western chains have risen in popularity introducing items such as pasta, Belgian waffles, and doughnuts, and iced coffees can be found on many retail-lined streets in Seoul.

Bulgogi tends to be a popular dish among Americans, partly because it is not as spicy as some other Korean foods. Also, it is usually served with rice and side dishes of *kimchi* that can be added according to the eater's tastes.

Bulgogi ("Fire Meat") or "Korean Barbecue"

Marinate overnight in the refrigerator:

- 1 to ½ pounds beef in paper-thin slices and small pieces. (Some mainstream American grocery stores actually sell "*Bulgogi* meat" in the deli section. Otherwise, it is usually the meat from the back, between the ribs. A little bit of marbling is good.)
- 4 green onions sliced long ways
- 4 cloves garlic, minced
- 4 teaspoons sesame seeds
- 4 teaspoons sesame oil
- 5 tablespoons soy sauce
- ½ cup brown sugar
- ¼ teaspoon black pepper

Mix all ingredients together to form a sauce. Pour it over the beef and mix it thoroughly. Let the meat marinate for at least 1 hour.

The traditional method of cooking is to grill on a special slotted pan over charcoal or an open flame (gas ranges work for this). Otherwise, you can either spread on a baking dish and broil or cook quickly in a frying pan with small amount of beef stock for extra "juice." (For a vegetarian version, use tofu or tempeh. The sauce is delicious on any kind of meat. Also, sliced mushrooms, onions, or other vegetables can be marinated and cooked along with the meat.)

Place in American Culture

Korean immigrants have brought with them the basis of traditional Korean foods such as *gochujang*, a paste made from the same chili peppers found in *kimchi*, and *doenjang*. Traditional dishes were re-created and new ones invented. One example is *soondubu jjigae*, a spicy, soft tofu soup that usually contains seafood such as oysters, mussels, clams, and shrimp, along with vegetables, onions, scallions, and *gochujang* and chili powder. The dish is served with a raw egg that is cracked into the boiling hot liquid. An immigrant, Hee Sook Lee, created the dish in Los Angeles when she opened BCD Tofu House in 1996. Lee went on to export the dish and her restaurant empire back to Korea and China.

Today Korean American food follows much the same trend of modern Korean food. While traditional Korean restaurants can be found in virtually every American city, along with an increase of large Korean supermarkets, such as the chain Hmart, Korean ingredients and culinary methods are influencing the American mainstream. This is in part due to Korean immigrants' role in the food industry. Many immigrants have established bodegas, greengrocers, and convenience stores in metropolitan areas. These shop owners began to serve traditional deli items with the addition of a few

Korean ones like *kimbap*, rice (*bap*), and vegetables, scrambled egg and/or seasoned beef, and pickled radish wrapped in sheets of dried seaweed (*gim*) or *jeon*, a pancake with meat, vegetables, and/or *kimchi*. Cheesesteaks were occasionally made with bulgogi. Now many delis serve more *bibimbap* (literally, mixed rice), a bowl of rice topped with seasoned vegetables, egg, and *gochujang* that is stirred together just prior to eating.

The Korean American supermarket chain, Hmart, has also helped familiarize the American public to Korean food and ingredients. Now located in eleven states, this large supermarket features a large *banchan* area where patrons can purchase their side dishes. Cooking demonstrations and sampling are promoted by the company to help teach consumers about the items in the store. However, Korean foods are not limited to small mom-and-pop markets or to Hmart; they are also found in mainstream American grocery stores. Along with *kimchi*, individual packs of roasted seaweed, called *gim*, were first found in health food stores and specialties stores such as Trader Joes but have moved into large national retailers.

Restaurants

While gaining in popularity, but still behind Chinese, Japanese, Thai, and Vietnamese, Korean restaurants in the United States traditionally catered to a Korean (or adventurous American) clientele. The food was often called too fishy or too garlicky, too smelly, or too spicy by those unfamiliar with the flavor profile. These ideas were reinforced by shows like *M*A*S*H* that emphasized the foreignness of *kimchi*. Many Korean immigrants opted to open Chinese, Japanese, or generic Asian fusion restaurants to cater to the American palate.

Like those found in Korea, Korean American foodways evolved over time, influenced by the American mainstream and the availability of ingredients, but also changes in Seoul restaurants and immigrant contact with other minority groups. Over the last ten years, Korean food has gained notoriety. Two Korean American chefs are focusing on bringing Korean flavors to the public at two ends of the culinary spectrum. Roy Choi's fusion Korean-Mexican food truck Kogi BBQ has popularized the Korean taco. The tortillas are topped with *galbi*, *daeji bulgolgi* (spicy thinly sliced pork), or tofu along with salsa and fresh *kimchi*. Iterations of Choi's famous taco can now be found across the country from hip New York eateries to Midwestern chain restaurants. On the other end of the spectrum, New York chef David Chang has elevated Korean American cuisine with his Michelin-stared Momofuku restaurant group. Both Choi and Chang use traditional Korean ingredients and techniques while departing from the traditional Korean meal.

Traditional Korean restaurants are also gaining in popularity. While early Korean establishments served a hodgepodge of Korean dishes, new restaurants are focusing on a specific type of dish—for instance, places that focus on *seolleongtang*, a soup made from slowly simmering ox bones until the broth is milky white. The plain soup is usually garnished with a few radishes and brisket in the restaurant; salt, ground pepper, and green onions are added by the diner at the table. Another style of Korean restaurant that is gaining popularity is Korean Chinese food. Due to geographical proximity, most Korean Chinese food is highly influenced by Northern cuisines from areas such as Beijing and Shandong. The dishes served in these restaurants are more closely identifiable as Korean rather than traditional Chinese. *Jajangmyeon* are noodles served with a salty black bean paste, diced beef or pork, and vegetables such as zucchini, potatoes, and onions. The dish is served with a side of pickled radish called *danmuji* and sliced raw onions that are dipped in bean paste. This dish is based on but is distinctly different from Chinese *zhajiang mian*. Other popular Korean Chinese dishes include a spicy seafood soup with thick chewy noodles called *jjamp-*

pong, a version of sweet and sour beef called *tangsuyuk*, and a sweet and spicy, deep-fried pork dish called *kkanpunggi*. In Korea, these dishes are delivered with the same frequency as pizza in America; however, in the United States most restaurants focus primarily on dining in.

Further Reading

Cwiertka, Katarzyna J. *Cuisine, Colonialism and Cold War: Food in Twentieth-Century Korea.* London: Reaktion Books, 2013.

Park, Kyeyoung. *The Korean American Dream: Immigrants and Small Business in New York City*. Ithaca: Cornell University Press, 1997.

Pettid, Michael J. *Korean Cuisine: An Illustrated History*. London: Reaktion Books, 2008.

Amanda Mayo

KUWAIT

(Western Asia) Kuwaiti American Food
See also: Saudi Arabia, Egypt, Iran, Iraq.

Background

Bordering the Persian Gulf, Iraq, and Saudi Arabia, Kuwait shares similarities in natural environment, history, and culture with other Gulf countries. Most residents live on the harbor in Kuwait City, and Kuwait's population is 60 percent Arab but includes large numbers of Indians, Egyptians, Bangladeshis, Filipinos, Syrians, and Pakistanis. The official language is Arabic, and the official religion is Islam (with a Sunni majority over Shias). Kuwait's harbor and natural oil reserves give it a strong economy. Kuwait was initially pro-Soviet, but since the Gulf War (officially August 2, 1990, to Januaury 17, 1991) it has hosted US military forces and is considered an ally, supporting a democratic government.

Kuwaiti citizens come to the United States primarily as students. Although they are spread across the country at different universities, a National Union of Kuwaiti Students helps them stay in contact with each other and navigate life in American society.

Kuwaiti food culture is similar to that of other Gulf countries, being a mixture of Mediterranean, Persian, Indian, and Arabian cuisines. As such, it is considered an important medium for hospitality, socializing, and family bonds. Tea, frequently flavored with mint or saffron, is ritually served after lunch, traditionally the largest meal of the day, and Arabic coffee is always offered to visitors. Kuwait's "signature" dish is *machboos*, which consists of chicken, mutton, or fish over rice cooked with special spices. Vegetables or eggs may also be added. The *zubaidi* fish, also called pomfret, is considered the national fish and is oftentimes featured at meals. *Khubz*, a large flatbread, is the traditional bread, and is substituted in the United States by other flatbreads from "Middle Eastern" bakeries. A fish sauce, *mahyawa*, accompanies meals, but it is not easily available in the United States. Kuwaiti Americans are also used to purchasing *falafel* (ground chickpea) and *shawarma* (skewer-roasted chicken or beef) sandwiches in their home country, and these are now frequently available in the United States, even from restaurants not associated with Middle Eastern cuisine.

Zubaidi (Pomfret Fish) and Rice

Ingredients:

- 1 kilogram (2¼ pounds) *zubaidi*; in the United States, they use tilapia, lamb, or chicken
- 1 tablespoon ground spices (ginger, dried lemon, cardamom, cumin, clove, cinnamon, black pepper)
- 1 cup olive oil
- 1 tablespoon lemon juice
- 4 cups water
- 3 onions, medium size
- 1 celery stalk, cut into chunks
- 1 carrot, cut into chunks
- 1 lemon, cut into slices

2 bay leaves
2 green peppers, cut into thin strips
¼ cup raisins
½ teaspoon saffron
3 cup stock
1 tablespoon corn oil
4 cups basmati rice, parboiled
2 cups yogurt
salt and pepper

Method:
1. Clean the fish and leave it in salted water with some flour for 30 minutes.
2. Rinse and drain in a colander.
3. Make slits on both sides of the fish using a sharp knife.
4. In a mixing bowl, mix half of the spices, half of the olive oil, and lemon juice and season with salt and pepper.
5. Marinate the fish, making sure that the marinade is covering all over the fish and into the slits. Set aside.
6. Boil water in a large pan. Cut one onion into big chunks, and add it to the water.
7. Add celery, carrot, lemon, and bay leaves.
8. Add the marinated fish and let boil for 5 minutes. Take out the fish and set aside.
9. Julienne the remaining onions. Heat the remaining oil in another pan over medium heat and sauté the onions.
10. Add green pepper, stirring the mixture for 5 minutes.
11. Add the remaining spices, raisins, saffron, and stock. Season with salt and pepper.
12. Let the mixture come to a boil, then lower the heat and let simmer for 7 minutes.
13. Grease a large, nonstick pan with corn oil.
14. In a large mixing bowl, mix 1 cup rice with yogurt. Spread to cover the bottom of the pan.
15. Assemble layers of the fish, onion mixture, and the remaining rice alternatively, seasoning each layer with salt and pepper, pressing down slightly.
16. Cook over medium heat for 5 minutes, lower the heat, cover and let cook for 15 minutes or until fully cooked.
17. Let cool. Invert the pan over a large serving plate.

Place in American Culture

Kuwait is now known to many Americans because of the Gulf War and continuing military operations in the region, but its cuisine is not distinguished in the United States from other Middle Eastern or Arabic cultures.

Restaurants

There seem to be no Kuwaiti restaurants in the United States, and because of their status as students or professionals, no Kuwaiti Americans work in food-related businesses. Kuwaitis in the United States generally seek out "Middle Eastern" or "Mediterranean" establishments, oftentimes purchasing catering services for special occasions.

Further Reading

Kuwait. http://iml.jou.ufl.edu/projects/spring06/eisa/index.html.

Nailam Elkhechen and Lucy M. Long

KYRGYZSTAN
See entry for Central Asia.